FAMILY LIFE IN AMERICA, 1620-2000

Edited by
Mel Albin
and
Dominick Cavallo

ADELPHI UNIVERSITY

Revisionary Press, St. James, New York 11780

Revisionary Press, March 1981
Copyright © 1981

Printed in the United States of America
ISBN 0960372606

Acknowledgements

David Burner provided both sage advice and saved us from more errors than we can calculate. Among those who provided able assistance were Karen Devlin, David Rubenstein, Rose Dunne, Terri Bose, Jo Cavallo, Bruce Wolfson, and Karen Tranchilla.

To Helene Bauman and Jack Albin,
for their love and support.

Cover Designer: Karen Devlin

Editors' Acknowledgments

Grateful acknowledgment is made to the following for permission to reprint previously published material:

Alfred Knopf Inc.: For excerpts from Anthony F. C. Wallace, *Rockdale: The Growth of an American Village in the Early Industrial Revolution* (New York, 1978).

Basic Books Inc: For excerpts from Christopher Lasch, *Haven in a Heartless World: The Family Beseiged* (New York, 1977).

Carnegie Mellon University: For excerpts from Carole Haber, "Mandatory Retirement in 19th Century America: The Conceptual Basis for a New Work Cycle," in *Journal of Social History* (Volume 12, No. 1, Fall 1978).

Carnegie Mellon University: For excerpts from Elaine T. May, "The Pressure to Provide: Class, Consumerism, and Divorce in Urban America, 1880-1920, in *Journal of Social History* (Volume 12, No. 2, Winter 1978).

Carnegie Mellon University: For excerpts from Robert F. Oaks, "'Things Fearful to Name': Sodomy and Buggery in Seventeenth-Century New England," in *Journal of Social History* (Volume 12, No. 2, Winter 1978).

Columbia University Press: For excerpts from Ulf Hannerz, *Soulside: Inquiries into Ghetto Culture and Community* (New York, 1969).

Feminist Studies: For excerpts from Johnny Farragher and Christine Stansell, "Women and There Families on the Overland Trail, 1842-1867, in *Feminist Studies* (Volume 2, No. 2/3, 1975).

Harcourt Brace Jovanovich, Inc.: For excerpts from Kenneth Keniston and the Carnegie Council on Children, *All Our Children: The American Family Under Pressure* (New York, 1977).

Lexington Books: For excerpts from Howard Feinstein, "Words and Work: Three Generations in the Family of William James," in Mel Albin, (ed.), *New Directions in Psychohistory: The Adelphi Papers in Honor of Erik H. Erikson* (Lexington, 1980).

Lexington Books: For excerpts from Edward Shorter, "Women's Diseases Before 1900," in Mel Albin, (ed.), *New Directions in Psychohistory: The Adelphi Papers in Honor of Erik H. Erikson* (Lexington, 1980).

Little Brown Inc.: For excerpts from Robert Coles, *Privileged Ones* (Boston, 1978).

Oxford University Press: For excerpts from John Demos, *A Little Commonwealth: Family Life in Plymouth Colony* (New York, 1971).

Oxford University Press: For excerpts from Paula Fass, *The Damned and the Beautiful: American Youth in the 1920s* (New York, 1979).

Oxford University Press: For excerpts from James Mohr, *Abortion in America: The Origins and Evolution of National Policy, 1800-1900* (New York, 1978).

Oxford University Press: For excerpts from Leslie Tentler, *Wage-Earning Women, Industrial Work and Family Life in the United States, 1900-1930* (New York, 1979).

Penguin Books Inc.: For excerpts from Linda Gordon, *Woman's Body, Woman's Right: Birth Control in America* (New York, 1977).

Sage Publications Inc.: For excerpts from Ken Libertoff, "The Runaway Child in America: A Social History" in *Journal of Family Issues* (Volume 1, No. 2, June 1980).

Simon and Shuster Inc: For excerpts from Kai T. Erikson, *Everything in Its Path: Destruction of Community in the Buffalo Creek Flood* (New York, 1976).

University of Pennsylvania Press: For excerpts from Dominick Cavallo, *Muscles and Morals: Organized Playgrounds and Urban Reform, 1880-1920* (Philadelphia, 1981).

College of William and Mary: For excerpts from James Axtell, "The White Indians of Colonial America," in *William and Mary Quarterly* (No. 32, Jan. 1975).

Table of Contents

INTRODUCTION

This book is not just another reader in family history, for it is not just about the family. While the theme of the volume is family life in America, our subject, in fact, is the American experience as seen through the history of the family. Each article in this volume has been selected because it acts as a prism through which it illuminates a rich and colorful spectrum of matters that have contemporary relevance.

In choosing selections we have steadfastly avoided succumbing to the current passion of most family historians, social scientists and policy-makers for quantitative analysis. We believe that the quantifiers are making the family a hostage of the computer. Some quantifiers forget that using a computer is a technique, not an explanation. Quantitative techniques can help analysts collect and collate data; they cannot, however, interpret data. The "new" social history, for example, with its "multivariate" and "aggregative" techniques, has been effective in isolating quantitative aspects of family history. We know more about how many people lived in households in the past, what they earned, how often they moved, and how their birth rates fluctuated than we did before quantifiers came on the scene. What we do not know is *what all this means*. To count is not necessarily to know, and to understand the meaning of family life in America we have to know not only how many people lived in households but how they related to one another; we must try to understand not only birth rate statistics but the nature of sexual encounters in American history, and how and why they have changed over time.

Traditional family history and sociology, on the other hand, is often replete with the prescriptive sermons of religious figures defining the "morally correct" family, the ruminations of family-dabbling philosophers (popular family "experts"), or the simplicity of the analysts themselves who assumed there was only *one meaning* to family life if family structure appeared to be the same.

In order to avoid these pitfalls, this book describes the shifting boundaries of family life, revealing the dialectics of the family's reaction to and on events outside of itself, inducing new relationships between the private and the public, the city and the country, the judicial and the administrative, wealth and poverty, medicine and education, the past and the future. Therefore, we have not sought to provide the reader with an eternally-fixed, one-dimensional snapshot of the family but an album of life in America. We do this through the family because that is where the action is.

We have chosen articles, then, that emphasize the incessant and intricate interactions between family and society, children and parents, husbands and wives, and feelings and behavior. How do the family, social institutions, and political and religious ideologies interact with one another? Together how do these phenomena help determine the individual's responses to natural disasters, sexuality, male and female social roles, authority, divorce, and race? Our attempt to integrate family matters with public behavior is, no doubt, far from perfect in execution. We believe, however, that this approach to family life in America will not only stimulate students to think about these issues but provide them with insight into the private (familial) origins of public aspirations and the impact of social events on family politics.

This book is divided into six sections. A discussion of critical issues is provided at the beginning of each section and of each article.

M.A.
D.C.
Garden City, N.Y. 1981

Section One:

The Structure of American Families
1620—1880

Historians of the family have engaged in heated debates about the structure of families in the past. Was there a time in the history of Western Civilization when most families were extended in structure—that is, consisted of several generations of kin living under one roof? Was the "modern" nuclear family, composed of a married couple and their children, a product of the Industrial Revolution? How do extended and nuclear families differ as purveyors of values from one generation to the next, or in their impact upon the social mobility of their progeny?

These issues are important, but an approach to family history that emphasizes the structure and composition of families tends to present historical issues from a narrow, quantitative and/or structural perspective. By so doing historians not only neglect, at times, to study the great variety of family forms that have existed in the United States and that cannot be neatly subsumed under the rubrics of "extended" or "nuclear" families, but they often forget that similarity of structure does not imply identity of function. Thus, as we shall see in the first article in this Section, the nuclear family in seventeenth-century Plymouth Colony was embedded in a cultural and economic context that differed greatly from that of a twentieth-century nuclear family and, therefore, performed very different functions for its members and its society than its twentieth-century counterpart. Finally, and perhaps most important, the emphasis on structure and quantification leads to a concerted ignorance of those aspects of family life that cannot be counted, calibrated, or measured, namely, the important ones, the ones related to how family members "feel" about each other and why.

In his essay on family membership in seventeenth-century Plymouth Colony, John Demos contends that the "Pilgrim settlers" who traversed the Atlantic Ocean on the **Mayflower** in 1620 were organized into nuclear families that, except for the occasional presence of a servant in the household, were similar in composition to families in our own day: the typical Plymouth family consisted of a married couple and their children living in their own home.

The resemblance in structure, however, does not necessarily imply an identification in values or functions. The households described by Demos differed from those of today in a number of important ways. In Plymouth the structure of the family, the length of women's child-bearing years, and the family's relationship to the world outside the home were vastly dissimilar to that of today's "typical" American family.

Why was this so? How do the families described by Demos differ in their composition, the interactions between parents and children, and their relationship with society from those of today?

Family Membership in Plymouth Colony

John Demos

Recent studies of colonial family life have sought to clear away some serious misconceptions about the size and membership of the typical household. It used to be thought that the norm was some sort of "extended family"—that is, a large assemblage of persons spanning several generations and a variety of kinship connections, all gathered under one roof. The change to our own "nuclear" pattern, with parents and children living apart from all other relatives, was in this view associated with the coming of the Industrial Revolution. It is now apparent, however, that small and essentially nuclear families were standard from the very beginning of American history, and probably from a still earlier time in the history of Western Europe.[1] The evidence for Plymouth is very much in line with these conclusions.

Our survey of Old Colony architecture surely implies some limits on the size of individual families: it is difficult to picture really large numbers of people managing to live together in such relatively modest houses. Such a situation might be conceivable in a warm climate, where most life could be carried on outdoors—but certainly not in New England.

The various deeds of gift and inheritance speak much more directly to the same point. They show beyond any possibility of reasonable doubt that one married couple and their own children always formed the core of the family—and often comprised its entire extent. There were, to be sure, some significant variants on this pattern, but probably no more than can be found in our own day. The most crucial single datum confirmed by the deeds is a clear assumption on all sides that married siblings would never belong to the same household. Contracts made between the families of a prospective bride and groom regularly provided for the building (or purchase) of a separate house for the new couple. The arrangements for the wedding of Joseph Buckland and Deborah Allen of Rehoboth apparently were typical: Buckland's father promised to "build the said Joseph a Convenient house for his Comfortable liveing with three score acrees of land ajoyning to it."[2] Many of the wills reveal a similar pattern. A man invariably left his house to some *one* of his sons—never to more than one. At the same time he sought to provide for the day his other sons would marry and would need to establish their own separate residences. So, for example, John Washburn of Bridgewater left a special bequest for a younger son "toward his building"[3]—the other children were already living in houses of their own. William Carpenter of Rehoboth, while making his first son (Samuel) his chief heir, did not forget his second one (Abiah). Samuel and Carpenter's widow were specially directed to "healp . . . [Abiah] to build an house; because Samuell hath an house built alreddy."[4] In all of the extant wills there is only one that proposes any kind of joint residence among different married couples, and it clearly recognizes that unusual and temporary nature of such arrangements. Thomas Bliss of

Plymouth, who died in 1647, left his "house and home lot" to his son Jonathan, on the condition that he assist a certain son-in-law in building a separate residence and in the meanwhile "let him peacably and quietly live in the house with him untell they shall bee able to set up a house for him."[5]

There is one more piece of evidence to introduce at this point: a rare and extremely valuable census for the town of Bristol, compiled in February, 1689.[6] The arrangement of the census is in itself significant. At one side there is a list of names of all the heads-of-household in the town. Three adjacent columns of figures (no names) are headed "Wife," "Children," and "Servants." In all, 421 persons are included in the census, and they are distributed through 70 families.

These figures suggest a rough average of six persons per family in the Bristol population of 1689. Closer examination shows that households of four, five, and six persons were most common, comprising some 47 per cent of the whole sample; 17 per cent were smaller than this (one to three people each), and 36 per cent were larger.[7] These results may seem surprisingly low, in the light of traditional notions about the size of the colonial family, but Bristol was not an unusual community. As I have tried to show elsewhere in greater detail, [8] the families of this town may have been slightly larger than the norm for some other parts of the colony. But if so, the discrepancy was extremely narrow, and for our purposes the Bristol materials should be regarded as typical.

The simple categories of "husband," "wife," "children," and "servants" are probably as accurate and useful as any more modern terms we might contrive for describing the colonial family. In fact, only the last one requires some explication in order to be intelligible today; the other three can be directly transposed. These continuities of language obviously say a good deal about the essential similarity of the structure of families then and now. But even so, it will be worthwhile to stop and consider each one of the categories separately. For while basic meanings may have remained the same, we must recognize certain changes through time in the environmental circumstances which surround family life.

Mortality is perhaps the most powerful of these circumstances, and unfortunately there are as yet few sound investigations of its exact dimensions in the colonial period. There are plenty of florid images floating about—images of marriage regularly cut short by death, and whole families of children wiped out by disease—but all this is quite unfounded. Indeed the Plymouth Colony records suggest a standard of life and health that would compare favorably with that of any preindustrial society today. My own work with these materials is not conclusive, but it does at least offer some working hypotheses. Three of them can be briefly stated: (1) A man reaching adulthood (defined for the moment as the age of twenty-one) could expect to live to about seventy. For a woman the average was some seven years less. (2) The lower figure for women does, of course, reflect the hazards inherent in bearing children. Yet this factor can easily be exaggerated. It seems that a bit less than 20 per cent of the deaths among adult women were owing to causes connected with childbirth. Or, to put it another way, something like one birth in thirty resulted in the death of the mother. (3) The rate of mortality among infants and small children was also much lower than we have traditionally supposed. This is a difficult matter to study systematically because some deaths among the very young were not recorded in the usual fashion. However, the evidence that does exist suggests a maximum of 25 per cent mortality for the entire age span between birth and maturity (age twenty-one), and the real figure may well have been substantially less.[9] Of course, in our own day the comparable rate would be close to 1 per cent—so there certainly *are* real differences here. Still, the point remains that death was not the "usual circumstance," even in these remote and essentially primitive colonial settlements. It was, to be sure, an even-present possibility, and few people can have gotten very far along in life without losing someone in their immediate circle of friends and relations. But in terms of the overall stability of family life it was not a factor of the first importance.

Death made its greatest impact when it struck at married adults, for the loss of one spouse obviously caused considerable dislocation within an individual family. Yet the problem was usually of limited duration, for many widows and widowers remarried within a relatively short space of time. Often the interval was less than a year, and in a few cases less than six months. We should not imagine here any lack of love for the departed spouse. It was rather a matter of custom, and indeed of sheer functional necessity. The man who lived out of the marital relation was rather awkwardly placed in terms of the larger community; moreover, he needed a wife's help in trying to maintain an efficient household. The same pressures worked with even greater force in the case of a widowed woman.

So it was that most families, within a given community at a given point in time, exemplified the basic model of husband, wife, and children. The situation in Bristol in 1689 can be precisely determined from the town census. Among the 70 families resident there, only two were headed by single adults (one widow, and one widower). The remaining 68 were fully "intact," at least at this (adult) level.

It may also be useful to calculate the portion of people who actually lived out this sequence of marriage, bereavement, and remarriage. It was, in fact, considerable, but nothing that even approached a majority of the community as a whole. My investigation of some 700 people who lived to be at least fifty years old has shown the following: Among the men some 60 per cent were married just once; for the women the comparable figure was 75 per cent. Moreover, most of the remainder were people with two marriages; only 6 per cent of the men and 1 per cent of the women were married *more* than twice.[10] Thus the old stereotype of the doughty settler going through a long series of spouses one after the other needs to be quietly set aside.

So much (temporarily) for husbands and wives; let us turn now to the category of children. What was the extent of *their* membership in the household of the Old Colony? Once again the Bristol census offers the most powerful single piece of evidence. It reveals, first of all, that a majority of the total population of the town comprised children; the exact figure was 54 per cent. It also shows that the average number of children per family was likely more than three, but that sets of one, two, three, four, and five were all common to a more or less equal degree. Above five children the sample tails off quite steeply. One-sixth of the families fall into this group (that is, over five children), and the largest single set is ten.[11] These results may seem a bit on the low side at first glance, but they must be viewed in context. It is important to remember that families grew rather slowly, and that the number of children in any particular household was a direct function of the age of the parents. There were certain very firm regularities in the spacing of births in the families of the colonists. The first child usually came along within fifteen months of the date of the marriage ceremony, often within twelve months—and occasionally, alas, within nine. (Of this, more later.)[12] Thereafter the normal spacing was about two years, though there was some tendency toward slightly longer intervals as the wife-and-mother grew older.

Note that young couples recently married were bound to contribute to the lower segment of any town sample, such as the one for Bristol. It was only as the parents neared middle age that their households might begin to show a really large number of children. But after middle age the process would reverse itself once again, since some of the older children would be leaving home to set up on their own. Thus there is nothing untoward about finding, simultaneously: (1) an average of three children per family for an entire community at any given point in time; and (2) a much higher average for children born to a particular couple during the whole span of their married lives. In actual fact, an examination of some 100 Old Colony couples for whom there is good information demonstrates that eight to nine children apiece was pretty standard.[13] Here, then, is one traditional belief about colonial family life which survives the test of the evidence—the notion, in short, that families reared extremely large numbers of children, at least by contrast to the norms of our own day.

There is one final point to mention with respect to the membership of children in these seventeenth-century households. Since births were usually spaced at intervals of two years or more, and since the whole period of childbearing for a given couple might encompass as much as twenty years, the children of each family comprised a community of persons of quite different ages and radically different stages of development. For example, the household of a man forty-five years old might well contain a full-grown son about to marry and begin his own farm, and an infant still at the breast, not to mention all of the children in-between. This is, of course, much in contrast to the situation that commonly prevails today, when parents not only have many fewer children all told but also try to have them within a certain limited space of time. (The age at which the average American mother now has her last child is twenty-six.) The modern pattern tends to highlight the distance between the generations, and to make of childhood a quite tangible, or at least visible, condition. But in Plymouth Colony, and indeed in any society where the same sort of family predominates, these differences were considerably blurred. The way to maturity appeared not as a cliff to be mounted in a series of sudden and precarious leaps, but as a gradual ascent the stages of which were quite literally embodied in the many siblings variously situated along the way.

The category of "servants" presents the major obstacle to a clear understanding of the membership of colonial families. The term itself was used in a very general and imprecise way, and covered many situations which we must try at least briefly to differentiate. First, and most easily recognized in the light of our own meanings today, there was the hired man or woman. This was a grown person, who contracted to work in some family for a specified period of time (anywhere from several months to several years). Such arrangements show up in the Colony Records under the following format: "Thomas Bunting . . . put himself as a servant to dwell with John Cooke, Junir, . . . during the terme of eight yeares."[14] This was, of course, the "indentured servitude" long familiar to historians of the seventeenth century.

In some cases men and women were obliged to become servants as an act of discipline initiated by the community at large. Petty criminals and idlers were often handled in this way. Thus, for example, in 1644 the General Court found James Till guilty of committing a theft and ordered him to serve in the household of Timothy Hatherly for two years; his earnings were to be used to pay off his fine.[15] Some years later a certain "Goodwife Thomas, the Welchwoman" was directed to work and live with the family of Robert Barker—he also to have control over the management of her estate and "to see that shee doe not live extravigantly as formerly."[16] Obviously in these special cases the wishes of the individuals involved were not considered, but in most other respects the arrangement resembled the standard model of servitude.

Occasionally men would "put" themselves in other households in order to learn a particular craft or skill. Thus in 1667 "Richard Handy, . . . woolcomber, hath covenanted, agreed, and put himselfe an apprentice to and with James Skiffe, Junir, . . . cooper, to live with the said James from the 25th of October next ensueing untill that hee judge in himselfe that hee hath fully attained the skill and craft of a cooper.''[17] Usually, however, the terms were less formal and specific than this. It must be said that the sum total of adult servants of all kinds, noted in some way in

The practice of "putting out" children touched a variety of different circumstances, only some of which can be reconstructed now. In certain instances the learning of a trade was central, and the terms of the contract defined a formal apprenticeship.[18] We know, moreover, that a master would ignore such terms only at his peril. In 1654 Jonathan Briggs, "sometimes servant to William Hailstone, of Taunton, complained agains his said mr that hee hath not pformed his covenants to him in that hee did not learn him the trad of a tayler.''[19] The General Court ruled for the plaintiff and directed Hailstone to pay 15 in damages. Conversely, in another Court case a servant formally released his master from an obligation to "learne mee . . . the trade of a cooper," since "it hath bine onely by my neglect the above said ingagement hath not yett bine pformed.''[20]

Yet in fact the actual records of this kind of specific training relationship are quite sparse; indeed the word "apprentice" was used as loosely as—and interchangably with—the vague term "servant." Most often the educational aspects of a contract were stated in quite general language. When John Phillips placed his son William in the household of John Bradford "after the manner of an Apprentice," Bradford agreed simply "to teach and instruct the said apprentice, to write and read and give him that education as becometh a master to a servant.''[21] Meanwhile Benjamin Savory went through two different "apprenticeships." In the first he was supposed to learn "whatsoever trad [his master] . . . can Doe";[22] in the second he was to be instructed "in learning that is to say to read and write" and also "in husbandry.''[23]

Still, we should not take lightly the clauses in these contracts which defined the obligation to teach at least two of the "three R's." For literacy was not widespread in this culture, and the ability to read and write must have been quite highly valued. Moreover, there was little formal schooling anywhere in the Old Colony until the last quarter of the century, [24] and the practice of placing children out may have constituted a functional equivalent for at least some of its young people. Perhaps, then, servants and apprentices were frequently the children of illiterate parents, moving into households which maintained a higher standard of education. But unfortunately these are very difficult relationships to prove.

It is easier, though, to analyze the standing of the different families involved, in terms of material wealth. And clearly, in certain cases, servants were leaving relatively poor families and going to wealthier ones. The indenture of Zachariah Eddy, for example, made all of this quite explicit. Eddy was only seven years old at the time, but his parents declared that they were obliged to put him out since they had "many children, & by reason of many wants lying upon them, so as they are not able to bring them up as they desire." The boy went into the household of Mr. John Browne of Rehoboth, "one of ye Assistants of this goument." Browne for his part promised to "bring him up in his imploymt of husbandry, or any busines he shall see meete for ye good of theire child.''[25] Yet there were also cases in which economic differentials could not have been an important factor. George Soule of Duxbury sent one of his daughters into the family of John Winslow—and *both* men were relatively well-to-do. Samuel Fuller's unusually complex household contained at the time of his death several servants of one type or another; but meanwhile his own daughter was living with "goodwife Wallen."

Still another factor behind many of these arrangements for putting children out was the death of one or both of the natural parents. In short, this was the way that seventeenth-century communities took care of orphans. Widow Mary Ring who died in 1631 left her young son Andrew to grow up in the family of her son-in-law Stephen Deane—requiring Deane "to help him forward in the knowledge & feare of God, not to oppresse him by any burthens but to tender him as he will answere to God."[26] Usually, when it was the husband who died first, the children were left in the day-to-day care of their mother. But if the widow remarried all of this might have to be changed. Some wills specifically anticipated this possibility: Anthony Besse's, for example, directed that, if his wife married again, "the five biggest [children] . . . bee put forth and theire Cattle with them according to the Descretion of the overseers."[27] In a few instances children were dispersed even though the widow lived on and did not remarry. Thus William Savill's will left only one of his three youngest children in the care of his wife; the other two were to be sent elsewhere.[28]

It must be confessed that when all of these reasons for transferring children from one household to another have been carefully laid out, there still remain some cases covered by none of them. That is, some of the children directly involved came from families that were very much intact, were relatively well-off, and had no lack of educational attainments; moreover, the contractual arrangements made no mention whatsoever of learning a particular trade. The possibility arises, therefore, that some broader social or personal values may have played into this whole pattern. Edmund Morgan has suggested that parents in this culture "did not trust themselves with their own children . . . [and] were afraid of spoiling them by too great affection"[29]—hence the impulse to send them away into other homes. Unhappily there is no way to confirm this with hard evidence. But among all the various speculations that might be offered here, Morgan's still seems the best one.

We should also like to know how common this practice was, how many children were directly affected. The impression created by reading dozens of wills and indenture contracts may well be misleading, for the question must really be posed in terms of some proportion of entire communities. Here again there is only one piece of evidence that directly fronts the issue, namely, the Bristol census for 1689. But if this is a representative source, it suggests that the number of children living in households other than those of their natural parents may not have been so great, at least at any single point in time. In the census, the "servants" category comprises some 56 persons, or 13 per cent of the total population of the town. More than two-thirds of all the families listed reported no servants at all; and only two showed a really large complement (eight and eleven respectively.)[30] Most important of all, there were four times as many "children" as "servants" reported in the whole census; and we should remember that the latter group must have included at least some adults who had hired themselves out. In short, the great majority of Bristol's young people were apparently living in the homes of their own parents in 1689—perhaps as many as 90 per cent of them.

Still, the same pattern should ideally be assessed *through* time as well, so as to reveal the proportion of children who spent *some part* of their early years living outside of the parental roof. This measure would serve to modify the picture somewhat, and might well take in as many as one-third of all the children. But without a sequence of several census reports there is no way to contrive an exact figure.

Hopefully it is now established that one married couple plus children and (in some cases) servants formed the model household unit in Plymouth Colony. But certain occasional variants on this pattern must be recognized at least briefly.

Most important was the residence in some households of aged grandparents. The community seems to have expected that old people no longer able to fend for themselves would find comfort and care in the families of their grown children. Husbands writing wills were particularly anxious to pin down these arrangements for the widows they would leave behind. William Carpenter of Rehoboth, for example, left his house to his son Samuel, with the stipulation that his widow "is to have the Rome I now lodge in and the Chamber over it and to have liberties to Come to the fier to Doe her occasions."[31] Thomas King's will provided much more detail: not only would his widow have "the East End of my dwelling house . . . with a liberty to make some use of the Cellars and and [sic] leantoos;" she would also receive "five pounds by the year paid to her and the one half of it in money the other half of it in Corne and other Provision also wood provided for her fire and winter meat and Sumer meat for two Cows."[32] Sometimes bequests to the children were made directly contigent on their performance of these filial duties. Josiah Winslow left all his movable properties to his wife, to be distributed at her death "to my Children accordingly as shee shall see cause and they Deserve, in thire Carryage and Care of her in her widdowes estate."[33] On other occasions when the dead man had failed to leave any will, his children might voluntarily agree to provide for their mother—witness the settlement of the estate of Thomas Crowell of Yarmouth, whereby his two sons "volluntory freely and willingly Condescended to maintaine our mother Agness Crowel . . . according to our abillities."[34]

There is also evidence that some men made arrangements of this kind even before their death—"retiring," in effect, on the "social security" provided by a willing child. The Colony Records contain a declaration by Lieut. Samuel Nash of Duxbury, who "being aged, and not in a capassety to live and keep house of himselfe, hath therefore put his estate into the hands of William Clarke, of Duxburrow, that thereby hee may have a comfortable livelyhood." Clarke, let it be noted, was married to Nash's daughter.[35] But occasionally these agreements were effected by men not formally related to one another. A pair of deeds from Marshfield in 1685 shows William White bestowing a large piece of land on John Branch, his "tenant," in exchange for L 50 and a pledge that Branch "shall . . . hereafter Maintaine me the said William White Providing for & allowing unto me Convenient & sutable Meat Drinke apparil washing & lodging both in Sickness & in health dureing the terme of my naturall life."[36] Sometimes a will offers a retrospective look at the same pattern. Thus Andrew Ring made a special bequest to a certain one of his sons named William "seeing his son William Ring had for divers yeares past taken the care of the family & bin the support of his old age & of his wife late deceased."[37]

The details of these arrangements often differed, but the outcome was presumably the same in all cases: the membership in some households of one or two older persons in addition to the central married pair. Another kind of variant showed the need in a few instances to find a place for unmarried adults, nearly always women. When a man died, leaving one or more daughters as yet unwed, he usually made special provision for them in his will. Stephen Hopkins, for example, left most of his estate to his son Caleb; but he also stipulated that his four daughters, who ranged in age from about fourteen to twenty-two "shall have free recourse to my house in Plymouth upon any occation there to abide and remayne for such tyme as any of them shall thinke meet and conveyent & they single persons."[38] These situations rarely lasted for any great length of time, for most girls were married before they got very far into their twenties. Near the end of the century, however, spinsters became somewhat more common, as demographic trends worked to create a surplus of females in certain of the older towns of the Colony.[39] And these spinsters could only have lived in the households of some relative, normally a parent or brother.

A young man, by contrast, was never subject to living arrangements of this type. For when he attained his majority he would normally move out from under the parental roof—either to marry and begin his own family, or else to "be for himself" while remaining single for a while longer.[40] It is important to stress both of these alternatives, since it is not widely recognized that single men could, and sometimes did, live in households of their own. Until 1669 [41] Plymouth had no laws comparable to those in the Massachusetts Bay Colony which compelled unmarried persons to live under regular "family government." It does seem that proper form required single men to obtain town permission before starting their own separate homes. Thus, for instance, Plymouth in 1639 allowed John Carew "to be for himself upon the continuance of the good report of his carriage & demeanr . . . Edmund Weston is lycenced to live wth John Carew, & to be ptner with him in workeing and planting."[42] Conversely, the authorities might act to break up an establishment of this type which did not conform to accepted standards of decent behavior. A Court Order of 1653 directed that "teag Jones, and Richard Berry, and others with them bee caused to part theire uncivell living together."[43]

Indeed, one senses that a degree of suspicion attached to households composed of unmarried men; but the point remains that for many years no actual statutes opposed the practice. It is clear, finally, that such households did exist and function—with or without the permission of local officials. Their significance is implicit in orders like the following one, issued by a Marshfield town meeting in 1653: "It is agreed upon that all young men who are in the township that are single persons, and are at their own hands, shall be liable to pay all the town's rates as the rest of the inhabitants do, after the value of ten pounds a head for every such person."[44]

Old people, spinsters, single men: here, then, are three social categories which were bound to create some modification of the basic nuclear family unit as previously described. But what can we say of the total importance of these alternative patterns? As usual, it is easy enough to illustrate that each alternative existed, but very hard to know what proportion of households were actually affected. Once again, the Bristol census in our only resource, and in this particular connection its utility is extremely limited. The census shows just one unmarrried man living in a house of his own, though it does also record in a very ambiguous way two other persons who may fall into the same category. It provides no evidence whatsoever for the residence of elderly people or spinsters in the homes of relatives. At first sight this seems an astonishingly meager result—so much so, indeed, that one begins immediately to cast about for some explanation in terms of the particular demographic configuration of Bristol at the time. Happily, there *are* certain facts which come close to meeting these specifications. Bristol was still a relatively new town in 1689, and as I have tried to show elsewhere in some detail, its citizenry was quite youthful overall.[45] Most of the settlers had been in their twenties or early thirties when they first came there, and were just a few years older at the time the census was taken. Elderly people and "old maid" sisters did not, presumably, wish to move to an entirely new community. We know from the wills and land deeds that such people did form a part of *some* Old Colony households—but mostly, it seems, in the older and more established settlements. In a broad sense, then, the average household may well have been more clearly nuclear in "new towns" than in those which dated from the earliest period.

There is one last category of people to be considered here—a category of "unfortunates" who needed placement in some particular households for their own care and protection. They never formed a large group numerically, but they do serve to point up rather vividly the wide range of functions which the family in this era was expected to serve. Here, for example, was an obvious way to handle some of the community's poorest citizens, people who simply could not make a living for and by themselves. A complicated set of Court deliberations in 1680-81 revolved around the case of John Harmon, a pauper who had been staying for some time with Robert Ransom of Plymouth. Harmon had lived previously in both Taunton and Plymouth, and there was some doubt as to which town should be responsible for the cost of his care (estimated by Ransom at three shillings per week).[46]

Harmon was not only poor—he was also "decriped," and it may be that most people in similar situations were suffering from a real physical disability. For, in a broad sense the treatment of serious illness was tied closely to the household setting. Of course, in the usual case a sick person would simply remain in his own home, under the watchful care of parents, spouse, or children. But occasionally illness came to someone who had no near relatives to look after him. Such a person would have to go to some other household, at least temporarily, and the town would pay for the arrangement.[47]

Moreover, certain men in the Colony acquired over time a reputation for medical knowledge, and probably took "patients" into their homes with some regularity. In the Marshfield records there is the notation (dated 1646) that "Josias Winslow and John Dingley were appointed by the town to take order that Roger Cooke be forthwith sent to Mr. Chauncey to cure, and for what they shall be at, either sending of him or in his cure, or for his diet and lodging, the town promist to save the said Josias and John Dingley harmless."[48] Roger Cooke was presumably a man without a family, and without the means to arrange for his own treatment. So the town stepped in, assumed financial responsibility, and sent Cooke to stay with Charles Chauncey of Scituate (whose talents as a physician were widely recognized).

It is, in sum, the combination of these two institutions—the family working *for* the town at large—that we must particularly notice. For in an era when there were no hospitals, no poorhouses, indeed no-specialized welfare insitutions of any kind, the *social* importance of the family was extremely large.

FOOTNOTES

1. On this point see Peter Laslett and John Harrison, "Clavworth and Cogenhoe," in H. E. Bell and R. L. Ollard, *Historical Essays, Presented to David Ogg* (London, 1963), 157-84. See also Peter Laslett, *The World We Have Lost* (New York, 1965), 89ff.

2. *Mayflower Descendant*, XVI, 82.

3. *Mayflower Descendant*, XV, 250.

4. *Mayflower Descendant*, XIV, 231.

5. *Mayflower Descendant*, VIII, 85.

6. Unfortunately, little is known about the origin of the census—by whom it was compiled, and for what purpose. It survives thanks to a copy made by George T. Paine of Providence, Rhode Island, and published in the *New England Historical and Genealogical Register*, XXX-IV (1880), 404-5. It has been republished in Richard LeBaron Bowen, *Early Reboboth* (Rehoboth, Mass., 1945), I, 75-76.

7. See Appendix, Table VI.

8. See John Demos, "Families in Colonial Bristol, Rhode Island: An Exercise in Historical

Demography," *William and Mary Quarterly,* 3d Ser., XXV (1968), 40-57. A brief description of the early history of Bristol is in order, since a good deal of the "quantitative" data presented hereafter comes from this one census. The town was taken from the Indians as a result of King Phillip's War, and regular settlement began around the year 1680. Most of the settlers came from adjacent Old Colony towns, such as Rehoboth and Swansea. They were a relatively young group and were presumably eager for the opportunities available to them in a new community. Bristol possesses a fine natural harbor, and in the eighteenth century it was to become a seaport of some consequence. However, in these early years it seems to have functioned chiefly as an agricultural town; the land was parceled out with this in mind, and only a few of the first generation of townsmen were active in trade. There are, in sum, three ways in which Bristol may have differed from other Plymouth Colony towns in 1689: the recency of its settlement, the relative youthfulness of its population, and its potentiality for a more commercial orientation. However, none of these factors is likely to have created serious distortions for our purposes: in terms of household size and structure Bristol may be regarded as a representative case. (For the modest exception to this statement, see below, p. 79.) For a more detailed account of the town's history see George L. Howe, *Mount Hope: A New England Chronicle* (New York, 1959), and George H. Munro, *The History of Bristol, R.I.* (Providence, 1880).

9. These conclusions are the outcome of considerable work with the vital records of the Old Colony. See Appendix, Tables II and III. For another, slightly more detailed statement, see John Demos, "Notes on Life in Plymouth Colony," *William and Mary Quarterly, 3d. Ser., XXII (1965), 271.*

10. See Appendix, Table V.

11. See appendix, Table VII.

12. See below, pp. 158-59.

13. See Appendix, Table I.

14. *Records of the Colony of New Plymouth, in New England,* ed. Nathaniel B. Shurtleff and David Pulsifer (Boston, 1855-61), II, 78. See also, *Plymouth Colony Records,* I, 8, for a similar, though short-term (seven months'), agreement between Richard Church and William Barker, And also, *ibid.,* 92, 100, 103, 104.

15. *Plymouth Colony Records,* II, 69.

16. *Plymouth Colony Records,* III 197. In 1633 the Court placed Thomas Higgens, "having lived an extravigant life," with John Jenney for a term of eight years. *Plymouth Colony Records,* I, 21. And five years later Web Adey was presented for "disorderly liveinge in idlenesse & nastynes," set in Court would find him one. The order also made Adey arrange to rent or sell his house and garden in order to buy clothes "fitt for service." *Ibid.,* 87.

17. *Plymouth Colony Records,* IV, 194.

18. See, for example, the agreement whereby Samuel Jenney was bound to Kenelm Winslow "in the joyners occupacon." *Plymouth Colony Records,* I, 24.

19. *Plymouth Colony Records,* III, 51.

20. *Plymouth Colony Records,* VI, 31.

21. This deed, from the Marshfield Town Records, is published in L. S. Richards, *History of Marshfield* (Plymouth, 1901), I, 28.

22. *Mayflower Descendant,* V, 91.

23. *Mayflower Descendant,* XII, 133.

24. See below, pp. 143-44.

25. *Plymouth Colony Records,* II, 112-13.

26. *Mayflower Descendant,* I, 30-31.

27. *Mayflower Descendant,* XIV, 152.

28. *Mayflower Descendant,* VII, 41-43.

29. Edmund Morgan, *The Puritan Family* (New York, 1966), 77.

30. See Appendix Table VIII.

31. *Mayflower Descendant,* XIV, 232.

32. *Mayflower Descendant,* XXXI, 100-101.

33. *Mayflower Descendant,* XXXIV, 34.

34. *Mayflower Descendant,* XI, 26.

35. *Plymouth Colony Records,* VI, 125-26. Not all of these "retirement" arrangements necessarily created joint households. In 1661, for example, Francis Sprague of Duxbury deeded his entire farm to his son John—on one condition. John was not to "enter upon the possession of house or land; till after the Decease of his father Francis Sprague but shall keep the house tenantable for his father During his fathers life." The son apparently would continue to live in another house of his own—exchanging a regular pattern of helpfulness for the pro-

mise of full ownership later on. See *Mayflower Descendant,* XVI, 206.

36. *Pilgrim Notes and Queries,* V. 88.

37. *Mayflower Descendant,* IV, 196.

38. *Mayflower Descendant,* XIII, 14.

39. For a somewhat larger discussion of this point see Demos, "Families in Colonial Bristol, Rhode Island: An Exercise in Historical Demography," 50-51.

40. See, for example, certain clauses in the will of John Churchill, Sr., in *Mayflower Descendant,* XVIII, 40-41.

41. In that year the following order was placed on the books: "Whereas great inconvenience hath arisen by single psons in this Collonie being for themselves and not betakeing themselves to live in well govrned families It is enacted by the Court that henceforth noe single pson be suffered to live of himselfe or in any Family but such as the Celectmen of the Towne shall approve of." William Brigham, *The Compact with the Charter and Laws of the Colony of New Plymouth* (Boston, 1836), 156.

42. *Plymouth Colony Records,* I, 135-36.

43. *Plymouth Colony Records,* III, 37.

44. Richards, *History of Marshfield,* I, 30.

45. This paragraph represents just a summary of certain matters discussed in more detail in Demos, "Families in Colonial Bristol, Rhode Island: An Exercise in Historical Demography," 44, 49-50.

46. *Plymouth Colony Records,* VI, 54, 74. It would be wrong, however, to suggest that this was the only, or even the major, way in which the settlers sought to provide for their poor. The more usual procedure was to encourage a poor man to keep his household together (assuming he had one to begin with), and to give him periodically some form of outside relief. Most towns, for example, seem to have maintained a common stock of cattle, which were farmed out to various poor families. Each family would have the milk from such cattle for its own use, and some portion of "the increase" (that is, calves born in the meantime). Occasionally, too, these procedures were supplemented by the direct allocation of money. For example of all this in the town of Plymouth, see *Records of the Town of Plymouth* (Plymouth, 1889), I, 3-4, 8-9, 12, 20, 27, 29.

47. *Records of the Town of Plymouth,* I, 172.

48. Richards, *History of Marshfield,* I, 27. A court order of March 2, 1647 recognized Mr. Chauncey as an "approved phisition."

The word "family" has an ideological as well as a quantitative dimension, for the family domicile is a psychological space ("our home") as much as it is a physical mass (the numbers of people living in the household). The words "my family" convey images of belonging and exclusivity, of ours and yours, of us and them. Most important, perhaps, the word family can imply that loving and caring are more likely to be derived from members of one's family than from those outside that circle. From this perspective, the term "family" can symbolize the relative openness or exclusiveness of a society.

In the following article James Axtell describes the experiences of some eighteenth-century white people who were captured in the war or kidnapped by northeastern Indian tribes. Although Axtell describes, at times in eloquent and moving prose seldom encountered in historical writing, the ways in which white captives were incorporated into Indian families, the article is not about the structure of families, Indian or white, as much as it is about the different ways Indians and whites perceived inclusion and exclusion—and how the symbolism of belonging and exclusion affected their respective perceptions of family.

There is much to ponder about this article, especially if we recall the European perception of Native Americans as "uncivilized."

The White Indians of Colonial America

James Axtell

The English, like their French rivals, began their colonizing ventures in North America with a sincere interest in converting the Indians to Christianity and civilization. Nearly all the colonial charters granted by the English monarchs in the seventeenth century assigned the wish to extend the Christian Church and to redeem savage souls as a principal, if not the principal, motive for colonization.[1] This desire was grounded in a set of complementary beliefs about "savagism" and "civilization." First, the English held that the Indians, however benighted, were capable of conversion. "It is not the nature of men," they believed, "but the education of men, which make them barbarous and uncivill."[2] Moreover, the English were confident that the Indians would want to be converted once they were exposed to the superior quality of English life. The strength of these beliefs was reflected in Cotton

Mather's astonishment as late as 1721 that

> Tho' they saw a People Arrive among them, who were Clothed in *Habits* of much more Comfort and Splendour, than what there was to be seen in the *Rough Skins* with which they hardly covered themselves; and who had *Houses full of Good Things,* vastly out-shining their squalid and dark *Wigwams;* And they saw this People Replenishing their *Fields,* with *Trees* and with *Grains,* and useful *Animals,* which until now they had been wholly Strangers to; yet they did not seem touch'd in the least, with any *Ambition* to come at such Desireable Circumstances, or with any *Curiosity* to enquire after the *Religion* that was attended with them.[3]

The second article of the English faith followed from their fundamental belief in the superiority of civilzation, namely, that no civilized, person in possession of his faculties or free from undue restraint would choose to become an Indian. "For, easy and unconstrained as the savage life is," wrote the Reverend William Smith of Philadelphia, "certainly it could never be put in competition with the blessings of improved life and the light of religion, by any persons who have had the happiness of enjoying, and the capacity of discerning, them."[4]

And yet, by the close of the colonial period, very few if any Indians had been transformed into civilized Englishmen. Most of the Indians who were educated by the English—some contemporaries thought *all* of them—returned to Indian society at the first opportunity to resume their Indian identities. On the other hand, large numbers of Englishmen had chosen to become Indians—by running away from colonial society to join Indian society, by not trying to escape after being captured, or by electing to remain with their Indian captors when treaties of peace periodically afforded them the opportunity to return home.[5]

Perhaps the first colonist to recognize the disparity between the English dream and the American reality was Cadwallader Colden, surveyor-general and member of the King's council of New York. In his *History of the Five Indian Nations of Canada,* published in London in 1747, Colden described the Albany peace treaty between the French and the Iroquois in 1699, when "few of [the French captives] could be persuaded to return" to Canada. Lest his readers attribute this unusual behavior to 'the Hardships they had endured in their own Country, under a tyrannical Government and a barren Soil," he quickly added that "the *English* had as much Difficulty to persuade the People, that had been taken Prisoners by the *French Indians,* to leave the *Indian* Manner of living, through no People enjoy more Liberty, and live in greater Plenty, than the common Inhabitants of *New-York* do." Colden, clearly amazed, elaborated:

> No Arguments, no Intreaties, nor Tears of their Friends and Relations, could persuade many of them to leave their new *Indian* Friends and Acquaintance[s]; several of them that were by the Caressings of their Relations persuaded to come Home, in a little Time grew tired of our Manner of living, and run away again to the *Indians,* and ended their Days with them. On the other Hand, *Indian* Children have been carefully

educated among the *English,* cloathed and taught, yet, I think, there is not one Instance, that any of these, after they had Liberty to go among their own People, and were come to Age, would remain with the *English,* but returned to their own Nations, and became as fond of the *Indian* Manner of Life as those that knew nothing of a civilized Manner of living. What I now tell of Christian Prisoners among *Indiana* [he concluded his history], relates not only to what happened at the Conclusion of this War, but has been found true on many other Occasions.[6]

Colden was not alone. Six years later Benjamin Franklin wondered how it was that

When an Indian Child has been brought up among us, taught our language and habituated to our Customs, yet if he goes to see his relations and makes one Indian Ramble with them, there is no perswading him ever to return. [But] when white persons of either sex have taken prisoners young by the Indians, and lived a while among them, tho' ransomed by their Friends, and treated with all imaginable tenderness to prevail with them to stay among the English, yet in s Short time they become disgusted with our manner of life, and the care and pains that are necessary to support it, and take the first good Opportunity of escaping again into the Woods, from whence there is no reclaiming them.[7]

In short, "thousands of Europeans are Indians," as Hector de Crevecoeur put it, "and we have no examples of even one of those Aborigines having from choice become Europeans!"[8]

The English captives who foiled their countrymen's civilized assumptions by becoming Indians differed little from the general colonial population when they were captured. They were ordinary men, women, and children of yeoman stock, Protestants by faith, a variety of nationalities by birth, English by law, different from their countrymen only in their willingness to risk personal insecurity for the economic opportunities of the frontier.[9] There was no discernible characteristic or pattern of characteristics that differentiated them from their captive neighbors who eventually rejected Indian life—with one exception. Most of the colonist captured by the Indians and adopted into Indian families were children of both sexes and young women, often the mothers of the captive children. They were, as one capitivity narrative observed, the "weak and defenceless."[10]

The pattern of taking women and children for adoption was consistent throughout the colonial period, but during the first century and one-half of Indian-white conflict, primarily in New England, it co-existed with a larger pattern of captivity that included all white colonists, men as well as women and children. The Canadian Indians who raided New England tended to take captives more for their ransom value than for adoption. When Mrs. James Johnson gave birth to a daughter on the trail to Canada, for example, her captor looked into her makeshift lean-to and "clapped his hands with joy, crying two monies for me, two monies for me." Although the New England legislatures occasionally tried to forbid the use of public moneys for "the Ransoming of Captives," thereby prolonging the Indians' "diabolical kidnapping mode of warfare," ransoms were constantly paid from both public and private funds. These payments became larger as inflation and Indians' savvy increased. Thus when John and Tamsen Tibbetts redeemed two of their children from the Canadian Indians in 1729, it cost them £105 10s. (1,270 livres). "Being verry Poore," many families in similar situations could ill afford to pay such high premiums even "if they should sell all they have in the world."[11]

When the long peace in the Middle Atlantic colonies collapsed in 1753, the Indians of Pennsylvania, southern New York, and the Ohio country had no Quebec or Montreal in which to sell their human chattels to compassionate French families or anxious English relatives. [12] For this and other reasons they captured English settlers largely to replace members of their own families who had died, often from English musketballs or imported diseases. [13] Consequently, women and children—the "weak and defenceless"—were the prime targets of Indian raids.

According to the pattern of warfare in the Pennsylvania theater, the Indians usually stopped at a French fort with their prisoners before proceeding to their own villages. A young French soldier captured by the English reported that at Fort Duquesne there were "a great number of English Prisoners," the older of whom "they are constantly sending . . . away to Montreal" as prisoners of war, "but that the Indians keep many of the Prisoners amongst them, chiefly young People whom they adopt and bring up in their own way." His intelligence was corroborated by Barbara Leininger and Marie LeRoy, who had been members of a party of two adults and eight children captured in 1755 and taken to Fort Duquesne. There they saw "many other Women and Children, they think an hundred who were carried away from the several provinces of P[ennsylvania] M[aryland] and V[irginia]." When the girls escaped from captivity three years later, they wrote a narrative in German chiefly to acquaint "the inhabitants of this country . . . with the names and circumstances of those prisoners whom we met, at the various places where we were, in the course of our captivity." Of the fifty-two prisoners they had seen, thrity-four were children and fourteen were women, including six mothers with children of their own.[14]

The close of hostilities in Pennsylvania came in 1764 after Col. Henry Bouquet defeated the Indians near Bushy Run and imposed peace. By the articles of agreement reached in October, the Delawares, Shawnees, and Senecas were to deliver up "all the Prisoners in [their] Possession, without any Exception, Englishmen, Frenchmen, Women and Children, whether adopted in your Tribes, married, or living amongst you, under any Denomination, or Pretence whatever." In the weeks that followed, Bouquet's troops, including "the Relations of [some of] the People [the Indians] have Massacred, or taken Prisoner," encamped on the Muskingum in the heart of the Ohio country to collect the captives. After as many as nine years with the Indians, during which time many children had grown up, 81 "men" and 12 "women and children" were returned. At the same time a list was prepared of 88 prisoners who still remained in Shawnee towns to the west, 70 were classified as "women and children." Six months later, 44 of these prisoners were delivered up to Fort Pitt. When they were captured, all but 4 had been less than sixteen years old, while 37 had been less than eleven years old.[15]

The Indians obviously chose their captives carefully so as to maximize the chances of acculturating them to Indian life. To judge by the results, their methods were hard to fault. Even when the English had the upper hand militarily, they were often embarrassed by the Indian educational power. On November 12, 1764, at his camp on the Muskingum, Bouquet lectured the Shawnees who had not delivered their captives: "As you are now going to Collect all our *Flesh,* and *Blood,* . . . I desire that you will use them with Tenderness, and look upon them as Brothers, and no longer as Captives.'' The utter gratuitousness of his remark was relected—no doubt purposely—in the Shawnee speech when the Indians delivered their captives the following spring at Fort Pitt. "Father—Here is your *Flesh,* and *Blood* . . . they have been all tied to us by Adoption, although we now deliver that up to you. We will always look upon them as Relations, whenever *Great Spirit* is pleased that we may visit them . . . Father—we have taken as much Care of these Prisoners, as if they were [our] own Flesh and blood; they are become unacquainted with your Customs, and manners, and therefore, Father we request you will use them tender, and kindly, which will be a means of inducing them to live contentedly with you.''[16]

The Indians spoke the truth and the English knew it. Three days after his speech to the Shawnees, Bouquet had advised Lt.-Gov. Francis Fauquier of Virginia that the returning captives "ought to be treated by their Relations with Tenderness and Humanity, till Time and Reason make them forget their unnatural Attachments, but unless they are closely watch'd,'' he admitted, "they will certainly return to the Barbarians.'' [17] And indeed they would have, for during a half-century of conflict captives had been returned who, like many of the Ohio prisoners, responded only to Indian names, spoke only Indian dialects, felt comfortable only in Indian clothes, and in general regarded their white saviors as barbarians and their deliverance as captivity. Had they not been compelled to return to English society by militarily enforced peace treaties, the ranks of the white Indians would have been greatly enlarged.

From the moment the Indians surrendered their English prisoners, the colonists faced a series of difficult problems. The first was the problem of getting the prisoners to remain with the English. When Bouquet sent the first group of restored captives to Fort Pitt, he ordered his officers there that "they are to be closely watched and well Secured'' because "most of them, particularly those whoe have been a long time among the Indians, will take the first Opportunity to run away.'' The young children especially were "so completely savage that they were brought to the camp tied hand and foot.'' Fourteen-year-old John McCullough, who had lived with the Indians for "eight years, four months, and sixteen days' (by his parents' reckoning), had his legs tied "under the horses belly'' and his arms tied behind his back with his father's garters, but to no avail. He escaped under the cover of night and returned to his Indian family for a year before he was finally carried to Fort Pitt under "strong guard.'' "Having been accustomed to look upon the Indians as the only connections they had, having been tenderly treated by them, and speaking their language,'' explained the Reverend William Smith, the historian of Bouquet's Expedition, "it is no wonder that [the children] considered their new state in the light of a captivity, and parted from the savages with tears.''[18]

Children were not the only reluctant freedmen. "Several women eloped in the night, and ran off to join their Indian friends.'' Among them undoubtedly were some of the English women who had married Indian men and borne them children, and then had been forced by the English victory either to return with their half-breed children to a country of strangers, full of prejudice against Indians, or to risk escaping under English guns to their husbands and adopted culture. For Bouquet had "reduced the Shawanese and Delawares etc. to the most Humiliating Terms of Peace,'' boasted Gen. Thomas Gage. "He has Obliged them to deliver up even their Own Children born of white women.'' But even the victorious soldier could understand the dilemma into which these women had been pushed. When Bouquet was informed that the English wife of an Indian chief had eloped in the night with her husband and children, he "requested that no pursuit should be made, as she was happier with her Chief than she would be if restored to her home.''[19]

Although most of the returned captives did not try to escape, the emotional torment caused by the separation from their adopted families deeply impressed the colonists. The Indians "delivered up their beloved captives with the utmost reluctance; shed torrents of tears over them, recommending them to the care and protection of the commanding officer." One young woman "cryed and roared when asked to come and begged to Stay a little longer." Some, who could not make their escape, clung to their savage acquaintance at parting, and continued many days in bitter lamentations, even refusing sustenance." Children "cried as if they should die when they were presented to us." With only small exaggeration an observer on the Muskingum could report that "every captive left the Indians with regret."[20]

Another problem encountered by the English was the difficulty of communicating with the returned captives, a great many of whom had replaced their knowledge of English with an Algonquian or Iroquoian dialect, and their baptismal names with Indian or hybrid ones. [21] This immediately raised another problem—that of restoring the captives to their relatives. Sir William Johnson, the superintendent of Indian affairs, "thought it best to advertise them [in the newspapers] immediately, but I believe it will be difficult to find the Friends of some of them, as they are ignorant of their own Names, or former places of abode, nay cant speak a word of any language but Indian." The only recourse the English had in such instances was to describe them "more particularly . . . as to their features, Complexion etc. That by the Publication of such descriptions their Relations, parents or friends may hereafter know and Claim them."[22]

But if several colonial observers were right, a description of the captives' physiognomy was of little help after they had been with the Indians for any length of time. Peter Kalm's foreign eye found it difficult to distinguish European captives from their captors, "except by their color, which is somewhat whiter than that of the Indians," but many colonists could see little or no difference. To his Maine neighbors twelve-year-old John Durell "ever after [his two-year captivity] appeared more like an Indian than a white man." So did John Tarbell. After thirty years among the Indians in Canada, he made a visit to his relatives in Groton "in his Indian dress and with his Indian complexion (for by means of grease and paints but little difference could be discerned)." When O.M. Spencer returned after only eight months with the Shawnees, he was greeted with a newspaper allusion "to [his] looks and manners, as slightly resembling the Indians" and by a gaggle of visitors who exclaimed "in an under tone, 'How much he looks like an Indian!'" Such evidence reinforced the environmentalism of the time, which held that white men "who have incorporated themselves with any of [the Indian] tribes" soon acquire "a great resemblance to the savages, not only in their manners, but in their colour and the expression of the countenance."[23]

The final English problem was perhaps the most embarrassing in its manifestations, and certainly was so in its implications. For many Indians who had adopted white captives, the return of their "own Flesh, and Blood" to the English was unendurable. At the earliest opportunity, after bitter memories of the wars had faded on both sides, they journeyed through the English settlements to visit their estranged children, just as the Shawnee speaker had promised Bouquet they would. Jonathan Hoyt's Indian father visited him so often in Deerfield, sometimes bringing his captive sister, that Hoyt had to petition the Massachusetts General Court for reimbursement for their support. In 1760 Sir William Johnson reported that a Canadian Indian "has been since down to Schenectady to visit one Newkirk of that place, who was some years a Prisoner in his House, and sent home after a year ago with this Indians Sister, who came with her Brother now purely to see Said Newkirk whom she calls her Son and is verry found of."[24]

Obviously the feelings were mutual. Elizabeth Gilbert, adopted at the age of twelve, "always retained an affection toward John Huston, her Indian father (as she called him), for she remembered his kindness to her when in captivity." Even an adult who had spent less than six months with the Indians honored the chief who had adopted him. In 1799, eleven years after Thomas Ridout's release, his friend and father, Kakinathucca, "accompanied by three more Shawanese chiefs, came to pay me a visit at my house in York town (Toronto). He regarded myself and family with peculiar pleasure, and my wife and children contemplated with great satisfaction the noble and good qualities of this worthy Indian." The bond of affection that had grown in the Indian villages was clearly not an attachment that the English could dismiss as "unnatural."[25]

Children who had been raised by Indian parents from infancy could be excused perhaps for their unwillingness to return. But the adults who displayed a similar reluctance, especially the women who had married Indian men and borne them children, drew another reaction. "For the honour of humanity," wrote Smith, "we would suppose those persons to have been of the lowest rank, either bred up an ignorance and distressing penury, or who had lived so long with the Indians as to forget all their former connections. For, easy and unconstrained as the savage life is, certainly it could never be put in competition with the blessings of improved life and the light of religion, by any persons who have had the happiness of enjoying, and the capacity of discerning, them." If Smith was struck by the contrast between the visible impact of Indian education and his own cultural assumptions, he never said so.[26]

To find a satisfactory explanation for the extraordinary drawing power of Indian culture, we should begin where the colonists themselves first came under its sway—on the trail to Indian country. For although the Indians were known for their patience, they wasted no time in beginning the educational process that would transform their hostile or fearful white captives into affectionate Indian relatives.

Perhaps the first transaction after the Indians had selected their prisoners and hurried them into cover was to replace their hard-heeled shoes with the footwear of the forest—moccasins. These were universally approved by the prisoners, who admitted that they traveled with "abundant more ease" than before. And on more than one occasion the knee-deep snows of northern New England forced the Indians to make snowshoes for their prisoners in order to maintain their pace of twenty-five to thirty miles a day. Such an introduction to the superbly adapted technology of the Indians alone would not convert the English, but it was a beginning.[27]

The lack of substantial food supplies forced the captives to accommodate their stomachs as best they could to Indian trail fare, which ranged from nuts, berries, roots, and parched corn to beaver guts, horseflank, and semi-raw venison and moose, eaten without the customary English accompaniments of bread or salt. When there was nothing to eat, the Indians would "gird up their loins with a string," a technique that at least one captive found "very useful" when applied to himself. Although their food was often "unsavory" and in short supply, the Indians always shared it equally with the captives, who, being hungry, "relished [it] very well."[28]

Sometimes the lessons learned from the Indians were unexpectedly vital. When Stephen Williams, an eleven-year-old captive from Deerfield, found himself separated from his party on the way to Canada, he "Hellowed" for his Indian master. When the boy was found, the Indian threatened to kill him because, as

Williams remembered five years later, "the Indians will never allow anybody to Hollow in the woods. Their manner is to make a noise like wolves or any other wild creatures, when they call to one another." The reason, of course, was that they did not wish to be discovered by their enemies. To the young neophyte Indian this was a lesson in survival not soon forgotten.[29]

Two other lessons were equally unexpected but instrumental in preparing the captives for even greater surprises when they reached the Indian settlements. Both served to undermine the English horror of the Indians as bloodthirsty fiends who defile "any Woman they take alive" before "putting her to Death." Many redeemed prisoners made a point of insisting that, although they had been completely powerless in captivity, "the Indians are very civil towards their captive women, not offering any incivility by any indecent carriage." Thomas Ridout testified that "during the whole of the time I was with the Indians I never once witnessed an indecent or improper action amongst any of the Indians, whether young or old." Even Smith admitted that "from every enquiry that has been made, it appears—that no woman thus saved is preserved from base motives, or need fear the violation of her honour." If there had been the least exception, we can be sure that this champion of civilization would have made the most of it.[30]

One reason for the Indians' lack of sexual interest in their female captives was perhaps aesthetic, for the New England Indians, at least, esteemed black the color of beauty. [31] A more fundamental reason derived from the main purpose of taking captives, which was to secure new members for their families and clans. Under the Indians' strong incest taboos, no warrior would attempt to violate his future sister or cousin. "Were he to indulge himself with a captive taken in war, and much more were he to offer violence in order to gratify his lust, he would incur indelible disgrace." Indeed, the taboo seems to have extended to the whole tribe. As George Croghan testified after long acquaintance with the Indians, "they have No [J]uri[s]diction or Law butt that of Nature yett I have known more than onest thire Council order men to be putt to Death for Committing Rapes, wh[ich] is Crime they Despise." Since murder was a crime to be revenged by the victim's family in its own way and time, rape was the only capital offense punished by the tribe as a whole.[32]

Captive testimony also chipped away at the stereotype of the Indians' cruelty. When Mrs. Isabella M'Coy was taken from Espom, New Hampshire, in 1747, her neighbors later remembered that "she did indeed find the journey [to Canada] fatiguing, and her face scant and precarious. But in her treatment from the Indians, she experience a very agreeable disappointment. The kindness she received from them was far greater than she had expected from those who were so oft distinguished for their cruelties." More frequent still was recognition of the Indians' kindness to children. Thomas Hutchinson told a common story of how "some of the children who were taken at Deerfield they drew upon slays; at other times they have been known to carry them in their arms or upon their backs to Canada. This tenderness," he noted, "has occasioned the beginning of an affection, which in a few years has been so rivetted, that the parents of the children, who have gone to Canada to seek them, could by no means prevail upon them to leave the Indians and return home." The affections of a four-year-old Pennsylvania boy, who became Old White Chief among Iroquois, seem to have taken even less time to become "rivetted." "The last I remember of my mother," he recalled in 1836, "she was running, carrying me in her arms. Suddenly she fell to the ground on her face, and I was taken from her. Overwhelmed with fright, I knew nothing more until I opened my eyes to find myself in the lap of an Indian woman. Looking kindly down into my face she smiled on me, and gave me some dried deer's meat and maple sugar. From that hour I believe she loved me as a mother. I am sure I returned to her the affection of a son."[33]

When the returning war parties approached the first Indian village the educational process took on a new complexion. As one captive explained, "whenever the warriors return from an excursion against an enemy, their return to the tribe or village must be designated by war-like ceremonial; the captives or spoils, which may happen to crown their valor, must be conducted in a triumphant form, and decorated to every possible advantage." Accordingly, the cheek, chin, and forehead of every captive were painted with traditional dashes of vermillion mixed with bear's grease. Belts of wampum were hung around their necks, Indian clothes were substituted for English, and the men and boys had their hair plucked or shaved in Indian fashion. The physical transformation was so effective, said a twenty-six-year-old soldier, "that I began to think I was an Indian." Younger captives were less aware of the small distance between role-playing and real acceptance of the Indian lifestyle. When her captor dressed Frances Slocum, not yet five years old, in "beautiful wampum beads," she remembered at the end of a long and happy life as an Indian that he "made me look, as I thought, very fine. I was much pleased with the beautiful wampum."[34]

The prisoners were then introduced to a "new school" of song and dance. "Little did we expect," remarked an English woman, "that the accomplishment of dancing would ever be taught us, by the savages. But the war dance must now be held; and every prisoner that could move must take its awkward steps. The figure consisted of circular motion round the fire; each sang his own music, and the best dancer was the one most violent in motion." To prepare for the event each captive had rehearsed a short Indian song on the trail. Mrs. Johnson recalled many years later that her song was "danna witchee natchepung; my son's was nar wiscumpton." Nehemiah How could not master the Indian pronunciation, so he was allowed to sing in English "I don't know where I go." In view of the Indians' strong sense of ceremonial propriety, it is small wonder that one captive throught that they "Seem[e]d to be Very much a mind I should git it perfect."[35]

Upon entering the village the Indians let forth with some distinctive music of their own. "When we came near the main Body of the Enemy," wrote Thomas Brown, a captive soldier from Fort William Henry, "the *Indians* made a Live-Shout, as they call it when they bring in a Prisoner alive (different from the Shout they make when they bring in Scalps, which they call a Dead-Shout)." According to another soldier, "their Voices are so sharp, shrill, loud and deep, that when they join together after one has made his Cry, it makes a most dreadful and horrible Noise, that stupifies the very Senses," a noise that naturally frightened many captives until they learned that it was not their death knell.[36]

They had good reason to think that their end was near when the whole village turned out to form a gauntlet from the entrance to the center of the village and their captors ordered them to run through it. With ax handles, tomahawks, hoop poles, clubs, and switches the Indians flogged the racing captives as if to beat the whiteness out of them. In most villages, significantly, "it was only the more elderly People both Male and Female wh[ic]h rece[iv]ed this Useage—the young prisoners of Both Sexes Escaped without it" or were rescued from any serious harm by one or more villagers, perhaps indicating the Indian perception of the captives' various educability. When ten-year-old John Brickell was knocked down by the blows of his Seneca captors, "a very big Indian came up, and threw the company off me, and took me by the arm, and led me along through the lines with such rapidity that I scarcely touched the ground, and was not once struck after he took me."[37]

The purpose of the gauntlet was the subject of some difference of opinion. A French soldier who had spent several years among the northeastern Indians believed that a prisoner "so unfortunate as to fall in the course of the bastonnade must get up quickly and keep on, or he will be beaten to death on the spot." On the other hand, Pierre de Charlevoix, the learned traveler and historian of Canada, wrote that "even when they seem to strike at random, and to be actuated only by fury, they take care never to touch any part where a blow might prove mortal." Both Frenchmen were primarily describing the Indians' treatment of other Indians and white men. Leininger and LeRoy drew a somewhat different conclusion from their own treatment. Their welcome at the Indian village of Kittanning, they said, "consisted of three blows each, on the back. They were, however, administered with great mercy. Indeed, we concluded that we were beaten merely in order to keep up an ancient usage, and not with the intention of injuring us."[38]

William Walton came closest to revealing the Indians' intentions in his account of the Gilbert family's captivity. The Indians usually beat the captives with "great Severity," he said, "by way of Revenge for their Relations who have been slain." Since the object of taking captives was to satisfy the Indian families who had lost relatives, the gauntlet served as the first of three initiation rites into Indian society, a purgative ceremony by which the bereaved Indians could exorcise their anger and anguish, and the captives could begin their cultural transformation.[39]

If the first rite tried to beat the whiteness out of the captives, the second tried to wash it out. James Smith's experience was typical.

> The old chief, holding me by the hand, made a long speech, very loud, and when he had done he handed me to three squaws, who led me by the hand down the bank into the river until the water was up to our middle. The squaws then made signs to me to plunge myself into the water, but I did not understand them. I thought that the result of the council was that I should be drowned, and that these young ladies were to be the executioners. They all laid violent hold of me, and I for some time opposed them with all my might, which occasioned loud laughter by the multitude that were on the bank of the river. At length one of the squaws made out to speak a little English (for I believe they began to be afraid of me) and said, 'No hurt you.' On this I gave myself up to their ladyships, who were as good as their word; for though they plunged me under water and washed and rubbed me severely, yet I could not say they hurt me much.[40]

More than one captive had to receive similar assurance, but their worst fears were being laid to rest.

Symbolically purged of their whiteness by their Indian baptism, the initiates were dressed in new Indian clothes and decorated with feathers, jewelry, and paint. Then, with great solemnity, the village gathered around the council fire, where after a "profound silence" one of the chiefs spoke. Even a hostile captive, Zadock Steele, had to admit that although he could not understand the language spoken, he could "plainly discover a great share of native eloquence." The chief's speech, he said, was "of considerable length, and its effect obviously manifested weight of argument, solemnity of thought, and at least human sensibility." But even this the twenty-two-year-old New Englander could not appreciate on its own terms, for in the next breath he denigrated the ceremony as "an assemblage of barbarism, assuming the appearance of civilization.''[41]

A more charitable account was given by James Smith, who through an interpreter was addressed in the following words:

> My son, you are now flesh of our flesh and bone of our bone. By the ceremony that was performed this day, every drop of white blood was washed out of your veins. You are taken into the Caughnewaga nation and initiated into a war-like tribe. You are adopted into a great family and now received with great seriousness and solemnity in the room and place of a great man. After what has passed this day you are now one of us by an old strong law and custom. My son, you have now nothing to fear. We are now under the same obligations to love, support and defend you that we are to love and to defend one another. Therefore you are to consider yourself as one of our people.[42]

"At this time," admitted the eighteen-year-old Smith, "I did not believe this fine speech, especially that of the white blood being washed out of me; but since that time I found that there was much sincerity in said speech; for from that day I never knew them to make any distinction between me and themselves in any respect whatever until I left them . . . we all shared one fate." It is a chord that sounds through nearly every captivity narrative: "They treated me . . . in every way as one of themselves."[43]

When the adoption ceremony had ended, the captive was taken to the wigwam of his new family, who greeted him with a "most dismal howling, crying bitterly, and wringing their hands in all the agonies of grief for a deceased relative." "The higher in favour the adopted Prisoners [were] to be placed, the greater Lamentation [was] made over them." After a threnodic memorial to the lost member, which may have "added to the Terror of the Captives," who "imagined it to be no other than a Prelude to inevitable Destruction," the mood suddenly shifted. "I never saw . . . such hug[g]ing and kissing from the women and crying for joy," exclaimed one young recipient. Then an interpreter introduced each member of the new family—in one case "from brother to seventh cousins"—and "they came to me one after another," said another captive, "and shook me by the hand, in token that they considered me to stand in the same relationship to them as the one in whose stead I was placed."[44]

Most young captives assumed the place of Indian sons and daughters, but occasionally the match was not exact. Mary Jemison replaced a brother who had been killed in "Washington's war," While twenty-six-year-old Titus King assumed the unlikely role of a grandfather. Although their sex and age may not always have corresponded, the adopted captives succeeded to all the deceased's rights and obligations—the same dignities, honors, and often the same names. "But the one adopted," reported a French soldier, "must be prudent and wise in his conduct, if he wants to make himself as well liked as the man he is replacing. This seldom fails to occur, because he is continually reminded of the dead man's conduct and good deeds."[45]

So literal could the replacement become at times that no amount of exemplary conduct could alter the captive's reception. Thomas Peart, a twenty-three-year-old Pennsylvanian, was adopted as an uncle in an Iroquois family, but "the old Man, whose Place [he] was to fill, had never been considered by his Family as possessed of any Merit." Accordingly, Peart's dress, although in the Indian style, was "in a meaner Manner, as they did not hold him high in Esteem after his Adoption." Since his heart was not in becoming an Indian anyway, and "observing that they treated him just as they had done the old worthless Indian . . . he therefore concluded he would only fill his Predecesor's Station, and used no Endeavours to please them."[46]

When the prisoners had been introduced to all their new relatives and neighbors, the Indians proceeded to shower them with gifts. Luke Swetland, taken from Pennsylvania during the Revolution, was unusually feted with "three hats, five blankets, near twenty pipes, six razors, six knives, several spoons, gun and ammunition, fireworks, several Indian pockets [pouches], one Indian razor, awls, needles, goose quills, paper and many other things of small value"—enough to make him the complete Indian warrior. Most captives, however, settled for a new shirt or dress, a pair of decorated moccasins, and abundant promises of future kindness, which later prompted the captives to acknowledge once again that the Indians were "a[s] good as their word." "All the family was as kind to me," related Thomas Gist, "as if I had really been the nearest of relation they had in the world." The two women who adopted Jemison were no less loving. "I was ever considered and treated by them as a real sister," she said near the end of a long life with them, "the same as though I had been born of their mother."[47]

Treatment such as this—and it was almost universal—left an indelible mark on every captive, whether or not they eventually returned to English society. Although captives like Mrs. Johnson found their adoption an "unnatural situation," they had to defend the humanity of the practice. "Those who have profited by refinement and education," she argued, "ought to abate part of the prejudice, which prompts them to look with an eye of censure on this untutored race. . . . Do they ever adopt an enemy," she asked, "and salute him by the tender name of brother?" It is not difficult to imagine what effect such feelings must have had in younger people less habituated to English culture, especially those who had lost their own parents.[48]

The formalities, purgations, and initiations were now completed. Only one thing remained for the Indians: by their daily example and instruction to "make an Indian of you," as the Delawares told Brickell. This required a steady union of two things: the willingness and gratitude of the captives, and the consistent love and trust of the Indians. by the extraordinary ceremonies through which they had passed, most captives had had their worst fears allayed. From a state of apprehension or even terror they had suddenly emerged with their persons intact and a solemn invitation to begin a new life, as full of love, challenge, and satisfaction as any they had known. For "when they [the Indians] once determine to give life, they give every thing with it, which, in their apprehension, belongs to it." The sudden release from anxiety into a realm of affirmative possibility must have disposed many captives to accept the Indain way of life.[49]

"By what power does it come to pass," asked Crevecoeur, "that children who have been adopted when young among these people, . . . and even grown persons . . . can never be prevailed on to re-adopt European manners?"[50] Given the malleability of youth, we should not be suprised that children underwent a rather sudden and permanent transition from English to Indian—although we might be pressed to explain why so few Indian children made the transition in the opporsite direction. But the adult colonists who became Indians cannot be explained as easily, for the simple reason that they, unlike many of the children, were fully conscious of their cultural identities while they were being subjected to the Indians' assiduous attempts to convert them. Consequently, their cultural metamorphosis involved a large degree of personal choice.

The great majority of white Indians left no explanations for their choice. Forgetting their original language and their part, they simply disappeared into their adopted society. But those captives who returned to write narratives of their experiences left several clues to the motives of those who chose to stay behind. They stayed because they found Indian life to possess a strong sense of community, abundant love, and uncommon integrity—values that the English colonists also honored, if less successfully. But Indian life was attractive for other values—for social equality, mobility, adventure, and, as two adult converts acknowledged, "the most perfect freedom, the ease of living, [and] the absence of those cares and corroding solicitudes which so often prevail with us." As we have learned recently, these were values that were not being realized in the older, increasingly crowded, fragmented, and contentious communities of the Atlantic seaboard, or even in the newer frontier settlements.[51] By contrast, as Crevecoeur said, there must have been in the Indians' "social bond something singularly captivating."[52] Whatever it was, its power had no better measure than the large number of English colonists who became, contrary to the civilized assumptions of their countrymen, white Indians.

FOOTNOTES

*Mr. Axtell is a member of the Department of History, Sarah Lawrence College. He wishes to thank Wilcomb Washburn for his suggestions and the American Council of Learned Societies for its support. A briefer version of this article was presented to the American Historical Association at its annual meeting in December 1872.

1. See, for example, Samuel Purchas, *Hakluytus Posthumus or Purchas His Pilgrimes, XIX (Glasgow, 1906 [orig. publ. London, 1625]), 406-409*, and Merrill Jensen, ed., *American Colonial Documents to 1776,* in David C. Douglas, ed., *English Historical Documents,* IX (New York, 1964), 65, 82, 85, 93.

2. Robert Gray, *A Good Speed to Virginia* (London, 1609), sigs. [Clv.] C2r. See also Michael Wigglesworth, *God's Controversy with New England* (1662), Massachusetts Historical Society, *Proceedings,* XII (1873), lines 57-68, 169; H. H. Brackenridge in Archibald Loudon, ed., *A Selection, of Some of the Most Interesting Narratives, of Outrages, Committed by the Indians, in Their Wars, with the White People* (Carlisle, Pa., 1808-1811), I, v; and [William Smith, D.D.], *Historical Account of Colonel Bouquet's Expedition Against the Ohio Indians, in 1764* (Cincinnati, 1868 [orig. publ. Philadelphia, 1765]), 77-78, herafter cited as *Bouquet's Expedition.*

3. Cotton Mather, *India Christiana* (Boston, 1721), 28-29. See also Solomon Stoddard, *Question, Whether God is not Angry with the Country for doing so little towards the Conversion of the Indians?* (Boston, 1723), 10.

4. *Bouquet's Expedition,* 80-81.

5. I am presently at work on a book entitled *The Invasion Within: The Contest of Cultures in Colonial North America* that will explore both the Europeans who ran away to join Indian societies and the many reasons for the English—and French—failure to convert the Indians to civilization and Christianity. Consequently, and for reasons of length, both subjects are omitted from the present essay.

6. Cadwallader Colden, *The History of the Five Indian Nations of Canada* (London, 1747), 203-204, 1st pagination.

7. Benjamin Franklin to Peter Collinson, May 9, 1753, in Leonard W. Labaree *et al.,* eds., *The Papers of Benjamin Franklin,* IV (New Haven, Conn., 1961), 481-482.

8. J. Hector St. John de Crevecoeur, *Letters from an American Farmer* (London, 1912 [orig. publ. 1782]), 215. Other contemporaries who recognized the disparity between Indian and European conversion results were Pierre de Charlevoix, *Journal of a Voyage to North-America* (London, 1761)), II, 108; Joseph Doddridge, *Notes on the Settlement and Indian Wars of the Western Parts of Virginia and Pennsylvania, from 1763 to 1783, Inclusive,* ed. Alfred Williams (Albany, N.Y., 1876 [orig. publ. Wellsburgh, Va, 1824]), 218; Adolph B. Benson, ed., *Peter Kalm's Travels in North America: The English Version of 1770,* II (New York, 1937), 456-457; Johann David Schoepf, *Travels in the Confederation [1783-1784],* trans. and ed. Alfred J. Morrison, I (Philadelphia, 1911), 283; J. P. Brissot de Warville, *New Travels in the United States of America, 1788,* trans, Mara Soceany Vamos and Durand Echeverria, ed. Durand

Echeverria (Cambirdge, Mass., 1964), 420; John F. Meginness, *Biography of Frances Slocum, the Lost Sister of Wyoming* (Willimasport, Pa., 1891), 196; and Flix Renick, "A Trip to the West," *American Pioneeer, I (1842), 79.*

Later students of the "white Indians" are John R. Swanton, "Notes on the mental assimilation of races," *Journal of the Washington Academy of Sciences,* XVI *(1926), 493-502;* Erwin H. Ackerknecht, "'White Indians': Psychological and Physiological Peculiarities of White Children Abducted and Reared by North American Indians," *Bulletin of the History of Medicine,* XV (1944), 15-36; A. Irving Hallowell, "American Indians, White and Black: The Phenomenon of Transculturalization," *Current Anthropology,* IV (1963), 519-531; and J. Norman Heard, *White Into Red: A Study of the Assimilation of White Persons Captured by Indians* (Metuchen, N.J., 1973). all four draw upon western captivities as well as colonial in a search for ethnological generalizations. A recent contribution is Richard Drinnon's sensitive *White Savage: The Case of John Dunn Hunter* (New York, 1972).

9. This generalization is based on a reading of over 100 captivity narratives and accounts.

10. [William Walton], *The Captivity and Sufferings of Benjamin Gilbert and His Family, 1780-83,* ed. Frank H. Severance (Cleveland, 1904 [orig. publ. Philadelphia, 1784]), 27, hereafter cited as *Captivity of Benjamin Gilbert.*

11. [Susannah] Johnson, A Narrative of the Captivity of Mrs. Johnson, reprint of 3d rev. ed. [1814] (Springfield, Mass., 1907 [orig. publ. Walpole, N.H., 1796]), 36; Emma Lewis Coleman, *New England Captives Carried to Canada* . . . (Portland, Me., 1925), I, 120-121, 132, II, 159-160, 261; Samuel G. Drake, ed., *Tragedies of the Wilderness* . . . (Boston, 1846), 100, 168, 280.

12. This is not to say that no expense was involved for the English in securing the release of captive colonists, but it was in the nature of modest presents rather than exorbitant ransoms. Sylvester K. Stevens and Donald H. Kent, eds., *The Papers of Col. Henry Bouquet* (Harrisburg, Pa., 1941-1943), XVIII, 182-184, hereafter cited as *Bouquet Papers.*

13. In the 1770s Guy Johnson and George Croghan, both authorities on the Indians of the Middle Atlantic colonies, thought that the English prisoners had been "generally adopted" rather than put to death. "The Opinions of George Croghan on the American Indians," *Pennsylvania Magazine of History and Biography,* LXXI (1947), 157; "Guy Johnson's Opinions on the American Indians," *ibid.,* LXXVII (1953), 322. See also Mary Jemison's remarks in James E. Seaver, *A Narrative of the Life of Mary Jemison,* ed. Allen W. Trelease (New York, 1961 [orig. publ. Canandaigua, N.Y., 1824]), 46-47, hereafter cited as *Life of Mary Jemison.* While older men and women could be ransomed from the Middle Atlantic tribes, most Indians who had adopted English children could not be persuaded to "sell [their] own Flesh and Blood," not even for "one thousand Dollars," as the Indian father of 12-year-old Elizabeth Gilbert put it. *Captivity of Benjamin Gilbert,* 103, 107.

14. "Further Examination of Michael La Chauvignerie, Jun'r, 1757," in Samuel Hazard *et al.,* eds, Pennsylvania Archives, III (1853), 306, hereafter cited as *Pa. Arch.:* "Examination of Barbara Liningaree and Mary Roy, 1759," *ibid.,* 634; "Narrative of Marie Le Roy and Barbara Leininger, for Three Years Captives Among the Indians," *PMHB, XXIX (1905), 417-420.*

15. James Sullivan *et al.,* eds., *The Papers of Sir William Johnson* (Albany, N.Y., 1921-1962), XI, 446, 484-491, 720-721, hereafter cited as *Johnson Papers; Bouquet Papers,* XVIII, 253; William S. Ewing, "Indian Captives Released by Colonel Bouquet," *Western Pennsylvania Historical Magazine,* XXXIX (1956), 187-203. On his two-month journey to a conference with the western Indians in 1760, John Hays saw 23 English prisoners; at least 14 were children. Their average age was 10 years. Two other prisoners were women, one aged 22 and the other "A[l]most Women," *Pennsylvania Archaeologist,* XXIV (1954), 63-83.

16. *Johnson Papers,* XI, 466, 728.

17. *Bouquet Papers,* XVII, 51.

18. *Ibid., 38;* "Provincial Correspondence: 1750 to 1765," in Samuel Hazard *et al.,* eds., *Register of Pennsylvania, IV (1829), 390, hereafter cited as Pa. Reg.; A Narrative of the Captivity of John McCullough, Esq.,* in London, ed., *Selection of Some of the Most Interesting Narratives,* I, 326-327; *Bouquet's Expedition,* 80.

19. "Provincial Correspondence," *Pa. Reg.,* IV (1829), 390-391; *Johnson Papers,* XI, 496-498.

20. *Bouquet's Expedition,* 76, 80; *Johnson Papers,* IV, 500; "Provincial Correspondence," *Pa. Reg.,* IV (1829), 390; "Relation by Frederick Post of Conversation with Indians, 1760," *Pa. Arch.,* III (1853), 742. I have translated Post's phonetic German spelling.

21. "Prisoners Delivered to Gov., by the Six Nations, 1762," *Pa. Arch.*, IV (1853), 100-101; *Johnson Papers*, IX, 720-721; Coleman, *New England Captives*, I, 323, II, 58. In a "List of Prisoners deliv[ere]d up by the Shawanese Nations of Indians at *Fort Pit, 10th May 1765,"* The following names were among those given for 14 captives who had been with the Indians from 2 to 10 years: Wechquessinah ("cant speak Eng[li]sh knows not from whence taken"), Joseph or Pechyloothume, Jenny or Ketakatwitch, Wapatenaqua, and Nalupeia, sister to Molly Bird. *Johnson Papers*, XI, 720-721. In an earlier list were Sour Mouth, Crooked Legs, Pouter of Wynima, David Bighead, Sore Knee, Sour Plumbs, *Bouquet Papers*, XVIII, 248. It would be important to know if these names were given in derision to resistant, older captives, or in good humor to accepting, younger ones.
22. *Johnson Papers*, XI, 812; *Bouquet Papers*, XVII, 39-41.
23. Benson, ed., *Peter Kalm's Travels*, II, 457; Coleman, *New England Captives* I, 196, II, II; O. M. Spencer, *The Indian Captivity of O. M. Spencer, ed.* Milo Milton Quaife, reprint of 1917 ed. (New York, 1968 [orig. publ. New York, 1835), 168-169, hereafter cited as *Indian Captivity of O. M. Spencer;* Samuel Stanhope Smith, *An Essay on the Causes of the Variety of Complexion and Figure in the Human Species,* 2d ed. (New Brunswick, N.J., 1810 [orig. publ. Philadelphia, 1787]), 70n-71n. See also Bernard W. Sheehan, *Seeds of Extinction: Jeffersonian Philanthropy and the American Indian* (Chapel Hill, N.C., 1973), Chap. 1, esp. 40-42, and Doddridge, *Notes on the Settlement and Indian Wars,* 91.
24. Coleman, *New England Captives,* II, 91, 117-118; *Johnson Papers,* X, 160, XI, 728. O.M. Spencer's Indian father for "several years" paid him an annual visit, *Indian Captivity of O. M. Spencer,* 171.
25. *Captivity of Benjamin Gilbert,* 181; Thomas Ridout, "An Account of My Capture By the Shawanese Indians . . . [1788]," *Blackwood's Magazine,* CCXXIII (1928), 313.
26. *Bouquet's Expedition,* 80-81.
27. Drake, ed., *Tragedies of the Wilderness,* 128; Stephen Williams, *What Befell Stephen Williams in his Captivity, ed. George Sheldon (Deerfield, Mass, 1889 [orig. publ. Greenfield, Mass, 1837]),* 5, herafter cited as *What Befell Stephen Williams;* John Williams, *The Redeemed Captive Returning to Zion (Springfield, Mass., 1908 [orig. publ. Boston, 1707]),* 14, 30.
28. Captivity Narrative of Joseph Bartlett in Joshua Coffin, *An Account of the Remarkable Occurrences in the Life and Travels of Col. James Smith* [1799], in Howard Peckham, ed., *Narratives of Colonial America, 1704-1765 (Chicago, 1971),* 82; *Samuel Lee to Nehemiah Grew, 1690, Colonial Society of Massachusetts, Publications,* XIV (1911-1913), 148.
29. *What Befell Stephen Williams,* 6; Drake, ed., *Tragedies of the Wilderness,* 61.
30. Charles H. Lincoln, ed., *Narratives of the Indian Wars, 1675-1699,* Original Narratives of Early American History (New York, 1913), 30; Drake, ed., *Tragedies of the Wilderness,* 125, 145; Ridout, "Account of My Capture," *Blackwood's Mag.,* CCXXIII (1928), 303; *Bouquet's Expedition,* 78; "Provincial Correspondence," *Pa. Reg.,* IV (1829), 390-391.
31. J. Franklin Jameson, ed., *Johnson's Wonder-Working Providence, 1628-1651,* Original Narratives of Early American History (New York, 1910), 150, 263; 'Morrell's Poem on New England," Mass. Hist. Soc., *Collections,* 1st Ser., I (1792), 135.
32. Charles Thomson in Thomas Jefferson, *Notes on the State of Virginia,* ed. William Peden (Chapel Hill, N.C., 1955), 200; "Opinions of George Croghan," *PMHB.* LXXI (1947), 157, See also *Life of Mary Jemison,* 73, and Sylvester K. Stevens *et al.,* eds., *Travels in New France by J. C. B.* (Harrisburg, Pa., 1941), 69.
33. Drake, ed., *Tragedies of the Wilderness,* 61, 115-116, 145, 158; Thomas Hutchinson, *The History of the Colony and Province of Massachusetts Bay,* ed. Lawrence Shaw Mayo, II (Cambridge, Mass., 1936), 104n; Mrs. Harriet S. Caswell, *Our Life Among the Iroquois* (Boston, 1892), 53. See also *Life of Mary Jemison,* 47, 57, and Timothy Alden, ed., "An Account of the Captivity of Hugh Gibson . . .," Mass. Hist. Soc., *Colls.,* 3d Ser., VI (1837), 153. The source of Hutchinson's information was Williams, *Redeemed Captive.* Jacob Lunenburg was bound so tightly on his captor's back that he was somewhat crippled for life. Coleman, *New England Captives,* II, 215.
34. Johnson, *Narrative of the Captivity of Mrs. Johnson,* 62; [Titus King], *Narrative of Titus King* . . . (Hartford, Conn., 1938), 10; Meginness, *Biography of France Slocum,* 65. See also Peckham, ed., *Narratives of Colonial America, 89;* Howard H. Peckham, ed., "Thomas Gist's Indians Captivity, 1758-1759," *PMHB,* LXXX (1956), 297; [Zadock Steele], *The Indian Captive; or a Narrative of the Captivity and Sufferings of Zadock Steele* . . .(Springfield, Mass., 1908 [orig. publ. Montpelier, Vt., 1818]), 68; Loudon, ed., *Selection of some of the Most Interesting Narratives,* I, 303-304.

35. Johnson, *Narrative of the Captivity of Mrs. Johnson,* 57-58; Drake, ed., *Tragedies of the Wilderness,* 129; King, *Narrative of Titus King,* 8.

36. *A Plain Narrative of the Uncommon Sufferings and Remarkable Deliverance of Thomas Brown, of Charlestown, in New-England,* 2d ed. (Boston, 1760), in *Magazine of History with Notes and Queries,* Extra Number No. 4 (1908), 8, 12; *The History of the Life and Sufferings of Henry Grace of Basingstoke in the County of Southampton,* 2d ed. (London, 1765 [orig. publ. Reading, Engl, 1764]), 12. See also Peckham, ed., *Narratives of Colonial America,* 81; Peckham, ed., "Thomas Gist's Indian Captivity," *PMHB,* LXXX (1956), 298; Drake, ed., *Tragedies of the Wilderness,* 269, 272; and *Captivity of Benjamin Gilbert,* 56, 121.

37. Beverley W. Bond, Jr., ed., "The Captivity of Charles Stuard, 1755-57," *Mississippi Valley Historical Review,* XIII (1926-1927), 66; "Narrative of John Brickell's Captivity among the Delaware Indians," *Am. Pioneer,* I (1842), 46.

38. Stevens *et al.,* eds., *Travels in New France by J. C. B.,* 68; Charlevoix, *Journal of a Voyage,* I, 369-370; "Narrative of Marie Le Roy and Barbara Leininger," *PMHB,* XXIX (1905), 409.

39. *Captivity of Benjamin Gilbert,* 56.

40. Peckham, ed., *Narratives of Colonial America,* 81. See also Alden, ed., "Captivity of Hugh Gibson," Mass. Hist. Soc., *Colls.,* VI (1837); Loudon, ed., *Selection of Some of the Most Interesting Narratives,* I, 306; and *Life of Mary Jemison,* 44.

41. Steele, *Indian Captive,* 70-71; Johnson, *Narrative of the Captivity of Mrs. Johnson,* 66.

42. Peckham, ed., *Narratives of Colonial America,* 91-92.

43. *Ibid.,* "John Brickell's Captivity," *Am, Pioneer,* I (1842). 46' Johnson. *Narrative of the Captivity of Mrs. Johnson,* 68.

44. *Life of Mary Jemison,* 44-47; *Captivity of Benjamin Gilbert,* 107, 123; Loudon, ed., *Selection of Some of the Most Interesting Narratives,* 307; Peckham, ed., "Thomas Gist's Indian Captivity," *PMHB,* LXXX (1956), 299; Luke Swetland, *A Very Remarkable Narrative of Luke Swetland . . . Written by Himself (Hartford, Conn., n.d.),* 7-8.

45. *Life of Mary Jemison,* 46; King, Narrative of Titus King, 14; Stevens *et al.,* eds, *Travels in New France by J. C. B.* 73. See also *Johnson Papers,* XIII, 191, and Charlevoix, *Journal of a Voyage,* I, 373.

46. *Captivity of Benjamin Gilbert,* 120-127, 135.

47. Swetland, *Remarkable Narrative,* 5; Peckham, ed., "Thomas Gist's Indian Captivity," *PMHB,* LXXX (1956), 299; *Life of Mary Jemison,* 47.

48. Johnson, *Narrative of the Captivity of Mrs. Johnson,* 67-68, 71, 76-77.

49. "John Brickell's Captivity," *Am, Pioneer,* I (1842), 44; *Bouquet's Expedition,* 78. The Canadian captors of Titus King told him that "I Should never go hum [home] that I was an Indian now and must be and Do as they Did." King, *Narrative of Titus King,* 14.

50. Ridout, "Account of My Capture," *Blacwood's Mag.,* CCXXIII (1928); John Leeth, *A Short Biography of John Leeth,* ed. Reuben Gold Thwaites (Cleveland, 1904 [orig. publ. Lancaster, Ohio, 1831]), 28, hereafter cited as *Biography of Leeth; Captivity of Benjamin Gilbert,* 109; Steele, *Indian Captive,* 72.

51. *Captivity of Benjamin Gilbert,* 81, 83.

52. Peckham, ed., "Thomas Gist's Indian Captivity," *PMHB,* LXXX (1956), 301; "John Brickell's Captivity," *Am. Pioneer,* I (1842), 54. Joseph Bartlett also lived with other white captives while a prisoner in Canada. Coffin, *Sketch of the History of Newbury, 332-333.*

{3} *Family structure is not random: it can, and frequently does, reflect the political, economic, or religious goals of the community. This is particularly true of the family structures characteristic of the utopian communities that have dotted the American cultural landscape from the Shakers of the eighteenth century to the hippie communes of the 1960s.*

In the following article Marlyn Dalsimer describes the concept of family membership promoted by the Oneida Community, one of the most famous utopian experiments in American history. The Oneida experiment in communal living was founded by John Humphrey Noyes in Putney, Vermont in 1837 and transplanted to Oneida, New York in 1848. According to Noyes, the purpose of Oneida was to fashion a heaven on earth by adhering to biblical injunctions about familial and communal organization. In his view the biblical way to a holy and redeemed society included group marriage, communal child care, a male-centered system of birth control, and a "scientific" concept of child breeding called "stirpiculture." Dalsimer analyzes these and other aspects of life at Oneida, focusing on the role of women as young girls, sexual partners, and mothers in a utopian commonwealth.

The Oneida experiment, which lasted until 1881, may appear "far out" by nineteenth-century standards (or by contemporary ones for that matter). There are, however, a number of themes in Dalsimer's article, particularly those related to sexual "freedom," the relationship between religious ideals and family organization, and the socialization of children that are relevant to contemporary problems and issues. How are Noyes's concepts of relations between the sexes related to our perceptions of male-female interactions?

Bible Communists:
Female Socialization and Family Life
in the Oneida Community

Marlyn Dalsimer

At Oneida John Humphrey Noyes attempted to fashion a collective family of 250-300 people. He envisioned himself as a modern Abraham who was the spiritual father of a new tribe of Bible Communists. He was the archetypical patriarch from whom all authority flowed. Throughout the community's history he was know as

"Father" Noyes. He took unto himself all the power of the tribe. He decided what economic activities the Community would engage in and who would work where; he dictated the substance and form of spiritual orthodoxy for all members; he decided which members could have children and when; and for some time he kept a close eye on sexual combinations in the Community. Into this collective patriarchal structure Noyes integrated a few "leading" men[1] whom he deemed worthy to carry out his directives. They were rather like younger brothers with whom the patriarch shared power. These men had several qualifications which fit them for the privilege. First, they were men. They were better educated or more spiritually developed, in Noyes's judgment, than most Community members. Most important, they were loyal to Noyes's vision of the "holy family". Sometimes these men were referred to by Oneida Community members as Noyes's "apostolic deputies" or "lieutenants," which indicates that they believed these men to be similar to Christ's disciples in function and prestige. The male leading members counseled with Noyes in his private living quarters concerning important decisions for the Community. They spoke at evening meetings of the Oneida family and wrote ideological articles for the Oneida publications. They took a prominent role in mutual criticism sessions, and controlled, through their apppointed representatives, the indoctrination of the children in spiritual matters.

In addition, Noyes consulted with a few leading women who occupied relatively powerless, but nonetheless prestigious, positions as "mother" and "aunts" to the Oneida family. These women were, in fact, Noyes's wife, favorite lover, and his two sisters,[2] whose task it was to interpret Noyes's ideology and decisions to the Oneida women and to secure female obedience to them. Both male and female "leading" members seem to have been exempted from the more mundane Community work assignments, but the nature of their contributions to Noyes's rule was dramatically different. Whereas the leading men were party to the decision-making process of the Community, it seems that the leading women relayed these decisions, made by the men, to their female constituency.

At the bottom of this family hierarchy was the vast majority of adults of both sexes at Oneida; they functioned as children in the collective family. They gave up their independence to "Father" Noyes, who, in their own best interests, directed their work and play, their education, their religious development, and their sexual activities. They believed implicitly in Noyes's wisdom as a prophet of God, and understood, as do most children, that obedience to the father's authority insured their economic security as well. Until the inevitabilities of Noyes's declining physical vigor and consequent challenge to his "first husband" privilege by dissident men, and the restive energies of Oneida's second generation of children combined in the last decade of the Community's existence to challenge the rule of Oneida's patriarch, Noyes was amazingly successful in forging unity and obedience from his communal family.

At the same time, Noyes made certain concessions to the relative power of all men over all women at Oneida. For example, individual men, no matter how insignificant in the total power relations of the Community family, retained the privilege of initiating sexual relationships with women and passed on their family names to the children born in the Community. They also dominated, as workers and supervisors, the income-producing labor activities of the Community. Thus, though the emphasis of Oneida theory and practice was aimed at replacing the smaller patriarchal nuclear family of the "world's people" with a collective, Biblically based patriarchy, Noyes maintained a somewhat contradictory, but successful, tension between these two forms of family in the Community. If these two forms clashed, however, Noyes was quick to assert the superior authority of his patriarchal rule of the Communal family.

Of the superiority of the collective family, Noyes was always certain. He took pleasure in pointing out that marriage and lonely old age decimated ordinary families, whereas in a holy community like Oneida one could enjoy "a perennial fount of childhood" and a constant sympathy of the generations which could "bid old age begone."[3] The Oneida Communists were proud to boast in 1873 that four families spanning four generations and ten families spanning three generations lived together under the Community roof. One child, "little Richard," in 1870 could count 21 blood relatives in the Community: "two grandfathers, one grandmother, one great-uncle, two great-aunts, two uncles, four aunts, one first cousin, six second cousins, father, and mother."[4] An ailing 86-year-old Community woman, who during her sickness benefited from "the attention of my *daughter and grandaughter* besides my other Community friends," rejoiced at the birth of her great-granddaughter:

> Dear little one! She is a new bud on an aged tree. I am eighty-six years and she is eight weeks, but we live under the same roof and belong to the same great family circle.[5]

The Oneida Communists stoutly defended themselves from critics who suggested that they were "home-breakers."[6] One woman wrote:

> . . . family groups [in the Community] can see each other daily; can love and serve one another in sickness and in health, and if faithful to Communism, may expect to live together, as the marriage service saith, "till death do them part." Where in the world can be found such unbroken families as here?[7]

In addition to these advantages of communal family living, some Community members noted the opportunity childless persons had to express love and affection toward the children of others. Perhaps these childless people were, in fact, freer to express their favoritism, for they were immune from criticism of "philoprogenitiveness," i.e., special love for one's own issue, considered a serious transgression of the standards of communal love. Pierrepont B. Noyes wrote of one such special adult in his life, Aunt Sarah Johnson, who was a "sort of foster mother to me," and remembered that various adopted aunts and uncles to Community children "petted them more than their own parents did."[8] At various times, Community adults other than the biological parents took individual guardianship of a child. During the winter of 1871, for example, each child spent an evening hour in the room of an adult, where they played, read stories, and looked at pictures together. Each week the child visited with a new adult.[9] This rotation was in keeping with Noyes's belief that children needed exposure to the "ascending fellowship" of those older and wiser.

Noyes's most imaginative argument for communism of family was that human society already practiced communism on a small scale by uniting in marriage two unrelated persons and their children. He argued that communism with non-relatives was "the strongest natural proclivity in adult life," and, typically, that it was the Oneida Communists' mission to enlarge this concept of family in the "spirit of progress and of the Pentecost." To allow "science and inspiration" to organize the family under communism was, therefore, but "returning home," not by the one-horse carriage, but by the "great railroad-train that carries a meeting house-full."[10] Noyes was never fond of partial solutions.

Central to an acceptance of Noyes's vision of the Biblical, communist family was his insistence that all true communists love each other equally. They were exhorted to enlarge their feelings of love and loyalty from a small family unit to include several hundred family members. Undoubtedly many Oneida members at first found it difficult to unlearn their previous socialization and training concerning proper familial love. Some, perhaps, held moral objections to communal sex. Mrs. Jonathan Burt, for example, whose husband and neighbors offered Noyes their land in the Oneida Reserve for the site of the original Community, balked at Noyes's complex marriage scheme. She eventually relented, however, and joined the Community with her husband and children.[11] Another woman, Louisa Easton, testified that she had trouble ridding herself of "an idolatrous love for my husband," and prayed to God "to remove all idols from my heart."[12] On the other hand, according to one source the men pleaded "hard and long" (presumably with their wives) for Community membership, only to find themselves hard pressed to give up "the petty authority that they had been accustomed to exercise in their family circles." This source hints rather delicately that these men could not concede "an enlargement of affectional happiness" to other family members, while "ready" for it themselves. Some men also found it painful to submit to criticism in which former wives participated.[13] Even though men and women joining the Oneida Community both experienced pain and difficulty in adhering to Community family standards, the men held one major consolation. They were, by explicit Community ideology, superior to women, and from this superiority accrued specific benefits in prestige, work roles, and sexual initiatives. While it was perhaps a relief to some women to get out from under the rule of a particularly tyrannical individual husband, Community women simply exchanged one smaller, patriarchal family structure for a larger, collective one.

Noyes's ideological pronouncements hammered constantly on the theme of the secondary, supportive role expected from women towards men in the Oneida family. In the ascending/descending fellowship at the heart of Community ideology, women were enjoined to accept Paul's remonstrance of Corinthians 11:3 that "the head of the woman is the man." Community writings frequently attributed family quarrels, discord and jealousy to two factors: first, that the man was estranged from God, and, therefore, could not fulfill his God-given duty to "inspire" the woman; and second, that the woman was overstepping her "natural" boundaries by attempting to rule and lead the man. According to Community ideology, the first dislocation had to be corrected before a man could put woman in her rightful place.[14]

The ideal woman/wife in the Oneida family was perhaps best described in an obituary which appeared in the Oneida *Circular* for Charlotte Noyes Miller, Noyes's sister, who died in the Community in October 1874. In the obituary Charlotte Miller was praised as a *"true woman"* because "there was not a suspicion of strong mindedness" about her. "She gave man his true place as head of woman, and felt no suppression or infringement from his superiority." All Community accounts mentioned Charlotte Miller's beauty and instinctive grace. Despite her many talents and contributions to the Community, which included receiving outside visitors, serving as a member of the Criticism and Stirpiculture Committees, and as "mother" to the class of younger girls, the strongest praise she drew was that "she would not have provoked your envy."[15] Here was the unmistakable message to Oneida women of their proper social role. They had to accede to an explicit male superiority and leadership, and hide any talents or abilities which might threaten the patriarchal assumptions of the Community.

PHILOPROGENITIVENESS

If Oneida women had difficulty adhering to this standard of true womanliness in relation to men, they had even more problems, judging from the number of references in the Community literature, in dealing with feelings of special love for their children. Affection for and control over one's children, often a source of comfort and power to women in patriarchal family structures, were removed from the hands of individual mothers in the Oneida Community and entrusted to the authority of adults judged particularly capable of moulding children to Community ideology and behavior. It was a Community woman, Mary E. Cragin, a favored lover and devoted disciple of Noyes, who first articulated Noyes's rejection of "sickly, family" love to Oneida women. While living at the Brooklyn branch commune with Noyes and their young son Victor while her three older children remained at Oneida, Cragin penned a letter to Oneida women on the dangers of "philoprogenitiveness." She argued that excessive love of children prevented women from loving God wholeheartedly. Philoprogenitiveness kept women's hearts "in a bleeding state, to the weakening of our whole character." This weakness could be fatal because it interfered with woman's salvation. Cragin suggested that as a tree needed pruning to grow vigorously, so might God take away children from mothers who were blinded by the passions of philoprogenitiveness. Cragin quoted the Biblical passage, "When I am weak, then I am strong," and exhorted her sisters to put God first. She concluded with a persuasive call: "I confess Christ my savior from the undue exercise of philoprogenitiveness. Who will join me?"[16] Apparently her exhortation won many female recruits, however reluctant and confused they felt about this ideological emphasis. Mary Cragin subsequently became a leader and teacher in the newly organized Children's House at Oneida where she and Noyes's wife, Harriet Holton Noyes, zealously socialized the children into Noyes's communal family.

Cragin's argument against philoprogenitiveness was buttressed by a variation of the ascending/descending fellowship theme developed by Noyes. The correct hierarchy of family inspiration under communism, according to Alfred Barron, then editor of the Oneida *Circular,* was the following: children should look up to the mother, the mother to the father, and the father to God. Barron warned of "false and divided counsels" in governing children when mothers diverted their love and attention "from husbands to *sons.*"[17] An early Community statement of "general principles" regarding the relationship of parents to children declared that love between adult men and women was a "superior passion" to love between adults and children. Parents "should not look so much to their children, as to the object of *pleasing God.*"[18] Another article discovered "two poles of influence" in parent/child relations: "the father's exacting and truthful severity," and the "mother's and grandmother's indulgent tenderness." It seemed that the Oneida children were getting too much of the female influence and not enough of the male, resulting in "insubordination and untruthfulness" among the children. To correct this intolerable imbalance, the article concluded that "children governed by mere motherly feeling [are] like a wheel with the hub left out. There must be masculine power and execution at the center and the mother's philoprogenitiveness must be loyally organized into that.''[19]

Just as the concepts of a traditional nuclear family and a family of Bible communists coexisted, sometimes easily and sometimes with difficulty, at the Oneida Community, so the individual parentage of children at Oneida was never completely suppressed. Nevertheless, Oneida women were exhorted to understand that they produced children not for their individual satisfactions, but for God and communism. At the Community christening of a newborn, for example, parents submitted their child and the name they had chosen for it to the whole Oneida family for approval, which, apparently, was routinely granted. An Oneida *Circular* description of such a christening reiterated that ''here the Church is the family, and the family is the Church, and the child that is born into the family is born into the Church . . . it is comely that parents of the new-born babe should make some recognition of the Community sponsorship.''[20] It is instructive that the article used the word ''sponsorship,'' rather than ''ownership,'' demonstrating that the Community did not insist on totally removing a child from identification with its biological parents. Nevertheless, it was abundantly clear that the Community took major responsibility for the socialization of its children, arguing that Community guardians were ''better able to discern and correct [children's] faults and encourage their virtues . . . than near relations would be.''[21] On another occasion the Oneida *Circular* did refer to the children as ''the property of the whole Community,'' and argued that they needed to ''communize the children . . . as completely as we have all other possessions.''[22]

Community militancy against maternal philoprogenitiveness waxed and waned during the 21 years before stirpiculture, depending upon specific conditions. Mr. Hatch, who worked in the Children's House in 1866, gave testimony that previously, when children were sick or irritable, their mothers would come to the children's quarters to give them special attention and care, probably becaue the women who worked in the Children's House ''had a great deal more respect for the mothers . . . than for Mr. Noyes's instincts.'' Hatch allowed that this permissiveness ''worked in the wrong direction . . . but . . . we have learned better now.'' He concluded that the children's ''department'' was paramount to ''the motherly spirit'' and that all Community members ''should feel that every child . . . belongs to the Community and not to the mother.''[23]

The advantages of Community care for children, particularly in relation to its effects on mothers, were often emphasized. Community literature pointed out that communal child care freed mothers from anxiety and fatigue which they would have suffered had they been wholly responsible for rearing their children. The main advantage of communal child care, however, was always that it freed mothers to pursue their highest calling—serving God. On one occasion ''Aunt'' Harriet Noyes Skinner solicited for publication in the Oneida *Circular* testimony from mothers about the advantages of Community care of children. Alice Ackley offered her opinion:

> I now realize . . . that the old way of each mother caring for her own child, begets selfishness and idolatry; and in many ways tends to degrade woman. . . . I appreciate the opportunity [communal child care] affords me of not only joining in public work but of self-improvement and ''going-home'' to God every day.[24]

She also felt released from a constant ''anxiety and worry lest [my daughter Corinna] should be sick.''[25]

In 1870, at the dedication of the new Children's Wing planned for the expected stirpiculture children, Augusta E. Hamilton spoke of the special advantages to mothers of Community care of children. She emphasized:

> . . . The prosperity and happiness, nay, salvation even, of our children, are insured to us, so far as the best of spiritual surroundings and instruction, . . . can secure it. . . . Our children have, as it were, a hundred loving fathers and mothers. . . . We mothers, too, are ennobled by the thought that we bare [sic] our children, not for ourselves, but for the good of the church.[26]

Another woman, "S.B.C.," emphasized woman's duties to man, and the unnatural interference which children often inserted into that relationship. She related that though she "struggled hard and long" against philoprogenitiveness toward her firstborn, "God found a way to have his truth." The child died. Through this experience she learned that it was "wicked to appropriate any of God's gifts," and concluded:

> This propensity in woman to have pets and worship them, seems barbarous to me now. It belittles her, distracts from her charms, her power of usefulness, and above all is an abuse of God. The desire of my heart is to rise out of this liability and separate myself entirely from the spirit of idolatry, and be what God designed woman should be—a true helpmeet to man.[27]

Philena B. Hamilton emphasized yet another theme. She wrote that she was grateful for Community child rearing because "I should never be able, myself, to secure in my children that obedience and respect necessary to their improvement and my happiness." She found that separation from her children better prepared her to accept them as God's gifts. After an absence of one year from her youngest daughter while Hamilton lived at the Wallingford branch, she noted that her child was "healthy, buoyant, and affectionate. I can see how a mother's fondness may be like a close, hot room to a child. . . ." She concluded that Community care released her from all anxiety about her children's futures and enabled her to "devote myself to the cause of the truth we have received [presumably, Bible communism], which is dearer to me than life."[28]

It is not surprising that these testimonials from Oneida mothers closely paralleled Noyes's ideas of correct family relations under Bible communism. Like the women's evaluations of complex marriage, these appraisals were solicited for publication in the Oneida *Circular* to prove to a skeptical outside world that all was well in the Oneida family. Curiously, however, several children's memoirs report considerably more ambivalence from their mothers in carrying out the lofty principles of the holy family. Harriet M. Worden, for example, once wrote of the "sickly, maternal tenderness" which damaged both mothers and children, but her son Pierrepont reported that she felt anguished by her separation from him. He believed that she surreptitiously gathered toys in her room for his weekly visit with her, and remembered that she sometimes interrupted his play in her room to ask: "Darling, do you love me? . . . I remember how tightly she held me and how long, as though she would never let me go."[29] Pierrepont Noyes felt that his mother was "trying to make up for lost opportunity, lavishing affection on me until . . . I half grudged the time taken from play.''[30] Several times Pierrepont Noyes heard his mother criticized for "idolatry" toward him and remembered periods of separation from her because of it. Occasionally her tenderness turned abruptly to severity if she feared he would be "sticky" at the end of a visit with her; this change of demeanor confused the child, who remarked years later, "the turbulence was mine, but the greater tragedy was my mother's.''[31] While writing his boyhood memoirs, Pierrepont Noyes tried to evaluate how Community militancy against philoprogenitiveness and separation from his mother had affected his development. He wrote:

> My conception of the grown folks' ideal was undoubtedly vague, but their antagonism to excessive human affection was neither vague nor meaningless. It came to us in the form of oppositions and prohibitions which affected our daily lives and whose intent even children would understand. A child has little capacity for loving that which it can neither see nor touch. Hence, the pressure to elevate the love emotion reacted with us as a suppression and, at least in my own case, oriented my interest toward material things.[32]

Though the Oneida *Circular* wrote that toddlers went to their communal nurseries "with eager zest" in a "real atmosphere of content,''[33] Corinna Ackley Noyes, daughter of Alice Ackley, remembered a less idyllic occasion of separation from her mother. Her own emotional reaction to the situation was undoubtedly heightened by her mother's ambivalence, which she communicated to the tot by some basic, non-verbal emotional mechanism. Corinna Ackley Noyes recalled:

> one two-week period of separation [when] I caught a glimpse of [my mother's] passing through a hallway near the Children's House and rushed after her screaming. She knew—what I was too young to know—that if she stopped to talk with me another week might be added to our sentence. Hoping, I suppose, to escape, she stepped quickly into a nearby room. But I was as quick as she. I rushed after her, flung myself upon her, clutching her around the knees, crying and begging her not to leave me, until some Children's House mother, hearing the commotion, came and carried me away.[34]

Even grandmothers were not immune from Community militance against philoprogenitiveness. Just as mothers were instructed to turn their primary attention to serving God and being "helpmeets" to men, so were grandmothers particularly enjoined to "recover [themselves] from the disorders" which years of family cares had brought upon them. A grandmother's highest duty was to bring upon her grandchildren "the care of God. In saving her own soul from the disorders of philoprogenitiveness, she becomes a medium of heavenly spirits to her descendants. . . .''[35] This advice notwithstanding, Corinna Ackley Noyes remembered her grandmother's love and care as a predominant force in her early life. In her memoirs she related a touching early memory of her grandmother's holding her in her arms, singing hymns with a "faith and fervor" that communicated "safety and peace" to the child.[36]

It is difficult to generalize about the cooperation Oneida women gave Noyes's ideals of the communist family. Certainly they tried courageously, if occasionally unsuccessfully, to separate themselves from feelings of philoprogenitiveness. The inaccessibility of Oneida women's private writings is unfortunate because one might glean from them deeper insights into women's feelings about themselves and their children. Likewise, only two written memories of Oneida childhood, by Pierrepont B. Noyes and Corinna Ackley Noyes (who married each other in 1894), provide material on children's reactions to the practical and emotional ramifications of Noyes's prohibition against excessive maternal love. As stirpicult children, their experiences are limited to the last decade of the Community's life when probably the rules of child care were most rigidly enforced. Though both autobiographies seem sensitive and honest, one must keep in mind that they were written from the hindsight of adulthood, after both authors had lived many years with traditional assumptions of family life. Nonetheless, the clarity and poignancy of Corinna and Pierrepont Noyes's accounts of early childhood emotions leads one to trust them. If true, these accounts, at the least, indicate considerable resistance and ambivalence on the part of their Oneida mothers to give up their children to the Community, the greater good of the church and their own spiritual development notwithstanding.

By contrast, no references to paternal philoprogenitiveness can be found in the Community literature. Corinna Ackley Noyes made no mention of her father in her memoirs, and wrote of her grandfather, Joseph Ackley, that, "during my early years in the old Community I seldom saw him and felt scarcely acquainted with him."[37] Likewise, Pierrepont B. Noyes had almost no contact with his father. He wrote:

> I revered him [as did all Oneida children, in the abstract], but he was much too far away, too near to heaven and God. He lived somewhere upstairs and, whenever I saw him, was usually surrounded by men . . . who were associated in my mind with the Apostles.[38]

Sometimes children developed close emotional ties with men who were not their biological fathers, as did Pierrepont Noyes with Abram Burt, the father of his half brother.

Fathers were free to visit with the children in the children's quarters and occasionally took care of their offspring for short periods of time, but apparently never felt the pain of separation from them or desired to control them more closely. One must ask why the burden of philoprogenitiveness fell so much more heavily on mothers than on fathers in the Oneida Community. Several concrete realities of male and female parental experiences in the Oneida Community offer some clues to explain female philoprogenitiveness in the Community.

First of all, Oneida women had exclusive care of their babies for the first year of the children's lives. They nursed their infants and watched over their waking and sleeping hours. From the intimate contacts of this first year of care, it is understandable that mothers developed strong ties with their children, who were totally dependent upon them for physical and emotional nurture. Just as likely is the fact that the abrupt change from their around-the-clock personal care of their children to their relinquishment to the Children's House probably caused a serious dislocation in the mothers' emotions and daily routines.

Secondly, women at Oneida were very nearly powerless, submitting to a male-dominated regime in ideology, work and sexual relations. It is, therefore, not surprising that they might resist loss of control in the one sphere in which they felt very needed and responsible—care of their children. On the other hand, for Oneida fathers the conception of children was but one aspect of Community living. They enjoyed some compensating privileges and responsibilities which mothers did not have.

In evaluating the concept of the communist family at Oneida, the small amount of evidence available suggests that women were reluctant to give up special feelings of love for their own children. In fact, they did not. They suffered for it, and perhaps the children did too. On the other hand, communal child care enabled Oneida women to enter the Community work force and to avail themselves of leisure time for study and cultural improvement. These advantages, however, were secondary to the ones most often mentioned in the Community literature, which instead emphasized women's greater accessibility to God and women's service roles as "helpmeets" to the men. One is struck by the threat to mothers that some Community pronouncements on philoprogenitiveness offered—that their children might die if the mothers made them too much the objects of "idolatry." This threat was unusual for the Oneida Communists who relied mainly on positive persuasion and loving understanding and criticism to achieve desired behavior. That this threat was occasionally resorted to is perhaps evidence of how strongly mothers clung to their children. One can imagine what terror this slightly veiled threat produced in persons accustomed to seeing God's "providence" in many mundane, daily occurrences. The other jarring aspect of Community child care ideology was that of Augusta Hamilton, who wrote that "our children have . . . a hundred loving fathers and mothers."[39] This was true only in a very abstract sense, for only a handful of carefully chosen Community guardians, predominantly women, had anything to do with the children after they left their mother's care. If an Oneida mother believed she gave up her children to Community care, she must have realized that this was only an abstract concept. Truer to say that she gave up her children to Noyes's ideology, carried out by his appointed representatives.

EDUCATION AND THE SOCIALIZATION OF GIRLS

In all, 135 children were brought to the Oneida Community by their parents, or born there before 1869.[40] The 58 "stirpicults" born in the last decade of the Community's existence brought the total number of children whom the Community reared to 193. After scientific breeding, the ensuing education of Community children became paramount. This priority was explicitly stated in the Oneida *Circular* of June 8, 1874: "As we value the future of Communism we must see to it that our children . . . are brought up in 'the nurture and admonition of the Lord,' else they will someday rise up against us and become a curse."

Generalizations about Oneida children's education are difficult to arrive at for two reasons. References to the Bible Communists' program for children are scanty and scattered, found mainly in isolated articles in the Oneida *Circular* and two published accounts of Oneida childhood by Pierrepont B. Noyes and Corinna Ackley Noyes. Secondly, conditions changed in the Community during its 44 years of existence, and with it the particulars of Oneida children's socialization. The material conditions of the Community, for example, dictated how long the children received formal schooling. In the lean years children left primary school and entered the adult work force of the Community at age 10; when the Community became more prosperous they continued their classroom work as children until age 12. The children to be educated, and the changing emphases of Noyes's interests themselves, also contributed to organic growth and changes in the children's program. At the same time a continuing commitment to Bible Communism and its indoctrination in the minds and hearts of the young permeated the children's education throughout the Community's history. In particular, the following discussion will examine as closely as possible the way in which Community education socialized girls to the Community standard of "true-womanliness."

Female and male children attended school together at Oneida until ages 10-12. They were usually graded according to age into three groups: toddlers, pre-schoolers, and primary school. For the primary school children, ages 6-12, formal classroom time was limited to the mornings, during which time they learned the three R's, geography, science, as well as "obedience, manners, and prayer."[41] The afternoons allowed ample time for work, outdoor play and a regular children's religious meeting. At the religious meetings Oneida children learned the idea of a "Providence"—"somebody bigger and wiser" who watched over them and their Community family. They received criticism from their elders on their behavior and attitudes, and occasionally administered criticism to each other. They often concluded their discussions by "'fess[ing] Christ a pure heart."[42]

In the early 1850's, when the Community was at the height of its religious fervor, even the children's secular education was heavily infused with religious themes. Mary Cragin, Noyes's enthusiastic lover and disciple, relied on Bible stories, pictures, prayer, and moral lessons in her teaching. During her tenure as Children's House leader, Cragin instituted a famous purge of dolls as playthings which provided the girls with their first lesson in the roles they would be expected to assume as Community women. The infamous doll purge coincided with the Community campaign against maternal philoprogenitiveness.

Mary Cragin gave the girls dolls, she explained, so that they would teach themselves to sew by making doll clothes.[43] The playthings, however, soon brought trouble to their young admirers. Harriet Worden, then one of the little girls who loved dolls, reported:

> The grown folks soon discovered that we were idolaters, worshiping our little waxen images, and becoming very heedless of our variously appointed chores about the house, as well as inattentive to the Bible and more serious matters.[44]

In typical Community style, Mary Cragin promptly formed a "committee" of herself and two girls, Sarah Burt and Mary Prindle, to study the "doll-question." Little Sarah dutifully reported that she was often late for breakfast because she tarried to dress her doll. Her doll drew her attention away from Christ, making her "frivolous" and inattentive to her studies. Mary Prindle testified that her doll offered similar temptations, and "then I have to be criticized."[45] Cragin summarized the trouble with the dolls in a four-point report submitted to Noyes, Erastus Hamilton and others, "who heartily approved of it."[46] First, playing with dolls as though they were living beings "is acting and speaking a lie, and we do not mean to speak or act lies." Secondly, dolls encouraged philoprogenitiveness, whereas the "fear of the Lord" should be the beginning of education "before we try to learn to become mothers." Playing with dolls, furthermore, encouraged baby talk and baby thoughts, and tended to make the girls forget "that our tongues belong to God." Finally, the "doll-spirit" seduced the girls from Community work tasks and diligent study. It was, Cragin concluded, the "same spirit that seduces women to allow themselves to be so taken up with their children that they have no time to attend to Christ, and get an education for heaven."[47] Clearly, the purge of the dolls paralleled the Community's attack on maternal philoprogenitiveness. Mary Cragin led both campaigns.

Noyes accepted Cragin's report and in his response likened the girls' attachment to their dolls to the "worship of graven images." The solution to the problem came swiftly. Cragin suggested burning the dolls. The Oneida *Circular* reported that the "little boys were loud in their clamors for the great massacre."[48] Harriet Worden recalled the subsequent ceremony in this way:

> We all formed a circle round the large stove, each girl carrying on her arms her long-cherished favorite, and marched in time to a song; as we came opposite the stove-door, we threw our dolls into the angry-looking flames, and saw them perish before our eyes. . . . It was some time before we could think of this wholesale slaughter without a slight emotion.[49]

Thereafter no dolls were permitted in the Community.

This incident very dramatically illustrated to girls one of their most important lessons in becoming Community women. God and the Community spirit came before everything else. Maternity was not an inevitability, but rather a privilege which a girl might attain after sufficient Community preparation for her womanly role.

In his memoirs of Oneida childhood, Pierrepont B. Noyes recorded the fullest details of life in the Children's House during the 1870's. From his descriptions one can conclude that boys and girls attended school and religious meetings together, with very little differentiation between the sexes, though he noted that the primary school teacher, Mr. Warne, was especially fond of boys[50] and often took them on nature hikes while the girls stayed behind. In outdoor play the children seemed to have segregated themselves voluntarily according to sex, for Pierrepont Noyes's descriptions of his childhood, with minor exceptions, mentioned only boys as companions. Yet Pierrepont Noyes cited no adult pressure for separation of the sexes in play. Boys seemed to have had more latitude for recreation and mischief than girls. In the class of boys 6-12 years old, for example, each was promised a coconut if able to swim across the creek by the end of the summer of 1877.[51] If girls had any part of the bargain, Pierrepont Noyes did not mention it, though one Community source noted that the branch commune at Wallingford did teach their girls to swim.[52] Likewise Oneida girls were excluded from the July 4, 1873, children's celebration. Mr. Woolworth gave each of the little boys a bunch of fire crackers; they also launched skyrockets and Roman candles from the top of the Mansion House's tower.[53]

Some toys, books, and facilities of the Oneida Children's House were regarded as the exclusive province of one sex or the other. In the rainy-day playroom, for example, the Oneida *Circular* boasted of a "carpenters bench, where the boys can learn the handling of tools."[54] The bookshelves in the children's quarters segregated reading material by sex. For the boys Pierrepont Noyes recalled the "Castlemon series of adventure stories, *Frank on the Prairie, Frank on the Gunboat. . . .*" Though he did not name the girls' books, probably because he never read them, Noyes noted that the boys "despised or at least affected to despise" the girls' books.[55]

Oneida boys and girls dressed simply but differently. The girls wore dresses covered by calico aprons; the boys, "pants-and-jackets," buttoned together.[56] One wonders why the little girls did not wear cotton pants, as adult women at Oneida did. The sleeping and dressing quarters of the children were also sex-segregated.[57] Pierrepont Noyes noted that "only the Girls' Room showed any attempt at decorative furnishing and for this very reason it always remained exclusively a girls' room."[58]

Children performed daily work for the Community as an integral part of their education. Sometimes the children helped at the various "bees" organized by the Community to gather potatoes or butternuts.[59] They pared and sorted apples, and once, in the animal trap-shop, sorted hundredweights of iron in a few hours, "a piece of work which would have occupied as many hired boys all day. . . ."[60] In the 1870's the children worked for an hour each day after lunch, making chains which were later attached to the steel traps manufactured by the Community. Older boys each had a "stent" of 100 chains to be completed before they could be excused. The girls and younger boys picked over the links, untangling them for the chainmakers.[61] At some time during this busy daily schedule one can conclude that the girls were taught sewing, since after age 12 they took full responsibility for making their own clothes as well as those of other Community members.

From these scattered descriptions one can glean some of the flavor of the purposes of Oneida children's education. Their young lives were not entirely free of distinctions and subtleties based on sex. These distinctions are not surprising, since they were perfectly in keeping with Noyes's clear delineation between the social roles of men and women which he believed necessary for "vital society."

If the sexual distinctions of early childhood at Oneida were somewhat subtle and restricted to certain activities and facilities, after graduation from primary school boys' and girls' experiences diverged sharply. After age 10-12, depending upon the period of Community history one examines, children became adults and moved into the adult quarters of the Mansion House. From that time until their middle twenties, young women and men were systematically separated from each other in work, study, and recreation by deliberate Community policy, which feared too much sexual attraction, or as the Oneida Communists called it, "horizontal fellowship." Moreover, for young women, opportunities for self-expression and growth shrank as they moved into the protecting arms of the "family circle" and the world of women's work, whereas young men's educational and work activities continued to expand, offering opportunities for intellectual growth and leadership training.

At about age 12, girls were introduced into the sexual practices of the Community. It was a sharp departure from life in the Children's House. Probably Oneida children knew little of the sexual arrangements in the Community, for they lived apart from the adult population and had little contact with adults other than their child-care workers. Likewise, Oneida children had no instruction in the rudiments of sex education or reproduction. They did not know where babies came from. The Oneida *Circular* printed an incident in which some curious outsiders tried to learn from a four-year-old boy who his parents were.

> "Where are your parents, little boy?"
> "My Papa Noyes and Mama Miller are at Wallingford."
> ....
> "Miller! That's a nice name; and what is your own name beside Miller?"
> The reply had such amplitude, such rolling fullness, such *naivete* and

simplicity, that we record it: "My name is Temple Noyes Dunn Burt Ackley!"[62]

The Community described this encounter approvingly, since it verified their considerable efforts to teach the children that they had many communal "pas and mas."

Because Oneida children were sheltered from almost all opportunities to see adults in social situations, they were probably extraordinarily naive about sex. Transition into adulthood was, therefore, more dramatically marked by knowledge of an initiation into complex marriage. Regretably, one can learn nothing from extant, public sources of how and by whom complex marriage was explained to Community girls. One Community writer mentioned that each primary school graduate came under the tutelage of a Community-appointed guardian for the transition into adulthood;[63] perhaps each guardian prepared her individual "pupil" for the realities of Community sex. Noyes himself might have instructed each girl before exercising his privilege of "first husband." Instruction by mothers was another possibility. Throughout the Community's history, one female leading member, Charlotte Noyes Miller, served as advisor to the class of young women. Possibly one of her duties was female tutelage in complex marriage. No matter from whom the girls received their instruction, they must have felt confused and puzzled by the new responsibilities of womanhood. Noyes initiated each virgin into sexual intercourse shortly after her first menses, and thereafter, from approximately ages 12-25, young women had sexual relations exclusively with much older Community men. According to one disgruntled older female member, some young women had intercourse with men daily, or even oftener.[64] By consenting to sexual "interviews" with older Community men, young women supposedly demonstrated their understanding of and cooperation with a correct Community spirit; sexual relations with older men also provided girls with spiritual tutelage in accordance with Noyes's "ascending fellowship" principle.

The other abrupt departure from the Children's House routine for girls was their work. From puberty they spent a majority of their time in the women's world of work at Oneida—home, laundry, printing office and silk spool factory. The Oneida *Circular* reported candidly that upon graduation from primary school, girls took up "household duties."[65] At this time a young woman also began to make her own clothing and possibly those of a child as well. Eventually she became "mother" to a man, mending and altering his clothing.

When Oneida girls moved into the adult world of work and sexual practices, their opportunities for education became limited to after-work hours. Formal educational instruction for young men continued, however, at least in the 1860's when the sons of the original Community members were in their twenties. Harriet Worden noted that "most of the boys continued their attendance at the school while the girls pursued their studies under special instructors, or attended the various evening classes."[66] The Oneida *Circular* of November 22, 1860, noted a school for young men ages 14-26 where they studied "reading, spelling, grammar and composition, arithmetic, algebra, and Latin." In 1862 Noyes inaugurated "an Institute with a system of professorships" for young men ages 12-20 which met 3-4 hours daily. They studied elocution, reading, spelling, geography, composition, mathematics, astronomy and languages. Noyes admonished the male scholars that they "should not consider their education finished when they had graduated from the school. . . . They could calculate to go on and become professors themselves. . . ."[67] Eventually five Community young men were sent to college, two earning degrees in medicine, two in engineering, and one in law.[68] No Community women attended college, nor did they receive formal classroom instruction after age 12. Evidently the

Community felt primary-school education adequate for women.

Shortly before her death at age 86, Polly Hayes Noyes, mother of John Humphrey Noyes, objected strenuously to the limited opportunities for young women in the Community. She wrote:

> I observe the young men in the Community are called out in various ways to new businesses and positions, and have new inducements and prospects to stimulate their activity, and I ask, is there anything like this for the girls? Is not the range of their operations very uniform and the extent of their opportunity for display of talent and genius too much confined?[69]

Perhaps Polly Hayes Noyes had in mind the fact that her grandsons Theodore Richards Noyes and Joseph Skinner were sent off to college; her granddaughters were not. Her criticism also alluded to the more stimulating work assignments available to young men. Polly Hayes Noyes correctly perceived that woman's world at Oneida constricted the abilities of young women. Though the Community printed the indomitable old woman's criticism, it did nothing to correct the inequalities she deplored. When Community girls entered womanhood, the boundaries of their existence were defined by home, work and female participation in complex marriage. An article in the Oneida *Circular* of August 11, 1873, perhaps best summarized the goals of female socialization in the Community:

> They [young women] are such a comfort to us; instead of being a trouble and a worry, they add so much beauty, harmony and happiness to our home. Obedient, industrious and enthusiastic for the Community, we have no fear for them, but everything to hope.

CONCLUSION

At Oneida, childhood appears to have been highly structured, but not oppressive, for the young. Following the strictures of Community ideology, Oneida children were not pampered or romanticized; rather they seem to have been cherished because they would someday become adult "Bible Communists" and carry on the social vision of their adult family. Boys and girls were raised and educated together until puberty; sexual distinctions among the children were present, but not particularly emphasized.

For an Oneida girl, the turning point in her life was puberty and her initiation into adult status, which included obligatory heterosexual activity, and dropping out of school into the world of women's work at Oneida. From then on, comely cooperation and "community spirit" were to be her main virtues. Through criticism sessions, evening meetings, and her relationships with leading adults, she learned that her primary responsibility was to serve God, and man, as a "helpmeet". To become a mother required patience and training in Community ideology; an Oneida woman did not control her own fertility or raise her children, were she awarded the privilege of becoming a mother. From the sketchy evidence available, the prohibition against philoprogenitiveness seems to have been the most difficult challenge to Oneida women.

FOOTNOTES

1. George Cragin, John Miller, Theodore R.Noyes, William Woolworth, Erastus Hamilton and Theodore Pitt.

2. Harriet Holton Noyes, Mary Cragin, Harriet Noyes Skinner and Charlotte Noyes Miller.

3. Oneida *Circular,* December 31, 1866. This is the Community's weekly newspaper, published continuously, 1851-1876, for distribution to the "outside world."

4. Ibid., February 21, 1870.

5. Ibid., August 18, 1873. My emphasis.

6. On occasion, membership in the Community did break up families, for example, in the instance of Mr. Herrick, "who left wife and children and a high church pulpit in New York City to come to the Community and thereafter his wife taught his children that their father was insane." P.B. Noyes, *My Father's House: An Oneida Boyhood.* (New York: Farrer and Rinehart, Inc., 1951), p. 28. Sometimes, too, some family members left the Community, and others chose to remain, e.g., Skinner, Hutchins, Mills, Worden, and Bailey. As frequently, perhaps, the Community provided a home for single parents with young children after a spouse's death, e.g., Marquis de Lafayette Worden and three daughters, Laura Burgess Smith and son, Albert Kinsley and sons. See ibid., pp. 75-76 and 26.

7. Oneida *Circular,* February 21, 1870.

8. P. B. Noyes, *My Father's House: an Oneida Boyhood,* p. 57.

9. Oneida *Circular,* November 27, 1871.

10. Barron and George Noyes Miller, eds., *Home-Talks by John Humphrey Noyes* (Oneida, N.Y.: Oneida Community, 1875), pp. 282-84.

11. Robert Allerton Parker, *A Yankee Saint: John Humphrey Noyes* and the Oneida Community (New York: G. P. Putnam's Sons, 1935), pp. 161-64.

12. *Daily Journal of the Onedia Community,* November 20, 1866.

13. Allan Estlake, *The Oneida Community: A Record of an Attempt to Carry Out the Principles of Christian Unselfishness and Scientific Race-Improvement.* (London: George Redway, 1900), pp. 33-34. "Allan Estlake" was a pseudonym for a former Oneida Community member.

14. Oneida *Circular,* September 5, 1865. In a particularly vicious attack on woman's independence, a male discussion in the Community once likened family disequilibrium to the American Civil War, referring to the Confederacy as the female half of the nation, bent on promoting discord in the country. Ibid.

15. Ibid., May 10, 1875. Emphasis in the original.

16. Ibid., October 5, 1868.

17. Ibid., April 1, 1867. My emphasis.

18. Ibid., January 29, 1863. Emphasis in the original.

19. Ibid., November 5, 1863.

20. Ibid., August 7, 1865.

21. Ibid., April 1, 1867.

22. Ibid., June 15, 1868.

23. *Daily Journal of the Oneida Community,* April 18. 1866.

24. Oneida *Circular,* June 23, 1873. See this issue for a full page of similar mothers' testimonials.

25. Ibid.

26. Ibid., October 3, 1870.

27. Ibid., May 18, 1868.

28. Ibid., December 16. 1867.

29. P. B. Noyes, *My Fathers House: An Oneida Boyhood,* p. 67.

30. Ibid., p. 65.

31. Ibid., p. 67.

32. Ibid., p. 72.

33. Oneida *Circular,* October 20, 1873.

34. Corinna Ackley Noyes, *The Days of My Youth,* (Kenwood, N.Y.: By the author, 1960), p. 16.

35. Oneida *Circular,* May, 1864.

36. C. A. Noyes, *The Days of My Youth,* p. 8.

37. Ibid., p. 5.

38. P. B. Noyes, *My Father's House: An Oneida Boyhood,* p. 70.

39. Oneida *Circular,* October 3, 1870.

40. Maren Lockwood Carden, *Oneida: Utopian Community to Modern Corporation.* (New York: Harper Torchbook, 1971), p. 63.

41. Oneida *Circular,* September 4, 1862.
42. Ibid., January 4, 1869, and May 13, 1872.
43. Constance Noyes Robertson, *Oneida Community: An Autobiography, 1851-1876.* (Syracuse, N.Y.: Syracuse University Press, 1970), pp. 331-32.
44. Harriet M. Worden, *Old Mansion House Memories. By One Brought Up in It.* (Kenwood, N.Y.: privately published, 1950; a reprint from articles written by Worden in the Oneida Circular, 1871-72), p. 80.
45. Robertson, *Oneida Community: An Autobiography,* p. 331.
46. Ibid., p. 332.
47. Ibid.
48. Ibid., p. 333.
49. Worden, *Old Mansion House Memories,* p. 80.
50. P. B. Noyes, *My Father's House: An Oneida Boyhood,* p. 100
51. Ibid., pp. 88-89.
52. Oneida *Circular, March 6, 1866.*
53. Ibid., July 14, 1873.
54. Ibid., December 1, 1873.
55. P. B. Noyes, My Father's House: An Oneida Boyhood, p. 90.
56. C. A. Noyes, *The Days of My Youth,* pp. 49-50.
57. P. B. Noyes, *My Father's House: An Oneida Boyhood,* pp. 44-45, and Oneida *Circular,* April 8, 1867.
58. P. B. Noyes, *My Father's House: An Oneida Boyhood,* p. 37.
59. Robertson, *Oneida Community: An Autobiography,* p. 312.
60. Ibid., p. 332.
61. P. B. Noyes, *My Father's House: An Oneida Boyhood,* p. 101.
62. Robertson, *Oneida Community: An Autobiography,* p. 321. Emphasis in the original.
63. Worden, *Old Mansion House Memories,* p. 60.
64. Ely Van de Warker, M.D., "A Gynecological Study of the Oneida Community," *American Journal of Obstetrics and Diseases of Women and Children,* XVII, no. 8 (August, 1884), p. 789.
65. Oneida *Circular,* October 29, 1851.
66. Worden, *Old Mansion House Memories,* p. 66.
67. Oneida *Circular,* September 4, 1862.
68. Robertson, *Oneida Community: An Autobiography,* p. 173.
69. Oneida *Circular,* June 18, 1866.

Section Two:

Passages: Growing Up and Growing Old in America

{4}

Few psychological theories are more compelling (or more confusing) than the notion of life-stages. Most of us assume that our lives are punctuated by stages of development, each with a definite beginning and ending, each bounded by an immutable time frame that separates it from the others. It is easier, however, to give these stages names, such as infancy, adolescence, adulthood, and old age, than to pinpoint either where one ends and the next begins, or how sensibilities and values that span a lifetime differ from one stage to the next.

One thing that can be said with certainty about life-stages is that their implications cannot be understood outside of an historical context. Life-stages are not universal. Modern adolescence as we know it, for example, is a product of urban-industrial culture—historians can find few traces of adolescence as a distinct stage of life before the nineteenth century. In addition, it must be kept in mind that life-stages are psychological, not biological, in character. While physical maturation is genetically programmed, the ways in which a society isolates specific aspects of the maturation process, and systematically ignores others, is not. "Old age" meant something very different in Confucian China, a society that valued the wisdom that springs from experience, than it does in contemporary America, a society that links mainstream values like social mobility and competitiveness with youth and vigor. Physically the "old" person in Confucian China resembled his counterpart in contemporary America; in terms of his social roles and the cultural implications of his stage of life he was very different.

Many factors contribute to a society's perception of the life-cycle, not the least of which is social class. In the following article, based upon interviews with contemporary parents and children, the distinguished psychologist Robert Coles describes the social, economic, and psychological worlds of the modern child born to wealth and position, Coles shows that even at a tender age the children of the rich are imbued with attitudes that distinguish them from their less fortunate age-peers: wealth is the dominant factor in their perceptions of self and others. Through his brilliant integration of the interview method and psychological insight, Coles provides us with valuable clues about the ways class differences influence the texture of life-stages.

How effectively does Coles make his case? Are all wealthy children alike? How can you account for differences between them? What is entitlement?

"How the *Other* Half Lives: Children of the Rich 1960-1980"

Robert Coles

The poor both are and are not all alike. On the one hand they struggle against the same odds—hunger and malnutrition in the worst instances, or a marginal life that poses constant threats. Yet Eskimos do not regard their poverty in the same way that Appalachian yeoman do, or Chicanos in Texas or southern California. In the four volumes that have preceded this one I have tried to show how the common social and economic vulnerability of the poor does not make for a uniform pattern of child rearing. Historical precedents, cultural experiences, religious convictions exert their influence on parents and children, make boys and girls differ in all sorts of respects, depending on where they live and who their parents are. The same holds for the well-to-do or the rich. It won't do to talk of *the* affluent ones in America (never mind the world!). It won't do to say that in our upper-middle-class suburbs, or among our wealthy, one observes clear-cut, consistent psychological or cultural characteristics. Even in relatively homogeneous suburbs, there are substantial differences in home life, in values taught, hobbies encouraged, beliefs advocated or virtually instilled.

But there are indeed distinct groups among the well-off—equivalent in their way to the various kinds of poor people. It is the obligation of someone who wants to know how children make sense of their lives—agricultural migrancy, Indian reservation life in the Southwest, the upper-income life of large homes amid ample acreage in rich towns or in wealthy urban enclaves—to document as faithfully as possible the way the common heritage of money and power affects the assumptions of individual boys and girls. Each child, however, is also influenced by certain social, racial, cultural, or religious traditions, or thoroughly idiosyncratic ones—a given *family's* tastes, sentiments, ideals, say. The issue is "class"; but the issue is not only "class."

Many of the influences, even some of the more idiosyncratic ones, that distinguish some children from others are themselves subject to side influences—a "rebound effect," one rather prosperous Illinois Mormon called it. He was anxious for me to know (just as he could not forget) that there was only so much his faith could resist. He took pains, constantly, to tell his children that he was not like his father; that he was not like his brother either, who lives in Salt Lake City and works for a bank. To live near Chicago and be a doctor, to be a Mormon living in a highly secular upper-middle-class world, was to be an exile. He felt stronger in his faith, but also weaker; he felt like his neighbors in many ways, but unlike them in critically important preferences and articles of faith.

What binds together a Mormon banker in Utah with his brother, or other co-religionists in Illinois or Massachusetts? What distinguishes such people, one from the other? Old New Orleans upper-class families are not in certain respects like families who live in, say, Wellesley Hills, Massachusetts, or Haverford, Pennsylvania, or up the hills outside San Antonio. There *are* resemblances, based on class, occupation, religion, common experiences, expectations, ideas conveyed to children. And yet, again, there are distinctions, shades of feeling and thinking, emphases of one sort or another—even within those families and well-to-do neighborhoods.

I use the word "entitlement" to describe what, perhaps, all quite well-off American families transmit to their children—and important psychological common denominator, I believe: an emotional expression, really, of those familiar, class-bound prerogatives, money and power. The word was given to me, amid much soul-searching, by the rather rich parents of a child I began to talk with almost two decades ago, in 1959. I have watched those parents become grandparents, seen what they described as "the responsibilities of entitlement" get handed down to a new generation. When the father, a lawyer and stockbroker from a prominent and quietly influential family, referred to the "entitlement" his children were growing up with, he had in mind a social rather than a psychological phenomenon: the various juries or committees that select the Mardi Gras participants in New Orleans' annual parade and celebration. He knew that his daughter was "entitled" to be invited here, to attend a dance there, to feel part of a carefully limited and sometimes self-important social scene.

He wanted, however, to go beyond that social fact; he wanted his children to feel obligated by how fortunate they were, and would no doubt always be, all things being equal—or unequal! He talked about what he had received from his parents and what he would give to his children, "automatically, without any thought," and what they too would pass on. The father was careful to distinguish between the social entitlement and "something else," a "something else" he couldn't quite define but knew he had to try to evoke if he were to be psychologically candid: "Our children have a good life ahead of them; and I think they know it now. I think they did when they were three or four, too. It's *entitlement*, that's what I call it. My wife didn't know what I was talking about when I first used the word. She thought it had something to do with our ancestry! Maybe it does! I don't mean to be snide. I just think our children grow up taking a lot for granted, and it can be good that they do, and it can be bad. It's like anything else; it all depends. I mean, you can have spoiled brats for children, or you can have kids who want to share what they have. I don't mean give away all their money! I mean be responsible, and try to live up to their ideals, and not just sit around wondering which island in the Caribbean to visit this year, and where to go next summer to get away from the heat and humidity here in New Orleans."

At the time he said no more. It was 1960, and I was interested mainly in what his son and his daughter thought about black children—and about the violence then being inflicted on a few black children brave enough and stubborn enough to walk past mobs into two elementary schools. But as months became years, I came back to that word "entitlement," especially because it was one I had heard years earlier, in Boston, when I was receiving my training in child psychiatry. "Narcisistic entitlement" was the phrase I had been taught to be familiar with, to use occasionally when speaking of a particular kind of "disturbed" child. The term could be used in place of more conventional, blunter ones that everyone else uses from time to time: a smug, self-satisfied child; or a child who thinks he (or she) owns the world, or will one day; or a self-centered child who expects a lot from just about everyone.

I recall a boy of eight I was treating in Boston, before I went South; my supervisor, a child psychoanalyst who had worked with a similar child for three years, and anticipated, alas, another year or two, at least, of thrice weekly office visits, told me that I was being naïvely hopeful, and a touch simpleminded, when I remarked upon the curiosity of the boy, his evident willingness to ask me questions about all sorts of persons, places, things—and so his capacity for engagement with the world around him. Yes, she pointed out, there was indeed a measure of that, but it was best that *we* ask questions about the nature of *his* questions. As we did, they all came back to him—to quite specific experiences he had gone through and wanted to talk about. And he had told me that, actually; he never asked a question out of intellectual interest—rather, in his words, "because I like to know what might happen next to me."

It is hard to describe the special fearfulness and sadness such a child struggles with. He was not the "ordinary" child; he was quite troubled. And I suppose the parents of such children (even if those mothers and fathers have other, relatively solid children, psychologically speaking) must be disqualified as "normal" or "average." They may be like anyone else on the street; may be rather knowing, psychiatrically—able to sense something "wrong" with a child's "behavior" and go do something about it by seeking out a doctor. But the analyst-supervisor I was myself "seeing" once a week was convinced that there was a "special narcissism," she called it, that a certain kind of parent offers a child: "Narcissism is something we all struggle with; but some people have more of it than others, and some children come from homes that have so much that all the money and possessions, all the rugs and furniture and toys and vacations and savings accounts and insurance policies come crashing on the child's head. There is a shift from narcissism to narcissistic entitlement."

I wasn't sure exactly what she meant, or how the "shift" she had mentioned did indeed take place. I know, because she is someone I still discuss psychoanalytic theory with, that she was not sure herself what the exact dimensions were of that childhood journey. But she knew even then, before there were "fields" like "social psychiatry" or "community psychiatry," that at some point a family's psychology and psychopathology engage with its social and economic life; and that when a migrant child or a ghetto child has to contend with narcissism, it will take on a certain flavor (narcissistic despair, for instance); whereas for a child who lives in a big house and whose parents have a lot and want to give a lot to their offspring, "narcissistic entitlement" may well be a possibility. The child withdraws not only into himself or herself but, by extension, into a certain world of objects, habits, and rituals—the comfortable world of a room, a home, a way of life. The child has much, but wants and expects more—only to feel no great gratitude, but a desire for yet more: an inheritance the world is expected to provide. One's parents will oblige, as intermediaries. And if underneath there lie apprehension and gloom and, not least, a strain of gnawing worthlessness, that is of no matter to many children whose "narcissistic entitlement" becomes what psychoanalytic theorists refer to as a "character trait," rather than a "symptom" that prompts a visit to a doctor. That is, the child is regarded by everyone, psychiatrists included, as "normal," as "all right," or different, but not all *that* different. One doesn't send every cocksure, greedy, self-centered child to a child psychiatrist.

In many other well-to-do homes I've visited, parents have known in their bones what child psychiatrists think and wonder as they talk with their children. Will a certain child get too much—so much that he or she runs the danger of turning away from life, forsaking people for a life of passionate involvement with objects? Less ominously, might a mild tendency in that direction become especially evident when things get tough, psychologically, for one reason or another? Will the child be willing to reach for people, and get along with them, but always with certain limits on the involvement? Often when children are four, five, and six, parents who have felt able to offer them virtually anything begin to pull back, in concern if not outright horror. A son not only has become increasingly demanding or petulant; even when he is quiet he seems to be sitting on a throne of sorts—expecting things to happen, wondering with annoyance why they don't, reassuring him that they will, or, if they haven't, shrugging his shoulders and waiting for the next event.

It was just such an impasse—not dramatic, but quite definite and worrisome—that prompted that New Orleans father to use the word "entitlement." He had himself been born to wealth, as will future generations of his family be, unless the American economic system changes drastically. But he was worried about what a lot of money can do to a person's "personality"; he uses that word as a layman, but he knows exactly what he has in mind. It isn't so much a matter of spoiling or indulging children; he is willing to let that happen, "within limits." But he knew precisely what those limits were: when the child begins to let his or her situation, the life that he or she lives, "go to the head." It is then that children begin "to act as if they have royal blood in them." And conservative though he is, for him each generation has to prove itself—not necessarily by finding new worlds to conquer or by becoming extraordinarily successful. He has wanted his children to show an interest in the world, to reach out and touch others, to develop their own initiatives, however circumscribed, undramatic, and conventional. It is those kinds of initiative he naturally finds appealing. He is rather satisfied with the life he was born to. He finds each day to be pleasant, interesting, and by his lights, quite useful. He has, however, worried at times that his children were taking *too* much for granted. When his young daughter, during a Mardi Gras season, kept *assuming* she would one day receive this honor and that honor—indeed, become a Mardi Gras queen—he realized that his notion of "entitlement" was not quite hers. *Noblesse oblige* requires a gesture toward others. Had a parent sensed the danger of what my supervisor referred to as a "shift" from "entitlement" to "narcissistic entitlement"?

He would not be the only parent to express such a concern to me in the course of my work. In homes where mothers and fathers profess no explicit reformist persuasions (to say the least!) they nevertheless worry about what happens to children who grow up surrounded by just about everything they want, virtually, on demand. And if much of the apprehension is conventional—that the child will become "spoiled"—there is an element of uneasiness that runs deeper. The parents may begin to regard spoiled behavior as but a symptom: "I don't mind if my children become a little spoiled. That's bound to happen. I worry that they will think that everything is coming to them; that they will grow up with the idea that if they're frustrated, or if they want something, then all they have to do is say a few words, and they'll have what they asked for. When they're like that, they've gone from spoiled to spoiled rotten—and beyond, to some state I don't even know how to describe."

When children are two and three they become increasingly conscious of what belongs to whom. They also become, usually, more and more willing and able to leave themselves behind, so to speak—reach out for objects as well as individuals. They develop their first friends, their first interests or regular and cherished activities. They learn too, most of them, a variety of restraints and frustrations. They must gain control of their bodies, manage without diapers, remember to empty their bladders before going to bed, and get up at night and do likewise in the bathroom rather than on the sheet and mattress. They must learn not to touch hot stoves; not to leave refrigerator doors open; not to spill things, break things, step on things; not to intrude on what belongs to others; not to confuse their prerogatives or possessions with the rights and property of parents, brothers and sisters, friends. At three and four, children from homes like those in New Orleans' Garden District have often started nursery school, have also started making visits to other homes or receiving visitors at their own homes. There are toys to share, games to play, a sandbox or a lawn or indeed a swimming pool or a paddock with its animals. All children have to struggle with themselves for the strength to offer as well as take, or to yield with tact and even a touch of gratitude what has been loaned rather than made an outright gift.

But for some children, a relative handful of the world's, such obligations and struggles are muted. Obviously it is possible for parents to have a lot of money yet avoid bringing up their children in such a way that they feel like members of a royal family. Yet even parents determined not to spoil their children often recognize what might be called the existential (as opposed to strictly psychological) aspects of their situation, and that of their children. A father may begin rather early on lecturing his children about the meaning of money; a mother may do her share by saying no, even when yes is so easy to say—but the child may well sense eventually what the parents know quite well: the difference between a voluntary posture and an utterly necessary one.

Such a child, by the age of five or six, has very definite notions of what is possible, even if not always permitted; possible because there is plenty of money that can be spent. That child, in conversation and without embarrassment or the kind of reticence and secretiveness that comes later, may reveal a substantial knowledge of economic affairs. A six-year-old girl in New Orleans knew that she would at twenty-one inherit half a million dollars. She also knew that her father "only" gave her twenty-five cents a week—whereas some friends of hers received as much as a dollar. She was vexed; she asked her parents why they were so "strict." One friend had even used the word "stingy" for the parents. The father, in a matter-of-fact way, pointed out to the daughter that she did, after all, get "anything she really wants." Why, then, the need for an extravagent allowance? The girl was won over, told her friends thereafter that it was no matter to her whether she even received an allowance; the important point was the future and what it had to offer. The friends then checked back with their parents, who were rather alarmed—that such young children were talking so freely and openly about family financial matters.

As a result the girl learned from her friends that she had disclosed what ought to be kept firmly under wraps. She decided on the basis of such declarations that her friends may well be "comfortable," but they are not as rich as her parents are or as she will on day be. They in turn explained to her that she had gone beyond the bounds of available evidence. The friends may simply have been told to keep quiet about their family's monetary status—a good idea, the girl was reminded by her parents. The girl agreed, but was not really prepared at the time to follow such advice. She had heard her parents talk with *their* parents about money matters and had been told that it is best that she, too, gradually understand what her financial situation is and will be. That being the case, she wondered out loud why it wasn't appropriate for her to share what she had learned about her future prospects with those she considered good friends. Her parents could only repeat their conviction that certain matters are quite definitely and properly kept within the confines of the family.

Such conversations between young children and their parents help consolidate in boys and girls a conviction of present and future affluence. It obviously never occurs to these children that they won't have food at some point in the near or distant future. Nor do they ever really lack for anything. There are differences in amount, and lectures and sermons may accompany parental acts of generosity. But admonitions don't modify the quite shrewd appraisal children make of what they are heir to, and don't at all diminish the sense of entitlement.

In an Appalachian mine-owner's home, for instance, a boy of seven made the following comment in 1963, after his father's mine had suffered an explosion, killing two men and injuring seriously nine others: "I heard my mother saying she felt sorry for the families of the miners. I feel sorry for them, too. I hope the men who got hurt get better. I'm sure they will. My father has called in doctors from Lexington. He wants the best doctors in all Kentucky for those miners. Daddy says it was the miners' fault; they get careless, and the next thing you know there's an explosion. It's too bad. I guess there are a lot of kids who are praying hard for their fathers. I wish God was nice to everyone. He's been very good to us. My Daddy says it's been hard work, running the mine and another one he has. It's just as hard to run a mine as it is to go down and dig the coal! I'm glad my father is the owner, though. I wouldn't want him to get killed or hurt bad down there, way underground. Daddy has given us a good life. We have a lot of fun coming up, he says, in the next few years. We're going on some trips. Daddy deserves his vacations. He says he's happy because he can keep us happy, and he does. If we want something real bad, we go tell him or Mum, and they oblige us almost all the time. That's what Daddy always says—that he's glad to oblige my sister and me!"

The father is not *always* "glad to oblige"; he can be quite stern at times, but the children have learned that his lectures have only a limited applicability to their life. Yes, there are restraints; not every request for money or a present is granted forthwith. On the other hand, their life is sufficiently comfortable to belie the parents' insistence on caution, lest there be nothing left. In fact, the lectures only seem to reinforce in the children a certain materialistic preoccupation. Having been told to make do with what they already have in such abundance, the boy and girl (and their counterparts in the homes I have visited in other parts of the United States) retreat to their respective rooms, get out their possessions, and begin to use them as well as simply gaze at them. The boy can be quite pointed and expressive about what he has—and is doing with what he has—at such moments: "I have my soldiers, and my trucks, and the tanks and the helicopters. I get them lined up. I build a fort. I have the blocks and the logs, and I make the fort strong. I have my helicopter pad. I make sure the pad is protected by tanks and some men with machine guns. Some terrorists might come and try to attack, and destroy the pad and the helicopter. It's best to keep a few planes in the air, to scout. You have to keep your eyes open, or there will be a surprise attack. I surround the fort with men, and I have these bushes and trees, and I put men behind them. And I have some men on horses."

He stops and look at what he has done. He is rather proud of himself. He has thought at times of working toward a military career, but he knows that he "most likely" will follow in his father's footsteps. There is a profitable coal company to run and his father has told him that, in the boy's words, "coal has a big future now because there's an energy problem." That observation prompts him to worry about his fort. Does *it* have enough energy or might there be one day be a shortage? No, he is sure that his fort will be able to manage successfully. There is a large stack of wood set aside in his stockade. As for the tanks, helicopters, airplanes, they will not lack fuel; there is an oil well nearby. And in the event that should give out, the boy is certain that oil can be flown in or, if necessary, a "secret pipeline" could be built, just in case some disaster should come upon the airfield-landing pad.

His sister has on some occasions become provocative, even truculent. She has asked him, after watching him "declare war" on an unseen enemy, why he always wins. He has replied that the answer is quite simple; he has the best army. She will occasionally express her misgivings: there might be, just *might* be, an army that could overcome his army, with its nineteenth-century fort and twentieth-century military hardware. The boy replies with scorn that his sister is being far too literal minded. Anyway, America has never lost a war, he knows for sure, and he is an American and does not intend to lose one either. Nor has his father, when brought into the argument later, been anything but encouraging. True, Vietnam was "a mess"; but the country was never "really determined" to win—and maybe never should have involved itself in such a struggle, waged in "distant jungles." The sister has by then lost all interest in her younger (by one year) brother's "game."

The boy is not obsessed with the war game, either. He has many other opportunities to play—other games or, more personally, friends to have over, to go visit. When he plays the war game with them, however, there is invariably a battle of wits, a stalemate. The boy and his friends are tireless in the resourcefulness they summon to their encounters. If necessary, they find themselves in possession of atomic bombs, supersonic planes, surprise tunnels, magical weapons of all kinds, secret supply bases, hidden contingents of men. Eventually, they each declare the other "a winner." The boy realizes: "I know there has to be a losing side. My sister is right. You can't win all the time. But she doesn't like to lose, either. She's always saying her guinea pig is the prettiest, and she says she can ride her bike faster than anyone. I hope I'll get a five-speed bike soon; as soon as I'm a little taller, I'll get one. Then you can really go zoom, zoom down the roads. They say that when I'm grown up, we'll be landing on the moon all the time and we'll be landing on the planets—Mars, for sure. This country will do it! Maybe I could be an astronaut for a while, and then come back and help Daddy in his business. He says he may buy a couple more mines, and by the time I'm out of college, there will be a lot to do. He says I should plan to be a lawyer, because it really helps you, if you have a business, to know how to go to court and protect yourself. The unions want to interfere a lot, and Daddy has to fight them. He has to give some ground, but he's the boss, and they can't push too hard or he'll close up his mines. Then they'd all be out of work! And Daddy could hire some other miners. There are a lot of people who would be glad to get a job!"

So it goes: an abundance of energy for his fort and air force base and an abundance of workers for his father's mines. Abundance is his destiny, he has every reason to believe. He may even land on the stars. Certainly he has traveled widely in this country. He associates the seasons with travel, among other events. In winter, for instance, there is a trip South, to one or another Caribbean island. Winters can be long and hard in Appalachia, and a respite is invigorating—and "healthy." The boy watches his father exercise, hears his mother talk about certain foods, and remarks upon something else that has to do with his future: he may well live to be over a century old. Why not?

His parents are not health faddists, or unusually self-preoccupied: given exercise, a careful diet, and medical progress, one will do (in the father's words) "right well." As an additional boost to the family's collective health, a sauna has been installed, and the children are entranced with it. They also are preoccupied with their two dogs, and their other animals—the guinea pigs, hamsters, rabbits, chickens. There is always someone in the house, a maid, a handyman. Still, it is sad to say good-bye. Now, if the family owned a plane, the animals could come along on those trips!

The boy doesn't really believe that his father ever will own a Lear jet; yet, at moments he can imagine himself wrong. And he can construct a fantasy: suddenly an announcement, most likely at breakfast, of a "surprise." It is a familiar sequence. The boy has come to associate breakfast with good news. What is ahead for the day? When does a certain vacation start? During one breakfast the father announced that he had a surprise. The children were all ears. So was their mother; she knew of no forthcoming surprise. The father paused, waited for a bit of suspense to build up, then made his announcement: a new car—a red MG, a fast car that takes curves well and seats only two, in which he would take his wife and children for rides, one at a time.

Yet the boy had apparently been hoping for another kind of surprise: "I woke up and it was very funny, I remembered that I'd just had this dream. In it I was walking through the woods with Daddy, and all of a sudden there was an open field, and I looked, and I saw a hawk, and it was circling and circling. I like going hunting with Daddy, and I thought we were hunting. But when I looked at him, he didn't have his gun. Then he pointed at the hawk, and it was coming down. It landed ahead of us, and it was real strange—because the hawk turned into an airplane! I couldn't believe it. We went toward the plane, and Daddy said we could get a ride any time we wanted, because it was ours; he'd just bought it. That's when I woke up, I think. I even forgot about the dream until I looked at my fort and the airplanes, and then I remembered the dream, and once I remembered it, I didn't forget it again."

Dreams evoke a social as well as psychological reality. Dreams show what a child can hope for, unashamedly expect. It so happens that among rich children one day's apparently fatuous, excessive fantasy or dream can turn into the next day's actuality. Four years after that boy had dreamed that his father owned a plane, the father got one. The boom of the 1970s in the coal fields made his father even richer. The boy was of course eager to go on flying trips; eager also to learn to fly. The family owned a horse farm by then, near Lexington, Kentucky, and when the boy and girl were not flying, they were riding. The girl learned to jump well, the boy to ride quite fast. At thirteen he dreamed (by day) of becoming an astronaut or of becoming the manager of his father's horse farm or of going to the Air Force Academy and afterward becoming a "supersonic pilot."

He would never become a commercial pilot, however; and his reasons were interesting: "I've gone on a lot of commercial flights, and there are a lot of people on board, and the polot has to be nice to everyone, and he makes all these announcements about the seat belts, and stuff like that. My dad's pilot was in the air force, and then he flew commercial. He was glad to get out, though. He says you have to be like a waiter; you have to answer complaints from the customers and apologize to them, just because the ride gets bumpy. It's best to work for yourself, or work for another person, if you trust him and like him. If you go commercial, like our pilot says, you're a servant. You can't really speak your mind. I'd like to fly, but I'm worried about going into the air force. Our pilot says it can be fun, or it can be murder, depending on your superior officer. If I got a bad one, I guess I'd just quit. They can't keep you in forever against your will."

He has only confidence about the future, no real sense of danger. At times he talks (at thirteen) as if he could simultaneously hold down several jobs. He would run the family horse farm. He would take part in any number of races and hunts. He would also fly his own plane. He would learn how to parachute; he might even become a professional parachutist. He met one at a fair, and found the man not only brave, but "real nice to talk to." In more restrained (realistic?) moments, he forgets the horse farm, forgets airplanes or just plain air; he talks about law school—the places his father would like him to race to, land upon. When only an eighth-grade student he imagined himself, one day, owning an airplane, flying it back and forth from law school (at the University of Kentucky) to his father's horse farm, some fifty miles away.

He has never had any patience for lines, for traffic jams, for crowded stores. Many of the children I have worked with are similarly disposed; they do not like large groups of people in public places—in fact, have been taught the distinct value not only of privacy but the quiet that goes with being relatively alone. Some of the children are afraid of those crowds, can't imagine how it would be possible to survive them. Of course, what is strange, unknown, or portrayed as unattractive, uncomfortable, or just to be avoided as a nuisance can for a given child become a source of curiosity, even an event to be experienced at all costs. An eight-year-old girl who lived well outside Boston, even beyond its suburbs, on a farm, wanted desperately to go to the city and see Santa Claus—not because she believed in him, but because she wanted to see "those crowds" she had in fact seen on television. She got her wish, was excited at first, then quite disappointed, and ultimately made rather uncomfortable. She didn't like being jostled, shoved, pushed, and ignored when she protested. She was only too glad when her mother suggested that they had gone through quite enough. Yes, they had, the daughter agreed. Soon they were in a cab, then on a commuter train. The latter was going to be the limit for the girl thereafter; if she would venture into the world, the train would be its microcosm. She would travel by train to Boston, then turn right around and travel back—unless, of course, she were going to a restaurant or an art gallery or to her parents' club. In those places one is not overcome by people who shout, and step on the feet of others, and ignore any protests made.

A week after the girl had gone through her Boston "adventure"(as she had called the trip *before* she embarked upon it), each student in her third-grade was asked to draw a picture in some way connected to the Christmas season, and the girl obliged eagerly. She drew Santa Claus standing beside a pile of packages, presents for the many children who stood near him. They blended into one another—a mob scene. Watching them but removed from them was one child, bigger and on a higher level—suspended in space, it seemed, and partially surrounded by thin but visible line. The girl wrote on the bottom of the drawing "I saw Santa Claus." She made it quite clear what she had intended to portray: "He was standing there, handing out these gifts. They were all the same, I think, and they were plastic squirt guns for the boys and little dolls for the girls. I felt sorry for the kids. I asked my mother why kids wanted to push each other, just to get that junk. My mother said a lot of people just don't know any better. I was going to force my way to that Santa Claus and tell him to stop being so dumb! My mother said he was probably a drunk, trying to make a few dollars, so he could spend it in a bar nearby that evening! I don't want to be in a store like that again. We went up to a balcony and watched, and then we got out of the place and came home. I told my mother that I didn't care if I ever went to Boston again. I have two friends, and they've never been in Boston, and they don't want go to there, except to ride through on the way to the airport. . . ."

With none of the other American children I have worked with have I heard such a continuous and strong emphasis put on the "self." In fact, other children rarely if ever think about themselves in the way children of well-to-do and rich parents do—with insistence, regularity, and, not least, out of a learned sense of obligation. These privileged ones are children who live in homes with many mirrors. They have mirrors in their rooms, large mirrors in adjoining bathrooms. When they were three or four they were taught to use them; taught to wash their faces, brush their teeth, comb their hair. Personal appearance matters and becomes a central objective from such children. A boy of eight expresses his rebelliousness by clinging to sloppy clothes, but leaves the house every day for school in a neat and well-fitted uniform. A good number of these children wear them—shirts or sweaters with a school's name and/or insignia on them. Even when the child relaxes, comes home, and changes into "old" clothes, there is an air of decisiveness about the act—and certainly, the issue is one of choice: to wear *this*, or *that*; to look a particular way, in keeping with a particular mood, time of day, event.

The issue also is that of the "self"—its display, its possibilities, its cultivation and development, even the repeated use of the word. A ten-year-old boy who lives in the outermost part of Westchester County made this very clear. I had originally met him because his parents, both lawyers, were active in the civil rights movement. His father, a patrician Yankee, very much endorsed the students who went South in the early 1960s and, nearer to home, worked on behalf of integrated schools up North. His own children, however, attended private schools—a source of anguish to both the father and the son, who do not lend themselves easily to a description that only emphasizes the hypocritical element in their lives.

The boy knew that he also *would* be (as opposed to wanted to be!) a lawyer. He was quick to perceive and acknowledge his situation, and as he did so he brought himself (his "self") right into the discussion: "I don't want to tell other kids what to do. I told my father I should be going to the public schools myself. Then I could say anything. Then I could ask why we don't have black kids with us in school. But you have to try to do what's best for your *own* life, even if you can't speak up for the black people. When I'm grown up, I'll be like my father; I'll help the black people all I can. It's this way: first you build *yourself* up. You learn all you can. Later, you can *give of yourself*. That's what Dad says: you can't help others until you've learned to help *yourself*. It's not that you're being selfish. People say you're selfish, if you're going to a private school and your parents have a lot of money. We had a maid here, and she wasn't right in the head. She lost her temper and told Daddy that he's a phony, and he's out for *himself* and no one else, and the same goes for my sister and me. Then she quit. Daddy tried to get her to talk with us, but she wouldn't. She said that's all we ever do—talk, talk. I told Daddy she was contradicting herself; because she told me a few weeks ago that I'm always doing something, and I should sit down and talk with her. But I didn't know what to say to her! I think she got angry with me because I was putting on my skis for crosscountry skiing, and she said I had too much, that was my problem. I asked her where the regular skis were, and she said she wouldn't tell me, even if she knew! It's too bad, what happened to her.

"I feel sorry for her, though. Like my sister said, it's no fun to be a maid! The poor woman doesn't look very good. She weighs too much. She's only forty, my mother thinks, but she looks as if she's sixty, and is sick. She should take better care of herself. She said my sister and I make big messes in the bathroom. But that's because we *use* the bathroom! And her breath—God, it's terrible. She isn't as clean as she should be. My mother wanted to get her some deodorant, but we were afraid she'd just blow up at us. But she did anyway. So it didn't make any difference! Like my Dad said, it's too bad about her; she didn't know how to take care of herself and now she's thrown away this job, and she told my mother last year that it was the best one she'd ever had, so she's her own worst enemy. I wonder what she'll think when she looks at herself in the mirror and tries to figure out what to do next."

He was no budding egotist. If anything, he was less self-centered, at ten, than many other children of his community or others like it. He was willing to think about, at least, others less fortunate than himself—the maid, and black people in general. True, he would often repeat uncritically his father's words, or a version of them. But he was trying to respond to his father's wishes and beliefs as well as his words. It was impossible for him, no matter how compassionate his nature, to conceive of life as other's live it—the maid, and yes, millions of children his age, who don't look in the mirror very often and may not even own one; who don't worry about what is worn, and how one looks, and what is said and how one sounds, and what is done (in the bathroom) and how one smells. . . .

All children struggle when very young—starting at a little under a year, in fact—to distinguish between themselves and their parents. They begin to realize, at two and three, that it is *they* who exist—individuals who crawl and walk and make noises and talk. As they separate, to a degree, from their mothers, especially then, at two or three, they first know loneliness. Certainly, thereafter, for most children, there are reattachments to the mother, new attachments to other persons—and to things. But the child turns inward too upon occassion, makes an effort to find comfort and even pleasure in a newfound solitariness. Freud, at one point, referred to "the purified pleasure ego"—by which he meant a child's delight in the various excitements or satisfactions he or she can manage to find. I recall a four-year-old boy in one home I visited, not far from that of the girl quoted just above, who slid up and down a wonderfully solid, circular staircase, shouting me, me, me; he was in love with the dizzying speed, with the feeling of control and power he had—with himself.

Later on, at five and six, such a child becomes quite conscious of rights and wrongs, of what ought to be done to please parents and teachers, not to mention one's own developing conscience. Psychoanalysts describe the "idealized parent image"—the part of a child's mind that holds up examples, insists upon directions. The child absorbs from significant persons his or her notions of what matters and how he or she should in general be trying to live—and tries to go along. The "you" that the girl mentioned above at age ten—a summary, almost, of which belongings had become part of her "self"—was preceded by the earlier "you" comprehended at the age of six: "I'd like to do good in school, and learn to ski, and ride my bike fast, and get to make real tasty cookies with the maid, and then I'll be good, and people will say, she's doing everything she should be doing, and I'll say that to myself. When I'm finished brushing my teeth, they'll be clean, and my mother will soon be upstairs and check me out, and I'll say to myself: you're doing okay. And a few minutes later my mother says the same thing: 'You're doing okay!'"

That child has had ample opportunities—beyond using a toothbrush well—to prove herself, as well as find pleasure in competence. She has been taught tennis and swimming by coaches, cooking by a maid, riding by her mother. The girl has also learned how to draw and paint, play the piano, "do" ballet. She has gone abroad often, has mastered words, used her own passport. She has become acquainted with forms of etiquette, with new protocols. She knows when to defer, when to speak up. She knows how to recognize various songs, symphonies operatic pieces. She knows how to walk the corridors of museums, recognize the work of certain artists. And too, she has acquired some of the psychological judgment good hostesses have: who is like whom, who belongs near whom at the table, who will be a "disaster" with whom. She used that word sometimes, when eleven and twelve, and in doing revealed more than a "prepubescent" affinity for a way of talking, or a superficial cleverness about people. In fact, she was indicating something significant about her sense of *herself*.

One such "disaster" was her mother's much younger cousin, and the girl knew why: "She's sloppy. She's always been sloppy. She speaks sloppy. She had a harelip, and that was what ruined her. The parents didn't take her to the right doctor, and the girl became shy, and she didn't want to talk to anyone, and when she was a teenager she became even worse. She just stayed in her room a lot. Then she got religious, in a weird way. She was always praying. My mother says they should have sent her to a doctor. She decided to become a nun, I think. She wanted to convert and be a Catholic, and then be a nun. They talked her out of that. She came to life a little. She began to go out and meet people. Then she met this guy, and he was a music teacher, and he was poor, and they fell in love, and they wanted to get married. He was a disaster, my mother says. He could barely open his mouth, and he didn't know which fork to use, and he wore real funny clothes, and he had a bad complexion, and the worst case of dandruff my mother had ever seen. He just sat there, and it didn't even seem to bother him that he didn't talk. But my mother's cousin was a disaster, too. She was just an oddball, that's what. They got married, and my mother says they've been good for each other."

"They would be poor now, if it wasn't that my mother's aunt left them some money. I think they have enough to get by. We see them sometimes; they come to visit my grandmother. We have to keep a straight face. We can't laugh. That would be bad. You should feel sorry for people who aren't as fortunate as you are. If you don't, then you are rude and you don't have charity. If you're not nice to someone, you've lost. You sink down to the other person's level. That's what Daddy tells us, and he gets angry if we don't pay attention. He says we've got a responsibility to show good manners at all times. I'd never call someone a 'disaster' in front of him; at least while we're having supper. Sometimes he'll be having a drink, and then even he will call someone a fool or *no good*; thats *his* way of calling someone he knows and doesn't like a 'disaster'. . . ."

For those "lucky," a sense of entitlement develops—the merger of what they have learned would be "ideal" and what they have actually experienced, into an ongoing attitude toward the world. Let others feel diminished, impeded, burdened; or let them long for a different kind of life, knowing all too clearly by the age of six or seven the difference between a castle in Spain and a ranch house in Levittown, or a ghetto tenement, or a tenant farmer's shack. For privileged children, there is every reason to feel entitlement. But let us not forget that entitlement is perfectly compatible with doubts, misgiving, despair. A child can feel—being realistic—entitled to a certain kind of life and yet have other reasons to be confused or hurt. Even schizophrenics experience the distinctions that have to do with class and caste, race and place of residence. . . .

For some of these children, the privileged life presents a danger of what clinicians have referred to as "secondary narcissism"—the "narcissistic entitlement" I mentioned at the beginning of this section. However, on the evidence of the privileged children I have come to know, I would emphasize the possibility that a feeling of "entitlement" may develop in a child without the potentially treacherous development of an excessively narcissistic tone. When a feeling of "entitlement" becomes "narcissistic," it has departed from what James Agee called "human actuality." Suppose [a] girl whose father had taken ill began, for her own reasons, to imagine that her father's illness would be associated with some extraordinary development: a call to the theater or television as a young actress; a medal of honor awarded by the school she attended; a party given her as an expression of her popularity. Suppose that girl, alternatively, expected the surgeon to cure her father, no matter *what* was discovered upon operating. Suppose that girl began crying constantly before her father entered the hospital; and did so petulantly, plaintively, as if less interested in her father's troubles than her own. At that point her narcissism would have taken its form from her private experiences, although the same child in other moments might lose her despairing self-centeredness. The point to emphasize is the mind's capacity to appreciate the reality of a certain kind of life. The mind can of course undercut a good thing, make a bad thing even worse, or make the best of it.

It is important that a privileged child's normal sense of "entitlement" be distinguished not only from pathological narcissism, but from the more common phenomenon known as being "spoiled." It is a matter of degree; "spoiled" children are self-centered all right, petulant and demanding—but not saddled with the grandiose illusions (or delusions) clinicians have in mind when using the phrase "narcissistic entitlement." The rich, the "well-to-do" are all too commonly charged with producing spoiled children. Yet one sees spoiled children everywhere, among the very poor as well as the inordinately rich. A child can be spoiled by a mother's attitude. What the child is "given" can be called excessive instinctual leeway or, in everyday words, however politicized in recent years, "permissive indulgence." I remember a migrant mother who knew precisely and uncannily what she was doing "wrong"—knew, indeed, to call it all "wrong." She told me one day that she had given birth to a particular child with more pain than usual and had been in lower spirits than ever before in her life during the first months of that child's life. When the baby began to notice the mother and the world, start crawling and separating himself from her, she felt a fierce desire within herself, expressed with unforgettable intensity, "to let that boy have anything he wants, anything he can lay his hands on." She was careful, for all her lack of education and her troubled spirits, to qualify herself. She moved quickly, immediately, from "anything he wants" to "anything he can lay his hands on." She knew that in the first or second year of life the child would have all he could do to reach and hold on to what he wanted.

But soon enough a child begins to see things that others have; on a rented, only half-working television set the migrant child saw a lot, and looked around the room and realized a lot. His was no blessed life! He continued, however, to want to take what little he could get. And of course children (or adults) can want things that are psychological in lieu of what is "material." They can become demanding, possessive, insistent, if allowed to be. They can compete with others for attention, push hard against others who try to assert themselves. They can make every effort to obtain center stage at all times. The migrant mother developed, deep within her hurt and sad self, a pride about her child and his stubborn, indulged, expropriative, loud-mouthed, and at times impossibly egotistical behavior.

⁂5⁂ *An enduring myth of the twentieth-century is that adolescents, especially males, are compelled by age-specific needs to congregate with their peers, blindly follow the dictates of the peer group, defy parental values and, consequently, create disciplinary problems for parents and school authorities. In novels, films, and scholary tracts the modern youth has often been portrayed as an uncritical follower of peer group-inspired fads in music, fashion, speech, and sexual mores.*

In this important article Paula Fass demonstrates that conformity to peer group values—at least in college fraternities during the 1920s—was less a result of biological urges than a consequence of social necessity. Fass argues that as Amercian society became economically complex and ethnically and socially diverse, it was impossible for the individual family to adequately prepare its children for the unexpected shifts in social perspective and economic prospects that inevitably accompany social diversity and industrial complexity. The family was too isolated and powerless to protect its young from, and prepare them for, the only certainty characteristic of modern life—uncertainty. The peer group, according to Fass, assumed, acted as an intermediary between the youth and society, and helped him adopt to the pressures and norms of modern life. The peer group, in short, assumed an important role traditionally accorded to the family.

What are the implications of Fass's thesis? Is the peer group bound to become stronger and the family weaker in modern society?

The World of Youth:
The Peer Society of the 1920's

Paula Fass

In the widening cracks of the social surface, a dense forest was growing up in the early twentieth century. At first only a shadow between the changing experiences of childhood and adulthood, youth blossomed into a full-grown experience in the 1920's. What was still in the popular imagination a mystical amalgam of fact and fancy had rapidly become a serious undertaking for the young. A tangle of work and play, career preparation, and mating games, the practice of youth became in the twenties a fully structured, directed, and effective social act. Observers saw it as a microcosm for good or ill, of America re-creating herself. And so it was. For youth incorporated the changes that were vividly but still strangely ushering in a new era.

Youth was, however, more than a microcosm. It was a social product made possible, even necessary, by those changes which historians have variously called the industrialization, modernization, or rationalization of American life. What the society experienced in large terms as a maturing economy, an urbanized geography, and a nationalized culture—all bewildering and threatening to those who remembered when things were otherwise—individuals born in the new century experienced on a more intimate (but no less significant) level in the changing experience of growing up. Advanced schooling, career choices, sexual anxieties, marriage decisions, political and social self-definition are all modern problems we have come to associate with a hybrid stage of life between family protection and adult autonomy, often called adolescence, but much better expressed in the elastic word "youth." Youth is an old term. But in the sense in which it means neither child nor adult but something strategically in between, it is as modern as the problems and pleasures with which it is associated.

Youth did not, of course, spring up simply because the need for it existed. It developed because the society gave it room to grow as institutions were reshaped to modern dimensions. As the family retreated to the private arena of emotion, two institutions—the school and the peer group—came to define the social world of middle-class youth. Neither was new in the 1920's, but each became more significant in the context of the changes in the family and the larger society. Together these institutions effected the transition from the family, where personal identity was formed, to the society, where social identity was expressed.[1] Between the two, the experience of youth took hold and took shape.

The role of the school in an urban industrial society is well known. Providing technical skills and training in social ideals and expectations, the school introduces the young to the material facts and social values of modern existence. Less well understood and far less commonly credited with importance in socializing the young is the adolescent peer group. But the two are profoundly related. For middle-class youths, going to school means going to school with peers and taking part with peers in a variety of formal and informal school-linked activities. A many faceted experience, modern education must be seen as a whole, as a social as well as, if not more than, an intellectual process.

Contemporary observers in the twenties rarely grasped the significant part peers played in directing individuals toward responsible adult behavior. Lay observers found them disturbing and threatening; professionals scarcely had room for them in a model of family practice which swallowed up all the significant features of child life in the concept of personality. But more recent sociological literature firmly places peer groups in the larger context of contemporary society. S. N. Eisenstadt especially has described the crucial role peers play in mediating the problems faced by individuals growing up in advanced industrial societies.[2] Unlike many sociologists in the twenties and thirties, Eisenstadt sees the transition from affectionate, responsive family life to a responsible adulthood in an impersonal, performance-geared society not as a smooth interpenetration but as a difficult confrontation. That confrontation, Eisenstadt contends, is softened through adolescent peer groups that provide many of the emotional supports of the family, especially the security of group identification and approbation, while they train the young to respond to extrapersonal performance standards similar to those that function in the larger, less personal social environment. Thus, the peer group provides emotional satisfactions in exchange for responsible action. It weans the adolescent from the freely given affection of the family and gradually introduces him to the demands of social roles.

By the 1920's, peers were already facilitating the transition from family nurture to social performance for middle-class adolescents. Reared in secure affectionate family environments where performance demands were minimal and emotional security freed from role specificity, young men and women engaged in a rich peer life at universities and colleges which was helping them to adjust to a new social environment. At the same time, the structure and mores of peer life on the campus helped to create the first modern American youth culture, a culture that was fed by the larger culture but that was also distinct and separate. What was happening to college youths was, of course, only one subset of youth experiences. In high schools, at work, and on the streets, peers were helping to lead individual youths into social maturity. But peer life at colleges was dense, isolated, and middle-class. The evidence is rich here, and it permits the historian to examine varieties of experience that the street corner rarely leaves behind. It also permits us to observe closely both the process of adjustment and the effects of peer influence on attitudes and behavior among a critical segment of the population. College students were a growing elite who would graduate to work and play, marry and vote in twentieth-century style. They also established patterns that both in youth and in adulthood others would soon follow, for better or worse, throughout much of the twentieth century.

Peer influence had grown in the interstices between older institutions and in response to new industrial and social conditions. And by the 1920's, the network of peer relations on the college campus had become a youth society—a mature and complex institution that took its place along with other radical new features of twentieth-century culture. Youth life in college had congealed into a distinct and identifiable social experience, still limited to the few in the twenties but already etching a pattern which would soon bite into the experience of more and more Americans.

Life for most students revolved around peer concern, activities, and values. Recalling his own experiences at the University of Chicago in 1919, Vincent Sheean proposed that the "social system of the undergraduate world" was made up of "a couple of thousand young nincompoops, whose ambition in life was to get into the right fraternity or club, go to the right parties, and get elected to something or other."[3] While Sheean's description of typical ambition was not far from the mark, the society he was attempting to describe was considerably more disciplined than the chaos of two thousand individual youths jockeying for position would suggest.

The actual structure of the campus society had little to do with the divisions and definitions used by the administration, such as academic class, course of study, or competitive standing. Rather it was based on residence, organizational affiliation, extra-curricular involvement, and behavioral conformity to peer standards. The administrative structure was a kind of progressive escalator from freshmen orientation to commencement that students automatically ascended on fulfilling academic requirements. The peer society had different criteria. The peer social structure can be visualized as a large circle, at the center of which were the fraternities and sororities or in the case of Harvard and Princeton, the eating clubs.[4] Often called the "organized," these students composed from 30% to 40% of the student body, with some variation by institution. Within this core group was a nucleus of the most prestigious and influential fraternities, usually the oldest ones on campus, and almost always those with national affiliation.

Tangential to the large mass circle were a number of much smaller circles representing closely knit groups of students with peculiar orientations or strong commitments shared by their members but generally outside or contrary to the interests of the mass of students. Usually formed around a specific interest, like religion, politics, or art, which members considered more important than being a "regular guy," these groups evolved an eccentric style different from that of the peer society.[5] Although these "fringe groups" powerfully controlled their own members, they had little influence on campus behavior, which usually responded to the centripetal force of fraternity standards. Those with strong religious convictions formed one such group on most college campuses and were normally attached to the campus YMCA and YWCA which sponsored social functions like dances and mixers, as well as church gatherings and Bible discussion groups. But while the Y's social functions were often attended by many students, the real church group was a small, highly motivated minority. At Syracuse University, for example, only about 5% of the students could be so characterized. The true Association loyalists were not liked by the general run of campus opinion, especially by the fraternities, because Y activists were considered overly earnest, uncomfortably committed, and self-righteous. "Many of the finest men on the campus will have nothing to do with the Association," one student leader at a large university volunteered, "because of this false emphasis" (self-righteousness).[6] The religious fringes and other such peripheral groups developed standards and ethics of their own. One of these appears to have been a high valuation of industry in scholarship, and there was also some tendency during the 1920's for many students with strong religious convictions to be committed to pacifism and to demonstrate pronounced political awareness of and concern for issues like war, race, and labor, which was not characteristic of the college world generally.[7]

The heart of the peer society lay in the network of fraternities and sororities that controlled group life on the campus. Prominent in all the major campus leadership positions, fraternity members controlled and directed the network of extra-curricular and social functions and through them set the standards in clothes, speech, amusements, and attitudes that the mass of the students (often called "barbs" for barbarians or non-Greeks) emulated.

How the fraternities gained this critical role on the American campus of the 1920's is part of the story of the expansion and development of American higher education. Fraternity influence is rooted in the many factors that changed the American colleges from elite academies to centers of mass education. And the growth of fraternity power paralleled the larger social experience of which this expansion was part. It sprouted at that juncture when a culture based on parochial communities was transformed into a mass society national in scale and increasingly unified and diverse. The fraternities were a centralizing force that cut across older fragmenting forms of campus identification like school class and replaced parochial campus rituals with collegiate style and active organizational participation. Through their emphasis on personal style and institutional activity they transformed individual campuses into sub-communities of a nationwide student culture.

Fraternities had existed on the American campus since the first chapter of Kappa Alpha was established at Union College in 1825. Founded as secret societies that incurred the suspicion of the faculty, they led a precarious existence and were insignificant as social organizations prior to the Civil War. Since few had lodges of their own, they used college facilities for their meetings. After the Civil War, they expanded rapidly, and the number of chapters grew. In the 1870's they began to establish their own lodges for meetings, and a few built student residences for members as well. This expansion took place during a period of increased student freedom as faculties, emulating European attitudes that permitted students greater latitude for self-determination in social and academic matters, released students from the once stringent supervision that obtained in American academies.[8] The student social organizations took over much of the social regulation relinquished by the faculty.

In 1883 there were already 505 fraternity chapters with a total of 67,941 active members and 16 chapters of women's sororities with 2038 members. By 1897 the fraternities had an estimated $2,660,000 worth of property. As fraternities grew during the 1880's and 1890's students organized more and more extra-curricular and social functions at the university in response to the increased independence granted to them. The fraternities, as tightly coordinated organizations, began to emerge as important social centers of student life and supported the new campus activities. The fraternities sponsored inter-organizational competitions in such things as athletics and held an increasing number of social affairs, like dances, dinners, teas, and smokers for their members.[9] They were ready-made organizations that could now take advantage of the new freedom for student initiative and for student self-discipline.

The important period of fraternity expansion did not come until the twentieth century, however, when, in response to ever larger numbers of students, fraternities grew rapidly. University administrations turned to fraternities for the housing and eating facilities which they offered and for which the schools had inadequate provision. Alumni, eager to highlight the prestige and standing of their college clubs, contributed heavily to expanding the facilities of these institutions. The most marked increase in fraternity membership and in the expansion of facilities took place in the decade of the twenties. In 1912 there were 1560 national fraternity and sorority chapters. The surging increase in enrollments during the twenties caused the number of chapters to more than double to 3900 in 1930. Fraternity building mushroomed. Fed by the worsening housing shortage on campus, the total number of fraternity houses increased from 774 in 1920 to 1874 in 1929. The value of reported property increased five-fold in ten years, reaching an estimated value of $90,000,000 in 1929.[10]

In the twenties, the demand for fraternities became so great that many local fraternities with no national affiliation were founded, and existing fraternities expanded the size of chapters. Whereas in the latter nineteenth century most chapters had from 10 to 15 members, this increased to 20 to 25 immediately prior to the war and often to 35 to 40 in the twenties. In many schools, especially the large state universities like Illinois, students and administrations consciously fostered an increase in the number of college fraternities. At Illinois, in the short period between 1918 and 1921, ten new sorority chapters were sponsored. The degree to which schools were "organized" is suggested by the fact that at Illinois, with a student population of about 10,000, there were 80 fraternities and 30 sororities. At Minnesota, with a student body of 7130, there were 67 academic and professional fraternities and 29 sororities. At the University of Michigan there were 93 fraternities and sororities.[11] The proportion of students who belonged to fraternities and sororities of the national or local variety varied from campus to campus. Usually, about 40% of the students belonged to the organizations, but the figure could vary from a scant one-third to a large two-thirds of the student body. By 1930, 35% of all students were fraternities or sororities. In most cases there was a somewhat larger proportion of men than of women in the organizations. Considerable variation in student membership in fraternities also existed between schools in the university complex; usually more students in the newly affiliated schools like commerce and business, rather than those in liberal arts, belonged.[12]

By the twentieth century the fraternities had already accumulated the prestige of being at the center of college life. Moreover, the fraternities now offered a ready mode of campus identity. As the campuses grew in size and complexity, it was no longer possible either to know or to be known by the majority of students in one's academic class. In the nineteenth century, the primary mode of differentiating the student body socially was by class—freshman, sophomore, junior, senior. Each class had rituals and identifying clothes, insignia, and well-defined customs for relating to superiors and inferiors in the academic class hierarchy. Most social events were organized by class, and there were inter-class activities like rushes, athletic meets, and dinners. Many of the traditions went back to the early days of the college in America, and some no doubt had medieval roots. Class affiliation was the primary mark of belonging, so class traditions carried an importance which practically disappeared in the twenties, except for some remaining rituals concerning freshman initiation.[13] In the twenties, the loss of class spirit was frequently lamented in the college papers, and the academic class rituals were everywhere on the decline as real regulators of student conduct. The size of classes precluded a meaningful identification with one's academic peers and the staged rituals between classes lost their effectiveness in controlling peer relations. It was, for example, almost impossible for the sophomore class as a unit any longer to keep the whole of the freshman class under vigilant supervision so that they in turn would maintain their defined position of subservience and learn the college traditions. The same was true of the traditional relations between the other classes. By the 1920's, all that remained of a once functioning social system were some superficial rites, especially those concerning freshmen. But the substance of most rites and the significance of class affiliation were gone. There was too little initial similarity in the school population for a really viable sense of affiliation to result from belonging to an academic rank alone, and the traditions were not strong enough to create a unity out of this diversity, as was their purpose. Repeated attempts to revive the system in the name of "tradition" and "spirit" failed at most universities.[14]

The more intimate fraternity group could, however, provide just such supervision and control over the initiation of new students into college life. The spirit which had attached itself to class affiliation devolved upon the fraternities by the twenties. The fraternities, maintaining the rituals of college life that had fallen away as school populations increased, became the watchdogs of campus mores and were by the twenties most closely identified with college life and traditions. This association of college life and fraternity membership was fed by alumni, who found the lodges and their identification with the organizations a convenient means of maintaining contact with their schools and a congenial place to which to return for alumni occasions. In a changing college world, the fraternities maintained those characteristics and rituals with which they, too, could continue to identify.

It was conformity, above all, that was the glue of campus life, the basis for group cohesion and identification on the campus, and while it was stickiest among members of fraternities and sororities, the whole campus seemed to be molded along similar lines. Most youths were eager not to be left out of participation in every passing fad. One professor at men's college noted, "The students are standardized and are much afraid of being called 'wets' and 'weirs'" (which was defined as "strange, queer, a genius"), and his institution was described as dominated by the "repressive influence of public opinion." As the editor of the *Daily Illini* explained, "The great college community has one standard of commonplaces."[15]

This conformity was not new in the twenties; it had elicited comment before then.

But in the twenties, if only for the sheer fact of numbers, the uniformity seemed more complete and widespread. Given the growth in numbers and the increased diversity of the population, it was also the more remarkable. It was, in fact, the fraternities who helped to press the larger and more heterogeneous populations of the twenties into what appeared to be a uniform mold. As the editor of the *Cornell Sun*, in one of his more iconoclastic moods, observed, "Our Greek Gods, waddling about their campus, compel uniformity even more than the gods of the plebeians. . . . Yes, it is the fraternity that compels the goose-step and allows no murmur against itself. Before we attack the college for producing types, let us look to the fraternity and break somehow this power that crushes individuality."[16]

The fraternities controlled the campus by controlling their own members. Through careful scrutiny and direction, fraternities homogenized behavior among affiliated students, required their campus participation, and forced the rest of the campus to associate itself with both the extra-curricular network and the behavioral norms of fraternities. The fraternities did this by utilizing the major mechanisms of peer control—election, supervision, ostracism, and prestige. By effecting strong group solidarity and peer identification, the fraternities were able, in the words of a far-ranging investigation of campus life to "control undergraduate social life wherever they are present in force." It was in the fraternity and sorority ranks that the campus "prominents," its athletic heroes and campus queens, were to be found.[17] An affiliated member, by securing election and maintaining his standing among associates, was in turn given those most treasured of possessions: personal security, peer recognition, and social esteem.[18] In the campus lingo, fraternity men and women were the "regulars," the greatest conformists, and therefore the most prestigious individuals. On the campus of the 1920's, individual merit came from group strength, personal identity resulted from rigid conformity, and social stratification bred community homogeneity. The key to this paradox was the campus peer network, a network in which fraternities maintained effective internal organizational conformity and promoted campus-wide emulation.

The control mechanisms began even before the freshman came to the fraternity house. Those who set great store by the "glamor" of college life (and few did not since it was drawing national attention) associated it from the first with fraternity membership. The fraternities were responsible for this association because of their conscious self-advertisement and their well-publicized control of social and extra-curricular activities. Often fraternity members or alumni were active in recruiting high-school students for specific schools, and fraternity members always made a point of conveying the importance of their own organizations. The incoming student knew that participation in student affairs made such membership necessary. "Many boys and girls know that their exclusion will mean being barred from most of the social life of the institution as well as from many privileges and extra-curricular activities," one investigator of campus life explained. He also knew that fraternities desired a certain "type."[19] Thus, freshmen arrived aping the mannerisms and styles associated with the college image. Conformity to what was believed to be the collegiate style epitomized by fraternity men and women was already self-imposed before a youth ever became a member.

The desire to be accepted by the inner group led to a voluntary assumption of the approved interests, manners, appearance, and behavior. Even those who would not be accepted for membership thus fitted themselves to the standard form. Indeed, many who had been rejected continued to nurture the hope of sophomore selection if they demonstrated the necessary conformity and gained a modicum of success in activities on their own. At Princeton, which had no fraternities but where social life was dominated by prestigious eating clubs, the self-imposed conformity was basic to club election. The selection took place at the end of the sophomore year, and students spent two years fitting themselves to an acceptable pattern. As the editor of the *Daily Princetonian* (always a member of such a club himself) noted, this encouraged "a barren conformity among the members of the two lower classes. By junior year this attitude is likely to have hardened into a habit of mind. The life of the underclassmen is tempered word and deed by the prospect of a day of reckoning when any peculiarities he may have will be paraded against him in the secret councils of the most high."[20]

The result for fraternity aspirants (and probably most college students entered with such aspirations)[21] was uniformity, a uniformity of manner and style that was maintained and improved upon by actual membership. A European student, after visiting a large number of American campuses, was amazed:

> In these societies you will find what is considered by themselves and others as the aristocracy among students on the campus. Here you find the typical student life. . . . The standard seems to be uniformity. Everyone who is different is "crazy," perhaps a bookworm or the like, and only those students are chosen who are believed to be able to become good fraternity brothers or sorority sisters and that of course means that they will have to measure up to what is considered "good form." . . . They dress alike, they do the same things at the same time and they think and speak in the same terms and have practically all the same interest.[22]

There were certain definite racial and religious limits of acceptability which automatically precluded fraternity selection, no matter what the success in cultivating the proper "style." In the twenties, there were already several national Jewish fraternities, with many local chapters, in response to the almost universal exclusion of Jews from the other organizations. There were also Negro fraternities and a trend toward the establishment of Negro chapters at various schools.[23]

But this exclusion did not confine or restrict conformity. On the contrary, it may well have accentuated the impulse toward imitation. Vincent Sheean recalled how he had mistakenly accepted the bid of a Jewish fraternity because the editor of the college newspaper was a member. It had not occurred to him that the fraternity to which the editor belonged and whose members seemed to have so much social polish and to have attained success in campus activities might in fact be restricted in religious affiliation. Once he accepted the bid, Sheean too was assumed to be a Jew. Much to his later embarrassment and regret, Sheean withdrew from the fraternity.[24] The incident points out two important features of college life: first, that certain very rigid social barriers to fraternity affiliation did exist and were well known on campus, so that Sheean would be mistaken for a Jew; but also that an uninitiated freshman found it difficult to recognize the difference. In some schools at least, Jews in fraternities of their own were to outsiders indistinguishable from others, and they too attained campus prominence. The campus was deeply stratified but so profoundly uniform that the ripples under the surface scarcely stirred the ocean calm. The same could not be true for blacks, whose own fraternities were often denied membership in the colleges' inter-fraternity councils.[25] Unquestionably discrimination existed on the campuses of the twenties, and the fraternities were often at the forefront of that discrimination because of their selectivity, but at the same time the peer system of emulation and imitation helped to assimilate diverse groups to a common pattern.

Beyond such limits, the criteria of fraternity membership except for very select organizations and schools like Princeton were nowhere so clearly defined. The editor of the *Cornell Sun* asserted that fraternity selection was based on "certain ineffable social qualifications," but these usually had more to do with superficial attractiveness and personality than rigid socio-economic class. Although family social prominence could almost always ensure selection, those without such connections were not automatically excluded. At Syracuse, for example, while the majority of fraternity members believed that there should be some financial or social requirements for admission, only a very small minority believed that these requirements should be rigid, and fraternity students indicated their willingness to live with working-class students. Max McConn, Dean of Lehigh University, noted, "If a lad has an agreeable exterior, a winning smile, and a pleasing manner, if he is a 'slick dresser' and a 'smooth talker' and he duly accredited as to purse, progenitors, and preparatory school, he is sure to be taken. Nay if his 'slickness' and 'smoothness' are exactly right, he will get in despite serious deficiencies in one or more of the other items."[26] The criteria of acceptability for most fraternities were attributes of manner, dress, and style. These were certainly related to family background, economic position, and prep-school training, but they could also be cultivated.[27]

Another basic criterion for fraternity membership concerned what McConn called "capabilities reported or displayed, for distinction in outside activities—athletics, the glee club, the annual comic opera, or even college journalism." This was very important. In order for fraternities to maintain their prominence on the campus they had to continue to dominate and control the activities, and they were careful to choose those who showed promise in extra-curricular leadership. For fraternity aspirants the support of an alumnus, a relative, or a friend from the same town or school was also a major asset. This alumni contact reinforced the reliance on social background, but by no means did all fraternity members have such connections. The very expansion in the size of fraternities precluded the possibility that the organizations would become family castes. The fraternities maintained a solid base of continuity that depended on class, family, and prep school, but went beyond these to include members with qualities of appearance, style, extra-curricular potential, and above all personality. They emphasized, above all, personal attributes that made an individual sociably agreeable and able to mix with others. These qualities, the vital core of David Riesman's other-directed modern personality, dominated the criteria of selection. They were best summarized by a fraternity leader who described the assets most valuable to fraternity selection: "Fraternities desire men who will make a fair appearance, be athletic or interested in campus activities; be good mixers who will help the fraternity internally, and be fair students, although this is often forgotten. Wealth counts, but one cannot get in on wealth alone."[28]

The importance of money and an individual's ability to spend lavishly on himself and his fraternity chapter seems to have varied by group and school, but it was never entirely excluded from consideration. If not valued for itself as a raw qualification, it was basic to many of the other characteristics that made for campus success. Fraternity affiliation was itself expensive. Nor would it hurt to come with a full purse to spend on clothes, autos, and entertaining. Despite frequent disavowals that fraternity life was luxurious and extravagant, inter-fraternity competition for grand houses and posh entertainments put a premium on the ability of members to spend freely on themselves and the social affairs and facilities of the chapter house. Max McConn included wealth among his four criteria but made it the least important. But a careful study of undergraduate life by R. H. Edwards, J. M. Artman, and Galen M. Fisher concluded otherwise, noting that "costly clothes and a car are at times the passport to membership in a sorority or a fraternity."[29]

Attractiveness, expensive display, personableness, and extra-curricular talents—a reactive mixture of personality and performance—were the qualities that counted most in fraternity selection. These were also the general solvent of peer relations on campus. "To many people," the *Daily Northwestern* observed, "the idea of being popular means that one must be good looking, have a 'line,' one must be able to dance 'divinely' and of course have money and a car. In fact, these are some of the first questions asked on inquiring about a prospective date."[30] Within the rigid limits of race and religion, popularity depended on attractiveness in style and manner and plastic amicability, aided and abetted by things money could buy rather than by rigid definitions of class, family, or social position.

The very nature of fraternity selection with its early rushing system[31] put a premium on a youth's appearance, expensive accoutrements, his ability to sell himself and be agreeable, the evidence of an already established reputation in activities like sports and dramatics, and connections with alumni. In the fraternities as on the campus as a whole, first acquaintance and superficial appearance colored future associations. Freshmen were greeted almost at the train station by representatives from the organizations. New students had almost no chance to become acquainted with the campus before they were hustled by fraternities to which they appeared attractive. And in choosing their organizations, freshmen too had to rely on alumni, friends, or the cultivated reputations that fraternities built up, the displays of wealth at the chapter house, or the visibility of fraternity members in campus organizations. "It is easy to fall in with a group because it has a fine house, or several cars hanging around, or because some of the members hold important campus offices," the Louisiana State *Reveille* warned new students[32] In each case, the stress was on readily identifiable marks of prestige and potential for campus popularity.

"Men and women are liked who contribute most to the pleasure of their companions," Robert Angell concluded about society at the University of Michigan, "and some of these have few more substantial qualities than being easy 'mixers.'" Of all the benefits reported to be derived from club life the one most frequently appreciated by students was training in meeting and cultivating people. It is not therefore surprising that those who already possessed these qualities or had the potential for developing them were looked upon favorably. And it was precisely these qualities that were developed through fraternity association. The ability to mix was regarded by the more optimistic as the quality of civilized sociability, and some proponents of fraternity life betrayed a certain snobbish appeal to social culture. But many, like the acerbic radical journal, the *New Student,* which believed that fraternities were opposed to individual excellence and especially deleterious to the cultivation of serious intellectual interests, saw it as the ability to adapt easily to one's social environment; to underplay personal intensities and interests of any kind; to shed personal identity altogether and float in the stream of group pressure.[33] Qualities of personality thus became the quality of personableness, of the agreeable exterior and slick sociability. Personality was one of the staples of fraternity relations; expensive consumption and extra-curricular achievements were the tickets to success.

As it fostered personality, the ethos of fraternity life consciously underplayed personal commitments or individual interests in anything that did not serve the needs of the group. A fellow who was too involved in non-campus politics or literature or music was somewhat strange; his interest precluded total devotion to group goals and good fellowship. Individual excellence in athletics was the exception, for athletic achievement symbolized the victory of the group in the intensely competitive world of the campus. Eccentricity or intensity of any kind was not readily subordinated to group dictates and was a dread quality because it also had the potential for being disagreeable. The fraternities, concluded one study of student life by the YMCA (a not-infrequent critic of the fraternity type), valued "receptivity, docility of mind, conformity, regimentation," because these promised "a stereotyped result from the acceptable neophyte."[34] The qualities found desirable in a man or woman and cultivated by the fraternity explain in part the decided anti-academic ethos of campus life in the twenties. Scholarship required commitment and emphasized individual, unassisted achievement. Peers subordinated the individual to group requirements and group success. On the campus of the 1920's, the emphasis was elsewhere than on booklearning—on extra-curricular activities that demonstrated allegiance to peer pursuits and on sociability that mediated peer relations.

FOOTNOTES

1. For a discussion of the psychological problems confronting the adolescent during this transition from what I call the personal to the social sphere, see Erik H. Erikson, "Youth: Fidelity and Diversity," in *The Challenge of Youth* (Garden City, N.Y., 1965), pp. 1-28. Erikson is, of course, primarily concerned with the problem of ego integration, but his identification of the two areas of acute concern, sexuality and "calling," are specifically problems of social role.
2. See S. N. Eisenstadt, "Archetypal Patterns of Youth," in *The Challenge of Youth*, ed. Erik H. Erikson, pp. 29-50, for a short discussion of what Eisenstadt has more completely dealt with in *From Generation to Generation: Age Groups and Scoial Structure* (New York, 1956).
3. Vincent Sheean, *Personal History* (Garden City, N.Y., 1934), p. 9.
4. There were no sororities at the elite Eastern women's schools during the period. See *Baird's Manual of American College Fraternities,* 13th ed., Francis W. Shepardson, ed. (Manasha, Wis., 1935).
5. For the general devaluation of literary-aesthetic interests and Bohemian styles among the mass of students, see, for example, *Ohio State Lantern*, December 7, 1925; *Daily Illini,* February 11, 1923. For the ostracism of those with radical views on politics or with intense political interests generally, Ohio State Lantern, April 3, 1924. An indication of the disdain for these fringe groups is the following advice: "For those of the intelligentsia, self-styled, who gather around their tea tables to lament the lack of American literature, we would prescribe a liberal dose of the best sports columns of the newspapers"; *Ohio State Lantern*, December 17, 1925. On the self-conscious literary circles, see also *Daily Illini*, review of *Town and Gown*, February 1, 1923.
6. Quoted in Edwards *et al., Undergraduates*, p. 283. For derisive comment about the funny habits and inhabitants of the UMCA, see *Daily Illini*, January 11, 1923, letter to editor. For the difference between students with strong religious orientations and others at Syracuse University, see Katz and Allport, *Students' Attitudes*, pp. 24-49. As one student president of the YMCA at a small university explained, "The YM reaches the ungrouped men better than the grouped. It provides rooms, jobs and some social life. . . . Few fraternity men come to the YM. I believe their lack of interest is due to fraternity men having homes of their own and being content with the fellowship of their own groups." Quoted in Edward *et al.,* p. 279. See also, Angell, *Adjustment,* p. 115.
7. See, for example, the article in the Duke *Chronicle*, March 7, 1928, which notes that religious idealism among students had been turned into active political channels, which was far better than a passive Christianity. For a discussion of this phenomenon, see Chapter 8 herein.
8. For early fraternities, see John Addison Porter, "College Fraternities," *The Century*, 36 (1888), 749-760. For the transition from the tight academies to the greater freedom of the colleges, see Frederick P. Keppel, *The Undergraduate and His College* (Boston and New York, 1917), pp. 12-18; William Clyde DeVane, *Higher Education in Twentieth-Century America* (Cambridge, Mass., 1965), pp. 14-33.

9. P. F. Piper, "College Fraternities," *Cosmopolitan Magazine*, 22 (1897), 646. Using one student newspaper, the *Rutgers Targum*, as a test case, the growing number of activities sponsored by fraternities toward the end of the century is clearly documented in its pages. In the 1870's there was practically no mention of meetings of fraternities, except as they met to issue a statement of condolence on the death of a member. By the late eighties and into the nineties, there were frequent teas, dances, dinners, etc.

10. See DeVane, *Higher Education*, pp. 19-21; C. H. Freeark, *A College Career and the American Fraternity System* (Lincoln, Neb., 1935), p. 9; R. J. Watts, "Development of University Residence Halls and the Effect Thereof on Fraternities and Sororities," *Central Association of College and University Business Officers, Twenty-fourth Annual Meeting, 1934*, p. 79. Watts' estimate of property values was based on only those ⸗rganizations which reported them.

11. Freeark, *American Fraternity system*, pp. 9-10; *Daily Illini*, December 7, 1921, January 14, 1922, and October 26, 1921. In another Midwestern school, Ohio State, ten new fraternity chapters were established in one year, *Ohio State Lantern*, april 20, 1923. Kenneth L. Roberts, "Smoldering Illini" *Saturday Evening Post*, 201 (January 12, 1929), 13; Chapin, *Extra-Curricular Activities*, pp. 8-9; Angell, *Adjustment*, p. 112.

12. See Chapin, *Extra-Curricular Activities*, Table 6, p. 28, for a breakdown by schools at Minnesota; Katz and Allport *Students' Attitudes*, p. 129, for Syracuse. *Which College?*, a handbook of colleges by Rita Halle, indicated those schools where fraternities were strong. Almost all state universities were so categorized. Of the more than 300 schools listed (including Catholic institutions where fraternities were weak), more than half were said to have strong fraternities.

13. See *Rutgers Targum*, April 21, 1897, for a story about school, fraternity, and class monograms. At this time there were still more demand for class insignia than for fraternity insignia. For further discussion, see Chapter 4 herein.

14. For the decline in "class spirit" because of the increase in class size, see *Daily Illini*, December 7, 1921; also, *Cornell Sun*, March 16, 1920. Attempts to re-establish senior garb, for example, never caught fire; see *Cornell Sun*, March 23, 1921. UCLA tried the most intricate set of class apparel, including "sombretos" for seniors and "cords" for juniors, but rather than distinguish classes, the articles became status symbols worn as a general fad; *UCLA Daily*, October 12, 1923. At Princton, a committee was appointed to reinstate "Certain Extinct Pattersn," but the editor of the *Daily Princetonian* noted that "A custom to be salutory must be a custom and not a rule," and that while development of class spirit was a worthy end, it was a lost cause (February 21, 1924). See also the Duke *Chronicle*, December 10, 1925, March 3, 1926.

UCLA provides an important demonstration of how fraternity life replaced the academic class structure. The transformation that had taken place over a period of 50 years elsewhere was here compressed into a short time because of the transformation of UCLA from a minor teachers institution to a major university and youth center. Before the war, the institution was a normal school with an almost exclusively female population. (In 1916, of 1675 students, only 86 were men; *UCLA Daily*, January 28, 1916.) By a series of legislative enactments, the school began first to offer a two-year liberal arts program in 1919, then a three-year, and finally in 1924 a full four-year program (December 12, 1923, p. 1). During this time, the college was still considered a minor division of the University at Berkeley, a feeder school, called the Southern Branch of the University of California. It had few clubs and very little sorority life, none of the sororities having a national affiliation. Almost from the first, when it began to offer liberal arts courses, the editors of the paper, invigorated by a new sense of the importance of the institution, began to campaign to make the college a youth center with a full contingent of traditions and rituals for creating student loyalty and a sense of group affiliation. "Traditions are to college spirit what the foundation is to a building," noted the editor on January 26, 1923. The first traditions that came to mind were those associated with the academic class system, and the fist attempts to establish traditions concerned freshman rules and regulations, distinctive apparel, and the granting of upper-class privileges. It was soon apparent that a social system based on class affiliation had failed. The last freshman class to be hazed officially was in 1925 (February 11, 1926).

In the meantime, a real social system based on fraternity affiliation and extra-curricular participation was growing on the campus. In 1922 the eight fraternities on campus formed an inter-fraternity council for the first time *(UCLA Daily*, September 15, 1922); the first nationally affiliated fraternity was established in 1923 and the first national sorority in the same year (February 27, 1923, April 17, 1923). The first all-fraternity-sorority dance was held in 1924

(January 19, 1924). In 1925, the newspaper began a series of articles on "prominent campus personalities" (November 13, 1925). By 1927, fraternity rushing had become a problem because of increased enrollment and the increase in fraternity chapters (February 7, 1927). By 1927, a UCLA editor was already talking about a very different kind of tradition, the tradition "that a man or woman who doesn't rate in the select group that hangs out in Millspaugh Hall between classes, has no chance of being one of the popular set on the campus. This tradition is being formed unconsciously but it is about the strongest we have" (November 2, 1927). The campus had evolved a social structure based on association and prominence.

15. Quoted in Edwards *et al., Undergraduate,* p. 14; *Daily Illini,* January 23, 1923.

16. *Cornell Sun,* December 7, 1925. Canby, *College Fathers,* and Keppel, *The Undergraduates,* describe college life in the prewar period.

17. Edwards *et al., Undergraduates,* p. 49. At Cornell in 1925, the fraternities, or "men on the hill," as they were called, published a "blue book" of BMOC's, or Big Men on the Campus; see *Cornell Sun,* March 26, 1925; also October 28, 1926.

18. In explaining why the distinction between the "ins" and the "outs" on the campus—those who were in fraternities and those who were not—was "so keenly felt," the LSU *Reveille* described it as "but natural that the pledge should look upon himself as one of the chosen few. Has he not been singled out from the multitude?" (October 7, 1927).

19. Rita S. Halle, "Greek or Barb?" *Good Housekeeping,* 91 (November, 1930), 43. At Duke University, the editor of *The Chronicle* was forced to assure freshmen who had not received fraternity bids that this did not automatically exclude them from campus prominence and leadership (October 26, 1927, February 18, 1925). Freshmen had associated the two so closely that it was necessary to make public statements to the contrary. See also Katz and Allport, *Students' Attitudes,* pp. 134-135; Angell, *Adjustment,* p. 115; Robert Cooley Angell, *The Campus* (New York, 1928), pp. 28-31, for "types" and conformity on the campus.

20. *Daily Princetonian,* December 8, 1926. Despite the common knowledge of social exclusivity practiced by the clubs, a referendum supported the continuation of the status quo; *Daily Princetonian,* April 23, 1926, p. 1. See also the interesting letter to the editor which notes that election to the clubs subsumes all other considerations, even taking precedence over previous friendships; March 10, 1926. The short story, "The Strangest Serenade," in Lois Montross and Lynn Montross, *Town and Gown* (New York, 1923), describes the effect of continuing fraternity aspirations. According to the *Ohio State Lantern,* April 26, 1921, many fraternities did in fact honor personal achievements by later election.

21. The following "joke" appeared in the Duke *Chronicle,* February 13, 1924:

> *Stranger:* "What do you think about fraternities?"
> *Freshman:* "I'm not booting one; I don't much believe in them."
> *Stranger:* "How about joining ours.?"
> *Freshman:* "Er-well-all-right. Which one do you belong to?"

The joke makes very plain that even most self-conscious opposition to fraternities was often a case of sour grapes. Note also that the freshman agrees even before he knows which organization he is accepting.

22. Jorgen Holck, "Fraternities," *The Survey,* 50 (1923), 391.

23. See *Braird's Manual,* which lists Jewish fraternities with the others, but lists the Negro fraternities separately (1935 edition). See *Ohio State Lantern,* May 2, 1924, for exclusion of Negro chapters.

24. Sheean, *Personal History,* pp. 11-19.

25. At Syracuse, for example, the bid of a black fraternity for membership in the Interfraternity Council was turned down (*New Student,* March 10, 1923, p. 3). Also, *Daily Illini,* May 3, 1924, May 7, 1924, letter to editor, and May 9, 1924 for the situation at Illinois. According to Katz and Allport, Negroes were the lowest on the list of those with whom fraternities and other student living associations would willingly room. This study makes clear that students were very exclusive in their choice of acceptable roommates. Katz and Allport found that fraternity members were the most exclusionary in their views *(Students' Attitudes,* pp. 143-157).

26. *Cornell Sun,* December 4, 1920; Katz and Allport, *Students' Attitudes,* pp. 183-184, 146; McConn, "Tired Business Men," 546.

27. At Princeton, the eating clubs were in fact very socially exclusive. Very few high school students, as opposed to those from the elite preparatory schools, were members of the organizations; see *Daily Princetonian,* February 28, 1924, p. 1. See *Cornell Sun,* December 13, 1921, for prep-school "type." But see also the story of Carl Peters, Hugh Carver's roommates

in *The Plastic Age*, by Percy Marks (New York, 1924). Peters appears to have all the earmarks of class but had merely learned to affect the mannerisms.

28. McConn, "Tired Business Men," 546; quoted in Edwards *el al., Undergraduates*, p. 53. See David Riesman with Nathan Glazer and Reuel Denney, *The Lonely Crowd*, abridged ed. (New Haven, 1964), for the characteristics of personality and sociability in the other-directed personality.

29. Edwards *et al., Undergraduates*, p. 18. See *Daily Illini*, March 27, 1925, on costly clothes as a means to popularity. Also, *Daily Illini*, February 1, 1924, p. 1, which notes that chapter house building amounting to one-half million dollars was under way among ten fraternities, and February 2, 1924, letter to editor.

30. *Daily Northwestern*, reprinted in *Daily Illini*, October 19, 1921. See also the *Ohio State Lantern*, April 25, 1923, p. 1, for the qualities that coeds desired in an ideal man. These included appearance, clothes, manner, ability to socialize, dancing skills, and ownership of a car.

31. Many administrators feared that early rushing prevented freshmen from first being introduced to the academic side of college before they were thrown into the social. Many schools moved to delay rushing. This was the case at Ohio State, where 24 creditors of acceptable academic work were required before a youth could belong to a fraternity; see *Ohio State Lantern*, October 6, 1921, p. 1.

32. LSU *Reveille*, October 7, 1924.

33. Angell, *Campus*, p. 7. For social culture, see Gerald Johnson, "Should Our Colleges Educate?" 723-727; also, Thomas Arkle Clark, *The Fraternity and the College*, (Menasha, Wis., 1915); Freeark, *Amercian Fraternity System, passim*. See *New Student*, November 15, 1924, p. 3, discussing the iconoclastic magazine *The Circle* published at the University of Chicago, and October 10, 1925 (editorial) reprinted from *The Dartmouth*, which gives a good summary of their criticisms.

34. *Present Position of the Student YMCA*, p. 37. Students with strong religious orientations and those who were active in the student Y's showed different patterns in their attitudes toward work, social life, extra-curricular activities, and athletics than did fraternity members. See Katz and Allport, *Students' Attitudes*, pp. 24-49.

One of the dangers of splitting human life into stages of development is that we tend at times to view each stage as a photograph—as an isolated, frozen frame of time and space. By thinking of life-stages in these terms we lose sight of their dynamic qualities and, equally important, we sometimes forget that a person's ideals, needs, aspirations, loves, and hates can traverse the life cycle: they appear during one phase of life, disappear during another, and re-appear (although perhaps in a different guise and for different reasons) in still another.

This dialectical quality of sensibilities is beautifully portrayed in the following study of one of America's foremost philosophers, William James. With a sensitivity equal to the subtlety of his subject, Howard Feinstein describes the interplay between James's difficulty in chosing a vocation, a problem that haunted him from his teenage years into his thirties, and the values of his imperious and famous father, Henry. Feinstein not only shows how the ideals of the elder James influenced his son's various career choices during these years, but how an imperious father linked his thoughts about science, art, religion and social change to his son's furture. Ultimately, Feinstein demonstrates that generations, as well as life-stages, are separated by soft shadows rather than impenetrable walls.

Words and Work: A Dialectical Analysis of Value Transmission between Three Generations of the Family of William James

Howard Feinstein

Introduction

I first had contact with Erik Erikson through reading *Childhood and Society* when I was in medical school in the early 1950s. I didn't understand much of what I read, particularly the sections on the life cycle. Since then my own life experience, analysis, clinical practice, and historical research have made his poetic construct of ego development more accessible to me. In the fall of 1967, I was a participant in his psychohistory seminar at Harvard. It is fitting that my work benefited from the critique of an early formulation in that seminar. This chapter is concerned with the transmission of ideas between generations, between father and son, between teacher and student. In this regard I will attempt to extend Erikson's ideas by putting them to a test that he himself has hinted at but not yet attempted. Whether my efforts clarify, creatively misunderstand, or transform the work that eluded me as a man in my twenties, I leave to the judgment of others.

I intend to focus my remarks on the generational transmission of values regarding work and vocational choice in the family of William James. Erikson has demonstrated the importance of this issue for identity formation in his biographical and theoretical works.[1] My aim will be to elucidate the process in which William James engaged with his father over this significant life decision. Biography is not my foremost concern in this discussion. Rather, I wish to use James family materials to demonstrate a method for uncovering the intergenerational exchange.

It is tempting for a historian to describe the transmission of values as a linear sequence between cohesive, stable entities. Henry James Senior believed that scientific work was appropriate for his eldest son. William became a scientist, ultimately concerning himself with the philosophic aspects of that subject. But such a view is far too simplistic. It fails to capture the complexity implied by Erikson's developmental psychology and the flux of social history. Henry James Senior, born in 1811, was not a monolith but a man who was vital and developing throughout his life. We cannot talk of him as the possessor of an inert block of ideas that he simply handed over to his son, however convenient this may be for literary clarity. Nor can we look at William James as the passive recipient of those values which, once in hand, were borne through a lifetime, hermetically sealed from his own changing experience. To do justice to our subject, we must talk not about the transmission of values, but value exchange between persons who are alive, as we are alive, and whose inner worlds may move to the rhythms of Erikson's developmental chronology, as our own seem to do.

Before turning to the James family intergenerational exchange, I would like to emphasize the methodological problem that we face by calling your attention to figure 10-1, borrowed from Klaus F. Riegel. It illustrates the nature of dialogue.[2] This figure represents the simplest kind of dialogue, but, as Riegel has pointed out, it is useful as a model for other types of exchange. Each of two speakers is shown relating his statements to those of the other and to his own previous statements. At A_1 a statement is made to B_2, but that is not the end of it, as a linear view would imply. A_1 is also directing his statement to the next step in his thought as well at to B_1, and that next step is shaped in response to B_1's answer, so that it becomes a new modal point in the process, or A_2. A_2 is also an anticipation of the next stages of the exchange as well as a reaction to previous stages. In this simplest exchange, A_2 is a thesis to which B_1 is the antithesis, and A_1 is the synthesis that completes the first unit of dialogue. To be sure, this simple case implies a level on consistency and attentiveness that is unfortunately rare when fathers and sons exchange words. But it will suffice to show the goal toward which we need to aspire if we are to reconstruct what happened in a value exchange.

This representation serves equally well for any interaction that involves two temporal sequences. I would like to adapt it for an exchange between father and son, where each of the nodal points represents that person at a different point in the life cycle. In other words, each point for *A* represents an anticipated or past self of

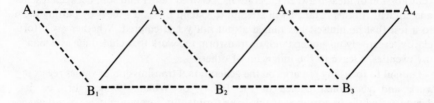

Figure 10-1. Diagram of the Nature of Dialogue.

Henry James Senior in relation to each point in the temporal sequence *B* that represents an anticipated or past self for his son William. Obviously, the very same diagram could represent either father or son in interaction with society or his historical moment (the state of development of a particular field, and so on). Each of the elements in this paradigm is constantly changing in relation to itself and the other. Although I have utilized a simpler diagram for this discussion, the paradigm is implicit in Erikson's epigenetic model.[3]

To bring this diagram to bear on the James family values regarding work choice, the problem can be formulated as follows: We want to reconstruct the dialogue between young Henry James Senior becoming middle-aged Henry James Senior becoming elderly Henry James Senior in relation to young William James becoming middle-aged William James becoming elderly William James. As if our task were not complicated enough, we have to keep in mind that young Henry James Senior developed his work values in relation to his father. Our work choice exchange thus becomes a trialogue engaging three generations.

Although our paradigm is simply diagrammed, the historical research required is complex and the literary task of reporting that interaction is very difficult, if not impossible, within the constraints of historical narrative. Film or music are media better adapted to the recreation of elements that are both synchronically and diachronically related. We are left with the option of retelling the same story over and over again, returning to enrich the context and shift the perspective so that the reader can appreciate the dialectical flux we have uncovered.

William James of Albany, an immigrant from Northern Ireland, amassed a huge fortune before his death in 1832. His son Henry refused to prepare himself for a career in the law as his father demanded. He was virtually cut out of his father's will as an unrepentant prodigal. This will was broken, but Henry smarted under the rejection. He avoided work and lived on his inheritance as his father had feared. When his son William chose his vocation, he did so in the shadow of his father's battle with his grandfather. One way that we can tap into this intergenerational exchange is by examining the shifting meanings of the words Henry used to map the world of work for himself and his son.

sient forays into painting, natural science, and medicine. He completed a medical degree but never practiced. His studies were frequently interrupted by trips abroad to recover from recurrent depressions that plagued, yet guided, his search for work. Belatedly, in 1873, he began teaching at Harvard, first anatomy and physiology, then psychology, and finally philosophy.

Henry James Senior wrote extensively, particularly during his Fourierest phase (1847-1855), about the nature of work. By the time his son considered a career as an artist, scientist, or philosopher, Henry had commented on each of these fields of endeavor—and he continued to develop his ideas about them throughout his life. The shifting language of vocation provides a map of the work world, as Henry James saw it. By studying the transformation of the father's specific meanings for the language of vocation, we can appreciate the difficulty William had in finding his way.

Had he been alive to read *The Harbinger* in 1848, William James of Albany would have been shocked to read his son Henry's declaration that, "No man dislikes labor." He would have been pleased, perhaps, that his son had finally come to his own conclusion that "it is in every man a divine inspiration which he can no more resist, than he can resist the attraction of the earth."[4] Work as a law of nature was close enough to work as a divine duty. But that apparent shift in Henry's thinking was illusory.

If he read on, William James of Albany would have discovered that his son Henry had not changed as much as he might have liked: "We repeat it: no man dislikes labor, free labor, labor which is the outgrowth of his own spirit, and expresses himself. But every man dislikes to labor for his *living*." The notion of force was anathema to James. "This is what disgusts him, *compulsory* labor in which the heart is not, labor which is dictated and enforced solely by the demands of bodily subsistence, or of social position." Work was an expression of God within, an act of self creation, or it was branded infernal labor. Writing on such an issue was always a personally significant act for Henry, and we can easily see how this deviation from the traditional Calvinist view suited his position as an independently wealthy man of letters who was freed of the necessity of earning a living because his father had labored so well.

Judging from his hortatory writings and humorous asides, Henry James never overcame a feeling of discomfort over not working successfully for money. His judgment became more severe as he grew older culminating in a flood of vituperation that could only signify deep self-loathing. Sixteen years after the *Harbinger* articles he declared. "No one of my readers is capable of feeling the least respect for an idle God anymore than for an idle man. Everyone respects labor; everyone respects the man who does something more to vindicate his human quality, *than just live upon his ancestral fat*" (my italics).[5] Henry James was in his fifties by then and still without gainful employment. William James of Albany had been dead for over thirty years; and this son that he had warned, and threatened, and finally punished, had come to pronounce his father's judgment on himself.

Henry James's view of work held contradictions within it that he never resolved. That failed resolution complicated his son's vocational development. He placed a high value on work that was self-expressive. Judging by his own example, work of this design required wealth and leisure. Yet he condemned those who lived on ancestral fat when others lacked the bare necessities of life. If a son wanted to follow his admired father's map of the work world, which way was he to go? Was it permissible (or admirable?) to use his grandfather's resources as his father had done, for

Work

The twelve years from 1860 to 1872 marked the period of William James's initial vocational floundering. Beginning as an eighteen-year-old student, he made tran- a prolonged search for vocation? What was to be the test of its value? Utility? Self-expansion? Should an eldest son make his forays brief to make way for the younger children? That might make way for others who lacked what was necessary for them, but why follow such worldly sign posts when the quest for authentic labor beckoned him down yet one more tantilizing path?

Henry James was not a methodical thinker. But it would be a mistake to conclude that he was unaware of the tension between his individualistic faith and his increas- ingly renaissant Calvinism. He was painfully torn between the push of desire to have his own way and the pull of social demands for productive work. His utopian solu- tion was to assume that conflict would disappear in a properly organized society in which "man will work no longer to live but only from it, no longer with a servile but only with a filial spirit."[6] Ideally, a man would want to do what he had to do, but as he knew all too well, this was not yet true. William James was about to discover this for himself. The lectures and books and table talk of a father, who seemed to urge both self-expression and religious duty with conviction on his son, compounded his dilemma. What if he did not want to do society's bidding? What if work performed in a filial spirit turned him to stone? What if he wanted to be like his father and avoid any lawful calling? As he approached each of his choices—art, science, and philosophy—William had to find his way through a labyrinth of contradictory pater- nal injunctions.

Art

For a brief period in his late thirties, Henry James thought art was the expression of divinity within man, and the artist was a hero grandly enthroned on the pinnacle of his hierarchy of spiritual development. The artist was the quintessential spon- taneous man. Yet when William decided to be a painter in 1859, he met vigorous resistance from his father. This apparent contradiction becomes a little less mysterious when we examine Henry James's usage. It is perfectly clear from his essays that he did not have painters or sculptors in mind. It is also obvious that he believed his *Harbinger* articles were art, and he himself was an artist in the pure (that is, his) sense of the term.

Art does not refer to any particular occupation but to a quality of spiritual rela- tionship to work. "The sphere of Art properly so called, is the sphere of man's spon- taneous productivity." Negatively stated, it was to be distinguished "on the one hand from his *natural* productivity, or that which is promoted by his physical necessities, and on the other by his moral productivity, or that which is prompted by his obligations to other men." In short, "Art embraces all those products of human genius, which do not confess the parentage either of necessity or duty."[7]

A painter was not necessarily excluded from the sphere of art. He might be an ar- tist in James's sense if he did not have to paint to support himself. If a painter had always been "Beyond the reach of want," and had been well educated "to ensure a comparatively free development of his faculty," and was devoted to his art, then James allowed that "the very highest happiness he is capable of lies in the untram- melled exercise of his calling."[8] By the time William was eighteen (1860) and had decided to launch himself in a painter's career, he fulfilled the criteria of his father's ideal case. He had never known want. He had been the subject of many experimental forays into the best schools his father could find in Europe and America. He had considerable talent for drawing, and this faculty had been developed under the guidance of his teachers. And he frankly described moments of artistic creation as high points of happiness for his inmost self. Yet his father balked, in 1860, at a plan that seemed to match his ideal itinerary of 1848. By the time William was old enough to fulfill that promise, his father's conception of the vocational world had changed.

Henry's paeon to art was orchestrated to his own vocational needs. To be sure he copied from Swedenborg, and Schopenhauer, and Shelling; but he was using them to make sense of his own life.[9] He offered himself as an example of the artist to his *Harbinger* audience. "Take for example, my present employment. It does not spring from any necessity of the natural life, for I have bread for all my physical wants. Nor does it spring from any sense of obligation to my neighbor, for being addressed to the universal reason of man, it is not fitted to promote any specific or individual interests. It is exclusively the offspring of my own delight or attraction towards this kind of labor."[10] If his journalism was art, then he was an artist in the grand sense. Rather than an unemployed writer without position in a work-oriented society, he was ensconced on the romantic heights where admiration was his due. Thus enthroned, Henry James could see himself as a prince rather than a failure.

The period of Henry James's enthusiasm for art and the artist covered William James's early school years. From the time when he was six until the time he was eleven or twelve, praise of aesthetic man flowed from his father's pen. We can only imagine how father's praise of the artist sounded to a boy with a talent for drawing. He was too young to be concerned with the question of his future vocation, although, in boyish fashion, he might have wanted to emulate Mr. Coe, his drawing teacher. It is doubtful that William was able to follow his father's philosophical view of art. What would have made an impression on him was the aura of excitement and parental approbation surrounding the word in his admired father's discussions. To be free, spontaneous, and creative was mysterious, grand, and admirable. To be an artist was something fine that might do some day.

In the next thirty years Henry James rarely wrote of art or the artist except in minor asides to compare the work of the artist unfavorably with the handiwork of God. In the scale of Henry James's adult life, this was a brief moment, a transient experiment in his own search for vocation. But as an artistically talented boy, with a strong affinity for his father, it was more important for William who was of an age when young people are eager to learn about the work world of adults as they imaginatively prepare themselves for the life that awaits them beyond childhood.[11] Career choice was not a real question but a playful possibility. Such is the disparity between time sense and ability to comprehend the adult world, that an ephermeral paternal experiment may become fossilized in an impressionable son's mind. What parent has not had the experience of having his own ideas recited back to him by a child who had made them his own, with an intensity that belies their source, and content that no longer represents the parent's current beliefs? Uneasily, one views a caricature encased in time—recognizable but no longer oneself. As Henry James struggled with his demons, the concept of aesthetic man was temporarily useful. When it came time for William to choose a career and he wanted to be a painter, he used his father's arguments. Henry did not make any note of recognition. He may have been too involved in the struggle to notice his old weapons being turned against him.

Science

In Henry James's map of the world of work, art was not a territory discrete from science. His earliest usage blended the two concepts. Science could be encompassed by art, and a scientist could be an artist. The bridging idea that linked art and science in his early *Harbinger* formulation was technology. Henry James looked upon technological advance as art, since it was expressive of "the actual life of God in man." He was convinced that this particular expression of the "perfect marriage between Creator and creature" had important theological implications. He claimed that, "every railroad refutes Calvinism, and the electric telegraph stultifies Apostolic succession." Technology authorized a new theology because it could bring about two important changes in man's condition: subjugation of nature, and through that subjugation, a solution of the problem of evil.

He reminded his fellow associationists that "science has at last brilliantly solved the problem of human destiny, and demonstrated in a thousand superb and palpable forms the truth of immemorial prophecies, that destiny involves the complete subjugation of nature." And he underscored the implications of that achievement, that radiant hope. "We find that science makes no advance but in the ceaseless direction of human welfare, in the ceaseless vindication of man's essential dignity; we find that the things which we have all along called evil and noxious, have at bottom a heart of the tenderest love to man, and exist only for the purpose of developing the otherwise inconceivable resources of his divine and omnipotent genius."[12] Thus rendered, a scientist was a worthy peer to share the pinnacle of James's spiritual hierarchy.

Henry used science in yet another sense. This second meaning found in his Fourierist writings also had theological implications. By science, he meant a rational program for political and social reorganization. A social program on the model of Fourier's phalanxes would overcome man's natural depravity and undermine this basic Calvinist tenet about human condition. Thus broadly conceived, science was a covering term for many different reform movements from temperance to antislavery. It held the promise of a society based on spiritual community rather than police, or convention, or legislation by men. And the movements of reform were sure signs that the promise would be fulfilled.

The advance of science authorized a new theology because it showed that the Calvinist vision of God was incorrect. Man was not evil, and God had not created an evil world. It was a view of science that made it natural for Henry James to welcome the scientist as an ally in his war on orthodoxy. He was happy to fight alongside fellow scientists (his affiliation with the associationist movement qualified him as a scientist) clearing vestiges of an outworn Calvinism (William of Albany was Presbyterian) from the American scene. He was also prepared to annoint his scientist ally into the priesthood of the new age. In an 1851 lecture, he actually suggested that professional ministers resign from their posts in favor of the priesthood of science. "Then at least *we* shall be well off: that is to say, we shall stand a chance at last of getting a capable or real priesthood of men of science, who ask no tithes, but are yet amply able to instruct us in all the conditions necessary to inaugurate the divine life on earth."[13] In Mr. James's confusing lexicon, a painter might not be an artist, and a scientist might be an artist or a priest.

As he moved beyond his Fourierist enthusiasm toward systematic speculation, Henry James changed the meaning of "science." Science became one element in his theory of knowledge. Briefly, he delineated three realms of human life: body, mind, and spirit. Each realm followed its own principle of organization. The organizing principle for body is sense. The principle for mind is science, and for spirit it is philosophy. In addition to having a separate principle of organization, each of the three realms is illuminated by its own unique light. The light of sense is the sun, for science it is reason, and for philosophy it is revelation. The three realms form a three-tiered hierarchy, building in ascending order from body-sense-sun, to mind-science-reason, to culminate in spirit-revelation-philosophy. Each level in the hierarchy builds on the knowledge of the one below but is not bound by the limitations of the inferior realm. Henry outlined this theory in the 1860s, and it demonstrates how much science had declined in his estimation. Before, the scientist was hailed as a priest. By the 1860s the scientist had given ground to the philosopher, who James now thought was the only man who could be trusted to speak authoritatively on matters of the spirit. Science was now placed in an ambiguous position. He appreciated its potency but insisted on the limitations of that power. As he grew older, there were still occasions when James emphasized the importance of science for the spiritual development of mankind with as much conviction as he had in the 1840s. But he more often reserved his enthusiasm for philosophy as the highest form of truth.

When he was enthusiastic about science, Henry James encouraged his son's scientific studies. He persisted in his preference for science over art, and William ultimately abandoned painting and entered the Lawrence Scientific School at Harvard in 1861. Even as William entered to halfheartedly prepare for a scientific career, Henry's high opinion of science had begun to wane. The hierarchy of knowledge that he explicated the year his son entered Harvard to become a scientist unseated science from its elevated position. At the outset, the shift was one of emphasis and left much that was admirable to science and the scientist. But the trend gathered momentum culminating in his frank declaration, in 1879 (six years after William began teaching science at Harvard), that "if a man's mind determine itself towards science or the senses, the result to one's spiritual understanding cannot help being disastrous in the extreme."[14] The priesthood of science was a glorious career, as Henry James mapped the work world in the 1850s. By the time his son gave in to his father and actually became a scientist, the lustre had tarnished. Indeed, rather than a glorious vocation, it had actually become dangerous for the soul.

Philosophy

Henry's usage of the term "philosophy" changed through his adult life along with the transformations in meaning of art and science. In the late 1840s it meant abstract thinking that "perpetually balks the intellect instead of satisfying it."[15] In the context of his Fourierist years, it was a term of opprobrium. In the 1860s, as he elaborated his formal doctrine of spiritual knowledge, philosophy became a field of the utmost importance, and it was transformed into a term of approbation. Philosophy was the most profound discipline that synthesized the lesser realms of science and sense into a reconciling form of truth. He contrasted it more and more with the narrowness of science. "Philosophy deals only with the essence of things, that is with the spiritual realm, . . . where science never penetrates—to which indeed she is incapable of lifting an eye."[16] There can be little doubt that as he reworked and expanded his doctrine of spiritual creation in his later years, Henry James thought of himself as a philosopher in the highest (his own) sense of the term.

Conclusions

When we place Henry James's writing on art, science, and philosophy in dialectical context, it is clear that he was intent on dramatizing his own vocational search and vindicating himself with his father. When he was most enthusiastic about art, it was because he could conceive of himself as an artist. He praised science when he considered himself one of the elect band publicizing Fourier's program of social science. He was happy to embrace the scientist as an admired ally laying waste the pretensions of conventional religion. He devalued science as he abandoned Fourier and directed his speculative efforts to his theory of spiritual creation. Then he admired philosophy and thought of himself as a practitioner of that elevated vocation. Each step along the way, William James had to cope with his father's confusing map of the world of work. He must have found it disheartening to discover that he could never catch his mercurial sire. When he aspired to be an artist, a heroic personage depicted by his beloved father in glorious hues, Mr. James was unhappy. When he shifted toward science, his father was no longer enthusiastic about scientists. When he changed from science to philosophy, it was merely technical philosophy that Mr. James considered inferior to his own spiritual doctrine. In effect, no matter how much acclaim the world would give William James, the development of his father's ideas kept him kneeling before him as the elder Henry gazed heavenward.

It would have been possible to present this as a history of ideas tracing Henry James Senior's participation in the currents of his times from Calvinism through Romanticism and Transcendentalism to Swedenborgianism. It would also have been possible to retell it, as many others have, as biography with the issue of work choice placed in the temporal sequence of a single life. Each has its merits, but if we are to recover the flux of value exchange between generations, the dialectical paradigm is closer to experience. Having undertaken this three generational, synchronic approach, I am painfully aware of all that has been left out. I appreciate the wisdom of Henry James's remark about his own literary omissions: "Really, universally, relations stop nowhere, and the exquisite problem of the artist is eternally but to draw, by a geometry of his own, the circle within which they shall happily appear to do so."[17]

FOOTNOTES

1. Erik Erikson, *Childhood and Society* (New York: W.W. Norton, 1950); *Young Man Luther: A Study in Psychoanalysis and History* (New York: W.W. Norton, 1958); *Gandhi's Truth: On the Origins of Militant Nonviolence* (New York: W.W. Norton, 1969).

2. Klaus F. Riegel, "Labor and Love: Some Dialectical Commentaries," unpublished manuscript; K.F. Riegel, "From traits and equilibrium toward developmental dialectics," in *1974-1975 Nebraska Symposium on Motivation*, ed. W.J. Arnold and J.K. Cole (Lincoln, Neb.; University of Nebraska Press, 1976), pp. 349-407; K.F. Reigel, "The dialectics of time," in *Life-Span Developmental Psychology; Dialectical perspectives of Experimental Research*, ed. H.W. Reece and N. Datan (New York: Academic Press, 1977).

3. Erikson, *Childhood and Society*, pp. 219-235.

4. Henry James, "Theological Differences in Association," *The Harbinger* 6 &1848):26.

5. Henry James, *Substance and Shadow; Or Morality and Religion in Their Relation to Life: An Essay upon the Physics of Creation* (New York: AMS Press 1977 reprint of 1863 ed.), p. 74.

6. Henry James, *The Church of Christ Not an Ecclesiasticism; A Letter of Remonstrance to a Member of the Soi-Disant New Church* (New York: AMS Press, 1977 reprint of 1854 ed.), p. 4.

7. Henry James, *Lectures and Miscellanies* (New York: 1852), p. 102.

8. Henry James, "The Divine Life in Man," *The Harbinger* 7 (1848):9.

9. Frederic Harold Young, *The Philosophy of Henry James, Sr.* (New York: College and University Press, 1951).

10. Henry James, "The Divine Life in Man," *The Harbinger* 8 (1848):9.

11. Erickson, *Childhood and Society*, pp. 226-227.

12. Henry James, "Theological Differences in Association," *The Harbinger* 6 (1848):26.

13. James, *Lectures and Miscellanies*, pp. 242-243.

14. Ibid., p. 314.

15. Henry James, *Society, the Redeemed Form of Man, and the Earnest of God's Omnipotence in Human Nature* (New York: Johnson Reprint, 1971 of 1879 ed.), pp. 296-297.

16. Henry James, "On the Philosophical Tendencies of the Age—J.D. Morell," *The Harbinger* 7 (1848):3.

17. James, *Substance and Shadow*, p. 305.

What does it mean to grow old? To feel the loss of physical prowess, to sense the decay of mental faculties, and to foresee the end of life are things that all who survive adulthood experience. The tragic dimension of this process is that we know it is inevitable: the road from birth to death is mapped indelibly in our consciousness.

If this aspect of old age is biological, inevitable and, therefore, even logical, there is another that is social, avoidable, and unreasonable: few groups of Americans suffer the stings of discrimination and aspersion as much as the elderly. In a way, the old are perceived as un-American, for the vocabulary Americans use to describe what they most value—"mobility," "initiative," "independence," "freedom from restraints," "competitiveness"—are seen as accoutrements of youth. And one phenomenon that cannot easily be integrated into this value system is symbolized by old age: failure. That the "failure" of the old is inevitable, that it is shared by all regardless of race, class, or sex does not seem to matter.

In this important article Carole Haber shows that discrimination against the elderly in the area of employment, and the evolution of retirement and pension plans in industry during the late nineteenth century, were, to a considerable degree, tied to the need of American businessmen to keep their labor costs down and to the desire of philanthropists and reformers to increase employment opportunities for younger workers.

Why was this so, according to Haber? Is she saying that capitalism and human dignity in old age are incompatible?

Mandatory Retirement in Nineteenth-Century America: the Conceptual Basis for a New Work Cycle

Carole Haber

In 1970, only about one in four of all American men over the age of sixty-five held full-time employment.[1] The great majority—over six million American men—were classified by the census as retired, formally nonemployed because of their advanced age. These proportions tend to obscure the fact that retirement is a relatively new development in American society. As late as 1890, in fact, only about one-quarter of all aged workers considered themselves permanently nonemployed.[2] By 1940, however, the elderly, out-of-work individual had become the rule rather than the exception.[3] As the proportion of workers surviving to age seventy rose sharply from 48.4% in 1890 to 74.9% in 1940,[4] retirement itself became a new stage of life, firmly established as part of the normal life cycle. In less than half a century, the prescribed roles for the old had undergone a major transformation.

To be sure, the concept of retirement was not an invention of the late 19th century. As early as 1713, Cotton Mather had noted the presence of retired old men whose unemployed state allowed them to devote their time to charity.[5] By 1870, about one-quarter of a million men over the age of sixty were no longer in the labor force.[6] What was new to the late 19th century was the growing demand by a wide variety of companies that their workers automatically retire at some specific, predetermined age. This arbitrary separation of the old from the young had a significant effect upon the life of every aging worker, both in terms of his own self-image and in the way he was perceived by others.

Economic historians have generally explained this phenomenon through an analysis of changes in the size, shape, and composition of the labor market.[7] With the aggregate work force as their accustomed unit of analysis, they discuss the tendencies that draw individuals into, or out of, the job market. This focus, however, fails to differentiate between those industries that established retirement and those that failed to do so; nor does it explain the motives behind these corporate decisions. If we assume that retirement is a necessary stage in the work course, this omission is in some sense irrelevant. If, however, we view mandatory retirement as an innovation of the late 19th century—and one that reflects specific attitudinal and institutional factors—such economic analysis explains neither the circumstances nor the beliefs that shaped this novel policy.

Those analysts who have considered retirement in historical terms have generally ascribed it to the forces of modernization.[8] Viewed in terms of statistical evidence, it is depicted as a consequence of urban and industrial growth. And the figures these experts cite certainly do reflect the marginal position of the old in modern America. In 1900, for example, although the old constituted 4.7% of the employed work force,[9] they held only 3-3.5% of the jobs in such growing industries as trade, manufacturing, mechanics, and transportation. Instead, they were overrepresented in agriculture (6.1%) and the professions (5.5%)—fields that allowed them to remain securely self-employed—and even more evident in the lowest status job of all, that of the unskilled laborer (12%).[10] Most ominously, as the country continued to urbanize, the aged became increasingly likely to be unemployed.[11]

This statistical approach vividly illustrates the trend toward retirement; it does little, however, to explain it. The creation of an industrial, urban environment did not, in fact, necessarily preclude employment for the old. Cities, rather than automatically limiting jobs, opened up new opportunities for millions. For this very reason, they attracted the immigrant and the displaced farmer. Moreover, the positions created by these new businesses often demanded far less physical strength than pre-industrial trades and crafts. Through technological innovations, women, children, and even old men possessed the necessary power to operate those machines requiring neither great skill nor advanced education. Thus, as a result, women and children (at least before legislative restrictions) rapidly filled industrial jobs, at times outnumbering men in the burgeoning factories.[12] For the elderly, however, an opposite trend developed. As they were increasingly phased out and replaced by new sources of labor, the aged began to form a distinct social category, separated by their advanced years and distinguished by their seeming inability to labor.

This paper will attempt to offer some explanations for this trend as well as suggest some of the motives underlying its original acceptance. This is not to imply that retirement was not shaped by rapid urban and industrial growth. These forces played an essential—if elusive—role in its formulation. But the precise shape and timing of mandatory retirement cannot be adequately explained in such general terms. Specific factors led to the creation of programs that demanded the retirement of the elderly worker. As this paper will show, this concept did not arise from the employee, at least in private industry. Instead it was devised and endorsed by charity reformers, large industrialists, and social and economic analysts. These interest groups were each willing to accept the restrictive aspects of such provisions in exchange for anticipated benefits. Mandatory retirement was, as we shall see, a measure of compromise that arose out of unique social and economic conditions. Moreover, the programs met with general public approval because they were consistent with assumptions that pervaded much of American society. Essential to the notion of age-related enforced retirement was a widely-shaped view of the capabilities of the old, a view based on past perceptions and future expectations of the elderly's role in society. These common conceptions—even if one construes them as a legitimation for economically-determined policies—became a fundamental element in the welfare and labor programs that increasingly came to structure the daily lives of the elderly. The following pages will trace the beliefs, motives, and decisions that transformed retirement from a measure of ad hoc charity for some of the indigent elderly into a mandatory prescription for all aged workers. Only through this focus can one begin to explain the rapid and overwhelming adoption of a practice that broadly discriminated against the old and, in effect, created a legitimately segregated class in modern society.

In America, problems of unemployment and discrimination against the elderly did not develop solely with the forces of industrialization; the old have experienced difficulties throughout the nation's history.[13] Even aged Puritans, whose status might logically have been assured through their society's hierarchical structure, rarely appeared truly confident that they would not be deserted in their dotage. Although the Biblical commandment to "honor thy father and thy mother" was law, civil authorities at times had to coerce young adults into supporting their parents.[14] As a safeguard against neglect, many aged landholders retained control of the property and thus exerted considerable authority over their children. Others, content to part with their estates before their own deaths, still wrote binding legal guarantees into the deeds that assured them lifelong familial care.[15]

As more and more individuals moved into the cities, however, many elderly persons faced magnified problems. Leaving their farms, migrants also left behind them the power and prestige inherent in the ownership of land and goods. Moreover, in highly populated urban areas, authorities were far less able to demand a family's continued support of an aged pauper or threaten him with deportation to his original county of residency.[16] By the early 19th century, in fact, most large cities possessed a large number of poverty-stricken individuals, a good many of whom had entered old age.[17] These persons faced few alternatives in their attempts to earn a living. Often unable to secure sufficient employment, they filled the rolls of private charities and, to the consternation of most welfare experts, applied to the city for outdoor relief.[18] Finally, as a last resort, many old people sought refuge in the almshouse, institutionalized alongside the sick, the orphaned, the drunk, and the petty criminal.

Charity organizations, therefore, were the first group to attempt to develop a systematic approach to the problems of the ages. Their awareness of the plight of many of the old tended to blur the fact that not all elderly urban dwellers were in need; the great majority sustained themselves without the reformer's aid. In granting alms to the elderly, however, welfare advocates often focused upon the strong correlation between age and dependency; the advanced years of the elderly became the key factor in the allocation of assistance. Like the blind, the deaf, or the orphan, the old were perceived to be a unique class, whose needs and abilities could be clearly differentiated from other types of paupers.

Yet there was nothing optimistic in this distinct characterization. Most mid-century reform groups found they could offer little real encouragement to the aged. Some welfare societies, in fact, refused to deal with the elderly at all. The New York Association for Improving the Condition of the Poor, for example, declined to assist the old as well as the handicapped, the infirm, and the immoral. In the opinion of the Association's representatives, these groups could never become fully productive members of society; instead, the charity workers believed, their fate lay in the almshouses and potter's fields of the cities.[19]

Organizations that allocated charity to the old were hardly more hopeful. Their approach was purely philanthropic; rarely did they attempt to help their elderly clients remain self-supporting.[20] Piecework employment was given to the young, while the old received alms and sympathy.[21] This distinction reflected ideas that had shaped mid-19th-century reform. The individuals who staffed benevolent societies were generally convinced that poverty would only be eradicated after the personalities of the poor had been transformed. Once the impoverished had become hardworking, thrifty, and temperate, they could not fail to be successful; their rise into the middle class would then be assured. In the early 1800s, evangelically-inspired volunteers believed this could be achieved through religious guidance and moral exhortation. Venturing into the slums, scores of friendly visitors sought to uplift the poor through their own enthusiasm and example. By mid-century, however, some of the leaders of the reform movement were beginning to reassess their earlier assumptions. The national depression of 1837-1844, and the massive immigration that followed revealed serious social problems. In many large urban centers, opportunities for the poor appeared harshly limited; often there were far more unskilled workers than available jobs.[22] Given such conditions, personality reform seemed almost hopeless; the downtrodden could hardly succeed while caught in a cycle of poverty, joblessness, and disease. Thus, the representatives of many charity organizations began to emphasize the importance of alotting work to the able bodied. Some associations, such as the Female Moral Reform Society and the Five Points Mission, sent caravans of youngsters into the countryside, where, they hoped, they might find both jobs and an uplifting environment. Other groups established urban workhouses and training centers to teach young adults how to profit by their own endeavors. Once these individuals had imbibed the values inherent in such labor, they would be able to start productive new lives away from the ominous tenements.[23]

For the indigent old, however, both the original philosophy and its modified successor were hardly applicable. Lacking the elastic personality of the child or the strength and agility of the adult, they could not be considered the most promising candidates for salvation. At least by uplifting the young, many charity workers reasoned, they might prevent old-age dependency in the future; once the impoverished adult had become thrifty and diligent, he would be able to save for his own senescence. Most experts conceded, however, that little could be done for the present generation of elderly paupers. With habits and ideas deeply engraved by time, their personalities seemed intractable; poverty had left a permanent mark upon their characters.[24] The most that could be achieved was to assure these individuals the basic necessities of life. Thus, while charity groups rescued other indigent persons from the almshouse, the old became the asylum's dominant inmate.[25] Characterized as unable to play a fully productive role in society, the elderly were sent to the poorhouse to spend their final days in destitution. Municipal policy took shape, if only as a consequence of the neglect of private philanthropy.

In the first half of the 19th century, a few charitable organizations attempted to save a small number of select individuals from this fate; yet the alternative they created was in no way a repudiation of the general policy of reform. In touring the cities' almshouses, charity volunteers had discovered elderly inmates who had not been born among the impoverished. Middle-class widows and spinsters, if suddenly without support, were often forced to seek shelter in the almshouse—a fact that alarmed some reformers. Thus, for those aged females "not inured to the struggles of penury," [26] concerned welfare advocates established a novel institution: the old age home. Sharply segregated on the basis of age, this new asylum was designed to meet all the needs of worthy women in their dotage, while allowing them to retain their dignity. In founding these homes, however, charity organizers only further underlined the nonproductive status of the old. Anxious to convince the public that they were not pauperizing their recipients, they portrayed the aged women as the most helpless and needy members of society. Lacking a past skill, and too ill to have a foreseeable future, these elderly individuals profited most from total isolation. In the late 1800s, many welfare advocates extended this characterization of the elderly to apply not only to poor women but to lonely old men and aged couples as well.[27] Removed from the mass of unemployed, the old had become segregated as the proper recipients of total care and benevolent consideration.[28]

This expansion of the old age home, as well as detailed studies on the elderly almshouse population [29] revealed the complexity of dependency in the aged. Contrary to the original beliefs of welfare experts, many among the elderly had never become "inured to penury." Along with widows and spinsters, the asylums filled with workingmen unable to save for their senescence. Paid only enough to survive, these individuals fell into destitution if they became unemployed. In the 19th century, very few workers had the financial resources necessary for a comfortable retirement. Regardless of their age, they had little choice; either they found work or faced institutionalization.

By the late decades of the 19th century, the predicament of the aged worker had attracted the attention of several industrialists as well as reformers. To guard against dependency in their laborers, they developed a new type of insurance: the old age pension. Like the solutions devised by charity organizations, these programs segregated the old and sharply limited their right to employment. But, compared with other welfare creations, these plans had a far-reaching effect. Through restrictions that included a mandatory age for retirement, they forced nonproductivity not only on the indigent old but on the still active, though elderly, wage earner as well.

In funding these programs, industrialists often emphasized their charitable motives; here was the gospel of wealth at its best, providing for those who had grown old and disabled. Yet these plans did not arise purely out of benevolent ideals. Instead, the development of pension systems, and the effect they had on the old, reflected the turbulent industrial conditions in which they initially developed.

The first businesses to adopt such programs were those connected with the railroads—a fact that was hardly accidental. In the late 19th century transportation executives confronted the best organized and most powerful brotherhoods of workers. These unions demonstrated their strength by calling for strikes that paralyzed the nation's business. Faced with the growing power of labor, and troubled by a highly unstable work force, the managers in this industry adopted paternalistic welfare programs, hopeful that they would pacify their disruptive employees. In the midst of the massive railroad strikes of 1877, the Chairman of the Board of Directors of the Chicago, Burlington, and Quincy Railroad, for example, explained the advantages of a relief program to the line's President. "I think," J.N.A. Griswald wrote to Robert Harris:

> that the sooner these plans are elaborated and adopted the better, in order to show the men that while we will not submit to their dictation we still have their interest at heart and are desirous of making them understand that the interests of the corporation and their own are mutual.[30]

The old age pension was one form of such relief. First proposed by the railroad-connected American Express Company in 1875, it was put into full operation in 1884 by the Baltimore and Ohio Railroad. Other transportation firms followed the B&O's lead, along with companies that dealt with mining, manufacturing, banking, and steel. Like the railroads, these were businesses that either faced strikes or were concerned about the stability of their workers.[31] By 1910, 49 such plans had been devised; in the next fifteen years the number rose to around 370.[32] Although most of the programs had been adopted in the early decades of the 20th century, they did not diverge from the initial design; in both form and effect, they reflected the origins of their 19th-century conception.

The great majority of these funds enacted similar provisions. The employee was required to work without interruption for a specified number of years, usually more than twenty or thirty. Upon reaching an advanced age, he could retire; after attaining a somewhat higher age, his departure became mandatory. He then received (in most cases) an annual pension of 1% of his average salary times the number of years he had been in the company's service. In making this provision, large industries often included a maximum age for hiring (usually between thirty-five and forty-five, though at times as low as thirty). Frequently this measure was presented as a charitable consideration; the management would hardly feel morally justified in forcing an aged worker to retire who could not qualify for his pension.[33]

Few workers, however, considered these programs a demonstration of their company's charitable instinct. Unlike other types of relief programs that were often jointly run by both management and labor, [34] pension funds remained firmly in the hands of the executives; workers neither contributed to their treasuries nor exerted any influence in their administration. This made the annuity a gift from the industrialist rather than a right earned through years of labor. The rules of the pension guaranteed that the laborer clearly understood this condition. Each plan included (in some form) a provision that read:

> No employee shall be considered to have a right to be retained in the service of the company, or any right or claim to any pension allowance, and the company expressly reserves its right and privilege to discharge any officer, agent or employee, when the interest of the company in its judgment may so require without any liability or any claim for a pension or their allowance other than salary or wages due and unpaid.[36]

To merit his pension, the worker, therefore, had to adhere closely to any regulations set by the management. Thus, he could neither make demands upon the firm nor quit to find more profitable employment. Most laborers, however, had been highly mobile; in the 19th century, the work force as a whole was extremely unstable. The majority of men employed by the railroads, for example, worked less than six months before seeking a transfer.[36] Once retirement plans were established, such mobility was no longer profitable. Basing their allotment on length of service, rather than establishing a flat rate or one based on merit, late-19th-century pension programs tied the worker's benefits directly to his own stability. Despite offers of better jobs or higher wages from other companies, the laborer then had an interest in remaining in the same position. "The pension," one bank president declared, "operates repeatedly as an incentive to hold men between the ages of forty and fifty when they have acquired the experience and skill which makes them especially valuable and prevents their being tempted away by slightly increased wages for a temporary period."[37]

Nor could the employee act in any way that might disturb the management. As each pension plan stated, the laborer who disrupted the company or provoked the executives would lose his pension—as well as his job. The management hoped that this would protect them against strikes; a worker, if he were anxious to receive an annuity in his old age, might be less willing to take part in a walkout. But pensions were more than an antistrike measure for they could exert control over other aspects of the worker's behavior. His conduct, not only while on the job, but after hours, and even well into the years of his retirement, had to meet with management approval if he expected to receive lifelong monthly payments. For example, the First National Bank of Chicago, which organized a pension fund in 1899, explained its definition of improper behavior explicit. Although it established a mandatory program that automatically collected 3% of the employee's wage, the management retained firm control over its administration. A *partial* listing of actions that might cause revocation of the pension privilege read:

> In the event a pensioned officer or employee shall engage in any other employment without the consent of the establishment's permission the pension will be forfeited. Any clerk who marries on a salary of less than $1,000 a year without the consent of the establishment forfeits all benefit rights and is subject to dismissal from employment. In case of bankruptcy of the pensioner, or of his taking the benefit of any insolvency law, or on his conviction for felony or misdemeanor, or on any judgment entered against, and in the case of any widow, in her misconduct being proved to the satisfaction of the bank, all benefit rights are forfeited provided, however, that the establishment may in its discretion renew the pension for any of the reasons named. Unwarrantable losses for which any officer or employee is responsible may, if they do not result in his dismissal result in his being punished in the discretion of the establishment by forfeiture of the offending officer's or employee's interest in the fund beyond what he himself has contributed to it without the interest. The benefits under the fund are not treated as vested rights: they are granted at the discretion of the establishment and continue only during the establishment's pleasure.[38]

The Grand Trunk Railway Company discovered an additional use for its pension.

Although the general manager of the line praised its system before the World's Railway Commerce Congress of 1893 for its "relief of the individuals from anxieties attendant upon the contemplation of the period of inability to provide for himself and his family . . .,"[39] the worries of its aged employees were far from over. In 1915, when its workers went out on strike, the management proceeded to recall these retired wage earners. The choice it gave the men was simple: either they returned to work or lost all their benefits.[40] With the pension as privilege, the employees would have to remain perpetually loyal to the firm.

Unions, therefore, viewed management-controlled pension plans with grave misgivings.[41] Not only did they attempt to regulate the daily behavior of the worker but placed an additional restriction on his future. According to these programs, when an employee reached a specified age he was automatically retired. Although prior to this many workers had left the labor force because of injury or ill health, their departure had not been based solely on age. The benefits granted by the workers' beneficial societies recognized this fact; while they allocated funds for death, accident, or disability, they did not provide for the older worker who merely decided to stop working. In the 19th century, the individual received aid if he were disabled; otherwise he was expected to obtain some type of employment.[42]

Traditionally, both management and labor had enacted measures to make the continued participation of the elderly possible. Some companies set aside less strenuous positions for the old and crippled. An elderly engineer might become keeper of the roundhouse; an old steel worker transferred into the position of plant watchman.[43] On the Chicago, Burlington, and Quincy Railroad, for example, one limited freight line, the Chariton branch, was reserved strictly for the elderly and disabled.[44] Often trade unions further adjusted their regulations to suit the needs of their elderly members. According to an early-20th-century report of the Commissioner of Labor:

> Many of the local unions of the various national unions that do not feel justified, under present conditions, in establishing old-age benefits have had in operation for many years provisions that permitted the old member to work for a wage rate lower than the rate fixed for younger members; in some local unions the member has been permitted to fix his own wage rate, the only condition being that he observe union rules. Many of the unions relieve the old member from the payment of all contributions except assessment for death benefits.[45]

Pensions that eliminated the old from the work force directly countered these measures. Yet, there was surprisingly little organized union resistance. In part, this occurred because the provisions created by the worker's societies for their elderly members did not keep the old worker employed. Even without mandatory age limitations, companies often released their workers when they advanced in age. Although most of these individuals remained in the labor force (and thus were not recorded as permanently unemployed or retired), they had difficulty obtaining new positions.[46] As we have seen, discrimination against hiring the old was not a late-19th-century innovation. Reduced from higher paying jobs, many of these workers searched for jobs as unskilled laborers.[47] At least with a pension, these individuals might escape dependency. Eventually, unions would also provide benefits for their members based on years of service and age. Although these plans did not demand that the worker retire and collect a pension, their adoption testified to the need to provide for an age-limited work cycle.[48]

But union opposition to retirement plans was muted for another reason as well. By accepting pensions, workers won an additional concession for their companies. A basic aspect of most pension plans was management's recognition of the seniority system. With employment practices based on years of service, workers felt they could eliminate the most extreme cases of managerial favoritism and nepotism.[49] (Even today, these two issues remain vitally interrelated. While the AFL-CIO opposes unilateral compulsory retirement, it accepts this condition when it hinges on the seniority system.)[50] Executives, in turn, saw advantages in accepting the plan. Although they lost some of their control over hiring, firing, and promotions, they exchanged this right in order to secure the further stability of their work force. As Robert Harris, President of the Chicago, Burlington, and Quincy Railroad, explained to his board chairman:

> It will not be disputed that it was the influence of the older men to which we owed the fact that the men at Aurora did not participate in the late troubles. The plan proposed [of graduated wages based on length of service] would operate to make the older men still more conservative..[They would earn extra money] which they would lose if they gave occasion for their discharge. I think that the difficulty that the Boston & Providence people experienced would be met by having the rule apply to those employed on stated service in the several departments.[51]

One drawback of this program, however, was the creation of a labor force staffed by older and highly-paid workers. According to the seniority system, any cutback would first affect the newest workers, leaving their elders employed and collecting relatively high wages. In adopting pension plans, companies responded in part to this dilemma; most programs included a mandatory retirement age. With the tacit cooperation of the unions, the elderly laborer was automatically pensioned at seventy or sixty-five, his place—as well as his seniority—vacated to make room for the promotion of the midlevel employee and the hiring of the younger worker.

Obviously industrialists would not have included this provision if they had anticipated a labor shortage.[52] At the end of the 19th century, however, European and country-to-city migration created an abundant supply of labor. To many Americans, this seemingly limitless pool of would-be industrial workers was vivid proof that the United States needed to reassess its immigration policy.[53] To industrial entrepreneurs, however, these migrants represented an unlimited source of employees who could easily and cheaply replace their higher-paid predecessors. They saw no need for immigration restriction. Thus, like middle-class reformers who had assigned available work to the young, industrialists followed a somewhat parallel course, setting strict age limits for the hiring and firing of workers. Through their pensions, they had clearly marked the point at which productive youth merged into incapacitated senescence.

Publicly, there was little opposition to this policy. Pensions, in fact, were entirely consistent with a growing emphasis in late-19th-century thought on a need to measure and categorize man's physical and mental capabilities. Experts from many fields incorporated the latest medical and protosociological theories into their disciplines in an attempt to define the proper role for each individual in mass society. In its extreme form, this ideological outlook led eugenics authorities to demand the sterilization of the measurably incompetent; only the most worthy were to sire future generations of Americans. Similarly, if somewhat less drastically, some labor experts rejected traditional laissez-faire principles in order to assure work to the most fit.[54] In their self-consciously rational design for the labor market, they automatically excluded the aged worker regardless of individual health or abilities. The popular view of aging held that, by the very process of becoming old, the aged employee necessarily had to be less productive than his younger counterpart. According to many physicians, aging could best be understood by conceiving of the body as a limited bank of vitality. At birth, the organism contained a store of energy that it used for growth and repair; by old age, however, this supply was all but gone. "The old man's bank is already overdrawn," wrote Dr. J.M. French in 1892. "He is living from hand to mouth."[55] Retirement became part of the medically endorsed prescription for conserving the elderly's rapidly dissipating strength "After sixty," admonished Dr. A.L. Loomis in 1888, "failure [of the old] to recognize the changing condition of their vital powers and continuance in their business habits of earlier life, after this period, are no better than suicide."[56]

Thus, when economic authorities recommended the mandatory elimination of the old from the job market, they relied upon the authority of medical science incorporating the language of the physician into their discussions. Francis A. Walker, one of the nation's leading late-19th-century economists, for example, viewed the overcrowded labor market with concern. As a partial solution he called for the creation of "factory acts prohibiting labor for all classes beyond the term which physiological science accepts as consistent with soundness and vigor."[57] This was a measure that would not only relieve the intense competition for jobs, but was in full accord with the physician's prescription for health and longevity. The elderly worker was advised to forget the "hurly-burly" of the active life and turn to rest and meditation. It was in his own best interest.[58]

As America entered the 20th century, an additional rationale supported the mandatory separation of old from young. Endorsers of pensions rephrased their arguments; they now not only referred to their programs as being highly ethical and benevolent, but, in addition, legitimated them with that by-word of the new industrial era: efficiency. In a period of increasing mechanical complexity, this had become a national craze. Efficiency experts invaded all fields and occupations, assured that they could bring rational order and simplicity to every human movement.[59] Armed with the omnipresent stopwatch, they set out to find the standard time for each job—that is, "the reasonable time for a good worker to accomplish the task set."[60] In this computation, experience and past knowledge were discounted, if not altogether disclaimed. The efficiency expert hoped to revolutionize work, completely re-educating the laborer as to the proper way to do each task. Eventually, publicists for this position contended the scientific manager would train employees who, like pieces of machinery, could by easily interchanged or, if need be, totally replaced. On the line, one leading efficiency authority asserted:

> the youngest member is as capable potentially as the highest, and whether he rises to supreme command in five years or forty-five depends on opportunity. When he has reached the age of retirement he gives way to a junior as one day gives way to another. There was nothing worth preserving, and the elimination of the temporary head produces a desirable wriggle of life all the way down the line.[61]

No expert would have disputed this assessment. The industrial pace, all agreed, used up the laborer, leaving him at sixty-five little more than a shell of his youthful self. In an era filled with tests and measures, however, this assumption remained unproven and significantly unexamined; few, if any correlations between age and efficiency were ever produced to convince the public of its validity.[62] Instead, experts often cited the 1873 study of Dr. George M. Beard who had crudely attempted to relate age to productivity. Compiling a list of the greatest geniuses of the past and present, Beard had declared that their composite biography scientifically proved their uselessness once they reached old age. "On the average," he wrote, "the last twenty years of the lives of original geniuses are unproductive . . . "[63]

In an overcrowded and increasingly seniority-based labor market, this became a generally accepted—and highly useful—conception. "Most employers," the President of the National City Bank of New York wrote, "regretfully acknowledge that it takes but a few years to use up a worker, so high is the pace at which work is now done. The employer is not to blame. He must keep his output up to the mark or be forced to the wall.[64]

One solution seemed clear enough: replace the aged worker with young and efficient through a system of retirement benefits. Explained in these terms, the rationale for pensions had significantly altered. Previously, relief was given to the totally disabled and dependent worker. His pension represented his only hope of escaping permanent almshouse residency. With pensions awarded chiefly to enhance the company's own efficiency, however, the definition of who should retire had considerably broadened. It now included not only those completely incapacitated, but all workers whose long years of service had become indisputable proof of their necessarily weakened and thus inefficient condition. These employees, efficiency experts cautioned, were just as much a threat to high production as the totally disabled; their slower pace and reduced output only inhibited the standard rate of the other wage earners.[65] Pensions, therefore, became a "wise business practice,"[66] ridding firms of their overpaid and underproductive members—the "dead weight," as one executive elected to term them.[67]

Moreover, in the first decade of the 20th century, while industrialists praised the economic merits of pensions and began to retire their employees, social analysts drew attention to federal, state, and city positions that daily served the public. Adopting the language of the efficiency expert, they set out to catalogue the waste inherent in these municipal jobs. Here, after all, were workers paid by taxes and expected to serve the public. Without a watchful industrialist to retire them when aged, and without a means of collecting a pension were they to retire voluntarily, municipal employees remained in their jobs far beyond their period of greatest usefulness. This, welfare experts cautioned, had important effects on everyone: children were not getting the best education, fires and crimes received less than full attention, and clerks and laborers paid by the government were backward and inefficient.[68] Nowhere was this point made clearer than in the influential *Report of the Massachusetts Commission on Old Age Pension Annuities, and Insurance* issued in 1910. A model for other states, the Massachusetts' *Report* went to great length to document the inefficiency evident in just one sector of Boston's municipal services:

> The returns show the following facts regarding the number of pensionable employees, their length of service, compensation and efficiency:
> The total number of employees over sixty-five is 491; over seventy years, 168. The amount of compensation paid to employees over sixty-five is $419,888.43; over seventy, $273,000. The number over sixty-five reported as inefficient is 296. The compensation paid to this group is

$200,194.35.

The percentage of inefficient employes among the employees over sixty-five is strikingly large in many departments. For example, in the cleaning and watering division of the street department 35 employed, of whom all are inefficient; in the cemetery department 16 persons over sixty-five are employed, of whom all are reported as inefficient; in the park department, 27 are employed, of whom 24 are inefficient.

The period of service is over 30 years in the case of 119 employees over sixty-five or 25 per cent of the total. Only 5 per cent, or 42 persons, have been in the employ of the city less than five years.

The leading departments, in respect to number of pensionable employees, rank as follows: 1) paving division of the street department, 109 over sixty-five years; 2) water department, 65; 3) sanitary division, street department, 58; 4) sewer division, street department, 47; 5) cleaning and water division, street department, 35; 6) park division, 27; 7) ferry division, street department, 26; 8) cemetery department, 16.

Although the *Report* indicated neither the measures used to determine inefficiency nor the number of substandard nonelderly laborers, its conclusion was clearly stated: the most economical solution was to pension off the inefficient and replace them with young, and unemployed, workers.[69]

Efficiency and welfare experts, therefore, joined economists and industrialists endorsing age-based pensions as a humane solution to widespread industry problems. They agree, after all on the principle behind it: the young would receive work while the elderly attained security away from the almshouse. Moreover, this had become a profitable solution for all; once production was no longer repressed by inefficient wage earners, the output of the country would multiply. "The effect of such a policy on the struggling millions of working people," prophesized Lee Welling Sequier in his often-quoted study on old age dependency, "would be little short of electric."[70] Retirement had now achieved the status of panacea for a whole host of social evils.

With this enthusiasm for the pension system came a recognition of a new, age limited work cycle. The laborer was no longer expected to continue to work until permanently disabled but merely until he attained a particular age. Mandatory retirement and the age-based pensions that justified it both reflected and furthered this transformation; the institution not only arose out of changing ideas about the elderly's need and ability to work, but legitimated the demand that the aged should no longer be employed.[71] With the Great Depression, the conception of the proper work cycle gained national recognition; in the social programs created to deal with severe unemployment, age became an important classification. For the young, welfare experts advocated work projects such as the W.P.A. and the Civilian Conservation Corps; for the old, they enacted the social security of age-based pensions.

Yet, as we have seen, this well-defined demarcation between old and young had not always existed. Instead, as this paper has attempted to show, it arose out of a complex set of problems stemming above all from an oversupply of labor in a rapidly industrializing society. Within this environment, traditional conceptions of work, poverty, and unemployment were often found wanting and were redefined to meet the changing times. No longer able to view poverty merely in terms of the habits of the poor, the members of many benevolent societies began to allot work to the young, convinced that their malleable personalities and energies would lead them to self-sufficient respectability. Industrialists also endorsed an age-structured work force, hopeful that it might control many of their labor difficulties. Mandatory retirement thus became a multifaceted solution: it promised work to the young, seniority to the unions, efficiency to the engineer, stability and discipline to the employer.

Enforced retirement also reflected widely-held notions about the abilities of the aged. The same set of beliefs that had segregated the elderly into old age homes and almshouses now restricted their right to employment. Basic to every aspect of the pension system was a conception of the old as incapacitated, inefficient, and, above all, the most powerless sector of society. To some degree, this characterization had a factual basis; the unemployed aged who were forced to seek refuge in institutions certainly did profit from the pension system. In addition, many elderly people gladly accepted their years of leisure.[72] But they did not leave the work force merely because they had grown old. The restrictions that limited the employment of the elderly were consciously devised in an attempt to regulate the labor market. As a result, in the late 19th century, mandatory retirement first developed into a new, economically-determined and culturally-legitimated stage of existence. Attitudes and institutions had converged in the creation of this significant innovation.

FOOTNOTES

I would like to thank Dr. Charles E. Rosenberg. Dr. Drew Gilpin Faust, and Dr. John Modell for their valuable comments and criticisms on this essay and Dr. Walter M. Licht for his assistance in obtaining railroad data. The publication was supported in part by NIH Grant LM02904 from the National Library of Medicine.

1. United States Department of Commerce, Bureau of the Census, *Detailed Characteristics. United States Summary: 1970*, Table 215. I have used the statistics from men for comparison with the 19th-century figures cited by social reformers and economists, which were always given for men only. For women, this statistic, of course, is much higher (89.8%), for both men and women it is 83.4% for about 17,000,000 individuals.

2. I. M. Rubinow, *Social Insurance* (New York, 1913), 305. This figure is 26.2%.

3. By 1940, only 45% of all men over sixty-five remained in the labor force.

4. These figures are for white males age twenty to seventy. Due to high infant mortality a much smaller percentage of the entire population survived to age seventy. In 1890, only about 32.1% of the population reached the advanced age of seventy: by 1940, 69.6% survived to this year. David Hackett Fischer, *Growing Old in America* (New York, 1977). Appendix: Table IV and V, 225-27.

5. Cotton Mather, *The Diary of Cotton Mather,* Vol. 2, 1709-1724 (Boston, 1912), 240.

6. *The Statistics of the Population of the United States.* Ninth Census. Vol 1 (Washington D.C., Government Printing, 1872). Table XXVIII, 698. In 1870, there were 989.516 men over sixty; of these, 634,837 were employed.

7. See, for example, Gertrude Bancroft, *The American Labor Force: Its Growth and Changing Composition* (New York, 1958): John Durand, *The Labor Force in the United States* (New York, 1948); Stanley Lebergott, *Manpower in Economic Growth: The American Record since 1800* (New York, 1964); and Clarence D. Long, *The Labor Force Under Changing Income and Employment* (Princeton, 1958).

8. These two approaches are neither contradictory nor exclusive. Bancroft, Durand, Lebergott and Long all discuss historical forces that caused a change in the size and composition of the labor force. See, in addition, Reinhard Bendix, *Work and Authority in Industry* (New York and Evanston, 1956); Juanita Kreps, "Economics of Retirement," in Ewald Busse and Eric Pfeiffer, eds., *Behavior and Adaptation in Later Life* (Boston, 1969; H. Orhbach, "Social Values and Institutionalization of Retirement" in Richard H. Williams, Clark Tibbits and Wilma Donahue, eds., *Processes of Aging* (New York, 1963), and Harris Schrank, "The Work Force," in Matilda W. Riley, Marilyn Johnson, and Anne Foner, eds., *Aging and Society: A Sociology of Age Stratification*, Vol. 3 (New York, 1972), 160-197.

9. At this time, the old comprised 4.2% of the population and 6.1% of the entire work force,

(males, 15 +), Rubinow, 365.

10. *Ibid,* 306.

11. By 1940, the location of the laborer seemed to influence his chances for employment. On the farm, the majority of workers aged sixty-five to seventy-four remained in the labor force (60.5%), while in the city only a minority of the same group could retain their employed positions (46.2%), Sixteenth Census of the United States, 1940, *Population Characteristics of Persons not in the Labor Force* (Washington, D.C., 1943), 4; also cited in Durand, 68.

12. Clarence Long has argued that it was precisely the entrance of these younger women that pushed old men out of the labor market. He cites that women's higher level of education as the most plausible reason for this trend. This explanation, however seems to me to be problematic on two levels. First, as Harris Schrank writes in his study on the work force, the figures do not confirm this hypothesis "for when education or level of skill is held constant, older workers are re-employed to a lesser extent than younger workers." (177) Secondly, when studied on an industry-to-industry basis (rather than viewing the labor force as a whole), mandatory retirement of old men does not seem directly influenced by the entrance of young women. The industries first adopting retirement policies were precisely those having the lowest level of women (i.e., transportation, mining, steel, and municipal positions such as policemen and firemen). This does not mean that the entrance of women did not push younger men into more male-oriented and higher-paying fields. As this paper will, aruge, an abundant supply of labor was instrumental in the adoption of age-based retirement policies. Long's equation, however, may be far more complex than he suggests, Long, 23-31; 159-180.

13. For a simplar view see Tamara K. Hareven. "The Last Stage: Historical Adulthood and Old Age," *Daedalus,* Vol. 105. No. 4 (Fall, 1976), 17; for an idealization of old age in the past, see, W. Andrew Achenbaum, "The Obsolesence off Old Age," *Journal of Social History,* Vol. 8, 48-62. (Fall, 1974) The author repeatedly accepts literary prescriptions as reality and ignores the actual living conditions of the old. This is also true of David Hackett Fischer's recently published study, *Growing Old in America* (New York, 1977). Fischer contends that before the transformation of western societies, (c. 1770-1820), the old were highly venerated in America. Yet the findings cited by Fischer seem to confirm that it was the elderly's ability to control the resources of the society—rather than their age—that caused them to be feared and respected. Fischer himself concedes that veneration "did not exist for the poor. To be old and poor and outcast in America was certainly not be venerated but to be despised." (60) For a more balanced view of attitudes towards aging in western societies see, Peter N. Stearns, *Old Age in European Society,* (New York, 1976), particularly chapter 1.

14. *A Report of the Record Commissioners of the City of Boston containing Boston Records from 1660-1701.* Vol 7 (Boston, 1881), Boston City Document 68 (1682); *A Report of the Record Commissioners of the City of Boston containing Boston Records from 1700-1728,* Vol. 8 (Boston, 1882), Boston City Document 77 (1722).

15. John Demos, *A Little Commonwealth* (New York, 1970), 177-78; Philip Greven, Jr., *Four Generations: Population, Land and Family in Colonial Andover* (Ithaca and London, 1970).

16. In colonial days, even an aged pauper was not permitted alms from a town of which he was not an official resident. Nicholas Warner, for example, was repeatedly warned in 1707 to leave the city of Boston. Although Mr. Warner protested that he was over the age of eighty and infirm, the selectmen held sternly to their judgment. *A Report of the Record Commissioners of the City of Boston containing the Records of the Boston Selectmen, 1701-1715* (Boston, 1884), 57; *A Report of the Record Commissioners of the City of Boston containing Miscellaneous Papers,* Vol. 10 (Boston, 1886), 113. For a similar case involving one William Smalcon, see *A Report of the Record Commissioners of the City of Boston containing the Records of the Boston Selectmen 1716-1736* (Boston, 1885), October 28, 1720, 76.

17. Mathew Carey, *Letters on the Condition of the Poor* (Philadelphia, 1835), February 22, 1835, 6.

18. The records of the Board of Guardians of Philadelphia for the year May 1829-May 1830 show that 549 individuals received weekly outdoor relief. Of these, 390, or more than 71%, were over the age of sixty, *Hazard's Register of Pennsylvania,* Vol. VI, No. 17 (October 23, 1830), 266-67.

19. A spokesman for the Association explained, "But it does not follow, that all applicants will be relieved by the Association: for some have claims on charities founded for specific objects: many are only fit subjects for the Alms-House; others are paupers by profession, and imposters . . . " *First Annual Report of the New York Association for Improving the Conditions of the Poor* (1845) (New York, 1845), 20; see also, Carroll Smith-Rosenberg, *Religion and the Rise of the City,* (Ithaca and London, 1971), 251.

20. In the early 19th century, charity organizations did report giving the old employment. for example, in 1835, Mathew Carey described the activities of the Provident Society that was supplying women—both old and young—with material for shirts. Carey made it clear that the elderly were receiving employment, although he assumed that their output, and their earnings, would be less than the young. Carey, *A Plea for the Poor* (Philadelphia, 1837), 5. Piecework employment was also evident in the early annual reports of the first private old age home in Philadelphia, The Indigent Widows' and Single Women's Society. These reports discussed the good spirits and feeling of self-sufficiency of the inmates. See, for example, the *Second Annual Report* (Philadelphia, 1818), 5; *Third Annual Report* (1819), 4; *Eleventh Annual Report* (1827), 5. By mid-century, however, this attitude had noticeably changed. In 1849, the managers of the home explained that their inmates could not possibly be productive as "all the beneficiaries here are very aged, the youngest considerably more than sixty years old, the rest beyond seventy, eighty and ninety, and that as a matter of course, they are rarely free from infirmity and disease and few are able to contribute by their industry to their support," *Thirty-third Annual Report* (1849), 4.

21. Some organizations felt they had to coax even this sympathy from the public. The managers of The Indigent Widows' and Single Women's Society complained. "But with the aged, we have few sympathies. They belong to a generation that has pased away, they can promise us neither reciprocation nor reward. Our reverence for them is rarely an active principle; and it is only the chastened spirit of Christianity that teachers us to revere the poor." *Twenty-seventh Annual Report (1942)*, 4.

22. In the midst of the national depression of the 1850s, for example, authorities in Philadelphia estimated that between 20,000 and 30,000 workers were unemployed; in New York City, the numbers rose to between 30,000 and 40,000. Leah Hannah Feder, *Unemployment Relief in Periods of Depression* (New York, 1936), 19.

23. This was the philosophy of such mid-century reform groups as the Female Moral Reform Society, the Children's Aid Society, the Five Points Mission, the Five Points House of Industry, and the Juvenile Asylum. Smith-Rosenberg, 251.

24. In explaining their emphasizing on youth, the Children's Aid Society stated a common prejudice against helping the aged. In their third annual report they wrote, "It is a grievous and laborious trial to strive against human evil on any side, but when to the effect of unfavorable circumstances and bad passions and selfishness is added the influence of time and habit, the labor under usual estimates, becomes almost hopeless." *Third Annual Report of the Children's Aid Society* (1856), (New York, 1856), 5.

25. By 1910, although the old made up only 4.3% of the population of the United States, they constituted about 33% of the national almshouse population. Moreover, as one study in Massachusetts showed, the aged almshouse population was far more stable than other inmates. While only 43% of all young asylum residents would be in the almshouse after one year, this was true for 70% of the elderly. Massachusetts Commission on Old Age Pensions, Annuities, and Insurance, *Report of the Commission on Old Age Pensions, Annuities, and Insurance* (New York, 1976 [originally published, Boston 1910]), 36-37. In New York City, in fact, the changed composition of the almshouse caused it to be renamed the City Home for the Aged and Infirm, I.L. Nascher, *Geriatrics: The Diseases of Old Age and their Treatment* (Philadelphia, 1914), 486.

26. the Indigent Widow's and Single Women's Society described their home as "especially designed to furnish an asylum for those whose earlier lives have been passed in the more refined walks of life, and whom experience, therefore, has not inured to the struggles of penury." *Twenty-eighth Annual Report* (1844), 3.

27. When the managers of an old age home for men opened their Philadelphia institution in 1865, they emphasized the total nonproductivity of ther inmates. ". . . our first duty," they wrote, "was to convince others of that which our own experience had taught us, namely that there is absolutely no class of humanity so sadly powerless to aid themselves, so useless in any of the ordinary duties of the household and so unwelcomed among strangers as destitute old men," *Annual Report of the Old Man's Home for 1866* (Philadelphia, 1867), 4.

28. For the origins of the old age home see Carole Haber, "The Old Folks at Home: The Development of Institutionalized Care for the Aged in Nineteenth-Century Philadelphia" *The Pennsylvania Magazine of History and Biography*, Vol. CI, No. 2 (April, 1977), 240-257: Ethel McClure, *More than a Roof: The Development of Minnesota Poor Farms and Homes for the Aged* (St. Paul, 1968).

29. See, for example, Charles Lawrence, *History of the Philadelphia Almshouses and Hospitals* (New York, 1976 [originally published Philadelphia, 1905]): Massachusetts Bureau

of Labor Statistics, *Tenth Annual Report, January, 1879* (Boston, 1879), 100-116; Massachusetts *Report of the Commission on Old Age Pensions, Annuities, and Insurance,* 35-45: *Report of the Pennsylvania Commission on Old Age Pensions,* (Harrisburg, Pa., 1919), 15-66.

30. J.N.A. Griswald to Robert Harris, October 5, 1877, in Thomas Cochran, *The Railroad Leaders, 1845-1890,* (Cambridge, 1953), 344.

31. Banks were one of the first totally white-collar organizations to establish pension funds, yet their motives did not differ greatly from other large industries. Bankers were concerned with the large turnover of their staffs, particularly when large amounts of money were handled by numerous employees unknown to the management (Bankers Trust, for example, had a staff of 1500 employees). With a pension, one bank president explained, the workers "are apt to devote their best efforts exclusively to their careers, and to be in less danger of diverting their energies into side channels of money making—channels which may easily lead them on dangerous grounds." E.A. Vanderlip, "Insurance from the Employers' Standpoint." *Proceedings of the National Conference of Charities and Corrections,* 1907, 462. Banks did differ from other large industries, however, in often making their funds contributory, automatically substracting 3% of their employees' wages.

32. Abraham Epstein, *The Problem of Old Age Pensions in Industry* (Harrisburg, Pa., 1926), 115-126.

33. See, for example, F. Spencer Baldwin, "Retirement Systems for Municipal Employes," *Annals of the American Academy of Political and Social Service,* Vol. 1 (July, 1911), 6-14: Epstein, *The Problem of Old Age Pensions in Industry,* 76-77.

34. Generally, these relief plans allocated benefits for accident, infirmity, and death. In 1908, there were about 350 company plans that were administered by the workers with management approval, if not direct intervention. More than 100 plans were jointly run by both the executives and workers. Another 30 programs were totally funded by the management. *Twenty-Third Annual Report of the Commissioner of Labor, (1908); Workman's Insurance and Benefit Funds in the United States* (Washington D.C., 1909), 271, 308, 607.

35. This particular restriction comes from the Western Electric Company Pension System (1906) as cited in the *Twenty-Third Annual Report of the Commissioner of Labor,* 646-47. Similar disclaimers can be found in all establishment-controlled programs.

36. Walter M. Licht, "Nineteenth-Century American Railway Men: A Study in the Organization and Nature of Work" (unpublished Ph. D. dissertation, Princeton University, 1977), chapter 2. Similar high turnover rates were reported in a number of large industries throughout the late 19th and early 20th centuries. In 1912, for example, 48% of the employees of the Ford Motor Company either quit or were fired; in 1907, ninety-one southern textile mills hired 57,000 new employees for 30,000 places. Daniel Nelson, *Managers and Workers: Origins of the New Factory System in the United States* (Wisconsin, 1975), 86.

37. Vanderlip, 462.

38. First National Bank of Chicago Pension Fund (1899) as reported in the *Twenty-Third Annual Report of the Commissioners of Labor,* 645-46.

39. L. J. Seargeant, "Superannuation of Railway Employes," *World's Railway Commerce Congress—Official Report* (Chicago, 1893), 175.

40. *Report of the Pennsylvania Commission on Old Age Pensions,* 114.

41. Frank Tracy Carlton, *The History and Problems of Organized Labor* (Boston, 1920), 315-16; E.E. Cummins, *The Labor Problem in the United States* (New York, 1932), 522; Henry Rogers Seager, *Social Insurance: A Program of Social Reform* (New York, 1910), 121-22.

42. In Pennsylvania, the law regulating and incorporating fraternal organizations (passed in 1893) also failed to consider the idea of pensions based solely on age. It allowed only for provisions in "case of sickness, disabily or death . . . " *Report of the Pennsylvania Commission on Old Age Pensions,* 198. This was also the case of the Massachusetts' law that incorporated fraternal organizations in that state. Massachusetts' *Report of the Commission on Old Age Pensions, Annuities, and Insurance,* 165. In the first decade of the 20th century, when unions did begin to adopt pension plans, they continued to make it clear that payment was for complete disability rather than for old age as such. The Order of Railroad Conductors (1908) demanded that the worker be "totally disabled and without means of support;" the Bricklayers, Masons, and Plasters International (1905), described their retirees as men "unable to secure sustaining employment; at any occupation." *Twenty-Third Annual Report of the Commissioner of Labor,* 204, 205.

43. See, for example, Massachusetts Board of Railroad Commissioners, *Twelfth Annual*

Report (1880), 59; Emory R. Johnson, "Railway Department for Relief and Insurance of Employes," *Annals of the American Academy of Political and Social Science,* Vol. VI (November, 1895), 68.

44. Paul V. Black, "The Development of Management Personnel Policies on the Burlington Railroad, 1860-1900" (unpublished Ph.D. dissertation, University of Wisconsin, 1972), 379-380.

45. *Twenty-Third Annual Report of the Commissioner of Labor,* 33.

46. Schrank, 177. In the 19th century, however, most men continued to see themselves as part of the labor market. In hospital death records—which surely recorded the most debilitated members of society—almost every elderly man reported some occupation. In the *Report of the Board of Administration of Charity Hospital (New Orleans) for the year 1876.* (Louisiana, 1876), for example, eighty-eight men over the age of sixty died during the year. Of these, only four, or less than 5%, were listed without occupations. Although one may logically question whether many of these men worked immediately before their deaths, they did not see themselves as retired.

47. A study done by the Pennsylvania Commission on Old Age Pensions that interviewed almost 4,000 aged workers in Pittsburgh, Reading, and Philadelphia concluded that "men past a certain age must quit even the skilled trades in which they have been engaged the greater part of their lives . . . While 36 per cent, stated that they were skilled or semi-skilled mechanics in their earlier days, only 23.8 per cent, of men past 50 years of age were still engaged in the same occupation." *Report of the Pennsylvania Commission on Old Age Pensions,* 101.

48. In 1919, Samuel Gompers explained, in part, why unions needed to recognize this new age-limited work cycle. In a letter to the Committee on Miners' Home and Pensions, he wrote, "Many of the proposals for social insurance are of a compulsory nature. Wage earners now find themselves confronted by this alternative: either labor organizations must make more comprehensive and more adequate provisions for trade union benefits or else they will have forced upon them compulsory social insurance under the control and direction of governmental agencies . . . " cited in the *Report of the Pennsylvania Commission on Old Age Pensions,* 200.

49. Dan H. Mater, "The Development and Operation of the Railroad Seniority System" *Journal of Business of the Univeristy of Chicago,* Vol. XII (1940), 399-402.

50. Harvey D. Shapiro, "Do Not Go Gently . . ." *The New York Times Magazine* (February 7, 1977), 36; on the connection between mandatory retirement and seniority see, Leonard Z. Breen, "Retirement—Norms, Behavior and Functions Aspects of Normative Behavior," in Williams, *et al., Processes of Aging,* 384.

51. Robert Harris, Letter to J.N.A. Griswald, December 10, 1877. Harris Letters, Chicago, Burlington & Quincy Papers, Newberry Library.

52. During war times, in contrast, companies loosened their regulations to adapt to the tightened labor situation. See Schrank, 163. During the Civil War, in fact, the efficiency of the Confederate railroad was disrupted by young workers being pressed into the military. To rectify this situation, the Board of Directors of the Virginia Central resolved "that the superintendant be instructed to employ men over forty years old in every case when a suitable person to perform the duties can be found, and that no assistant agent be retained who is between the age of eighteen and forty-five unless he is exempt from military duty," Charles W. Turner, *Chessie's Road* (Richmond, 1956), 45.

53. Labor unrest, unemployment, and the growth of the cities' slums were all cited as visible evidence that America was no longer able to absorb all the world's hunger and poverty. John Higham, *Strangers in the Land* (New York, 1972), chapter 7.

54. Frank J. Furstenberg and Charles A. Thrall have noted the presence of a "job rationing ideology" in a limited job market. This, a "system of shared beliefs about who should have the greatest access to the limited supply of jobs," tended the eliminate the elderly from the legitimate job market. Furnstenberg and Thrall cite the Social Security system and private pension plans as means of making the old feel "less obligated to work and less entitled to a job." Furstenberg and Thrall, "Counting the Jobless: The Impact of Job Rationing in the Measurement of Unemployment," *The Annals of the American Academy of Political Science,* Vol. 418 (March, 1975), 45-59; see also Kreps, "Economics of Retirement," 81.

55. J.M. French, "Food and Hygiene of Old Age," *The Journal of the American Medical Association,* Vol. XIX, No. 21 (November 19, 1892), 596.

56. A.L. Loomis, "The Climate and Environment Best Suited to Old Age in Health and Disease," *Transactions of the Fifth Annual Health Meeting of the American Climatological Association,* (1888), 8-9.

57. Francis A. Walker, *The Wages Question* (New York, 1876), 414-15.

58. J. Madison Taylor, "The Conservation of Energy in those of Advancing Years," *The Popular Science Monthly,* Vol. LXIV (February, 1904), 345. The ideas of American physicans such as French, Loomis, and Taylor will be explored in depth in a study on the medical conception of aging in the 19th century in which the author is presently engaged.

59. Samuel Haber, *Efficiency and Uplift: Scientific Management in the Progressive Era 1890-1920.* (Chicago, 1964)

60. Harrington Emerson, *Efficiency as a Basis for Operations and Wages* (New York, 1909), 98.

61. *Ibid.,* 68.

62. At least, I have not been able to find any. This has also been the conclusion of Robert Atchley. *The Sociology of Retirement* (Massachusetts, 1976), 15.

63. George M. Beard, *Legal Responsiblity in Old Age based on Researches into the Relation of Age to Work* (New York, 1873), 8.

64. Vanderlip, 458; see also, *The Carnegie Foundation for the Advancement of Teaching,* "The Moral Influence of a Pension System," Vol. 6 (1911), 23-31.

65. Bendix, 279; Emerson, 70, 159-60; Epstein, *Facing Old Age Dependency in the United States and Old Age Pensions* (New York, 1922), 162; Epstein. *The Problem of Old Age Pensions in Industry,* 6: Rubinow, 389).

66. Vanderlip, 458.

67. Baldwin, 14.

68. Ibid, 6-8; *Carnegie Foundation for the Advancement of Teaching,* Vol. 4 (1909), 70; Vol. 6 (1911), 23, and Vol. 7 (1912), 71; Epstein, *Facing Old Age,* 183; F. MacVeagh. "Civil Service Pensions," *The Annals of the American Academy of Political and Social Science,* Vol. 38, No. 1 (July, 1911), 305-06.

69. Massachusetts *Report of the Commission on Old Age Pensions, Annuities, and Insurance,* 270-71.

70. Lee Welling Squier, *Old Age Dependency in the United States* (New York, 1912), 321.

71. Companies without pension plans tend to retain a much higher percentage of workers over sixty-five than do companies with such plans. The adoption of these policies, therefore, tends to legitimatize the release of the aging employee, Long, 167.

72. There is a great deal of variation in the elderly's attitude towards retirement. Many individuals who lack the financial security necessary for a comfortable retirement dread losing their full incomes; others dislike being forced to withdraw from their occupations; still others look forward to retirement. This is true today as it was in the early 20th century. See, Breen, 384; J. Hamilton Crook and Martin Heinstein, *The Older Workers in Industry* (California, 1958), 45; Durand, 35; Eugene A. Friedman and Robert J. Havigurst, *The Meaning of Work and Retirement* (Chicago, 1953), esp. chapter 1; for attitudes in the early 20th century see, *Carnegie foundation for the Advancement of Teaching,* Vol. 4 (1909), 67.

Section Three:

Sexuality and the Family

{8}

Few historical topics are shrouded in as much mystery, or elicit as much curiosity, as sexuality. The more we learn about the clinical and emotional aspects of sexuality, past or present, the more its implications as a mode of interpersonal expression eludes us. One thing is certain, however. Sexual drives, manifestations, and modes of gratification are so diverse and idiosyncratic that it is virtually impossible to either determine what constitutes "normal" sexual expression or to characterize particular historical communities (such as the New England Puritans) or eras (the Victorian period, for example) as sexually repressive. Human beings, whether Puritan, Victorian or contemporary are far too diverse, and their societies far too complex, to be readily subsumed under convenient (and facile) rubrics, particularly in the area of sexuality. In spite of the massive psychological, historical, and sociological investigations into the nature of sexual expression in American society conducted in this century, the only thing we can say with certainty about this compelling and elusive topic is that it remains shrouded in ambiguity.

The first essay in this Section provides fascinating insights into the ambiguity and diversity of sexual expression in seventeenth-century New England. Robert F. Oaks confirms what Edmund Morgan suggested in his seminal book **The Puritan Family**, first published in 1940s: Puritans were not necessarily Puritanical about sexuality. But Oaks goes one step further than Morgan, and contends that, for a variety of reasons, Puritan magistrates and the general community may have tolerated, if not condoned, homosexuality.

Is Oaks convincing? Is his data too narrow? If the Puritans were even remotely as tolerant of "deviant" sexuality as Oaks suggests, then why has the word "Puritan" become synonymous with sexual repression?

"Things Fearful to Name": Sodomy and Buggery in Seventeenth-Century New England

Robert F. Oaks

In recent years, historians have begun to study the long neglected story of human sexuality. The previous neglect of a subject that affects virtually every individual stemmed both from a reluctance to discuss such a sensitive topic and from the difficulties involved in research. Several demographic studies of 17th-century New England recently have begun to probe such questions as the incidence of adultery, divorce, and pre-marital sex, but as yet there is very little information on variant sexual activity such as homosexuality and bestiality.[1]

Research into these areas is more difficult because one of the major sources for the historian of heterosexual activity—birth records—is obviously absent. The most important source for variant sexual activity in colonial New England is court records. This evidence should be used cautiously since it provides information only about people caught in specific acts. One could argue that court records for this period no more reflect the true nature of homosexuality and bestiality in Puritan society than the records of the New York Police Department do of homosexuality in late 20th-century New York City. Nevertheless, these records do show that this type of activity existed in colonial New England and also suggest that some of the few speculations that historians have made are inaccurate. It is not true, for instance, as Edmund Morgan claimed many years ago, that "Sodomy [was] usually punished with death."[2] Nor do the records of Plymouth substantiate Geoffrey May's claim that "between one-fifth and one-fourth [of all sex offenses] were for various homosexual practices."[3] On the other hand, these records do reveal Puritan attitudes toward variant sexual activity and suggest that even extreme attempts to suppress it could not eliminate it.[4]

There was some confusion over terminology in describing variant sex crimes in colonial America. The two terms used most often—buggery and sodomy—sometimes meant different things to different people. Usually, the Puritan colonies used the term sodomy to refer to homosexuality and buggery to refer to bestiality. But occasionally, buggery also meant homosexuality, sodomy referred to bestiality, and, on one occasion, Massachusetts authorities tried without much success to stretch the definition of sodomy to apply to heterosexual child molestation.[5]

Both crimes were capital offenses in all the New England colonies. Homosexuality had been capital in England since the days of Henry VIII, but the Puritan colonies, where laws regulating moral behavior were often severe, patterned their laws not on the English statutes, but on the Old Testament.[6] Plymouth, the first colony specifically to make sodomy and buggery punishable by death (1636), included these crimes with other capital offenses, such as murder, rape, treason, witchcraft, and arson.[7] The law only applied to men, however. Lesbianism usually did not come under the definition of sodomy. John Cotton wanted to include lesbianism as a capital crime in a proposed legal code he drew up for Massachusetts in 1636, but his code was not accepted. Only in New Haven after 1655, when the colony did accept Cotton's code, was female homosexuality a capital crime, and even that exception ended when Connecticut incorporated the colony ten years later.[8]

Yet despite the harsh penalties for sodomy and buggery, Puritan leaders often refused to apply them, especially for homosexual activity. As with other types of crimes, the courts often employed the concept of remission of sentences for many sex crimes. Remission may have resulted from an enlightened attempt to move away from the traditional concept of punishment for retribution, it may have reflected economic realities in an area where labor was scarce, or it may have stemmed from a reluctance to apply capital punishment to crimes feared to be rather common. It is significant that Puritan authorities, despite the penalties on the books, apparently regarded homosexuality—though not bestiality—as not much worse than many "ordinary" sex crimes. Adultery, for example, was also a capital offense, but the death penalty was rarely inflicted in New England for that crime either.[9] This reluctance to punish illicit sexual activity of all types grew stronger in the latter decades of the 17th century.

The first recorded incident of homosexuality in New England occurred in 1629, when the ship *Talbot* arrived in Massachusetts. During the voyage, "5 beastly Sodomiticall boyes . . . confessed their wickedness not to be named." Unwilling to deal with anything so distasteful, Massachusetts authorities sent the boys back to England, arguing that since the crime occurred on the high seas, the Bay Colony had no jurisdiction.[10]

The colony of Plymouth seemed to have more homosexuality than other areas of New England, though this may simply indicate a greater willingness to prosecute such crimes, or, perhaps, less opportunity for privacy. There may have been problems with homosexuality in Plymouth as early as the mid-1620s. The well-known story of Thomas Morton of Merrymount could have homosexual overtones. William Bradford's description of the "great licentiousness" of Morton and his men hints that such activity may have taken place:

> And after they had got some goods into their hands, and got much by trading with the Indians, they spent it as vainly in quaffing and drinking, both wine and strong waters in great excess. . . .They set up a maypole, drinking and dancing about it many days together, inviting the Indian women for their consorts, dancing and frisking together like so many fairies, or furies, rather; and worse practices. As if they had anew revived and celebrated the feasts of the Roman goddess Flora, or the beastly practices of the mad Bacchanalians.[11]

Morton does not specify their "worse practices," but it is not unreasonable to assume that some of those Englishmen voluntarily living in isolation from all women except a few Indians would have practiced homosexuality. For some, it may have been situational, stemming from limited opportunities for heterosexual activity; but for others, homosexuality may have been the preference, as it undoubtedly was for

English pirates in the West Indies later in the century.[12]

Several years later, in 1636, Plymouth held the first trial for homosexuality in New England. John Alexander and Thomas Roberts were "found guilty of lude behavior and uncleane carriage one [with] another, by often spendinge their seede one upon another." The evidence was conclusive, since the court had a witness and confessions from the accused. Furthermore, Alexander was "notoriously guilty that way," and had sought "to allure others thereunto." This was a clear-cut case, and, it would seem, an obvious time to apply the death penalty, adopted by the colony only a few months earlier. But instead, the court issued a more lenient sentence. Alexander was stripped, burned in the shoulder with a hot iron, and banished from the colony. Roberts, a servant, was whipped, returned to his master to serve out his time, and forbidden from ever owning land in the colony. Apparently there was some dispute over this last restriction, because the phrase "except hee manefest better desert" was inserted in the records, then crossed out.[13]

The leniency extended to the two men is perhaps surprising. Alexander's banishment suggests that the court was not worried about a labor shortage. Nor would a death sentence be out of line with penalties in other areas of England rule. In the mid-1629s, Virginia executed Richard Cornish for sodomy. Though there is some evidence that the charges may have been trumped up to rid the colony of a troublesome individual, the fact that sodomy was even chosen as an excuse for execution indicates that the 17-century Englishman had few qualms about imposing death as punishment for that crime.[14] And in England, in 1631, the Earl of Castlehaven was found guilty and executed for crimes "so heinous and so horrible that a Christian man ought scarce to name them." Not only did Castlehaven abet the rape of his wife by one of his servants, but he also committed sodomy with several servants. This latter act brought the death sentence. Here, too, there was some remission when the Earl appealed directly to Charles I for mercy, but not nearly to the same degree granted by Plymouth to Alexander and Roberts. The King commuted the Earl's sentence from hanging to the more humane beheading, and then postponed the execution for a month to give Castlehaven "time for repentence."[15]

The Roberts and Alexander case also suggests that Plymouth officials prosecuted with some reluctance. They "often" engaged in such conduct, and Alexander was "notoriously guilty that way." If Alexander was so notorious, why had he not been punished before? Perhaps the magistrates were willing to overlook homosexuality unless it became too obvious, an attitude not unlike that of 20th-century America. It is even possible that the death penalty was an attempt to discourage widespread activity. The fact that it was not applied to such an obvious case only a few months after it went on the books suggests that it was meant only as a warning, and no one seriously throught of using it.

Another Plymouth sodomy case, in 1642, resulted in even more lenient treatment. The court found Edward Michell guilty of "lude and sodomiticall practices" with Edward Preston. Michell was also playing around with Lydia Hatch, and Preston attempted sodomy with one John Keene, but was turned down. To complicate matters ever further, Lydia was caught in bed with her brother Jonathan. The sentences imposed for these various activities are particulary interesting since homosexuality in this case received approximately the same punishment as illicit heterosexuality. Lydia Hatch was publicly whipped. Michell and Preson were each whipped twice, once in Plymouth and again in Barnstable. John Keene, because he resisted Preston's advances and reported the incident, was allowed to watch while Michell and Preston were whipped, though the record intriguingly states that "in some thing he was faulty" too. Jonathan Hatch, regarded as a vagrant, was whipped and then banished to Salem.[16] These penalties were not only extremely light, but were not much harsher than penalties imposed for the relatively common heterosexual crime of fornication.[17]

Lesbian activity was scarcely punished at all. There were no prescribed penalties on the books, which may explain why there is only one recorded case in New England. In 1649, Mary Hammon and Sara Norman, both from Yarmouth, were indicted for "leude behavior each with other upon a bed." Mrs. Norman was also accused of "divers Lasivious speeches." Her sentence required that she make a public acknowledgement "of her unchast behavior" and included a warning that such conduct in the future would result in an unspecified harsher punishment. Inexplicably, Mary Hammon was "cleared with admonision." It is difficult to understand how one woman could be guilty and the other innocent, though it is possible that the court was more disturbed by Mrs. Norman's "lasivious speeches" than they were by her "leude behavior."[18]

There was undoubtedly much more homosexual activity than the court records indicate. By the early 1640s, Governor Bradford lamented the great number of sex crimes, not only heterosexual offense, "But that which is even worse, even sodomy and buggery (things fearful to name) [which] have broke[n] forth in this land oftener than once." Bradford tried to explain what seemed to be a virtual crime wave. He suggested that the Devil was particularly active in those regions that attempted "to preserve holiness and purity." But he had nonreligious explanations as well. Because laws were so strict regarding sex crimes, they produced a lot of frustration "that it may be in this case as it is with waters when their streams are stopped or dammed up. When they get passage they flow with more violence." The dams of sexual wickedness obviously had broken in New England. On the other hand, Bradford suggested, perhaps contradicting himself, there was no more evil activity in Plymouth than elsewhere, "but they are here more discovered and seen and made public by due search, inquisition and due punishment."[19]

In addition to Bradford's suggestion that sex crimes were rampant, the court records hint at homosexual activity in addition to the three obvious cases described above. One of the earliest historians to study homosexuality in New England claimed that the Plymouth records "show that of the prosecutions for all sex offenses, between one-fifth and one-fourth were for various homosexual practices."[20] This estimate is very exaggerated. While there are numerous references to "uncleanness" or "unclean practices," the majority of them do make it clear that these were definitely heterosexual. A somewhat hasty count of sexual offenses in Plymouth records produced the following results: there were 129 definite heterosexual offenses including fornication, "licivious going in company of young men", kissing a married woman, adultery, prostitution, and rape; there were 3 definite homosexual offenses; 2 definite buggery cases; one accusation each for sodomy and buggery; and only 15 unspecified cases that might have been either homosexual or heterosexual. Out of a total of 151 sex offenses, then, there were at the most 19 cases of homosexuality, and probably fewer than that. These figures, however, should not in any sense be interpreted as reflecting the percentage of homosexual activity in Plymouth. It was undoubtedly easier, even in such a close knit society, to escape detection for homosexual activity than for heterosexual activity. The most common crime, by far, was fornication, and it was usually detected when pregnancy resulted, a risk obviously absent for homosexuals.

Some of the possible homosexual cases in the Plymouth records do allow interesting speculation. Most suggestive is the case of Richard Berry and Teage Joanes. In 1649, Berry accused Joanes of sodomy, and both were ordered to attend the next court for trial. Berry also claimed that Joanes committed "unclean practisses" with Sarah Norman, the woman involved in the lesbian case. In the intervening six months between the accusation and the trial, however, Berry changed his mind and testified that he had lied, for which he was sentenced "to be whipte at the poste." If Berry's original intention had been merely to smear Joanes, it is difficult to understand why he would do it in such a way as to implicate himself. It is possible that the two men were lovers. Perhaps they had quarrelled, leading to the accusation, but later reconciled. Berry then decided to suffer the penalty for lying rather than have Joanes suffer the penalty for sodomy. Further evidence for this interpretation stems from a court order three years later when Joanes and Berry "and others with them" were required to "part theire uncivell liveing together." Ten years later, one Richard Beare of Marshfield, a "grossly scandalouse person . . . formerly convicted of filthy, obsceane practises," was disenfranchised. It is possible that this "Beare" is an alternate spelling of Richard Berry.[21] Berry did have a wife, by the way, a rather unsavory woman named Alice. She was accused of several crimes herself. Once she milked someone's cow, another time she stole a "neckcloth" and on another occasion some bacon and eggs.[22]

There are several other cases of "disorderly liveing" or "lude carriage" that suggest the possibility of homosexual activity, but the evidence is far from conclusive. In 1637, for instance, Abraham Pottle, Walter Deuell, Webb Adey, and Thomas Roberts, accused of "disorderly liveing," were required "to give an account how they live." Adey, in particular, got into trouble on several other occasions. He "profaned the Lord's Day" several times by working, for which he was whipped. By 1642, still practicing "his licentious and disorderly manner of liveing," Adey went to jail.[23]

In another case, one John Dunford, "for his slaunders, clamors, lude & evell carriage," was banished from Plymouth. The records are silent as to the exact nature of his "evell carriage," but the rather unusual and severe punishment, especially in light of John Alexander's banishment two years earlier, may suggest homosexual activity.[24] The same may be said of William Latham, fined 40s for entertaining John Phillips in his house, contrary to the court's order.[25] John Emerson was also fined for "entertaining other mens servants," though the sex of the servants is unmentioned.[26] Anthony Bessie was indicted for "liveing alone disorderly, and afterwards for takeing in an inmate [boarder] without order."[27] James Cole was acquitted of the charge of "entertaining townsmen in his house."[28] But Edward Holman was fined for entertaining another man's servant, John Wade, and for taking Wade to Duxbury in his boat.[29]

Other possible homosexual cases include Tristram Hull's, indicted for unspecified "unclean practises." The charge, however, did not keep Hull from being chosen constable of Yarmouth five years later.[30] There was also John Bumpas, whipped for "idle and lasivius behavior."[31] A final possible homosexual case involves Hester Rickard. Convicted of "laciviouse and unaturall practices" in 1661, she was ordered to sit in the stocks, wearing a paper on her hat decribing her crime in capital letters. It is likely, however, that her "unnatural practice" was adultery (she was married). On the same day, Joseph Dunham was sentenced to sit in the stocks with a paper on his hatt for "divers laciviouse carriages." Dunham was also fined 200 pounds. Though the records do not specifically connect the two, the timing suggests that their cases were related.[32]

The one execution for homosexuality in New England occurred in the colony of

New Haven in 1646, when William Plaine of Guilford was convicted of "unclean practices." Though a married man, Plaine reportedly committed sodomy with two men in England before coming to America. Once in Guilford, "he corrupted a great part of the youth . . . by masturbations, which he had committed and provoked others to the like above a hundred times." To make matters worse, this "monster in human shape," as John Winthrop called him, expressed atheistic opinions. Plaine received the death penalty, though it was probably his corruption of youth and his "frustrating the ordinance of marriage" that weighed more heavily on the magistrate than the sodomy.[33]

Though the Puritans nearly always meant homosexuality when they used the term sodomy, one time when it was not used in that context is the exception that proves the rule, while shedding additional light on the practical legal setting for homosexuality itself. In 1641, Massachusetts authorities were horrified to learn that for the previous two years, three men had regularly molested two young girls, beginning when the elder was only seven.[34] The revelations produced outrage and calls for the death penalty, but no one knew exactly how to define the crime. Since the girls apparently consented to the treatment, could it be considered rape? Even if it were rape, at that time there was no specific law against it in Massachusetts, and "there was no express law in the word of God" for a sentence of death. So the authorities tried to stretch the definition of the capital crime of sodomy to fit this case. But this created several legal problems inherent in all accusations for sodomy. English precedent for solomy and buggery convictions generally required proof of actual penetration. The accused men confessed to molestation, but denied penetration. The magistrates had only the girls testimony to go on, leading to yet other legal restrictions that provided no man could be compelled to testify against himself, and that two witnesses were needed to any crime that resulted in a death sentence.[35]

In an attempt to solve these problems, the magistrates wrote for advice to other New England colonies, soliciting written opinions from ministers, the nearest equivalent to legal experts.[36] The majority of the respondents concluded that evidence of actual penetration was necessary for the crime to be sodomy. This made the other questions all the more important: could the accused be forced to testify against himself, and, if not, were two witnesses always necessary for a capital conviction? There was disagreement on the former question, though nearly everyone ruled out torture as means of exacting a confession. As to the number of witnesses, the ministers generally held out for two, except where there was a confession by the accused or "concurrent and concluding circumstances."[37]

Because of the confusion, when the General court met in May, 1642, they were divided on the sentence. Several magistrates did want the death penalty, but, after much dispute, they finally agreed on a lighter sentence only because the "sin was not capital by any express law of God." The attempt to define it as sodomy had simply not worked. So instead of death, the three were sentenced to severe whippings, confinement to Boston, and in the case of one of them, multilation of his nostrils and imprisonment.[38]

This whole scandal and the difficulties involved in applying capital punishment are directly related to the whole question of homosexuality. The disagreement over the necessity for penetration, self-accusation, and the number of witnesses applied in those cases as well. A new statutory rape law did nothing to eliminate the legal difficulties in obtaining sodomy convictions. Perhaps the almost rigorous standards of evidence dissuaded authorities from trying to obtain the death penalty for ordinary sodomy cases, falling back instead on more lenient sentences which were possible when the evidence was not totally conclusive.

But if the Puritans were willing to bend over backwards to apply scrupulous legal guarantees to cases involving homsexuality and child molestation—making the imposition of the death penalty practically impossible—they were often willing to forgo these guarantees when presecuting for buggery. Sodomy and buggery were usually linked together both in the Bible and in Puritan legal codes, but despite the connection between the two crimes, the penalties imposed in 17th-century New England were often quite different. There was little reluctance to impose the death penalty for buggery even though the legal problems were often identical with those inherent in sodomy. Before speculating as to why this discrepancy existed, it might be helpful to describe specific cases and the penalties imposed.

In the same year as the discovery of the mistreatment of the young girls, one William Hackett (or Hatchet) "was found in buggery with a cow, upon the Lord's day." A woman absent from church because of some illness, "espied him in the very act." When Hackett, a boy of about 18 or 20 years of age, came before the magistrates, he confessed to attempted buggery "and some entrance, but denied the completing of the fact." Many of the same problems came up in this case as in the child molestation case. There was only one witness, and the evidence of penetration was sketchy at best, since the boy denied completing the act. But eventually the court agreed "that his confession of some entrance was sufficient testimony with the woman," and the majority of the magistrates sentenced him to death. Governor Richard Bellingham, who still doubted some of the evidence, refused to pronounce the sentence, but Deputy Governor John Endecott had no such qualms and sentenced the boy to die. After the sentencing, the boy, described as "ignorant and blockish," finally confessed "completing this foul fact, and attempting the like before, with other wickedness." On the day of the execution, the cow was first slain in front of the boy, and then after a prayer by the Rev. Mr. John Wilson of the Boston Church, Hackett, " with a trembling body," was hanged.[39]

A few months later, New Haven executed George Spencer on even flimsier evidence. A sow, previously owned by a man for whom Spencer had worked as a servant, gave birth to a deformed fetus, "a prodigious monster." Unfortunately, some people saw a resemblance between the fetus and poor George Spencer. It pearle in itt, is whitish & deformed" like that of the fetus. Furthermore, Spencer was notorious for "a prophane, lying, scoffing and lewd speritt."[40]

Spencer, when examined, first said that he did not think that he had committed buggery with the sow in question. Then he denied it outright, but he was sent to prison because of the "strong possibilities." Spencer continued to deny guilt in prison until visited by one of the magistrates, who reminded him that confession sins would bring mercy. Spencer then confessed to the crime, though later he claimed he did so merely to please the magistrate. On another occasion, when several other magistrates visited him, Spencer again confessed to that crime as well as several others, such as lying, scoffing at the colony's laws, and profaning the Lord's Day ("calling itt the ladyes day"), though he denied other "acts of filthynes, [homosexual?] either with Indians or English." When brought to trial, Spencer denied all that he had formerly confessed, but the court was "aboundantly satisfied in the evidence," even though there were no witnesses and Spencer refused to confess under oath. Despite these legal problems, Spencer, according to the law of Leviticus 20:15, was put to death.[41]

Perhaps the most famous New England buggery trial was that of Thomas Granger, a 16- or 17-year-old youth in Plymouth. In 1642, Granger was indicted for buggery "with a mare, a cow, two goats, five sheep, two calves and a turkey." Somebody saw Granger committing buggery with the mare. Unfortunately, Governor Bradford, who recorded the incident in his history of Plymouth, decided to "forbear particulars." Nevertheless, upon examination, Granger "confessed the fact with that beast at that time, [and] sundry times before and at several times with all the rest of the forenamed in his indictment." The court had some difficulty determining which sheep were involved, so they staged a lineup for Granger, where "he declared which they were they and which were not." The court then sentenced Granger to death. The animals were "killed before his face, according to the law, Leviticus xx.15; and then he himself was executed."[42]

With some relief, Bradford reported that both Granger and another man who "had made some sodomitical attempts upon another"—probably Edward Michell or Edward Preston—had learned these things in England. But the Governor warned that these cases showed "how one wicked person may infect many," and cautioned families to choose their servants wisely.[43]

A few months later, in Massachusetts, the Court of Assistants found Teagu Oerimi guilty of "a foule, & divilish attempt to bugger a cow of Mr. Makepeaces." Fortunately for Ocrimi, his attempt did not succeed. The court ordered him "to be carried to the place of execution & there to stand with an halter about his necke, & to be severely whipped."[44]

And in the same colony in 1646, Robert Miller went to jail, after being accused of buggery. The witnesses disagreed, however, and when the weather turned cold, Miller was released on bond, and ordered to appear at the next court. There is not further mention of Miller, however, so perhaps the charges were dropped for insufficient evidence.[45]

Perhaps the most interesting buggery case occurred in New Haven in 1647. Again, it involved a sow who bore a deformed fetus and a man with the thoroughly improbable name of Thomas Hogg. The fetus "had a faire & white skinne & head, as Thomas Hoggs is." Hogg, a servant for the woman who owned the sow, denied guilt. But the case grew stronger when the court learned that on more than one occasion Hogg had been guilty of indecent exposure: "he said his breeches were rest." Hogg claimed that "his belly was broake . . . & he wore a steel trusse, & so it might happen his members might be seens," though Goodie Camp testified that she had given him a needle and thread "to mend his breeches." After imprisoning Hogg for the crimes of bestiality and exposure, the court decided to seek additional evidence. The governor and deputy governor accompanied Hogg to the barnyard and ordered him to fondle ("scratt") the sow in question. The official records tell us that "immedyatly there appeared a working of lust in the sow, insomuch that she powred out seede before them." The magistrates then order him to fondle another sow, "but that was not moved at all." If that was not evidence enough, "Lucretia, the governors neagar woeman," testified that she had seen Hogg "act filthiness with his hands by the fier side." Other witnesses testified that he had at various times stolen a dumpling and some cheese. The court decided to consider the buggery charge later on, but in the meantime, for his "filthynesse, lyeing & pilfering," Hogg was severely whipped and sent to prison "with a meane dyet & hard labour, that his lust may not bee fedd." For some reason, the records do not indicate any further consideration of the bestiality charge. Apparently the charge was dropped, because Hogg was alive and out of jail the following year, when the court warned him for not showing up for watch.[46]

In 1662, another case in New Haven, by then incorporated into Connecticut, suggests the difficulties involved in detecting buggery. In that year, a 60-year-old man named Potter was executed for bestiality, even though "this Wretch, had been for now Twenty years, a member of the Church in that Place, and kept up amoung the Holy People of God there, a Reputation for Serious Christianity." This pillar of the community (or as Cotton Mather preferred, this "Pillar of Salt"), engaged in such practices on and off for 50 years, since age 10, with a wide variety of animals. The fact that he could do this without detection for half a century suggests that even in a close knit society some discreet individuals could indulge whatever sexual passions they had. Ten years before his execution, Potter's wife discovered him "Confounding himself with a *Bitch,*" but he managed to convince her to keep silent. But when his son "saw him hideously conversing with a *Sow,*" the story came to light. Apparently the shocked son reported his father. Before his execution, "A *Cow, Two heifers,* Three *Sheep,* and Two *Sowes,* with all of which he had committed his Brutalness," were killed while Potter watched.[47]

These cases indicate that the Puritans were less hesitant to punish buggery with death than they were sodomy. Again, since they usually linked the two crimes, the differences in the severity of punishment is puzzling. It is possible that the Puritans suspected that homosexuality was so widespread that a strict application of the law would lead to very unpleasant consequences. Edmund Morgan suggests that this is the reason why the full penalties were generally not applied for heterosexual sex crimes.[48] Bestiality, on the other hand, may have been less common in the 17th century (as in the 20th century), and thus easier to control. Then again, one might speculate that the opposite was the case. In the mid-20th century, Kinsey researchers found that the incidence of bestiality was highest in farming communities—similar to 17th-century New England. Kinsey reported that 40 to 50% of all farm boys had some sort of animal contract. Perhaps, then, Puritan leaders suspected that bestiality was a much more widespread phenomenon than homosexuality and imposed harsher sentences in order to suppress the far more serious of the two crimes.[49]

There is another possibility. The harsh punishments for buggery may reflect a general 17th century revulsion with animal contacts. The cases mentioned above provide some clues for such an interpretation. The two pig fetus cases indicate that the Puritans believed it was possible for a man to impregnate an animal, an obvious impossibility in sodomy. This possibility may have made buggery even more heinous. The Puritans were not far removed from the middle ages, when reports of man-like creatures were common. Even more relevant were contemporary accounts written by Englishmen visiting Africa, where, they believed, there was a close connection, including sexual intercourse, between Africans and apes.[50] Even more than homosexuality, bestiality dehumanized man. The horror with which the 17th-century Englishman regarded buggery helped them to rationalize racism toward blacks. In New England, it explains why a son would report his own father to the authorities, and why even the man's wife apparently had considered it a few years earlier. The horror may also explain why New Englanders were willing to dispense with some of the rules of evidence to obtain the death penalty for buggery.

But attitudes toward buggery apparently began to soften as the century wore on. The subject still cropped up occasionally in the court records, but convictions declined. In 1666, William Honywell, jailed in Plymouth on suspicion of buggery, was released for insufficient evidence.[51] The same was true in Massachusetts in 1676 and 1677, when juries found insufficient evidence to convict Jack, a black servant, of buggery with a cow and John Lawrence of buggery with a mare.[52]

The last execution for buggery by the Massachusetts Court of Assistants was that of Benjamin Goad in 1673. This youth, accused of buggery with a mare "in the highway or field" in broad daylight, apparently confessed at first, but then denied it at his trial. The jury, confused by the legal technicalities, decided that if Goad's confession when first arrested plus the testimony of one witness were sufficient for conviction, then he was guilty. But if his denial under oath during the trial took precedence, then Goad was guilty only of attempted buggery. The magistrates then declared that Goad was indeed "Capitolly Guilty." The mare was "knockt on ye head," and then Goad was hanged.[53]

This case provides evidence of changing attitudes, since the execution created some controversy. An increasing tolerance for illicit sexual activity of all kinds in the latter decades of the 17th century apparently produced a corresponding decline in the willingness of many citizens to accept strict enforcement of the moral code.[54] The Rev. Samuel Danforth felt compelled to preach and publish a sermon defending Goad's execution. Danforth admitted that some people objected to "making such a *Youth*, a childe of Relgious Parents, and that in his tender years, such a Dreadful Example of Divine Vengeance." But while others pitied Goad's youth, Danforth pitied "the holy Law of God." Remember, Danforth told his flock, "Goad gave himself to Self-pollution, and other Sodomitical wickedness. He often attempted Buggery with several Beasts, before God left him to commit it . . . and he continued in the frequent practice thereof for several months.[55]

But the tide was running against those who held Danforth's views. In Plymouth in 1681, Thomas Saddeler was arraigned for buggery with a mare. Though he denied it, the jury found him guilty, but of the lesser charge "of vile, abominable, and presumptuous attempts to buggery with a mare." His punishment was rather severe, but it was not capital as it probably would have been earlier in the century. Saddeler was whipped, forced to sit on the gallows with a rope around his neck, branded in the forehead with letter "P" (for pollution), and banished from the colony.[56]

Saddeler's is the last buggery case in any of the published records of New England. Just as prosecutions for sodomy ended 30 years earlier, buggery too dissappeared from the records. There may be additional cases in the records of countless local courts and these sources must be searched before we will have a more accurate picture of variant sexual activity in colonial America, but for now it seems reasonable to conclude that sexual behavior, of whatever kind, gradually became more a matter of personal conscience and less a concern for the courts. It may be true, as Edmund Morgan suggested, that the "Puritans became inured to sexual offenses, because there were so many."[57] The decline of religious fervor toward the end of the century, the inability of earlier repression—actual or threatened—to stop illicit sex, and the increasing secularization of the state—resulting in less concern for enforcing moral law—combined to make prosecutions for variant sexual activity a thing of the past.[58] Not even the Puritans could prevent men and women from practicing many forms of sexual activity officially regarded as sinful. Perhaps nothing is more symbolic of the failure of the "city upon a hill" than the history of variant sexual activity in 17th-century New England.

FOOTNOTES

1. See particularly John Demos, *A Little Commonwealth: Family Life in Plymouth Colony* (New York, 1970); Demos, "Families in Colonial Bristol, Rhode Island," *William and Mary Quarterly*, 3d Ser., XXV (1969), 40-57; Philip J. Greven, Jr., *Four Generations: Population, Land, and Family in Colonial Andover, Massachusetts* (Ithaca and London, 1970); Kenneth A. Lockridge, *A New England Town: The First Hundred Years* (New York, 1970); Robert Higgs and H. Louis Stettler, III, "Colonial New England Demography: A Sampling Ap-

proach," *Wm. and Mary Qtly.*, 3d Ser., XXVII (1970), 282-294.

2. Edmund S. Morgan. "The Puritans and Sex," *New England Quarterly, XV* (1942), 603.

3. Geoffrey May, *Social Control of Sex Expression* (New York, 1931), 247.

4. Two recent pioneering works on the history of homosexuality are Vern L. Bullough, *Sexual Variance in Society and History* (New York, 1976); and Johnathan Katz, *Gay American History: Lesbians and Gay Men in the U.S.A.* (New York, 1976).

5. Louis Crompton, "Homosexuals and the Death Penalty in Colonial America," *Journal of Homosexuality, I* (1976), 277-278: Katz, *Gay American History, 24.*

6. Crompton, *"Homosexuals and the Death Penalty,"* 277-278; David H. Flaherty, *"Law and the Enforcement of Morals in Early America,"* in Donald Fleming and Bernard Bailyn, eds., *Perspectives in American History,* V (1971): *Law in American History,* 213.

7. *Records of the Colony of New Plymouth in New England,* eds. Nathaniel B. Shurtleff and David Pulsifer (Boston, 1855-1861), XI, 12.

8. Katz, *Gay American History,* 20, 22: Crompton, "Homosexuals and the Death Penalty," 278-279.

9. For more on the concept of remission, see George I, Haskins, *Law and Authority in Early Massachusetts: A Study in Tradition and Design* (New York, 1960), 204-205; and Jules Zanger, "Crime and Punishment in Early Massachusetts," *Wm. and Mary Qtly.,* 3d Ser., XXII (1965), 473-474. For the death penalty and adultery, see Flaherty, "Law and Morals in Early America." 213-214.

10. *Records of the Governor and Company of the Massachusetts Bay in New England,* ed, Nathaniel B. Shurtleff (Boston, 1853-1854), I, 52,54: "Francis Higginson's Journal," in Stuart Mitchell, ed., *The Founding of Massachusetts* (Boston, 1930), 71.

11. William Bradford, *Of Plymouth Plantation 1620-1647,* ed. Samuel Eliot Morison (New York, 1970), 204-206.

12. See B.R. Burg. "Pirate Communities in the Seventeenth Century: A Case Study of Homosexual Society," forthcoming in the *Journal of Homosexuality.* Professor Burg kindly provided me with a manuscript copy of his article.

13. *Records of Plymouth,* I, 64.

14. Crompton, "Homosexuals and the Death Penalty," 290-292, Katz, *Gay American History,* 16-19.

15. Caroline Bingham, "Seventeenth-Century Attitudes Toward Deviant Sex." *Journal of Interdisciplinary History,* I (1971), 44-472. Dutch New Netherland also executed two individuals for sodomy in 1646 and 1658. In 1646, the guilty party (a black man) was sentenced to be choked to death and then burned. In the second case, the man was tied in a sack and thrown into a river to drown: Katz, *Gay American History,* 22-23, 570n.

16. *Records of Plymouth,* II, 35-36.

17. See Demos, *A Little Commonwealth,* 157-158, 158n.

18. *Records of Plymouth,* II, 137, 163.

19. Bradford, *Of Plymouth Plantation,* 316-317.

20. May, *Social Control of Sex Expression,* 247.

21. *Records of Plymouth,* II, 146, 148, III, 37, 177.

22. *Ibid.,* III, 28, 36, 75, 82.

23. *Ibid.,* I, 68 to 92; II, 36, 42.

24. *Ibid.,* I, 128.

25. *Ibid.,* I, 87.

26. *Ibid.,* I, 118.

27. *Ibid.*

28. *Ibid.,* III, 17.

29. *Ibid.,* III, 126.

30. *Ibid.,* II, 36, 115.

31. *Ibid.,* II, 170.

32. *Ibid.,* III, 210.

33. John Winthrop, *The History of New England from 1630 to 1649,* ed. James Savage (Boston, 1853), II, 324: Katz, *Gay American History,* 22.

34. *Records of Massachusetts Bay,* II, 12-13; Winthrop, *History of New England,* II, 54-58.

35. *Ibid.,* Bullough, *Sexual Variance,* 437.

36. Withrop, *History of New England,* II, 54-58; Bradford, *Of Plymouth Plantation.* Appendix X, 404-443.

37. Winthrop, *History of New England,* II, 54-58.

38. *Ibid., Records of Massachusetts Bay,* II, 12-13. On the same day the court handed down

these sentences, they adopted several laws to eliminate some, though not all, of the confusion. Developing the concept of statutory rape, the court decreed that any man having "carnall copulation" with any "woman chld under ten years old" would be put to death, regardless of whether or not the girl consented. Rape of a married or engaged woman also carried the death penalty. Rape of an unmarried woman over ten years old could be punished by death, but the judges were given the discretion of applying a lesser penalty. And finally, a man who committed "fornication with any single woman," with her consent, could be punished by forcing them to marry, a fine, corporal punishment or any or all of these at the discretion of the judge, *Records of Massachusetts Bay,* II, 21-22.

39. Winthrop, *History of New England,* II, 58-60; *Records of Massachusetts Bay,* I, 334.

40. *Records of the Colony and Plantation of New Haven, from 1638 to 1649,* ed. Charles J. Hoadly (Hartford, 1857), 62-69.

41. *Ibid.,* Winthrop, *History of New England,* II, 73.

42. Bradford, *Of Plymouth Plantation,* 320-324; *Records of Plymouth,* II, 44.

43. Bradford, *Of Plymouth Plantation,* 324.

44. *Records of the Court of Assistants of the Colony of Massachusetts Bay, 1630-1692* (Boston, 1904-1928), II, 121.

45. *Records of Massachusetts,* I, 79.

46. *Records of New Haven,* 295-296.

47. [Cotton Mather], *Pillars of Salt: An History of Some Criminals Executed in this Land Capitol Crimes. With Some of their Dying Species* . . . (Boston, 1699), 63-66, Evans No. 877.

48. Morgan, "The Puritans and Sex," 602.

49. See Alfred C. Kinsey, Wardell B. Pomeroy, and Clyde E. Martin. *Sexual Behavior in the Human Male* (Philadelphia and London, 1948), 623- 669-670.

50. Winthrop D. Jordan, *White Over Black: American Attitudes Toward the Negro, 1550-1888,* (Chapel Hill, 1968), 28-32.

51. *Records of Plymouth,* IV, 116.

52. *Records of the Court of Assistants,* I, 74, 87.

53. *Ibid.,* I, 10-11.

54. Flaherty, "Law and Morals in Early America," 229.

55. [Samuel Danforth], *The Cry of Sodom Enquired Into: Upon Occasion of the Arraignment and Condemnation of Benjamin Goad, For His Prodigious Villany* . . . (Cambridge, 1674), Evans V, 186.

56. *Records of Plymouth,* VI, 74-75.

57. Morgan, "The Puritans and Sex," 595.

58. Flaherty, "Law and Morals in Early America." 228-233, 244.

Abortion is one of the most volatile political and moral issues in our society. But it is not a new one. Until the middle of the nineteenth century abortion was not a topic of concern to most Americans, both because it was confined to cases of rape or illicit affairs and because most Americans, including medical specialists, assumed that the fetus was not a human being until it "quickened," that is became capable of movement, usually around the fourth month of pregnancy. Abortions done prior to the fourth month were not considered criminal.

In an enlightening articles James Mohr explores the parameters of what he calls the "great upsurge" in the incidence of abortion during the mid-nineteenth century. Mohr contends that the incidence of abortion rose dramatically during this period, a result of a desire for birth control on the part of white, married, middle class women who wished both to limit the size of their families and avoid the risks of childbearing. Mohr describes in fascinating detail the growth of a new and powerful abortion industry during these years.

How does the issue of abortion differ today from the period investigated by Mohr? Is abortion in today's society primarily a method of birth control? Is it still a prerogative of the affluent classes?

The Great Upsurge of Abortion, 1840-1880

James Mohr

In the early 1840s three key changes began to take place in the patterns of abortion in the United States. These changes profoundly affected the evolution of abortion policy for the next forty years. First, abortion came out into public view; by the mid-1840s the fact that Americans practiced abortion was an obvious social reality, constantly visible to the population as a whole. Second, the overall incidence of abortion, according to contemporary observers, began to rise sharply in the 1840s and remained at high levels through the 1870s; abortion was no longer a marginal practice whose incidence probably approximated that of illegitimacy, but rather a widespread social phenomenon during the period. Third, the types of women having recourse to abortion seemed to change; the dramatic surge of abortion in the United States after 1840 was attributed not to an increase in illegitimacy or a decline in marital fidelity, but rather to the increasing use of abortion by white, married, Protestant, native-born women of the middle and upper classes who either wished to delay their childbearing or already had all the children they wanted. This chapter will examine the evidence for the first two of these crucial changes.

The increased public visibility of abortion may be attributed largely to a process common enough in American history: commercialization. Beginning in the early 1840s abortion became, for all intents and purposes, a business, a service openly traded in the free market. Several factors were involved in the commercialization of abortion, but the continued competition for clients among members of the medical profession stood out.[1] Because that competition was so intense, many marginal practitioners began in the early 1840s to try to attract patients by advertising in the popular press their willingness to treat the private ailments of women in terms that everybody recognized as signifying their willingness to provide abortion services.[2] Abortion-related advertising by physicians, which was not prohibited during this period, quickly became a common practice in the United States and was encouraged by members of the also fiercely competitive press corps, hungry for advertising revenue. Abortion-related advertisements appeared in both urban dailies and rural weeklies, in specialty publications, in popular magazines, in broadsides, on private cards, and even in religious journals. To document fully the pervasiveness of those open and obvious advertisements would probably require the citation of a substantial portion of the mass audience publications circulated in the United States around midcentury.

During the 1840s Americans also learned for the first time not only that many practitioners would provide abortion services, but that some practitioners had made the abortion business their chief livelihood. Indeed, abortion became one of the first specialties in American medical history. Even its opponents considered it "a regularly-established money-making trade" throughout the United States by 1860.[3] Preeminent among the new abortion specialists was Madame Restell of New York City. Restell, an English immigrant whose real name was Ann Lohman, had begun performing abortions on a commercial scale late in the 1830s, but did not gain public attention until the early 1840s.[4] In 1841 her first arrest placed both her name and her occupation before the public. Although at least one irate citizen made unveiled public suggestions about "a recourse to Lynch law," and although Restell's prosecutor warned that "lust, licentiousness, seduction and abortion would be the inevitable occurrences of every day" if her activities were not stopped quickly and completely, she was convicted only of two minor infractions of the law.[5] The publicity she gained more than offset any temporary inconvenience, and by the middle of the 1840s Restell had branch agencies in Boston and Philadelphia. Salesmen were on the road peddling her abortifacient pills and, if the pills failed to work, her salesmen were authorized to refer patients to the main clinic in New York.[6] Restell's enterprise would remain lucrative and successful into the late 1870s, when Madame Restell herself was destined to be one of the most celebrated victims of America's sharp shift on abortion policy.

It is important to note that Restell was no isolated aberration, but only the most flamboyant and the most publicized of the abortionists who began to appear during the 1840s. In the week beginning January 4, 1845, to cite but a single example, the *Boston Daily Times* contained the advertisements of a Dr. Carswell: "particular attention given to all Female complaints, such as Suppressions. . . . Dr. Carswell's method of treating these diseases, is such as to remove the difficulty in a few days. . . . Strict secrecy observed, and no pay taken unless a cure is performed''; a Dr. Louis Kurtz of Leipsic, who would treat "private diseases" in the same manner and had the additional selling point of speaking English, German, and French; a Dr. Dow, whose advertisement was similar to Carswell's, but added: "N.B. Good accommodations for ladies"; and for Madame Restell's Boston branch.[7] "Sleeping Lucy", a Vermont clairvoyant, had opened a small business in the abortion trade in 1842; her expanded enterprise would remain vigorous through the 1870s.[8] In its first major statement on abortion in the United States, the prestigious *Boston Medical and Surgical Journal* noted with alarm in 1844 that abortionists had come out into the open and were thriving. "The law has not reached them," the *Journal* rightly observed, "and the trade of infanticide [i.e. abortion] is unquestionably considered, by these thrifty dealers in blood, a profitable undertaking."[9]

The popular press began to make abortion more visible to the American people during the 1840s not only in its advertisements but also in its coverage of a number of sensational trials alleged to involve botched abortions and professional abortionists. In Massachusetts, New York, New Jersey, and Iowa such cases evoked direct legislative responses, which will be examined in a subsequent chapter, but in the present context the very fact of public coverage indicated an increased awareness of abortion in the United States. Prior to 1840 virtually nothing had been mentioned about abortion in the popular press; during the period when the first laws concerning abortion were being passed in state legislatures, the practice had not been a public issue. By the early 1840s, however, the press had become interested in the phenomenon. When Madame Restell was arrested for a second time in 1845, the New York City dailies and the new *National Police Gazette* covered the story closely and expressed concern about the lack of restriction on abortion in the United States.[10] Freed once again, Madame Restell herself took to the columns of the *New York Tribune* in August of 1847 to counter what she regarded as unjustified slurs upon her and her line of work.[11]

By 1850, then, commercialization had brought abortion out into public view in the United States, and the visibility it gained would affect the evolution of abortion policy in American state legislatures. At the same time a second key change was taking place: American women began to practice abortion more frequently after 1840 than they had earlier in the century. As a reasonable guess, abortion rates in the United States may have risen from an order of magnitude approximating one abortion for every twenty-five or thirty live births during the first three decades of the nineteenth century to an order of magnitude possibly as high as one abortion for every five or six births by the 1850s and 1860s.[12] Clearly, a change like that was also likely to have some effect upon the evolution of abortion laws.

One indication that abortion rates probably jumped in the United States during the 1840s and remained high for some thirty years thereafter was the increased visibility of the practice. It is not unreasonable to assume that abortion became more visible as least in part because it was becoming more frequent. And as it became more visible, more and more women would be reminded that it existed as a possible course of action to be considered. The advertisement of abortion services remained vigorous from the early 1840s, when it first appeared, through the late 1870s, when anti-advertising and anti-obscenity laws drove it from the market place. Madame Restell's empire alone was reported in 1871 to be spending approximately $60,000 per year on advertising.[13] Economists argue that advertising both responds to a perceived market and helps to expand that market. Hence, abortifacient advertising was presumably aimed throughout the period from 1840 through 1880 at a clientele large enough to justify its expense, it presumably helped to maintain the size of the clientele, and it may actually have been a factor in expanding the clientele in certain areas.

A second piece of evidence for high abortion rates for the period was the existence during that time of a flourishing business in abortifacient medicines. The *Boston Medical and Surgical Journal* asserted that there were a least six practitioners openly retailing abortifacient preparations in Boston by the summer of 1844, and before midcentury the abortifacient drug business would become a major and apparently very profitable enterprise.[14] Moreover, and this point is important in the present context, the effectiveness of nineteenth-century abortifacient preparations is not really an issue. It is probable that these preparations helped to trigger a relatively small number of actual abortions.[15] But the booming business in abortifacients indicated that a significant number of American women were trying to have abortions. After all, they did not know that the drugs were incapable of doing what their advertisers claimed they could do. And it is likely that many of the women who failed to get results with medicines would turn next to surgical methods of terminating their pregnancies.

During the week of January 4, 1845, the *Boston Daily Times* advertised Madame Restell's Female Pills; Madame Drunette's Lunar Pills; Dr. Peter's French Renovating Pills, which were sold as " 'a blessing to mothers' . . . and although very mild and prompt in their operations, pregnant females should not use them, as they invariably produce a miscarriage"; Dr. Monroe's French Periodical Pills, also "sure to produce a miscarriage"; and Dr. Melveau's Portuguese Female Pills, likewise "certain to produce miscarriage." These ads, to repeat, were from a single paper for a single week in 1845.[16] The "meaning and intent" of advertisements like that, it was widely acknowledged, were well known to "every schoolgirl" in America, and the fact that abortionists frequently advertised in the "personal" columns as astrologers and clairvoyants were also clearly understood by nineteenth-century newspaper readers.[17]

A physician who had grown up in France and studied medicine there before emigrating to New England confirmed, with a good deal of shock, that abortifacient ads in "the press of the United States . . . [were] intelligible not only to fathers and mothers, but also to boys and girls!" The "licentiousness" of the newspapers appalled this Frenchman, who blamed the press for creating an impression in young girls' minds that abortion was a common, acceptable practice. He believed that "a large proportion of the increase of abortion" could "be traced to the dissemination of immoral and criminal advertisements in daily journals".[18]

The abortifacient drug industry that emerged as a large-scale business in the 1840s continued to boom through the 1870s, and was not completely dead even in the early twentieth century. Nevertheless, the industry is difficult to deal with historically. No business records from the small abortifacient manufacturing firms have survived, and none of the in-house narrative histories of major drug companies mentions abortifacient preparations. The best information about the commercial abortifacient preparations that became so common on the American market after 1840 comes from research conducted by a remarkable physician-pharmacologist named Ely Van de Warker in Syracuse, New York, in the late 1860s and the early 1870s.

In an effort to discover what was in the commercial abortifacients that his female patients used so extensively, Van de Warker purchased samples of eleven of the leading brands available in his local area and did two things. First, he took a dose of each according to the directions on the wrappers and described the symptoms. Second, he made what chemical analysis he could of each of them, given the state of chemical analysis generally at that time and the limitations of his own laboratory facilities. Two of the eleven seemed "perfectly inert." Three others were reasonably mild laxatives and, in Van de Warker's opinion, "would not cause an abortion unless used by women very liable to external and mental influences." Such purgatives might, in other words, have considerable powers of suggestion, but were chemically harmless and not really abortifacients. The remaining six, however, could be dangerous drugs in the hands of desperate women willing to try large doses rather than the recommended amounts. The active ingredient in one seemed to be ergot, in another a mixture of ergot with oil of tansy and oil of savin. Aloes appeared to be the chief ingredient of the last four. Van de Warker also mentioned that a twelfth popular brand of abortifacient that he knew about probably depended upon black hellebore.[19]

In addition to the brisk trade in commercial abortifacients, what was probably an even larger business in abortifacient drugs was being conducted over-the-counter between women and local apothecaries. The story of cottonroot is instructive in this context. Beginning in 1840 several Southern physicians drew attention to the fact that slave women used cottonroot as an abortifacient, and they considered it both mild and effective.[20] Although regular physicians never prescribed cottonroot for any purpose in normal practice, druggists around the country were soon beginning to stock it. By the late 1850s, according to the *Boston Medical and Surgical Journal,* cottonroot had "become a very considerable article of sale" in New England pharmacies.[21] In 1871 "a druggist in extensive trade" informed Van de Warker "that the sales of ext[ract of] cotton-wood had quadrupled in the last five years" and that it was "purchased very extensively by small miscellaneous country merchants, who always have the extract among their stock of drugs."[22] Cottonroot remained available to American women in pharmacies and retained its "popular reputation as an abortive agent" into the early 1880s.[23]

Cottonroot, however, was only one of the drugs involved in the informal trade between women and apothecaries. "Having been part owner of a drug store, in a populous city," wrote Ely Van de Warker, "I speak from personal knowledge":

> The apothecary usually compounds from two to five drugs, which he regards as emmenagogue, in the form of mixture, bolus, or pill. I have known of perfectly inert drugs being mixed and sold to women who applied for abortifacient drugs for a criminal purpose. But generally druggists do not thus trifle with their reputations as skilful abortionists. The temerity with which even respectable druggists will sell violent and noxious drugs to women far advanced in pregnancy forms one of the most alarming features of this trade.[24]

Van de Warker added that he was always astounded at "the cool effrontery of young girls and women" in discussing sexual matters with their local druggists. Throughout the 1860s and early 1870s local apothecaries wrote their national trade journal for the latest emmenagogic recipes and the *Druggists' Circular* complied by publishing several for their readers to try.[25]

Along with the suddenly striking public visibility of abortion and the existence of a booming business in abortifacient preparations, a third source of indirect evidence for the likelihood of increased abortion rates in the United States after 1840 was the accelerated proliferation of materials that allowed American women an ever widening access to possible methods of aborting themselves. While popular health manuals continued to supply some of this information, as they had earlier in the century, the number of specific tracts directed at women and their sexuality increased dramatically in the middle decades of the nineteenth century as well. Some of the latter had begun to appear in the 1830s, when the first serious public discussions of contraception and family limitation were published in the United States.[26]

Richard Reece's *Lady's Medical Guide,* published in 1833, was a harbinger of later developments. Reece advanced autoabortive techniques by recommending for suppressions of menstrual flow, in addition to the ingesting of aloes, black hellebore, or savin, the use of a syringe to administer vaginally solutions of pennyroral, the favorite folk emmenagogue of the British Isles. Reece had patented a female syringe himself and urged readers to send for one.[27] These syringes were doubtless ineffective as uterine probes and hence not directly abortive instruments, but their availability to the public beginning in the 1830s must have accustomed many women to the idea that instruments could be used safely and effectively to control their reproductive functions. In a similar vein, private clinics for women, like the one which opened at the corner of Lynde and Cambridge Streets in Boston in 1834, began to advertise pointedly during the 1830s their willingness to treat any and all female complaints.[28] Although these early private clinics probably catered primarily to women concerned about venereal disease, such businesses were the forerunners of what would become a substantial number of private abortion clinics by the 1840s and 1850s. . . .

Contemporary writers on medical jurisprudence offered another source of evidence that abortion rates in the United States soared during the middle decades of the nineteenth century. Virtually all of the nation's experts on forensic medicine in the years from 1840 through 1880 concurred in this opinion. Amos Dean of the Albany Medical College noted in 1850 that the abortion business had "long since been reduced to a system," that women concealed pregnancies in order to obtain medical treatments that would abort them, and that death from savin poisoning was abnormally high in the United States.[29] R. E. Griffith, who edited an 1845 American edition of Alfred S. Taylor's standard British publication, *Medical Jurisprudence,* believed that ergot was very frequently used on his own side of the Atlantic as a abortifacient.[30] Clement B. Penrose, who edited another edition of Taylor twenty-one years later, interjected in brackets the note: "The frightful frequency of intentional abortion in this country has long been notorious, no less than the extraordinary ignorance as to its criminality, even among well-educated persons."[31] In other words, in 1866 Penrose considered it both common and condoned, notwithstanding several new laws that had appeared by then. Francis Wharton and Moreton Stille, in their 1855 *Treatise on Medical Jurisprudence,* likewise affirmed the high incidence of abortion in the United States.[32] So did both John Reese and Geroge W. Field in jurisprudence texts they wrote in the 1880s.[33]

Through all of the jurisprudence books, moreover, ran the unanimous opinion that little could be done to combat the practice, even by forensic experts like themselves. Abortion remained essentially impossible to prove at law on the basis of the knowledge and technology available to medical examiners in the nineteenth century. As Wharton and Stille reluctantly concluded:

> The signs of abortion, as obtained by an *examination of the female,* are not very certain in their character. It is seldom, indeed, that an examination of the living female is had, and especially at a period early enough

to afford any valuable indications. When abortion occurs in the early months, it leaves but slight and evanescent traces behind it.[34]

That meant prosecutors would have to rely on witnesses, which put them in a wretched position. If the abortion succeeded, action would not be brought since nothing remiss could be proved and the woman would not testify; if the woman was injured, it was her word, already compromised by her willingness to accept the risks, against that of the abortionist, who would claim the woman deceived him into believing it a case of ammenorrhea; if the woman died, her body could not testify on her behalf because pathologists could not determine for certain that an abortion had taken place. And the party with the greatest stake in the whole business, the fetus, did not exist as a human being either in the eyes of the law or in the collective opinion of the majority of Americans at midcentury, unless it had quickened and there was somebody left to testify that it had quickened.*

The enduring resiliency of the quickening doctrine throughout the period from 1840 through the 1870s indirectly substantiates further the likelihood of high abortion rates during that period. Writer after writer expressed the opinion that the American public simply did not consider the termination of pregnancy prior to quickening an especially serious matter, much less as some form of murder. To document fully the pervasiveness of the quickening doctrine in the United States through the 1870s would take scores, if not hundreds, of pages of references. It was simply a fact of American life. An especially striking example of the moral neutrality with which most Americans viewed abortion before quickening was recorded by a female school teacher in 1868. She attended a lecture series by a woman physician, Dr. Anne Densmore, in which Dr. Densmore argued that abortion was murder. Struck by the possibility that the doctor might be right, "several" of the women in the audience who had practiced abortion fainted at the thought of having committed murder.[35] Homer Hitchcock's straightforward statement to the Michigan State Board of Health in 1876 was representative of countless similar declarations during the middle period of the nineteenth century: "There is very generally current among the people the notion that before a pregnant woman 'quickens,' *i. e.* before the fourth month of pregnancy, there is no real life in the foetus, or at least that it is not a 'living soul,' and to destroy it is no real crime."[36]

As a consequence of the quickening doctrine, the vast majority of American women during the middle decades of the nineteenth century, when contemplating the possibility of an abortion, never had to face seriously the moral agonies so characteristic of the twentieth century's attitude toward the subject of abortion. The chief concerns of nineteenth-century women were probably centered on their own health and safety, as the nation's first wave of abortion laws suggested, not upon the inherent morality or immorality of what they were doing. In the minds of most Americans at the time, abortion was probably much closer morally to contraception, with which it was explicitly linked in several of the laws to be discussed in later chapters, than it was to murder or manslaughter. The point is important, and almost unanimously supported by all contemporary observers; twentieth-century observers, regardless of their own moral preconceptions, can believe that the incidence of abortion in the United States was very high between 1840 and 1880 without having to believe that a large proportion of American women were morally bankrupt on an issue of life and death. For these women the issue was *not* life and death prior to

*[ed. note: "Quickened" referred to the felt movement of the fetus months after conception. Prior to "Quickening" abortion was not considered illegal before the mid-nineteenth-century.]

quickening. . . .

The Medical Society of Philadelphia, aware of declining birthrates in the United States since 1840, declared itself in 1867 "ready to urge and prove" that the decline was "the result mainly of the practice of criminal abortion." Toward this end they conducted a survey of Philadelphia's regular physicians by mailing out to every one of them an "interrogatory circular." Though only 59 physicians returned the questionnaire, the respondents comprised, according to the secretary of the society, a representative cross section of the city's regulars. One of the questions asked: "What proportion of your cases of abortion do you believe to have been criminally produced?" Nineteen of the doctors answered one-half, 21 replied a quarter; 11 thought it "a large majority," presumably well over half; one doctor thought 75 percent of all abortion cases he saw had been induced; and 7 did not answer that question. Unfortunately, the questionnaire did not ask for specific figures on the numbers of abortions relative to the numbers of pregnancies or live births, but it inquired whether the Philadelphia regulars were of the "opinion that abortions are on the increase in our community?" All 59 answered affirmatively in 1868-69.[37]

Dr. P. S. Haskell, in a report to the Medical Association of Maine, claimed that "not less than *two thousand*" abortions were performed in his state each year during the early 1870s.[38] According to the 1880 census, there were approximately 12,000 births per year in Maine at that time. Haskell was thus suggesting a ratio of one abortion for every six live births at minimum.[39] Horace Knapp wrote in 1873, "There can be no doubt that more children are destroyed annually in their mother's womb than are born alive," and quoted the opinion of a Cincinnati Methodist minister that there was not a block in his city without a woman who had had an abortion and "thought it nothing."[40]

By the end of the decade of the 1870s, medical writers began to suggest earlier estimates had been, if anything, too low. In 1878 physicians testifying in the closely watched murder trial of an abortionist in southern Illinois set the ratio at 25 percent of all pregnancies.[41] In Wisconsin the situation seemed even worse. According to the state medical society's report to AMA headquarters in 1879, "where one living child is born into the world, two are done away with by means of criminal abortion."[42] The Wisconsin report was greater by a factor of two than any other medical estimate of the period, and can probably be discounted. But less easily dismissed was still another upward revision of the Storer and Heard ratio of one abortion in every five pregnancies made by the Michigan State Board of Health two years later. . . .

The record of birthrates in the United States during the nineteenth century underlies all the foregoing contemporary evidence and offers final reasons to believe that the United States experienced a great upsurge in the incidence of abortion that began around 1840 and continued roughly through the 1870s. The data are circumstantial to be sure, but striking nonetheless, especially when combined with the conclusions of modern demographers about population trends in other societies. In 1810 there were 1358 children under the age of 5 for every 1000 white women of childbearing age in the United States. That extraordinarily high birthrate exceeded any ever recorded in a European nation. By 1890 the figure had fallen to a moderate 685 children per 1000 women. Put differently, the average American woman bore 7.04 children in 1800; 3.56 by 1900. The steepest decennial drop in this long decline, which had been slight through the first three decades of the century, occurred between 1840 and 1850, exactly when abortion information, abortion services, and abortion itself came out into the open. American birthrates continued to drop thereafter more steeply than they had earlier in the century, and the United States completed a demographic transition from high birthrates and high deathrates at the end of the eighteenth century to lower birthrates and lower deathrates at the beginning of the twentieth.[43] Similar patterns have been discerned by historical demographers in other nations as modernization has reshaped successive societies around the world.[44]

The decline in American birthrates, of course, even during the 1840s and 1850s, cannot be attributed wholly or even primarily to the practice of abortion. Recent research makes clear the fact that contraceptive information was also being disseminated throughout the United States from the early 1830s through the end of the century, and some of the techniques advocated were at least partially effective even by modern standards.[45] The adoption of these new contraceptive techniques by Americans no doubt played a large role in the nation's falling birthrates from the 1830s onward, and it is reasonable to assume that the role of contraception increased in relation to the role of abortion as the century wore on. Yet the probability of very high abortion rates for several decades around midcentury cannot be dismissed, the advent of contraceptive techniques notwithstanding.

First, modern demographers assert that abortion has played a major role in the demographic transitions of other developing nations that have moved from populations characterized by high deathrates and high birthrates to populations characterized by low deathrates and low birthrates. Professor Abdel Omran of the University of North Carolina, for example, declared in 1971 that it was his "opinion that when developing societies are highly motivated to accelerate their transition from high to low fertility, induced abortion becomes such a popular method of fertility control that it becomes a kind of epidemic."[46] While Omran's opinion was based upon data drawn primarily from the experiences of Japan and Chile in the twentieth century, his conclusion also seems appropriate to the United States in 1840, when it was a developing nation making the kinds of transitions Omran was discussing. Certainly most observers a hundred years ago would have believed Omran's observation to be applicable to nineteenth-century America, and they would probably also have agreed with his characterization of the phenomenon as an epidemic. Thus, regardless of the availability of early contraceptive techniques, abortion appears likely to have been, just as contemporaries claimed it was, a quantitatively significant factor in the demographic transition to lower birthrates in the United States that was increasingly evident after 1840.[47]

Second, modern demographers have noticed the paradox that an increased use of contraceptive techniques has frequently led to an *increase* rather than a decrease in abortion rates, at least in the short run. This is explained by the theory that people beginning to use contraceptive techniques have made a commitment to limit the size of their families, but lack experience with the methods of contraception they have decided to try. The result is a high rate of "mistakes," or unwanted conceptions, and a consequent turning to abortion to erase them. This occurred in twentieth-century societies when the contraceptive techniques themselves were extremely effective once mastered.[48] But consider the situation in the United States at the middle of the nineteenth century. Not only were several successive generations of Americans being introduced to new contraceptive techniques over a period of several decades and making mistakes with them, they were also burdened with the additional handicap that the techniques themselves were frequently unreliable even when mastered. This must have greatly extended the period of reliance on abortion as a quantitatively significant backstop for women who sought to limit the number or to determine the spacing of their children in nineteenth-century America. Consequently, the gradual commitment of Americans to contraceptive practices after the 1830s paradoxically increases, rather than decreases, the likelihood that contemporary observers who testified to the existence of a great upsurge of abortion in the United States between 1840 and 1880 were right.

Either the commercialization and attendent visibility of abortion, on the one hand, or the great upsurge in the incidence of abortion, on the other, might have prompted American state legislators to reconsider their policies toward the practice after 1840. But a third change in the patterns of abortion in the United States, which made reassessments even more likely, was also taking place. That change involved a shift in the perception of who was having abortions for what reasons in the United States after 1840.

FOOTNOTES

1. On the intensity of competition during this period and the effects of that competition on the behavior of the medical profession, see, in addition to the standard histories of medical practice in America, the following two articles: Barnes Riznik, "The Professional Lives of Early Nineteenth-Century New England Doctors," *Journal of the History of Medicine and Allied Sciences,* XIX, No. 1 (Jan. 1964), 1-16 and Edward C. Atwater," The Medical Profession in a New Society, Rochester, New York (1811-1860)," *Bulletin of the History of Medicine,* XLVIII, No. 3 (May-June 1973), 221-235.

2. Atwater, "Medical Profession in a New Society," 228; Joel Shew, *Midwifery and the Diseases of Women* (New York, 1852), 155-157.

3. J. M. Toner, *Abortion in Its Medical and Moral Aspects* (privately prepared pamphlet from a journal reprint, 1861), 445. Toner Collection, Rare Book Room, Library of Congress.

4. [William F.] Howe and [A. H.] Hummel, *In Danger; or Life in New York, a True History of a Great City's Wiles and Temptations, True Facts and Disclosures* (New York, 1888), 155-167; "Madame Restell, and Some of Her Dupes," editorial in the *New York Medical and Surgical Reporter,* 1, No. 10 (Feb. 21, 1846), 158-165; A Physician of New-York, *Trial of Madame Restell, for Producing Abortion on the Person of Maria Bodine, to Which is Added, a Full Account of Her Life and Horrible Practices: Together with Prostitution in New York; Its Extent—Causes—and Effects upon Society* (New York, 1847), 68 pp., Raimo Collection.

5. *Trail of Madame Restell, Alias Ann Lohman, for Abortion and Causing the Death of Mrs. Purdy; Being a Full Account of All the Proceedings on the Trial, Together with the Suppressed Evidence and Editorial Remarks* ([New York], 1841). The quotes are from pages 8 and 21.

6. *Boston Daily Times,* Jan. 4, 1845; George Ellington, *The Women of New York, or the Under-World of the Great City* (New York, 1869), 395-411; Howe and Hummel, *In Danger,* 155-167.

7. *Boston Daily Times,* Jan. 4, 1845-Jan. 11, 1845.

8. See her broadside in the Undercurrents in Medicine, I, No. 2, scrapbook collection at Countway Library, Harvard University.

9. *Boston Medical and Surgical Journal,* XXX, No. 15 (May 15, 1844), 302-302.

10. *National Police Gazette* mentioned Restell often. See Vol. 1, 98, 100, 97, 204-205, 212, 220, 228, 236-237; Vol. II, 212, 412. On February 7, 1846, the *Gazette* mentioned that the daily papers had "teemed" with abortion-related stories for the previous several days.

11. See her letter to the editor, *(New York Tribune,* Aug. 26, 1847).

12. The first of these two estimates is the more frankly speculative. There is virtually no quantitative data, good, bad, or indifferent, on the actual incidence of abortion in the United States prior to the 1830s. Hence the first figures used here had to be inferred from tangential information such as fertility rates of the states in the Union in 1800 and from the known fact that abortion was associated almost exclusively at the turn of the nineteenth century with illegitimacy. Unfortunately, at this point there are no very reliable estimates of illegitimacy in the United States in the early nineteenth century either, and figures had to be calculated, at least in part, from the recently published research of British demographers and then corrected for the differences in the timing of population shifts in the British Isles, on the one hand, and among the largely British population of North America at the end of the eighteenth century, on the other. Consequently, even though the author believes, on the basis of several years of reading original sources on the around the subject of abortion in the United States for the early nineteenth century and on the basis of reading many of the available demographic studies for the United

States and Great Britain, that the first figures are entirely reasonable, they should not be taken as anything more than speculative—though informed—estimates. The second of the two estimates offered here, while also speculative, is much firmer than the first. The chief types of evidence upon which it was based are presented in this and the following chapter. While much of the evidence is necessarily inferential or "soft" or biased or limited in scope, its cumulative implications—in the author's judgment—are strong enough to sustain the estimates offered here for the midcentury period.

13. "The Evil of the Age," *New York Times,* Aug. 23, 1871.

14. *Boston Medical and Surgical Journal,* XXXI, No. 6 (Sept. 11, 1844), 124.

15. The nineteenth century had no preparations capable of directly producing abortions, though contemporary physicians and the public believed otherwise. On the other hand, as Professor Lonnie S. Burnett of the Johns Hopkins Medical School observed to the author, the compounds contained in nineteenth-century abortifacient preparations might occasionally have initiated abortions in women prone to miscarry, and the belief that women were taking abortifacient drugs might have exerted enough psychological pressure on some of them to produce an abortion regardless of the inherent effectiveness or lack of effectiveness of the medicine itself. See also Anne Colston Wentz, Lonnie S. Burnett, and Theodore M. King, "Methodology in Premature Pregnancy Termination," *Obstetrical and Gynecological Survey,* 28, No. 1 (Jan. 1973), especially 3 and 9, and Bernard N. Nathanson, "Drugs for the Production of Abortion," *Ibid.* 25, No. 8 (Aug. 1970), 727-731.

16. *Boston Daily Times,* Jan. 4, 1845-Jan. 11, 1845.

17. On the fact that every women in the county understood abortifacient advertisements for what they were, see "Criminal Abortion," editorial in *Buffalo Medical Journal and Monthly Review, XIV,* No. 4 (Sept. 1858), 248. The quote is from Ely Van de Warker, "The Criminal Use of Proprietary or Advertised Nostrums," *Papers Read before the Medico-Legal Society of New York from Its Organization,* 2d Ser., 1882, 78. The paper had been read in June 1872 and published in the *New York Medical Journal,* XVII, No. 1 (Jan. 1873), 23-25. A great many other observers all agreed. Shew, *Midwifery,* 155-157, confirms the recourse of abortionists to clairvoyant and astrologist advertisements as early as the 1840s, and the practice continued into the 1870s, when advertising curbs made such ploys more frequent than ever.

18. Ed. P. Le Prohon, *Voluntary Abortion, or Fashionable Prostitution, with Some Remarks upon the Operation of Craniotomy* (Portland, Maine, 1867). Quotes and from 3, 8, and 9.

19. Van de Warker, "Criminal Use of Proprietary Nostrums," 77-89.

20. *The Journal of Materia Medica,* n. s. III, No. 1 (Jan. 1861), 20-21, quoted four physicians, one from Mississippi, one from South Carolina, and two from Tennessee, all of whom noted in various journals between 1840 and 1860 that cottonroot" was habitually and effectively resorted to by the slave of the South for producing abortion, and this, too, without seriously affecting the general health." One of them, a Dr. Shaw, reported in the *Nashville Journal of Medicine,* that it was the best and most gentle emmenagogue extant. Cottonroot remained a popular folk abortifacient in the South through the 1870s. See Johnson, "Puerperal Convulsions," 274-280.

21. *Boston Medical and Surgical Journal,* LXIII, No. 11 (Oct. 11, 1860), 212.

22. Van de Warker, "Detection of Criminal Abortion, Part. II," 241.

23. J. C. Gleason, "A Medico-Legal Case of Abortion, Followed by Conviction of the Accused Abortionist," *Boston Medical and Surgical Journal,* CI, No. 6 (Aug. 7, 1879), 188. See testimony of Dr. J. W. Spooner in the trial. Gleason was the Rockland County Medical Examiner; David Wark, *The Practical Home Doctor for Women and Children to Which Is Added a Valuable Appendix Containing a List of Medicinal Herbs and Their Value, with Chapters Explaining Poisons and Their Antidotes, How To Resusciate the Drowned, How To Process in Cases of Accidents and Emergencies, the Skin and Its Care, the Teeth and their Care, Etc.* (New York, 1882), 173.

24. Van de Warker, "Detection of Criminal Abortion, Part. II," 231-232.

25. *American Druggists' Circular and Chemical Gazette,* IV, No. 3 (March 1860), 68; V, No. 1 (Jan. 1861), 13; XVI, No. 11 (Nov. 1872), 192, XVII, No. 3 (March 1873), 64. These recipes involved the old favorites: ergot, aloes, savin, and black hellebore. In November of 1875 the *Circular* published a story about an abortion conviction in Illinois and ceased publishing recipes for local druggists to make up their own abortifacients.

26. James W. Reed, "Contraceptive Practice in the Nineteenth Century" (draft chapter of a forthcoming study of birth control in the United States from 1830 to 1970). The author would like to acknowledge Mr. Reed's help and generosity in making his findings available prior to their publication.

27. Richard Reece, *The Lady's Medical Guide; Being a Popular Treatise on the Causes, Prevention, and Mode of Treatment of the Diseases to Which Females Are Particularly Subject (Philadelphia, 1833)*, 46-48, 50. Reece cautioned, in obvious fashion, *"the remedies we have recommended for suppression should not be employed, if there be present any symptom strongly indicating impregnation."*

28. Mrs. Mott, *The Ladies' Medical Oracle; or, Mrs. Mott's Advice to Young Females, Wives, and Mothers* (Boston, 1834.

29. Dean, *Principles of Medical Jurisprudence*, 40, 127-140.

30. Alfred S. Taylor, *Medical Jurisprudence*, R. E. Griffith, ed. (Philadelphia, 1845), 472-473.

31. Alfred S. Taylor, *A Manual of Medical Jurisprudence*, Clement B. Penrose, ed. (Philadelphia, 6th American ed., 1866), 444-446. Quote is from an editor's note on p. 460.

32. Wharton and Stille, *Treatise on Medical Jurisprudence*, 267-277.

33. John J. Reese, *Test-Book of Medical Jurisprudence and Toxicology* (Philadelphia, 1884), 442-454; George W. Field, *Field's Medico-Legal Guide for Doctors and Lawyers* (Albany and New York, 1887), 147-188.

34. Wharton and Stille, *Treatise on Medical Jurisprudence*, 277.

35. *The Revolution*, I, No. 11 (March 19, 1868), 170.

36. Homer Hitchcock, "Report on Criminal Abortion," *Fourth Annual Report of the Secretary of the State Board of Health of the State of Michigan* (Lansing, 1876), 60-61.

37. Andrew Nebinger, *Criminal Abortion: Its Extent and Prevention* (Philadelphia, 1870), and Nebinger, "Criminal Abortion: Its Extent and Prevention," *Transactions of the Medical Society of the State of Pennsylvania at its Twenty-Seventh Annual Session*, XI, Part I (Philadelphia, 1876), 119-140.

38. P. S. Haskell, "Criminal Abortion," *Transactions of the Maine Medical Association, 1871-1873*, IV (Portland, 1873), 465-473.

39. *Compendium of the Tenth Census* (Washington, 1883), Part I, 609.

40. Horace Knapp, *Women's Confidential Adviser on the Health and Diseases of Women* (Providence, R.I., 1873), 72, 78-79.

41. W. J. Chenoweth, "A Case of Criminal Prosecution for Murder by Causing Abortion," *Cincinnati Lancet and Clinic*, XLI (1879), 361-364. The abortionist, a woman, eventually won dismissal of her case after a hung jury failed to convict.

42. Stanford E. Chaille, "State Medicine and State Medical Societies," *Transactions of the American Medical Association*, XXX, (1879), 355.

43. Wilson H. Grabill, Clyde V. Kiser, and Pascal Whelpton, *The Fertility of American Women* (New York, 1958), 14-19; Yasukichi Yasuba, *Birth Rates of the White Population in the United States, 1800-1860* (Baltimore, 1962), 32.

44. The question of why modernizing societies undergo this common and characteristic transition is, of course, one of the cardinal questions faced by historical demographers. The literature on that question, most aspects of which lie beyond the scope of this study, is extensive to say the least. For a representative discussion of the theory of demographic transition see Petersen, *Population*, 8-15, and for a heuristic reconsideration of "why"—which fits rather well with the evidence here—see Robert V. Wells, "Family History and Demographic Transition," *Journal of Social History*, IX, No. 1 (Fall 1975), 1-10.

45. Reed, "Birth Control and the Americans," *passim;* Wilson Yates, "Birth Control Literature and the Medical Profession in Nineteenth Century America," *Journal of the History of Medicine and Allied Sciences*, XXXI, No. 1 (Jan. 1976), 42-54.

46. Abdel R. Omran, "Abortion in the Demographic Transition," in *Rapid Population Growth: Consequences and Policy Implications*, report of a study committee of the National Academy of Sciences (Baltimore, 1971), 481.

47. David V. Glass makes a not dissimilar point with reference to the importance of abortion in demographic transitions in Germany. *Population Policies and Movements in Europe* (New York, [1940] 1967), 278-282. Cf. also the statement of the historical demographer Richard A. Easterlin in a paper entitled "Factors in the Decline of Farm Fertility in the United States: Some Preliminary Results," which he read before a session of the American Historical Association convention on December 29, 1974: "The methods of deliberate fertility control [in the United States during the 1850s] cannot be determined, but coitus interruptus and perhaps abortion are the most likely candidates."

48. Omran, "Abortion in the Demographic Transition," 508-511.

10

>Abortion, free love, homosexuality and birth control are not
>only politically and morally volatile terms, they are ambiguous
>as well: their implications can and do change from one historical
>era to the next. Just as the designations "nuclear family" and
>"extended family" are meaningful only when applied to specific
>historical settings, the cultural implications of sexual attitudes
>and orientations attain meaning only when placed in a historical
>context.
>   In the following article Linda Gordon demonstrates that the
>terms "free love" and "birth control" had distinctly different
>meanings to feminists in the mid nineteenth century than they do
>to feminists in the late twentieth century. For the earlier
>feminists birth control and free love were not necessarily
>strategies of sexual liberation. On the contrary, according to
>Gordon, birth control and free love were means through which
>some feminists sought to liberate themselves *from* sexuality.
>   How does Gordon prove this point? Can a person be both a
>feminist and anti-sexual?

Voluntary Motherhood
The Beginnings of the
Birth-Control Movement

Linda Gordon

By the 1870s the feminist movement in the United States was divided into many
different organizations and loose reform tendencies. Yet among these groups there
was a remarkably coherent ideology on major questions—marriage and divorce, suffrage, employment opportunity, for example—and on no question so much as on
that of birth control. The standard name applied to the demand for birth control was

"voluntary motherhood"—incorporating a political statement about the nature of *involuntary* motherhood and child-rearing in women's lives and a solution to the problems they presented.

The feminists who advocated voluntary motherhood were of three general types: suffragists (divided between two national organizations and many local groups), moral reformers (in causes such as temperance, social purity, church auxiliaries, and women's professional and service organizations), and members of small free-love groups. The political distance between some of these feminists was great—as between the socially conservative churchwomen and the usually atheistic and anarchistic free lovers, for example. Thus their relative unity as feminists and voluntary-motherhood advocates seems the more remarkable.

Free-love groups in the 1870s were the closest successors to the perfectionist reform groups of the first half of the century. The free-love movement was always closely related to free thought, or agnosticism, and was characterized by a passionate resentment of the Christian established churches, especially in their power to influence law and create restrictive social and cultural norms. They called themselves free lovers as a means of describing their opposition to legal and clerical marriage which, they believed, stifled love. Free-love groups were always small and sectarian and were usually male-dominated, despite their ideological feminism. They never coalesced into a large or national organization, but represented the dying remnants of a preindustrial period of utopian reform. Their very self-definition built around their iconoclasm and isolation from the masses, the free lovers could offer intellectual leadership in formulating the shocking arguments that birth control in the nineteenth century required.[1]

The suffragists and moral reformers, on the other hand, concerned to win mass support, became increasingly committed to social respectability; as a result they did not generally advance far beyond prevalent standards of propriety in discussing sexual matters publicly. Indeed, as the century progressed the social gap between these people and the free lovers grew, for the second and third generations of suffragists had become increasingly respectable (whereas in the 1860s and 1870s the great feminist theoreticians, such as Elizabeth Cady Stanton, had been intellectually closer to the free lovers, and at least one of these early giants, Victoria Woodhull, was for several years a member of both the suffragist and the free-love camp). But even the quest for respectability did not stifle these feminists completely, and many of them said in private writings—in letters and diaries—what they were unwilling to utter in public.

The similarities between free lovers and suffragists on the question of voluntary motherhood should be understood then not as minimizing the political distance between them, but as showing how their analyses of the social meaning of reproduction for women were converging. The sources of that convergence, the common ground of their feminism, were their similar experiences in the changing conditions of nineteenth-century America. Most were educated Yankees of professional, farm, or commercial families, responding to severe threats to the stability, if not dominance, of their class position. Both groups were disturbed by the consequences of rapid industrialization—the emergence of great capitalists and a clearly defined financial oligarchy, the increased immigration that provided cheap labor and further threatened the dignity and economic security of the Yankees. Above all they feared and resented the loss of their independence and would have undone the wage-labor system entirely had they been able. Free lovers and suffragists, as feminists, welcomed the decline in patriarchal power within families that followed upon industrialization, but they worried, too, about the possible disintegration of the family and the loosening of sexual morality. They saw reproduction in the context of these larger social changes and in the context of a movement for women's emancipation; and they saw that movement as an answer to some of these large social problems. They hoped that giving political power to women would help to reinforce the family, to make the government more just and the economy less monopolistic. In all these wishes there was something traditional as well as something progressive. Their voluntary-motherhood ideas reflected this duality.

Since we bring to our concept of birth control a twentieth-century understanding of it, it is important to stress the fact that neither free lovers nor suffragists approved of contraceptive devices. Ezra Heywood, patriarch and martyr, thought "artificial" methods "unnatural, injurious, or offensive."[2] Tennessee Claflin, feminist, spiritualist, and the sister of Victoria Woodhull, wrote that the "washes, teas, tonics and various sorts of appliances known to the initiated" were a "standing reproach upon, and a permanent indictment against, American women. . . . No woman should ever hold sexual relations with any man from the possible consequences of which she might desire to escape."[3] *Woodhull and Claflin's Weekly* editorialized: "The means they [women] resort to for . . . prevention is sufficient to disgust every natural man. . . ."[4]

On a rhetorical level the main objection to contraception was that it was unnatural, and the arguments reflected a romantic yearning for the "natural," rather pastorally conceived, that was typical of many nineteenth-century reform movements. More basic, however, in the women's arguments against contraception was an underlying fear of the promiscuity that it could permit. And that fear was associated less with any woman's fear for her own virtue than with her fear of other women—"fallen women"—who might undermine her husband's fidelity.

To our twentieth-century sensibility it would seem that a principle of voluntary motherhood that rejects contraception is a principle so theoretical as to be of little real impact. What gave it substance was that it was accompanied by another, potentially explosive, conceptual change: the reacceptance of female sexuality. Both free lovers and suffragists, interestingly, staked their claims here on the traditional grounds of the natural. Free lovers argued, for example, that celibacy was unnatural and dangerous—for men and women alike. "Pen cannot record, nor lips express, the enervating, debauching effect of celibate life upon young men and women. . . . "[5] Asserting the existence, legitimacy, and worthiness of female sexual drive was one of the free lovers' most important contributions to sexual reform; it was a logical correlate of their argument from the "natural" and appeal for the integration of body and soul.

Women's rights advocates, too, began, timidly, to argue the existence of female sexuality. Isabella Beecher Hooker wrote to her daughter: "Multitudes of women in all the ages who have scarce known what sexual desire is—being wholly absorbed in the passion of maternity—have sacrificed themselves to the beloved husbands as unto God—and yet these men, full of their human passion and defending it as righteous & God-sent lose all confidence in womanhood when a woman here and there betrays her similar nature & gives herself soul & body to the man she adores."[6] Alice Stockham, a spiritualist and feminist physician, lauded sexual desire in men and women as "the prophecy of attainment." She urged that couples avoid reaching sexual "satiety" with each other in order to keep their sexual desire constantly alive, for she considered desire plesant and healthful.[7] Elizabeth Cady Stanton, commenting in her diary in 1883 on the Whitman poem "There is a Woman Waiting for

Me," wrote, " . . he speaks as if the female must be forced to the creative act, apparently ignorant of the fact that a healthy woman has as much passion as a man, that she needs nothing stronger than the law of attraction to draw her to the male."[8] Still, she loved Whitman, and largely because of that openness about sex that made him the free lovers' favorite poet.

According to the system of ideas then dominant, women, lacking sexual drives, submitted to sexual intercourse in order to please their husbands and to conceive children. There was a nervousness about this view, however, expressed in the ambivalence of asserting both that women naturally lacked sexual drive and that they must be protected from exposure to sexuality lest they "fall" and become depraved, lustful monsters. This ambivalance perhaps came from a subconscious lack of certainty about the reality of the sexless woman, which was a construct laid only thinly on top of an earlier conception of woman as highly sexed, even insatiably so, that prevailed until the late eighteenth century. Victorian ambivalence on this question is nowhere more tellingly revealed than in the writings of physicians, who viewed woman's sexual organs as the source of her being, physical and psychological, and blamed most mental derangements on disorders of the genitals.[9] Indeed, they saw it as part of the nature of things, as Rousseau had written, that men were male only part of the time, but women were female always.[10] In a system that limited women's opportunities to make other contributions to culture, it was inevitable that women should be more strongly identified with sex than were men. Indeed, females were frequently called "the sex" in the nineteenth century.

The concept of the maternal instinct helped to make Victorian sexual attitudes more consistent. In many nineteenth-century writings we find the idea that the maternal instinct was the female analog to the male sex instinct; as if the two instincts were seated in analogous parts of the brain, or soul. Thus to suggest, as these feminists did, that women might have the capacity for being sexual subjects rather than mere objects, feeling impulses of their own, automatically tended to weaken the theory of the maternal instinct. In the fearful imagination of the self-appointed protectors of the family and of womanly innocence, the possibility that women might desire sexual contact not for the sake of pregnancy—that they might even desire it at a time when they positively did not want pregnancy—was a wedge in the door to denying that women had any special maternal instinct at all.

Most of the feminists did not want to open that door either. Indeed, it was common for nineteenth-century women's rights advocates to use the presumed special motherly nature and sexual purity of women as an argument for increasing their freedom and status. It is no wonder that many of them chose to speak their subversive speculations about the sexual nature of women privately, or at least softly. Even among the more outspoken free lovers, there was a certain amount of hedging. Lois Waisbrooker and Dora Forster, writing for a free-love journal in the 1890s, argued that although men and women both had an "amative" instinct, it was much stronger in men, and women—only women—also had a reproductive, or "generative," instinct. "I suppose it must be universally conceded that men make the better lovers," Forster wrote. She thought that it might be possible that "the jealousy and tyranny of men have operated to suppress amativeness in women, by constantly sweeping strongly sexual women from the paths of life into infamy and sterility and death," but thought also that the suppression, if it existed, had been permanently inculcated into woman's character.[11]

Modern birth-control ideas rest on a full acceptance, at least quantitatively, of female sexuality. Modern birth control is designed to permit sexual intercourse as often as desired without the risk of pregnancy. Despite the protestations of sex counselors that there are no norms for how often people should engage in intercourse, the popular view always had such norms. Most people in the mid-twentieth century think that "normal" couples indulge several times a week. Given this concept of sexual rhythms, and the accompanying concept of the purpose of birth control, the free lovers' rejection of artificial contraception and "unnatural" sex seems to eliminate the possibility of birth control at all. Nineteenth-century sexual reformers, however, had different sexual norms. They did not seek to make an infinite number of sterile sexual encounters possible. They wanted to make it possible for women to avoid pregnancy if they badly needed to do so for physical or psychological reasons, but they did not believe that it was essential for women to be able to indulge in sexual intercourse under those circumstances.

In short, for birth control they recommended periodic or permanent abstinence, and the tradition of "magnetation" theories of sex among the perfectionists made this seem a reasonable, moderate procedure. The proponents of voluntary motherhood had in mind two distinct contexts for abstinence. One was the mutual decision of a couple; the other was the unilateral decision of a woman. Let us consider them one at a time.

In the context of the nineteenth century's patriarchal society, the "mutual decision of a couple" often meant the will of the male. Thus abstinence chosen by a couple normally meant that the husband accepted self-imposed celibacy, either continuous or through a form of rhythm method. Some medical observers had correctly plotted the woman's fertility cycle, but the majority of physicians, accepting a logic of analogy from lower mammals rather than direct observation of humans, had got it quite wrong. (It was not until the 1920s that the ovulation cycle was correctly plotted, and the 1930s before it was generally understood among American doctors.) Ezra Heywood, for example, recommended avoiding intercourse from six to eight days before memstruation until ten to twelve days after it.[12] Careful use of the calendar could also provide control over the sex of a child, Heywood believed: conception in the first half of the menstrual cycle would produce grils, in the second half, boys.[13] These misconceptions functioned, conveniently, to make arguable Heywood's and others' ideas that celibacy and contraceptive devices were *both* dangerous.

Some voluntary-motherhood advocates explored another form of abstinence—male continence, or avoidance of ejaculation. Ezra Heywood, for example, endorsed the Oneida system, but was repelled by Noyes's authoritarian ledership and his ban on monogamous relationships.[14] Dr. Alice Stockham developed a more woman-centered approach to male continence, "Karezza," in which it was necessary for the woman as well as the man to avoid climax.[15]

Concern with sexual self-control was characteristic of the free lovers' point of view. It came to them mainly from the thought of the utopian communitarians of the early nineteenth century, but it was most fully developed theoretically by Ezra Heywood. Beginning with the assumption that people's "natural" instincts, left untrammeled, would automatically create a harmonic, peaceful, ecological society—an optimism certainly deriving directly from liberal philosophical faith in the innate goodness of man—Heywood applied it to sexuality, arguing that the natural sexual instinct was innately moderated and self-regulating. Heywood denied the social necessity of sublimation. On one level, Heywood's theory may seem inadequate as a psychology, since it cannot explain phenomena such as repression and the fact that adults have greater self-control than children. As a social critique, however, it has power. It argues that the society and its attendant repressions have distorted the animal's natural self-regulating mechanism and have thereby created excessive and obsessive sexual drives. It offers a social explanation for these phenomena usually described in psychological terms and holds out the hope that they can be changed.

Essentially the same as Wilhelm Reich's theory of "sex-economy," the Heywood theory of self-regulation went beyond Reich's in providing a weapon against one of the ideological defenses of male supremacy. Self-regulation as a goal was directed against the prevalent attitude that male lust was an uncontrollable urge, an attitude that functioned as a justification for rape specifically and for male sexual irresponsibility generally. We have to get away from the tradition of "man's necessities and woman's obedience to them," Stockham wrote.[16] The idea that men's desires are irrepressible is merely the other face of the idea that women's desires are nonexistent. Together the two created a circle that enclosed woman, making it her exclusive responsibility to say No, and making pregnancy her God-given burden if she didn't, while denying her both artificial contraception and the personal and social strength to rebel against male sexual demands.

Heywood developed his theory of natural sexual self-regulation in answer to the common anti-free-love argument that the removal of social regulation of sexuality would lead to unhealthy promiscuity: ". . . in the distorted popular view, Free Love tends to unrestrained licentiousness, to open the flood gates of passion and remove all barriers in its desolating course; but it means just the opposite; it means the *utilization of animalism,* and the triumph of Reason, Knowledge, and Continence."[17] He applied the theory of self-regulation to the problem of birth control only as an afterthought, perhaps when women's concerns with that problem reached him. Ideally, he believed, the amount of sexual intercourse that men and women desired would be exactly commensurate with the number of children that were wanted. Since sexual repression had had the boomerang effect of intensifying human sexual drives far beyond "natural" levels, effecting birth control now would require the development of the inner self-control to contain and repress sexual urges. But he expected that in time sexual moderation would come naturally.

Heywood's analysis, published in the mid-1870s, was concerned primarily with excessive sex drives in men. Charlotte Perkins Gilman, one of the leading theoreticians of the suffrage movement, reinterpreted that analysis two decades later to emphasize its effects on women. The economic dependence of woman on man, in Gilman's analysis, made her sexual attractiveness necessary not only for winning a mate, but as a means of getting a livelihood too. This is the case with no other animal. In the human female it had produced "excessive modification to sex," emphasizing weak qualities characterized by humans as "feminine." She made an analogy to the milk cow, bred to produce far more milk than she would need for her calves. But Gilman agreed entirely with Heywood about the effects of exaggerated sex distinction on the male, producing excessive sex energy and its excessive indulgence to an extent debilitating to the whole species. Like Heywood she believed that the path of progressive social evolution ran toward monogamy and toward reducing the promiscuous sex instinct.[18]

A second context for abstinence was the right of the wife unilaterally to refuse her husband. This idea is at the heart of voluntary motherhood. It was a key substantive demand in the mid-nineteenth century when both law and practice made sexual submission to her husband a woman's duty.[19] A woman's right to refuse is clearly the fundamental condition of birth control—and of her independence and personal integrity.

In their crusade for this right of refusal the voices of free lovers and suffragists were in unison. Ezra Heywood demanded "Woman's Natural Right to ownership and control over her own body-self—a right inseparable from Woman's intelligent existence. . . ."[20] Paulina Wright Davis, at the National Woman Suffrage Association in 1871, attacked the law "which makes obligatory the rendering of marital rights and compulsory maternity." When, as a result of her statement, she was accused of being a free lover, she accepted the description.[21] Isabella Beecher Hooker wrote her daughter in 1869 advising her to avoid pregnancy until "you are prepared in body and soul to receive and cherish the little one. . . ."[22] Elizabeth Cady Stanton had characteristically used the same concept as Heywood's, that of woman owning her own body. Once asked by a magazine what she meant by it, she replied: ". . . womanhood is the primal fact, wifehood and motherhood its incidents. . . . must the heyday of her existence be wholly devoted to the one animal function of bearing children? Shall there be no limit to this but woman's capacity to endure the fearful strain on her life?"[23]

The insistence on women's right to refuse often took the form of attacks on men for their lusts and their violence in attempting to satisfy them. In their complaints against the unequal marriage laws, chief or at least loudest among them was the charge that they legalized rape.[24] Victoria Woodhull raged, "I will tell the world, so long as I have a tongue and the strength to move it, of all the infernal misery hidden behind this horrible thing called marriage, though the Young Men's Christian Association sentence me to prison a year for every word. I have seen horrors beside which stone walls and iron bars are heaven. . . . "[25] Angela Heywood attacked men incessantly and bitterly; she was somewhat ill-tempered, though not necessarily inaccurate. "Man so lost to himself and woman as to invoke legal *violence* in these sacred nearings, *should have solemn meeting with, and look serious at his own penis until he is able to be lord and master of it, rather than it should longer rule, lord and master, of him and of the victims he deflowers.* "[26] Suffragists spoke more delicately, but not less bitterly. Feminists organized social-purity groups and campaigns, their attacks on prostitution based on a larger critique of the double standard, to which their proposed remedy was that men conform to the standards required of women.[27]

A variant of this concern was a campaign against "sexual abuses," which in Victorian euphemistic language could mean deviant sexual practices or simply excessive sexual demands, but not necessarily violence or prostitution. The free lovers in particular turned to this cause because it gave them an opportunity to attack marriage. The "sexual abuses" question was one of the most frequent subjects of correspondence in free-love periodicals. For example, a letter from Mrs. Theresa Hughes of Pittsburgh:

> . . . a girl sixteen, full of life and health when she became a wife. . . . She was a slave in every sense of the word, mentally and sexually, never was she free from his brutal outrages, morning, noon and night, up almost to the very hour her baby was born, and before she was again strong enough to move about. . . . Often did her experience last an hour or two, and one night she will never forget, the outrage lasted exactly four hours.[28]

Or from Lucinda Chandler, well-known moral reformer:

> This useless sense gratification has demoralized generation after genera-

tion, till monstrosities of disorder are common. Moral education, and healthful training will be requisite for some generations, even after we have equitable economics, and free access to Nature's gifts. The young man of whom I knew who threatened his bride of a week with a sharp knife in his hand, to compel her to perform the office of "sucker," would no doubt have had the same disposition though no soul on the planet had a want unsatisfied or lacked a natural right.[29]

From an anomymous woman in Los Angeles:

> I am nearly wrecked and ruined by . . . nightly intercourse, which is often repeated in the morning. This and nothing else was the cause of my miscarriage . . . he went to work like a man a-mowing, and instead of a pleasure as it might have been, it was most intense torture. . . .[30]

Clearly there was a level of hostility toward sex here. The observation that many feminists hated sex has been made by several historians,[31] who have usually failed to perceive that their hostility and fear of it came from the fact that they were women, not that they were feminists. Women in the nineteenth century were urged to repress their own sexual feelings, to view sex as a reproductive and wifely duty. But they also resented what they had experienced, which was not abstraction, but a particular, historical kind of sexual encounter: intercourse dominated by and defined by the male in conformity with his desires and in disregard of what might bring pleasure to a woman.

Furthermore, sexual intercourse brought physical danger. Pregnancy, childbirth, and abortions were risky and painful experiences in the nineteenth century; venereal diseases were frequently communicated to women by their husbands. Elmina Slenker, a free lover and novelist, wrote, "I'm getting a host of stories (truths) about woman so starved sexually as to use their dogs for relief, and finally I have come to the belief that a CLEAN dog is better than a drinking, tobacco-smelling, venereally diseased man!"[32]

Sex-hating women were not simply misinformed, or priggish, or neurotic. They were often responding rationally to their material reality. Denied even the knowledge of sexual possibilities other than those dictated by the rhythms of male orgasm, they had only two choices: passive and usually pleasureless submission, with high risk of undersirable consequences, or rebellious refusal. In that context abstinence to ensure voluntary motherhood was a most significant feminist demand. There was a medical superstition that women could not conceive unless they felt sexually aroused; it is understandable that Dr. Alice Stockham, for example, proposed deliberate sexual coldness as a form of birth control.[33]

What is remarkable is that some women recognized that it was not sex, but only their husbands' style of making love, that repelled them. One of the women who complained about her treatment went on to say: "I am undeveloped sexually, never having desires in that direction; still, with a husband who had any love or kind feelings for me and one less selfish it *might* have been different, but he cared nothing for the torture to *me* as long as *he* was gratfied."[34]

Elmina Slenker herself, the toughest and most crusty of all these "sex-haters," dared to explore and take seriously her own longings, thereby revealing herself to be a sex-lover in disguise. As the editor of the *Water-Cure Journal,* and a regular contributor to *Free Love Journal,* she expounded the theory called Dianaism, or Nonprocreative Love, sometimes called Diana-love and Alpha-abstinence.[35] It meant free sexual contact of all sorts except intercourse.

> We want the sexes to love more than they do; we want them to love openly, frankly, earnestly; to enjoy the caress, the embrace, the glance, the voice, the presence & the very step of the beloved. We oppose no form or act of love between any man & woman. Fill the world as full of genuine sex love as you can . . . but forbear to rush in where generations yet unborn may suffer for your unthinking, uncaring, unheeding actions.[36]

Comparing this to the more usual physical means of avoiding conception, *coitus interruptus* and male continence, reveals how radical it was. In modern history general public awareness of the possibilities of nongenital sex and of forms of genital sex beyond standard "missionary position" intercourse has been a recent, post-Freudian, even post-Masters and Johnson phenomenon. The definition of sex in terms of heterosexual intercourse has been one of the oldest and most universal cultural norms. Slenker's alienation from existing sexual possibilities led her to explore alternatives with a bravery and a freedom from religious and psychological taboos extraordinary for a nineteenth-century Quaker reformer.

In the nineteenth century neither free lovers nor suffragists ever relinquished their hostility to contraception. Free speech, however, was always an overriding concern,* and for that reason Ezra Heywood agreed to publish some advertisements for a vaginal syringe, an instrument the use of which for contraception he personally deplored, or so he continued to assure his readers.[37] Those advertisements led to Heywood's prosecution for obscenity, and Heywood defended himself with his characteristic flair by making his position more radical than ever before. Contraception was moral, he argued, when it was used by women as the only means of defending their rights, including the right to voluntary motherhood. Although "artificial means of preventing conception are not generally patronized by Free Lovers," he wrote, reserving for his own followers the highest moral ground, still he recognized that not all women were lucky enough to have free lovers for their sex partners.[38]

> Since Comstockism makes male will, passion and power absolute to *impose* conception, I stand with women to resent it. The man who would legislate to choke a woman's vagina with semen, who would force a woman to retain his seed, bear children when her own reason and conscience oppose it, would waylay her, seize her by the throat and rape her person.[39]

Angela Heywood, Ezra's wife, enthusiastically pushed this political line.

> Is it "proper," "polite," for men, real *he* men, to go to Washington to say, by penal law, fines and imprisonment, whether woman may continue her natural right to wash, rinse, or wipe out her own vaginal body

---

*Radicals were usually united in their opposition to Comstock's censorship. The National Liberal League, for example, formed in 1876 to promote secularism, mounted a petition campaign for repeal of the Comstock law and collected over fifty thousand signatures.

opening—as well as legislate when she may blow her nose, dry her eyes, or nurse her babe. . . . Whatever she may have been pleased to receive, from man's own, is his gift and her property. Women do not like rape, and have a right to resist its results.[40]

Her outspokenness, vulgarity in the ears of most of her contemporaries, came from a substantive, not merely a stylistic, sexual radicalism. Not even the heavy taboos and revulsion against abortion stopped her: "To cut a child up in woman, procure abortion, is a most fearful, tragic deed; but *even that* does not call for man's arbitrary jurisdiction over woman's womb."[41]

It is unclear whether Heywood, in this passage, was actually arguing for legalized abortion; if she was, she was alone among all nineteenth-century sexual reformers in saying it. Other feminists and free lovers condemned abortion and argued that the necessity of stopping its widespread practice was a key reason for instituting voluntary motherhood by other means. The difference on the abortion question between sexual radicals and sexual conservatives was in their analysis of its causes and remedies. While AMA doctors and preachers were sermonizing on the sinfulness of women who had abortions,[42] the radicals pronounced abortion itself as undeserved punishment, and women who had them as helpless victims. Woodhull and Claflin wrote about Madame Restell's notorious abortion "factory" in New York City without moralism, arguing that only voluntary conception would put it out of business.[43] Elizabeth Cady Stanton also sympathized with women who had abortions, and used the abortion problem as an example of women victimized by laws made without their consent.[44]

Despite stylistic differences, which came from differences in goals, nineteenth-century American free-love and women's rights advocates shared the same basic attitudes toward birth control: they opposed contraception and abortion but endorsed voluntary motherhood achieved through periodic abstinence; they believed that women should always have the right to decide when to bear a child; they believed that women and men both had natural sex drives and that it was not wrong to indulge those drives without the intention of conceiving children. The two groups also shared the same appraisal of the social and political significance of birth control. Most of them were favorably inclined toward Neo-Malthusian reasoning (at least until the 1890s, when the prevailing concern shifted to the problem of underpopulation rather than overpopulation).[45] They were also interested in controlling conception for eugenic purposes. They were hostile to the hypocrisy of the sexual double standard and, beyond that, shared a general sense that men had become oversexed and that sex had been transformed into something disagreeably violent.

But above all, their commitment to voluntary motherhood expressed their larger commitment to women's rights. Elizabeth Cady Stanton thought voluntary motherhood so central that on her lecture tours in 1871 she held separate afternoon meetings for *women only* (a completely unfamiliar practice at the time) and talked about "the gospel of fewer children & a healthy, happy maternity."[46] "What radical thoughts I then and there put into their heads & as they feel untrammelled, these thoughts are permanently lodged there! That is all I ask."[47] Only Heywood had gone so far as to defend a particular contraceptive device—the syringe. But the principle of women's right to choose was accepted in the most conservative parts of the women's rights movement. At the First Congress of the Association for the Advancement of Women in 1873 a whole session was devoted to the theme "Enlightened Motherhood," which had voluntary motherhood as part of its meaning.[48]

The general conviction of the whole feminist community that women had a right to choose when to be pregnant was so strong by the end of the nineteenth century that it seems odd that they were unable to overcome their scruples against artificial contraception. The basis for this reluctance lies in their awareness that a consequence of effective contraception would be the separation of sexuality from reproduction. A state of things that permitted sexual intercourse to take place normally, even frequently, without the risk of pregnancy, inevitably seemed to nineteenth-century middle-class women to be an attack on the family. In the mid-Victorian sexual system, men normally conducted their sexual philandering with prostitutes; accordingly prostitution, far from being a threat to the family system, was a part of it and an important support of it. This was the common view of the time, paralleled by the belief that prostitutes knew of effective birth-control techniques. This seemed only fitting, for contraception in the 1870s was associated with sexual immorality. It did not seem, even to the most sexually liberal, that contraception could be legitimized to any extent, even for the purposes of family planning for married couples, without licensing extramarital sex. The fact that contraception was not morally acceptable to respectable women, was from a woman's point of view, a guarantee that such women would not be a threat to her own marriage.

The fact that sexual intercourse often leads to conception was also a guarantee that men would marry in the first place. In the nineteenth century women needed marriage far more than men. Lacking economic independence, women needed husbands to support them, or at least to free them from a usually more humiliating economic dependence on fathers. Especially in the cities, where women were often isolated from communities, deprived of the economic and psychological support of networks of relatives, friends, and neighbors, the prospect of dissolving the cement of nuclear families was frightening. In many cases children, and the prospect of children, provided that cement. Man's responsibilities for children were an important pressure for marital stability. Women, especially middle-class women, were also dependent on their children to provide them with meaningful work. The belief that motherhood was a woman's fulfillment had a material basis: parenthood was often the only creative and challenging activity in a woman's life, a key part of her self-esteem.

Legal, efficient birth control would have increased men's freedom to indulge in extramarital sex without greatly increasing women's freedom to do so. The pressures enforcing chastity and marital fidelity on middle-class women were not only fear of illegitimate conception but a powerful combination of economic, social, and psychological factors, including economic dependence, fear of rejection by husband and social-support networks, internalized taboos, and, hardly the least important, a socially conditioned lack of interest in sex that may have approached functional frigidity. The double standard of the Victorian sexual and family system, which had made men's sexual freedom irresponsible and oppressive to women, left most feminists convinced that increasing, rather than releasing, the taboos against extramarital sex was in their interest, and they threw their support behind social-purity campaigns.

In short, we must forget the twentieth-century association of birth control with a trend toward sexual freedom. The voluntary-motherhood propaganda of the 1870s was associated with a push toward a more restrictive, or at least a more rigidly enforced, sexual morality. Achieving voluntary motherhood by a method that would have encouraged sexual license was absolutely contrary to the felt interests of the very group that formed the main social basis for the cause—middle-class women.

Separating these women from the early-twentieth-century feminists, with their interest in sexual freedom, were nearly four decades of significant social and economic changes and a general weakening of the ideology of the Lady. The ideal of the free lovers—responsible, open sexual encounters between equal partners—was impossible in the 1870s because men and women were not equal. A man was a man whether faithful to his wife or not. But women's sexual activities divided them into two categories—wife or prostitute. These categories were not mere ideas but were enforced in reality by severe social and economic sanctions. The fact that so many, indeed most, free lovers in practice led faithful, monogamous, legally married lives is not insignificant in this regard. It suggests that they instinctively understood that free love was an ideal not to be realized in that time.

As voluntary motherhood was an ideology intended to encourage sexual purity, so it was also a pro-motherhood ideology. Far from debunking motherhood, the voluntary-motherhood advocates consistently continued the traditional Victorian mystificantion and sentimentalization of the mother. It is true that at the end of the nineteenth century an increasing number of feminists and elite women—that is, still a relatively small group—were choosing not to marry or become mothers. That was primarily because of their increasing interest in professional work, and the difficulty of doing such work as a wife and mother, given the normal uncooperativeness of husbands and the lack of social provisions for child care. Voluntary-mothhood advocates shared the general belief that mothers of young children ought not to work outside their homes but should make mothering their full-time occupation. Suffragists argued both to make professions open to women and to ennoble the task of mothering; they argued for increased rights and opportunities for women *because* they were mothers.

The free lovers were equally pro-motherhood; they only wanted to separate motherhood from legal marriage.[49] They devised pro-motherhood arguments to bolster their case against marriage. Mismated couples, held together by marriage laws, made bad parents and produced inferior offspring, free lovers said.[50] In 1870 *Woodhull and Claflin's Weekly* editorialized, "Our marital system is the greatest obstacle to the regeneration of the race."[51]

This concern with eugenics was characteristic of nearly all feminists of the late nineteenth century. At the time eugenics was mainly seen as an implication of evolutionary theory, which was picked up by many social reformers to buttress their arguments that improvement of the human condition was possible. Eugenics had not yet become a movement in itself. Feminists used eugenic arguments as if they instinctively felt that arguments based solely on women's rights had not enough power to conquer conservative and religious scruples about reproduction. So they combined eugenics and feminism to produce evocative, romantic visions of perfect motherhood. "Where boundless love prevails, . . . " *Woodhull and Claflin's Weekly* wrote, "the mother who produces an inferior child will be dishonored and unhappy . . . and she who produces superior children will feel proportionately pleased. When woman attains this position, she will consider superior offspring a necessity and be apt to procreate only with superior men."[52] Free lovers and suffragists alike used the cult of motherhood to argue for making it voluntary. Involuntary motherhood, wrote Harriet Stanton Blatch, daughter of Cady Stanton and a prominent suffragist, is a prostitution of the maternal instinct.[53] Free-lover Rachel Campbell cried out that motherhood was being "ground to dust under the misrule of masculine ignorance and superstition."[54]

Not only was motherhood considered an exalted, sacred profession, and a profession exclusively woman's responsibility, but for a woman to avoid it was to choose a distinctly less noble path. In arguing for the enlargement of woman's sphere, feminists envisaged combining motherhood with other activities but never rejected motherhood. Victoria Woodhull and Tennessee Claflin wrote:

> Tis true that the special and distinctive feature of woman is that of bearing children, and that upon the exercise of her function in this regard the perpetuity of race depends. It is also true that those who pass through life failing in this special feature of their mission cannot be said to have lived to the best purposes of woman's life. But while maternity should always be considered the most holy of all the functions woman is capable of, it should not be lost sight of in devotion to this, that there are as various spheres of usefulness outside of this for woman as there are for man outside of the marriage relation.[55]

Birth control was not intended to open the possibility of childlessness but merely to give women leverage to win more recognition and dignity. Dora Forster, a free lover, saw in the fears of underpopulation a weapon of blackmail for women:

> I hope the scarcity of children will go on until maternity is honored at least as much as the trials and hardships of soldiers campaigning in wartime. It will then be worth while to supply the nation with a sufficiency of children . . . every civilized nation, having lost the power to enslave woman as mother, will be compelled to recognize her voluntary exercise of that function as by far the most important service of any class of citizens.[56]

"Oh, women of the world, arise in your strength and demand that all which stands in the path of true motherhood shall be removed from your path," wrote Lois Waisbrooker, a feminist novelist and moral reformer.[57] Helen Gardener based a plea for women's education entirely on the argument that society needed educated mothers to produce able sons (not children, *sons*).

> Harvard and Yale, not to mention Columbia, may continue to put a protective tariff on the brains of young men: but so long as they must get those brains from the proscribed sex, just so long will male brains remain an "infant industry" and continue to need this protection. Stupid mothers never did and stupid mothers never will furnish this world with brilliant sons.[58]

Clinging to the cult of motherhood was part of a larger conservatism shared by free lovers and suffragists: acceptance of traditional sex roles. Even the free lovers rejected only one factor—legal marriage—of the many that defined woman's place in the family. They did not challenge conventional conceptions of woman's passivity and limited sphere of concern.[59] In their struggles for equality the women's rights advocates never suggestd that men should share responsibility for child-raising, housekeeping, nursing, or cooking. When Victoria Woodhull in the 1870s and Charlotte Perkins Gilman in the 1900s suggested socialized child care, they assumed that only women would do the work.[60] Most feminists wanted economic independence for women, but most, too, were reluctant to recommend achieving this by turning women loose and helpless into the economic world to compete with men.[61] This preference was conditioned by an attitude hostile to the egoistic spirit of capitalism; but since the attitude was not transformed into a political position, it often appeared in the guise of expressing women's failings rather than the system's faults. Failing to distinguish, or even to indicate awareness of a possible distinction, between women's learned passivity and their equally learned distaste for competition and open aggression, these feminists also followed the standard Victorian rationalization of sex roles, the idea that women were morally superior. Thus the timidity and self-effacement that were the marks of women's powerlessness were made into innate virtues. Angela Heywood, for example, praised women's greater ability for self-control, and, in an attribution no doubt intended to jar and titillate the reader, branded men inferior on account of their lack of sexual temperance. Men's refusal to accept women as human beings she identified, similarly, as a mark of men's incapacity: ". . . man has not yet achieved himself to realize and meet a PERSON in woman. . . . "[62] In idealistic, abstract terms, no doubt such male behavior is an incapacity. In the historical context it was an expression of false consciousness on Heywood's part because she omitted to mention the power and privilege to exploit women that the supposed "incapacity" gave men.

This omission reveals a false consciousness characteristic of the cult of motherhood: a consciousness that ignored or denied the privileges men received from women's exclusive responsibility for parenthood. For the "motherhood" of the feminists' writings was not merely the biological process of gestation and birth, but a whole package of social, economic, and cultural functions. Although many of the nineteenth-century feminists had done substantial analysis of the historical and anthropological origins of woman's social role, they nevertheless agreed with the biological-determinist point of view that woman's parental capacities had become implanted at the level of instinct, the famous "maternal instinct." That concept rested on the assumption that the qualities that parenthood requires—capacities for tenderness, self-control and patience, tolerance for tedium and detail, emotional supportiveness, dependability and warmth—were not only instinctive but sex-linked. The concept of the maternal instinct thus also involved a definition of the normal instinctual structure of the male that excluded these capacities, or included them only to an inferior degree; it also carried the implication that women who did not exercise these capacities, presumably through motherhood, remained unfulfilled, untrue to their destinies.

Belief in the maternal instinct reinforced the belief in the necessary spiritual connection for women between sex and reproduction and limited the development of birth-control ideas. But the limits were set by the entire social context of women's lives, not by the intellectual timidity of their ideas. For women's "control over their own bodies" to lead to a rejection of motherhood as the *primary* vocation and measure of social worth required the existence of alternative vocations and sources of worthiness. The women's rights advocates of the 1870s and 1880s were fighting for those other opportunities, but a significant change had come only to a few privileged women, and most women faced essentially the same options that existed fifty years earlier. Thus voluntary motherhood in this period remained almost exclusively a tool for women to strengthen their positions within conventional marriages and families, not to reject them.

FOOTNOTES

1. The interested reader may refer to the following major works of the free-love cause: R. D. Champman, *Freelove a Law of Nature* (New York: author, 1881); Tennessee Claflin, *The Ethics of Sexual Equality* (New York: Woodhull & Claflin, 1873), pamphlet; Claflin, *Virtue, What It Is and What It Isn't; Seduction, What It Is and What It Is Not* (New York: Woodhull & Claflin, 1872); Ezra Heywood, *Cupid's Yokes: or, The Binding Forces of Conjugal LIfe* (Princeton, Mass. Co-operative Publishing Co., 1876); Heywood, *Uncivil Liberty: An Essay to Show the Injustice and Impolicy of Ruling Woman Without Her Consent* (Princeton, Mass: Co-operative Publishing Co., 1872); C. L. James, *The future Relation of the Sexes* (St. Louis: author, 1872); Juliet Severance, *Marriage* (Chicago: M. Harman, 1901); Victoria Claflin Woodhull, *The Scare-Crows of Sexual Slavery* (New York: Woodhull & Claflin, 1874); Woodhull, *A Speech on the Principles of Social Freedom* (New York: Woodhull & Claflin, 1872); Woodhull, *Tried as by Fire or, The True and the False Socially: An Oration* (New York: Woodhull & Claflin, 1874), pamphlet.

2. Heywood, *Cupid's Yokes,* p. 20.

3. Claflin, *Ethics of Sexual Equality,* pp. 9-10.

4. *Woodhull & Claflin's Weekly* 1, no. 6 (1870): 5.

6. Letter to her daughter Alice, 1874, in the Isabella Beecher Hooker Collection, Beecher Stowe mss. This reference was brought to my attention by Ellen Dubois of SUNY-Buffalo.

7. Alice Stockham, *Karezza: Ethics of Marriage* (Chicago: Stockham, 1898), pp. 84, 91-92.

8. Theodore Stanton and Harriot Stanton Blatch, eds., *Elizabeth Cady Staton as Revealed in Her Letters, Diary and Reminiscences* (New York: Harper & Brothers, 1922), 2:210 (Diary, September 6, 1883).

9. For a good summary of the medical literature, see Carroll Smith-Rosenberg and Charles Rosenberg, "The Female Animal: Medical and Biological Views of Woman and Her Role in Nineteenth-Century America," *Journal of American History 60, no. 2 (September 1973): 332-56.*

10. J. J. Rousseau, *Emile* (New York: Columbia University Teachers College, 1967), p. 132. Rousseau was, after all, a chief author of the Victorian revison of the image of woman.

11. Dora Forster, *Sex Radicalism as Seen by an Emancipated Woman of the New Time* (Chicago: M. Harman, 1905), p. 40.

12. Heywood, *Cupid's Yokes,* pp. 19-20, 16.

13. Ibid., pp. 19-20; *Woodhull & Claflin's Weekly* 1, no. 18 (September 10, 1870): 5.

14. Heywood, *Cupid's Yokes,* pp. 14-15.

15. Stockham, *Karezza,* pp. 14-15.

16. Ibid., p. 86.

17. Heywood, *Cupid's Yokes,* p. 19.

18. Charlotte Perkins Gilman, *Women and Economics* (New York: Harper Torchbooks, 1966) pp. 38-39, 42, 43-44, 209.

19. In England, for example, it was not until 1891 that the courts first held against a man who forcibly kidnapped and imprisoned his wife when she left him.

20. Ezra Heywood, *Free Speech: Report of Ezra H. Heywood's Defense before the United States Court, in Boston, April, 10, 11, and 12, 1883* (Princeton, Mass: Co-operative Publishing Co., 1883), p. 16.

21. Quoted in Nelson Manfred Blake, *The Road to Reno: A History of Divorce in the United States* (New York: MacMillan, 1962), p. 108, from the *New York Times,* May 12, 1871 and July 20, 1871.

22. Letter of August 29, 1869, in Hooker Collection, Beecher-Stowe mss. This reference was brought to my attention by Ellen Dubois.

23. Elizabeth Cady Stanton mss. no. 11, Library of Congress, undated. This reference was brought to my attention by Ellen Dubois.

24. See for example, *Lucifer, The Light-Bearer,* ed. Mosses Harman (Valley Falls, Kansas: 1894-1907) 18, no. 6 (October 1889): 3.

25. Victoria Woodhull, *The Scare-Crows,* p. 21. Her mention of the UMCA is a reference to the fact that Anthony Comstock, author and chief enforcer for the U.S. Post Office of the antiobscenity laws, had begun his career in the YMCA.

26. *The Word* (Princeton, Mass.) 20, no. 9 (March 1893): 2-3. Emphasis in original.

27. See for example, the National Purity Congress of 1895, sponsored by the American Purity Alliance.

28. *Lucifer,* April 26, 1890, pp. 1-2.

29. *The Next Revolution, or, Woman's Emancipation from Sex Slavery)* (Valley Falls, Kansas:

Lucifer Publishing Co., [1890]), p. 49, pamphlet, unsigned but probably by Mosses Harman.

30. Ibid., pp. 8-9.

31. Linda Gordon et al., "Sexism in American Historical Writing," *Women's Studies* 1, no. 1 (Fall 1872).

32. *Lucifer 15, no. 2 (September 1886): 3.*

33. *Alice Stockham, Tokology: A Book for Every Women* ([1883]) New York: R. F. Fenno, 1911), pp. 153-53.

34. *The Word* 20 (1892-93), passim, for example.

35. For example, *Lucifer* 18, no. 8 (December 1889): 3; 18, no. 6 (October 1889): 3.

36. Ibid. 18, no. 8 (December 1889): 3.

37. Heywood, *Free Speech,* p. 17.

38. Ibid., p. 16.

39. Ibid., pp.3-6. "Comstockism" is again a reference to Anthony Comstock. Noting the irony that the syringe was called by Comstock's name, Heywood wrote: "To name a really good thing 'Comstock' has a sly, sinister, wily look, indicating vicious purpose; in deference to its N.Y. venders, who gave it that name, the Publishers of *The Word* inserted an advertisement. . . .which will hereafter appear as 'the Vaginal Syringe'; for its intelligent, humane and worthy mission should no longer be libelled by forced association with the pious scamp who thinks Congress gives him legal right of way to an control over every American Woman's Womb." At this trial, Heywood's second, he was acquitted. At his first trial, in 1877, he had been convicted, sentenced to two years, and served six months; at his third, in 1890, he was sentenced to and served two years at hard labor, an ordeal that probably cuased his death a year later.

40. *The Word* 22, no. 9 (March 1893): 2-3.

41. Ibid.

42. For example, Horatio Robinson Storer, M.D., *Why Not? A Book for Every Woman* (Boston: Lee and Shepard, 1868). Note that this was the prize essay in a contest run by the AMA in 1865 for the best antiabortion tract.

43. Claflin, *Ethics of Sexual Equality;* Emanie Sachs, *the Terrible Siren, Victoria Woodhull, 1838-1927* (New York: Harper & Brothers, 1928), p. 139.

44. Elizabeth Cady Stanton, Susan Anthony, Matilda Gage, eds., *History of Woman Suffrage,* 1:597-98.

45. Heywood, *Cupid's Yokes,* p. 20; see also American Journal of Eugenics, ed. M. Harman, 1, no. 2 (September 1907); *Lucifer,* February 15, 1906; June 7, 1906; March 28, 1907; and May 11, 1905.

46. Elizabeth Cady Stanton to Martha Wright, June 19, 1871, Stanton mss. This reference was brought to my attention by Ellen Dubois of SUNY-Buffalo; see also Stanton, *Eight Years After, Reminiscences 1815-1897* (New York: Schocken, 1971), pp. 262, 297.

47. Stanton and Blatch, *Stanton as Revealed in Her Letters,* pp. 132-33.

48. *Papers and Letters,* Association for the Advancement of Women, 1873. The AAW was a conservative group formed in opposition to the Stanton-Anthony tendency. Nevertheless Chandler, a frequent contributor to free-love journals, spoke here against undersired materni- ty and the identification of woman with her maternal function.

49. *Woodhull & Claflin's Weekly* 1, no. 20 (October 1, 1870): 10.

50. Woodhull, *Tried as by Fire,* p. 37; Lillian Harman, *The Regeneration of Society.* Speech before Manhattan Liberal club, March 31, 1898 (Chicago: Light Bearer Library, 1900).

51. *Woodhull & Claflin's Weekly* 1, no. 20 (October 1, 1870): 10.

52. Ibid.

53. Harriot Stanton Blatch, "Voluntary Motherhood," *Transactions,* National Council of Woman of 1891, ed. Rachel Foster Avery (Philadelphia: J. B. Lippincott, 1891), p. 280.

54. Rachel Campbell, *The Prodigal Daughter, or, the Price of Virtue* (Grass Valley, Califor- nia, 1885), p. 3. An essay read to the New England Free Love League, 1881.

55. *Woodhull & Claflin's Weekly* 1, no. 14 (August 13, 1870): 4.

56. Dora Forster, *Sex Radicalism,* pp. 39-40.

57. From an advertisement for her novel, *Perfect Motherhood: or, Mabel Raymond's Resolve* (New York: Murray Hill, 1890), in *The Next Revolution.*

58. *Helen Hamilton Gardener, Pulpit, Pew and Cradle* (New York: Truth Seeker Library, 1891), p. 22.

59. Even the most outspoken of the free lovers had conventional, role-differentiated images of sexual relations. here is Angela Heywood, for example: "Men must not emasculate themselves for the sake of 'virtue,' they must, they will, recognize manliness and the life element of

manliness at the fountain source of good manners. Women and girls demand strong, well-bred generative, vitalizing sex ability. Potency, virility, is the grand basic principle of man, and it holds him clean, sweet and elegant, to the delicacy of his counterpart." From *The Word* 14, no. 2 (June 1885): 3.

60. Woodhull, *The Scare-Crows; Charlotte Perkins Gilman, Concerning Children* (Boston: Small, Maynard, 1900).

61. See for example Blatch, "Voluntary Motherhood," pp. 283-84.

62. *The Word* 20, no. 8 (February 1893): 3.

11

According to many contemporary feminists, one of the most persistent, and inimical, myths of Western history is that women are not sexual beings, that they do not crave sexual pleasure with the vim, vigor and (all too often) vitriol displayed by men. From the feminist perspective, men have utilized women's alleged aversion to sexuality as an excuse for various types of exploitation and domination, including the double standard and the existence of prostitution.

In this controversial article Edward Shorter contends that the feminists may be wrong. Shorter argues that the combination of the biological peculiarities of female reproductive organs and the inadequacies of pre-twentieth-century medicine exposed women to a wide variety of genital disorders which made sexual activity extremely painful for them. According to Shorter, because of this disability a large number of women did have an aversion to sexuality. While not denying the bane of sexism, Shorter contends that the notion of sexual aversion was less a figment of the male chauvinist imagination than a reality generated by the vulnerability of female reproductive organs.

Does Shorter's argument make sense? Do you have a different perspective on Linda Gordon's thesis about the origins of the birth control movement after reading Shorter?

Women's Diseases Before 1900

Edward Shorter

If women in past times have been unequal to men, it is partly because they have been so vulnerable to their own bodies. Their inferior status in the eighteenth and nineteenth centuries resulted, in some measure, from their victimization by their reproductive organs in a way that men have never been victimized. This vulnerability has several dimensions:

1. Women's exposure to an unending series of pregnancies, as a result of both their husbands' "conjugal rights" over their bodies and rape, which makes them immediately vulnerable to male violence.

2. Women's exposure to death, terrible pain, and mutiliation in childbirth, a vulnerability to the forces of nature that men, of course, escape, and that is inflicted on women as a consequence of their sexual contact with men.

3. Women's vulnerability to a whole range of diseases of the reproductive system

for which there is no male counterpart in urology. If the first two aspects of misadventure have received some treatment in the scholarly literature, women's diseases have, among historians of women, excited no attention at all. They are the subject of this chapter.

Even today women are more exposed to illness than men as a result of the reproductive system. In 1976, for example, a survey recorded forty-eight days of "restricted activity" owing to acute genitourinary disorders for every hundred women interviewed, only twelve for every hundred men.

Another survey of "chronic" conditions of "prostate" and "female trouble except breasts," as the survey put it, uncovered a similar difference.[1] I shall argue in the following pages that in North America and Western Europe before 1900 the difference in "morbidity" status between men and women was even more glaring and that if women were obliged to take secondary roles in traditional society, it was partly because they were constant prey to nutritional disorders and pelvic diseases that left them more enervated than men in their daily lives; that made them highly apprehensive about their sexual relations with men; and that helped convince them that femininity was a curse imposed on womankind by God.

Of course other reasons exist for the subordination of women in times past, such as the teachings of the Catholic Church or the formidable networks of male bonding arrayed against women. My purpose is not to make physical vulnerability the chief explanation of women's ritual subservience, their legal status as minors, or the constant victimization of their daily lives. It is rather to show that at the level of disease they were not only worse situated than men but often the direct victims of male sexuality. This is a more modest undertaking than documenting the roots of sexual subservience and often benumbingly technical. But I remind the reader of two larger perspectives in "mentalities," which I hope the medical evidence in this chapter will help open up: (1) that women themselves felt deeply debased and humiliated by these gynecological afflictions that were their lot all along, a further spur for them to comply voluntarily with patriarchy; and (2) that a precondition for the explosion of modern feminism has been the abolition of these various vulnerabilities, through birth control, through what has become virtually risk-free childbearing, and through the medical alleviation of most of the pelvic pathology we shall encounter here. Alas, not all. I shall not discuss gynecological cancer, that "angel of death of the woman's world," because the historical evidence on prevalence rates is just too skimpy.[2] And I shall omit all those new "diseases of civilization," such as anorexia nervosa, to which women have been newly subject.[3] Two other disease conditions will also be omitted from consideration:

1. Hysteria—simply because the diagnosis was too unreliable. When nineteenth-century doctors use the term, they lump together a number of different psychiatric symptoms and then hopelessly discredit their own usefulness as observers by attributing the whole thing to the uterus. What is one to make, for instance, of the following utterance, from a "medical topography" of Wurzburg in 1805:

> Among the female gender the so-called nervous diseases are to be encountered among all classes, yet with some differentiation. Marriage, with all its consequences, is often the best remedy for hysteria. Often, however, the disease makes such strides, especially among single women, that all efforts of the doctors are unable to prevent its transition into an incurable malady. . . . Hysterical women suffer especially in the

period of the monthly cleaning, which often is combined with great pain.[4]

We have no way, moreover, of knowing how common hysterical symptoms were among men. I am inclined to dismiss as hopeless any effort to reconstruct the epidemiology of women's mental health from sources like these. (My confidence in this whole range of psychiatric labels has been further shaken by the recent discovery that a specific "menopausal" syndrome, on which doctors have until recently relied heavily, simply does not exist.[5])

2. Uterine malpositions—especially retroversion, which is the backward-tilting of the uterus. Nineteenth-century medicine was obsessed with malpositions, but we now know that how the uterus rests in the body is responsible for very few symptoms perceived by the women themselves. (Gravest is that a retroverted uterus might drag down the ovaries into the "pouch of Douglas," resulting in painful coitus.) I have decided simply to ignore the whole question.

Let me avert a possible misunderstanding or two. My aim is not to write a puff piece for the "marvels of medical science," which (it could be argued) has inflicted a sort of cultural diseaster on attitudes to our bodies and to death in the twentieth century. Nor is it to present evidence of women's attitudes to their bodies in traditional times, because we have no way of knowing what most of these women actually thought as their uteruses started to prolapse or as the dull pains of cervical cancer started to announce themselves. At present we are reduced to inferring what they might have felt about their relations with men, about the "joy of sex," and about the very nature of femininity itself as they brushed against the various disease conditions that are the subject of this chapter. Ultimately, whoever wants to write about the impact of disease on women's lives will be obliged to find information on the attitudes of the women themselves. By declaring as "provisional" and "interim" my findings, and by clearly posting as "speculative" the bridges to mentalities constructed here, I have hoped for the moment to elude this responsibility.

A brief word about the sources. Historians have paid little attention to several varieties of medical treatises that convey considerable information about the lives of women in times past. We have, for one thing, the hundreds of medical topographies written in the years after 1778, when the French Royal Academy of Medicine asked provincial doctors to send in reports on the diseases, hygienic conditions, and folkways of the local populations.[6] A similar kind of literature seems to have started out quite independently in Germany and in other countries as well.[7] Then too, around 1840 numerous doctors began to publish statistical reports on the patients in their clinics. Remember that only in the first half of the nineteenth century does the "clinic," as opposed to the general hospital for the poor, really get going. So thereafter a quite rich literature on, let us say, the epidemiology of the contracted pelvis or the ovarian tumor becomes available. Previous students of women's health have dwelt almost entirely on gynecology and obstetrics textbooks, to the exclusion of this rich data on the incidence of disease in the female population as a whole.[8]

Well, the reader might object, were the lives of women in past times really so different from our own days? Have "narrowly defined sex roles" and "male chauvinism" not been the main affliction of women since time out of mind? The following description of women's health in the small town of Sigmaringen early in the nineteenth century suggests that women's problems may have been more complicated than their inability to get into law school:

The main causes of poor (female) health here are:

The laborious field and house work, which generally fall upon the women and from which otherwise women even in primitive societies are exempt.

You can see pregnant women here reaping the grain harvest, bundling up and hauling away the sheaves, mowing, carrying fodder, wood and water, and during the winter they're constantly threshing.

Intercourse right up to the end of pregnancy.

The mean, insufficient diet of the women, in that the men spend every evening at the tavern, and the women and children content themselves at home, year in and year out, with a miserable *Wassersuppe.*

Lack of proper rest, care and treatment when they get sick, whereby they continue to work, without any help at all, as long as possible before . . . the doctor is called.

The delay in summoning the midwife.

Their impregnation again immediately after birth, whereby the completely recovered uterus receives the ovum not in the proper place, not in the fundus, but on one side, or deeper down in the lower uterine segment.[9]

(This latter is apparently a reference to a complication of pregnancy called "placenta previa," in which the placenta implants itself near or across the mouth of the cervix, making the mother liable to sudden hemorrhaging.)

The point running through this chapter is that if women in places like Sigmaringen were callously treated by their husbands, weary of the burden of children, and attentive to the parish priest's declamations about the special burden God had placed on Eve, it was partly because the illnesses of their own frail bodies had ground much of the joy of life, the young confidence, the easy autonomy, out of their existence.

Sigmaringen, and many accounts like it, help us to construct a larger picture of the health of women before the twentieth century. My discussion will center on four areas: (1) diseases arising from the nutritional deficiencies to which women were more subject than men; (2) "Leukorrhea," a whitish, glutinour vaginal discharge; (3) such sequellae of pregnancy as fistulas and perineal tears; (4) a whole range of uterine and ovarian pathology, such as giant tumors, painful menstruation, and uterine prolapse.

DEFICIENCY DISORDERS

A prefatory point—the most serious deficiencies of nutrition fell on women during pregnancy and in the puerperium, which I have omitted from this chapter on the grounds that they erupted only momentarily—although often with fatal results—rather than dragging on the life long. Of the many diseases arising from vitamin and mineral shortages that we could consider here, such as women's higher susceptibility to tuberculosis, I focus on two: iron-deficiency anemia and pelvic contractions arising from childhood rickets.

So rare has iron-deficiency anemia become in our own time that we are inclined to ascribe its physical symptoms in the past to Victorianism or to the oppression of women. In fact, many of the real world counterparts of these literary heroines, with their pale faces, their easy fatiguability, and their inconstant appetites, were suffering from anemia, the chronic depletion of the body's iron stores (although the cause was unknown). This deficiency, as seen in young women, was called "chlorosis."[10] The same pattern of description appears again and again: pallid color, irregular menstruation, weariness, and some kind of puslike vaginal discharge indicating the presence of an infection (which would further exacerbate the anemia).[11] Hysteria is often mentioned too, although whether the doctor understands by that wide swings of personality, the tremor arising from some kind of functional disease, or the muscular rigidity associated with classical descriptions of hysteria is impossible to say. A typical quote is that of Dr. W.W. Johnson of Washington, D.C. written in 1888: "Confirmed ill health . . . is common after the establishment of the marriage relations and after childbirth among American women. . . . The principal manifestations of this persistent ill health are chronic anemia, with malnutrition, and impaired or altered function in all the organs, especially in those of the nervous system."[12] And just to show that these descriptions are not merely the sexist fantasies of a gaggle of society gynecologists, anemia was endemic toward the turn of the century also among working-class women. For example in Leipzig female subscribers to the local Health Insurance Fund missed work much more frequently than male subscribers because of "weak blood" and "anemia" *(Blutarmut und Bleichsucht)*: ages fifteen through nineteen fifty times as often, ages fortynine and older seven times as often. These were mainly women working in the textile and garment industries.[13]

I think it possible that many of these early accounts confuse anemia with early tuberculosis, and the real incidence may therefore be somewhat lower. But the fatigued, undernourished women we encounter recovering from childbirth in Lyon's Croix Rousse suburb, where they worked in the silk industry, show too clearly the hallmarks of anemia.[14] A vast pool of iron-deficient women clearly existed among the working classes.

But just women? To the extent that worms of chronic infection were the source of the anemia, we have no reason for thinking that men as well were not anemic. One factor in anemia, however, was exclusively female: iron loss through pregnancy and childbirth. Today an average, well-nourished North American woman will be unlikely to store in her own bone marrow the 800 milligrams or so of iron she needs for a typical pregnancy, and to offset the huge iron demands that both the fetus and her own hemoglobin mass make, women currently ingest large amounts of supplementary iron.[15]

Now, let us recall the following:

1. Even though iron as a cure for anemia has been used since time out of mind, in traditional dosages it seems to have done little good. And the biochemistry of anemia was not understood until the 1890s.[16]

2. The intestinal worms that plagued much of the population prevented the gut from absorbing a good deal of the natural iron that people got in their diets. Although in England (at least) normal iron intake was sufficient by modern standards, worms would have prevented the body from utilizing it.[17] The natural history of worms has yet to be written, but so many medical topographies comment casually upon "Wurmer" or "vers" in infants and adults that we must conclude the incidence was substantial.[18]

The average woman was likely to have between six and twelve pregnancies in her lifetime, her iron deficit deepening with each (and further exacerbated to the extent that she breastfed).[19]

The conclusion is inescapable that iron-deficiency anemia was another of those burdens that nature had allocated especially to women, making them more irritable, more anorexic, more tired, more flatulent, more subject to vasomotor disturbances such as "hot flashes," more prey in general than men to nameless aches and pains and unspecific tinglings—all of which are the classic symptoms or iron-deficiency anemia.

Only around 1918 was it established that vitamin D and sunlight are essential to the intestine's absorption of calcium, which, in turn, is vital for proper bone growth.[20] The "beading" of the ribs and the bowlegs symptomatic of rickets occur, of course, among both boys and girls. But only among women does the twisted growth of the pelvis have such grisly consequences—in childbirth. Victims of rickets exhibit a "flat" pelvis, in which the sacrum at the rear grows too close to the pubic bone at the front, narrowing the space through which the infant's head may pass in its descent along the birth canal. These deformed pelves give rise to the nightmare of "dystocia," protracted, agonized labors, as in endless hours of bearing down the mother is simply unable to force the infant's head through the birth canal. Or the fetal head might not even engage in the pelvic inlet, so narrow are the bones. When this happens, her birth attendant has to either tug the fetus out with forceps, or reach in and pull out manually the infant's feet. Or in extreme cases simply let the mother die undelivered.

Here is Guillaume Mauguest de la Motte, a small town doctor in late-seventeenth-century Normandy, encountering a typical contracted pelvis: "On 23 March, 1694, I was called to deliver a woman in the parish of Teil, two leagues from here (Vallognes), who had started in labor the previous day and whose waters had burst, the hand of the fetus protruding." We have here, in other words, an "arm presentation," in which the mother is unlikely to deliver the child spontaneously because its neck and shoulder are lodged against her pelvic inlet. "I introduced my hand in her vagina easily and pushed it up to the top part of her sacrum . . . which I found curved inward, leaving so little space between it and the pubic bone that I was obliged to try more than four times to get hold of the infant's feet." De la Motte was trying to perform an obstetrical operation known as "version," turning the infant feet first, to prepare it for delivery, the mother's pelvis being highly contracted. Finally however he succeeded in getting one foot between his two fingers and the other foot, lying close by, foilowed. He then pulled the child slowly from the womb. The mother survived, but the baby died a quarter of an hour later.[21]

It is thus clear that contracted pelves represented a serious problem for women: they increased the incidence of malpresentations in childbirth, which in turn increased the maternal mortality; a flat pelvis, or a pelvis with severe inlet or outlet contractions, would almost certainly cause labor to be protracted, stretching possibly over several days, further increasing the risk of death or infection; and a contracted pelvis might oblige the midwife or accoucheur to use instruments in the delivery, indeed to cut the fetus into pieces in order to extract it, thereby enhancing again the mother's risk. (Only about half of mothers with contracted pelves delivered spontaneously.)[22] Although the problem is, strictly speaking, obstetrical, the woman whose pelvis had grown badly in childhood would remain deformed all her life. A permanent organic lesion, these pelves distinguished women clearly from men in terms of risking medical misadventure.

What percentage of women before World War I had contracted pelves? Here we must renounce any pretense at precision because, even though a "pelvimeter" had been devised late in the eighteenth century, only in the 1850s did studies on how to classify pelvic abnormality begin to appear.[23] Before then, contractions were spotted only if they were grossly apparent to the naked eye, the mother's hips twisted and misshapen, or if they became evident as a result of obstructed labor. Even later on, measurements are difficult to compare because different obstetricians report different kinds of pelvic diameters.

I am going to advance the view that a sizeable minority of all women in those pre-1900 centuries suffered serious contractions, but it should first be observed that the distribution of pelvic deformities was highly uneven, both by class and by region. In some areas local doctors reported no pelvic bone problems at all, such as Berlin's H. Wollheim, writing in 1844. Only 1.6 percent of his clinic patients had contracted pelves, "and also in private practice, according to the experience of the busiest accoucheurs, obstetrical operations arising from pelvic deformities belong to the rarest of cases." Women in the Swiss valley of Lotschental had traditionally been free of pelvic problems, and in eighteenth-century Chambery local mothers were reported as having "large and well shaped pelves." The obstetricians at Avignon's lying-in hospital reported in 1905 that "pelvic contractions are unusual in the Midi, and seldom observed at the *Maternite* of the Vaucluse." And less than 2 percent of the women birthing at Munich's lying-in hospital, 1859 to 1879, were found to have deformed pelves.[24]

Although the biochemistry of rickets is still not entirely clarified, we do know that to grow properly, bones require calcium salts, and calcium is metabolized in the body through the aid of vitamin D. Of the possible sources of vitamin D, such as fish-liver oil, not least important is exposure of the skin to the sun's ultraviolet rays. Hence social historians have, for a long time, associated rickets mainly with the smoky industrial cities of Victorian England, where dirt particles in the air presumably filtered out much ultraviolet radiation, and where children got out relatively little to play in parks and such (hitched, as they were, to pullcarts in the mines).

But that view is incomplete. Rickets abounded in parts of Europe hundreds of miles from the nearest smoking chimney. Here, for example, is Doctor Olivet, reporting in 1819 on the town of Montereau (Seine-et-Marne): "Children become liable at the age of 8, 10, 14, 16 or 20 years to rachitic deviations of the spine, to the turning inward of the sternum, two circumstances which give rise to a number of hunchbacks quite considerable for a town as small as Montereau. This bone disease, when it arrives late, strikes almost exclusively young women . . . who experience difficult menstruation, deforming their shape. Nature will suffice to cure them, provided they endure their fate with corsets . . . " But it was most unlikely that nature "cured" the pelves of many, which doubtless had been misshapen from birth. (Some people do, however, recover from childhood rickets.) How else are we to interpret the information that among infants in Montereau rickets were "almost universal," that at the age of twelve months many children had as yet made no effort to walk, and that others still experienced difficulty at twenty-four months. Their dentition was "irregular." Their "pelvic bones appear greatly emaciated, and the skin of their thighs forms folds that are disagreeable to the eye."[25]

These accounts could be multiplied by the dozens for other parts of Europe, for staid administrative cities like Konigsberg where "very many" young girls were considered "deformed," for schoolchildren in Victoria (Australia), of whom in 1910 to 1915, 20 to 30 percent were estimated to suffer from rickets. The proportion of rachitic infants toward the end of the nineteenth century in Europe's big cities ranged from 8 percent in Basel to 28 percent in London, to 31 percent in Prague.[26]

Unlike leukorrhea or uterine prolapse, rickets leaves telltale skeletal remains, which permit us to plot a rough history of the disease. The late Calvin Wells, a paleopathologist, commented on the "very low incidence" of rickets in prehistoric and early historic times, seeing then a slow increase through the Middle Ages and a dramatic explosion in England during the period of the industrial revolution. "A major factor in this was that owing to the gravitation of women to the factories, few infants were breast-fed."[27] In view of the substantial implantation of rickets during the nineteenth century in decidedly unindustrial rural and artisanal areas, I am disinclined to share Wells' emphasis on the "industrial era." Yet to go by a Swedish time series, the disease does seem to peak in the mid-nineteenth century, in Hamburg evidently several decades earlier.[28]

I should like to be able to argue that the difference in rickets between males and females supports the proposition that women have been historically less well nourished than men, a proposition for which there exists, I think, independent evidence.[29] Unfortunately, the data on bone diseases do not unambiguously support this hypothesis. Paleopathological studies of several early populations have shown the kinds of bone defects normally associated with malnutrition to be higher in female skeletons than male.[30] In late nineteenth-century Europe, however, boys suffered from rickets more often than girls, which suggests that at least female children, (whatever the nutritional lot of adult women might have been), were not systematically underfed.[31] Unlike men, however, women paid the price of their rickets in childbirth.

LEUKORRHEA

Leukorrhea means simply some kind of whitish or puslike vaginal discharge, and is not, in contrast to what eighteenth- and nineteenth-century doctors thought, a disease in itself. The wide range of illnesses that give rise to these discharges may be divided into two categories, vaginal infections and infections elsewhere in the pelvis, which drain through the vagina. Consider, for example, the multitude of microorganisms in the vagina itself which can cause leukorrhea:

1. Trichomonads, tiny flagellate protozoa that cause a yellow-greenish or purulent discharge, constant itching, painful urination, general pelvic pain, and a fetid odor.

2. Candida albicans, a yeastlike organism that produces a thick, caseous, yellow-white discharge that resembles cream cheese. The disease is called "moniliasis," and is experienced as a sharp burning sensation, together with itching and pain in intercourse. Infants born to women with candida infections often developed a similar fungal growth in their mouths called "thrush," and, in the eighteenth century, died of it in massive numbers.[32]

3. Hemophilus vaginalis, and a host of other bacteria called staphylocci and stretococci, that infect the vagina, causing itching and burning, pain on pressure, and unpleasant exudates: white in the case of hemophilus vaginalis, sticky and purulent for "staph" infections.

Those are just the chief pathogens that can produce "vaginitis," the market-basket term for all the pelvic itching we have been discussing. Infections elsewhere in the pelvis can produce another long series of leukorrheas, but since the doctors of the time were incapable of diagnosing any of them on the basis of the agent involved, little point is served in detailing all the things that can go wrong with the cervix and the uterus, or in describing the pockets of pus that accumulate alongside the ligaments in the pelvis. For the time being we just note that many different infections, not the least of which is gonorrhea, produce the cervicitis and endometritis that eighteenth-century doctors, with their unsterilized probes and primitive speculums, lumped together as the single disease "leukorrhea." (They did, however, distinguish gonorrheal infections from other varieties).

I wish to make two larger points about vaginal infection. The first is that the existence of leukorrhea may point to some more fundamental organic disease of interest to us. And even though their doctors often dismissed their complaints as "hysterical," and thus automatically the lot of women, the women themselves who had leukorrhea seemed to have known that something graver was wrong. In the folklore of Finland around 1914, for example, it was said that leukorrhea was "a serious sickness, a defect which weakens the woman generally, finally rendering her infertile."[33]

The second point is that leukorrhea was enormously widespread. Today perhaps one of every four gynecology patients has some kind of leukorrhea, which is quickly treated and cured.[34] Estimates for pre-1900 Europe appear considerably higher. Consider, for example, Berlin at the end of the eighteenth century: "The female sex here suffers commonly from a disease which more than any other has recently increased among the general population. There are, among all classes, only a few women entirely exempt from this condition. . . . The consequences of leukorrhea are by no means insignificant . . . in that the patients look pale and sickly, are plagued by attacks of hysteria, and are usually infertile."[35] Before we dismiss this as the exaggeration of a society gynecologist describing a clientele of languishing bankers' wives, let's listen to Dr. Zengerle, investigating fifty years later the cottage-industrial workers around Wangen in Wurttemberg: "One of the most frequent diseases among our female population is the so-called 'white-flowers' [leukorrhea], and there are perhaps few regions in our fatherland where one encounters so many female individuals suffering from this malady, young girls as well as married women. . . . The cause of the high incidence of this disease [is] the lifestyle of constant sitting, and the accompanying enormous consumption of food. For the female part of our population is, from October until April, almost continually occupied with spinning, sewing or knitting from early morning until late evening, in overheated living quarters. . . ."[36]

I am unable to put my finger on a single doctor who, in commenting on women's diseases, does not mention how common leukorrhea is: Schubler and Cless in Stuttgard called it "very widespread"; Schneider in Ettlingen remarks on its "stubborness" and how it often makes women infertile; Rouger in Vigan, Gard department, considers it "highly frequent at all ages and among all classes"; Metzger in Konigsberg, Klinge in the mining districts of the Oberharz, Herz in Prenzlau, Crouzet in Lodeve, all comment on its typicality.[37] Dr. Ely van de Warker, who in 1877 did a gynecological survey of about a quarter of the women in the Oneida Community (before he was stopped by John Humphrey Noyes), reported that 42 percent of the women had more than "small" amounts of leukorrhea.[38]

Some of these cases are clearly consequences of infected abortions, others of gonorrhea, others of "trich" infections, which husbands had picked up from prostitutes and transmitted to their wives. We learn, in short, little about the history of disease from studying leukorrhea, for these discharges represented so many different diseases. But for the women afflicted with them, the pruritis and vaginitis, the malodor, and the embarrassment they may have felt from their husbands, doubtless made these infections a major moment in their intimate lives, a moment for which there is no real male equivalent.

PERINEAL TEARS AND FISTULAS

In poorly managed deliveries the mother's birth canal and perineum are often torn, and although this type of injury would normally belong in a discussion of obstetrics, the scars and lesions of these tears may remain with the woman all her life, an enduring reminder of the potential consequences of sexuality. I have therefore decided to include them among the maladies that may affect women's attitudes to men and to their own bodies.

Our sources speak of two kinds of childbirth lesions in particular: tears of the birth canal, including ruptured uteruses, torn cervixes, and lesions in the septum between vagina and bladder (vesico-vaginal fistulas) or between vagina and rectum (recto-vaginal fistulas), to scarred-over vulvas; and ruptures of the perineum, which is the skin extending from the base of the vagina to the anus. Tiny perineal tears are quite common in childbirth even today, and to make their repair easier, accoucheurs often perform routinely "episiotomies," which means cutting a small incision into the perineum with a pair of scissors, to facilitate the passage of the fetal head, then stitching it up again afterwards. Major perineal tears are another problem, however.

Because most births, in the years before 1900, were managed by midwives, who intervened rarely with forceps to accelerate an obstructed labor (or who, when they intervened, would wreak considerable damage), the incidence of lesions in childbirth seems to have been fairly high. This is a sensitive subject, the competence of midwives and "grannies."[39] And while the midwives of traditional Europe do indeed seem to have been competent to handle normal deliveries (having a stillbirth rate of 5 percent, perhaps, and a maternal mortality of 1 percent), they were usually at a loss to manage birth complications, especially dystocias, when the fetus ceases to advance along the birth canal, its head lodged in the vagina perhaps, or pounding repeatedly against the pelvic floor, or stuck in some malposition in the pelvic outlet.[40] An obstructed labor of this nature can result in ruptures and tears in several ways:

1. The accoucheur (or midwife) reaches into the uterus to perform version, grabbing the infant's feet and pulling it out. A clumsy version can easily rupture the mother's uterus or her incompletely dilated cervix.[41]

2. The midwife attempts manually to dilate the vagina (doctors, whatever their flaws, had enough training at least to realize the vagina was undilatable) and bruises and tears the whole vulvar area. De la Motte, for example, tells of a woman he went to deliver in 1698 who had been "all torn up" *(toute dechiree)* at the hands of an incompetent midwife. Three months later he was again summoned because the woman's vagina had sealed together completely as a result of the scars. "I found a woman in terrible convulsions, complaining in the intervals that these convulsions caused her intolerable pain in her private parts and in her whole abdomen." De la Motte opened her up again with a lance, a huge quantity of "thick, black blood" flowed out, and she became well again, going on to bear another child.[42]

3. As the fetal head lodges in the vagina, the cells on the membranous wall dividing the vagina from the bladder start to die and slough off, finally opening up a hole, called a "fistuala." Although holes between vagina and rectum may be opened too, leaving women with vaginas "full of feces," the most common variety by far is

the bladder-vagina lesion.[43] Here is a German doctor's description of fistulous women, around 1836: "A sadder situation can hardly exist than that of a woman afflicted with a vesicovaginal fistula. A source of disgust, even to herself, the woman beloved by her husband becomes, in this condition, the object of bodily revulsion to him; and filled with repugnance, everyone else likewise turns his back, repulsed by the intolerable, foul, uriniferous odor." The basic problem with this sort of fistula, it must be explained, is that the urine trickles uncontrollably from the vagina, rather than from the urethra.

> The labia, perineum, lower part of the buttocks, and inner aspect of the thighs and calves are continually wet, to the very feet. The skin assumes a fiery red color and is covered in places with a pustular eruption. Intolerable burning and itching torment the patients, who are driven to frequent scratching to the point of bleeding, as a result of which their suffering increases still more. . . . The refreshment of a change of clothing provides no relief, because the clean undergarment, after being quickly saturated, slaps against the patients, flopping against their wet thighs as they walk, sloshing in their wet shoes as though they were wading through a swamp. The bed . . . is quickly impregnated with urine and gives off the most unbearable stench. Even the richest are usually condemned for life to a straw sack, whose straw must be renewed daily. One's breath is taken away by the bedroom air of these women, and wherever they go they pollute the atmosphere.[44]

How common were such fistulas? A cure had already been developed for them, and obstetrics in general enormously improved, by the time we get systematic statistics. Only two vesico-vaginal fistuals were reported to the Medical Society of the Middlesex East District of Massachusetts, for example, among 2,666 childbirth cases between 1855 and 1882. But those were all physician-assisted deliveries.[45] Another study during the 1890s at the Vanderbilt Clinic in New York found only one vesico-vaginal fistula among 398 gynecology patients (and one rectovaginal fistula too). The author speculated that "the early use of the forceps probably accounts for the rarity of this accident at the present time."[46] Other North American doctors argued late in the nineteenth century that vaginal fistulas were becoming uncommon.[47] And a 1920's survey of women in New York City seeking birth control advice found vaginal fistulas in only 1.5 percent of the 8,300 clients examined.[48]

But in traditional Europe, at least, fistulas seem to have been quite common. Although a statistical estimate is impossible, in 1860, the Finistere's Dr. Caradec included fistulas in a list of accidents of delivery that he considered "frequent." The British obstetrician Fleetwood Churchill, writing earlier on, declared them "not very rare." And the seventeenth-century Parisian accoucheur Paul Portal included fistulas among the horrors that happened easily if too much force were used in the delivery.[49]

What these fistulas represented for the lives of common women can scarcely be imagined today. Women were reduced to desperate extremities to avoid them, subjecting themselves to incredibly painful operations (likely to be unsuccessful at best, fatal at worst) for their repair. One Austrian woman, for example, whose fistula had been operatively closed underwent caesarean section rather than risking another, at a time when the mortality from caesarean sections was around 25 percent.[50]

4. The cleaving open of the perineum from vagina to anus was a possible consequence of bearing an infant with a large head. In contrast to fistulas, these perineal ruptures were highly frequent. Philadelphia's Barton Hirst, writing in 1917, speculated that "of the 2,500,000 women delivered in the United States annually, a million or more or less are added every year to the ranks of the comparatively unfit from this preventable cause."[51] He includes the genital canal as well as the pelvic floor in this estimate.

These injuries often happened because the fetal head was permitted to pop out too quickly; and their consequences endured because the birth attendant failed to stitch the mother back up. Both are signs of incompetent obstetrics, and both happened often among the women of the popular classes. As Thomas Madden wrote in the 1870s of Dublin:

> The after-effects of lacerations of the perinaeum are even more distressing with patients of the working class than is the case with women of a higher social condition. . . . Increased experience of the intimate domestic habits of the wretched denizens of the crowded tenements of the lanes and back streets of the capital of the poorest country in Europe has confirmed the observation—the wives of our artisans and labouring men undergo far more hardship and privation, and at the same time perform as much labor as their husbands. The whole of the domestic duties of women of this class, such as washing, cooking, carrying children, etc., all act as powerful predisposing causes of prolapse of the womb; and, therefore, when the support that should be afforded by the perinaeum is taken away by the accident we are now considering . . . the tendency to prolapse [is] increased. . . .[52]

We shall consider uterine prolapse in more detail in a moment. The points I wish to make here are that (1) perineal tears were quite common, and (2) their long-term effects on the lives of women could be devastating.

In 1671, for example, a woman who had given birth nine years earlier, came to see the Parisian accoucheur Francois Mauriceau. Evidently as a result of the large size of her infant's head, she seems to have suffered a third-degree perineal tear, which would mean that her anal sphincter muscle had torn in two, leaving her unable to control defecation. Mauriceau describes this as a "simple deformity" which gave her "une extreme chagrin." But by the time she saw him the rupture had formed a rigid scar, and could not be reopened and repaired properly without "une incision tresdouloureus." So she went away resigned. But, just imagine, for nine years she had endured this torment in silence.[53]

UTERINE-OVARIAN DISORDERS

Given the medical ignorance of the doctors, the embarrassment of the women afflicted, and the primitive means of diagnosis available, we can say little about the epidemiology of uterine and ovarian disorders. A minimal solution is simply to review the most common complaints that women would mention to the doctors.

First, there were anomalies of menstruation. If we may take Marie Kopp's survey of New York women seeking birth control advice in the 1920s as a "modern" baseline, around one fifth of all older married women complain of "irregular menstruation."[54] Whether that is intracycle bleeding, which would be extremely useful in diagnosing tumors or cancer, heavy periods, or just lack of regularity in their arrival is unclear.

We may infer from earlier doctors' qualitative accounts that considerably more than a fifth of their patients complained of menstrual irregularity. Berlin's Dr. Wollheim wrote in 1844 that "disorders of menstruation are extremely common; the suppression or delay (of the menses) happens more often than does an excessive flow." Doctor Lavergne of Lamballe indicated in 1787 that "nothing was more common than irregular menses and amenorrhea (a missed period). This latter accident afflicts above all the women of the lower classes, who are exposed to it by their work." Similar remarks could be quoted from late-eighteenth- and nineteenth-century medical topographies for the mining communities of Klausthal and the Oberharz, Stuttgard, Wurzburg, Hamburg, and Hanau.[55] Whether in all these cases more than a fifth of all married women had such complaints is impossible to say. We know only that these problems appear often in the patients' minds, and in the doctors'.

Painful menstruation, another harbinger of some graver problem, appears often in these accounts. Only 6 percent of all older married women suffered it in the 1920s birth control survey.[56] For the cottage workers of early-nineteenth-century Wangen it was "quite frequent"; De la Motte reports "some" young unmarried women suffering the kind of pain and vomiting in menstruation that a mother endures in labor.[57] And so on. Nothing systematic can be made of such testimony, but we are alerted that dysmenorrhea is, at least, not a "disease of civilization."

And what of the whole complex pathology of tumors and growths in the ovaries and uterus? The world of pain that contemporary gynecology texts take hundreds of pages just to classify? Here we descend into the truly unknown. The Kopp survey put noncancerous uterine tumors at 4.2 percent of the 8,300 women examined; the birth-control doctors didn't classify ovarian tumors separately, probably because they're so difficult to palpate in a routine bimanual examination.[58] Other gynecologists, writing around the turn of the century, found 12 to 14 percent of their patients to have fibroid tumors (the most common variety of uterine growths).[59]

Fehling comments that before 1800 the medical literature contains almost no reference to ovarian cysts as a pregnancy complication and speculates that during the nineteenth century they may have become more common. And Lubben's study of morbidity early in the nineteenth century in Germany's impoverished Rhon district found uterine disorders, most of which were (presumably) tumors, "exceptionally frequent."[60] Aside from these wisps of smoke, the medical literature I have seen reports only isolated case studies of ghastly ovarian cysts that swelled up to 40 pounds and the like. We are left puzzling to what extent this pelvic pathology represented a debilitating irritant in the lives of normal women.

Given the large number of births to older married women, the gruelling regimen of work to which they were subjected, and custom of not sparing oneself of all during pregnancy, we would expect a high incidence of uterine prolapse, which in fact happened. Prolapse occurs through the weakening of the cardinal ligaments, which hold the uterus in place within the abdomen, or through the weakening of the muscles on the pelvic floor, which gives support from below. The result is that the uterus begins to slide down the vagina, in extreme cases (called "procidentia") making the woman look as though she had an elephant's trunk hanging down between her legs. The condition represents both a serious medical problem, involving leakage of urine or infection of the ulcerated cervix and collapsed vaginal walls, and a striking dilemma in the psychodrama of sexual relations. What must a woman with a badly prolapsed uterus feel about sexual relations with her husband or imagine that he feels about her?

The 1920s Kopp survey of New York women found 8.6 percent of them to have prolapsed uteruses.[61] Although the repair of prolapse had become, by that time, a simple procedure in gynecological surgery, we might assume that most of the poorish, immigrant women on whom these birth control clinics drew put this kind of surgery low on their list of priorities. So the one-in-ten figure for prolapse approximates roughly the "traditional" level.

So common was prolapse among the working-class in Manchester that the first major procedure for its repair, developed in the 1890s by two local gynecologists named Archibald Donald and William Fothergill, was called the "Manchester Operation."[62] Indeed, prolapse might result in part from the demands of factory life where women could pass their pregnancies standing interminably in front of their machinery. Elsewhere uterine prolapse was associated with roughly managed deliveries, incompetent midwives, and the ensuing weakening of the pelvic floor (as, for example, through major perineal tears).[63] Prolapse has, par excellence, been one of those constants in women's lives that reminded them how much more vulnerable they were than men to the blank face of fate.

Antibiotics have made us forget today about that vast armada of pathogens that invaded uterus and adnexa to produce infections, the mildest of which merely created a sensation of "heaviness," the most severe of which—as in "puerperal fever"—might often end in the woman's death. They were a daily affliction for lower-class women, as Max Hirsch testified in his survey of the occupational diseases of factory women early in the twentieth century: "The uterus becomes swollen, painful on pressure; the patients claim about congestion in the lower abdomen and about pains up and down the back . . . All these conditions, from simple endometritis (an infection of the lining of the uterus), to chronic metritis, retroflexio and parametritis (pockets of pus accumulating in the uterine ligaments) are to be found among female workers who spend long hours sitting with their upper bodies bent over or who just stand for long periods. . . ."[64]

Rather than assailing the reader with further quotations about uterine and adnexal infections, I shall make just one brief point: many of the infections from which these women suffered were undiagnosable by the medicine of the time and instead dismissed as "neurotic symptoms." Chronic pelvic infection produces no external signs, such as leukorrhea; nor are its victims likely to have a high temperature or high sedimentation rates (tests of infection available to late-nineteenth-century medicine). Yet movement, intercourse, and defecation are all likely to be painful for them. They will feel enervated and inclined (if possible) to take to their beds for rest. They will in short, exhibit all the symptoms that nineteenth-century women's doctors were inclined to write off as "neurosis" or "hysteria," which some twentieth-century historians have accepted as evidence of doctors convincing women they were invalids to better dominate them.[65] If in fact these middle-class valetudinarians really were suffering from "endometriosis" (the spread of endometrial tissue outside the lining of the uterus to attack other pelvic organs, first diagnosed in 1922) or from pelvic inflammatory disease, it would behoove us as historians to be more sympathetic to the doctors, who guilty mainly of a sort of condescending incompetence, and to their patients, who knew that they themselves were experiencing genuine pain, and that they were not "overanxious," although no one would believe them.

CONCLUSION

Much speculation has recently been devoted to the evident sexual uninterest of married women in their husbands during times past. The scholarly journals have bulged with tales of nineteenth-century women "who aren't supposed to feel sexual desire," or who were counseled "surtout ne bougez pas" during intercourse. Three explanations have offered for this:

1. That a chauvinistic male society systematically repressed women's sexuality, persuading them that the world of eros was soiled and disgusting, and that female purity could only be maintained through failure to lubricate.[66]

2. That men were normally so brutal and clumsy in intercourse that women's best interest would be preserved in avoiding the entire business entirely and retreating instead to the company of one's sisters.[67]

3. That women felt uneasy about sex because of the grim physical consequences that pregnancy, birth, and abortion could have for their bodies and their lives in general.[68]

The purpose of this chapter is to reinforce the third interpretation, by stressing that not only were women vulnerable to men through the sex act and the impregnation likely to ensue, but they were also vulnerable to men at many somatic levels: in being subjected to nutritional disorders that men did not experience; in having a whole range of genital equipment liable to fall into disrepair in a way that did not happen to men; and in being liable to various pelvic exudates and prolapses that would make them feel uneasy about their naked bodies in intimate contact with men. I argue that among the historical consequences of this vulnerability were a female preference for abstinence as a means of birth control, for the company of other women as opposed to "family togetherness," and for an intense religiosity, which maintained that if God had imposed such burdens on womankind, it could only be because He was testing them.

FOOTNOTES

1. See U. S. Department of Health, Education, and Welfare, *Acute Conditions: Incidence and Associated Disability, United States, July 1975-June 1976* (Vital and Health Statistics: series 10; Data from the National Health Survey, no. 120; US-DHEW publication no. /PHS/ 78-1548, National Center for Health Statistics, Hyattsville, Md., January 1978), p. 10. See also U.S. Department of Health, Education and Welfare, *Prevalence of Chronic Conditions of the Genitourinary, Nervous, Endocrine . . . Systems and Other Selected Chronic Conditions, United States, 1973* (Vital and Health Statistics: series 10: Data from the National Health Survey, no. 109; US-DHEW publication HRA 77-1536), pp. 44-45.

2. Hermann Fehling, *Entwicklung der Geburtshilfe und Gynakologie im 19 Jahrhundert* (Berlin: 1925), p. 233. "Wurgengel der Frauenwelt."

3. See, for example, A.H. Crisp et al., "How Common Is Anorexia Nervosa? A Prevalence Study," *British Journal of Psychiatry* 128 (1976):549-554. Calvin Wells argued, however, in a letter to me, "I think there is substantial evidence of anorexia nervosa in earlier case histories, though it may not have been common."

4. Phil. Jos. Horsch, *Versuch einer Topographie der Stadt Wurzburg in Bexiehung auf den allgemeinen Gesundheitszustand* (Arnstadt: 1805), p. 185.

5. See the review of research by J.R.W. Christie Brown and M.E. Christie Brown, "Psychiatric Disorders Associated with the Menopause," in *The Menopause: A Guide to Current Research and Practice,* ed. R.J. Beard (Baltimore: University Park Press, 1976), pp. 57-80.

6. See *Travaux proposes aux Medicins et physicians regnicoles et etrangers, par la Societe Royale de Medicine . . . 1778;* chap. 1 is entitled "Sur la Description Topographique et

Medicale de la France," p. 1.

7. Alfons Fischer, *Geschichte des deutschen Gesundheitswesens,* vol. 2 (Berlin: 1933), pp. 37-38, 113-120. Fischer claims that the idea originated in Germany and seems unaware of the entire French contribution. Arthur Imhof has recently begun an extensive analysis of the German topographies. See pp. 50-62 of the introduction to the volume he edited, *Biologie des Menschen in der Geschichte: Beitrage zur Sozialgeschichte der Neuzeit aus Frankeriech und Skandinavien* (Stuttgard-Bad Cannstatt: Friedrich Fromann Verlag, 1978).

8. See G.J. Barker-Benfield, *The Horrors of the Half-Known Life: Male Attitudes toward Women and Sexuality in Nineteenth-Century America* (Champaign-Urbana, Ill.: University of Illinois Press, 1974); Stephen Kern, *Anatomy and Destiny: A Cultural History of the Human Body* (Indianapolis, Ind.: Bobbs-Merrill, 1975).

9. Franz Xaver Mexler, *Versuch einer medizinischen Topographie der Stadt Sigmaringen* (Freiburg: 1822), pp. 155-156.

10. For a historical overview see W.M. Fowler, "Chlorosis: An Obituary," *Annals of Medical History* 8 (1936): 168-177. For more recent literature, see Karl Figlio's excellent article, "Chlorosis and Chronic Disease in Nineteenth-Century Britain: The Social Constitution of Somatic Illness in Capitalist Society," *Social History* 3 (1978): 167-197, and Robert P. Hudson, "The Biography of Disease: Lessons from Chlorosis," *Bulletin of the History of Medicine 51 (1977):448-463, who argues that "iron played only a small role in the disappearance of the disease" (p. 459).*

11. Among many accounts, here is D. Pfieninger, writing in 1834: "For the female gender anemia and interruptions in menstruation which stand in a reciprocal relationship with hysteria are very common in Stuttgart. The widespread belief that hysteria is to be found more among the upper than the lower classes appears to be without foundation." *Beschriebung von Stuttgard hauptsachlich nach seinen naturwissenschaftlichen und medicineisch Verhaltnissen* (Stuttgard: 1834), p. 116.

12. "Chronic Anemia and Wasting in Newly Married Women: Some of the Causes of their Persistence and Incurability," *American Journal of Obstetrics* 21 (1888):113.

13. Max Hirsch, "Frauenarbiet und Frauenkrankheiten," in Josef Halban and Ludwig Seitz (eds.), *Biologie und Pathologie des Weibes: Ein Handbuch der Frauenheilkunde und Geburtshilfe,* vol. 1 (Berlin: 1924), p. 940.

14. "Nous noterons ici le nombre tres-restreint de femmes qui ont nourri leurs enfants, soit par faiblesse, soit per necessite de travailler; il est inutile de parler de la faible constitution de ces malheureuses meres de famille, la population de la Croix-Rousse est assez connue par sa mauvaise conformation et le grand nombre de ses phthisiques." F. Guyenot and Ch. Pujo, *Etude clinique sur les suites de couches: Compte-rendu de la maternite de l'hopital de la Croix-Rousse durant l'hiver 1867-68* (Lyon: 1869), p. 76.

15. 800 megagrams figure from Louis Hellman and Jack A. Pritchard, *Williams Obstetrics,* 14th ed. (New York: Appleton-Century-Crofts, 1971), pp. 763-764.

16. Fowler, "Chlorosis," p. 172.

17. Jack C. Drummond and Anne Wilbraham have estimated that the diet of better-off people in seventeenth-century England would have provided perhaps 6 to 12 megagrams in available iron a day, depending on the proportion of bread in the diet. Men in twentieth-century English middle-class families have access to virtually the identical amount of available iron (11 mg.), women 8 mg. *The Englishman's Food: A History of Five Centuries of English Diet* (London: Cape, 1939), p. 156.

18. J.W. Consbruch, for example, wrote of the county of Ravensberg, "Worms and their traces are very frequently found among the rustics, a consequence of the numerous flour-based dishes they consume. In some regions . . . a strikingly large number of tapeworms are to be noted." *Medicinische Ephemeriden, nebsi einer medicineisch Topographie der Grafschaft Ravensberg* (Chemnitz: 1793), pp. 57-58.

19. The average number of live births in family reconstitution studies of French and German villages ranges from about five to eight. If we add on an additional 30 percent to represent pregnancy wastage and stillbirths, we get six to twelve as the average number of pregnancies of a typical married woman who survives to the menopause.

20. For the story see recently (Dame) Harriette Chick, "Study of Rickets in Vienna, 1919-1922," *Medical History* 20 (1976):41-51.

21. *Traite complet des acouchemens,* rev. ed. (Leiden: 1729), p. 344.

22. For various clinical reports see Carl von Hecker, *Beobachtungen und Untersuchungen aus der Gebaranstalt zu Munchen, 1859-1879* (Munich: 1881), pp. 84-129; Franz Torggler, *Bericht uber die Thatigkeit der geburtshilfichgynakologischen Klinik zu Innsbruck, 1881-1887*

(Prague: 1888), pp. 84-96; Ernst Kummer, "Die Prognose der Geburt bei engem Becken," *Zeitschrift fur Geburtshulfe und Gynakologie* 12 (1186):418-429.

23. The classic treatise in Gustav Adolf Michaelis's, *Das enge Becken nach eigenen Beobachtungen und Untersuchungen* (Leipzig: 1851).

24. H. Wollheim, *Versuch einer medicinischen Topographie und Statistik von Berlin* (Berlin: 1844), p. 69; Carl Muller, *Volksmedizinisch-geburtshilfliche Aufzeichnungen aus dem Lotschental* (Stuttgart: Hans Huber, 1969), p. 136; Joseph Daquin, *Topographie medicale de la ville de Chambery* (Chambery: 1787), p. 79; Emile Estachy, *La Maternite de Vaucluse: Historique, statistiques* (Montpellier: 1905), p. 37; Hecker, *Gebaranstalt zu Munchen,* p. 10.

25. Ms. in Paris Academie de medecine, Societe de l'ecole de medecine de Paris, memoires OP, received 25 February 1819.

26. Joh. Dan. Metzger, "Medicinische Topographie von Konigsberg," *Archiv der parktischen Arzneykinst* 2 (1786):299; Milton James Lewis, "'Populate or Perish': Aspects of Infant and Maternal Health in Sydney, 1870-1939" (Australia National University, diss., 1976), p. 37; August Hirsch, *Handbuch der historisch-geographischen Pathologie, vol. 3: Die Organkrankheiten,* 2d ed. (Stuttgart: 1886), p. 516.

27. "Prehistoric and Historical Changes in Nutritional Diseases and Associated Conditions," *Progress in Food and Nutrition Sciences* 1 (1975):753-754.

28. Jonas Frykman, *Horan i bondesamhallet* (Lund: Hum. diss., 1977), p. 77, graph of "horeskaver. Meddelare med angivna fodelsear, 1824-1890"; Johann Jakob Rambach, *Versuch einer physisch-medizinischen Beschreibung von Hamburg* (Hamburg: 1801), pp. 175-176.

29. For detailed evidence that women in, for example, Norway and Iceland were not only thought to need less but actually got less food at table before World War I, see Lily Weiser-Aall, "die Speise des Neugeborenen," in Edith Ennen and Gunter Wiegelmann (eds.), *Festschrift Matthias Zender: Studien zu Volkskultur, Sprache und Landesgeschichte,* vol. 1 (Bonn: Rohrscheid, 1972), pp. 543-544.

30. See Calvin Wells, "Ancient Obstetric Hazards and Female Mortality," *Bulletin of the New York Academy of Medicine* 51 (1975):1235-1249. Wells concludes that "the pattern of illness in these children reflects the difference between relatively well-fed boys—the up-and-coming warriors and patriarchs—and the marginally fed or frankly undernourished girls—the future drudges and mothers" (p. 1248).

31. See the statistics in Friedrich Prinzing, *Handbuch der medizinischen Statistik,* 2d ed. (Jena: 1931), pp. 212-215.

32. In the manuscripts of the "Vicq d'Azyr" collection in the Paris Academie de Medecine there are, for example, numerous reports from local doctors writing late in the eighteenth century that "le muguet," the French word for "thrush" (Monilia, candida albicans) was exacting a heavy mortality toll among the neonates of their locality. See especially the cartons SRM 175-185.

33. E. Pelkonen, *Pelkonen, Uber volkstumliche Geburtshilfe in Finnland* (Helsinki: 1931), p. 30.

34. "Open in four," see Robert W. Kistner, *Gynecology: Principles and Practice,* 2d ed. (Chicago: Year Book Medical Publishers, 1971), p. 79.

35. Ludwig Formey, *Versuch einer medicinischen Topographie von Berlin* (Berlin: 1796), p. 196.

36. (Dr.) Zengerle, "Auszug aus einer . . . statistisch-medicinischen Topographie des Oberamtsbezirks Wangen (Schluss,)" *Medicinisches Correspondenz-Blatt des wurtembergischen arztlichen Vereins* 18 (1848):255.

37. G. Cless and G. Schuber, *Versuch einer medizinischen Topographie . . . Stuttgart* (Stuttgart: 1815), p. 76; P.J. Schneider, *Versuch einer medizinisch statistischen Topographie von Ettlingen* (Karlsruhe: 1818), p. 339; Francois-Alexandre Rouger, *Topographie statistique et medicale de la ville et canton du Vigan* (Montpellier: 1819), pp. 99-100; Metzger, "Konigsberg," p. 305; Johann Heinrich Wilhelm Klinge, *Fragmente aus dem Tagebuch eines Arztes auf dem Oberharz* (Stendal: 1812), p. 34; Simon Herz, *Versuch einer medicinischen Ortbeschreibung . . . Prenzlau* (Berlin: 1790), p. 83; Jean-August Crouzet, *Topographie medicale et statistique comparee de Lodeve* (Montepellier: 1912), pp. 128, 217, written 1898.

38. "A Gynecological Study of the Oneida Community," *American Journal of Obstetrics* 17 (1884):785-810, leukorrhea data on p. 804.

39. There is a fiercely partisan feminist literature designed to redeem the midwives from the reproaches of male doctors. See recently, for example, Jean Donnison, *Midwives and Medical Men: A History of Inter-Professional Rivalries and Women's Rights* (New York: Schocken, 1977); Ann Oakley, "Wise-women and Medicine Man: Changes in the Management of

Childbirth," in *The Rights and Wrongs of Women,* ed. Juliet Mitchell and Ann Oakley (Harmondsworth: Penguin, 1976), pp. 17-58; and for a flagrant example, Suzanne Arms, *Immaculate Deception: A New Look at Women and Childbirth in America* (Boston: Houghton-Mifflin, 1975), chap. 1.

40. While stillbirth statistics are readily available, maternal mortality in home deliveries is much harder to determine for pre-1900 Europe. My own investigations, however, show the normal range to have fluctuated between perhaps 0.5 per cent of all births. In a group of Baden counties around 1800, to take one example, maternal mortality was perhaps 1 percent of all births. Karlsruhe, Generallandesarchiv, 74/9071.

41. Among many horror stories, see for example that in De la Motte, *Traite complet des acouchemens,* p. 275.

42. Ibid., pp. 508-510.

43. See, for example, J. DeLee, "Six Cases of Caesarean Section," *American Journal of Obstetrics* 51 (1905):738.

44. J.F. Dieffenbach, quoted by Harold Speert, *Essays in Eponymy: Obstetric and Gynecologic Milestones* (New York: Macmillan, 1958), pp. 442-443.

45. "A Summary of Obstetric Cases Reported by Members of the Middlesex East District Medical Society, and Compiled by Dr. Samuel W. Abbott," *Boston Medical and Surgical Journal* 57 (1882-1883):5.

46. William S. Stone, "A Review of Five Years' Experience with Pelvic Diseases at the Vanderbilt Clinic (cont'd)," *American Journal of Obstetrics* 41 (1900):803, 805.

47. See Thomas Addis Emmet, "The Necessity for Early Delivery, as Demonstrated by the Analysis of 161 Cases of Vesico-Vaginal Fistula," *American Gynecological Society, Transactions* 3 (1878):124, 126. This kind of evidence, unhappily, provided an overly vigorous push for the kind of "meddlesome midwifery" that was endemic among American obstetricians in the first half of the twentieth century.

48. Marie E. Kopp, *Birth Control in Practice: Analysis of Ten Thousand Case Histories of the Birth Control Clinical Research Bureau* (first ed. 1934; reprint New York: Arno Press, 1972), p. 156.

49. Louis Caradec, *Topographie medico-hygienique du department du finistere* (Brest: 1860), p. 80; Churchill, *On the Theory and Practice of Midwifery,* 3d American ed. (Philadelphia: 1848), p. 467," . . . one of the most distressing and intolerable accidents to which females are subject; and the more so, as a cure is but seldom affected" (p. 467); Paul Portal, *La Pratique des accouchemens* (Paris: 1685), p. 10.

50. Torggler, *Bericht Klinik Innsbruck,* p. 141.

51. "Fifteen Years' Experience with the Intermediate Repair of the Injuries of Childbirth," *American Journal of Obstetrics* 75 (1917):755.

52. "On Lacerations of the Perinaeum, Sphincter Ani, and Recto-Vaginal Septum: Their Prevention and Surgical Treatment," *American Journal of Obstetrics* 5 (1872-73):53.

53. *Observations sur la grossesse et l'accouchement des femmes* (Paris:1694), pp. 39-40.

54. *Birth Control in Practice,* p. 84.

55. Wollheim, *Topographie Berlin,* p. 310; Luis Marie Lavergne, *Topographie medicale de Lamballe et de ses environs en 1787* (Lehon: les presses d'Entre-Nous: journal de l'hopital psychiatrique Saint Jean de Dieu, 1959), p. 33; Friedrich Benjamin Lentin, *Merkwurdigkeiten von der Witterung, der Einwohner zu Klausthal, in den Jahren 1774 bis 1777;* I have quoted from passages excerpted in *Archiv der praktischen Arzneykunst* 1 (1785):312; Klinge, *Oberharz,* p. 34; Cless and Schubler, *Stuttgart,* p. 75; Horsch, *Topographie Wurzburg,* p. 185; Rambach, *Beschreibung Hamburg,* p. 335; Johann Heinrich Kopp, *Topographie der Stadt Hanau, in Beziehung auf den Gesundheits—und Krankheitszustand der Einwohner* (Frankfurt/Main: 1807), p. 160.

56. Kopp, *Birth Control in Practice,* p. 88.

57. Zengerle, "Topographie Wangen," 255; *Traite complet des acouchemens,* p. 71.

59. James N. West, "What Shall We Perform Myomectomy and When Hysterectomy in Uterine Fibromyomata?," *American Journal of Obstetrics* 56 (1907):701, 702 for the two estimates of 12 and 14 percent.

60. *Entwicklung der Geburtshilfe,* pp. 116-117; K.H. Lubben, *Beitrage zur Kenntniss der Rhon in medizinischer Hinsicht* (Weimar: 1881).

61. *Birth Control in Practice,* p. 156.

62. Speert, *Essays in Eponymy,* pp. 108-115; see also De la Motte, *Traite complet des acouchemens,* p. 651, who saw a good deal of prolapse among unmarried women.

63. See, for example, Metzger, "Topographie von Konigsberg," p. 305. For a world over-

166

view see Hinrich Ploss and Max and Paul Bartels, *Das Weib in der Natur- und Volkerkunde,* rev. ed. by Ferd. v. Reitzenstein, vol. 3 (Berlin: 1972), pp. 105-106.

64. "Frauenarbeit," p. 961.

65. Ann Douglas Wood, for instance, writes of " . . . a nightmare vision of sick women dependent on male doctors who use their professional superiority as a method to prolong their patients' sickness and, consequently, the supremacy of their own sex." The cure for many of these diseases turns out, unsurprisingly, to be "female strength." '"The Fashionable Diseases': Women's Complaints and Their Treatment in Nineteenth-Century America," *Journal of Interdisciplinary History* 4 (1973): quotes from pp. 43-47.

Barbara Ehrenreich and Deirdre English go even further in their discussion of "male" medicine in nineteenth-century America. "[It] made very little sense as *medicine* [italics in original], but it was undoubtedly effective at keeping certain women—those who could afford to be patients—in their place." They go on to say that "prescribed bed rest was obviously little more than a kind of benign imprisonment." Finally they declare, "The more the doctors 'treated', the more they lured women into seeing calls, the tonics and medicines, the health spas—served, above all, to keep a great many women busy at the task of doing nothing." *Complaints and Disorders: The Sexual Politics of Sickness* (Old Westbury, N.Y.: The Feminist Press, Glass Mountain Pamphlet no. 2, 1973), pp. 35-37.

66. Most recent in a long line of authors to take this approach is Lawrence Stone, *The Family, Sex and Marriage in England, 1500-1800* (New York: Harper and Row, 1977), pp. 673-677.

67. Again, in a venerable historiographical tradition, see most recently Linda Gordon, *Woman's Body, Woman's Right: A Social History of Birth Control in America* (New York: Viking/Grossman, 1976), pp. 104-105.

68. This, generally, is the approach I have taken in *The Making of the Modern Family* (New York: Basic Books, 1975), and in "maternal Sentiment and Death in Childbirth: A New Agenda for Psycho-Medical History," in Patricia Branca (ed.), *The Medicine Show: Patients, Physicians and the Perplexities of the Health Revolution in Modern Society* (New York: Science History Publications, 1977), pp. 67-68.

Section Four:

The Family and Socialization

The process of "socialization," that is, the way individuals are taught social roles, moral values, and obedience to authority, is complex. While the family is an important agency of socialization, and the child's first learning environment, it does not monopolize this process. Other institutions exert a powerful influence on the individual during his early years. Religion, the demands and restraints of social class, ethnicity, political institutions, and the ideologies of educators affect socialization of the young. Together with the family, these and other institutions teach the child what his society expects of its men, women, parents, workers and leaders. In retrospect, it may appear as though a person had to become what he is; in reality, however, (especially in a democratic society) so many institutions have input to this process that the individual is frequently sent conflicting and contradictory signals about his future roles and responsibilities.

The first article in this Section, by the renowned anthropologist Anthony F. C. Wallace, exemplifies the ambiguities of the socialization process. In his incisive descriptions of life in a mid-nineteenth century mill town in southeastern Pennsylvania, Wallace shows how the often conflicting values of mill owners influenced the atmosphere in the mills, and conveyed contradictory signals about their present and future prospects and roles to child laborers. The owners' capitalistic beliefs tended at times to conflict with their religious values, and their paternalistic desire to control the lives of their workers did not rest easily alongside their belief in democracy.

How would these conflicts surface in the everyday lives of the child workers? Would the values of mill owners contradict those of the child's family? If so, which set of values meant most to the youngsters?

"Childhood, Work, and Family Life in a 19th-Century Cotton Mill Town"

Anthony F. C. Wallace

THE FORMS OF THE FAMILY
IN A COTTON-MANUFACTURING DISTRICT

The American doctrine of family, sanctioned in religion, morality, and law, and almost universally accepted in the 1850's, held that the married pair and their children constituted the natural basis of human society. From this fundamental unit, the simple nuclear family, radiated lines of ascent and descent and affinal connection that bound each nuclear family together with others in loose aggregations of kinship. The nuclear family itself might also exist in several more or less incipient or modified forms: as a married couple whose children had not yet been born or who had died or moved away; as a surviving spouse with children; as surviving children whose parents had died. Such a family, however modified, lived together in a house. There might, however, be others who shared the house with its proprietary family: individual grandparents, uncles and aunts, cousins, nephews and nieces, grandchildren, or even more remotely connected relatives; domestic servants; and boarders who paid rent. A household thus consisted of at least one nuclear family (simple or modified) and, usually, various kinsmen, servants, or boarders.

Within the outlines of this basic pattern, several different styles of family organization were possible. In the Rockdale manufacturing district (and in other, similar manufacturing districts nearby, as on the Brandywine), two of these different styles—workers' and the managers'—must be noted, because they functioned very differently in the economic life of the community.

Among the workers, the nuclear family was vitally necessary to the economic welfare of most adult individuals. An unmarried working-class adult of either sex could live alone. There were no small apartments or dormitories, and even if there had been, and the person could have afforded to pay the rent, there was not enough time in view of the long working hours to keep house and cook for oneself. Thus the unmarried adult either lived with his parents and siblings (in which case he either paid rent or put his earnings into the common fund) or moved out to live as a paying boarder in the household of another nuclear family. He or she could not live indefinitely as a boarder, however. The single person was expected to marry; there was little opportunity for sexual activity outside marriage, and much risk attached to it; and, if one were eager to improve one's situation in life, it was clear that the quickest way for the working-class person to do so was to form a nuclear family partnership. Such partnership was fundamental to the survival-and-advancement strategy of the people of the working class. Among the mill workers, the members of a nuclear family (simple or modified) constituted an effective economic partnership. Each person above infancy contributed either work or money to the unit; cash was saved and pooled as a capital fund for future travel and investment, usually in land or tools and equipment for a trade (or even manufacturing). Any combination of members might work in the factory, including husband, wife, or children, so long as there was a female at home to cook, mind the children, and take care of boarders.

The boarders were a crucially important factor in the financial plans of many working-class households, for they paid good money—$2 per week if male, $1.25 per week if female. The wife, who cooked for the boarders and did their housekeeping (which probably included laundry services), could bring in as much as $24 per month by caring for three male boarders—very likely more than the rest of the family earned as the mill. At the time of the 1850 census, between a quarter and a half of all mill workers' households were keeping boarders. The nuclear family partnership thus used the house which it rented from the mill owner as capital with which to make money.

In this working-class system it is difficult to see marriage as a means of establishing an alliance between groups. Although an extended family might—as in the case of the Morrises—travel together, it was essentially traveling as a large, dispersed nuclear family, consisting of aged parents and their married children. The in-laws came along as spouses rather than as representatives of the families of their parents. Marriage and procreation established a partnership among individuals; the nuclear family partnership was the necessary condition for the renting of capital equipment (a house) and the pooling of factory income.

The implications of the partnership family system for social attitudes within the working class at this time are interesting. A hardworking and well-disciplined family could in a few years, if not impeded by illness or unemployment, save enough money to travel west, buy land, and become farmers (where the family partnership concept was equally applicable)—or, alternatively (and far less frequently), establish credit, borrow money, and become merchants or manufacturers. The mother and teen-age children evidently were almost as productive financially as the father; and, since the partnership could remain even if the father (or mother) died or moved away, many working-class widows and widowers were heads of families and of households. As on the farm, the labor of children, even small children, was essential in household and baby-minding chores. The system did tend to reduce the amount of schooling the children received (only about half of the eligible working-class children in 1850 were listed as having attended school in the previous year). But it also probably tended to minimize the patriarchal quality of family life—a quality that only the wealthy manufacturer or merchant was able to support. In many families the wife, in addition to being a wage or rent earner, was also the partnership's business manager, collecting the family paycheck directly from the manufacturer, or from her husband and children, and formulating and administering the family budget. This situation should, theoretically, have been conducive to tension between a working father whose contribution to the partnership was not worth much more than, if as much as, that of his wife and children. And such tension in turn should have contributed to a centrifugal tendency that would, as it were, spin off discontented young unmarried men and women to live as boarders with other working-class families, thus perpetuating that most necessary aspect of the whole system.

In the managerial class, where income was the profit of a business or a large farm owned and administered by the father, the nuclear family partnership was not economically necessary for the survival and progress of the individual. The father—the businessman—could take care of himself and his wife and children. Bachelors could live comfortably on their fathers' profits and spinsters remain at home happily with their parents and sisters. Sons might go into the family business or they might turn to one of the professions or to benevolent and charitable activities. And instead of paying boarders, the nonfamily members of the household were paid servants. Indeed, the nonpartnership aspect of the marital relationship might be most emphatically demonstrated, as in the care with which the Sellers family kept the estate of their sister, Peter Hill's wife, separate from his estate by putting it in trust.

In contrast to the working-class concept of the marital economic partnership, the managerial class thought in terms of the potential alliance implications of marriage. Nathan Sellers and James Knowles objected to their daughters' marriages to men with whom a family connection seemed economically perilous. When Sallie Knowles married John P. Crozer without her father's consent, he made it plain that no financial claims could be made on him by her new family. And when Hannah Sellers finally did receive permission to marry Peter Hill, there was thereafter a continuing financial alliance (an irritating one to the Sellers') between the two families. The Lammots and Du Ponts were intimately joined by the marriage of Lammot's daughter to E. I. Du Pont's son; the business connections and friendships of the Smiths and the Du Ponts were cemented by no less than two marriages. And we shall later note the importance of affinal connections to Henry Moore, John S. Phillips, and John P. Crozer in acquiring the capital to carry out their plans for manufacturing.

Among the managerial class, furthermore, the patronymic descent group was far more important than among the workers. Such a group was formed of the successive generations of persons patrilineally descended from and bearing the name of an original male ancestor or ancestors (if they were a group of brothers) who had become established in America many years before. Living members of such patronymic descent groups considered them to be in some sense great families, and marriages were sometimes actually recognized as alliances between patronymic groups (as in the case of the Lammots and Du Ponts). One of the members would keep the genealogical records and be able to trace the family's ancestry back deep into European history. Great families, often maintained contact with kinsmen in Europe and exchanged visits occasionally. To the list of such old great family names as Sharpless, Phillips, Smith, Lewis, Sellers, Gilpin, Du Pont, Dutton, and Darlington would in the next generation be added those of the managers who had become successful in this—Crozer, Lammot, Riddle. This emphasis upon a descent group identity, represented by a name and a genealogy, no doubt contributed to the members of the group a sense of being a meaningful member in an immortal corporate entity—as estimate of self far different from the identity gained as a member of a nuclear family partnership, which eventually would be dissolved by the death of its members. And it had different implications for social attitudes, too: it emphasized the value of age and of the male line, and treated women as peripheral (the daughters' children, bearing another patronym, were forever lost); indeed, in this class they were peripheral in an economic sense, being engaged in financially nonproductive tasks. Women served as the links that joined men in systems of descent and alliance, which were of course economically significant relations; but their own primary work was neither heavy housework nor factory production but rather the administration of servants, church activity, and the cultivation of artistic and literary interests.

But the working-class family style and the managerial-class family style, however different in some ways, were precise complements to one another. The managers, in order to make the profits required to support their own extended family alliances, needed a stable and contented work force, composed of nuclear family partnerships and unmarried boarders in households that provided the proper mix of males and females of various ages. They attracted such a work force by paying relatively high wages, by providing houses at very low rents, by allowing workers to raise vegetables on company land and even keep a cow or some chickens, by reducing the rents during hard times, and by helping them in many small ways with credit, banking services, and transportation. The workers, in order to save the cash needed to buy land in the west, worked hard and for the most part without complaint in the managers' mills, enduring periods of unemployment, partial employment, and reduced wages, foregoing the prospect of education for many of their children, and even allowing the evangelical women of the managerial class to find respectable and interesting work in saving their souls. . . .

THE HOUSEHOLDS ROCKDALE

The seven hamlets were in many respects very similar to one another. Each was a cluster of houses nestled around a mill; or strung out along the road that passed the mill, with a few extra structures to serve as community centers: Calvary Church at Rockdale, the Baptist chapel at West Branch, the inn at Lenni, the schoolhouses, the blacksmiths' shops (but most of the craftsmen and shopkeepers plied their trade in a room or two of their residences). The population of the hamlets ranged from 186 at Parkmount to 411 at Crozerville; the number of houses varied accordingly, from 32 to 77. The house—whether the usual two-rooms-plus-attic-plus-half-cellar stone tenement, constructed in blocks of two to four units, or the much larger farmhouses and mansions—was the natural enumeration unit, because it partitioned the population neatly into a finite number of households.

But the household was not conceived—even by the census enumerator—to be the fundamental social unit. The fundamental social unit was the simple nuclear family, composed of a mother and a father (who were assumed to be legally married, of course) and their natural children. Of the 351 houses in the district, 156 were occupied by such families living by themselves; another 96 were occupied by simple nuclear families who had taken in other people, sometimes relatives (like an aging parent or the sibling of one of the spouses or the orphaned child of a kinsman) and sometimes boarders (from individuals to whole families). If one includes all those households where the central unit was a simple nuclear family, then fully 72 percent of all the houses were occupied and headed by simple nuclear families. Most other households were composed of anticipations or remnants of the simple nuclear family: recently married couples who had not yet had children, older married couples whose children had moved away, a set of unmarried adult siblings whose parents had died, and—more common than any of the rest—one-parent families.

> The temperature of their atmosphere is generally high, approaching a medium of from sixty to seventy degrees in winter, and rising to eighty and even ninety degrees in summer. Their atmosphere is constantly filled with floating particules of cotton; the finer the yarns to be spun,

the higher the temperature must be. Cotton yarns cannot be spun in any atmosophere other than this. The cotton wool, when impregnated with the oil used to diminish friction in the machinery, and in the usual temperature of the rooms, emits a most offensive fetor. This fetor, acted on by the azote and hydrogen abounding in the rooms, gives an atmosophere which none but those accustomed to it can respire without nausea.

In the rooms where the cotton wool undergoes the first process of carding and breaking, the atmosophere is one floating mass of cotton particles, which none but those accustomed to it, can breathe, for an hour together, without being nearly suffocated.

No doubt this odoriferous effect was intensified in some mills (not the Riddles') by the provision of loosely partitioned water closets on the working floors (usually but not always separate for males and females). Other observers noted that new employees experienced "a little nausea at first and their appetite for food is lessened."[2]

Another factor significantly affecting the comfort and ease of the work was the quality of the early stages of preparation. American factories generally devoted less attention to the carding and preparation of the roving than did English factories. The result was an inordinately high frequency of breakage, starting with the sliver emanating from the finisher card, continuing with the various drawing and stretching frames, and culminating in the throstle and mule rooms. An experienced spinner reported that in English factories, where one piecer attended two miles, the child walked twenty-five miles per day. With only one mule to attend in America, the distance theoretically would be halved; but this advantage was more than overbalanced by the effects of poor quality in the preparation of the rovings. An experienced English carder, employed by Joseph Ripka of Manayunk, testified: "I consider the work of piecers, here, at the mule, greater than in England, although here the children attend but one mule; the reason is, that the work in England is much better prepared, and requires less piecing."[12] Thus, ideally, a child might sit a large part of the day, if the work were well prepared; but in general it was not possible, and the child, like the other workers, had to stand and walk for the full twelve to fourteen hours per day.

The effect of the long hours of constant physical labor, attending the continuously operating machines, was fatiguing enough for adults. Some spinners, being piece workers, preferred to work less. A Scottish spinner, for instance, testified, "I consider a great evil in the business the length of time we have to labor; I consider eight hours labor per day, as much as I can bear, in justice to myself; I work by the piece." The effect on children was striking, particularly upon first entering the mill. The ankles tended to swell, the appetite to decline. William Shaw, erstwhile Parkmount employee and afterward one of Crozer's workers, testified succinctly in 1837 about the effect on children of conditions in the factories he had known:

> The children are tired when they leave the factory; has known them to sleep in corners and other places, before leaving the factory from fatigue. The younger children are generally very much fatigued, particularly those under twelve years of age; has not heard frequent complaints of pain; more of being worried; has known the children to go to sleep on arriving home, *before* taking supper; has known great difficulty

in keeping children awake at their work; has known them to be struck, to keep them awake. . . .[3]

The mule was one of the largest and most complex mechanical devices ever made by man; larger machines, like locomotives and stationary steam engines, were power generators. The maximum size of the mules of this period was about 280 spindles. Such mules were about 60 feet long, and the size limitation was based on the physical strength required of the spinner to push, and control, the massive carriage on its inward course. The mule spinner—invariably a man—was the highest paid operative in the mill. Each spinner was assisted in operating his mule by a small team of two or even three lower paid boy or girl operatives: a piecer, whose job it was to repair the broken threads (five or six a minute) at the end of a run, when the carriage was briefly motionless; a creel attender, keeping the mule supplied with bobbins of roving (which meant carrying baskets of bobbins up and down stairs); and the scavenger, who scurried about under the sheet of yarn between the carriage and the frame, sweeping up dirt, picking up broken ends, and picking fuzzballs off the yarn. The scavenger's situation was graphically described by the English novelist Charlotte Elizabeth:

> "And what is scavenging?"
> "Oh, that made me laugh. You see, bits of cotton wool will stick to the thread, and they mustn't go on the reels; so there is a little girl huddled up under the frame and she snatches off all the loose wool, and throws it down so fast! and when the machine runs back, if the little scavenger did not bob and duck, and get very low, she would have a fine knock on the head."
> "Poor thing!" said Helen, "she can nver stretch herself out, hardly; and she is almost choked and smothered in the dust of the light cotton bits that she has to pull and scatter about.". . .[4]

Perhaps the most difficult and controversial aspect of discipline had to do with children. In the first place, the young piecers, creel attenders, and scavengers were not technically the manufacturer's employees at all; their discipline was the responsibility of the mule spinner who hired them. Riddle, in recalling his youth in Ireland ("I have been working in a cotton factory since I can recollect. . . . I was not more than nine years old when I was put into a factory, and have been raised in one"), observed, "There was a great deal of whipping there, we have not here." Crozer, speaking in a similar vein in 1837, said, "when factories were first established in this vicinity, severe whipping was often practised, but it was found not to be the best mode of management, and has been, in a great degree, abandoned." Riddle even claimed that if the children who worked for the mule spinners "were oppressed in any way, they would tell me, of course." Certainly the children not working for spinners were disciplined by foremen and carding masters. But probably the most effective measure in maintaining both the general level of efficiency, cleanliness, and propriety and a not-too-severe mode of discipline for "the little ones" (as Riddle called them) was the informal culture of the workers. It must be remembered that all of the people who worked in the mill lived within easy walking distance, and most in the sixteen tenement houses located within 100 yards of the mill. The spinner's team, the carding masters' assistants, the young hands in the preparation room, were, if not their own children, then the children of neighbors who also worked in the same mill.

Real brutality, made visible by bruises, welts, tears, and headaches, would not only offend the abused child's parents but also interfere with the work, for an injured or panic stricken child would not be able to do good work. And a large proportion of the piecers were, the daybook makes plain, not the children of the spinners. The record shows, for instance, that Joseph Pedrick pieced for Fancis Bonner, Mary Fredd pieced for Richard Bates and later for Sarah Cochrane (in the card room), Sarah McDade pieced for James McBride. Lydia Wier and later Joseph Pedrick for Hugh McMunn, Charles McNamee for David Crummer, and so on. One may suspect that, at least by the 1830's, the manufacturer and his agents must have avoided, as much as possible, involving themselves in any direct way with the physical discipline of "the little ones," leaving that arena to the community of workers. This meant, as other witnesses in the Philadelphia area testified, discipline by ridicule and "taunting," occasionally supplemented as required by cuffs, slaps, kicks, and ear-boxings. . . .

Rules about punctuality therefore were rigid. Tardiness was punished by docking wages or, if repeated, by dismissal—even in the case of the small children. Working conditions in the mills of two of the Chester Creek manufacturers were described in the 1837 Pennsylvania Senate investigation, and the witnesses (including Riddle and Crozer and William Shaw, one of their past employees) all agreed on the severity of the punctuality requirements. William Shaw, who worked two years for the Riddles and then for Crozer, reported:

> I have known work to commence as early as twenty minutes past four o'clock, in the summer season, and to work as late as half an hour before eight, P.M.; an hour and a-half allowed for breakfast and dinner, when the hands all leave to go to dinner—children and all; the ringing of the bell was the notice to begin, and docking wages the penalty; the foreman rings the bell and stops the machinery. In the cities, the engineer rings the bell and stops the machinery.
>
> The period of labor is not uniform; in some cases, from sun to sun. It is most common to work as long as they can see; in the winter they work until eight o'clock, receiving an hour and a-half for meals; an hour and a-half is the entire time allowed for going, eating and returning; and that time is often shortened by the ringing of the bell too soon.
>
> Punishment, by whipping, is frequent; they are sometimes sent home and docked for not attending punctually; never knew both punishments to be inflicted; generally the children are attentive, and punishments are not frequent.

Riddle felt that the factory regimen in Northern Ireland, when he worked there as a youth, was more strict than in the Chester Creek factories: "Children suffered very much under that system. They got to adhere to their regular hours, pretty much. The time was still severe on them. There was a great deal of whipping there, we have not here." And Crozer noted that the children, if they were to be employed at all, had to work under the same discipline as adults: ". . . the work of children cannot be shortened, without also abridging that of adults, as the labor of one is connected with that of the other, being part of a system, which, if broken in upon, destroys a connecting link in the chain of operations.[5]

A related work rule mentioned by the Chester Creek witnesses was that children should be constantly attentive and not sleep in the mill (even if not at the moment actively employed). Violations of such rules were punished in a variety of ways: notifying the parent, sending home, docking wages, pulling ears, slapping, whipping, and outright dismissal.

Not even mentioned, but implicit throughout the testimony, was the assumption that the orders of managers to overseers, overseers to spinners and weavers, spinners to piecers and scavengers, and in general orders from bosses to operatives, were to be obeyed promptly and efficiently. Also unmentioned was the assumption that there were some limits to the power of the manager to discipline workers. In 1833 there had been a precedent-setting case in the nearby Montgomery County's Court of Quarter Sessions. An overseer in the cotton factory of Bernard McCready had been indicted on the charge of beating one of the young operatives under his direction, a lad of fourteen. The jury found him guilty, fined him $1, and assessed him the costs of prosecution. *Hazard's Register* intoned:

> By this trial a principle has been established for the government of those "clock-work institutions," which will deprive certain petty tyrants of much of their usurped authority, and secure to the operatives a degree of protection under the laws of our country, which will tend to render their situation less onerous, because they will feel themselves more secure from oppression. The march of free principles is onward, and the time is fast approaching when the rights of the working-man shall be respected, and his person be protected from wrong and outrage.[6]

But for less obviously work-related moralties, the practice differed from factory to factory. Thus, speaking of cleanliness, one of the traditional Protestant virtues, William Shaw declared that "no attention is paid by the manufacturer, or others in the factory, to the personal cleanliness of the children." Robert Craig, the manager at John S. Phillips' mill at Fairmount in Philadelphia, reported, "No attention is bestowed by the managers or proprietors, to the personal or bodily cleanliness of the children." But Crozer said that the children in his mill were "generally cleanly." Another object of varying concern on the part of manufacturers was the possibility of undue intimacy between the sexes. No manufacturer attempted to segregate the sexes by room or even by type of machine, except for putting males at the more strenuous or more skilled jobs. But there was concern about the provision of water closets. The Senate committee regularly asked about sanitary conveniences. Shaw observed: "No particular attention is paid to morals; the boys and girls are not kept separate in the factories; they have different water closets, generally separated only by a partition. . . ." Craig also noted that "the water closets of the boys and girls are separate. "The Riddles went a little further, separating workers by age as well as sex: "The boys and girls at our mill have different water closets; the boys and girls in different parts of the yard; the men and women the same house, but a partition between them." Crozer did not mention the subject of toilets in his testimony.

Still more various was the attitude toward profane and obscene language. Although the one was deemed wrong because blasphemous, and the other because it implied—or might lead to—loose sexual conduct, the mills varied in their concern. Crozer was emphatic: "no improper conduct or conversation is allowed in well conducted factories—at least there is not in mine." But Samuel Riddle was indifferent to the whole question, putting it on a "Boys will be boys" level: "I do not think that boys in factories are more in the habit of using profane and obscene language, than those out of doors; when a number of boys get together out of doors, they always do these things. I think that the girls do not use such language." Shaw's experience was that the typical manufacturer did not care: "No particular attention is paid to morals . . . obscene language is frequently used, not often by females; profane language is frequently used; care is seldom taken to prevent these things; if their work is done, it is all that is required. . . ." And Craig contradicted himself, declaring in one passage that "no attention is paid to the morals of the children in the factory; they are neither advised nor reprimanded, unless they neglect their work," yet in another place testifying that children were dismissed for using bad language: "Profane and obscene language is too frequent in the absence of the superintendent, and happens between boys and girls, and is injurious to the morals in a great degree; no other means to prevent it is resorted to other than dismissal when the superintendent hears them at it."[7]

Crozer, indeed, as might have been expected, was the most moralistic of the local manufacturers whose factories were the subject of testimony. He had, he said, a policy of dismissing any female employee who had a doubtful reputation:

> The young women employed, are possessed of a proper self-respect, and depatures from chastity are not common. Females of loose character, if known, or *even suspected* as such, would be immediately dismissed from my factory, and I think could not get employment in any of the neighboring factories.[8]

None of the written regulations survive from any of the Rockdale mills, but the "Rules and Regulations of the Matteawan Company" in 1846 have been preserved. Matteawan, as we noted earlier, was one of the most successful of the cotton manufactories, and a center of machine-making. When it was visited by Robert Owen in 1824, the proprietor had made a point of his high moral expectations, informing Owen's party, when they praised the appearance of the workers, "that when a girl did not shew a disposition to be clean & neat in her dress they turned her off."[9] The rules in 1846 had not been relaxed; their severity certainly exceeded that of the Rockdale district (perhaps as a result of the hard Calvinist convictions of the proprietors, who were members of the Dutch Reform Church):

> No person will be admitted into the yard during working hours, except on business, without permission of an agent. At all other times, the watchmen will be invested with full control.

> The work bell will be rung three minutes, and tolled five minutes; at the expiration of which, every person is expected to be at their work, and every entrance closed, except through the office, which will at all times be open during the working hours of the factory.

> No person employed in the manufacturing departments can be permitted to leave their work without permission from their overseer. All others employed in and about the factory are requested to give notice to the agent or superintendent, if they wish to be absent from their work.

> No talking can be permitted among the hands in any of the working departments, except on subjects relating to their work.

No spirituous liquors, smoking, or any kind of amusements, will be allowed in the workshops or yards.

Those who take jobs will be considered as overseers of the persons employed by them, and subject to these rules.

Should there exist among any of the persons employed, an idea of oppression on the part of the company, they are requested to make the same known in honorable manner, that such grievances, if really existing, may be promptly considered.

To convince the enemies of domestic manufactures that such establishments are not "sinks of vice and immorality," but, on the contrary, nurseries of morality, industry, and intelligence, a strictly moral conduct is required of every one. Self-respect, it is presumed, will induce every one to be as constant in attendance on some place of divine worship as circumstances will permit. Intemperance, or any gross impropriety of conduct, will cause an immediate discharge of the individual.

The agent and other members of the company are desirous of cultivating the most friendly feeling with the workmen in the establishment, believing they are to rise or fall together. Therefore, to promote the interest and harmony of all, it is necessary there should be a strict observance of these rules and regulations.[10]

CREATING AN ETHICAL SYSTEM FOR THE WORKERS

It is clear, from the consideration of work rules, that the manufacturers, whether ardent evangelicals or stubborn infidels, all gave to the requirements of technology and economics the first priority in designing factory discipline. They were willing, in fact, to require the workers to behave in ways, and to labor under conditions, that they themselves, and the community generally, conventionally regarded as conducive to immorality. They recognized that the system of long hours prevented the children who worked in factories from getting any education at all—even though the spirit of the Revolution, and the rhetoric of Jacksonian democracy, favored educating all the young people of the commonwealth. Illiteracy, by rendering religious instruction more difficult and Bible-reading impossible, was in itself an obstacle to the moral improvement of the working class. Both Riddle and Crozer therefore testified in favor of prohibiting the labor of children under twelve in cotton factories, in order to free the early years for basic education and to protect the very young from the immoral influences of factory life. And both Riddle and Crozer favored an overall reduction in hours of labor. But they were not willing to introduce these reforms into their own factories, and opposed unilateral legislation by the Pennsylvania legislature on the subject, because, they said, they feared that manufacturers in other states, lacking such laws, would have a competitive advantage and would drive the Pennsylvania manufactories out of business. The demands of conventional morality, when they conflicted with the iron laws of technology and economics, regularly were accorded second place.

Samuel Riddle was eloquent and direct on the problem of balancing economic interest against child welfare:

I think that it would be better to prohibit the employment of children under twelve years of age; the children under that age, would then have a better chance of going to school. I don't think it would increase the wages of labor; I don't think it would make any difference in this respect. The parents of children employed in factories, would be generally opposed to it, I think. A great many widow women have no other way of support, and they would want to get their children into factories at an earlier age. There are too many fathers who are themselves idle, and live by the work of their little children; they would be opposed to it. If children over twelve only, went into factories, the time of labor as now practised, would not make any odds. No system could be established about factories by which children could be required to be schooled a portion of time; when children are employed, the men could not do the work the little ones does; we can't dispense with the work of children in factories. I believe the manufacturer would be better if the hours were shortened—if they were shortened all over the U. States; otherwise I would fear the competition of other States. The children might be instructed under such a system, by night schools.

I should think that it would be good, that boys should not be employed until they can read and write. I think it would be better all round; it would not increase the wages of labor; it would be good for the rising generation, and better for the factory. Generally, the children in factories are not able to read and write; they would be inclined to learn, if they had the opportunity. It would be preferable to have girls put on the same footing, but as to age of employement we do not consider it so important.

A system, such as I suggest, would operate very hardly on the poor people, unless you gave it time, by providing that it should commence a year or two as the public schools have been commenced.

. . . I think that a length of labor of sixty-six hours a week in Pennsylvania alone, would effect us so that we could not compete with other States. We pay higher for wages here than they do at the Eastward, and when times are bad, they can under-sell us, so that we have to stop.[11]

Crozer was also eloquent, but somewhat more defensive than Riddle, blaming the resistance to reform even more explicitly on the parents:

The adults emplyed in manufactories, have, within the last few years, expressed much anxiety to shorten the hours of labor, and have made application for this purpose, to their employers; no direct grant has been made, but the time has been somewhat shortened generally; the parents of children employed, have not, I think, taken an active part on this subject, probably from the fear, that a corresponding reduction of wages would follow; I think many employers might oppose abridging the hours of work, because it would then be necessary to increase the fied capital of buildings and machinery, to obtain the same amount of work—but the strongest objections arise from the apprehension that a change in time of work, would give other States an advantage over us.

Education is much neglected about manufactories; a large portion of the families employed, are those of indigent widows, who require the work of their children for support, or of idle, intemperate fathers, who do little or nothing themselves towards supporting their families: and these, especially the latter, have but little inclination to school their children, and it is frequently the case, when employers encourage the schooling of the children, the parents object and postpone, with the complaint of being "unable, *for the present*, to lose the labor of the child"; employers have not always encouraged education; small operatives have often been scarce, and employers were therefore, desirous to retain the children in the factories; this difficulty has mostly disappeared on Chester Creek, and perhaps in other places as small children have become more abundant.

I think legislative action, for the protection and education of factory children, desirable—yet, I am constained to say, the necessity of the case arises more from the conduct of parents, than that of employers.[12]

The manufacturers evidently were experiencing a moral dilemma. They were committed, at least as responsible citizens if not also as evangelical religionists, to the moral and mental improvement of the people, and especially of the children, who were connected with their mills. But successful management of a factory in a competitive market economy in their opinion required them to tolerate, or even create, noxious working conditions for their employees: denial of educational opportunity, exposure to profane and obscene language, promiscuous association of the sexes and of different age groups in intimate working arrangements.

The solution was to urge reform, not in the mill but in the institutions of the community, and particularly in the educational system. The Pennsylvania Senate investigating committee in 1838 reported a bill which provided that no children under ten would be permitted to work in factories; that children over ten who did work in factories, but could not read, write, or keep accounts, should be sent to school three months in every year of employment; and that children under sixteen should not be allowed to work more than ten hours per day.[13] But the bill did not pass; in fact it was never brought to a vote.

The manufacturers relied on the community to resolve the problem: on the parents to bring up their children properly; on the Sunday School to educate them and give them elementary religious instruction and moral guidance; on the newly created system of public schools (instituted in 1836 as a result of the Commonwealth law of that year) to provide free education to all children; and on the Sunday School teachers and clergy to instruct both children and adults in Christian duty. . . .

CHILD LABOR:
WORKERS AS OBJECTS OF PITY AND THE TEN HOURS LAW

When the struggle between management and labor began in the 1820s, the cotton mill workers, despite their anomalous position in the roster of trades, had generally had a high opinion of themselves as a radical reforming element in society. By the mid-forties, despite a practical improvement in their material conditions, the textile workers had become objects of public sympathy and of the religious reformer's condescending concern. They were now for the most part children, and, as Clementina once put it, "poor girls that work on the looms."[14] The mode of passage and enforcement of the ten hours law symbolize the transformation.

One of the standing complaints of cotton factory workers was the long working day, on the order of fourteen hours, including about an hour for meals. The Pennsylvania Senate committeee's investigation in 1837 had included testimony from operators and manufacturers alike alleging that the protracted hours of work were injurious to the health of children and left them so tired that they could not pay attention in night school or sometimes even in Sunday School. Poor factory children could not of course take advantage of all of the free public schools, which thus, in effect, were observed for the children of more affluent parents. The turnouts in 1835 and 1836 in Philadelphia had won the journeymen of that city a ten hours agreement with the master tradesmen; but nothing had happened to benefit the operatives as a result of either their own strikes in 1836 and 1842 or the Pennsylvania Senate investigation of 1837.

In 1846, the operatives of Philadelphia, inspired by a brief strike of the factory girls at Pittsburgh in support of a ten hours law, formed their own "Ten Hours Association." They wrote an address to "The Working Classes of the Country," which urged it as beneficial to employers and employees alike that the ten hours system be universally adopted. The address was printed in the *Upland Union*. It described the evil consequences of the long hours in graphic terms:

> We see the laborer in the morning approach his toil with a dread of its long protraction and excess, that even a sound night's slumber, and long continued habit have failed to wear away. We see him as the day declines with wearied limbs, and gloomy thoughts, and cheerless spirits, casting upon the setting sun a lingering and heart-sick glance, or after it is gone from view, listening in despondency to hear, through the clattering of machinery, the hour of his delivery from toil. We see him unable to fulfill towards his family the offices and duties of his station, because his wearying labors have substituted petulance and gloom for the feelings of affection; and languor and indifference for the power of instruction. We see him producing wealth by perpetual exertion, yet living a life of unceasing anxiety and want. We see him subjected to continual privations, inconvenience and suffering, and cut off from the ordinary sources of gratification and enjoyment. We see him in ignorance, servility and degradation, and deprived of the time, the taste, the energy, necessary for his elevation and improvement. We see him losing all interest in matters of general importance, and degenerating into a mere machine, with intelligence to guide him in his labor, and compensation enough to keep him in profitable working order and economical repair.

Invoking the welfare of mankind, the spirit of the age, and the evidence of progress in justification, the paper called upon the nation to fix a date for "the general change."

A second, related, complaint was that children of tender years ought not to be employed at all. Although many widows were supported by their children's wages, and although the nimble little fingers of the young were supposedly uniquely qualified for handling delicate yarns, there was a persistent argument in favor of keeping younger children out of the factories. The considerations advanced in support of restrictions on the age of labor included the hazard to health, the threat to morals, and the need for education. These arguments also had been expressed by witnesses before the Senate committee in 1837 but had seen no result.

Precedent existed for government intervention. England had had legislation on the

the books since 1802 that aimed to protect the health and morals of factory children. In 1834 a new Act of Parliament provided that no person under the age of eighteen was permitted to work at night or to labor more than twelve hours per day or for more than a total of sixty-nine hours per week. In 1840 President Van Buren by executive order had put federal employees on a ten-hour basis. And in 1847 the New Hampshire legislature became the first in the nation to pass a law specifying that ten hours was a legal day's work (although its effectiveness was reduced by a clause permitting special contracts which extended that limit). . . .

The whole matter came in for a public airing next year in the Senate's abortive investigation of the working conditions of children employed in cotton mills. Crozer and Riddle both testified, more or less blandly, that they would like to see the hours of child labor reduced nationally, not just in Pennsylvania. The more extreme positions were taken by William Shaw, the discharged ringleader from West Branch, on the operatives' side, who testified first, and by Joseph Ripka, the principal manufacturers in Manayunk, who testified last. Shaw was forthright in condemning the manufacturers for the overworking of children and the neglect of their educational needs:

> The greatest evils known are, first, the number of hours of labor, and the number of children employed. . . . The proportion of children varies in different establishments; has known more than one-fourth to be children under twelve years of age: under twenty years, would include in many cases, three-fourths; not many are apprenticed; they are usually hired to employers by parents and guardians. The hours vary in different establishments; in some I have worked fourteen and a-half hours. . . . The labor of the children is in some cases excessive—in other it is not. The children are employed as spinning and carding. The question of excessive labor is more upon the kind of work; carding is the hardest work; their work is regulated by the operation of the machinery, at carding; and they must stand during the whole time; considers twelve or fourteen hours labor excessive at either branch for a child. I have known children of nine years of age to be employed at spinning; at carding, as young at ten years. . . . I think no attention is paid to education during the time they are employed in factories, except what they receive from Sabbath schools, and some few at night schools, when they are in an unfit condition to learn; the children attend Sabbath school with great reluctance; many will not attend in consequence of the confinement of the week.

But Joseph Ripka saw the matter in a completely different light, claiming that the only reason for labor strife was the evil "Trades' Union" and that he employed children mostly as an act of charity:

> If any evil exists in the factory system, it is the principles of the Trades' Union, which has been introduced amongst the laboring classes in general; it has been imparted to this country by English and Irish men within a few years, and has the tendency to destroy the good feeling

which has, heretofore, existed between the employer and the workman in this country, and the leaders are men, either of low character or designing politicians. To show that the principle is a bad one, the leaders are always trying to keep the working people in an excitement, to have them always ready for a turn-out, they lay contribution ont he working classes, and expend the money amongst themselves, by going about from place to place to make speeches, and encourage them to turn out. when labor is plenty, the workingmen will get good wages and find plenty employment without the aid of the Trades' Union, and in hard times, the Trads' Union cannot keep up wages or find employment for the working classes. If they could do it, why don't they do it at the present time. . . .

I employ twenty-five children under twelve years of age, and they are pressed on me by widows, or by mothers of dissipated husbands; and when I do employ them, it is for mere charity than any thing else. Children, under twelve years of age, are of no profit to the employers in cotton factories, it is the age when they ought to be educated, and I have always been against to employ them. . . .

The labor for children is not excessive.

The children do not appear tired when they leave work.[15]

The general economic decline, beginning with the financial panic of 1837, placed the unions in a poor position to call for strike actions against employers who reduced wages or otherwise failed to meet the expectations of operatives. Some of the manufacturers kept their mills operating more to provide wages than to produce cotton goods, for although the yarn and cloth might be unsalable now, it would probably be sold later, and if starving operatives left the district to find work elsewhere, the manufacturer would be hard-pressed to find new, trained operatives at a time when all the mills would again be seeking them. Besides, providing work was a matter of Christian charity in an age when there was no source of public relief but the poorhouse, which separated husbands and wives and children, and exposed the respectable poor to the influence of the immoral, the improvident, and the insane. . . .

FOOTNOTES

1. "Testimony of the Witnesses, accompanying the Report of the Committee of the Senate, appointed to investigate the subject of the Employment of Children in Factories," *Pennsylvania State Journal*, 1837-38, Part 2, p. 306.
2. *Ibid.*, pp. 347-8, 292.
3. *Ibid.*, pp. 329, 280-1.
4. Charlotte Elizabeth (Tona, Mrs. Charlotte Elizabeth.) *Helen Fleetwood in The Works of Charlotte Elizabeth*, vol. 1, (New York: Dodd, 1847), pp. 537-8.
5. *Pa. Senate Journal*, 1837-38, Part. 2, pp. 280, 300, 304.
6. *Hazard's Register of Pennsylvania*, vol. 12, p. 16 (April 19, 1834).
7. *Pa. Senate Journal*, 1837-38, Part 2, pp. 279-81, 283-5, 299-307.
8. *Ibid.*, p. 305.
9. Carol D. Snedeker, (ed.), *The Diaries of Donald MacDonald, 1824-1826*, (Indianapolis, Indiana Historical Society, 1942), p. 195.
10. *Hunt's Merchant's Magazine*, 1846, pp. 370-1.
11. *Pa. Senate Journal*, 1837-38, Part 2, pp. 301-2.
12. Ibid, pp. 304-6 "Report of the Committee by Mr. Peltz, Feb. 7, 1838."
13. *Pa. Senate Journal*, 1837-38, Part. 1, p. 326.
14. John R. Commons *et al. (eds.) A Documentary History of American Industrial Society.* (Cleveland, Ohio: A. H. Clark, 1900-11), vol. 8, pp. 200-5.
15. *Pa. Senate Journal*, 1837-38, Part 2, pp. 208-1, 357-9.

Because the family is the primary institution of socialization, many assume that it has sole "input" in determining how boys and girls grow into their future social and sex roles. But institutions other than the family play important roles in the socialization of the young—the school, the peer group, religious institutions, the media and the work-place, to name a few. To understand how the young learn what it means to be a woman or man in a given society, we have to know not just the dynamics of family life, but how family activities and values intersect with various social institutions and ideologies.

In this article Leslie W. Tentler describes how the values, perceptions of woman's roles, and economic prospects of urban, working-class (mostly) ethnic families from 1900 to 1930 intersected with the daughter's world of work. Tentler shows how the desire of most of these families to imbue a sense of domesticity and loyalty to the family in their working daughters affected both the nature of work chosen by the young women and the ways they disposed of their incomes.

How did the experiences of these women differ from those of their brothers'? Would attitudes of working class families toward their daughters differ significantly from middle-class families? Why?

The Working-Class Daughter 1900-1930

Leslie Woodcock Tentler

The working-class daughter who lived in the parental home was the typical female wage earner in the years between 1900 and 1930. And the working-class daughter in this period was overwhelmingly likely to be employed at some time before she married. In Chicago in 1920, nearly 88% of unskilled workers' children at least sixteen years old and living with their parents were estimated to be working; for families of skilled workers, the estimate was close to 85%. Girls were less likely than boys to be employed, it is true, but a large majority of daughters in these families were certainly wage earners. And even in 1920, nearly one-third of the fourteen-and fifteen-year-old in unskilled workers' families in Chicago held jobs.[1]

The adolescent girl's experience of work was inevitably influenced in important ways by her experience of family life. It was within the family that she acquired her initial understanding of the place of paid work in her life, and it was principally within the family that she formed the self-image that shaped her work behavior. If she often ventured excitedly into work as into exotic terrain, she was nonetheless an explorer heavily weighted with conservative cultural values. To understand the worker she became, we must try to understand working-class family relationships and the economic realities that supported those relationships.

The complexities of this family life can never be certainly known, but contemporary observers speak with some degree of unamimity about relationships and attitudes in working-class families. What they seem to say is this: working-class family life, while often marked by conflict, was also characterized by a high degree of cohesiveness and by strong and controlling bonds of obligation and loyalty, deriving at least in part from the marginal economic situation of many families. These ties were especially strong for daughters. For most young women, wage earning was an essentially domestic obligation; their wages belonged to the family. Neither the emotional nor the economic realities of working-class life prepared them to assume a role independent of this loyalty.

In this chapter we shall examine what contemporaries recorded about family life in urban working-class neighborhoods, both its economic and its emotional dimensions. We shall try to discover what young women experienced as they matured, attended school, and found employment. Beyond question this is a risky business; evidence is neither abundant nor free from the distortions of class prejudice. And inevitably there is distortion of reality when generalizations are made about so individual and intimate an experience as family life.

This history of domestic experience, however, will never claim precision as its forte. What a good historian can do is read the best contemporary evidence in a sensitive and imaginative way and construct a reasonable picture of what life was like—in its broad outlines—for a great many people. We cannot know the nuances of individual experience, but we can assess what observers have said about the behavior and attitudes of a group—whether that group is based on occupational, economic, or ethnic similarities—and decide whether the evidence is consistent and plausible. The exceptional individual is sometimes lost in this approach, but we approximate another truth: we learn something, however fragmentary, about the quiet routine of ordinary life and people.

It is, fortunately, not difficult to describe the economic dimension of working-class family life in the early twentieth century, even though income statistics for the period are not absolutely reliable, especially with regard to annual family income.[2] But two important facts about the economic situation of the urban working-class family are well documented, and they are facts that shaped profoundly the life options of the working-class girl. One is that the majority of working-class families throughout the period, and especially before the First World War, earned incomes that hovered near what contemporaries defined as a poverty line. The other is that even such inadequate incomes generally depended on the contributions of more than one family breadwinner.

Hence, the apparent willingness of many working-class parents to "sacrifice" the younger generation for immediate material gain, to terminate their children's education as soon as legally possible, and to forego vocational training for sons and daughters. A majority of parents seemed prepared to condemn their children to the near-poverty of the undereducated and the unskilled.[11] But this did not happen through the parents' volition alone: many working-class children were willing, indeed eager, to assume the burden of wage earning at an early age, to dispense with formal education even where parents were anxious for a grammar school or high school diploma.[12] The reasons for this were many. They included the unhappy school experience of many working-class children, peer group pressure, and children's own sense of frustration at a cramped and penurious home environment.[13] In many working-class communities, moreover, the fact that a majority of children left school at fourteen meant that to do so seemed natural and inevitable. In these communities, the first job was widely regarded as a rite of passage to adulthood, especially for boys; even unskilled work was initially endowed with an aura of excitement. But also important was a child's strong sense of obligation to parents and family.

Many contemporary observers were particularly impressed by the intense family loyalties of working-class girls. Although they were generally more successful in school than boys, daughters left school for work or to assist at home about as frequently as their brothers. They worked at dull, ill-paying jobs more steadily than adolescent boys; they usually surrendered their entire wage to their mothers—males often returned only a portion of their pay; and they had more household responsibilities than wage-earning sons. Investigators often reported tension between parents and daughters in working-class families, especially over spending money and social freedom, but most daughters stayed essentially obedient: they remained in the parental home, they surrendered their wages, they compromised with parents on standards of behavior.[14] Interviewing working daughters of Polish families in Chicago, Louise Montgomery noted:

"Poor people, not as the charity visitor knows them, but poor, as the rank and file of wage earners are poor," wrote Crystal Eastman in 1909.[3] Every major investigation of working-class family income, from 1900 to 1924, verified this poverty. Before 1915, investigators asserted, average annual incomes in families of urban wage earners ranged between $700 and $800, a sum generally described as a subsistence budget for a family of four.[4] With incomes below $800 per year, argued Robert Chapin in 1909, the families of New York City wage earners were underfed, underclothed, and inadequately housed. A yearly income of $800 permitted sufficient food and clothing, though it did not materially relieve congested housing conditions. Other investigators supported his contention.[5]

After 1915, when a dramatic decrease in European immigration and a temporary increase in industrial production due to war demand caused a general rise in wages, some investigators argued that increases in the cost of living more than offset wage earners' new prosperity.[6] Moreover, several observers claimed, the postwar decade saw a change in working-class expectations with regard to living standards. Wage earners' families, as well as families of the middle class, began to define as "necessities" a whole range of goods hitherto considered luxuries. With an expanded definition of need, a sense of economic marginality might persist despite a rise in real income.[7]

Chapin noticed in 1909 that families of New York City wage earners generally reached annual incomes above $800 only when more than one family member was at work.[8] Other investigators verified this: generally fewer than 50% of urban working-class households studied were willing or able to subsist on the income of the father alone. Many such families took lodgers; in some, the mother went to work; but the most important source of additional income in urban working-class families was the wages of adolescent children, both sons and daughters. These wages were necessary—often to insure subsistence, sometimes to provide a modest measure of comfort or security when a father's income was sufficient for food, clothing, and shelter.[9]

Many working-class families experienced the period of greatest privation when children were small and only the father was able to work. This was especially true if sickness or unemployment reduced his already inadequate wage. By the time a working-class child reached adolescence, he well understood the importance to his family of extra income, even the small contribution an unskilled young worker might make. . . .[10]

> Girls sometimes complain that they do not have enough "returned" to them in spending money and in "the kind of clothes the other girls wear." If the mother is indulgent with her daughter's desire for evening pleasures and some of the novelties and frivolities of fashion, there is little friction; if she fails to recognize these legitimate demands of youth, the distance between mother and daughter is widened, though among the 500 girls their instinctive devotion to family claim has been strong enough to keep them obedient.

Indeed, Miss Montgomery asserted, even in those rare families where daughters earned more than sons or fathers, they generally accepted "a position in the household that forces them to coax, cry, or quarrel with the mother whenever they wish independent spending money."[15]

Jane Addams, among others, believed that the docility of the wage-earning daughter stemmed from authoritarian child-rearing patterns in working-class families. Where family income was close to the poverty line, she argued, children were inevitably regarded primarily as potential wage earners, and parental behavior was dominated by the need to produce compliant offspring. She offered an illustrative anecdote:

> The head of a kindergarten training-class once addressed a club of working women, and spoke of the despotism which is often established over little children. She said that the so-called determination to break a child's will many times arose from a lust of domination, and she urged the ideal relationship founded upon love and confidence. But many of the women were puzzled. One of them remarked, "If you did not keep control over them from the time they were little, you would never get their wages when they are grown up." Another one said, "Ah, of course she (meaning the speaker) doesn't have to depend on her children's wages. She can afford to be lax with them, because even if they don't give money to her, she can get along without it."[16]

Other observers of working-class family life concurred: the absence of serious rebellion among adolescent wage earners, especially daughters, resulted from the strict discipline that characterized the treatment of children.[17] But such observations, while describing an important element in family life, neglected the bonds of affection and loyalty that also help to explain adolescent behavior. The working-class mother, usually a strong and controlling figure, was frequently the vital emotional center of the household. She created a sense of obligation in her children through her nurturant role as well as through harsh and arbitrary discipline. Certainly when working daughters themselves described the meaning and purpose of their work, the desire to "help mama" was often important.[18] "It was assumed as a matter of course that the girls' pay envelope should be turned over to the mother intact. It wouldn't look nice to pay board to the mother that raised you,' was the common view of the girls," wrote Louise Odencrantz of Italians in New York.[19] "The great majority of girls turn over their income without question to the family, and are proud and happy to be able to do so," echoed the compiled testimony of two thousand social workers in 1913.[20] The intimate relationship between habits of obedience and strong family affection is well illustrated in an essay written in 1926 by a Pennsylvania working woman:

> One day I ran into the house from school and found my mother looking very tired and depressed. She usually wore a look of anxiety these days, since my father had gone to the hospital, but her depression was very marked today.
>
> "What's the matter, mama," I asked. "Is papa worse?"
>
> "No, my child, he is improving, but the doctor told me this afternoon it will be at least six months before he will be able to leave the hospital."
>
> I knew at once what had made my mother so very sad now. My father's income had been cut off when he became injured, and my mother knew the little money she had would last only a short time, with four growing children to feed.
>
> Although I was but fifteen years old, I suddenly realized it was my duty as the oldest child to go to work. I tried to fight off the idea, by telling myself I probably wouldn't after all.
>
> I slept little that night and as I rolled and tossed my conscience seemed to be shouting at me, "Would you see your mother go to the factory for the sake of your school? Would this be fair?"
>
> The next morning I awoke with my mind resolved to take the step which I would do anything to avoid. Instead of telling the principal at once when I got to school, I went to all the classes that day, and after my last class at three-ten, I told her with much reluctance.
>
> I shall never forget how, as I walked home that hot day, my heart seemed to sink lower with each step. I walked along seeing nothing, for the thought that I had left school forever was driving me mad. Thus, the next day I entered the factory with the door to education slammed in my face.[21]

Less articulate, but no less eloquent, was the young Italian girl who confided to Louise Odencrantz, probably in 1913: "Last summer when I was laid off for nine weeks, I couldn't sleep nights. It was awful." "She tried to bridge the gap with work in other industries," added Odencrantz, "and the best that she could find was a job in a large plant preparing spices, where she worked from 7:30 in the morning until 6:30 at night for $4.00 a week." The Italian daughter "works because her family relies on her to do her part. . . . She feels her responsibility keenly and slack time is a season of horror for her."[22]

Working-class parents themselves stressed aid in family support as a natural, normal, and important element of filial loyalty. Noting that more than 84% of 347 New York City department store employees interviewed in 1910 were surrendering their entire earnings to their families, federal investigators declared:

> While many of these girls were the sole or the partial support of their families, others, especially foreigners, pay the entire earnings into the family fund from a sense of filial duty. It would never occur to some of the daughters of foreign parents to withhold even a part of their wages?" To a question, "How much does your daughter pay for board?" There frequently came an answer: "She gives me all of her

money, of course. She is my child. When she wants to pay board she can go somewhere else to live.''[23]

During the 1920s the custom of giving the entire wage to the mother was probably abandoned in many families, even for daughters. More families could afford to indulge their children, and certainly the better-educated adolescent, alert to the heightened consumption standards of the decade, was a more formidable bargainer for personal privilege than the very young wage earner of the prewar years. Even in conservative Italian and Irish families, Caroline Ware discovered in Greenwich Village in the 1920s, some working children were permitted to pay board and keep the rest of their pay for personal spending. But in Greenwich Village most working-class parents expected the children to contribute most of their pay to the family. The old norm of filial devotion was not easily surrendered, for to do so required a radical change in the parents' understanding of what a family was. "The older Irish women felt that it didn't seem right 'to make a boarding-missus out of the mother.' ''[24] Indeed, throughout the 1920s, it is likely that most working-class daughters contended with parents who were reluctant, for economic and emotional reasons, to grant them much personal economic freeedom.

When a working-class girl left school, then, and ventured into work, she did so more in the service of family and home than in search of personal independence. Her sense of family obligation placed severe limits on her sense of personal autonomy and her life options. Despite the adventure of adolescent employment, it was the working-class girl, rather than her wealthier sister, who remained more closely tied to home, more deeply committed to a familial rather than an individualistic ethic. Her life at school, at work, and in the home illustrates this clearly.

SCHOOLING IN THE WORKING CLASS

Poverty meant undereducation for nearly all working-class youth. It was very common, as late as the First World War, for working-class children to leave school before grammar school graduation. Often they left as soon as the legal school-leaving age—usually fourteen—was attained, and sometimes before. ("I started to work when I was twelve—six years ago," a Chicago garment worker remembered in 1910, "and I was so small that the boss could cover me with his coat when the factory inspector came around.")[25] In New York City the State Factory Investigating Commission found in 1914 that nearly 75% of factory women studied had left school before the eighth grade, as had nearly 40% of the female store employees interviewed.[26] And the Immigration Commission in 1908 demonstrated conclusively that not only high school but often the upper grades of the grammar school were beyond the reach of a heavily immigrant working-class. Excessive concentration of children in the early primary grades reflected not only the youthfulness of an immigrant population but also a severe degree of school retardation for many older children, especially but not exclusively those from immigrant families.

By 1920 rising family income, more stringent child labor laws, and heightened educational standards even routine jobs caused many working-class children to remain in school until they were sixteen. But with the sixteenth birthday, the majority of these children left school, and most of them went to work. In New York in 1920, only 27% of the city's sixteen- and seventeen-year-olds remained in school; in Chicago all but 29% in this age group were school-leavers. And although high school attendance nationally increased sharply during the 1920s, working-class children continued to be seriously disadvantaged educationally, girls perhaps more so than boys. In three of the four cities with which this study is principally concerned, girls in 1930 failed to enjoy access to high school in as large proportions as their brothers. In Chicago and New York the discrepancies were most pronounced: 62% of Chicago's sixteen- and seventeen-year-old males were in school, as opposed to 54% of the girls in this age group. In New York 60% of the boys and only 54% of the girls of sixteen and seventeen were enrolled in school. In Philadelphia boys in this age group enjoyed a small advantage over girls, although enrollments in the upper grades in Philadelphia were unusually low for both sexes. Only in Boston were girls as likely as boys to be in school at sixteen and seventeen years of age. In 1920, however, girls had been slightly more likely than boys of this age to be in school.[27]

It is not immediately clear why working-class girls in 1930 were evidently less educationally advantaged than their brothers. When only a small number of working-class children attended high school, girls were at least as likely as boys to be enrolled. Even in 1920 rough equality prevailed between the sexes in terms of school enrollments for sixteen- and seventeen-year-olds in the four cities under study. Perhaps many working-class parents in the 1920s, with limited financial resources but an increasing respect for extended education as essential to adult security, came to regard education as necessary to sons but merely desirable for daughters. Girls, as we shall see, had few persuasive grounds on which to argue for their rights to an education.[28]

And this is significant, for girls suffered more grievously than boys from undereducation. By the 1920s, even routine retail sales jobs generally required education beyond the legal minimum, and movement into high-status, "clean" clerical work could not occur without extended education. "Girls who have not had some high-school work should not be encouraged to take business 'college' courses in stenography and typewriting," warned a 1911 Chicago study. "In general there seems to be little hope for the grammar school girl who has gone to 'college.' After a weary and most discouraging search for a position, the best that is open to her is an undesirable place at a low wage from which she cannot advance."[29] White-collar occupations rarely offered the chance to master skills through on-the-job training or formal apprenticeship; employers depended on the school to teach the rudiments of clerical employment. But white-collar jobs represented for most working-class women the only escape from the monotony and physical exhaustion of unskilled factory work, however illusory that mobility ultimately proved to be in terms of promotion opportunities and wages. The undereducation of many working-class women was thus a greater handicap in the job market than the undereducation of working-class men, for whom apprenticeship, promotion within an industrial occupation, or union protection of seniority rights could make mobility or security possible within the blue-collar ranks.

The limited educational opportunities of working-class girls, moreover, placed them at a serious disadvantage in competition for the best paid and most interesting clerical employment. Working-class men rarely contended for skilled jobs with well-educated men from the middle class, but the rapidly expanding job market for clerical workers attracted middle-class as well as working-class women. Clerical workers with limited or inferior educations became, in effect, members of a vast white-collar proletariat. Although they escaped the factory in increasing numbers after the First World War, most working-class women found open to them only those white-collar jobs too routine and low status to be of interest to better-educated women.

Despite the economic disadvantages of early school-leaving, however, probably a large majority of working-class girls gladly left school to go to work. They, like their brothers, often found the schoolroom dull; the workroom was generally less rigorously supervised than the authoritarian, academically-oriented urban schoolroom of the early twentieth century. (Theories of child-centered education had had little impact on the public schools of Greenwich Village, Caroline Ware noted as late as 1930: "During the first six weeks of each school year, the front blackboard in the lower-grade classrooms of one school was devoted to the instructions, 'Eyes front, Hands in lap. Heads straight.'")[30] And although there were bright and eager children whose abilities and interests made early school-leaving a personal tragedy, most working-class pupils probably experienced school in terms of humiliation and fustration. In underfunded educational systems, which were ill-prepared to teach large populations of non-native speakers of English, failure for many children was inevitable. Throughout the 1920s large numbers of urban school children were, because of academic deficiencies, in grades for which they were too old.[31]

Against the frustrations of school stood the enticements of the job. At work, the young were given easily mastered tasks, and they enjoyed, at least initially, an unprecedented sense of achievement. The first job represented a long step toward adulthood. And the prospect of spending money, no matter how little, was a powerful incentive to go to work. For those working-class girls who remained in school after most of their friends had taken jobs, a New York investigator commented in 1911, "the dresses of their employed friends are constant sources of envy." Wage earning, moreover, generally secured for the young entry into an exciting world of evening entertainments and social life with the opposite sex. The high school student, without economic leverage within the family and burdened with homework, was often isolated from his neighborhood peers. "The young high school pupil cannot help contrasting his own daily and nightly routine with that of his friend who is employed 'downtown'. In every way his own life seems hard, confined, and unnatural."[32] Indeed, for most working-class adolescents, extended schooling was probably not a happy choice until there were sufficient numbers of working-class children in high school to cause the school to become a major focus of their social lives, much as the job had once been for most youngsters in this age group. Even in 1930, however, the lure of the job generally proved greater than the lure of the high school diploma. Most working-class youth left high school before graduation.

In most working-class communities, moreover, much school policy, even in the 1920s, assumed and encouraged pupil failure. Many teachers, school administrators and politicians were actively involved in reinforcing family decisions about early termination of education. Early in the century, big city school systems were seriously overcrowded, and frequently lacked sufficient facilities for the populations they were legally obligated to serve. One solution to this problem was to discourage extended use of the schools by working-class children, and typically, in 1912, the Chicago Board of Education opposed an amendment to the compulsory education law of Illinois prohibiting the employment of children at fourteen years of age.[33] Children who decided to leave school were usually not questioned by school authority about their decision, and they sometimes understood the ease with which they could leave as official approval of the decision to do so.[34] There was, moreover, in many classrooms a palpable cultural gulf between the teacher and her pupils. Teachers often assumed that working-class children could not master the standard curriculum, which was generally so far removed from the values and experiences of working-class children that mastery was indeed difficult for most. Even classroom discipline was made more troublesome by the failure of many teachers and educational policymakers to comprehend the cultural worlds from which their students came. Caroline Ware wrote of Italian children in Greenwich Village in the 1920s:

> The initial impact of the school upon the children often was very confusing to them. When these children first came to school, they had already learned in their homes certain habits and attitudes, and they had been punished for failure to conform to certain standards of conduct. But the school's disregard for any home training which differed in its assumptions from that of the school frequently resulted in the children being treated as though they were personally misbehaving when actually they were conducting themselves as they had been taught. The effect of having to bear the burden of blame for cultural differences between home and school often set the children vigorously against the school.[35]

And while the tensions between Italian families and the public schools were often especially strong, these tensions were evident in virtually all working-class communities. Children were not only pulled from school by family need; many were also driven from school by inflexible and unsympathetic educational policies.

The inadequacies of the schools, however, were but partially responsible for the frequent educational failure of working-class children. The attitudes toward education that many children absorbed at home ensured that school would not often be taken seriously as a means to social mobility or self-discovery. Many working-class parents, including the foreign born, expressed to investigators the hope that their children would exceed the parents' life achievements by entering a skilled trade or obtaining clean "indoor work", generally clerical employment.[36] But fewer parents believed that education beyond the legal minimum provided a reliable means to occupational mobility, certainly not sufficiently reliable to do for years without the wages of a child of age to go to work. And the very real material needs of the family meant that respect for education was more often than not a value that, however rhetorically honored, had little to do with daily life. Louise Boland More, writing about wage earners' families in New York, commented in 1907:

> In regard to child labor, there seems to be a general feeling among parents that they would like to keep the children in school longer if they could afford it, but that they cannot, and the result to be gained did not seem worth the sacrifice. This feeling was expressed by one woman when she said: "I know Josie (13) ought not to stay out of school, but what could I do? I needed the money and she had the chance." She promised to send her back to school in a few weeks, but unless the truant officer appears, these promises are soon forgotten! With an intimate knowledge of the family struggle for existence, it is easy to understand this eagerness to put a child to work as soon as possible. . . . Yet there is a universal desire that the children should become skilled workers and "learn a trade."[37]

In addition to profound mistrust of the practicality of academic eduction, a mistrust that had some basis in fact, the attitudes of many working-class parents toward their children's education were complicated by the immigrant's misperception of the culture. Louise Montgomery discovered in Chicago that many Polish parents believed education beyond the compulsory age was appropriate only to the "upper classes."[38] Polish, Italian, and Jewish parents alike expressed a fear that "excessive" education would render daughters unfit for marriage.[39] Many traditional Catholic parents retained an Old World ecclesiastical ideal of education, believing that formal schooling ought to terminate at the age of confirmation, generally twelve or thirteen. In a 1917 study Edith Abbott and Sophonisba Breckinridge interviewed the mother in a "very prosperous" Chicago immigrant family:

> When it was suggested that they were sufficiently prosperous to keep the boy in school until he graduated from the eighth grade, she seemed greatly surprised to know that children were allowed to stay in school after they were fourteen; her other children, she said, had all left the parochial school when they were confirmed, and she had never understood that children could go to school when they were old enough to work.[40]

Finally, in many families, the desire to own property was an important motive force toward early wage earning, for even when a father's wage could adequately feed and clothe his family, the parents' fear of old-age poverty made property ownership imperative. Few working-class parents, it seems, trusted their sons, or their sons' abilities, to contribute to the parents' support once the sons themselves were married. And the self-respect attendant on an independent old age was apparently worth a considerable price to the older generation.[41]

Hence, many working-class children received little encouragement to regard education as serious, future-oriented work, or to resist peer pressure to quit school and find a job as soon as legally possible. Girls in particular suffered from lack of parental support. Especially but not exclusively in immigrant families, the education of daughters was considered of distinctly secondary importance to that of sons. Girls, ran conventional reasoning, would inevitably marry and commence an occupation for which academic training was irrelevant; since social mobility for a woman depended almost solely on her marriage prospects, extended education for daughters had no practical justification.[42] The inexperienced fourteen-year-old rarely possessed compelling counter-arguments to the seasoned logic of her elders. An articulate Brooklyn woman remembered in 1922 her own particularly female experience of school-leaving:

> I started out quite alone and unrecommended at the age of thirteen to seek my first job. Having finished grammar school at that age decided that. Coming of a family in which each member would, as a matter of course, be expected to contribute his or her share to the family exchequer just as early as possible, and who considered industry almost a religion, it was the thing to do, as inevitable as eating and breathing and finally dying. It was just part of the scheme of life.
>
> I did not have other dreams, it is true. But a child of thirteen has little command over her own existence, or at least I hadn't at that time. It wasn't so much that I was ambitious as that I had a passionate love for books . . .and I begged my mother to permit me to go to high school. I

went so far as to register at one of the local high schools in order to be able to attend should mother relent by the beginning of the fall term. . . . To do mother justice, she understood, a little, my longing to go and would have liked to have me continue, but it seemed neither practical nor sensible to her. She looked at the world about her (our world) and reasoned it out. I was to earn my living of course, for a time at least, and it was up to me to get as great a return as possible in the shortest time.

Had I been a boy instead of a girl, with my natural love for my studies, mother might have struggled to send me ahead, much as she needed what little I could earn. But a girl didn't need an education. In fact it might very well be a mistake to teach her too much, for several reasons. First, she would no doubt be married by the time she was twenty. That gave her family only a few years in which to expect financial return from her, and the years spent at school would be wasted. One could get the same return, in some cases a greater return, by starting out as early as one could be hired and getting practical experience that way.[43]

These assumptions about women's education were made manifest to girls throughout their brief school careers. It was common, observers claimed, for school-age girls to be kept home to do housework and care for children if the mother—or even a relative or neighbor—were ill or unusually busy.[44] Such interruptions necessarily impeded academic progress, increasing the likelihood of failure in school with its attendant humiliation for the normally compliant girl, anxious to please her middle-class teacher. And the willingness of many parents to keep a daughter from school served to reinforce the most important lesson of her socialization: that women's primary loyalty was to the family. "The claims of the school weigh against the claims of the family," wrote Josephine Roche of Italians in New York City:

> While she is a little girl in the grades, having difficulty perhaps with her lessons, the disadvantages to her of being "kept out" a few days does [sic] not weigh an instant against some temporary family need in which she may be of help. Illness, financial loss, trouble of any kind, not merely in her own home but in that of an aunt or uncle, keep many a young girl out of school if only to lament the afflicted.[45]

The moment of school-leaving—an important rite of passage in working-class life—communicated very conservative messages about sexual identity. Although the age at which a majority of children left school had advanced from fourteen to at least sixteen by 1930, the reasons that young people left school were throughout the period expressed in terms of conventional sex roles. Because high school would not significantly increase their wage-earning abilities, boys left school to begin a life's work and become men. Girls left school to help the family, often as wage earners, and to wait for marriage. Girls might, it was true, argue for extended education on the ground that white-collar work increased their chances of marrying well. ("When a clerical worker at a local clinic married one of the doctors," noted Caroline Ware, "the clinic was besieged with applications for jobs, and parents who had been doubtful about permitting daughters to work there began insisting that they get clerical training on the chance of their getting in.")[46]

But when a family made sacrifices to insure the further education of a son rather than a daughter, the young girl had little choice but to accept an educational double standard: schooling beyond the legal minimum was ultimately justified by future occupational achievement, and such achievement for women was apt to be modest and temporary. High school for girls was essentially an indulgence, a luxury within the reach of many upwardly-mobile, working-class families who might choose to buy the prestige of clerical employment for their daughters, but it was rarely regarded as a young woman's right.[47] Mary Van Kleeck recalled a New York flower maker, an Italian girl whose wages helped to send a brother through a medical course. "'When he graduated,' she said, 'I cried all day and was as happy as though I had graduated myself. I often say to my mother that we treat my brother as if he were a king. But I can't help it.'" Van Kleeck added:

> In the same spirit the oldest daughter of a Russian family left normal school after the second year in order that her older brother might attend college. Her father was a tailor. Two younger children were in school. She explained that she wanted to go back to normal college, but for her brother a college education was "a matter of life position," while for her it was not.[48]

Thus, even in families that regarded education as a serious matter and were willing to forego adolescents' wages for an extended period of schooling, daughters were often taught that their sex made personal ambition unnecessary or inappropriate. Only when the demand for women in clerical employment became sufficiently great that continued education for girls seemed to parents a sound family investment did most working-class girls attend high school as a matter of course. And even in major cities as late as 1930, their claims to a high school education, as we have seen, were less strong than the claims of their brothers. . . .[49]

THE WAGE-EARNING DAUGHTER AT HOME

In the home, the wage-earning daughter was encouraged to understand herself and her future in terms of the domestic role. We have seen that young women usually remained completely dependent economically on their families and that wage earning did not relieve them of household responsibilities. But when an adolescent boy went to work, he rapidly assumed something like adult status: often, he began to pay board, freely disposing of his additional income; he was not burdened with domestic chores; his activities were rarely restricted or questioned. A 1911 investigation of female laundry workers offers an illustrative example:

> "Eighteen years, single, Polish. Five years laundry experience. Went to work at thirteen in laundry. Lives at home with parents and gives them wages, $5.50 a week. Father earns $55 a month, nine children in family, two besides this girl working. Brother pays $1 a week room and board. Sister earns $6 a week and gives it to parents. Rent six-room flat in brick row. Comfortably furnished and modern conveniences, but very crowded."[50]

Some observers even claimed that periodic voluntary unemployment was tolerated for sons but not for daughters.[51]

The privileges that sons enjoyed appear to derive primarily from the conviction of working-class women that men—especially young men—were unreliable, headstrong, freedom-loving creatures who had to be indulged in order to insure continued family support. Many mothers admitted that working sons were given freedom because discipline might cause them to leave home, depriving the family of needed income.[52] Relatively few working-class boys actually did so; mothers managed rebellious youths with considerable effectiveness. And husbands, secured by the bonds of matrimony and thus by the sanctions of religion, custom, and law, usually gave all or most of their pay to their wives, as we shall see. Nevertheless anxieties about the loyalties of sons were often translated into a mystique of male privilege: "Of course they don't give you all they make," an Italian mother told Louise Odencrantz, "They're men and you never know their ways."[53] Daughters, however, presented no threat. Their wages were sufficiently low that life outside the family would have been extremely difficult, and the social climate in working-class communities did not normally sanction a young woman's separate residence.

The relative freedom that many women experienced at work also helped to secure daughters to a dependent role within the family. One of the intangible benefits of employment was escape from the hot, crowded flat, from the press of domestic duties and the inevitable adolescent conflicts with parents. And this advantage was valued, for girls normally had fewer means of escape from the family than boys did. Many young women preferred work to life at home, and often failed to see in their wage earning a sacrifice justifying fundamental change in their domestic status. By the time the job became more irksome than diverting, the possibilities of escape through an early marriage were real and appealing to most young women.

That working-class daughters remained under family control in the most important matters of wages and residence does not, however, mean that their relations with parents were without conflict. Wage earning changed many adolescent girls. With employment, a young woman inevitably assumed a more powerful family role; her monetary contributions were usually accompanied by a new, if reluctant, willingness on the part of parents to bargain with her on issues of personal privilege. Most frequently, the young wage earner desired greater social freedom, increased spending money, and, sometimes, changes in the decor of the home or the parents' traditional style of life. Her parents, often deeply conservative, with close ties to an immigrant generation or immigrants themselves, generally found her demands a source of painful conflict.[54]

Contemporary observers indicate, however, that in these painful struggles over standards of female social behavior it was the young working daughter who usually emerged victorious: "Those who faithfully hold to a difficult and uncongenial occupation, bringing home the entire wage to the family and submitting to an almost patriarchal control in other matters, will demand a freedom in the use of their evening hours before which the foreign parents are helpless," noted Louise Montgomery in Chicago.[55] Indeed, with the exception of many Italian girls, young working-class women throughout the period appear to have enjoyed active social lives quite independent of direct family control. Both before and after the First World War, watchful investigators recorded—often with dismay—the gay sociability of adolescents in the industrial city. "They want something entirely different from the day's occupation," wrote Mary McDowell of Chicago working girls. "The movies and the jazz dance seem to be the only outlet offered them at a cheap rate. They turn to these and soon do not care for the quiet of home or clubs and classes offered."[56]

Adolescents in the Hull House area, Jane Addams noted in a 1909 book, were utterly fascinated by the dance hall and the cheap theater. These defined an exclusively peer-oriented world that excluded adults and eluded adult control:

> This spring a group of young girls accustomed to the life of a five-cent theater, reluctantly refused an invitation to go to the country for a day's outing because the return on a late train would compel them to miss one evening's performance. They found it impossible to tear themselves away not only from the excitement of the theater itself but from the gaiety of the crowd of young men and girls invariably gathered outside discussing the sensational posters.[57]

It was probably inevitable that working daughters should defy their parents over this sort of freedom. Adolescent girls were normally interested in the opposite sex, in clothes, in good times with friends. And it was the promise of freedom in the evening, often, that helped to make bearable long hours of a dull job. "Girls are rushing all day long," explained a New York investigator in 1910. "But in spite of [their] weariness, many seek the stimulus of exciting pleasures and thus feel that they are getting something out of life."[58]

The circumstances of working-class life in the industrial city made a social life away from home especially important. Wage earners' families usually lived in severely congested housing: the privacy essential to courtship was distinctly lacking.[59] Lacking as well was a sense of spiritual space, of relief from the pressures of a near-poverty existence. "The circle of the working girl's life is cramped and limited," wrote Mary McDowell in a private paper. "A cramped home to eat and sleep in, a cramped place for work, a cramped public dance hall, where, on Saturday night, she has her only social outlet."[60]

But it was the "cramped public dance hall," the movie theater, and amusement park that provided the space and privacy essential to many working-class adolescents. Commercial amusement places were free from parental and neighborhood surveillance. They permitted the young to explore the city and, at the same time, to observe and appropriate more daring standards of sexual conduct. Working-class adolescents in Greenwich Village in the 1920s, according to Caroline Ware, longed to escape the neighborhood in the evening. Trips "uptown" were trips to an exotic world, and the expansive youth who took his date to an expensive movie house might justifiably hope for a reward: "The distinction between taking a girl to Times Square or to the local house was pointed out by one young man, who carefully explained that if you took a girl to a Times Square movie, you could try to kiss her good night, but if you only took her to a local movie, it would be presumptuous to attempt to kiss her."[61] And once recreation had become a highly profitable business, the movie palace and the dance hall provided an element of luxury normally absent from everyday life. "These commercialized places are far lighter, airier, and more beautiful than any small home can be," noted a New York settlement worker as early as 1910. "They represent roominess, freedom, grandeur . . ."[62] Very likely the heightened consumption standards evident even among working-class families by the 1920s were to some degree shaped by adolescent exposure to this mass-produced glamour.

Certainly the adolescent girl who went freely, often from the age of fourteen, to the theater, the dance hall, or to promenade a brightly lighted shopping street was enjoying a freedom her immigrant mother had never experienced and a freedom her mother often could not reconcile with traditional requirements of feminine respectability. And there is little doubt that the increased personal power in the family that wage earning guaranteed young women helped to make this new freedom a reality. But whether the greater social freedom of adolescence represented a genuine break with the past, a radical change in the status of women in the home and the community, is a complicated question. The change is real—apparently dramatic—but it is not clear that this behavior represents something totally new.

It is well to remember that the most daring of working daughters enjoyed at best a partial freedom. She was not economically independent, and in all probability never would be. Her ultimate dependence on the protection of home and parents represented a powerful check on her behavior; so, too, did openly inegalitarian family and community standards for male and female behavior. Middle-class observers might believe that some young working girls were as free in their social lives as their brothers, but most young women were aware that improprieties could damage their ability to attract suitable male companions and, eventually, mates. Young women were not unaware that the frenetic social life—seemingly an end in itself—was also, perhaps primarily, an elaborate prelude to engagement and marriage. Noted Caroline Ware in Greenwich Village: "Various places at which dances were held were rated according to the kind of crowd—i.e., the chances that one might have of finding a good match."[63]

To some extent the new social freedom enjoyed by the working daughter simply represents an adaption of traditional courtship customs to the realities of city life. Certainly, in many instances, rebellion was necessary even to secure privacy for free association with peers, to meet available young men, to initiate properly romantic relationships with those known from school and neighborhood. The repressiveness of many immigrant parents toward adolescent daughters, argued Jane Addams, was cruel and pointless, since a changed social environment made it impossible for parents to provide appropriate husbands for their daughters. The dance hall, theater, park, and street represented the urban marriage market, definitely free enterprise in its workings but traditional in its goals.[64]

Courtship in this new setting did not necessarily generate radically altered relationships between men and women. Females remained dependent on males both in an economic sense—for the pleasures of evening entertainment—and in a more important emotional sense. In defining her life goal as the attraction of an eligible male and, eventually, marriage, the adolescent girl depended on a man to give meaning to her adult existence. As she pursued that happy goal, she was much less concerned with establishing equality between the sexes than with securing for herself the freedom to win a mate without parental sponsorship. She wished, in short, to be herself the sum of her dowry, to be desirable for reasons wholly other than those of family connection. And she largely succeeded, for personal attractiveness, stylishness, and the ability to be an easy participant in an increasingly standardized adolescent culture were, in the eyes of her contemporaries, the important criteria for choosing a bride. Her success won her greater personal freedom; it may have infused the early months or even years of marriage with a tenderness and romance her parents had no known. But his does not mean that the marriage relationship became an equitable one, or that early romance evolved into genuine companionship. Freedom from parental restraints was the single-minded goal of most young women; their vision did not normally extend beyond adolescent "good times" to include a serious reevaluation of their lives as adults.

This is not to say, however, that the experience of adolescent freedom was unimportant, or that this experience did not change young women in significant ways. The working-class daughter in the early twentieth century did not mature into the same woman that her mother had been, especially if her mother was an immigrant. But the change between generations probably appeared to be more dramatic than it actually was. Certainly, the greater freedom in dress, manners and morals that came about in the early twentieth century altered the self-image of many women, altering too their sense of what was possible in the lives they led. Young women absorbed from popular culture a highly romantic view of marriage. They hoped, according to Caroline Ware, for "'True Story Magazine's version of 'love' and the 'Ladies' Home Journal' style of a 'lovely home.'"[65] Girls who had experienced a pleasurable adolescence and who assumed that pleasure was a veritable right doubtless anticipated a measure of leisure and self-indulgence as wives. Their heightened expectations—or the disappointment of their expectations—could not help but affect relationships with husbands and children, and very likely they affected such critical choices as the decision to limit and space the birth of children. But greater social freedom without corresponding economic freedom did not fundamentally change the life possibilities of young women. Marriage—indeed, marriage at progressively earlier ages—remained necessary to most young women in our period, necessary both economically and psychologically. Their life choices reflected directly this most basic dependence.

FOOTNOTES

1. Day Monroe, *Chicago Families: A Study of Unpublished Census Data* (Chicago: University of Chicago Press, 1932), pp. 173-174.
2. W. Jett Lauck and Edgar Sydenstricker, *Conditions of Labor in American Industries: A Summarization of the Results of Recent Investigations* (New York and London: Funk and Wagnalls Company, 1917), pp. 138-139.
3. Crystal Eastman, "The Temper of the Workers Under Trial," *Charities and the Commons,* XXI (January 2, 1909), p. 563.
4. Lauck and Sydenstricker, *Conditions of Labor,* p. 248.
5. Robert Coit Chapin, *The Standard of Living Among Workingmen's Families in New York City* (New York: Russell Sage Foundation, Charities Publication Committee, 1909), pp. 245-247; Louise Bolard More, *Wage-Earners' Budgets: A Study of Standards and Costs of Living in New York City* (New York: Henry Holt and Company, 1907), pp. 269-70; Margaret F. Byington, *The Households of a Mill Town,* The Pittsburgh Survey, Vol. 4, ed. Paul Underwood Kellogg (New York: Russell Sage Foundation, Charities Publication Committee, 1910), p. 105; Montgomery, *The American Girl in the Stockyards District,* p. 7; J. C. Kennedy, *Wages and Family Budgets in the Chicago Stockyards District, with Wage Statistics from Other Industries Employing Unskilled Labor,* A Study of Chicago's Stockyards Community, Vol. 3 (Chicago; University of Chicago Press, 1914), pp. 7-8; New York *Fourth Report of the Factory Investigating Commission,* Vol. 4, pp. 1625, 1668, 1671; Dorothy W. Douglas, "The Cost of Living for Working Women: A Criticism of Current Theories," *Quarterly Journal of Economics,* XXXIV (February 1920) p. 247; Esther Louise Little and William Joseph Henry Cotton, "Budgets of Families and Individuals of Kensington,Philadelphia" (Ph. D. dissertation, University of Pennsylvania, 1920), p. 145.
6. Douglass, "Cost of Living for Working Women," p. 247.
7. Ormsbee, *The Young Employed Girl,* pp. 56-57, 63, 103.
8. chapin, *The Standard of Living,* pp. 55-57.
9. U.S., Congress, Senate, *Reports of the Immigration Commission.* Vol. 19: *Immigrants in Industries, part 23: Summary Report on Immigrants in Manufacturing and Mining.* Vol. 1, S. Doc. 633, 61st Congr., 2nd sess. (Washington, D.C.: Government Printing Office, 1911), pp. 129-130. *See also* Van Kleeck, *Artificial Flower Makers,* p. 76; Van Kleeck, *Women in the Bookbinding Trade,* pp. 89-90; Kennedy, *Wages and Family Budgets,* p. 66; Van Kleeck,

Working Girls in Evening Schools, p. 112; Van Kleeck, *A Seasonal Industry,* p. 60; Odencrantz, *Italian Women,* p. 17; Little and Cotton, "Budgets of Families," p. 147; U.S., Department of Labor, Women's Bureau, *The Share of Wage-Earning Women in Family Support,* Bulletin of the Women's Bureau No. 30 (Washington, D.C.: Government Printing Office, 1923), pp. 74-75; Leila Houghteling, *The Income and Standard of Living of Unskilled Laborers in Chicago* (Chicago: University of Chicago Press, 1927), p. 86; Monroe, *Chicago Families,* p. 150.

10. Van Kleeck, *Artificial Flower Makers,* pp. 79-80; Anthony, *Mothers Who Must Earn,* pp. 129-130 Monroe, *Chicago Families,* p. 157.

11. Robert A. Woods, ed., *Americans in Process: A Settlement Study by Residents and Associates of the South End House* (Boston and New York: Houghton Mifflin Company, 1903), p. 125; *Wage-Earners' Budgets,* p. 87; Byington, *Homestead,* p. 126; Talbert, *Opportunities in School and Industry,* pp. 16, 40; Odencratz, *Italian Women,* pp. 168, 205; Little and Cotton, "Budgets of Families," p. 146.

12. Montgomery, *The American Girl in the Stockyards District,* pp. 11, 20; True, *The Neglected Girl,* p. 41; R. R. Lutz, *Wage-Earning and Education,* p. 34; Ormsbee, *The Young Employed Girl,* p. 30.

13. Addams, *The Spirit of Youth and the City Streets,* pp. 125-126; Talbert, *Opportunities in School and Industry,* p. 14; Van Kleeck, *Artificial Flower Makers,* p. 204; New York, *Fourth Report of the Factory Investigating Commission,* Vol. 4, p. 1485; Odencrantz, *Italian Women, pp. 251-253.*

14. Addams, *Democracy and Social Ethics,* p. 46; Jane Sheldrick Howe, *All Work and No Play: A Plea for Saturday Afternoon: Stories Told by Two Hundred Department Store Girls* (Chicago: Juvenile Protective Association of Chicago, 1910), no pagination; MacLean, *Wage-Earning Women,* p. 82; U.S., Congress, Senate, *Report on Condition of Women and Child Wage-Earners,* Vol. 5, pp. 21-22, 106; Massachusetts, *Report of the Commission on Minimum Wage Boards,* pp. 7, 140; Mongomery, *The American Girl in the Stockyards District,* p. 57; Van Kleeck, *Artificial Flower Makers,* pp. 84-87; Van Kleeck, *Women in the Bookbinding Trade,* p. 100; Woods and Kennedy, *Young Working Girls,* p. 55; Anthony, *Mothers Who Must Earn,* p. 46; Ture, *The Neglected Girl,* pp. 19, 20, 104; New York, *Third Report of the Factory Investigating Commission,* pp. 150-153; New York, *Fourth Report of the Factory Investigating Commission,* Vol. 4, p. 1538; U.S., Department of Labor, Woman's Bureau, *Summary of the Report on Condition of Women and Child Wage-Earners,* p. 20; Annie Marion MacLean, *Women Workers and Society* (Chicago: A. C. McClung Company, 1916), pp. 41-42; Odencratz, *Italian Women,* p. 21; Little and Cotton, "Budgets of Families," p. 2; U.S. Department of Labor, Women, Bureau, *Women in Illinois Industries,* p. 7; Ormsbee, *The Young Employed Girl,* pp. 49-50; Consumers' League of New York, *Candy Factories,* p. 2.

15. Montgomery, *The American Girl in the Stockyards District,* pp. 57-58.

16. Addams, *Democracy and Social Ethics,* pp. 45-46.

17. Talbert, *Opportunities in School and Industry,* p. 23; Woods and Kennedy, *Young Working Girls,* pp. 46-47.

18. Josephine Roche, "The Italian Girl," in True, *The Neglected Girl,* p. 109; Amy Hewes, *Women as Munition Workers: A Study of Conditions in Bridgeport, Connecticut* (New York: Russell Sage Foundation, 1917), p. 165; Odencrantz, *Italian Women,* p. 254; Manning, Immigrant Women and Her Job, p. 58.

19. Odencrantz, *Italian Women,* p. 176.

20. Woods and Kennedy, *Young Working Girls,* p. 55.

21. Edythe Greth, "The Open Door," *Bryn Mawr Light,* Vol. 2, Summer 1926, mimeographed (Hilda Smith Papers), no pagination.

22. Odencratz, *Italian Women,* p. 179.

23. U.S. Congress, Senate, *Report on Condition of Women and Child Wage-Earners,* Vol. 5, p. 148.

24. Ware, *Greenwich Village,* p. 416.

25. "Statements of Six Garment Strikers," n.d., but c. 1910, typewritten (National Women's Trade Union League Collection, Schlesinger Library, Radcliffe College), p. 2.

26. New York, *Fourth Report of the Factory Investigating Commission,* Vol. 4, p. 1484.

27. U.S., Department of Commerce, Bureau of the Census, *Fourteenth Census of the United States,* 1920, Vol. II: *Population: General Report and Analytical Tables* (Washington, D.C.: Government Printing Office, 1920), pp. 1091, 1099, 1111; idem, *Fifteenth Census of the United States,* 1920, Vol. II: *Population: General Report: Statistics by Subjects* (Washington, D.C.: Government Printing Office, 1933), pp. 1145-1146.

28. U.S., Congress, Senate, *Reports of the Immigration Commission,* Vol. 2, pp. 190-193, 564-568; ibid., Vol. 16: *Children of Immigrants in Schools,* Vol. 4, pp. 626-627, 786-790.

29. Chicago School of Civics and Philanthropy, *Finding Employment for Children,* p. 18.

30. Ware, *Greenwich Village,* p. 329; Massachusetts, *Report of the Commission on Industrial and Technical Education,* pp. 5, 87; Talbert, *Opportunities in School and Industry,* p. 18; Montgomery, *The American Girl in the Stockyards District,* pp. 12-13; Perry, *The Millinery Trade in Boston and Philadelphia,* p. 99; Ormsbee, *The Young Employed Girl,* p. 35.

31. Montgomery, *The American Girl in the Stockyards District,* p. 16; Van Kleeck, *Working Girls in Evening Schools,* pp. 32-33; New York, *Fourth Report of the Factory Investigating Commission,* Vol. 5, pp. 2910-2911; Pennsylvania, State Department of Public Instruction, *Report of the Survey of the Public Schools of Philadelphia,* Book II: *Organization and Administration: Pupils* (Philadelphia: The Public Education and Child Labor Association of Pennsylvania, 1922), pp. 183-187; Ormsbee, *The Young Employed Girl,* pp. 16-17, 19, 20; George D. Strayer, *Report of the Survey of the Schools of Chicago, Illinois,* Vol. V: *Summary of Findings and Recommendations* (New York: Bureau of Publications, Teachers College, Columbia University, 1932), pp. 75-76, 79-80.

32. Joseph King Van Denburg, *Causes of the Elimination of Students in Public Secondary Schools of New York City* (New York: Teachers College, Columbia University, 1911), p. 185.

33. Chicago, Board of Education, *Fifty-Eighth Annual Report of the Board of Education,* 1912, in Montgomery, *The American Girl in the Stockyards District,* p. 27.

34. Bryner, *The Garment Trades,* p. 137; Ormsbee, *The Young Employed Girl,* p. 37.

35. Ware, *Greenwich Village,* p. 69.

36. Women's Educational and Industrial Union, "Industrial Opportunities for Women in Somerville," pp. 14-15; Talbert, *Opportunities in School and Industry,* pp. 43-44; Montgomery, *The American Girl in the Stockyards District,* p. 6; Anthony, *Mothers Who Must Earn,* pp. 4, 47.

37. More, *Wage-Earners' Budgets,* p. 148.

38. Talbert, *Opportunities in School and Industry,* p. 15; Montgomery, *The American Girl in the Stockyards District,* p. 3.

39. Montgomery, *The American Girl in the Stockyards District,* p. 3: Odencrantz, *Italian Women,* pp. 255-256.

40. Edith Abbott and Sophonisba P. Breckinridge, *Truancy and Non-Attendance in the Chicago Schools* (Chicago: University of Chicago Press, 1917), p. 142; Elizabeth Beardsley Butler, "Sharpsburg: A Waste of Childhood," in *Wage-Earning Pittsburgh,* ed. Paul Underwood Kellogg, The Pittsburgh Survey, Vol. 6 (New York: Russell Sage Foundation, Charities Publication Committee, 1911), p. 285; Montgomery, *The American Girl in the Stockyards District,* pp. 3, 6.

41. Byington, *Homestead,* p. 160; Talbert, *Opportunities in School and Industry,* p. 15; Montgomery, *The American Girl in the Stockyards District,* p.15.

42. Woods, *Americans in Process,* pp. 296-297; Montgomery, *The American Girl in the Stockyards District,* pp. 7, 15-17.

43. Lillian Wolfe, "How and Why I Chose My First Job, " *The Bryn Mawr Daisy,* July 8, 1922, mimeographed (Hilda Smith Papers), no pagination.

44. Elsa G. Herzfeld, *Family Monographs: The History of Twenty-Four Families Living in the Middle-West Side of New York City* (New York: James Kempster Printing Company, 1905), pp. 55-56, 142-143; True, *The Neglected Girl,* p. 35; Elizabeth A. Irwin, *Truancy: A Study of the Mental Physical, and Social Factors of the Problem of Non-Attendance at School (New York: n. pub., 1915), pp. 26-27.

45. Roche, "The Italian Girl," in True, *The Neglected Girl,* p. 102.

46. Ware, *Greenwich Village,* p. 69.

47. Montgomery, *The American Girl in the Stockyards District,* pp. 7, 8; Van Kleeck, *Artifical Flower Makers,* p. 85.

48. Van Kleeck, *Artificial Flower Makers,* p. 86.

49. On the relationship between economic opportunity and the schooling level of working-class girls, *see* Miriam Cohen, "Italian-American Women in New York City, 1900-1950: Work and School," *Class, Sex, and the Women Worker,* ed. Milton Cantor and Bruce Laurie, Contributions in Labor History, No. 1 (Westport, Conn.: Greenwood Press, 1977), pp. 120-143.

50. U.S., Congress, Senate, *Reports on Condition of Women and Child Wage-Earners,* Vol. 12, p. 99. *See also* More, *Wage-Earners' Budgets,* p. 87; Addams, *The Spirit of Youth and the City Streets,* pp. 54-55; Montgomery, *The American Girl in the Stockyards District,* p. 58; Woods and Kennedy, *Young Working Girls,* p. 53; Anthony, *Mothers Who Must Earn,* p. 45;

Odencrantz, *Italian Women,* pp. 21, 176, 204; U.S. Department of Labor, Women's Bureaus, *Share of Wage-Earnig Women in Family Support,* pp. 60, 80, 163; Hughes, *Mothers in Industry,* pp. 205.

51. Woods and Kennedy, *Young Working Girls,* pp. 53-54; Anthony, *Mothers Who Must Earn,* p. 123; True, *The Neglected Girl,* p. 51; Odencrantz, *Italian Women,* p. 179.

52. Montgomery, *The American Girl in the Stockyards District,* p. 58; Little and Cotton, "Budgets of Families," p. 76.

53. Odencrantz, *Italian Women,* p. 176.

54. Montgomery, *The American Girl in the Stockyards District,* pp. 59-60; Woods and Kennedy, *Young Working Girls,* pp. 36-37; True, *The Neglected Girl,* p. 51; New York, *Fourth Report of the Factory Investigating Commission,* Vol. 4, p. 1543; Hewes, *Women as Munitions Workers,* p. 65; Mary McDowell, "The Foreign Born," n.d., typewritten (Mary McDowell Papers), p. 5-6; McDowell, "The Young Girl in Industry," p. 3.

55. Montgomery, *The American Girl in the Stockyards District,* p. 32.

56. McDowell, "The Young Girl in Industry," p. 1.

57. Addams, Spirit of Youth and the City Streets, p. 91. On the social lives of working-class girls, *see also* John M. Gillette, "The Cultural Agencies of a Typical Manufacturing Group: South Chicago," *American Journal of Sociology,* VII (September 1901), p. 207; Bushnell, "Some Social Aspects of the Chicago Stockyards: The Stock Yard Community at Chicago," p. 306; Albert Benedict Wolfe, *The Lodging House Problem in Boston,* Harvard Economic Studies, Vol. 2 (Boston and New York: Houghton Mifflin Company, 1906), pp. 30-31; Addams, *The Spirit of Youth and the City Streets,* pp. 18-19, 46, 84, 86-87; Margaret F. Byington, "The Family in a Typical Mill Town," *American Journal of Sociology,* XIV (March 1909), p. 657; Belle Lindner Israels, "The Way of the Girl," *The Survey,* XXII (July 3, 1909), pp. 486-497; Louise Dekoven Bowen, *The Public Dance Halls of Chicago* (Chicago: Juvenile Protective League of Chicago, 1910), no pagination; Hapgood, *Types from City Streets,* pp. 131-136. U.S. Congress, Senate, *Report on Condition of Women and Child Wage-Earners,* Vol. 5, p. 120; Montgomery, *The American Girl in the Stockyards District,* pp. 32, 59, 68; Woods and Kennedy, *Young Working Girls,* pp. 106-107; MacLean, *Women Workers and Society,* pp. 109-110; illinois, Senate, *Report of the Senate Vice Committee, Created Under the Authority of the Senate of the 49th General Assembly* (n. pub., 1916), p. 495; Leroy E. Bowman and Maria Ward Lambin, "Evidence of Social Relations as Seen in Types of New York City Dance Halls," *Journal of Social Forces,* III (January 1925), p. 286; Ormsbee, *The Young Employed Girl,* pp. 6-7; William J. Blackburn, "A Brief Report of a Study Made of the Organization, Program and Services of the University of Chicago Settlement, 1927-1928," n.d., typewritten (May McDowell Papers), pp. 5-6.

58. MacLean, *Wage-Earning Women,* pp. 44-45.

59. Woods, *The City Wilderness,* pp. 101-102; Emily W. Dinwiddie, *Housing Conditions in Philadelphia* (Philadelphia: Octavia Hill Association, 1904), pp. 19-20, 26; More, *Wage-Earners' Budgets,* pp. 130-131; U.S., Congress, Senate, *Reports of the Immigration Commission,* Vol. 26: *Immigrants in Cities,* Vol. 1, S. Doc. 338, 61st. Cong., 2nd sess. (Washington, D.C.: Government Printing Office, 1911), pp. 184, 197; Van Kleeck, *Artificial Flower Makers,* p. 83; Lauck and Sydenstricker, *Conditions of Labor,* pp. 291-293; Odencrantz, *Italian Women,* pp. 15, 197; Mary McDowell, "Housing," 1921, typewritten (Mary McDowell Papers), p. 1; Hughes, *Mothers in Industry,* p. 185; Houghteling, *Income and Standard of Living,* pp. 106-107; National Industrial Conference Board, *The Cost of Living in Twelve Industrial Cities* (New York: National Industrial Conference Board, Inc., 1928), pp. 23-24.

60. McDowell, "Our Proxies in Industry," p. 1.

61. Ware, *Greenwich Village,* p. 368.

62. Mary Kingsbury Simkhovitch, "A New Social Adjustment," in *Proceedings of the Academy of Political Science in the City of New York: The Economic Postion of Women,* Academy of Political Science, Columbia University (New York: Columbia University, 1910), p. 87.

63. Ware, *Greenwich Village,* p. 405.

64. Addams, *The Spirit of Youth and the City Streets,* pp. 44-45.

65. Ware, *Greenwich Village,* p. 187.

⁓{14}⁓

How young boys grew into men (that is, come to reflect how society expects "men" to act) and young girls become women is an exceedingly difficult question to answer. The sources from which individuals derive models of masculinity and femininity are multi-dimensional and do not necessarily comport with cultural, sociological or biological stereotypes.

This does not mean that cultural stereotypes do not affect socialization. In this article Dominick Cavallo traces the complex process of female socialization that characterized the life of one of America's most notable women, Jane Addams. In the first-third of the twentieth-century Addams not only won fame and a Nobel Peace Prize because of her social settlement work and her activities to promote world peace, but she did so in a manner that symbolized to her society what an "ideal" woman was supposed to be—self-sacrificing, maternal, caring, and full of boundless love for all. Cavallo demonstrates, however, that the road to ideal femininity was not an easy one for Addams, that as a child and young woman she was confused about how cultural symbols of masculinity and femininity related to her behavior and moral values, and that her road to gender identity was an idiosyncratic one strewn with innumerable twists, turns, and obstacles. Most important, Cavallo shows that gender stereotypes are not mutually exclusive but can adaptively merge as a result of social or personal problems.

Growing Up Female in a Middle Class Family: The Early Years of Jane Addams

Dominick Cavallo

In 1880 one of the ablest members of the Rockford College debating team, twenty-year-old Jane Addams, addressed her schoolmates on a subject which in one way or another would engage the curiosity, passion and anxiety of Americans for the next hundred years, the "new woman." Addams told her audience at this small, northern Illinois woman's college that educated woman must perceive themselves as more than future homemakers and mothers. Though more "intuitive" and emotional in their thinking than men, educated women had the same responsibility as their male

203

counterparts to direct their intellectual energies into the mainstream of modern empirical and scientific thinking. Addams told her listeners that new social roles and careers for women would embellish rather than diminish the new woman's femininity. Indeed, far from denying her femininity the new woman

> wishes not to be man, nor like a man, but she claims the same right to independent thought and action. . . . (O)n the one hand, as young women of the nineteenth-century, we gladly claim these privileges, and proudly assert our independence, on the other hand we still retain the old ideal of womanhood—the Saxon lady whose mission it was to give bread unto the household.[1]

As these last lines indicate, young Addams, along with many Americans of her day, assumed that one's sexual characteristics by and large determined one's social role and moral style.[2] Woman—particularly those of the "Saxon lady" persuasion—were vessels of piety, solicitous of the weak and dispossessed, emotional, empathic, loving, maternal and, above all, incurably domestic.[3] On the other hand, men were empirically oriented, rational, curious about the world, aggressive, ambitious, profane, political, polemical—in a word, worldly.[4]

The problem with Addams' "independent" new woman was that she did not mesh with these prevailing sexual stereotypes. Clearly, Addams was exhorting her young female listeners to summon the courage to venture into what for too long had been a man's world. The educational achievements and social sophistication of educated, middle class women entitled them to a place in that world. At the same time, however, Addams demanded that they retain and refine their commitment to their "households." But how could educated women achieve and maintain this delicate balance between worldliness and domesticity? At what point would immersion in worldly ambition and realities lead to a diminution of "true womanhood" and a loss of feminine identity? This was a thorny problem, one which generated pain, anxiety and disillusionment among late-nineteenth-century educated middle class women like Addams.[5]

Some historians have suggested that the flood of reform movements which swept the country after 1890 to some extent resolved this dilemma. According to these historians, the social settlement movement in particular—in which settlement residents nursed the sick, fed the hungry, and helped immigrants accommodate themselves to the strains of life in their new land—allowed middle class women such as Addams to mobilize their considerable intellectual skills in a war against the staggering social, economic, and political problems confronting American cities. But while the social settlement was a forum for heated ideological debates about, and coldly objective sociological analyses of, urban society, it was also a kind of neighborhood household. Through settlement work female residents whose ambitions transcended homemaking found an opportunity to nurture an entire neighborhood and thus expand their "innate" maternal propensities beyond the confines of the nuclear family. In other words, the social settlement was a kind of middle ground in that it allowed talented women like Ellen Gates Starr (co-founder with Addams of Hull House), Julia Lathrop, Florence Kelley, Vida Scudder and others to think scientifically and politically (i.e., like men) but confined their thinking within a distinctly feminine (i.e., household) setting.[6]

On the surface there is much to be said for this interpretation.[7] However, it lacks explanatory depth for a number of reasons, not the least of which is that it cannot account for the large number of males who participated in the social settlement movement. We will not understand the roles played by middle class men and women in the social settlement movement if we assume the mutual exclusivity of the cluster of stereotypes embodied in nineteenth-century images of "true womanhood" and aggressive masculinity. For example, between 1889 and 1914 forty-percent of settlement residents were male.[8] Unlike their female colleagues male settlement workers like Robert Woods of Boston's South End House and Graham Taylor of Chicago Commons were not subjected to sex role identity confusion simply because they went to college. Nor, of course, did they have to face the crudities of sex discrimination or the subtler slings and arrows of the domestic piety syndrome. Yet these men saw their social settlement work in much the same light as Addams and other female reformers.

Thus, if Addams exhorted Hull House residents to exhibit a kind of maternal empathy with people of the slum, to be "swallowed" and "digested" by the people,[9] so too Robert Woods used nurturant-empathic symbols to describe the moral role of South End House residents. The resident (male or female) must not only be concerned with the welfare of those in his/her neighborhood, he/she must achieve "absorbtion" into "the momentum of the personality which is to be influenced." The settlement house should strive to revive the flow of "moral menstruum" into the city's morally desiccated streets and tenements.[10] Politically, however, Woods perceived the settlement as a "scientific laboratory" whose purpose was to devise social policy based upon a hard-headed, empirical sociological analysis of pertinent social "facts."[11] As we shall see, Addams was equally committed to the ideal of the settlement as a kind of scientific half-way house between the laboratory and society. Thus, like Addams, Woods blended supposedly antithetical feminine and masculine qualities in the ideal settlement resident.

This confluence of culturally prescribed gender characteristics becomes less confusing if we approach the concept of culture from the perspective provided by the sociologist Kai T. Erikson. Erikson defines culture as a "moral space" which both shapes and delimits the behavior of people. Culture is a cluster of inhibitions, rules, languages and values "that promote uniformity of thought and action."[12]

Thus far Erikson's definition of culture is hardly unique. But he goes on to argue that forces besides those generating uniformity are at work in all cultures. Culture not only affects how people think and feel, but how and what they imagine as well, and "it is one of the persisting curiosities of human life that people are apt to imagine the complete contrary of the ideas and attitudes that figure most significantly in their view of the world."[13] That is, the counterpart of a value is implicit in the minds of its adherents, so that wherever "people devote a good deal of emotional energy to celebrating a certain virtue . . . they are sure to give thought to its counterpart." Value and counter-value, then, become cultural partners, leading to what Erikson calls an "axis of variation that cuts through the center of a culture's space" attracting "attention to the diversities arranged along it."[14]

The stereotyping of feminine and masculine moral and social styles common in nineteenth-century America can be seen as an example of Erikson's axis of variation hypothesis. The demand that men be assertive and ambitious implied the fear that they might fall short of these ideals and succumb to a "feminine" passivity. The notion that women were emotionally and intellectually suited to be masters of the household contained, however implicitly, the fear that under certain circumstances they might aspire to be masters of the world outside the household. In short, these stereotypes contained ambiguities, and Erikson's analysis of how individuals and societies deal with ambivalence is worth noting.

> These contrary tendencies are reflected at many different levels within the social order. At the individual level . . . they are experienced as a form of ambivalence. When a person is caught between two competing strains in his cultural surroundings and can find no way to resolve the dilemma, he can be said to suffer from inner conflict. When he is able to attune himself comfortably to one or another of these strains, *or manages somehow to combine them into a new and more coherent whole,* he can be said to have achieved ego-integration.[15]

In this essay I will argue that from early childhood Jane Addams was exposed to this type of cultural ambiguity with regard to masculine-feminine moral styles, that the ambiguity was implicit in her broader cultural milieu as well as in her idiosyncratic familial setting, and that her decision to found the Hull House social settlement was, for her and her society, a creative resolution of this ambiguity. During childhood and adolescence Addams walked the tightrope of a feminine-masculine "axis of variation," and experienced intense moral and social conflict because of an inability to adaptively integrate within her personality competing feminine-masculine moral prescriptions; that is, she was not consistently sure when or how she should act like a "true" woman. But as her personal crisis deepened during the 1880s, so too did the social and moral crisis of urban America. Her response to the urban crisis not only led to the founding of Hull House in 1889, but helped her achieve what Kai Erikson calls "ego integration." In Addams' case, ego integration consisted of a viable synthesis of feminine-masculine ethical strains into a new and dynamic moral vision of urban America, one which combined a commitment to what she called a "social" (feminine) morality, with an equally intense faith in the social and moral utility of the scientific method and bureaucratic techniques (with their aura of hard-headed masculinity).

Of course, Addams conflicts and crises were idiosyncratic, and we cannot assume that all social settlement workers experienced the same conflicts in the same fashion. Settlement workers were a disparate group characterized by a variety of political and economic persuasions,[16] and further research is needed to ascertain the relevance of Addams' conflicts to the experience of other settlement workers.

Finally, a word about the methodology employed in this study. Although aspects of psychoanalytic theory are used to interpret Addams' opinions and behavior as a youth and adult, it must be made clear at the outset that no simple, linear correlation exists between the problems of her youth and her adult behavior and political opinions. Addams' behavior as an adult was not simply a product of youthful problems, conflicts, or traumas. Adult patterns of behavior are not necessarily echoes of infantile psychosexual or psychosocial "oral," "anal," or "phallic" experiences, notwithstanding the genetic approach to life histories employed by many psychoanalysts and psychohistorians.[17]

This is not to say, of course, that a person's past is irrelevant to her future. The issue is not the relevance of past to present, but the meaning of that relevance. The responses of a child to parental treatment, developmental changes, or social pressures may develop into more or less stable structural patterns of coping with inner stresses and external stimuli. These patterns, however, are neither one dimensional nor inflexible. Their meaning and value within the "psychic economy" change as the person's internal and social environments change. In short, past and present have an interactional rather than a linear relation to each other.

This means that the psychobiographer must not only isolate the subject's significant psychological patterns, but must also be sensitive to their transformations over time. In Addams' case, her life history to 1889 provided her with a repertoire of *potential* values and behaviors. At various moments in her development these potentials intersected with specific social events or psychological developments which were independent of, and not contingent upon, the events or problems of her earlier years. Taken together these two independent factors provided the groundwork for her development of a social philosophy as well as for her participation in the social settlement movement. The social events and psychological patterns of her early years did not—could not—determine how she would respond to unanticipated future events.[18]

THE EARLY YEARS

Addams was born in 1860 in Cedarville, Illinois, a small town in the northwestern corner of the state. Her mother, Sarah Weber Addams, who died two years later in giving birth to her ninth child, came from a middle class background in Pennsylvania. Although Sarah Addams entertained "no thought of a 'career' excepting that of mother and homemaker," she had attended boarding school and obtained what for those days was considered a good education for a woman.[19]

Because her mother died when Jane Addams was two years old, and her father remained unmarried until 1868, she centered upon him "all that careful imitation which a little girl ordinarily gives to her mother's ways and habits."[20] According to his daughter, John Addams became the "dominant influence" in her life. It was her idealized image of his character, behavior and status which "first drew me into the moral concerns of life."[21]

Addams' childhood attachment to her father was so intense that her nephew said it amounted to a "possession."[22] As a child she was continually abashed by what she perceived as her unappealing physical appearance, and by the physical contrast between herself and her handsome father. She was horrified at the thought that strangers might guess "the ugly, pigeontoed little girl, whose crooked back obliged her to walk with her head very much to one side," was the daughter of such a dignified, respected, and handsome man.[23] These inferiority feelings towards her father were a constant theme of Addams' childhood ruminations. One Sunday during her eighth year (it may be significant that it was the same year John Addams planned to remarry) she appeared before him in a new cloak "gorgeous beyond anything I had ever worn before." For some reason she wanted to appear particularly attractive when they went to church. However, her father admonished her that the cloak was too ostentatious and might make the other girls at Sunday school feel inferior. Sorely disappointed, Addams agreed to leave her new garment at home.[24]

The man whose character his daughter idolized was in many respects the embodiment of his era's ideal of success. John Addams was a miller's apprentice prior to settling in Cedarville in the 1840's, but he quickly took advantage of the many opportunities offered by a burgeoning economy. By the late-1850s Addams was president of the Second National Bank of Freeport, Illinois. He was president of a life insurance company and owner of lumber and flour mills as well. Politically he was conservative and very influential in Illinois politics. He was a friend and political ally of Lincoln and served as a Republican member of the state legislature from 1854 to

1870. Addams was a "practical" man who spurned political and religious extremism. His political philosophy revolved around the ideals of equal opportunity, individual initiative, and local control of the economy. As a father he has been described as "austere" in his relations with his family: he expected, and usually received, the obedience and loyality of his children.[25]

John Addams' in fact, exemplified the virtues of the nineteenth-century "rugged individualist." As a young pioneer he exhorted himself in his diary to ignore opinions and enticements which threatened his principles. He was a man who took advice "only from his own conscience."[27] Since he seldom troubled himself over questions of religious dogma, his description of himself as a Quaker assumes meaning when viewed from the perspective of his moral individualism. Nor, except in business affairs, did he offer advice to others. Accustomed to living by his private "inner light," and convinced that the great duty of man was to secure and preserve his moral integrity, " 'Honest John Addams' refused to interfere with the spiritual affairs of others."[27]

As she neared adolescence Addams' moral precepts were dominated by an idealized image of her father's character. She identified with, admired, and tried to emulate those facets of his character which made him socially and economically successful.

> I doubtless contributed my share to that stream of admiration which our generation so generously poured forth for the self-made man. I was consumed by a wistful desire to apprehend the hardships of my father's earlier life in that faraway time when he had been a miller's apprentice.[28]

Accordingly, she sought out the books, ideas, and ideals which influenced him as a young man. Whenever possible she emulated him. Sometimes her passion for emulation assumed extreme form, such as waking at three in the morning because he did so. Addams wanted to expose herself to her father's experiences in order to "understand life as he did."[29]

Her father's ideals may have dominated Addams' childhood values and behavior, but they did not monopolize them. Although Sarah Addams died when Jane was two years old, Sarah, or at least her death, had considerable impact on her daughter. Death at any age was a common occurrence in the world Addams grew up in. Of nine children born to Sarah and John only four lived beyond sixteen years of age.[31] But death's pervasiveness did not dull its impact on Addams when her mother died. Indeed, her nephew James Weber Linn said that Addams remembered her mother's final hours and, in her desire to be at her mother's side, she pounded on the bedroom door.[31]

Half a century later Addams provided indirect evidence of the impact her mother's death had on a vulnerable two years old. In 1916, at the age of 56, she published a book called *The Long Road of Woman's Memory*, a sensitive, moving description of the physical and psychological degradation experienced by Western women. In the final chapter Addams discussed an eerie experience she had while visiting Egypt some years after founding Hull House. The ancient Egyptians' religious and artistic responses to death aroused within her "an unexpected tendency to interpret racial and historic experiences through personal reminiscences."[32] Perhaps this feeling was a natural response to the artistic splendor of Egyptian tombs.

> Nevertheless, what I, at least, was totally unprepared to encounter, was the constant revival of primitive and over powering emotions which I had experienced so long ago that they had become absolutely detached

from myself and seemed to belong to someone else—to a small person with whom I was no longer intimate, and who was certainly not in the least responsible for my present convictions and reflections. It gradually became obvious that the ancient Egyptians had known this small person quite intimately and had most seriously and naively set down upon the walls of their temples and tombs her earliest reactions in the presence of death.[33]

In their tombs the Egyptians "painstakingly portrayed everything that a child has felt in regard to death." In their ardor to overcome the finality of death, the ancient Egyptians and the modern child "often become confused" and "curiously inter-related."[34] Children and "primitive" peoples shut out death, the child through magical thinking, the "primitives" by erecting "massive defences" like the pyramids.[35]

These thoughts sparked another memory in Addams. When she was six or seven the mother of a classmate had died, and the students were brought to the cemetery for the final rites. Young Addams had believed the dead went to heaven and was "totally unprepared to see what appeared to be the person herself put deep down into the ground." She became "suddenly and brutally" aware of the finality of death, and for weeks her "days were heavy with a nameless oppression and the nights filled with horror." During these painful weeks the question of what her motherless classmates could do to help themselves haunted her. But not for long. That dread was soon "translated into a demand for definite action on the part of the children against this horrible thing which had befallen their mother."[36]

What are we to make of these memories? It may seem odd that Addams' memory of her first confrontation with death's finality occurred at the funeral of someone else's mother. Nevertheless, it is understandable. The memory awakened in Egypt was that of her classmate's mother because the visual impact of the internment "suddenly and brutally" brought six-year-old Addams face to face with something she hitherto denied: the finality of the loss of her own mother. It also resuscitated the memory of her response to that loss. Her feelings were translated, as she put it, into definite "action." She was now a child of six or seven and infinitely more capable than four years earlier of feeling adrift in the absence of a mother, of feeling different from children whose mother had not "deserted" them, and of feeling vaguely culpable that she was somehow unworthy of having a mother.

Such feelings are not unusual in a motherless or fatherless six years old.[37] What is significant was Addams' capacity to cope with her crisis, to respond realistically (within the parameters allowed by her culture) to the fact that she and her siblings were motherless and her father a widower. She coped with this situation by identifying with the virtues, attitudes and duties her society associated with femininity and motherhood. As we have seen, during these years she doted on her father, adored him, and wanted to appear attractive to him. In her autobiography she recalled feeling "a curious sense of responsibility" during her sixth or seventh year. Her almost missionary solicitousness was pervaded by feelings of "feminine" sensitivity and maternity, and was made even more intense because it coincided with unresolved Oedipal tensions, and with her recent discovery at the "other" mother's funeral that Sarah Addams was gone forever.

I dreamed night after night that everyone in the world was dead excepting myself, and that upon me rested the responsibility of making a wagon wheel. The village street remained as usual, the village blacksmith shope was 'all there.' Even a glowing fire upon the forge and the anvil in its customary place near the door, but no human being was within sight. They had all gone around the edge of the hill to the village cemetary, and I alone remained alive in the world. I always stood in the same spot in the blacksmith shop, darkly pondering as to how to begin, and never once did I know how, although I fully realized that the affairs of the world could not be resumed until at least one wheel should be made. The next morning would often find me, a delicate little girl of six, with the further disability of a curved spine, standing in the doorway of the village blacksmith shop, anxiously watching the burly, red-shirted figure at work. I would store my mind with such details of the process of making wheels as I could observe, and sometimes I plucked up courage to ask for more. 'Do you always have to sizzle the iron in water?' I would ask, thinking how horrid it would be to do so.[38]

This recurring dream, along with recollections of her confrontation with death, indicate that however powerful her identification with her father's aggressive, "inner light" moral style may have been, "feminine" counter-identifications were active in Addams quite early. And while one need not be a Freudian to discern the sexual symbolism in her dream, along with the not very subtle hints that she had taken her mother's place in the household, of much greater significance is that Addams' dream conveys, albeit impressionistically, one way socially prescribed feminine roles became intertwined with the idiosyncratic experiences of a female child left "alone" with her widowed father.

This material does not indicate that Addams was neurotic. Her attempts to cope with death appear to have been adaptive—given the society she lived in. They also appear to have initiated a process of learning to cope with the inevitability of death. By the time she was fifteen, Addams saw death as a "relentless and elemental" force. "(O)nce to be young, to grow old and to die, everything came to that!"[39] But as we shall see, this was not her last brush with the anguish of death, and only the beginning of her confusion over feminine and masculine moral styles.

THE ADOLESCENT YEARS

When she was seventeen Addams entered nearby Rockford Seminary, a non-degree granting woman's college which specialized in missionary training. She wanted to go to Smith College because it was one of the few institutions offering the B.A. to women, but her father insisted she attend nearby Rockford. As usual she obeyed him.[40]

On the surface at least, Addams appeared as attached as ever to the moral, social, and political ideals of John Addams through most of her four years at Rockford. She resisted her teachers' attempts to "convert" her, because she believed that like her father she could live a morally upright life without adhering to externally imposed denominational discipline. Also, her social and political views, as expressed in her school work, for the most part faithfully reflected the critical elements of the elder Addams' world-view: hard work, personal initiative, and asceticism. As late as the mid—1880s she still throught of herself as a high tariff Republican.[41]

But alongside these "masculine" identifications "feminine" counter-identifications were reawakened during the Rockford years. Perhaps it would be more precise to say her feminine identifications attained a new level of development and began to assume a form quite alien to the pliant, would-be mother of the blacksmith dream. Addams could no more accept Rockford's conventional ideals about woman's social roles as either homemaker or missionary than she could accept its conventional religious wisdom. Her exposure to the major intellectual currents of the day, particularly Darwinism, convinced her that the study of science might open social and political doors hitherto closed to women. By studying science woman's "intuitive" mind could be trained to function empirically and concretely. The educated woman should not limit her aspirations to traditional social roles, but "convert" her "wasted force to the highest use."[42]

If Addams' vision of woman's expanded role in American society went far beyond the prevailing "domestic piety" image of women, it did so, as J.O.C. Phillips has pointed out, in terms of women's social rather than sexual roles. While higher education provided some women with skills that allowed them to seek rewards outside the home, it also expanded the scope of their alleged innate nurturant propensity. An enlarged social role for women gave them the opportunity to bring their nurturant skills to bear on perplexing social and political issues.

Once Addams began to think of feminine nurturance as a *political* force instead of a means of exerting a benign influence on children and husbands within the home, she ran the risk of open conflict with her father's moral style. In almost every way, the nurturant propensities of what Addams called the "truest womanhood" that "can yet transform the world,"[44] clashed with the moral consciousness of John Addams. The notion of feminine nurturance was far removed from the morally privatized world of her father. Indeed, the ideals of the socially oriented, "Saxon lady" moral style she increasingly identified with during her college years were explicitly opposed to the "masculine" traits of social individualism, unrestrained ambition, and a subjective "inner light" moral style. Thus, even before she graduated from Rockford in 1881, the year her father died, Addams was already reassessing her commitment to John Addams' moral style and, consequently, found herself in the midst of a struggle between antipodal masculine and feminine moral styles.

It is difficult to pinpoint the reasons why this conflict surfaced at Rockford. Undoubtedly, the college's missionary atmosphere was permeated with visions of woman's destiny as savior of a forlorn, materialistic world. And though Addams was relatively immune to the religious-messianic ambiance within which Rockford's image of woman's destiny was immured, it would be a short step for this rather secular young person to apply feminine nurturant themes to social and political issues.

But a more compelling reason for the surfacing of moral conflict in these years was that she *was* in college. Addams was a member of the first generation of middle class women to attend college in significant numbers.[45] Because she was a college student the possibility existed that she might develop skills and ambitions that would make her dissatisfied with traditional feminine social roles. In fact, her college experience might make those roles singularly unattractive, and spark a desire to explore vocational possibilities previously monopolized by men.

Had Addams resigned herself to becoming a mother and homemaker, conflicting masculine-feminine moral styles might be handled with relative ease. Her nurturant propensities would be exercised within the home and there would be little conflict in her believing, for example, in a high tariff since this was a wordly, non-domestic issue which fell within the masculine (non-nurturant) sphere. On the other hand, if for some reason Addams as homemaker opposed a high tariff, she could exert her feminine influence in the home and try to change the opinions of "her men." In either case she would remain within the bounds of her assigned feminine sphere. But once Addams confronted the possibility that as a college trained woman she might have to find a place for herself in the masculine world, the struggle between feminine and masculine moral styles could become acute. If college broadened her vocational horizons, if it created the potential for careers previously unavailable to a woman, it inevitably forced Addams to deal head-on with the conundrum of masculine and feminine roles and values. Could she be a "true" woman and work in the "outside" world? Could she adhere to John Addams' moral style and maintain her femininity? If she went into the masculine world armed with the nurturant values she said could "yet transform the world," would she thereby have to turn away from her beloved father's moral style—a style she had cherished and tried to emulate all her life?

The dilemma would be intensified by the crisis of adolescence. Indeed, the adolescent experience must have been far more painful for young women in Addams' situation that it had been for women in other classes or in earlier years. An educated middle class woman and adolescent living in the last quarter of the nineteenth-century was confronted with the difficult task of becoming something other than her mother had been, and perhaps something other than she herself had envisioned becoming a few short years before. In Addams' case, the combination of moral ambivalence and adolescent uncertainty provided the foundation for her prolonged existential crisis which began in 1881 and persisted until 1889.

As profound as her confusion over these issues had been during the Rockford years, the death of her father in 1881 exacerbated the problem. In that year she entered a phase in which she felt herself "absolutely at sea as far as any moral purpose was concerned." Following a one year residence at Woman's Medical College of Philadelphia, Addams became mired in a prolonged period of lassitude and "melancholy." To an extent her suffering derived from a chronic spinal deformity, but the depth of her depression and her profound confusion about vocational goals and moral styles convinced her that the malaise was not caused by physical problems.[46]

> However, it could not have been due to my health for as my wise little notebook sententiously remarked, 'In *his* own way each *man* must struggle, lest the moral law become a far-off abstraction utterly separated from *his* active life.'[47]

Year by year during the 1880s her inability to transcend depression, or make her moral life less "abstract," increased. In a letter of 1884 to her former Rockford classmate Ellen Gates Starr, Addams confided that her ill health and vocational uncertainty were symbols of a failure of will: she lacked the confidence to make a vocational choice.[48] Two years later she complained to Starr that her "faculties, memory, receptive faculties and all" had become "perfectly inaccessible locked up away from me." That year she reached "the nadir of my nervous depression and sense of maladjustment."[49]

Passivity and inertia were accompanied by a revulsion against the "cultural" attainments of young men and women of her class. The literary and artistic world she was exposed to at school and during trips to Europe enhanced her alienation from the "real" world. Literary and artistic endeavors seemed to "cloud the really vital situation spread before our eyes," especially when intellect was perceived as distinct from moral concerns and consequences.[50]

Addams' late-adolescent crisis lasted eight years. During this period she was unable to make vocational plans, which is to say she could not confront her future. Why? Is there a connection between her inability to face the future on the one hand, and her adolescent crisis and the masculine-feminine moral conundrum which left her morally at "sea" on the other?

There is a connection between time—psychic time—and the moral dilemmas confronting adolescents. The superego, particularly the ethical values of the ego ideal, stands for the person's future. Conscience "speaks to us from the viewpoint of an inner future," pointing in the direction of what the person should *become*, and generating anxiety and loss of self esteem should she fall short of the idealized future. In this sense, superego represents the young person's future.

Addams' prolonged time of troubles represented a need to suspend her future. It was, therefore, a profoundly moral crisis. She was unable to make a final choice between the moral styles reflected in feminine nurturance and her father's ethical individualism. Consequently, she lacked the will to be anything but passive. Not only were her cognitive and moral faculties "inaccessible," but she was pendant in time, unable to respond autonomously or actively to the "external" world. The psychoanalyst Paul Seton has aptly described the relationship between this passivity and the crumbling of parental ideals during adolescence.

> Without past or future or both, there can be no experience of duration and no sense of one's own history. The timelessness had not been an eruption of the unconscious or a decomposition of ego functioning, but is frequently a suspension of superego operations because one needs to suspend a sense of closure, which nothing can convey as ineluctably as time does. Adolescence is a psychedelic period, a time of dedifferentiation and expansion beyond the up-until-then abiding constrictions of the parental superego and ego ideal.[52]

In Addams' case, these normal difficulties were compounded by her father's death, which occurred in the midst of her moral reassessment. Feelings of loss and mourning inherent in the adolescent task of turning away from at least some paternal ideals, was heightened for her by John Addams' death. The inevitable guilt experienced by a youth who, like Addams, was reevaluating significant aspects of her father's values, was exacerbated by loss of the one who personified those values. The anxiety and fear of abandonment which often accompanies the adolescent moral reevaluation was intensified by the guilt Addams may have felt because her doubts about the paternal system of values appeared to be answered by his death.[53] For her to turn away from those values now was tantamount to having wished his death. In short, Addams could neither let go of the paternal moral style nor subscribe to it. The result was her long bout with depression.

While her crisis was not fully resolved until the opening of Hull House, the outline of her resolution assumed shape by the mid-1880's. As we have seen, nineteenth-century Americans associated John Addams' privatized moral consciousness with the "masculine" traits of rationality, inner control, and a cool, objective analysis of social reality. By contrast, the "feminine" moral style was "social" because it was rooted in an intuitive, emotional, and empathic insight into the needs and feelings of others, particularly one's children and husband. Thus, there was a spatial as well as a gender dimension associated with specific forms of moral evaluation: an "inner," personal (masculine) form, and an "outer," empathic, social (feminine) orientation. Addams, in effect, commented on this spatial bi-polarity in 1883 when she wrote

Starr that from "babyhood" the altruistic impulses of female children were cultivated, and they were "taught to be self-forgetting and self-sacrificing, to consider the good of the [social] whole before the good of the ego." As Addams took the first tentative steps in the mid-1880's to resolve her moral dilemma, her ideas about moral evaluation tended to be broached in terms of this inner-outer moral bipolarity.

For example, the spatial parameters of her crisis were poignantly revealed in her correspondence with Starr during these years, especially when they discussed religion. "I am always blundering," wrote Addams,

> When I deal with religious nomenclature . . . simply because my religious life has been so small; for many years it was my ambition to reach my father's moral requirements, and now when I am needing something more, I find myself approaching a crisis.[55]

The significance of Addams' religious speculations lies in its spatial imagery. Her letters to Starr are replete with images depicting tensions between inner (masculine) and outer (feminine) moral styles. For instance, on one occasion she confessed to Starr that the difference in their approaches to religion was that Starr desired to experience an inner "beautiful faith," while Addams felt only the need for "religion in a practical sense" as a guide to social action.[56] According to Addams, Starr needed religion to attain inner peace and harmony, while she instead sought a practical faith useful for arbitrating everyday moral problems. The inner-outer bi-polarity in Addams ethical perspective was reflected in her discussion of the Incarnation.

> I don't think God embodied himself in Christ to reveal himself, but that he did it considering the weakness of man; that while man might occasionally comprehend an abstract diety he couldn't live by it, it came to him only in his more exalted moments, and it was impossible for his mind to retain his own conception of God . . . If a man can once see God through Christ then he is saved for he can never again lose him as Christ is always with him.[57]

In other words, a God that is wholly-other and can be "seen" only through an abstract, subjective, blind act of faith is inadequate as an ethical guide. Only a divinity embodied in Jesus—in the life of a real person engaged in a network of social and moral relationships—could be relevant to ethics because the individual can "see" Jesus and use the facts of his life as a behavioral model. "I believe more and more," she wrote Starr in 1885, "in keeping the . . . facts of Christ's life before us and letting the philosophy go."[58] Facts, in short, were inexorably objective, outer and social, and thus far removed from the inner-directed subjectivity of faith.

Addams' confusion, at least on the religious front, was eased somewhat in 1885 when she became a Presbyterian. Although her conversion was bereft of intense emotional upheaval, joining the church alleviated to some degree her morbid sense of a discrepancy between "What I am and what I ought to be," as she put it. Significantly, Addams also felt that by becoming a Presbyterian she entered a community of "fellowship" that was "almost early Christian in its simplicity." This bond of fellowship allowed her to "give up one's conceit or hope of being good in one's own right," a conceit John Addams would never have surrendered. By opting for a modern counterpart to primitive Christianity, instead of becoming a Quaker like her father, Addams in effect was calling into question his privatized, "inner light" perception of moral rectitude. Instead, she chose a church that satisfied her craving for "an *outward* symbol of fellowship, some bond of peace, some blessed spot where unity of spirit might claim right of way over all differences."[59]

Perhaps the most striking and significant insight into Addams' adolescent crisis is provided by a letter she wrote Starr in August, 1879. Characteristically, Addams was discussing her moral dilemma: how could personal religious values be related to everyday social encounters? She then described a short-lived psychic experience of "peace" during which the dualisms and conflicts of her moral crisis were temporarily eased. Her description of this transient experience provides us with precious insights into the phenomena at the root of her crisis: adolescence and confusion over masculine and feminine moral styles.

> Lately, it seems to me that I am getting back of it—superior to it, I almost feel—Back to a great Primal Cause, not Nature exactly, but a fostering mother, a necessity, brooding and watching over all things, above every passion and yet not passive, the mystery of creation . . . the idea embodied in the Sphinx—peace.[60]

It is essential to understand what an adolescent torn between conflicting moral configurations meant by saying she was going "back to Primal Cause . . . a fostering mother." As mentioned earlier, the ego ideal represents the ethical dimension of the individual's future, and it is important to keep in mind that its origins can be traced to the second half of the child's first year. We have also noted that through childhood and adolescence Addams' ego ideal was the "scene" of a battle between masculine and feminine moral styles, although until her final two years at Rockford the masculine style appears to have dominated. What, then, is the connection between her experience of being pulled "back" to a primal cause and her moral dilemma?

Adolescent regression to pre-ego ideal states is both normal and common.[61] Because superego becomes less efficient in fulfilling its roles as regulator of self esteem and appraiser of behavior during adolescence, the ego, whose task is to guide the person through the maze of often conflicting demands made by her "inner voice" and external reality, is "left weak, isolated and inadequate."[62] Set adrift, with little guidance from superego, the ego may seek refuge at one or another pre-adolescent levels of development, probably a level where her doubts and conflicts were less intense. This form of regression is necessary for the youth's stability and future development, because it allows her to re-visit (in a sense re-live) those infantile interactions with parental figures which generated superego in the first place.[63] In effect, regression allows the youth to reevaluate past moral commitments in light of her present needs.

Addams' regression took the form of going back to a "fostering mother" because it is upon the "earliest wishful fantasies of merging and being one with the mother" that "the foundations on which all object relations as well as all future types of identifications are built."[64] Once the primal union of mother-infant begins to crumble around the second half of the infant's first year, and the child begins to realize, however vaguely, that she is a separate entity from what Addams called her primal cause, the ego ideal emerges as a substitute for the lost ideal state of unity. From now on the child's self esteem is based on the congruence between her behavior and the internalized "omnipotent" parental images with which she identifies.[65]

In getting back of it all through reunion with her primal cause (and in her later conversion to Presbyterianism as well) Addams recreated the experiences of union, separation and reunion which preceded formation of her ego ideal. That is, she mingled present and past. Regression and recreation allowed her to discard questionable aspects of the paternal superego, re-externalize them as it were,[66] and create the possibility of reevaluating her commitment to his moral style.

As the 1880s wore on she discarded those aspects of John Addams' moral style that encouraged moral autonomy. Paternal moral patterns were gradually replaced by "feminine" social-organic concepts of morality. Her conversion to a denomination which in her eyes evoked images of early Christian communitarianism symbolized her desire to live by "the simple proposition that man's action is found in his social relationships in the way in which he connects with his fellows."[67]

By creating what she called a "code of social ethics," or a "social" (non-individualistic) morality, the dualisms at the heart of her crisis, masculine-feminine, inner-outer, and subjective-objective, could be resolved. Addams was convinced that such dualisms caused many of her middle class contemporaries to experience the same difficulties in relating private ideals to social behavior.[68]

We must, of course, keep in mind that Addams' moral crisis was rooted in her idiosyncratic childhood and family experiences. Yet we should also remember that the moral vocabulary (if I might put it that way) of her crisis was social as well as personal: changes in her moral vocabulary had echoes in the changing structure of American society. The increasingly corporate tendencies of American business, the monumental problems spawned by overcrowded and unsanitary conditions in cities, and the social, economic, and educational problems generated by the presence of "unassimilated" immigrants from Asia and southern and eastern Europe had to affect the sensibilities of this intelligent young woman. Specifically, these conditions indicated that the country was becoming too complex and, as she would put it, too "interdependent" to accommodate the moral individualism and subjectivity of her father. The old frontier virtues of "thrift, industry, and sobriety," she later wrote, pertained only to the individual and to a decentralized economy in which "each man had his own shop." But as society and industry become more organized "life becomes incredibly complex and interdependent" and, therefore, moral values must shift away from personal needs or beliefs and toward society "as a whole."[69] It was her desire to extend her own "social," empathic, organic (feminine) morality to the rest of society, as a means of making "social intercourse express the growing sense of economic unity" in society,[70] that prompted her to open Hull House. And it is to this relationship between her personal crisis and her perception of urban-industrial problems that I will direct my final remarks.

CONCLUSION: *THE MASCULINE AND FEMININE DIMENSIONS OF SOCIAL REFORM*

Addams found an ideal forum to express what she called "both a creed and a practice of social morality" in 1889 when she and Starr opened Hull House in Chicago. Unquestionably, the social settlement symbolized for Addams the domestication of her wordly skills. She and Starr were "ready to perform the humblest" services, "wash the new-born babies, and prepare the dead for burial, nurse the sick and mind the children." [71] When discussing the role of the settlement in urban society she often employed images consistent with her adolescent recreation of union with her fostering mother. She informed Hull House residents that they must be "swallowed," and "digested" and "disappear into the bulk of the people."[72] The residents should view the city as "organic" and sedulously strive to prevent it from becoming "over-differentiated." They must persuade urbanites that "individual morality" and pride in personal achievements were irrelevant "in an age demanding social morality and social adjustment."[73] She was certain that these aspects of the reform impulse were rooted in feminine, maternal sentiments.

> Maternal affection and solicitude, in woman's remembering heart, may at length coalesce into a chivalric protection for all that is young and unguarded. This chivalry of women expressing protection for those at the bottom of society, as far as it has already developed, suggests a return to that idealized version of chivalry which was the consecration of strength to the defense of weakness.[74]

Hull House represented Addams' rejection of her father's moral insularity in favor of a social morality. On the other hand, her equally compelling belief that social settlement workers should undertake "objective" analyses of social data, constituted a rejection of the stereotypically passive, emotional female role in favor of an allegedly masculine rationality needed to make scientific, objective evaluations of people and things. Settlement workers should make scientific studies of the causes and consequences of urban proverty, political corruption and the like, because only unprejudiced, rational, objective analyses of the "facts" could uncover the underlying causes of urban problems.[75] More significantly, residents must focus their attention on the concreteness, factuality, and immediacy of the social experiences of their clients, for "we do not believe that genuine experience can lead us astray any more than scientific data can."[76]

Thus Addams' social philosophy blended a spatially outward, or communal (feminine), moral style with a (masculine) empirical orientation. Both tendencies pointed in the same direction: *each emphasized the centrality of facts, objectivity, and experience, while implicitly denigrating the personal and the subjective,* especially in the areas of morality and social analysis. "Action" she wrote, "is indeed the sole medium of expression for ethics."[77] What people did, in contrast to what they felt or thought, was what mattered ultimately, because "the deed often reveals when the idea does not."[78] What the deed reveals is the actor; and what the abstraction of personal morality and intellectual ideas often conceal are the private, insular moral precipitates of behavior. Addams' "pragmatic" interest in results, her quest to have the social settlement "test the value of human knowledge by action and realization,"[79] was a reflection of the shift from "inner" control to "external" conformity which occurred in her moral and social perspectives during the 1880s. Nor were these sentiments peculiar to Addams. As Allan Davis has pointed out, social settlement workers, male and female, exhibited an unmitigated faith in the truth-revealing power of unadorned facts and statistics, as well as in the reform potential of administrative techniques.[80]

At any rate, once the masculine empirical and feminine moral orientations converged, as they did in Addams' moral style and social philosophy, it was a short step to the notion that "scientific," bureaucratic control of the person's enviroment could determine his personality development, thus creating an atmosphere conducive to social reform. "We don't expect to change human nature," Addams said of social workers shortly before her death in 1935, "but we do expect to change human behavior."[81]

FOOTNOTES

1. Addams quoted in J.O.C. Phillips, "The Education of Jane Addams," *History of Education Quarterly*, 14 (Spring, 1974), p. 63.
2. On the issues of masculine and feminine social roles and sentiments see Peter Gabriel Filene, *Him, Her, Self: Sex Roles in Modern America* (N.Y., 1974); Ann Douglas, *The Feminization of American Culture* (N.Y., 1977); Barbara Welter, "The Feminization of American Religion: 1800-1860," in Mary Hartman and Lois W. Banner, eds., *Clio's Consciousness Raised* (N.Y., 1974); "The Cult of True Womanhood: 1820-1860," *American Quarterly*, 18 (1966), 151-174; Christopher Lasch, *The New Radicalism in America* (N.Y., 1965), pp. 3-68; Anne Kuhn, *The Mother's Role in Childhood Education: New England Concepts, 1830-1860* (New Haven, 1947).
3. *Ibid.*
4. Douglas, *Feminization,* p. 176.
5. Jane Addams, *Twenty Years at Hull House* (N.Y., 1910), pp. 94-95.
6. Lasch, *New Radicalism,* pp. 3-37; John Rousmaniere, "Cultural Hybrid in the Slums: The College Woman and the Settlement House," in Michael Katz, ed., *Education in American History* (N.Y., 1973), 122-138; Phillips, *History of Education Quarterly,* pp. 50-60; Jill Conway, "Jane Addams: An American Heroine," *Daedalus,* 93 (Spring, 1964).
7. Particularly Rousmaniere's which is extraordinarily subtle and perceptive.
8. Rousmaniere, "Hybrid," p. 123.
9. Addams quoted in Morton White and Lucia White, *The Intellectual Versus the City* (Cambridge, Mass., 1962), p. 154.
10. Robert Woods, *The Neighborhood In Nation-Building* (Boston, 1923), pp. 106-109.
11. *Ibid.,* pp. 9, 43.
12. Kai T. Erikson, *Everything In Its Path* (N.Y., 1976), p. 81.
13. *Ibid.*
14. *Ibid., pp. 81-82.*
15. *Ibid., p. 82 (emphasis added).*
16. *Allen F. Davis, Spearheads for Reform: The Social Settlements and the Progressive Movement* (N.Y., 1967), pp. 111-112.
17. For an incisive discussion of these issues, see Lois B. Murphy and Alice E. Moriarty, *Vulnerability, Coping and Growth* (New Haven, 1976), pp. 171-198.
18. *Ibid.,* pp. 171-175.
19. Marcet Halderman-Julius, "The Two Mothers Of Jane Addams," *Addams Papers*, Swarthmore College Peace Collection, pp. 3-5.
20. Addams, *Twenty Years,* p. 25.
21. *Ibid.,* pp. 1-2.
22. James Linn, *Jane Addams, A Biography* (N.Y. 1938), p. 26.
23. Addams, *Twenty Years,* p. 7.
24. *Ibid., pp. 26-27.*
25. *Ibid.,* p. 16; Allen Davis, *American Heroine: The Life and Legend of Janer Addams* (New York., 1973), p. 4-6.
26. Linn, *Addams,* p. 16.
27. *Ibid., pp. 17-18.*
28. Addams, *Twenty Years,* pp. 12-13.
29. *Ibid.*
30. Halderman-Julius, "Two Mothers," pp. 4, 11.
31. Linn, *Addams,* p. 22.
32. Jane Addams, *The Long Road Of Woman's Memory* (N.Y., 1916), p. 141.
33. *Ibid.,* p. 142
34. *Ibid.,* pp. 145-146.
35. *Ibid.,* pp. 147-149.
36. *Ibid.,* pp. 154-157.
37. Gregory Rochlin, "The Dread Of Abandonment," *Psychoanalytic Study of the Child,* 16 (1961), pp. 452-453.
38. Addams, *Twenty Years,* p. 22.

39. Addams quoted in Linn, *Addams*, p. 39.
40. Lionel C. Lane, "Jane Addams As Social Worker," unpublished Ph. D. dissertation (University of Pennsylvania, 1963), pp. 6-7.
41. Addams, *Twenty Years*, pp. 49-50; Davis, *Heroine*, pp. 20, 35-36.
42. J.O.C. Phillips, "The Education Of Jane Addams," *History Of Education Quarterly*, 14 (Spring, 1974), pp. 50-60.
43. Addams quoted in *Ibid.*, p. 63.
44. Linn, *Addams*, p. 63.
45. John Rousmaniere, "Cultural Hybrid In The Slums: The College Woman And The Settlement House," in Michael Katz, ed., *Education In American History* (N.Y., 1973), pp. 124-127.
46. Addams to Ellen Gates Starr, Jan. 7, 1883, *Starr Papers*, Sophia Smith Women's Collection, Smith College.
47. Addams, *Twenty Years*, p. 16.Italics added. It is significant that Addams used masculine pronouns to describe her moral dilemma.
48. Addams to Starr, June 8, 1884, *Starr Papers.*
49. Addams to Starr, Feb. 7, 1886, *Starr Paper;* Addams, *Twenty Years,* p. 77.
50. Addams, *Twenty Years,* pp. 70-77.
51. Paul Seton, "The Psychotemporal Adaptation of Late Adolescence, "*Journal of the American Psychoanalytic Association,* 22 (1974), pp. 797-804.
52. *Ibid.*, p. 816.
53. Rochlin, *Psychoanalytic Study of the Child*, 16, p. 461; Martha Wolfenstein, "How is Mourning Possible," in *ibid.,* 21 (1966), pp. 113-115.
54. Addams to Starr, Dec. 2, 1883, *Starr Papers.*
55. Addams to Starr, Dec. 6, 1885, *Starr Papers.*
56. Addams to Starr, Jan. 29, 1880, *Starr Papers.*
57. *Ibid.*
58. Addams to Starr, March 30, 1885, *Starr Papers.*
59. Addams, *Twenty Years,* pp. 78-79. [Italics added.]
60. Addams to Starr, Dec. 2, 1883, *Starr Papers.*
61. Peter Blos, "Character Formation in Adolescence," *Psychoanalytic Study of the Child,* 23 (1968), p. 253; Edith Jacobsen, "Adolescent Moods and the Remodeling of the Psychic Structure in Adolescence," in *ibid.,* 16 (1961), p. 180.
62. Peter Blos, *On Adolescence* (N.Y., 1962), pp. 73, 193.
63. Blos, *Psychoanalytic Study of the Child,* 23, p. 253.
64. Edith Jacobson, *The Self and the Object World* (N.Y., 1968), p. 39. One need not take this genetic sentiment literally to justify the act of regression.
65. Calvin Settlage, "Cultural Values and the Superego in Late Adolescence,"*Psychoanalytic Study of the Child,* 27 (1973), pp. 80-81.
66. Jacobson, *Self,* p. 121.
67. Addams, *Twenty Years,* p. 96.
68. Jane Addams, *Democracy and Social Ethics* (N.Y., 1902), p. 4.
69. *Ibid.*, pp. 212-213.
70. Jane Addams, *Philanthropy and Social Progress* (N.Y., 1893), p. 1.
71. Addams quoted in Lane, "Addams," p. 59.
72. Addams quoted in White and White, *Intellectual,* p. 154.
73. Addams, *Twenty Years,* p. 100; *Democracy,* pp. 2-3.
74. Addams, *Long Road*, pp. 82-83.
75. Addams, *Democracy*, pp. 64-68.
76. *Ibid.*, pp. 6-7, 273-275.
77. *Ibid.*, p. 273.
78. Jane Addams, "A Function of the Social Settlement," *Annals of the American Academy of Social and Political Sciences,* 13 (May 1899), p. 236.
79. *Ibid.*
80. Davis, *Spearheads*, p. 173.
81. Addams quoted in Linn, *Addams,* p. 416.

⋆⁅15⁆⋆

There are many ways to inflict pain. The experience of black people in the United States has been notable not only because racists have systematically excluded most of them from the physical comforts and the joys of achievement offered others, but because the unique and vital familial life-style developed by blacks has been de-valued, most often by those who do not fit the "redneck" racist stereotype. Before and since the end of slavery, ostensibly intelligent observers have insisted that the black family was essentially matrifocal, that black men were incapable of living in a stable family union, and that, therefore, black male youngsters grew up without a cohesive model of "maleness" upon which to construct their identities as breadwinners committed to the vitality and stability of their families.

That these perceptions are riddled with half-truths and nonsense is deftly demonstrated in this important article by Ulf Hannerz. During the 1960s Hannerz, an anthropologist, made a study of black family and community life in Washington, D.C. He concluded that black youngsters in the Washington ghetto do have meaningful masculine role models, even if they are reared in households headed by a female, and that while these models differ radically from those praised by white, "mainstream," society, they are nonetheless effective and adaptive.

Among other things, this article forces us to re-think the whole question of cultural definitions of "masculinity" and "femininity." What is a "male" role? Aside from obvious sexual functions, do men and women differ at all? Are all, or most, perceptions of masculinity and femininity socially-imposed fictions?

Growing up Male in a Black Ghetto

Ulf Hannerz

In this final chapter on sex roles, and in particular on the male role, we will take a look at some social and cultural data concerning the life of ghetto boys as a context for raising anew a question to which some people apparently feel they already have a satisfactory answer. The question, in its most general form, is, "What is the character of sex role socialization for young lower-class black males in a community where matrifocality is common?" It seems important to point out that we are really only raising the question and examining it. To give a definite answer to it, for one thing, one would need a degree of psychological sophistication which is outside the area of competence of at least this social anthropologist. The reason for taking another look at this complex question, then, is that some of the pronouncements on it have been somewhat deficient in their considerations of culture and social relations, and these are the facets which will be examined here.

Our point of departure is the commonly accepted opinion that a boy growing up in a household where the father is more or less absent comes to suffer from confusion over his sexual identity. First of all, the person with whom the boy ought to identify is missing, so the boy has no appropriate model for his sex role. The information about the nature of masculinity which a father would transmit unintentionally to his sons merely by going about his life at home is lacking. Furthermore, the adult who is available, the mother, is inappropriate as role model for him; if he starts to identify with her, he will sooner or later find out that he has made a mistake. ("Identification" is here taken, perhaps somewhat simplistically, to stand for perception of real or desired similarity between model and observer, leading to the observer's acting in imitation of the model.) This misidentification with mother would lead the young males to become more feminine. Some commentators on black family structure do indeed cite examples of men out of matrifocal families of orientation inclined toward feminine behavior: Dai (1949:450) writes of a psychiatric patient who ever since early childhood had wished to be a girl and who acquired such feminine interests as playing with dolls, doing house work, and being his mother's helpmaid. Rohrer and Edmonson (1964: 165-167) describe more extensively the case of Roland who stayed with his mother until her death and devoted his life completely to caring for her. He took a "womanly pride", as the two authors put it, in the furnishings of his apartment and their care, and seemed to have little to do with other men. His psychological test responses showed confusion over his sex role, and it appeared that he had largely taken over his mother's position in the home and in the family.

Cases such as these would serve as examples of rather overt tendencies toward femininity among some men coming out of matrifocal families. Very casual observations in the ghetto also lead one to believe that male homosexuality is not particularly infrequent in the community. Small ghetto boys are well aware of what a "faggot" is (but also of what a "bulldagger"—lesbian—is; there are obviously sociopsychological forces propelling toward female homosexuality as well[1]). However, all sex role confusion does not take this course. Brody and his collaborators (Brody 1961; Derbyshire *et al.* 1963) mention such identification problems as a contributing cause of schizophrenia (sometimes occurring in conjunction with homosexuality) among black mental patients. Many more writers, however, see as the final consequence of this early misidentification and confusion a compulsively masculine reaction, in that males from matrifocal families of orientation come to embrace a very conspicuously male role definition.[2] In this view, the male peer group, as the locus of anxious masculinity, has developed as a response to the male need for a forum where identity problems of this kind can be resolved. Walter B. Miller is one of those scholars who have pointed to such a relationship between matrifocality and the type of masculine expression we find in the black ghetto (1958:9; 1959:227). Roger D. Abrahams (1964:32 ff.) is another. Rohrer and Edmonson write that although the peer group is a necessary institution, it is only a poor substitute for family security and stability. Yet without the group, the self-doubts and insecurity of the male would be even stronger and more crippling; in the peer group they can be shared by the frightened and confused little boys and the tough but embattled "mama's men" they grow into (Rohrer and Edmonson 1964:167-168).

This is the kind of depiction of the process of growing up male in the ghetto which we will discuss here. It is rooted in an implicit or explicit microsociological notion of what goes on in domestic life under matrifocality. Restated in a perhaps somewhat extreme form, the interpretation is that there is a male model vacuum, and even a risk that the little boy will start striving to become more feminine like his mother. When he belatedly discovers his mistake—and this "discovery", of course, need not be on a high level of awareness—he strives hard to compensate by being extremely masculine, but traces of the identification with mother are hard to destroy, so the process of ostentatious male identity definition has to go on continuously, as a kind of rhetoric of behavior directed as much at oneself as at anybody else.

Are we to believe this?

In the face of a lot of evidence, this view of male identity development cannot easily be rejected altogether. There are points in the story, however, where modifications may be suggested, question marks inserted, and alternative interpretations proposed.

First of all one may want to point out that the problems of identification and re-identification are not qualitatively unique to the boy in the black ghetto matrifocal family. It is, of course, a commonplace and generally accepted tenet of psychoanalytic theory that infants first identify with the mother and that boys later have to change their identification to the father as the major available male. The necessity of some kind of change of identification for boys is thus far from peculiar to the ghetto; what is unusual, if we follow the interpretation summarized above, is the problem of finding someone to reidentify with. Furthermore, however, and more noteworthy, there have been claims set forth that precisely this kind of difficulty in finding a useful model is characteristic of white urban middle class in American society. Parsons points out that girls can be initiated into a female role from an early age because their mothers are usually continuously at home doing things which are tangible and meaningful to the children, while fathers do not work at home so that their role enactment remains to a large extent unobserved, inaccessible and relatively unknown. Girls can help their mothers with many domestic activities and thus get sex role training; the boys have little chance to emulate their fathers in action, partly because of the abstract and intangible nature of many middle class male tasks (Parsons 1942:605). Elsewhere Parsons views the peer groups of white middle class boys quite similarly to the way other commentators have looked at the peer groups of boys from black matrifocal families; these groups are seen as a focus of compulsive masculinity where boys reinforce one another's reaction formations (in Parsons and Bales 1955:116).

The gap between white mainstream and ghetto matrifocality thus appears to have narrowed down even more as far as the socialization experiences of boys are concerned. Yet the observers of matrifocal families cited above obviously consider this difference great enough for the boys involved to have particular problems in arriving at a satisfactory definition of their male identity. To give some opportunity for evaluating this view, we will take a look at the typical contexts of potential sex role socialization of ghetto boys from matrifocal families, starting by paying particular attention to that extreme case of matrifocality, the husbandless household.

SOCIALIZATION AT HOME

Several factors are obviously involved in determining what kind of sex role learning for young males goes on in the household. One of them is whether adult male role models are really as unavailable as they are presumed to be, although the father is absent. In previous chapters we have indicated that husbandless households need not be maleless—many of them have boarders, others include a mother's brother. In a great many cases, the boys' mothers have male friends who make regular visits; some households are not strictly husbandless in that the mother has a resident male friend, common-law husband or ordinary husband, who is not her children's father. Quite frequently, then, the adult male vacuum within the household is less than complete. It should be possible to some extent to use these men as role models, so that the boys can make some sense of what is "typically male" from their behavior. The question to what extent the boys really fashion their own behavior after these potential models cannot be conclusively answered here. As we have noted earlier, the relationship between these men and the children of the dominant woman (or women) in the household is not usually particularly close. (It may be added here too that in many cases the difference between such households and matrifocal families with a resident husband-father may not be great. In the household of Harry and Patricia Jones of Winston Street, the closest relationship is undoubtedly that of Patricia Jones and her teenage daughter. This is not at all balanced by Harry Jones' relationship to his sons, for as he readily admits, he seldom speaks to them except to ask them to run errands, keep quiet, or get out of his way. On the other hand, he is also quite attached to the teenage daughter, whom he often takes along when he goes for a car ride with a friend or when he goes bowling. The sons tend to turn to their mother or older sister for help or advice rather than to their father.) It may be that this relatively non-nurturant quality of the relationship of men to boys in matrifocal families makes it unlikely that it will be a basis for identification and role modeling, but there is also some evidence that in general, nurturance is not a necessary antecedent of imitative learning (cf. Bandura and Walters 1963:95). Other writers on identification, like Parsons (in Parsons and Bales 1955), have assumed that the person of power in the household is the major model for the children, everything else held equal. If this is valid for the ghetto matrifocal family, the mother may indeed be a more important model for the boys than any domestically peripheral male figure. Yet it should be noted here that the woman in a matrifocal household far from always is in a position of uncontested dominance over the adult males—husband, male friend, or brother in residence—and this could tend to blur her image of power for the children. In addition, we should remind ourselves that the degree of control a woman in a matrifocal household really has over members in the household oriented toward participation in street life is often quite limited. Thus even if there is no other adult in the household, the children may not become overawed by maternal powerfulness.

Burton and Whiting (1951) present another approach to the nature of identification in what they call the "status envy hypothesis", according to which identification consists of the covert practice, in fantasy or in play, of the role of an envied status. In a husbandless household, they see the mother as the person to be envied, as she controls the resources sometimes withheld from children—resources which are thus to be envied. Burton and Whiting cite the studies of Miller and of Rohrer and Edmonson which were discussed above, and accepting the interpretations of compulsive masculinity in peer groups as made by these authors, they see this as evidence for the status envy hypothesis; obviously the boys must have overidentified with their mothers to arrive at such a strong reaction formation.

However, even here the evidence from ghetto matrifocality is not quite as clearcut as it may seem. Burton and Whiting point out that the Oedipal situation is only a special case of the status envy hypothesis, and if ghetto mothers have male friends on whom they spend some of their affection because they are, if nothing else, desirable company, then there is an Oedipal situation in which the boys' object of envy is another male—to be identified with according to the hypothesis. Again the necessity of identifying only with mother is not quite as obvious as it might have appeared at the outset.

Another issue which we will leave largely unresolved is whether the relatively asymmetrical character of a functioning father-son relationship, as in a mainstream American family, really provides the optimal conditions for a son to learn his male role. As the father assumes his leader and authority role, the son becomes assigned to a complementary dependent and submissive role. The central position of an adult male in the household could also conceivably lessen the boy's chance of practicing his male role by providing too stiff competition.[3] Yet it may be that we are introducing a red herring here. First of all, father-son relationships are not necessarily forced into a rigid mold of dominance and submission; according to an early paper by Gregory Bateson (1942), there is a noticeable difference in this respect between English and American mainstream culture in that American children are encouraged by their parents toward independence and even a certain boastfulness. Furthermore, and at least as important, the child's imitation of the adult need not take place in the direct interaction with that adult. Rather, he may pick up the adult's behavior covertly in the process of role taking which goes on continuously in interaction, rehearse it to himself, and display it in quite different relationships. Even in a dominance-submission relationship can thus the submissive party learn to be dominant. Finally, as Parsons points out (in Parsons and Bales 1955:59), the socializing agent plays at least a dual role in relation to the socializee. In his direct relationship he may motivate the latter to take him for a model, but the modes of behavior he models may be taken out of quite different social contexts and relationships which the socializee may observe only as a non-participant or a participant not directly interacting with the model.

These points may lead us to doubt that the mainstream household is inferior to the matrifocal household as a male role socialization milieu as far as the influence of paternal presence is concerned. But neither can we state conclusively that the matrifocal household is devoid of potential role models, or that these potential models do not really function as such, even if circumstances are such that their modeling efficiency is probably not optimal.

Another major question is what kind of influence the mother (or any other adult woman in the household acting in some way like a mother) actually has on a boy. For one thing, there seems to be some danger here that those commentators who have most strongly drawn the attention toward the possibility of socialization into non-masculine behavior in a female-headed household have made too facile an inference from childrearing in female-headed households which are possibly quite different from those in the ghetto. Pettigrew, for instance, cites evidence from studies of white American boys whose fathers were absent from family life during World War II, and of Norwegian sailors' sons. These boys were reported as clearly more immature, submissive, dependent, and effeminate than other boys. (Pettigrew 1964:18). But here the strong possibility must be noted that these boys had very different relationships to their mothers than many ghetto boys in matrifocal families have. A housewife with few children and relatively limited everyday contacts with other adults is likely to devote a great deal of time to nurturant interaction with the children, and her relationship to them is thus likely to become intensive and quite possibly overprotective. If the boys then turn out as described by Pettigrew there is little reason for surprise. Obviously there are instances of such motherchild relationships in the ghetto; the case of Roland described by Rohrer and Edmonson and cited above may well have been one of them. But those who worry about ghetto boys becoming more immature, submissive, dependent, and effeminate on account of mother's influence might have done well to give more heed to the comment on this topic in one of the pioneering anthropological studies of black Americans, Hortense Powdermaker's *After Freedom*. Writing of a Mississippi town, Powdermaker points out that the black mother in households where there is no father either works outside the home or is busy at home with her own work, thus having little spare time and energy to lavish on her children. Powdermaker also notes that the women have outside sexual contacts and thus do not make the children emotional substitutes for a mate (Powdermaker 1939:197).

The matrifocal households in the Winston Street neighborhood are in many ways like those described by Powdermaker. They often contain large numbers of children, and taking care of domestic chores for such large households—and with so limited resources—makes it rather difficult for the mother to engage actively in very intensive emotional relationships with the children. Furthermore, many of the mothers have—aside from possible male friends—female friends among relatives and neighbors with whom they tend to spend spare time. Thus the possibility that boys would continue to identify too strongly with the mother is somewhat weakened by the quality she gives—willingly or not—to her interaction with them.

Another facet of maternal influence on the identity of young males involves her actions in instructing them, knowingly or not, about masculinity. Cannot the mother, in her domestic behavior, get her distinction between her own sex category and that of her son across to him, and thereby contribute to having him choose other models? Of course she can, to some extent, and we have already in an earlier chapter noted that the ghetto-specific public imagery about sex roles tends to influence mothers in their behavior toward their children; for instance, they appear to prefer to have daughters, and they have other expectations for their sons' behavior than for that of their daughters. This is how one single mother of three boys and two girls expresses it:

> "You know, you just got to act a little bit tougher with boys than with girls, 'cause they just ain't the same. Girls do what you tell them to do and don't get into no trouble, but you just can't be sure about boys. I mean, you think they're OK and next thing you find out they're playing hookey and drinking wine and maybe stealing things from cars and what not. There's just something bad about boys here, you know. But what can you say when many of them are just like their daddies? That's the man in them coming out. You can't really fight it, you know that's the way it is. They know, too. But you just got to be tougher."

So the women are tougher toward their sons, and they expect their sons to be tougher than their daughters. They feel this is as it should be; a boy who is not tough in his overt behavior may be ridiculed as a "sissy" not only by his peers but also by the women of his household, and his mother admonishes him to act like a boy.

This should not be taken to mean that women consciously and exclusively socialize their sons toward ghetto-specific masculinity. On the contrary, one may be quite certain that most of the instruction mothers are aware of giving is in line with mainstream norms. But even in the domestic context there is some ghetto-specific male role socialization because the women in the household—primarily the mother, but also a grandmother, an aunt, or sister if they are present—have their behavior toward boys colored by the implicit or explicit notions of the typical characteristcs of masculinity. As the socialization relationship in some ways comes to reflect the generalized relationship between men and women in the community, it is to a certain extent a question of an antagonistic socialization. The women are much more concerned to warn sons than daughters against drinking, stealing, staying away from school, and so forth, as they perceive these as male activities; they warn both boys and girls against having too much to do with the other sex, but they make it perfectly clear that boys should refrain from initiatives, while girls need only be on guard against such initiatives. One may speculate that there is an element of self-fulfilling prophecy in such instruction, as the women thus make explicit to the boys what can be expected from a male. This suspicion would seem to have much less support if all mothers were quite consistently and unambiguously negative in their response when such behavior occurs. However, like their older counterparts, young ghetto males, correctly or not, seem rather often to perceive some ambivalence and contradictoriness in the views held by women concerning what males should be like. One may in fact occasionally discern an admiring undertone in complaints by mothers about their sons, just as in those by women about their male friends. One young man in his late teens, still living at home, made this comment about his mother:

> "Sometimes my mother makes a big deal out of it when I have a taste and says I shouldn't drink and I'm turning into a bum and that kind of stuff, you know what I mean. And she acts real angry and says I shouldn't be running around so much, and one day I might get in trouble and all that stuff, you know. And then I hear her talking to all her old women friends about how I go out with all those girls and how I'm really going strong, and once she came and offered me a taste, big smile on her face you know, and then she said she found the bottle in my room a week ago! Shi-it, I'm sure I'm just the way she wants me to be. Women just want to make themselves look good, you know, so they keep fussing about you and showing off."

For an additonal fragment of evidence that ghetto women's response to shows of ghetto-specific masculinity on the part of young males is not uniformly rejective one may turn again to ghetto entertainment; there is an enthusiastic reception from the female audience, adolescent and upwards, to youthful stage personalities showing such behavior. For instance, the child prodigy Little Dion—a song and dance boy—and the youngest member of the young rock-and-roll group Alvin Cash and the Registers, both sometime stars of that series of ghetto stages known as "the chitterling circuit", had a choreography with a heavy sexual load, entered into agressive verbal contests with the emcees, and put on a *blasé* air about affairs with women, while the mothers in the audience rocked with laughter at this expression of masculinity.

There seems to be some indication, then, that ghetto mothers differentiate between the sexes in the socialization which goes on within the domestic domain; perhaps they do so more strongly than other mothers because the social cleavage between the sexes is so pronounced in the ghetto and is seen as a very fundamental social fact. This differentiated socialization can at least make it obvious to the boy that the mother is not an appropriate role model for him; to some extent it may, largely quite unintentionally, show the road to ghetto-specific masculinity. Rohrer and Edmonson note this (1964:161-162), but they attach little weight to it in their over-all view. Yet, all in all, the phenomena we have pointed to here may lead us to believe that the sex role vacuum for the socialization of males in the matrifocal family is considerably less than complete. This need not mean that a ghetto family of such a structure is just as efficient as the mainstream family in socializing males toward a culturally appropriate form of masculinity. But perhaps we may find it reasonable to doubt that the difference between them is as great as it is sometimes made out to be.

SOCIALIZATION IN THE STREET

Anyway, these notes on what goes on in the matrifocal family as far as male role socialization is concerned are of somewhat marginal importance when compared to the point at which the absent-model view of male role development can be most strongly criticized. In an earlier chapter, we cited Birdwhistell's (1966) comment on what he called the "sentimental model" of family life; Birdwhistell pointed out that much thinking about the family, among social scientists as well as among the general public, is based on an idealized image which need not be a very accurate reflection of family life in reality. One of the characteristics of the "sentimental model" is that the family is depicted as relatively self-sufficient. It is implied that most of the members' psychological needs are met in interaction with other members.

Theoretical frameworks for socialization research seem often to be based on the unquestioned assumption that the "sentimental model" is a correct representation of reality—see for instance Kagan's review article (1964:145). This assumption may be reinforced by the strong influence that Freudian thinking has had on the study of family processes; it may be, of course, that this model was closer to real life in Freud's days, and in Freud's milieu, than it may be now, particularly in the ghetto community. According to the "sentimental model" it is natural that if the family does not socialize its boys to masculinity, nobody does. But as we have already pointed out, it is characteristic of many ghetto dwellers, in particular of that segment of the community where matrifocality occurs most frequently, that they participate intensively in the social life of the street, and they start to do so at an early age. And when young boys start taking part in street life, they are exposed to a great number of males, even if there is little by way of an adult male presence at home. As we have noted before, there is no lack of males in the ghetto community, although many of them are no more than loosely attached to any childrearing household. True, in seeing the behavior of their adult male neighbors, young boys get a number of potential role models who show great variability in behavior between themselves, as several life styles co-exist in the community. This may well contribute to variation, compromises, and drift in the boys' behavior. But the men showing ghetto-specific masculinity are in a majority among those who hang out at the street corner, in the alley, or at the carry-out. Thus there is a tendency for the boys to be more strongly exposed to this kind of masculinity than to any other as they start to spend much of their lives away from the household, in territory they share with these men. Again, of course, we come back to the question whether the interaction between the boys and the men is such that it will influence the boys significantly in ordering their behavior. Here we can only note that the men are at least no amorphous mass of anonymous individuals, seen once and then never again; many of them are known neighborhood residents whom the children see practically every day. The men are also familiar with the children. As we have said before, they often keep a watchful eye on the children's play; they tell the children not to play too close to the traffic, they serve as an audience for games, they break up a fight occasionally, and sometimes they give a little instruction for instance in boxing. Now and then they send a boy away on an errand to the store, for a nickel or a dime. Such interaction may lead the boys to experience these men as significant others and perhaps as role models. And in the context of the street corner, if nowhere else, these men—or some of them, at least—may have their share of power and success which might make them seem enviable persons.

THE COMPANY OF PEERS

However, adult men are not the only role models ghetto boys may find in street life. The peer group is a highly influential phenomenon in the patterning of their existence, and its importance begins to be felt early in life. Mothers in ghetto families, both matrifocal and others, often have many children and much to do, so they frequently let older children take care of their younger siblings; particularly often, it seems, those of the same sex. This may mean that one older male whom a small boy may take as a role model is his older brother.[4] More generally, however, the boy is thus introduced at an early age to the all-male peer group. For other boys the link to such a group may be slightly more difficult to achieve so early, but even for them the initiation into the peer group context soon comes. Peer group life, of course, brings boys into contact with others of the same age, so that they can seek concealed solutions to common problems. However, the groups are not severely age graded; the members' ages span over a few years. Thus boys may participate both in groups where they are among the younger members and in groups where they are among the older, and a great many boys are in both positions at the same time, in relation to different groups.

In these groups, of course, there is intensive interaction between members. Much of the activity in the boys' groups may be viewed as "just ordinary children's play"—ball games, roller skating, and so forth. It is noticeable, however, that much of the behavior evinced in the peer group context is of the type we have described as ghetto-specific masculinity, typical of many adult men in the community. There is the concern with sex; already boys less than ten years old talk in the group context about "getting some pussy" (or "some leg" as boys in Washington started saying about 1967), and although there is undoubtedly the same kind of exaggeration in their claims of which one might suspect some of the older males, there is little question that many of the boys start sexual experimentation early, with the girls who form separate but somewhat more loosely knit groups parallel to those of the boys. Many boys also eagerly grasp for opportunities to taste liquor. A streetcorner man may let them have a little, but they many also manage to get it some other way, from somebody's house, from a parked car, or from some intoxicated streetcorner alcoholic who is in no shape to guard his belongings. There is fighting for fun or in all seriousness, and there are intensive involvements in verbal contests, as we shall discuss at greater length below. The interest in male clothing fashions is also there—this is the comment of a man in the Winston Street neighborhood on his young neighbors:

> "These kids criticize your clothes even if their own clothes are the raggediest things you ever saw. Leroy kept talking about my shoes the other day, and there wasn't one thing right about them the way he carried on. And his own shoes hardly got soles underneath!"

The proponents of that view of male role socialization which emphasizes the lack of paternal role models at home interpret these masculine concerns in the peer group in a manner consistent with their over-all analysis, as we have already seen. Peer group formation is seen to be simply a response to the discovery that the identification with mother is all wrong; the boys get together to enhance their masculinity. According to the vocabulary in which this kind of interpretation is usually formulated, this is a reaction formation of compulsive masculinity. Rohrer's and Edmonson's delineation of the characteristcs of peer group members were cited above; they couch it in such terms as "self-doubts", "insecurity", and "frightened and confused little boys". The peer group is seen as a "second-rate substitute" for family life.

There seems to be a certain weakness in this kind of view of peer group life, at least in its most clearcut form. First of all, one may wonder whether the "sentimental model" of the family is not rearing its head from below the surface of the analysis here. Is this model not a significant ideological underpinning for the judgment of the peer group's worth relative to that of the family? Despite the strength of the mainstream family model in the ghetto community, it is obvious that many of its male members, on the basis of their experience, turn the entire thing around and consider the family a poor substitute for the peer group as far as satisfactions are concerned. Furthermore, the interpretation exemplified by Rohrer and Edmonson seems to contain a fair amount of psychological reductionism in the explanation of the genesis of peer groups, and this reductionism may be open to some questioning. In this view of ghetto male behavior, it appears that the peer group is born again and again, like a Phoenix arising from those ashes of mother identification perhaps not completely burned to the end, out of a sheer psychological need for a place where masculinity can be celebrated. An alternative or at least complementary view of peer group functioning ought to be stated.

We may speculate that peer groups originally became an important component of the structure of the black community precisely because there was a need for them of this kind, and we can assume that they continue to meet such a need. It is very questionable, however, if it is an accurate representation of the continuity of the ghetto social structure to claim that peer groups emerge repeatedly independently of one another. As we pointed out above, small children are usually inducted into relationships with already existing groups of slightly older children, and there is constantly the idea of the peer groups as a natural context of children's life. Parents, neighbors, and older siblings contribute in making boys members of peer groups. The young males easily end up in these whatever are their families of origin and their psychological needs, and as ghetto-specific masculinity tends to be an idiom of interaction in the peer groups these serve as cultural equalizers for boys starting from different points and moving toward different goals. We have noted in an earlier chapter that generations of one family may show different life styles, and that peer groups may have an important influence in causing such changes; but even if boys later move toward mainstreamer lives, a great many of them have established some competence in ghetto-specific masculinity during their period of more intensive peer group participation. This may be helpful even for a mainstreamer member of the ghetto community, for instance in interaction with streetcorner men.

The craving for an arena for masculinity need thus not be *the* motive for entering into the first stage of that series of age graded groups which always exists in the ghetto. Any thoroughgoing psychological reductionism in accounting for the existence of male peer groups is, if not unfounded, at least too onesided.

At this point one may also ask whether some of the psychological characterizations of peer group members are not couched in too strong terms in order to make them fit with the rest of the interpretation. The fact that children of large ghetto families are left to take care of their own entertainment, or in the company of an older sibling rather than in that of the mother, seems to constitute an independence training, intended or not, which seems quite successful in the case of most children in the Winston Street neighborhood. (It was an early impression in field work that the small children's way of life reminded one of the *Peanuts* comic strip. Later it was realized that this was probably because most of them seemed very independent and self-confident, and handled their interaction without much of the parental mediation which has a relatively large place in small middle-class white children's play.) Thus it seems hard to vouch for the general applicability of a description of small ghetto boys as "frightened" and "confused."

The other view of how boys come to participate in peer groups, as stated above, does not explain the intensity of masculine expression, as does the reaction formation view. It is necessary, therefore, to interpret this in some other way. The most obvious explanation is again that of role modeling. The older members of a peer group tend to be somewhat dominant to the younger ones, and it is thus likely that the older ones are perceived as role models; but at the same time these older boys participate as junior partners in relationship to boys older than them. It is likely, therefore, that adult concepts of masculinity are continuously trickling down through the age grades through a series of role model relationships where the boy who is the socializee in one relationship is the model in the next. At the same time, of course, there is the direct influence of adult role models.

We may also note that peer groups may take up the masculine theme and elaborate on it in their own way because their members can easily perceive that public imagery is preoccupied with the differences and the relationships between the sexes. There is probably a less significant discontinuity between childhood and adulthood in this regard in the ghetto than there is in mainstream society. While mainstream children are often somehow "protected" from knowledge of adult interest in matters of sex, ghetto children easily learn a great deal about this topic by listening to adult conversations. Even if the adults try to avoid this, the lack of privacy in ghetto homes makes it difficult to shield the children both from overhearing such exchanges and from witnessing sexual behavior of one type or another. Besides, ghetto children are intensively exposed to the broadcasts of black radio stations, blaring continuously in many households and often out on the sidewalks as well—one index of this exposure is that they often know the texts of the top tunes word for word. The rock-and-roll tunes as well as the disc jockey's talk are primarily aimed at adults and older teenagers and have some rather obvious sexual content. In this way, too, the younger boys may learn their concern with masculinity and sex from age groups above them. Borrowing a concept from Cloward and Ohlin (1960), we may say that the ghetto community provides a relatively open learning structure for the ghetto-specific male role. . . .

THE ALTERNATIVES IN REVIEW

This chapter has been openly partisan in order to point out what looks like weak points in a well-known view of the process of growing up male in the ghetto. We would not serve this purpose well by denying or passing over points in favor of that argument altogether; it should be noted, therefore, that many of the streetcorner men out of matrifocal families of orientation have a strong attachment to their mothers, although the relationship is not free from conflicts. Fats, unemployed, a heavy drinker, and a streetcorner strongman, claims he is a Muslim and is in constant conflict with his mother who is an old-fashioned Baptist. Yet he leaves the rent for his apartment for her to keep for him over the weekend before he goes out on Friday night; "So I can't take from it," he explains with a slightly embarrassed smile. Another Friday evening, the two Preston brothers were fighting and threatening each other, in the family's house and all the way down Winston Street. The neighbors explained it in terms of their mother's illness: "They never got along good, but they're very upset now 'cause their mother is in the hospital, and so they just break down you see." Both brothers are close to sixty years old and alcoholics. One may note, also, that when a marriage breaks up, it is often the man who moves home to mother; and many streetcorner men readily condemn their fathers who left their mothers alone, although they have behaved similarly themsleves. Finally, we may observe with Abrahams (1964:261-261) that the word "motherfucker" and its derivatives are used in a curiously ambivalent way, sometimes in statements of admiration and at other times in a thoroughly pejorative sense.

In this context it should also be pointed out that there are expressions of a kind of fascination with sexual deviation. "Faggot" is in frequent use as a term of abuse among men, "sissy" and "punk" (with a less clear reference to homosexuality) more often among boys. The "Jewel Box Revue", a transvestite show, travels regularly on the chitterling circuit, including appearances at the Howard Theatre. Thus it can hardly be denied that there is an apparent concern with sex role problems in the ghetto.

It is questionable, however, whether they can all be laid at the door of matrifocality. It would seem rather likely that sex role deviations, and a concern with such deviations, could occur rather frequently in a community where ambivlent and conflict-ridden relationships between the sexes are understood to be prevalent, where one of the alternative male roles is difficult to live up to because of severe macrostructural constraints, and the other alternative is as personally demanding as the ghetto-specific role may be to some. If there is anything in the guess that such factors may also be at work, the influence of matrifocality may have been overestimated even in the shaping of those sexual deviations which ghetto dwellers themselves recognize.

The major goal of this chapter, however, is not to pose an alternative explanation of a "pathology", but to throw in doubt the existence of much of it. For it seems that the thesis which has been criticized throughout this chapter is one which constantly views the ghetto-specific male role as a kind of psychopathology; because the matrifocal family does not conform to the mainstream model and because the ghetto-specific male role does not either, one "deviation" is said to cause the other by way of first a lack of role models, then a compulsive masculine reaction continuing into adulthood. To reach this result one employs a framework of interpretation loaded with mainstream assumptions, about what a man should be like—a mainstream male, of course—and about the kind of relationship which sex role socialization needs if it is to occur—the father-son relationship, of course. In both cases, it seems likely that the normative bias makes the scheme of interpretation unfair to a community with a different social organization and different cultural norms. To a considerable extent, it seems to be a spurious claim that ghetto boys have no role models, and it seems quite possible that the ghetto-specific male role recurs in generation after generation in the manner sex roles are usually transmitted, through role modeling and in other ways. In the interpretive scheme of sex role confusion and compulsive male reaction formation, little or nothing is said about the ghetto-specific male role as a cultural entity in its own right, because adult males are largely absent from the picture until they appear as grown boys, embattled "mama's men"—the imagery here seems to have the child as the father of the man, as reaction formation seems to carry on into infinity. The existence of a ghetto-specific male pattern of behavior seems to by only a recurrent accident caused by matrifocality.

The alternative perspective set forth here and foreshadowed in the preceding chapter holds that the ghetto-specific male role is dependent on macrostructural factors not just because these make males disappear from the arena where they should be role models, but because these factors have forced ghetto men to redefine their sex role in a ghetto-specific way. After this role has been defined in accordance with circumstances, however, the man may well be the father of the child, in a socializing sense—that is, the role modeling process is at work.

The criticisms made in this chapter may well have been shaped by the typical predilections of a social anthropologist, vaguely uneasy with a more complex use of psychological arguments in explaining social forms while at the same time ready to challenge any point of view which takes cultural invariance for granted and which assumes that a certain function, such as role modeling, can only be vested in a particular structure, such as the nuclear family. Obviously the ghetto is not the most clearcut possible example of cultural difference; the picture is complicated by the fact that the community has so little autonomy but is under pressure to idealize a set of cultural norms to which many of its members can hardly conform. Thus ghetto boys, according to this social anthropological perspective, are socialized not only into their ghetto-specific sex role—rather, they are biculturated.[5] At home and in school, and through diverse mass media, they are instructed in mainstream culture, with its attendant proper behavior for boys. There are also the ghetto's own mainstreamers who acquaint the boys with this cultural alternative by their sheer presence, and furthermore there is some personal contact with the surrounding society.[6] Yet this involvement with mainstream culture on the part of ghetto dwellers provides no excuse for ignoring the facts of life peculiar to the ghetto, or taking such a narrow view of which of them are relevant that possibly significant social and cultural relationships are left out. If the kind of argument about male growth which has been questioned here is carried too far, it lends itself to facile judgments about "solving the masculinity crisis" which are more than a little bizarre. It may be claimed, for instance, that since the father is not around, the model vacuum can be filled with male school teachers and social workers.[7] Whether ghetto boys would really be given to modeling themselves on the representatives of these two categories seems highly uncertain, and one may wonder why they should be able to beat all other men outside the family out of the competition. But it may well be that the commentators who suggest such solutions see in the mainstream manner of man not just the only proper model, but also possible model—persons differing from it are seen as "confused", and thus nobody would bother to take them as models.

The lack of awareness of the possibility of ghetto-specific culture can also be seen in attempts to measure the "femininity" of ghetto males with far from culture-free psychological instruments, according to which it is feminine to agree with such statements as "I think that I feel more intensely than most people do" and "I would like to be a singer" (cited by Pettigrew 1964:19). The first index ignores the fact that black people have simply had a great deal to feel intensely about, something they now identify quite consciously in their self-conception, as embodied in the vocabulary of "soul" (see chapter 7). The other takes no note of the general great concern with music in the black community, nor of the fact that singing is generally recognized as a road to success, more open to a black man than are many others.

There is no need to claim that all interpretations of ghetto masculinity in terms of misidentification with mother, followed by compulsive masculinity, are so culturally naive. As we have pointed out above, facts remain which favor such an interpretation. We must also be aware that boys from matrifocal families may have quite different experiences, and that individuals may evince the same behavior and participate in the same institutions for quite different reasons. It may well be that neither the thesis criticized here nor the one outlined as an alternative can alone provide an understanding of how ghetto boys become ghetto men; they, and perhaps other interpretations as well, may be needed as complementary perspectives rather than as alternatives.[8] But even so—or perhaps particularly in such a case—it is necessary to point out exactly how far one single mode of interpretation may go, and what are its weaknesses. This is particularly necessary when the correctness and completeness of one of them become taken for granted, and when there is a tendency to pursue it to extreme and untenable positions, as seems to have happened in this case.

FOOTNOTES

1. Although overt lesbians are sometimes taunted for their deviance, there appears to be a rather high degress of tolerance toward them among people who know them; in general higher, probably, than toward male homosexuals. Since it is a focal concern among many ghetto dwellers to find an angle for making a profit of one kind or other, deviants are sometimes also drawn into such schemes, as this field note from a conversation between a few men shows:

> The men were reminiscing as usual about past acquaintances and encounters, and somebody mentioned Martha, a woman who used to live a few blocks away and who has had a career of secual deviations. Lee said that although one is inclined not to like "people like that", many of them are actually quite nice. Martha is now a bulldagger (lesbian), but earlier she wanted young men. Alfred, speaking about Martha: "She looked more like a man than I do . . . She had a moustache . . . In fact, she looked like a gorilla! Well, at this time when she wanted young fellows, you know, she wanted me, so this friend of mine was constantly bringing me to her house, 'cause that way we got free drinks. She always had a lot of whiskey at home. But then, you know, after that we had to get out of their quick!"

2. "Role embracement" is defined by Goffman (1961:106) as consisting of an admitted attachment to the role; a demonstration of role competence; and a visible investment of attention and effort.
3. Keil (1966: 23) suggests that this might be the case.
4. Of course, one should be aware that role-taking in interaction with same-sex and cross-sex siblings can have an influence on sex role socialization quite generally—see for instance an alysis by Brim (1958).
5. The concept of biculturation was coined by Polgar (1960) in a study of Indian boys.
6. Of course, this parallel socialization according to two sets of standards can cause some ambivalence for the boys, as the continued contrast between mainstream culture and the ghetto-specific situation does for adult men. To the boys, however, the ghetto-specific male role may seem to be more tangible, and more relevant for their own self-conception, than the mainstream role. Nor are they likely to feel the moral pressure of mainstream culture as strongly as those adult men may do who do not function as providers and family heads.
7. This is suggested by Whitaker (1967: 47); there is a curious paradox in that, as she acknowledges, other men than a father can serve as role models, but she takes into no account the possibility that they already do.
8. It should also be noted that the two perspectives are not so different as they may seem, for obviously when boys allegedly become compulsive about their masculinity they must give cultural content to their concern by modeling their own behavior on that of other men. The issues remain whether there is really a "normal" notion of masculinity (that is, the outside observer's) or adopting a ghetto-specific form.

Section Five:

Families in Crisis

One of the enduring myths of American history is that the family is a refuge from the innumerable social storms and stresses to which the individual is exposed. According to the myth, while American society stresses economic, social, and sexual competition, forcing the individual to compete and perform, the family is a haven of love and security, a "place" that values the person because of who he is rather than for what he has achieved. The family, in short, is a retreat from the interpersonal wars of the American social and economic battlefields.

To a great extent, this is nonsense. From its inception American society has been characterized by incessant geographical and social mobility. In a variety of ways, these phenomena force the individual to think and behave as if he had no family—that is, no permanent social anchor, no stable physical or spiritual "place," no ultimate security. If mobility and family stability are, to some extent, incompatible, the texture of twentieth-century life in America has placed further limits upon the family's capability to shelter the individual. The public school, not the family, now has the primary responsibility to teach the child how to navigate the stormy waters of American social and economic life; government, not the family, has evolved a vast array of programs, ranging from child labor laws and the food stamp program to medicare and social security, to secure the health and welfare of individuals. As American society becomes more complex the family becomes less capable of building a protective wall of love and security around its members.

Nonetheless, many Americans persist in believing that the family can accomplish what the American way of life, for good or ill, relentlessly denies: social and personal stability. In this Section we see families enmeshed in a host of social crises, the causes and resolutions of which are beyond their volition or control. As we read these articles it becomes evident, however, that American families have tried their best to perform an impossible task. That they have failed to produce miracles is not their fault. Families have done no worse—indeed, they have done a good deal better—than most institutions to protect and nurture the individual.

This quality is beautifully portrayed in the following article by one of America's primier historians, Eugene D. Genovese. Genovese's article deals with one of the most stressful family crises and social situations imaginable, human slavery. What was the "function" of black families during slavery? Why did slaveholders simultaneously denigrate and, to some degree at least, support the cohesiveness of slave families? What was the legacy of these families to Afro-American culture?

Husbands and Fathers, Wives and Mothers, During Slavery

Eugene D. Genovese

Husbands and Fathers

According to the slaveholders, slave men had little sense of responsibility toward their families and abused them so mercilessly that Ole Massa constantly had to intervene to protect the women and children. Skeptics might wonder how these allegedly emasulated men so easily dominated the strong-willed and physically powerful women of the matriarchal legend, but the slaveholders never troubled themselves about such inconsistencies. "Negroes are by nature tyrannical in their dispositions," Robert Collins of Macon, Georgia, announced, "and, if allowed, the stronger will abuse the weaker; husbands will often abuse their wives and mothers their children.' Thus, he concluded, masters and overseers must protect the peace of the quarters and punish aggressors.[1] "Foby," writing on the proper way to manage servants, proudly announced: "The husbands are taught by sad experience to know that they shall not abuse their better halves." Planters frequently instructed their overseers to protect the poor black women against their unfeeling husbands.[2] The great white fathers spoke without a touch of irony. . . .

Life in the quarters, like lower-class life generally, sometimes exploded in violence. Court records, plantation papers, and exslave accounts reveal evidence of wife-beating but do not remotely sustain the pretension that without white interference the quarters would have rung with the groans of abused womanhood. Too many black men did not believe in beating their wives, and too many black women, made physically strong by hard field work, were not about to be beaten. So, why should slaveholders, who thought nothing of stripping a woman naked and whipping her till she bled, express so much concern? The pontificating of the ideologues might be dismissed as politically serviceable rubbish, but the concern of the slaveholders who wrote in agricultural journals primarily for each other's eyes and who penned private instructions for overseers demands explanation.

The slaveholders needed order and feared that domestic abuse would undermine the moral of the labor force. But, then, why not require the drivers to enforce peace and quiet? Why not refrain from intervening unless plantation morale actually sagged? After all, the intervention and whipping might easily provoke a worse reaction than the incident itself. But, by asserting himself as the protector of black women and domestic peace, the slaveholder asserted himself as *paterfamilias* and reinforced his claims to being sole father of a "family, black and white." In this light, the efforts of the drivers or plantation preachers or other prestigious slaves to restrain abusive husbands represented an attempt by the quarters to rule themselves.

When a driver intervened and usurped the role of *paterfamilias,* he may have thereby underscored the paternalist ideology of the plantation; but, by keeping the white man out of the picture, he set limits to the slaves' internalization of racist norms.

The slaveholders intuitively grasped something else. A black man whose authority in the house rested on his use of force may have picked the worst way to assert himself, but in a world in which so much conspired to reduce men to "guests in the house" and to emasculate them, even this kind of assertion, however unmanly by external standards, held some positive meaning.

The slave women did not often welcome Ole Massa's protection. They preferred to take care of themselves or, when they needed help, to turn to their fathers, brothers, or friends. As any policeman in a lower-class neighborhood, white or black, knows, a woman who is getting the worst of a street fight with her man and who is screaming for help usually wants relief from the blows; she does not want her man subjected to an outsider's righteous indignation and may well join him in repelling an attack. When Ellen Botts's mother—the much-respected Mammy of a sugar plantation—showed up with a lump on her head inflicted by her hot-tempered husband, she told her master that she had had an accident. She would deal with her husband herself and certainly did not want to see him whipped. When James Redpath asked a slave woman in South Carolina if slave women expected to leave their husbands when they fell out, he got the contemptuous answer meddlers in other people's love lives ought to expect: "Oh, no, not allus; we sometimes quarrel in de daytime and make up at night."[3]

The slaveholders did not want their slaves to abuse each other. Rather, they could not abide their slaves' living together without outside interference. They therefore read the signs as they wished. The slaves, for their part, did not live like saints but did take care of each other quite as well as any other people raised in a less than genteel world.

The slaveholders, in their tender concern for black women who suffered abuse from their husbands, remained curiously silent about those who fell back on their husbands' protection. Laura Bell's father won her mother's hand by volunteering to take a whipping in her place. Most slaveholders had the sense to prohibit such gallantry, but no few black men braved their wrath by interposing themselves between their wives or daughters and the white man who sought to harm them.[4] Not only husbands but male friends killed, beat, or drove off overseers for whipping their women.[5]

Black women fell victims to white lust, but many escaped because the whites knew they had black men who would rather die than stand idly by. In some cases black men protected their women and got off with a whipping or no punishment at all: in other cases they sacrificed their lives. Knowledge of their inevitable response prevented many outrages from happening.[6] Eliza Frances Andrews need not have expressed surprise when one of the first acts of the freedmen in Georgia was to organize a "Sons of Benevolence" to protect "female virtue." And Kate Stone should have known better than to say of the battle of Milliken's Bend, "It is said the Negro regiments fought like demons but we cannot believe that. We know from long experience they are cowards.[7]

In view of the risks, the wonder is not that more black men did not defend their women but that so many did, especially since the women had to caution restraint or risk their men's lives. With children and each other to consider, the slaves had to strengthen each other in a course of acceptance of what could be prevented only at too hight a price. If submission to outrage sometimes revealed cowardice, so did it often reveal a far greater strength than most men and women are ever asked—or ever should be asked—to display.[8]

Even short of death, the pride of assertive manliness could reach fearful proportions. An overseer tried to rape Josiah Henson's mother but was overpowered by his father. Yielding to his wife's pleas and the overseer's promise of no reprisal, the enraged slave desisted from killing him. The overseer broke his promise. Henson's father suffered one hundred lashes and had an ear nailed to the whipping post and then severed.

> Previous to this affair my father, from all I can learn, had been a good-humored and light-hearted man, the ringleader in all fun at corn-huskings and Christmas buffoonery. His banjo was the life of the farm, and all night long at a merry-making would he play on it while the other Negroes danced. But from this hour he became utterly changed. Sullen, morose, and dogged, nothing could be done with him.

Threats of being sold south had no effect on him. The thoughts running through his mind as he came to prefer separation from the wife he loved to enduring life there must remain a matter of speculation. His master sold him to Alabama, and he was never heard from again.[9]

What kind of evidence and how much of it is needed to convince skeptics that the essential story of black men in slavery lay with the many who overcame every possible hardship and humiliation to stand fast to their families? Elizabeth Keckley's father, sold away a long distance from her mother, returned to visit his family every Christmas and Easter. Later sent to the Caribbean, he regularly exchanged letters with the wife he was never to see again. A slave in Georgia prevailed on his master to sell him to Jamaica so that he could find his wife, despite warnings that his chances of finding her on so large an island were remote. Renty, a slave on that George Noble Jones plantation in Florida, divorced his wife and married again only when his new favorite promised to take care of his children. George Payne of Virginia wept when his child was sold away from him, and another slave in Virginia chopped his left hand off with a hatchet to prevent being sold away from his son. Stepfathers everywhere reportedly treated the newly acquired children as if they had been their own. Freedmen in Louisiana stubbornly resisted impressment by the Union army because, as their old master explained, their families were suffering. John Blassingame has convincingly demonstrated how the slave men of the Union border states flocked into the army once their families were guaranteed freedom in return for their enlistment.[10]

Slave men provided for their families to a greater extent than has been appreciated. The overwhelming majority of the masters gave their slaves enough to eat but did not err on the side of generosity; and the fare was coarse and monotonous. The slaves would have suffered much more than many in fact did from malnutrition and the hidden hungers of nutritional deficiencies if the men had not taken the initiative to hunt and trap animals. "My old daddy," recalled Louisa Adams of North Carolina, "partly raised his chilluns on game. He caught rabbits, coons an' possums. He would work all day and hunt at night. . . ."[11] The men took pride in their effort. Edgar Bendy of Texas boasted, "I used to be plumb give up to be de best hunter in Tyler and in de whole country. I kilt more deer dan any other man in de country. . . . " And the boys took pride in their fathers, grandfathers, and uncles. A half century later John Glover of South Carolina remembered his grandfather as "a great 'possum hunter."[12] The men had some justification for their boasting.

Trapping wild turkeys, for example, required considerable skill; not everyone could construct a "rabbit gum" equal to the guile of the rabbits; and running down the quick, battling raccoon took pluck.[13] For a boy growing up, the moment when his father thought him ready to join in the hunting and to learn to trap was a much-sought recognition of his own manhood.

For the slaves fishing was much more than the lazy pastime of white plantation romance. They varied monotonous and inadequate diets by catching fish, crabs, and gathering oysters, clams, conchs, turtles, terrapins, shrimp, and prawns, and anything else available. The coastal lowlands of Maryland, Virginia, South Carolina, and Georgia as well as the bayou country of Louisiana offered special opportunities, but most regions had some kind of stream with something worth catching. According to Mrs. Schoolcraft, every black man on the South Carolina coast made his own canoe "by burning the inside, and then scraping out a great oaken log, some ten or twelve feet long."[14]

The archaeological excavation of a slave cabin in Georgia by Robert Ascher and Charles H. Fairbanks turned up evidence of a wide assortment of animals, birds, and fish. "The animals," they write, "were young, old, and in-between, suggesting that their pursuer took whatever he could find." Their study supports the insistence of ex-slaves and antebellum travelers that the men put much effort into supplementing their families' diet. As they conclude: "In sum, through excavation, we have learned that the people in one cabin managed to add considerable protein to their diet, apparently through their own efforts."[15]

Many slaves had Saturday afternoons free for hunting and trapping, but many more had to find time after a long day's work during the week. A free afternoon did not always avail anyway since opossum and raccoon, the slaves' great favorites, run at night. When the masters allowed the slaves to roam about at night, they turned the hunt into a great collective sport and shared the spoils. When the masters frowned on this activity, they had to go singly or in pairs and risk punishment. Although few masters wanted their slaves to run about at night instead of resting for the next day's work, most saw the advantage in allowing the slaves to get some of their own food, and the masters also needed these efforts to help control the ravages of raccoons, squirrels, and crows in their fields. . . .[16]

Sensible masters actually encouraged a limited sexual division of labor among their slaves and saw some advantage in strengthening the power of the male in the household. Many planters identified slave women by their husbands' names: Tom's Sue or Joe's Mary. A strong man who kept his wife and children in line contributed to social peace and good order. William Ervin of Lowndes Country, Mississippi, laid down the following as the second point in his Rules for the Plantation:

> 2nd. Each family to live in their own house. The husband to provide fire wood and see that they are all provided for and wait on his wife. The wife to cook & wash for the husband and her children and attend to the mending of clothes. Failure on either part when proven shall and must be corrected by words first but if not reformed to be corrected by the Whip.[17]

Hugh Davis, whose scrupulous biographer considers him typical of the bigger planters of the Alabama Black Belt, included among his rules:

> Men alone are required to feed and perform all lot work [animal care] at

the close of every day. The women are required, when work is done in the field, to sweep their houses and yards and receive their supper [communally prepared] at the call of the cook, after which they may sew or knit but not leave their houses otherwise.[18]

On the large plantations, which displayed a greater division of labor than the small plantations and farms, men did heavy work on rainy days or in slack periods while the women sewed, cleaned up the grounds, and did assorted lighter tasks. Even then, the foreman of the women's crew was often a man.[19]

This division of labor and the strengthened male role within it, which so many planters encouraged, helped shape the kind of men who might prove more independent than slaves were supposed to be. The slaveholders, therefore, here as elsewhere, had to live with a contradiction: dispirited slave men could not keep the good order necessary for efficiency and, besides, might become troublesome in their very irresponsibility; spirited slaves with a sense of being men would help keep good order and render the plantation more efficient, but they too, in different ways, might become troublesome in their very responsibility. Slaves remained a troublesome property.

Meanwhile, in ways wholesome and not so wholesome, the men asserted themselves. If Nancy Williams's mother spent extra hours in making quilts for the family, her father built the shelves and closets to house them. If Mary Ann Lipscomb's mother had to weave when tired from a day's labor, her father did his best to help. Other men asserted themselves at the expense of their wives by contemptuously refusing to do "women's work."[20]

The struggle to become and to remain men, not the "boys" their masters called them, included some unattractive manifestations of male aggression. The freedmen, Miss Botume noted, spoke affectionately of their wives but in such a way as to suggest that they were property, virtually slaves, helpless children who had to be taught everything.[21] Almost everywhere in the south the freedmen demanded wages high enough to allow them to support their families. They wanted their women home with the children, and the women supported the demand vigorously. Many women may have preferred housekeeping to the rigors of farm work and thought they were choosing an easier life, but most seem to have felt a great need to give their children a full-time mother. In any case, these tough women, who so often proved militant during the political struggles of Reconstruction, displayed not merely a willingness but a desire to defer to their husbands both at home and in the new political world they were entering together. For all the deformations introduced by slavery, they knew that many of their men were strong and dependable and wanted the others to become so.

The slaveholders deprived black men of the role of provider; refused to dignify their marriages or legitimize their issue; compelled them to submit to physical abuse in the presence of their women and children; made them choose between remaining silent while their wives and daughters were raped or seduced and risking death; and threatened them with separation from their family at any moment. Many men caved in under the onslaught and became irresponsible husbands and indifferent fathers. The women who had to contend with such men sometimes showed stubborn cheerfulness and sometimes raging bitterness; they raised the children, maintained order at home, and rotated men in and out of bed. Enough men and women fell into this pattern to give rise to the legends of the matriarchy, the emasculated but brutal male, and the fatherless children. These legends did not merely arise from contemporary proslavery propagandistic fantasies or from the ethnocentricity of later historians and social scientists; they rest on unquestionable evidence, which, being partial, has misled its interpreters.

The inability of the slave men to protect their women against the insults and abuse of masters and overseers hardly put them in a unique or unusual position. For centuries, the mass of European serfs and dependent peasants suffered such indignities at the hands of lords and warlords, yet no one questions their masculinity. Men cannot define the tests of masculinity in a manner abstracted from the web of class power in which they find themselves; women do not normally expect their men to get themselves killed in a fruitless attempt to prevent what cannot be prevented. In a paternalistic system men defer to their lords in a variety of ways without losing a sense of themselves as men in relation to their women. Although slave men suffered deeply, their is no evidence that most felt themselves less than men. But white racism did undermine them in other ways. It created among them and their women a tendency to doubt that black men could play all the roles that white could, but these generally concerned matters of political, economic, and intellectual leadership rather than male-female relations.

Many men and women resisted the "infantilization," "emasculation," and "dehumanization" inherent in the system's aggression against the slave family. How many? No one will ever know. At issue is the quality of human relationships, which cannot be measured. But these exists as much evidence of resistance and of a struggle for a decent family life as of demoralization. A brutal social system broke the spirit of many and rendered others less responsible than human beings ought to be. But enough men came out of this test of fire whole, if necessarily scarred, to demonstrate that the slaves had powerful inner resources. A terrible system of human oppression took a heavy toll of its victims, but their collective accomplishment in resisting the system constitutes a heroic story. That resistance provided black people with solid norms for family life and role differentiation, even if circumstances caused a dangerously high lapse from those norms. The slaves from their own experience had come to value a two-parent, male-centered household, no matter how much difficulty they had in realizing the ideal.

The role of the male slave as husband and father therefore requires a fresh look. If many men lived up to their assigned irresponsibility, others, probably a majority, overcame all obstacles and provided a positive male image for their wives and children. An ex-slave recalled his boyhood:

> I loved my father. He was such a good man. He was a good carpenter and could do anything. My mother just rejoiced in him. Whenever he sat down to talk she just sat and looked and listened. She would never cross him for anything. If they went to church together she always waited for him to interpret what the preacher had said or what he thought was the will of God. I was small but I noticed all of these things. I sometimes think I learned more in my early childhood about how to live than I have learned since.[22]

Protective fathers appeared in the lullabies slave mothers sang to their children.

> Kink head, wherefore you skeered?
> Old snake crawled off, 'cause he's a-feared.
> Pappy will smite hime on de back

With a great big club—Ker whack! Ker whack![23]

Many ex-slaves recalled their fathers as stern disciplinarians, and the slaveholders' complaints about fathers' abusing their children may be read as supporting evidence. Other slave men left their children a memory of kindness and affection that remained through life. Will Adams's father, a foreman on a Texas plantation, came in exhausted after a long day's work but never failed to take his son out of bed and to play with him for hours.[24] The spirituals and other slave songs reflected the importance of the father in the lives of the children; many of them sang of the reunification of the family in heaven and of the father's return.[25]

Men knew that they might have to part from their wives and children, but that knowledge did not engender indifference so much as a certain stoical submission to that which had to be endured. Under painful conditions, many did their best even while others succumbed. Mingo White's father, upon being sold, did nothing unusual when he charged a male friend with responsibility for looking after his son.[26] A principle of stewardship had arisen in the quarters. Even in the absence of a father, some male would likely step in to help raise a boy to manhood. When the war ended, men crisscrossed the South to reclaim their families and to assert authority over their children.[27]

Slave children usually did have an image of a strong black man before them. Critical scholars have made the mistake of measuring the slave family by middle-class norms; naturally, they have found it wanting. Even when a slave boy was growing up without a father in the house, he had as a model a tough, resourceful driver, a skilled mechanic or two, and other field hands with some time for the children of the quarters. Some of those men devoted themselves to playing surrogate father to all the children. They told them stories, taught them to fish and trap animals, and instructed them in the ways of survival in a hostile white world. The norm in the quarters called for adults to look after children, whether blood relatives or not. Every plantation had some men who played this role. Under the worst of circumstances, one or two would have been enough; usually, however, there were a number. And there were the preachers. To the extent that the slaves heard their preachers, the children saw before them influential black men whose eloquence and moral force commanded the respect of the adults.

A positive male image existed even in those cabins without resident fathers. In the urban ghettos of the twentieth century, where the one-parent household has taken on greater prominence, the children have not suffered from a lack of a masculine presence. Ulf Hannerz observes: "More or less steady boyfriends (sometimes including the separated father) go in and out. Even if these men do not assume a central household role, the boys can obviously use them as source material for the identification of male behavior."[28] And more sharply, Charles Keil:

> Clearly, lower-class Negro culture includes a concept of manhood that differs in kind from the white middle-class definition of a man as a head of household, who holds down a steady job and sends his kids to college. . . . But as far as he and his women are concerned, he spends his money freely, dresses well, and is great in bed. That's just the way he is—*a man*—and they like him that way, despite the fact that he's obviously "no good."[29]

However outsiders may judge the kind of masculinity projected by these circumstances, claims of emasculation and infantilization do not ring true. The slave children, like the ghetto children of later decades, saw a pattern of behavior that implied clear sexual differentiation and a notion of masculinity with its own strengths and weaknesses.

What happened to a slave boy who witnessed, as many did, his father's being whipped by a white man, or worse, his father's standing helplessly while his mother was being whipped? Clearly, the moment had to be traumatic and the boy's confidence in his father had to be shaken. Children apparently did not often witness such scenes: most masters preferred to discipline their slaves at times and in places unavailable to the children, and the slave parents conspired to keep their children ignorant. As for those children who saw and suffered, many possibly never got over the shock. But there is no evidence that many despised their fathers, especially since their mothers tried to explain the acquiescence and instruct their children in the ways of survival. Nor do we know how many children reacted like that Mexican peasant boy who saw his father collapse helplessly in tears when a treacherous landowner expropriated his land. Emiliano Zapata did not despise his father. He swore vengeance.[30]

Peter Poyas, Denmark Vesey's lieutenant in the abortive rising of 1822, is remembered as the man who showed his troops how to face execution: "Do not open your lips; die silent, as you shall see me do." He might also be remembered for his restrained comment to the judge who sentenced him to death: "I suppose you'll let me see my wife and family before I die?"[31]

Wives and Mothers

Elizabeth Hyde Botume in her wonderful book, *First Days Amongst the Contrabands,* tells of the black women recently emancipated by the Yankee invasion:

> When the women found me so unsuspicious, they exhibited their handicraft with no small degree of pride. It was not an unusual thing to meet a woman coming from the field, where she had been hoeing cotton, with a small bucket or cup on her head, and a hoe over her shoulder, contentedly smoking a pipe and briskly knitting as she strode along. I have seen, added to all these, a baby strapped to her back. The patient devotion of these negro women was most admirable.[32]

The women field hands generally had a longer day than their men. Even the critical Fanny Kemble thought that the middle-aged men did not appear overworked but that the women did. She particularly drew attention to the effects of hard field work in combination with childbearing.[33] Ex-slaves said much more. In addition to the usual work load, the women had to cook for their families, put the children to bed, and often spin, weave, and sew well into the night. On many plantations masters and overseers released them from field work early to attend to their household chores, but on many others they did not, except perhaps on Saturday to get the week's washing done. Many of the women rose early to feed their men, although most masters sensibly preferred to arrange for communal preparation of the morning's meal. Harrison Beckett of Texas grimly recalled his mother's coming in exhausted from the fields and having to cook for her husband and children: "Lots of times she's so tired she go to bed without eatin' nothin' herself."[34]

Usually men, not women, plowed on the large plantations, but when the minority of plantation women who did plow are added to those on smaller units who had to work alongside their men or even alone, it would appear that the rigors of plowing engaged the efforts of a substantial minority of southern slave women.[35] On many plantations the women proved superior to the men in picking cotton; in general, men and women did about equally well. Not unusually a woman would rate as the most valuable field hand on the place or as the single most physically powerful individual. Some excelled in such exacting roles as logrollers and even lumberjacks.[36] And if the men often helped their wives to keep up with their tasks, the roles could be reversed. "My daddy was a field hand," recalled Pierce Harper, who had been a slave in North Carolina, "and my mother worked in the field, too, right 'longside my daddy, so she could keep him lined up." Her mother had a reputation as the best field hand on the place and her father as the worst. "My mother," she explained, "used to say he was chilesome."[37]

White southerners, who usually knew better, sometimes pretended that black mothers cared little about children. The whites might have been referring to that stoicism toward the death of an infant which appears in all societies with high infant mortality, especially among the poor; yet even upper-class southern whites suffered too often from death of their own infants not to understand the necessity for a certain amount of fatalism and self-control. They did not confuse their own self-discipline with lack of grief. The white women and even the men frequently commented on the grief felt by particular slave parents when they lost a child.[38] The sadistic mistress who whipped a slave girl to death fully appreciated the maternal affection of her slaves: she sent for the girl's mother to watch her die.[39]

The calmness of many slave mothers and fathers in the face of the death of their infants and young children recalls that of many other peoples who simply had to live with the probability of losing some of their children. Keith Thomas writes: "In Tudor and Stuart England men were fully accustomed to disease and a low expectation of life. Parents were slower to recognize the individuality of their children, for they well knew that they might lose them in their infancy."[40] Philippe Aries adds that such conditions existed in France well into the nineteenth century: "Nobody thought, as we ordinarily think today, that every child already contained a man's personality. Too many of them died."[41]

Mrs. Kemble, commenting on the apparent indifference of parents to the death of a boy, recounted a telling incident: "The mother merely repeated over and over again, 'I've lost a many; they all goes so'; and the father, without a word or comment, went out to his enforced labor."[42] This self-protective hardening of parents' attitudes toward their children, reinforced under slavery by fear of sale, did not appear in the quarters any more noticeably than elsewhere under conditions of high infant mortality; it may even have appeared less often. Most black women welcomed their babies as a joy, loved them, and braced themselves for inevitable losses and heartaches.

Some slave women took little interest in their children either because they succumbed to the terrific pressures of overwork, insufficient time for child care, and general demoralization or because they did not want to raise them as slaves.[43] But much of what has been called indifference was no more than the effects of exhaustion of women who loved the children they could not always find patience for. Women who had been forced into cohabitation might especially have resented the children of these unions; yet there is no evidence that even they usually did so.

Women who did not want children knew how to abort or to arrange to have a child die soon after birth. With childbirth deaths so common from natural causes, the deed could not easily be detected. But birth and reproduction rates remained high. Slave abortions, much less infanticide, did not become a major problem for the slave holders or an ordinary form of "resistance" for the slaves. Infanticide occurred, but so far as the detected cases reveal anything, only in some special circumstance. The white citizens of Virginia petitioned in 1822 to spare a slave condemned to death for killing her infant. The child's father was a respectable, married white man, and the woman insisted she would not have killed a child of her own color. Lou Smith, an ex-slave from South Carolina, recalled a woman who had had one child after another sold away from her. Finally, she poisoned her next child and swore to have no more. The other slaves knew what she had done but protected her.[44] For the most part, however, the slaves recognized infanticide as murder. They loved their children too much to do away with them; courageously, they resolved to raise them as best they could, and entrusted their fate to God. Nothing like the widespread infanticide of, say, nineteenth-century Japan, with its economic rationale, ever swept the quarters.[45]

Particularly humane or closely calculating masters released their slave women from field work for a full month before and after childbirth, but many fell short of this model. Normally, the women would have their tasks lightened or cut in half during the last month of pregnancy and then would not be expected back at work until a month after delivery.[46]

Plantation midwives usually attended the deliveries, although mistresses sometimes helped. Slaveholders turned to physicians rarely, but the substantial fees recorded in physicians' account books suggest that they regularly attended the difficult cases.[47] The women often complained bitterly that they needed more time before and after delivery, but they may have been more concerned about the care of their infants than about their own health. The slaveholders thought a month's rest after delivery ample and pointed out, accurately, that the peasant and working-class women of Europe had no such good fortune.[48]

Black women supposedly needed less consideration than the weaker white women anyway, but the statistics on death in childbed as well as on disease and deformity following childbirth provide no support for this rationalization.[49] Nor did lectures on the superiority of their treatment relative to that of, say, English peasant and working-class women who had to endure the physical and psychological hardships attendant upon pregnancy, delivery, and nursing. Kenneth Stampp, admittedly working from shaky data, plausibly estimates many more spontaneous abortions and stillbirths in black women than in white. Whatever the precise differential, the slave women's particular vulnerability to this group of maladies largely resulted from overwork, inadequate prenatal care, and enforced performance of tasks beyond their strength.[50]

The women complained especially about the inadequate conditions for nursing. Landon Carter permitted his slaves to leave the fields three times a day to attend to their babies; the women thought five times would be proper and caused themselves no little trouble by lying or trying to maneuver the overseer into giving them more time. During the nineteenth century three or four times became standard. On M. W. Philips's plantation in Hinds County, Mississippi, the women went into the cookhouse to nurse at breakfast, at 9:30 A.M., at noon, and once during the afternoon. On some plantations mothers could remain with their infants for two hours at midday.[51] Often, the nurses brought the children to their mothers in the field. Overseers and nurses had instructions to keep mothers from nursing their children for fifteen minutes or so after they had stopped working in hot weather or had walked the long distance from the fields. Such instructions could not readily be enforced; too often, hot and tired mothers picked their children up eagerly and nursed them under conditions that might easily have done psychological and physical damage.[52]

If slave mothers viewed their infants with indifference as many slaveholders claimed, they had some strange ways of showing it. Notwithstanding the objective difficulties in nursing, they showed, by more recent standards, a marked unwillingness to wean them early. "We sucked till we was a fair size," said Mary Reynolds of Louisiana in expressing a common view. The Gullah slaves, like the West Africans to whom they remained culturally closer than did other slaves, nursed their children two or three years and even longer. The slaves' practice did not vary greatly from southern practice in general, especially that of the lower classes. Mrs. Kemble, Olmsted, and others were taken aback at the prolonged nursing among the whites. The little evidence we have indicates that the blacks followed the same course and nursed their babies as long as they reasonably could.[53]

Many women saw their children only for a few minutes at night and then on weekends. That some became indifferent ought to cause no surprise; and yet, clearly, most did not.

> My mammy [recalled Fannie Moore of South Carolina] she work in de field all day and piece and quilt at night. . . . I never see how my mammy stand such hard work. She stand up for her chillen though. De old overseer he hate my mammy, 'cause she fought him for beatin' her chillen. Why she get more whippin' for dat dan anythin' else.[54]

Fannie Moore's mother had plenty of company in slave mothers who forcibly defended their children against white abuse.[55]

Although often accused of indifference to their children, slave mothers could hardly have made a deeper impression on the children themselves. The lifelong love of the children, male and female, for their mothers shines through the narratives, as it does through the earlier writings of successful runaways and the occasional observations of whites. Martha Schofield recorded in her diary the dying words of her male cook: "Lord forgive them. I am coming mother, I am coming. Oh! This is plesant, my mother's grave."[56] William Wells Brown reflected on his mother's having been sold south and on the probability of her early death: "As I thought of my mother, I could not but feel that I had lost, 'The glory of my life/My blessing and my pride!/I half forgot the name of slave/When she was by my side.' "[57] Josiah Henson wrote of the mother from whom he was separated by sale only to be reunited by repurchase after he had fallen ill:

> We have been in the main very happy. She was a good mother to us, a woman of deep piety, anxious above all things to touch our hearts with a sense of religion. . . . Now, I was once more with my best friend on earth, and under her care. . . .[58]

George Teamoh of Virginia recalled his mother in a letter to Carter G. Woodson that might have spoken for numerous others:

> My mother—whom I well remember—bore the common name "Winnie."

She died when I was quite small. My father, who was not her husband by the usages of custom died some time after. She was the mother of three or four children, whether all by the same man I am not prepared to say, but what I do know is, she was a kind and affectionate mother and true to her offspring. She was raised with my old mistress, to whom we both belonged.[59]

These were not occasional pronouncements. When added to the powerful image of the mother that comes through the spirituals, as well as to the overwhelming evidence of maternal devotion in the plantation records and the slave narratives, they compel the conclusion that the children felt loved and experienced their mothers' tenderness and warmth. In view of how much conspired to thwart the maternal instincts of these black women, their achievement reached heroic proportions.

The story of the slave women as wives requires indirect examination. To deduce from it an assumption that the man was a guest in the house will not do. A review of the actual position of the men as husbands and fathers suggests that the position of the women was much more complex than usually credited. The women's attitude toward house work, especially cooking, and toward their own femininity by itself belies the conventional wisdom according to which the women unwittingly helped ruin their men by asserting themselves in the home, protecting their children, and assuming other normally masculine responsibilities.[60]

A remarkable number of women did everything possible to strengthen their men's self-esteem and to defer to their leadership. What has usually been viewed as a debilitating female supremacy was in fact a closer approximation to a healthy sexual equality than was possible for whites and perhaps even for many postbellum blacks. The men did not play the provider for their families in a full and direct sense, but they did everything they could to approximate it. They could have scored few successes without the sympathetic cooperation of their women, many—by no means all—of whom yielded their own prerogatives. This female deference represented an effort by the women to support their men—an effort that could only have flowed from a judgment on what men ought to be and an awareness of the terrible ravages being wrought by slavery. On whatever level of consciousness, many women—perhaps a substantial majority—understood that the degradation of their men represented their own degradation as black women and that of their children. They wanted their boys to grow up to be men and knew perfectly well that, to do so, they needed the example of a strong black man in front of them.

The struggle of the women to define a feminine role for themselves and to strengthen their men's sense of their own masculinity came to fruition after the war when the women so readily deferred to their men without surrendering their own opinions and activities, which were often militant. Black people found themselves in a brutal battle for genuine freedom in a postwar world in which certain norms reigned. They knew that in order to win, they would have to accommodate to those norms—specifically, the norms according to which men, not women, controlled the political process and supported the family. The ease with which black men and women made that transition, when not prevented by forces beyond their control, demonstrates how well prepared they already were.

The slave family had, however, rested on a much greater equality between men and women than had the white family. It had bred strong women. The strength of the women did not necessarily undermine the men; often, it supported them. It took enormous strength for a woman to keep her man from avenging an insult or a beating she had suffered and to convince him that the test of his masculinity was self-restraint, not some action that would deprive her of a husband and her children of a father. He needed that assurance to survive, and only she could give it to him. But with freedom the women had to strengthen their men in ways that separated themselves from some of the major sources of their own strength, especially their place in the economy. Their withdrawal from field work undoubtedly would have gone much further if new systems of exploitation had not forced many of them to help their tenant-farmer and sharecropper husbands. The subsequent history of the black family is another matter. New conditions of oppression made it difficult for black men and women to build on their past and create the new and more sexually equitable family inherent in it.

The postbellum record should not be projected backward. A substantial number of black women came out of slavery just as strong as some historians insist. But, in a sense, they had always been even stronger: strong enough to know that their own dignity required having strong men who could meet their responsibilities; strong enough to support their men in those very aspirations.

FOOTNOTES

1. Robert Collins, "Essay on the Management of Slaves," *SC,* XII (July, 1854), 206.
2. Foby, "Management of Servants," *SC,* XI (Aug., 1853), 226-228; Sitterson, *Sugar Country,* p. 57.
3. Radwick. ed., *Texas Narr.,* IV (1), 76; Redpath, *Roving Editor,* p. 66. See also Kemble, *Journal,* p. 167.
4. Rawick, ed., *S.C. Narr.,* II (2), 36; *Okla. Narr.,* VII (1), 28; *Ark. Narr.,* IX (3), 231; *N.C. Narr.,* XIV (1), 101; *Ga. Narr.,* XII (2), 13; Greene, ed., *Diary of Col. Landon Carter,* II, 777; J. H. Johnston, *Race Relations and Miscegenation,* pp. 306-307.
5. See, e.g., Scarborough, *Overseer,* pp. 90-100; Weld, *Slavery as It Is,* p. 47; Radwick, ed., *Mo. Narr.,* XI, 171.
6. See Martineau, *Society in America,* II, 142; Catterall, ed., *Judicial Cases,* III, 362-363; Fisk University, *Unwritten History of Slavery,* pp. 1-2; and in general, James Hugo Jonston, "A New Interpretation of the Domestic Slave System," *JNH,* XVIII (Jan., 1933), 42.
7. E. F. Andrews, *War-Time Journal of a Georgia Girl,* p. 349; Kate Stone, *Brokenburn,* p. 219.
8. This problem long outlived slavery and cast a shadow over black male-female relations, discussion of which would best be reserved for blacks. See esp. Joyce Ladner, *Tomorrow's Tomorrow: The Black Woman* (New York, 1971).
9. *Father Henson's Story of His Own Life,* pp. 6-7.
10. Keckley, *Behind the Scenes,* pp. 22, 25-28; Mrs. Smith Journal, 1793, pp. 17-18; Phillips and Glunt, eds., *Florida Plantation Records,* p. 63; Trollope, *Domestic Manners,* pp. 246-247; Radwick, ed., *S.C. Narr.,* III (3), 17; J. M. McPherson, *Negro's Civil War,* pp. 62-63; Minor Plantation Diary, Sept. 28, 1863; Blassingame, "Recruitment of Colored Troops in Kentucky, Maryland, and Missouri," *Historian,* XXIX (Aug., 1967), 539-540.
11. Rawick, ed., *N.C. Narr.,* XIV (1), 3; also *S.C. Narr.,* III (3), 193; I have found only one reference to hunting by women; see *Ark. Narr.,* IX (4), 6.
12. Rawick, ed., *Texas Narr.,* IV (1), 67; *S.C. Narr.,* II (2), 138.
13. Dick, *Dixie Frontier,* p. 35; Hundley, *Social Relations,* p. 343; Rawick, ed., *S.C. Narr.,* II (2), 215.
14. Schoolcraft, *Plantation Life,* pp. 42-43; House, ed., "Deterioration of a Georgia Rice Plantation During Four Years of Civil War," *JSH,* IX (Feb., 1943) 108; G. G. Johnson, *Social History of the Sea Island,* pp. 85-86; Sydnor, *Slavery in Mississippi,* p. 34, n. 58, Wall, "Founding of Pettigrew Plantations," *NCHR,* XXVII (Oct., 1950), 409; Fisk University, *Unwritten History of Slavery,* p. 136; Hundley, *Social Relations,* pp. 343-344.
15. Ascher and Fairbanks, "Excavation of a Slave Cabin," *Historical Archeology* (1971), pp. 3-17. See also Dick, *Dixie Frontier,* p. 96; Lyell, *Second Visit,* II, 17; Northup, *Twelve Years a Slave,* p. 200; Saxon *et al., Gumbo Ya-Ya,* p. 238; Yetman, ed., *Life Under the "Peculiar Institution,"* pp. 61, 268, 331; Fisk University, *Unwritten History of Slavery,* p. 44; Rawick, ed.,

250

S.C. Narr., II (3), 56; *N.C. Narr.,* XIV (1), 105.

16. See, e.g., the correspondence between Joseph Bieller of Louisiana and his father, Jacob, in the Snyder Papers.

17. Ervin Journal, p. 46.

18. W. T. Jordan, *Hugh Davis,* p. 95.

19. F. L. Riley, ed., "Diary of a Mississippi Planter," pp. 343-344; Seale Diary, March 7, 1857; Monette Day Book and Diary, *passim;* LeBlanc Record Book, 1859-1866.

20. WPA, *Negro in Virginia,* pp. 88-89; Rawick, ed., *S.C. Narr.,* III (3), 104; Scott, *Southern Lady,* p. 30.

21. Botume, *First Days Amongst the Contrabands,* pp. 221, 226.

22. Fisk University, *God Struck Me Dead,* p. 161.

23. Yetman, ed., *Life Under the "Peculiar Institution,"* p. 71.

24. Rawick, ed., *Texas Narr.,* IV (1), 2.

25. Odum and Johnson, *Negro and His Songs,* pp. 54, 55; Higginson, *Army Life,* p. 211.

26. Yetman, ed., *Life Under the "Peculiar Institution,"* pp. 310-311.

27. See, e.g., the account in Fisk University, *Unwritten History of Slavery,* p. 105.

28. Ulf Hannerz, "Another Look at Lower-Class Black Culture," in Rainwater, ed., *Soul,* p. 173.

29. Keil, *Urban Blues,* p. 26.

30. John Womack, *Zapata and the Mexican Revolution* (New York, 1969), p. 6. See also Pennington, *Fugitive Blacksmith,* in Bontemps, ed., *Great Slave Narratives,* p. 211; Rawick, ed., *S.C. Narr.,* III (3), 260; *Ark. Narr.,* X (5), 27; *N.C. Narr.,* XIV (1), 5.

31. Thomas Wentworth Higginson, *Black Rebellion* (New York, 1969), pp. 148, 144.

32. Botume, *First Days Amongst the Contrabands, p. 53.* Also Rawick, ed., *Ga. Narr.,* XIII (3), 53.

33. Kemble, *Journal,* p. 263.

34. Rawick, ed., *Texas Narr.,* IV (1), 54. Also *S.C. Narr.,* II (2), 66, 114: *Texas Narr.,* V (3), 190; *Ga. Narr.,* XII (2), 41, 187; WPA, *Negro in Virginia,* p. 65; Kiser, *See Island to City,* p. 60.

35. For general surveys see Bonner, *Georgia Agriculture,* p. 87; J. B. Sellers, *Slavery in Alabama,* p. 66; J. G. Taylor, *Negro Slavery in Louisiana,* p. 62; Phillips and Glunt, eds., *Florida Plantation Records,* p. 515; and Myers, ed., *Children of Pride, passim.* For the recollections of ex-slaves see Jeremiah W. Loguen, *Reverend J. W. Loguen as a Slave and as a Freeman* (New York, 1970) [1859]), p. 18; Rawick ed., *S.C. Narr.,* II (2), 80; III (4), 36; *Texas Narr.,* IV (1), 223; *Miss. Narr.,* VII (2), 158, 165; *Mo. Narr.,* XI, 130, 261; *Ga. Narr.,* XII (1), 93, 180, 215, 312, 313; XV (2), 57, 130, 149, 159. Fogel and Engerman doubt that many women plowed, but I fear that they have been misled by the records of the larger plantations, which exhibited a greater sexual division of labor; see *Time on the Cross,* p. 141.

36. Sydnor, *Slavery In Mississippi,* p. 96; Bonner, ed., "Plantation Experiences of a New York Women," *NCHR,* XXXIII (July, 1956), 400; *Life and Times of Frederick Douglass,* p. 142; Rawick, ed., *Ala. Narr.,* VI (1), 46, 338; Fisk University, *Unwritten History of Slavery,* p. 13; Northup, *Twelve Years a Slave,* pp. 155-156; Yetman, ed., *Life Under the "Peculiar Institution,"* p. 252.

37. Rawick, ed., *Texas Narr.,* IV (2), 109.

38. See, e.g., Kate Stone, *Brokenburn,* p. 87; John Palfrey to William Palfrey, May 30, 1832.

39. Drew, *Refugee,* p. 259.

40. K. Thomas, *Religion and the Decline of Magic,* p. 17.

41. Aries, *Centuries of Childhood,* p. 39. Aries may well push hs argument too far. See Natalie Zemon Davis, "The Reasons of Misrule: Youth Groups and Charivaris in Sixteenth-Century France," *Past and Present,* No. 50 (Feb., 1971), pp. 55-56.

42. Kemble, *Journal,* p. 95. For some illustrations of white concern about the high death rate of the slave children see Elizabeth Manigault, Gowrie, and Silk Hope Plantations, Slave Records, Sept.-Oct., 1834; K. W. Skinner to C. M. Manigault, July 12, 1851, in the Manigault Papers; J. H. Randolph to Mosses Liddell, Nov. 13, 1851, in the Liddell Papers.

43. This argument has been pressed as far as it can go—much too far in fact—by Raymond and Alice Bauer, "Day to Day Resistance to Slavery," *JHN,* XXVII (Oct., 1942), 415-417.

44. J.H. Johnson, *Race Relations and Miscegenation,* p. 308; Rawick, ed., *Okla. Narr.,* VII (1), 302. Also Catterall, ed., *Judicial Cases,* V, 139; C. C. Jones to Charles C. Jones, Jr., Dec. 10, 1859, in Myers, ed., *Children of Pride,* pp. 544-545.

45. For a discussion of the economic pressures for infanticide in Japan see Johannes Hirschmeier, *Origins of Entrepreneurship in Meiji Japan* (Cambridge, Mass., 1964), pp. 73,

121; G. B. Sansom, *Japan: A Short Cultural History* (New York, 1931), pp. 516-517.

46. Ingraham, *South-West*, II, 125; Lyell, *Second Visit*, I, 264; Weld, *Slavery as It Is*, p. 12; R. R. Gibbes, "Southern Slave Life," *DBR*, XXIV (Jan., 1858), 324; G. G. Johnson, *Social History of the Sea Islands*, p. 96; Sydnor, *Slavery in Mississippi*, p. 64.

47. See William B. Price Books, I (1836-1843) and II (Aug. 14-22, 1846); B. B. Jones Book, III (1838); Turner Physician's Record Book, 1857.

48. See, e.g., E. P. Thompson, *Making of the English Working Class*, p. 38.

49. M. C. Mitchell, "Health and the Medical Profession in the Lower South, 1845-1860," *JSH*, X (Nov., 1944), 434.

50. Stampp, *Peculiar Institution*, p. 316.

51. Greene, ed., *Diary of Col. Landon Carter*, I, 494; Olmsted, *Seaboard*, pp. 658, 698, and *Back Country*, p. 47; J. B. Sellers, *Slavery in Alabama*, p. 128; Sydnor, *Slavery in Mississippi*, pp. 64-65.

52. Willie Lee Rose has suggested, in an unpublished paper, that the consequences of this practice were far-reaching and require expert medical and psychological review. At the moment we can only note the possibilities. Some planters worried about it; see, e.g., J. Channing to Edward Telfair, Oct. 3, 1787, in the Telfair Papers.

53. Rawick, ed., *Texas Narr.*, V (3), 237; for an extreme case see V (2), 220. Also Bascom, "Acculturation Among the gullah Negroes," *American Antropologist*, XLIII, no. 1 (1941), 39; Kemble, *Journal*, p. 254; Olmsted, *Back Country*, p. 199; Frazier, *Negro Family*, p. 112.

54. Yetman, ed., *Life Under the "Peculiar Institution,"* p. 277.

55. See, eg., Rawick, ed., *Texas Narr.*, IV (1), 37; *Ark. Narr.*, XI (7), 193.

56. Schofield Diary, Feb. 5, 1966.

57. *Narrative of William Wells Brown*, p. 35; also pp. 2, 10.

58. *Father Henson's Story of His Own Life*, pp. 10, 14.

59. George Teamoh Journal, Pts. 1-2, pp. 27, 29, in the Woodson Papers.

60. For an able defense of this view with which I cannot agree, see Bernard, *Marriage and Family Among Negroes*, pp. and esp. 73.

⋅❋{18}❋⋅ *Regardless of its "official" ideological position on a given issue, no society ever achieves absolute commitment to a moral, economic, or social value. Although Americans have always been committed to the notion of geographic mobility, especially when it fosters the economic advancement of the individual, they have also maintained a belief in its opposite, the notion of stability in time and space. The concept of stability has often been symbolized by an idealized, frequently unrealistic, perception of family cohesiveness, by a glorification of small town life, or by a nostalgic longing (most frequently displayed by transplanted suburbanites) for the ethnically homogeneous urban neighborhood of their youths. These antipodal ideals of mobility and stability, of movement and community, have parried with each other throughout American history. Indeed, this struggle may be one of the most significant causes of value conflict in American society.*

In this article Johnny Farragher and Christine Stansell trace this conflict during the great western migrations of the nineteenth-century. The Overland Trail was more than a route to a new life or economic improvement. It was also the scene of an intense struggle between the ideals of family cohesiveness and stability—represented for various reasons by the women in the migration—and "movement," mobility and ambition—symbolized by "masculine" attitudes.

Why did women and men in the nineteenth-century symbolize the values of stability and mobility respectively? Did territorial expansion lesson family cohesiveness?

Women and Their Families on the Overland Trail to California and Oregon, 1842-1867

Johnny Faragher and Christine Stansell

*I am not a wheatfield
nor the virgin forest*

*I never chose this place
yet I am of it now*

Adrienne Rich
"From an Old House in America"

From 1841 until 1867, the year in which the transcontinental railroad was completed, nearly 350,000 North Americans emigrated to the Pacific coast along the western wagon road known variously as the Oregon, the California, or simply the Overland Trail. This migration was essentially a family phenomenon. Although single men constituted the majority of the party which pioneered large-scale emigration on the Overland Trail in 1841, significant numbers of women and children were already present in the wagon trains of the next season. Families made up the preponderant proportion of the migrations throughout the 1840s. In 1849, during the overwhelmingly male Gold Rush, the number dropped precipitously, but after 1851 families once again assumed dominance in the overland migration.[1] The contention that "the family was the one substantial social institution" on the frontier is too sweeping, yet it is undeniable that the white family largely mediated the incorporation of the western territories into the American nation.[2]

The emigrating families were a heterogeneous lot. Some came from farms in the Midwest and upper South, many from small Midwestern towns, and others from Northeastern and Midwestern cities. Clerks and shopkeepers as well as farmers outfitted their wagons in Independence, St. Louis, or Westport Landing on the Missouri. Since costs for supplies, travel, and settlement were not negligible,[3] few of the very poor were present, nor were the exceptionally prosperous. The dreams of fortune which lured the wagon trains into new lands were those of modest men whose hopes were pinned to small farms or larger dry-goods stores, more fertile soil or more customers, better market prospects and a steadily expanding economy.

For every member of the family, the trip west was exhausting, toilsome, and often grueling. Each year in late spring, west-bound emigrants gathered for the journey at spots along the Missouri River and moved out in parties of ten to several hundred wagons. Aggregates of nuclear families, loosely attached by kinship or friendship, traveled together or joined an even larger caravan.[4] Coast-bound families traveled by ox-drawn wagons at the frustratingly slow pace of fifteen to twenty miles per day. They worked their way up the Platte River valley through what is now Kansas and Nebraska, crossing the Rockies at South Pass in southwestern Wyoming by midsummer. The Platte route was relatively easy going, but from present-day Idaho, where the roads to California and Oregon diverged, to their final destinations, the pioneers faced disastrous conditions: scorching deserts, boggy salt flats, and rugged mountains. By this time, families had been on the road some three months and were only at the midpoint of the journey; the environment, along with the wear of the road, made the last months difficult almost beyond endurance. Finally, in late fall or early winter the pioneers straggled into their promised lands, after six months and over two thousand miles of hardships.[5]

As this journey progressed, bare necessity became the determinant of most of each day's activities. The primary task of surviving and getting to the coast gradually suspended accustomed patterns of dividing work between women and men. All able-bodied adults worked all day in one way or another to keep the family moving. Women's work was no less indispensable than men's; indeed, as the summer wore on, the boundaries dividing the work of the sexes were threatened, blurred, and transgressed.

The vicissitudes of the trail opened new possibilities for expanded work roles for women, and in the cooperative work of the family there existed a basis for a vigorous struggle for female-male equality. But most women did not see the experience in this way. They viewed it as a male enterprise from its very inception. Women experienced the breakdown of the sexual division of labor as a dissolution of their own autonomous "sphere." Bereft of the footing which this independent base gave them, they lacked a cultural rationale for the work they did, and remained estranged from the possibilities of the enlarged scope and power of family life on the trail. Instead, women fought *against* the forces of necessity to hold together the few fragments of female subculture left to them. We have been bequeathed a remarkable record of this struggle in the diaries, journals, and memoirs of emigrating women. In this study, we will examine a particular habit of living, or culture, in conflict with the new material circumstances of the Trail, and the efforts of women to maintain a place, a sphere of their own.

The overland family was not a homogeneous unit, its members imbued with identical aspirations and desires. On the contrary, the period of westward movement was also one of multiplying schisms within those families whose location and social status placed them in the mainstream of national culture.[6] Child-rearing tracts, housekeeping manuals, and etiquette books by the hundreds proscribed and rationalized to these Americans a radical separation of the work responsibilities and social duties of mothers and fathers; popular thought assigned unique personality traits, spiritual capacities, and forms of experience to the respective categories of man, woman, and child.[7] In many families, the tensions inherent in this separatist ideology, often repressed in the everyday routines of the East, erupted under the strain of the overland crossing. The difficulties of the emigrants, while inextricably linked to the duress of the journey itself, also revealed family dynamics which had been submerged in the less eventful life "back home."

A full-blown ideology of "woman's place" was absent in pre-industrial America. On farms, in artisan shops, and in town marketplaces, women and children made essential contributions to family income and subsistence; it was the family which functioned as the basic unit of production in the colony and the young nation. As commercial exchanges displaced the local markets where women had sold surplus dairy products and textiles, and the workplace drifted away from the household, women and children lost their breadwinning prerogatives.[8]

In Jacksonian America, a doctrine of "sexual spheres" arose to facilitate and justify the segregation of women into the home and men into productive work.[9] While the latter attended to politics, economics, and wage-earning, popular thought assigned women the refurbished and newly professionalized tasks of child-rearing and housekeeping.[10] A host of corollaries followed on the heels of these shifts. Men were physically strong, women naturally delicate; men were skilled in practical matters, women in moral and emotional concerns; men were prone to corruption, women to virtue; men belonged in the world, women in the home. For women, the system of sexual spheres represented a decline in social status and isolation from political and economic power. Yet it also provided them with a psychological power base of undeniable importance. The "cult of true womanhood" was more than simply a retreat. Catharine Beecher, one of the chief theorists of "woman's influence," proudly quoted Tocqueville's observation that "in no country has such constant care been taken, as in America, to trace two clearly distinct lines of action for the two sexes, and to make them keep pace with the other, but in two pathways which are always different."[11] Neither Beecher nor her sisters were simply dupes of a masculine imperialism. The supervision of child-rearing, household economy, and the moral and religious life of the family granted women a certain degree of real autonomy and control over their lives as well as those of their husbands and children.

Indeed, recent scholarship has indicated that a distinctly female subculture emerged from "woman's sphere." By "subculture" we simply mean a "habit of living"—as we have used "culture" above—of a minority group which is self-consciously distinct from the dominant activities, expectations, and values of a society. Historians have seen female church groups, reform associations, and philanthropic activity as expressions of this subculture in actual behavior, while a large and rich body of writing by and for women articulated the subcultural impulses on the ideational level. Both behavior and thought point to child-rearing, religious activity, education, home life, associationism, and female communality as components of women's subculture. Female friendships, strikingly intimate and deep in this period, formed the actual bonds.[12] Within their tight and atomized family households, women carved out a life of their own.

At its very inception, the western emigration sent tremors through the foundations of this carefully compartmentalized family structure. The rationale behind pulling up stakes were nearly always economic advancement;[13] since breadwinning was a masculine concern, the husband and father introduced the idea of going west and made the final decision. Family participation in the intervening time ran the gamut from enthusiastic support to stolid resistance. Many women cooperated with their ambitious spouses: "The motive that induced us to part with pleasant associations and the dear friends of our childhood days, was to obtain from the government of the United States a grant of land that 'Uncle Sam' had promised to give to the head of each family who settled in this new country."[14] Others, however, only acquiesced. "Poor Ma said only this morning, 'Oh, I wish we never had started,' " Lucy Cooke wrote her first day on the trail, "and she looks so sorrowful and dejected. I think if Pa had not passengers to take through she would urge him to return; not that he should be so inclined."[15] Huddled with her children in a cold, damp wagon, trying to calm them despite the ominous chanting of visiting Indians, another woman wondered "what had possessed my husband, anyway, that he should have thought of bringing us away out through this God forsaken country."[16] Similar alienation from the "pioneer spirit" haunted Lavinia Porter's leave-taking:

> I never recall that sad parting from my dear sister on the plains of Kansas without the tears flowing fast and free. . . . We were the eldest of a large family, and the bond of affection and love that existed between us was strong indeed . . . as she with the other friends turned to leave me for the ferry which was to take them back to home and civilization, I stood alone on that wild prairie. Looking westward I saw my husband driving slowly over the plain; turning my face once more to the east, my dear sister's footsteps were fast widening the distance between us. For the time I knew not which way to go, nor whom to follow. But in a few moments I rallied my forces . . . and soon overtook the slowly moving oxen who were bearing my husband and child over the green prairie . . . the unbidden tears would flow in spite of my brave resolve to be the courageous and valiant frontierswoman.[17]

Her dazed vacillation soon gave way to a private conviction that the family had made a dire mistake: "I would make a brave effort to be cheerful and patient until the camp work was done. Then starting out ahead of the team and my men folks, when I throught I had gone beyond hearing distance, I would throw myself down on the unfriendly desert and give way like a child to sobs and tears, wishing myself back home with my friends and chiding myself for consenting to take this wild goose chase."[18]

Men viewed drudgery, calamity, and privation as trials along the road to prosperity, unfortunate but inevitable corollaries of the rational decision they had made. But to those women who were unable to appropriate the vision of the upwardly mobile pilgrimage, hardship and loss only testified to the inherent folly of the emigration, "this wild goose chase."

If women were reluctant to accompany their men, however, they were often equally unwilling to let them go alone. In the late 1840s, the conflict between wives and their gold-crazed husbands reveals the determination with which women enforced the cohesion of the nuclear family. In the name of family unity, some obdurate wives simply chose to blockbust the sexually segregated Gold Rush: "My husband grew enthusiastic and wanted to start immediately," one woman recalled, "but I would not be left behind. I thought where he could go I could and where I went I could take my two little toddling babies."[19] Her family departed intact. Other women used their moral authority to smash the enterprise in its planning stages. "We were married to live together," a wife acidly reminded her spouse when he informed her of his intention to join the Rush: "I am willing to go with you to any part of *God's Foot Stool* where you think you can do best, and under these circumstances you have no right to go where I cannot, and if you do you need never return for I shall look upon you as dead."[20] Roundly chastised, the man postponed his journey until the next season, when his family could leave with him. When included in the plans, women seldom wrote of their husbands' decisions to emigrate in their diaries or memoirs. A breadwinner who tried to leave alone, however, threatened the family unity upon which his authority was based; only then did a wife challenge his dominance in worldly affairs.[21]

There was an economic reason for the preponderance of families on the Trail. Women and children, but especially women, formed an essential supplementary work force in the settlements. The ideal wife in the West resembled a hired hand more than a nurturant Christian housekeeper.[22] Narcissa Whitman wrote frankly to aspiring settlers of the functional necessity of women on the new farms: "Let every young man bring a wife, for he will want one after he gets here, if he never did before."[23] In a letter from California, another seasoned woman warned a friend in Missouri that in the West women became "hewers of wood and drawers of water everywhere."[24] Mrs. Whitman's fellow missionary Elkanah Walker was unabashedly practical in beseeching his wife to join him: "I am tired of keeping an old bachelor's hall. I want someone to get me a good supper and let me take my ease and when I am very tired in the morning I want someone to get up and get breakfast and let me lay in bed and take my rest."[25] It would be both simplistic and harsh to argue that men brought their families West or married because of the labor power of women and children; there is no doubt, however, that the new Westerners appreciated the advantages of familial labor. Women were not superfluous; they were workers. The migration of women helped to solve the problem of labor scarcity, not only in the early years of the American settlement on the coast, but throughout the history of the continental frontier.[26]

In the first days of the overland trip, new work requirements were not yet pressing and the division of labor among family members still replicated familiar patterns. Esther Hanna reported in one of her first diary entries that "our men have gone to build a bridge across the stream, which is impassable," while she baked her first bread on the prairie.[27] Elizabeth Smith similarly described her party's day: "rainy . . . Men making rafts. Women cooking and washing. Children crying."[28] When travel was suspended, "the men were generally busy mending wagons, harnesses, yokes, shoeing the animals etc., and the women washed clothes, boiled a big mess of beans, to warm over for several meals, or perhaps mended clothes."[29] At first, even in emergencies, women and men hardly considered integrating their work. "None but those who have cooked for a family of eight, crossing the plains, have any idea of what it takes," a disgruntled woman recalled: "My sister-in-law was sick, my niece was much younger than I, and consequently I had the management of all the cooking and planning on my young shoulders."[30] To ask a man to help was a possibility she was unable even to consider.[31]

The relegation of women to purely domestic duties, however, soon broke down under the vicissitudes of the Trail. Within the first few weeks, the unladylike task of gathering buffalo dung for fuel (little firewood was available *en route*) became women's work.[32] As one traveler astutely noted, "force of surroundings was a great leveler";[33] miles of grass, dust, glare, and mud erased some of the most rudimentary distinctions between female and male responsibilities. By summer, women often helped drive the wagons and the livestock.[34] At one Platte crossing, "the men drawed the wagons over by hand and the women all crossed in safety"; but at the next, calamity struck when the bridge collapsed, "and then commenced the hurry and bustle of repairing; all were at work, even the women and children."[35] Such crises, which compounded daily as the wagons moved past the Platte up the long stretches of desert and coastal mountains, generated equity in work; at times of Indian threats, for example, both women and men made bullets and stood guard.[36] When mountain fever struck the Pengra family as they crossed the Rockies, Charlotte relieved her incapacitated husband of the driving while he took care of the youngest child.[37] Only such severe afflictions forced men to take on traditionally female chores. While women did men's work, there is little evidence that men reciprocated.

Following a few days in the life of an overland woman discloses the magnitude of her work. During the hours her party traveled, Charlotte Pengra walked beside the wagons, driving the cattle and gathering buffalo chips. At night she cooked, baked bread for the next noon meal, and washed clothes. Three successive summer days illustrate how trying these small chores could be. Her train pulled out early on a Monday morning, only to be halted by rain and a flash flood; Mrs. Pengra washed and dried her family's wet clothes in the afternoon while doing her daily baking. On Tuesday the wagons pushed hard to make up for lost time, forcing her to trot all day to keep up. In camp that night there was not time to rest. Before going to bed, she wrote, "Kept busy in preparing tea and doing other things preparatory for the morrow. I baked a cracker pudding, warm biscuits and made tea, and after supper stewed two pans of dried apples, and made two loaves of bread, got my work done up, beds made, and child asleep, and have written in my journal. Pretty tired of course." The same routine devoured the next day and evening: "I have done a washing. Stewed apples, made pies and baked a rice pudding, and mended our wagon cover. Rather tired." And the next: "baked biscuits, stewed berries, fried meat, boiled and mashed potatoes, and made tea for supper, afterward baked bread. Thus you see I have not much rest."[38] Children also burdened women's work and leisure. During one quiet time, Helen Stewart retreated in mild defiance from her small charges to a tent in order to salvage some private time: "It exceeding hot . . . some of the men is out hunting and some of them sleeping. The children is grumbling and crying and laughing and howling and playing all around."[39] Although children are notably absent in women's journals, they do appear, frightened and imploring, during an Indian scare or a storm, or intrude into a rare and precious moment of relaxation, "grumbling and crying."[40]

Because the rhythm of their chores was out of phase with that of the men, the division of labor could be especially taxing to women. Men's days were toilsome but broken up at regular intervals with periods of rest. Men hitched the teams, drove or walked until noon, relaxed at dinner, traveled until the evening camp, unhitched the oxen, ate supper, and in the evening sat at the campfire, mended equipment, or stood guard. They also provided most of the labor in emergencies, pulling the wagons through mires, across treacherous river crossings, up long grades, and down precipitous slopes.In the pandemonium of a steep descent,

> you would see the women and children in advance seeking the best way, some of them slipping down, or holding on to the rocks, now taking an "otter slide," and then run til some natural obstacle presented itself to stop their accelerated progress and those who get down safely without a hurt or a bruise, are fortunate indeed. Looking back to the train, you would see some of the men holding on to the wagons, others slipping under the oxen's feet, some throwing articles out of the way that had fallen out, and all have enough to do to keep them busily occupied.[41]

Women were responsible for staying out of the way and getting themselves and the children to safety, men for getting the wagons down. Women's work, far less demanding of brute strength and endurance, was nevertheless distributed without significant respite over all waking hours: mealtimes offered no leisure to the cooks. "The plain fact of the matter is," a young woman complained,

> we *have no time for sociability*. From the time we get up in the morning, until we are on the road, it is hurry scurry to get breakfast and put away the things that necessarily had to be pulled out last night—while under way there is no room in the wagon for a visitor, nooning is barely long enough to eat a cold bite—and at night all the cooking utensils and provisions are to be gotten about the campfire, and cooking enough to last until the next night.[42]

After supper, the men gathered together, "lolling and smoking their pipes and guessing, or maybe betting, how many miles we had covered during the day,"[43] while the women baked, washed, and put the children to bed before they finally sat down. Charlotte Pengra found "as I was told before I started that there is no rest in such a journey."[44]

Unaccustomed tasks beset the travelers, who were equipped with only the familiar expectation that work was divided along gender lines. The solutions which sexual "spheres" offered were usually irrelevant to the new problems facing families. Women, for example, could not afford to be delicate: their new duties demanded far greater stamina and hardiness than their traditional domestic tasks. With no tradition to deal with the new exigencies of fuel-gathering, cattle-driving, and cooking, families found that "the division of labor in a party . . . was a prolific cause of quarrel."[45] Within the Vincent party, "assignments to duty were not accomplished without grumbling and objection . . . there were occasional angry debates while the various burdens were being adjusted," while in "the camps of others who sometimes jogged along the trail in our company . . . we saw not a little fighting . . . and these bloody fisticuffs were invariably the outcome of disputes over division of labor."[46] At home, these assignments were familiar and accepted, not subject to questioning. New work opened the division of labor to debate and conflict.

By mid-journey, most women worked at male tasks. The men still retained dominance within their "sphere," despite the fact that it was no longer exclusively masculine. Like most women, Lavinia Porter was responsible for gathering buffalo chips for fuel. One afternoon, spying a grove of cottonwoods half a mile away, she asked her husband to branch off the trail so that the party could fell trees for firewood, thus easing her work. "But men on the plains I had found were not so accomodating, nor so ready to wait upon women as they were in more civilized communities." Her husband refused and Porter fought back: "I was feeling somewhat under the weather and unusually tired, and crawling into the wagon told them if they wanted fuel for the evening meal they could get it themselves and cook the meal also, and laying my head down on a pillow, I cried myself to sleep."[47] Later that evening her husband awakened her with a belated dinner he had prepared himself, but despite his conciliatory spirit their relations were strained for weeks: "James and I had gradually grown silent and taciturn and had unwittingly partaken of the gloom and somberness of the dreary landscape."[48] No longer a housewife or a domestic ornament, but a laborer in a male arena, Porter was still subordinate to her husband in practical matters.

Lydia Waters recorded another clash between new work and old consciousness: "I had learned to drive an ox team on the Platte and my driving was admired by an officer and his wife who were going with the mail to Salt Lake City." Pleased with the compliment, she later overheard them "laughing at the thought of a woman driving oxen."[49] By no means did censure come only from men. The officer's wife as well as the officer derided Lydia Waters, while her own mother indirectly reprimanded teenaged Mary Ellen Todd. "All along our journey, I had tried to crack that big whip," Mary Ellen remembered years later:

> Now while out at the wagon we kept trying until I was fairly successful. How my heart bounded a few days later when I chanced to hear father say to mother, "Do you know that Mary Ellen is beginning to crack the whip." Then how it fell again when mother replied, "I am afraid it isn't a very lady-like thing for a girl to do." After this, while I felt a secret joy in being able to have a power that set things going, there was also a sense of shame over this new accomplishment.[50]

To understand Mrs. Todd's primness, so incongruous in the rugged setting of the Trail, we must see it in the context of a broader struggle on the part of women to preserve the home in transit. Against the leveling forces of the Plains, women tried to maintain the standards of cleanliness and order that had prevailed in their homes back East:

> Our caravan had a good many women and children and although we were probably longer on the journey owing to their presence—they exerted a good influence, as the men did not take such risks with Indians . . . were more alert about the care of teams and seldom had accidents; more attention was paid to cleanliness and sanitation and, lastly, but not of less importance, meals were more regular and better cooked thus preventing much sickness and there was less waste of food.[51]

Sarah Royce remembered that family wagons "were easily distinguished by the greater number of conveniences, and household articles they carried."[52] In the evenings, or when the trains stopped for a day, women had a chance to create with these few props a flimsy facsimile of the home.

Even in camp women had little leisure time, but within the "hurry scurry" of work they managed to recreate the routine of the home. Indeed, a female subculture, central to the communities women had left behind, reemerged in these settings. At night, women often clustered together, chatting, working, or commiserating, instead of joining the men: "High teas were not popular, but tatting, knitting, crochetting, exchanging recipes for cooking beans or dried apples or swopping food for the sake of variety kept us in practice of feminine occupations and diversions."[53] Besides using the domestic concerns of the Trail to reconstruct a female sphere, women also consciously invoked fantasy: "Mrs. Fox and her daughter are with us and everything is so still and quiet we can almost imagine ourselves at home again. We took out our Daguerrotypes and tried to live over again some of the happy days of Auld Lang Syne."[54] Sisterly contact kept "feminine occupations" from withering away from disuse: "In the evening the young ladies came over to our house and we had a concert with both guitars. Indeed it seemed almost like a pleasant evening at home. We could none of us realize that we were almost at the summit of the Rockey Mountains."[55] The hostess added with somewhat strained sanguinity that her young daughter seemed "just as happy sitting on the ground playing her guitar as she was at home, although she does not love it as much as her piano."[56] Although a guitar was no substitute for the more refined instrument, it at least kept the girl "in practice with feminine occupations and diversions": unlike Mary Ellen Todd, no big whip would tempt her to unwomanly pleasure in the power to "set things going."

But books, furniture, knick-knacks, china, the daguerrotypes that Mrs. Fox shared, or the guitars of young musicians—the "various articles of ornament and convenience"—were among the first things discarded on the epic trash heap which trailed over the mountains. On long uphill grades and over sandy deserts, the wagons had to be lightened; any materials not essential to survival were fair game for disposal. Such commodities of woman's sphere, although functionally useless, provided women with a psychological lifeline to their abandoned homes and communities, as well as to elements of their identities which the westward journey threatened to mutilate or entirely extinguish.[57] Losing homely treasures and memorabilia was yet another defeat within an accelerating process of dispossession.

The male-directed venture likewise encroached upon the Sabbath, another female preserve. Through the influence of women's magazines, by mid-century Sunday had become a veritable ladies' day; women zealously exercised their religious influence and moral skill on the day of their families' retirement from the world. Although parties on the Trail often suspended travel on Sundays, the time only provided the opportunity to unload and dry the precious cargo of the wagons—seeds, food, and clothing—which otherwise would rot from dampness. For women whose creed forbade any worldly activity on the Sabbath, the work was not only irksome and tedious but profane.

> This is Sabath it is a beautiful day but indeed we do not use it as such for we have not traveled far when we stop in a most lovely place oh it is such a beautiful spot and take everything out of our wagon to air them and it is well we done it as the flower was damp and there was some of the other ones flower was rotten . . . and we baked and boiled and washed oh dear me I did not think we would have abused the sabeth in such a manner. I do not see how we can expect to get along but we did not intend to do so before we started.[58]

Denied a voice in the male sphere that surrounded them, women were also unable to partake of the limited yet meaningful power of women with homes. On almost every Sunday, Helen Stewart lamented the disruption of a familiar and sustaining order of life, symbolized by the household goods strewn about the ground to dry: "We took everything out the wagons and the side of the hill is covered with flower biscut meat rice oat meal clothes and such a quantity of articles of all discertions to many to mention and childr[n] included in the number. And hobos that is neather men nor yet boys being in and out hang about."[59]

The disintegration of the physical base of domesticity was symptomatic of an even more serious disruption in the female subculture. Because the wagon trains so often broke into smaller units, many women were stranded in parties without other women. Since there were usually two or more men in the same family party, some male friendships and bonds remained intact for the duration of the journey. But by midway in the trip, female companionship, so valued by nineteenth-century women, was unavailable to the solitary wife in a party of hired men, husband, and children that had broken away from a larger train. Emergencies and quarrels, usually between men, broke up the parties. Dr. Powers, a particularly ill-tempered man, decided after many disagreements with others in his train to make the crossing alone with his family. His wife shared neither his misanthropy nor his grim independence. On the day they separated from the others, she wrote in her journal: "The women came over to bid me goodbye, for we were to go alone, all alone. They said there was no color in my face. I felt as if there was none." She perceived the separation as a banishment, almost a death sentence: There is something peculiar in such a parting on the Plains, one there realizes what a goodbye is. Miss Turner and Mrs. Hendricks were the last to leave, and they bade me adieu the tears running down their sunburnt cheeks. I felt as though my last friends were leaving me, for what—as I thought then—was a Maniac."[60] Charlotte Pengra likewise left Missouri with her family in a large train. Several weeks out, mechanical problems detained some of the wagons, including those of the other three women. During the month they were separated, Pengra became increasingly dispirited and anxious: "The roads have been good today—I feel lonely and almost disheartened. . . . Can hear the wolves howl very distinctly. Rather ominis, perhaps you think. . . . Feel very tired and lonely—our folks not having come—I fear some of them ar sick." Having waited as long as possible for the others, the advance group made a major river crossing. "Then I felt that indeed I had left all my friends," Pengra wrote, "save my husband and his brother, to journey over the dreaded Plains, without one female acquaintance even for a companion—of course I wept and grieved about it but to no purpose."[61]

Others echoed her mourning. "The whipporwills are chirping," Helen Stewart wrote, "they bring me in mind of our old farm in pensillvania the home of my childhood where I have spent the happiest days I will ever see again. . . . I feel rather lonesome today oh solitude how I love it if I had about a dozen of my companions to enjoy it with me."[62] Uprootedness took its toll in debilitation and numbness. After a hard week, men "lolled around in the tents and on their blankets seeming to realize that the 'Sabbath was made for man,'"[63] resting on the palpable achievements of miles covered and rivers crossed. In contrast, the women "could not fully appreciate physical rest, and were rendered more uneasy by the continual passing of emigrant trains all day long. . . . To me, much of the day was spent in meditating over the past and in forebodings for the future."[64]

The ultimate expression of this alienation was the pressure to turn back, to retrace steps to the old life. Occasionally anxiety or bewilderment erupted into open revolt against going on.

> This morning our company moved on, except one family. The woman got mad and wouldn't budge or let the children go. He had the cattle hitched on for three hours and coaxed her to go, but she wouldn't stir. I told my husband the circumstances and he and Adam Polk and Mr. Kimball went and each one took a young one and crammed them in the wagon, and the husband drove off and left her sittin. . . . She cut across and overtook her husband. Meantime he sent his boy back to camp after a horse he had left, and when she came up her husband said, "Did you meet John?" "Yes," was the reply, "and I picked up a stone and knocked out his brains." Her husband went back to ascertain the truth and while he was gone she set fire to one of the wagons. . . . He saw the flames and came running and put it out, and then mustered spunk enough to give her a good flogging.[65]

Short of violent resistance, it was always possible that circumstances would force a family to reconsider and turn back. During a cholera scare in 1852, "women cried, begging their men to take them back."[66] When the men reluctantly relented, the writer observed that "they did the hooking up of their oxen in a spiritless sort of way," while "some of the girls and women were laughing."[67] There was little lost and much regained for women in a decision to abandon the migration.

Both sexes worked, and both sexes suffered. Yet women lacked a sense of inclusion and a cultural rationale to give meaning to the suffering and the work; no augmented sense of self or role emerged from augmented privation. Both women and men also complained, but women expanded their caviling to a generalized critique of the whole enterprise. Margaret Chambers felt "as if we had left all civilization behind us"[68] after crossing the Missouri, and Harriet Ward's cry from South Pass—"Oh, shall we ever live like civilized beings again?"[69]—reverbated through the thoughts of many of her sisters. Civilization was far more to these women than law, books, and municipal government; it was pianos, church societies, daguerrotypes, mirrors—in short, their homes. At their most hopeful, the exiles perceived the Trail as a hellish but necessary transition to a land where they could renew their domestic mission: "Each advanced step of the slow, plodding cattle carried us farther and farther from civilization into a desolate, barbarous country. . . . But our new home lay beyond all this and was a shining beacon that beckoned us on, inspiring our hearts with hope and courage."[70] At worst, temporary exigencies became in the minds of the dispossessed the omens of an irrevocable exile: "We have been travelling with 25-18-14-129-64-3 wagons—now all alone—how dreary it seems. Can it be that I have left my quiet little home and taken this dreary land of solitude in exchange?"[71]

Only a minority of the women who emigrated over the Overland Trail were from the Northeastern middle classes where the cult of true womanhood reached its fullest bloom. Yet their responses to the labor demands of the Trail indicate that "womanliness" had penetrated the values, expectations, and personalities of midwestern farm women as well as New England "ladies." "Woman's sphere" provided them with companionship, a sense of self-worth, and most important, independence from men in a patriarchal world. The Trail, in breaking down sexual segregation, offered women the opportunities of socially essential work. Yet this work was performed in a male arena, and many women saw themselves as draftees rather than partners.

Historians have generally associated "positive work roles"[72] for women with absence of narrowly defined notions of "woman's place." In the best summary of literature on colonial women, for example, the authors of *Women in American Society* write: "In general, neither men nor women seemed concerned with defining what women were or what their unique contribution to society should be. . . . Abstract theories about the proper role of women did not stand in the way of meeting familial and social needs."[73] Conversely, the ascendancy of "true womanhood" and the doctrine of sexual spheres coincided with women in a rapidly expanding market economy. On the Overland Trail, cultural roles and self-definitions conflicted with the immediate necessities of the socioeconomic situation. Women themselves fought to preserve a circumscribed role when material circumstances rendered it dysfunctional. Like their colonial great-grandmothers on pre-market subsistence farms, they labored at socially indispensable tasks. Yet they refused to appropriate their new work to their own ends and advantage. In their deepest sense of themselves they remained estranged from their function as "able bodies."

It could be argued that the time span of the trip was not long enough to alter cultural values. Yet there is evidence that the tensions of the Trail haunted the small and isolated market farms at the journey's end.[74] Women in the western settlements continued to try to reinstate a culture of domesticity, although their work as virtual hired hands rendered obsolete the material base of separate arenas for women and men.

The notion of subculture employed in this and other studies of nineteenth-century women is hazy and ill-defined. We need to develop more rigorous conceptions of society, culture, and subculture, and to clarify the paradoxes of women's position, both isolated and integrated, in the dominant social and cultural movements of their time. Nonetheless, the journals of overland women are irrefutable testimony to the importance of a separate female province. Such theorists as Catharine Beecher were acutely aware of the advantages in keeping life divvied up, in maintaining "two pathways which are always different" for women and men.[75] The women who traveled on the Overland Trail experienced firsthand the tribulations of integration which Beecher and her colleagues could predict in theory.

FOOTNOTES

We wish to thank Howard Lamar for his continuing support and Peter H. Wood, Ann Douglas, and Michele Hoffnung for their help and criticism. C. Stansell wants to acknowledge the importance of the experiences she shared with Joan Nueman Fleming and Katherine Fleming in this interpretation of women's history in the West. A National Endowment for the Humanities Youth Grant AY-7451-72-482 supported J. Faragher's portion of the research for this article.

[1]The 1841 Bidwell-Bartelson party of about fifty people included only five women—three of them wives—and ten children. Contemporary figures for the forties' migrations indicate that men made up roughly 50 percent of the parties, women and children the other 50 percent. These proportions prevailed until the Gold Rush. In contrast, the composition of the 1849 emigration was men-92 percent, women-6 percent, and children-2 percent; in 1850, men-97 percent, women and children-3 percent. In 1852 the proportions shifted toward the pre-1849 norm: men-70 percent, women-13 percent, children-20 percent. These percentages are rough estimates, and indicate no more than trends.

For overall figures see Merrill Mattes, *The Great Platte River Road* (Lincoln, Nebraska: Nebraska State Historical Society, 1969), p. 23. For the early forties' on the Oregon Trail, see

David Lavender, *Westward Vision: The Story of the Oregon Trail* (New York: McGraw-Hill, 1963), pp. 349-50, 365. For the California branch: George R. Stewart, *The California Trail: An Epic With Many Heroes* (New York: McGraw-Hill, 1962), pp. 8, 54-55, 85, 147, 187, 195, 232, 303, 310. For the Gold Rush: Georgia Willis Read, "Women and Children on the Oregon-California Trail in the Gold-Rush Years," *Missouri Historical Review 34* (1944-1945): 6.

[2]Arthur W. Calhoun, *A Social History of the American Family from Colonial Times to the Present* 3 vols. (New York: Barnes & Noble, 1945) 2:11. Calhoun's statement has stood up well to demographic tests; after analysis of nineteenth-century census data, Jack Eblen concludes that "the deeply entrenched ideal and institution of the family provided the mechanism by which people were bound together during the process of cultural transplantation and adaptation" ("An Analysis of Nineteenth Century Frontier Populations," *Demography* 2, no. 4 [1965]: 341).

[3]A simple enumeration of the special equipment necessary for the trip indicates the expense. Each family needed a light wagon, harnesses, and a team, usually oxen; the team alone could easily cost two hundred dollars. Arms and ammunition were purchased specially for the trip; such weapons as shotguns and rifles cost around twenty-five dollars. Since there was practically no chance for resupply along the route, a family had to stock for the entire six-month trip, a considerable investment that only the economically stable could afford. For discussion and details see Mattes, *Great Platte River Road,* pp. 37-50; Stewart, The California Trail, pp. 106-26.

[4]Neighbors and friends often moved as a "party," later joining a larger train. Brothers, cousins, and their families, or parents and one or two married children and their families, might set out together. Conjugal and parental ties usually survived under stress, while other relations disintegrated or exploded. Interestingly, the most enduring extrafamilial bonds may have been between nuclear families and the single men who traveled with them. The latter saved money by attaching themselves to family parties rather than outfitting a wagon alone. Some paid for their passage, while others worked as drivers or cattle drovers. For examples of various groupings, see Phoebe Goodell Judson, *A Pioneer's Search for an Ideal Home* (Bellingham, Washington: United Printing, Binding and Stationery Co., 1925), pp. 15-17; Mary E. Ackley, *Crossing the Plains and Early Days in California* (San Francisco: the author, 1928), p. 17; Sarah J. Cummins, *Autobiography and Reminiscences* (Walla Walla, Oregon: The Walla Walla Bulletin, 1920), p. 22; Mrs. J. T. Gowdy, *Crossing the Plains: Personal Recollections of the Journey to Oregon in 1852* (Dayton, Oregon: n.p., 1906), p. 1; Nancy A. Hunt, "By Ox Team to California," *Overland Monthly* 67 (April 1916): 10; Mrs. M. A. Looney, *A Trip Across the Plains in the Year of 1852 with Ox Teams* (McMinnville, Oregon: n.p., 1915), p. 8; and Mrs. Lee Whipple-Halsam, *Early Days in California: Scenes and Events of the '60s as I Remember Them* (Jamestown, California: n.p., 1923), p. 8.

[5]For a recent revision of work on the Overland Trail see Mattes, *The Great Platte River Road.*

[6]Most of the research on the Victorian family has been based on middle- and upper-class northeastern and midwestern families. We do not yet know to what extent the ideology of domesticity affected poor, proletarianized, or southern families.

Although our suggestions about the geographic and class composition of the migrations are generally accepted ones, they remain hypothetical in the absence of demographic research. An overwhelming majority of the women who kept the journals upon which much of our research is based *did* come from the northeastern and midwestern middle class. Nevertheless, until we know much more about the inarticulate families from backwoods Missouri, we cannot pretend to describe the "normative" experience of the overland family. Our interpretation is limited to families whose structure and consciousness were rooted in American bourgeois culture.

[7]The ten volumes of Sarah Hale's *Ladies' Magazine* (1828-1837) are rich primary sources for antebellum ideals of sex roles and the family. For secondary works see the introductory pieces in Nancy Cott, ed., *Root of Bitterness* (Boston: E. C. Dutton, 1972), and Kathryn Kish Sklar, *Catharine Beecher* (New Haven: Yale University Press, 1973). A relatively inaccessible essay remains one of the most illuminating treatments of the period: Nancy Osterud, "Sarah Josepha Hale: A Study of the History of Women in Nineteenth Century America" (unpublished honors thesis, Harvard College, 1971).

[8]See Cott, *Root of Bitterness,* pp. 11-14; Alice Clark, *Working Life of Women in the Seventeenth Century* (London: G. Routledge & Sons, 1919); Elisabeth Dexter, *Colonial Women of Affairs: Women in Business and Professions in America Before 1776* (Boston: Houghton Mifflin Co., 1924); Alice M. Earle, *Home Life in Colonial Days* (New York: McMillian Co.,

1899); and Nancy Osterud, "The New England Family, 1790-1840" (unpublished manuscript, Old Sturbridge Village Education Department; Sturbridge, Mass., n.d.).

[9]We do not use "productive" as a value judgement but as a historically specific concept: labor which produces surplus value within the capitalist mode of production. Within the work process itself, both men's *and* women's labor was "useful," but only men's, in the accepted sex-division, resulted in the creation of commodities. For a provocative discussion of this problem see Ian Gough, "Marx's Theory of Productive and Unproductive Labor," *New Left Review* 76 (November-December 1972): 47-72, and Lise Vogel, "The Earthly Family," *Radical America* 7 (July-October 1973): 9-50.

[10]See Sklar, *Catharine Beecher,* and Ann D. Gordon, Mari Jo Buhle, and Nancy E. Schrom, "Women in American Society," *Radical America* (1972): 25-33.

[11]Quoted in Catharine Beecher, *A Treatise on Domestic Economy* (New York: Harper Brothers, 1858), p. 28.

[12]The most comprehensive account to date of domesticity, culture, and sexual spheres is Sklar, *Catharine Beecher;* see especially pp. 151-67 and 204-16. For the cultural importance of reform to women, see Carroll Smith-Rosenberg, "Beauty, the Beast, and the Militant Woman: A Case Study in Sex Roles in Jacksonian America,;; *American Quarterly* 23 (Fall 1971): 562-84 and Gail Parker, *The Oven Birds: American Women on Womanhood 1820-1920* (New York: Doubleday and Co., 1972), pp. 1-56. Nancy Cott's argument in *Root of Bitterness,* pp. 3-4, is a concise summary of the subculture argument. See Ann Douglas Wood, "The 'Scribbling Women' and Fanny Fern: Why Women Wrote," *American Quarterly* 23 (Spring 1971): 1-24, and "Mrs. Sigourney and the Sensibility of the Inner Space," *New England Quarterly* 45 (June 1972): 163-81 for women's cultural impulses in literature.

[13]The Great Pacific migration began in the wake of the depression of 1837-40. The Pacific Northwest and California seemed to offer unfailing markets at Hudson's Bay forts, Russian settlements, even the massive Orient. The Pacific itself was to be the great transportation network that backwoods farmers needed so desperately. The 1841 migration was the result of the work of the Western Emigration Society, specifically organized to overcome the economic problems of the depressed Midwest. In short, the coast was rich in fertile, free land and unlimited chances for economic success. See Lavender, *Westward Vision,* pp. 327-28. The major exception to this generalization is the Mormon emigration.

[14]Judson, *A Pioneer's Search,* p. 9.

[15]Lucy Rutledge Cooke, *Crossing the Plains in 1852 . . . as told in Letters Written During the Journey* (Modesto, California: the author, 1923), p. 5. See also James Robertson, *A Few Months in America* (London: n.p., 1855), p. 150; Nancy A. Hunt, "By Ox-Team," p. 9; and Elias Johnson Draper, *An Autobiography* (Fresno, California: the author, 1904), p. 9.

[16]Margaret M. Hecox, *California Caravan: the 1846 Overland Trail Memoir of Margaret M. Hecox* (San Jose, California: Harlan-Young Press, 1966), p. 31.

[17]Lavinia Honeyman Porter, *By Ox Team to California: A Narrative of Crossing the Plains in 1860* (Oakland, California: author, 1910), p. 7; see also Margaret White Chambers, *Reminiscences* (n.p.: n.p. 1903), pp. 5-7.

[18]Porter, *By Ox Team,* p. 41.

[19]Luzena Stanley Wilson, *Luzena Stanley Wilson, '49er* (Oakland, California: The Eucalyptus Press, 1937), p.1.

[20]Mary Jane Hayden, *Pioneer Days* (San Jose, California: Murgotten's Press, 1915), pp. 7-8.

[21]Our sample of women's diaries and memoirs is by definition biased toward those women who successfully challenged their husbands. A more comprehensive view requires reading another set of journals—those of men who left their families behind. This work, as a part of a general history of the family, women, and men on the Overland Trail, is now in progress: John Faragher, "Women, Men and Their Families on the Overland Trail" (Ph.D. thesis, Yale University, in progress).

[22]For a particularly striking record of marriage proposals, see *Mollie: The Journal of Mollie Dorsey Sanford in Nebraska and Colorado Territories, 1857-66* (Lincoln, Nebraska: University of Nebraska Press, 1959), pp. 20, 58, 59, 74, 91.

[23]Quoted in Nancy Ross, *Westward the Women* (New York: Alfred A. Knopf, 1944), p. 110.

[24]Mrs. John Wilson, quoted in Read, "Women and Children on the Oregon-California Trail in the Gold-Rush Years," p. 7.

[25]Ross, *Westward the Women,* p. 11.

[26]See Mari Sandoz's biography of her father, *Old Jules* (Lincoln, Nebraska: University of

Nebraska Press, 1955) for a dramatic illustration of a male homesteaders' functional view of wives and children.

The conventional view that the American west was predominantly male dies hard. Jack Eblen, in "Nineteenth Century Frontier Populations," conclusively demonstrates that the sex ratio in the West was little different from that in the East: women were nearly always present in numbers equal to men. See Christine Stansell, "Women on the Plains." *Women's Studies* (forthcoming).

[27]Esther Allen, *Canvas Caravans: Based on the Journal of Esther Belle McMillan Hanna* (Portland, Oregon: Binfords & Mort, 1946), p. 18.

[28]Mrs. Elizabeth Dixon Smith Geer, "Diary," in Oregon Pioneer Association, *Transactions of the Thirty-fifth Annual Reunion* (1907), p. 169.

[29]Catherine Margaret Haun, quoted in Read, "Women and Children on the Oregon-California Trail in the Gold-Rush Years," p. 9.

[30]Chambers, *Reminiscences,* p. 8.

[31]See Adrietta Applegate Hixon, *On to Oregon! A True Story of a Young Girl's Journey Into the West* (Wesler, Idaho: Signal-American Printers, 1947), p. 17, for one of the few instances in the diaries when men took on women's work.

[32]See Charles Howard Crawford, *Scenes of Earlier Days: In Crossing the Plains to Oregon, and Experiences of Western Life* (Chicago: Quadrangle, 1962), p. 9, for an account of women's resistance to assuming this particular responsibility.

[33]Cummins, *Autobiography and Reminiscences,* p. 28.

[34]See Gowdy, *Crossing the Plains,* p. 2; John Barnett, *Long Trip in a Prairie Schooner* (Whittier, California: Western Stationery Co., 1928), p. 105; and Lydia Milner Waters, "A Trip Across the Plains in 1855," *Quarterly of the Society of California Pioneers* 6 (June 1929): 66.

[35]Charlotte Emily Pengra, "Diary of Mrs. Byron J. Pengra," (unpublished typescript in Lane County Historical Society, Eugene, Oregon, N.D.), p. 8.

[36]Mary Burrell, "Mary Burrell's Book" (manuscript diary, Beinecke Library, Yale University), no pagination; Cummins, *Autobiography,* p. 27; E. Allene Dunham, *Across the Plains in a Covered Covered Wagon* (Milton, Iowa: n.p., n.d.), p. 10.

[37]Pengra, "Diary," p. 5.

[38]Ibid., pp. 6, 8-9, 12.

[39]Helen Marnie Stewart, "Diary," (unpublished typescript at Lane County Historical Society, Eugene, Oregon, 1961), p. 13.

[40]The place of children in the structure of the overland family is an intriguing question that we are reserving for more research and reflection. On the basis of their infrequent appearance in the journals, it seems that in this area, too, nineteenth-century patterns were modified. Many historians have pointed the antebellum period as the time when "the child" emerged from obscurity to a special status. In the overland sources, however, children over the age of five are rarely discussed except as younger and more vulnerable members of the working group, requiring little extra or special attentions.

[41]Elizabeth Wood, "Journal of a Trip to Oregon, 1851," *Oregon Historical Society Quarterly* 17 (1926): 4.

[41]Helen M. Carpenter, "A Trip Across the Plains in an Ox Wagon, 1857" (manuscript diary, Huntington Library, San Marino, California), pp. 27-28.

[43]Hixon, *On to Oregon!* p. 17.

[44]Pengra, "Diary," p. 5.

[45]Emery T. Bray, ed., *Bray Family Geneology and History* (n.p.: n.p., 1927), p. 10.

[46]Ibid.

[47]Porter, *By Ox Team to California,* p. 43.

[48]Ibid., p. 118.

[49]Waters, "A Trip Across the Plains in 1855," p. 77.

[50]Hixon, *On to Oregon!* p. 45.

[51]Catherine Haun in Read, "Women and Children During the Gold-Rush Years," p. 9. See also Hixon, *On to Oregon!* p. 15 and *passim;* and William Smedley, "Across the Plains in Sixty-two," *The Trail* 19 (March 1927): 11.

[52]Sarah Royce, *A Frontier Lady: Recollections of the Gold Rush and Early California* (New Haven: Yale University Press, 1932), pp. 8-9.

[53]Haun in Read, "Women and Children During the Gold-Rush Years," p. 9.

[54]Harriet Sherril Ward, *Prairie Schooner Lady: The Journal of Harriet Sherril Ward* (Los

Angeles: Westernlore Press, 1959), p. 60.

[55]Ibid., p. 95. See also Celinda E. Hines, "Diary of Celinda E. Hines," in Oregon Pioneer Association, *Transactions of the Forty-sixth Annual Reunion* (1918, pp. 82-83 and *Passim).*

[56]*Ward, Prairie Schooner Lady,* p. 69.

[57]See Narcissa Whitman, "Diary," (manuscript, Beinecke Library, Yale University), p. 18, or in any one of its many published versions—e.g., *Oregon Historical Quarterly* 35 (1936). Also Esther and Joseph Lyman, "Letters About the Lost Wagon Train of 1853" (unpublished typescript in Lane County Historical Society, Eugene, Oregon), p. 6; and Georgia Read and Ruth Gaines, eds., *Gold Rush: the Journals, Drawings, and Other Papers of J. Goldsborough Bruff . . . April 2, 1849—July 20, 1851* (New York: n.p., 1949), p. 45 and *Passim.*

[58]Stewart, "Diary," entry for June 6, 1853. See also Whitman, "diary," p. 21; Pengra, "Diary," p. 3; and Royce, *Frontier Lady,* p. 11.

[59]Stewart, "Diary," entry for June 12, 1853.

[60]Mrs. Mary Rockwood Power, "The Overland Route: Leaves from the Journal of a California Emigrant," *Amateur Book Collector* 1 (November 1950): 6.

[61]Pengra, "Diary," entries for May 2, 3, 8, and 10, and entries for June 5, 24, and July 7, 1853. See also, Royce, *Frontier Lady, p. 9;* and Mrs. *Mary A. Frink, Journal of the Adventures of a Party of California Gold-Seekers* (Oakland, California: n.p. 1897), p. 67.

[62]Stewart, "Diary," entry for May 1, 1853.

[63]Judson, *A Pioneer's Search,* p. 23.

[64]Ibid.

[65]Geer, "Diary," pp. 165-66.

[66]Hixon, *On to Oregon!* p. 18.

[67]Ibid.

[68]Chambers, *Reminiscences,* p. 7.

[69]Ward, *Prairie Schooner Lady,* p. 128. See also Allen, *Canvas Caravans,* p. 28.

[70]Judson, *A Pioneer's Search,* p. 18.

[71]Maria Parsons Belshaw, "Diary of a Bride Written on the Trail in 1853," *Oregon Historical Society Quarterly* 33 (March-December 1932): 334.

[72]Cott, *Root of Bitterness,* p. 5.

[73]Gordon, Buhle, and Schrom, *Women in American Society,* p. 22.

[74]Stansell, "Women on the Plains."

[75]Catharine Beecher, *Domestic Economy,* p. 28.

19

Many Americans like to think of the family as an anchor of security in a world suffused with indifference and anxiety. When they are confronted with evidence that significant numbers of young people run away from home, Americans, unwilling to believe that anyone in his right mind would forsake the comforts of a "good" home, tend to see nefarious forces at work: the child has been victimized by parental cruelty, or been lured away by evil companions, or, when all other explanations fail, the child is seen as victim of the destiny that befalls those possessed of a "bad seed."

The truth is, however, that the problem of runaway children is as old as America and cannot be dismissed as a product of delinquency or bad environment. As Ken Liebertoff shows in the following article, reasons for running away from the family are multi-faceted and, in many cases, reflections of routine economic and social conditions. In this sense, running away from home is a logical result of the "normal" American environment, not a reaction against it.

From this perspective, is the family really a haven from the "cruel" world or a reflection of it?

The Runaway Child In America

Ken Libertoff

There is little, if any, doubt that adolescents[1] who run away from home in our society are considered a significant social issue. Since the mid-1960s there has been increased interest in and concern for the growing numbers of children who leave their parents (or guardians) before they are of legal age. Unfortunately, in recent years there has been a tendency to perceive and perhaps even to dismiss this behavior as a delinquent activity or as a mental disorder despite the fact that there is little agreement about the cause and meaning of this social phenomena. In doing so, many law enforcement, mental health, social welfare, and youth advocacy professionals have contributed to the creation of a viewpoint which inhibits reasonable and wise social policies for these adolescents. In order to develop an accurate theoretical perspective, therefore, it is crucial to examine the larger social, historical, political and economic context of running away in America.

Long before the American War of Independence, the runaway child was a familiar fixture in the settlement and development of the original 13 colonies. Some experts seemingly believe that this issue is of recent vintage. However, runaway children were among the earliest immigrants to the eastern shores of this nation during the seventeenth and eighteenth centuries. Running away to and, more significantly, running away in America has traditionally grown out of a mixture, of youthful expectations and hope for a better life away from home as well as out of frustrations and despair over current life circumstances.

While there certainly are numerous accounts of young and daring boys who ran to America attracted by a sense of excitement, fascination, and adventure that permeated this distant land, there are also historical references to many poor children, particularly those from English, Scottish, Irish, Dutch, and Portuguese families, who ran away from dreary, miserable, and often oppressive conditions in Europe (Aries, 1962; Bremner, 1970). Seeking work, if not fortunes, and with the simple expectation of better circumstances in a new land, these youths left their families (or masters) and ran to port cities where arrangements could be made for passage to the colonies. Frequently, this commerce was transacted through a contract called "indentures," which committed the young person to an American employer for a specified number of years (Abbott, 1908). Even wealthy sons of upper-class families ran away to America during this period. It was not unusual to find that these upper-class offspring were particularly spirited or rebellious youths whose behavior had seriously offended their elders.

The inhabitants of the earliest colonies struggled to survive and to gain stability during those early years, and the faltering economic conditions exacerbated the demand for and promoted the influx of youthful workers. There is no doubt that labor was in short supply, not only in the southern colonies but in the northern regions as well. Since English traditions made child labor a social fact, not a social problem, children as young as six were considered part of the production force (Bremner, 1970). This child labor concept was readily accepted in the labor-starved American colonies.

Another British creation, the Poor Law of 1601, indirectly added to the flow of young people to America (Bremner, 1970). This law made English municipal authorities responsible for the care of orphans and abandoned children throughout the country. By the late 1600s the law had resulted in considerable expenditures because there were increasing numbers of poor children in England's large cities. Many of these young people were runaways and street urchins. It did not take long for English officials to realize that it might be more profitable (or at least less expensive) to send some of these youths to the colonies as indentures or servants rather than providing for them in the homeland. Many of these youths became part of an overseas business venture in which merchants and shipowners contracted with English commission agents called "spirits" who would arrange for the indentures or contact of service (Bremner, 1970). The demand for these children was strong and constant. Not surprisingly, the Public Record Office of England registered several complaints against overzealous commission agents who, in 1638, were reported to "by lewd subtitles entice away youth against the consent of their parents, friends or masters" (Bremner, 1970: 9). There is little doubt that runaway children were involved in this business system.

If running away to this country was part and parcel of the founding of this nation, then there is much evidence to suggest that the runaway child in America has played an important role in the growth and development of the country. In Massachusetts, for example, where the patriarchal family structure and strict Puritan moral code reinforced strict child-rearing practices, young people still managed to run away with regularity. It must be noted that disobedience to the family was such a serious matter in the Commonwealth that, in 1646, a law was enacted which called for the death penalty for "stubborn or rebellious sons of sufficient years of understanding . . . sixteen, which will not obey the voice of his father or the voice of his mother" (Shurtleff, 1854: 335). Two years later, the Commonwealth passed a law which affected many young people, since it was aimed at controlling indentured servants. (Many youths in colonial days were indentured servants or apprentices.) The law of 1648 marked the first piece of legislation in America that specifically prohibited runaway behavior.

> It is also ordered that when any servants shall run away from their masters or any other inhabitants shall privily go away with suspicion of ill intention, it shall be lawful for the next magistrate . . . to pass men and boats or pinnaces at the publick charge to pursue such person by sea or land and bring them back by force of arms [Bremner, 1970: 115].

Although similar legislative provisions would be made in the other colonies, many young people did run away during the seventeenth and eighteenth centuries. It is important to note that during these formative years in American history most adolescents were employed. Many of them served as apprentices, learning a specific trade. Boys were most frequently apprenticed between the ages of 10 and 14 and served until they were 21. Girls served to age 18 or until they married. Not infrequently, children of poor families worked from early childhood to age 21.

Many young people became disenchanted, bored, or oppressed by these arrangements and ran away before the designated time of departure. Several of these episodes have been captured in news pamphlets or county records. In 1682, for example, Thomas Betts, a servant of John Simmons in Ipswich, Massachusetts, was sentenced to be whipped and fined for often running away and being incorrigible (Bremner, 1970). William Sanford, an apprentice of Daniel Dutton in West New Jersey, was charged and punished for running away in 1696 (Bremner, 1970). Another more extreme case was that of William Battin, whose final speech was recorded in the *American Weekly Mercury* in 1722, shortly brfore he was hanged. Battan had run away from his apprentice master in Chester County, Pennsylvania, and subsequently became involved with an arson and murder case. Battin referred to his "gross actions . . . committed before and after the time of . . . running away from [his] parents" (Bremner, 1970: 25). The Boston *Evening Post* ran many advertisements offering rewards for runaway servants and apprentices during the early decades of the eighteenth century. One particularly amusing runaway announcement appeared in the Pennsylvania Gazette, March 1, 1776, by William Moode:

> This present instant on the fourteenth day
> My apprentice boy did run away
> Thomas Stillenger he is called by name
> His indentures further testifies the same.
> He has always been a vexatious lad
> One reason why his is so meanly clad
> [Bremner, 1970: 153]

While many obscure and unknown young people were engaged in runaway behavior, other participants were to become leading figures in American history and folklore. None other than Benjamin Franklin provides an excellent account of how a spirited nature, a desire for travel, and the need to assert personal independence led to an important runaway experience. Like most youths of this time, Ben began working in his father's tallow shop at the age of 10. Two years later he became an apprentice, signing his indentures (until age 21) to an older brother who had a printer's shop in Boston. As related in his autobiography, Ben considered running away on many occasions because of a "strong inclination for the sea." After becoming proficient in his trade, Ben finally did resolve to run away. Helped by a friend, Ben managed to arrange his leave by securing passage with a ship captain sailing for New York. The captain only agreed to take Ben as a passenger after being falsely told that an escape from Boston was critical because the boy had gotten a "naughty Girl with Child." Ben, like many runaways, enjoyed his travels and the experience of being in New York City. Penniless and unknown, he soon made his way to Philadelphia and began an illustrious career (Bremner, 1970).

Throughout American history, periods of war and social upheaval have always spurred runaway activity. Certainly this was true during the Revolutionary War. Numerous youths ran away to join the army while other New England boys found their way to American warships. One New Hampshire youth captured the excitement and emotions of the time in his diary, which described the activity in Portsmouth Harbor on the New Hampshire seacoast.

> Ships were building, prizes taken from the enemy unloading, privateers fitting out, standards waved on the forts and batteries, the exercising of soldiers, the roar of cannon, the sound of martial music and the call for volunteers so infatuated me that I was filled with anxiety to become an actor in the scene of war. . . . Though not yet fourteen years of age, like other boys, I imagined myself almost a man. I had intimated to my sister that, if my Father would not consent that I should go to sea, I would run away and go on board a privateer (Sherburne, 1831: 18]

Running away was not confined to urban locations or even the more populated sections of the country. By way of illustration, it is instructive to note that in the late 1790s the poor young son of a revolutionary war soldier ran away from his frontier home in the northeastern part of Tennessee. He was leaving home in order both to escape a beating from his father and to explore the surrounding region. After several years of wandering, the boy returned home, only to leave again soon there after. This 13 year-old boy was Davy Crockett, who was to become, according to noted historian Daniel Boorstein, "the most important and for some time, the most widely-known popular candidate for national hero-worship" (Boorstein, 1965: 328).

Until the mid-1800s there were relatively few social and legal distinctions between children and adults. However, the impact of both industrialization and urbanization had a tremendous influence on the nation. This period in history marked a distinct change in the role of and expectations for young people. One result was to place increased restrictions on American youths.

While teenagers, many of whom were runaways, heeded Horace Greely's (1850) advice to "Go West, young man," the industrial development on the nation's east coast created a new and in many ways different system of child labor. The generally stable but exceedingly long apprentice system which had been so prevalent and necessary for learning a trade in the colonial period was now replaced by a new order. Factory work was generally routine, simple, and mechanical, often requiring exhausting hours but little skill. Although major technological advances in the late nineteenth century would eliminate many unskilled positions held by child laborers, prior to and even after the Civil War young people were attracted to factory work. There are many reports of sons and daughters of poor, rural families from small New England towns running away to seek employment in these industrial plants. This occurred despite the fact that, according to the Boston *Evening Transcript* of March 24, 1832, "the time of labor is from the break of day until eight o'clock in the evening" (Bremner, 1970). During this period the vast richness of the American west, the allure of the sea, the excitement of city life, and the outbreak of the Civil War all contributed to the runaway syndrome (Thernstrom, 1964; Wittke, 1939; Handlin, 1951).

Urbanization was most evident on the eastern shores in the nineteenth century. The population of Massachusetts, for example, increased from 523,287 in 1820 to well over one million people in 1860. During a comparable period, more than 5,000,000 immigrants journeyed to this country (Bremner, 1970). It was during this time that leaders in American cities, especially those in the northeast, became aware of the growing numbers of poor and immigrant children who were in evidence on almost every street corner. Many of these young people were either incapable or unwilling to work, while others lacked proper adult supervision. Only a small percentage of these immigrant youths participated in the developing public education system which had been introduced by, among others, Horace Mann, Henry Barnard, James Carter, and Samuel Lewis. These conditions became even more noticeable after compulsory education laws were passed in 1836.

Although immigrant children did not import delinquency to America, the growing poverty, idleness, and crime rates were most prevalent in those locations where the new arivals lived. The basic family institution was under great stress, and numerous observers described with alarm the prevalence of uncontrolled and unproductive youth. Josiah Quincy, who was the mayor of Boston and the former President of Harvard College, reported in 1820 on the poor, idle and vicious children of that city (Bremner, 1970). Many of these youths were found wandering and begging in the streets. These and similar types of runaway and street children were vividly described by George Matsell, a police chief New York City:

> I allude to the constantly increasing numbers of vagrant, idle and vicious children of both sexes, who infest our public fares, hotels, docks . . . wherever ther inclination leads them, a large proportion of these juvenile vagrants are in the daily practice of pilfering whatever offers, and begging where they cannot steal. . . . The female portion of the youngest class, those who have only seen some eight or twelve summers, are addicted to immoralities of the most loathsome descriptions [Bremner, 1970: 755].

In response to, and perhaps in anticipation of, these changes in economic and social conditions during this period, several important new reform measures were adopted which had considerable impact on young people. As early as 1830, Joseph Tuckerman, a Unitarian clergyman in Boston, argued that child labor was leading to moral ruin, ignorance, and general delinquency (Bremner, 1970). Efforts were made to regulate and control child labor, while at the same time reformers were proposing that formal public schooling be made mandatory as a way of ensuring that social and moral values as well as skilled trades could be taught to all children. The Massachusetts statute of 1836, the earliest compulsory school attendance law in the nation, declared that children under the age of 15 could be employed in manufacturing only if they had received three months of schooling in the year preceding their employment (Bremner, 1970). Fourteen years later Horace Greeley proposed a law reform which was hailed as a major liberal measure. It called for a limit of a 10-hour work day for children under the age of 12 (Greeley, 1850).

The society at large was becoming increasingly alarmed about those adolescents who departed from home prematurely. Unlike their earlier predecessors, these children were particularly noticeable, not only because they were of immigrant parents, but also because they would congregate in significant numbers on urban street corners. Most of them were neither wanted nor needed in the labor force and many of them turned to a life of crime. These factors led to the imposition of state control in the affiars of the once-sancrosanct family unit. This new relationship marked a profound change for adolescents and resulted in increased intervention on the part of police and social workers who frequently interceded on behalf of these children. Many a parent of a runaway or street child was found to be incapable of providing adequate guidance for their offspring during the latter stages of the nineteenth century, and as a result some youngsters were placed in alternative living arrangements.

Contemporary programs of delinquency control can be traced back to the end of the nineteenth century, when social reformers helped to create special judicial and correctional institutions for the labeling, processing, and management of troublesome youth. The "invention" of delinquency, according to Anthony Platt (1969), was very much the work of reform-minded middle- and upper-class women who were particularly concerned about poor immigrant children living in large American cities. Because these humanitarians were dedicated to rescuing those who were less fortunately placed in the social order, their orientation confirmed a growing tendency to view children as naturally dependent and in need of constant adult supervision. By fostering the creation of a juvenile court system, the child-savers not only reaffirmed old categories of deviant behavior, but they identified and invented new ones. In many of these behaviors, such as running away, the "actor" was a participant in a victimless crime. Such classifications as "stubborn child" or "wayward minor" would later become known as status offenses during the twentieth century. These behaviors were actions that were illegal only for persons under 18 years of age. The reformers of this period, therefore, played a major role as social engineers for middle-class moral values and they were viewed as upholders of traditional social institutions such as the family and the school (Platt, 1969).

The juvenile justice system, which took hold only at the turn of this century, was designed to be a benevolent and paternalistic one. Given the ideological underpinnings of the child-savers' movement, it is not surprising that this developing court system diminished the civil rights and the privacy of youth. The following comments by Judge Julian Mack, one of the early proponents of the juvenile court system, relect not only the fatherly tone but the authoritarian posture of those in charge.

> The problem for determination by the judge is not, Has this boy or girl committed a wrong but what is he, how has he become what he is and what had best be done in his interest and in the interest of the state to save him from a downward career [Mack, 1909: 119]

The concept of *"parens patriae"* not only authorized the courts to use wide discretion in resolving the problems of youthful offenders, but it formalized the increased power of the state in family matters.

Young delinquent children, be they runaways or street children in America's cities, were now sent to special institutions for youthful offenders. Although Platt cites 1899 as the year in which the first juvenile court was developed (in Illinois), Massachusetts was already operating similar institutions as early as the 1830s. The Farm School, for example, was established on Thompson's Island outside of Boston in 1833 for "children between the ages of seven and fourteen who were growing up in idleness and hastening to crime" (Bremner,1970: 127). Magistrates like William Sayer were reluctant to convict delinquents as criminals. He commented about his responsibilities in the following manner:

> During the past nine years, I have been frequently called upon to issue warrants against juvenile offenders . . . the complaints are for petty thefts, pilfering from gardens and orchards . . . for being runaways, stubborn children, idlers and vagabonds. . . . But there is seldom a case of a juvenile offender in which I am not well satisfied that the parents, or person having the child in charge is most blamable [Bremner, 1970: 696].

The runaway youth phenomenon was greatly exacerbated during the Great Depression years. This period of economic diseaster, more than any event (except that is, for the countercultural movement of the 1960s), was responsible for publicizing the plight of runaway and transient youth. During the 1930s great numbers of boys and girls from varied socioeconomic backgrounds left home, often running away or departing with the tacit consent of impoverished parents. In response to this highly visible and well-publicized young army of transient youths, the United States government established the Federal Relief Administration in 1933. As a result of this legislation, some camps and shelters for young people were established.

In 1934, the National Conference of Social Workers examined the issue of transient youth and found it to be an important concern.

They described the transient boy in the following manner:

> He is a small-town boy either seeking adventure or withdrawing from a home situation where relief is inadequate and from a community which affords no opportunity for employment. . . . Because he is denied the maturing influence which a job would yield, the period of his adolescence is being unduly extended [Bremner, 1974: 29].

Transient Service Bureaus were opened in order to provide lodgings for young people on the road. In selected locations, education and vocational training were provided in addition to recreation and work programs. Most of these projects were designed with the hope that these teenagers would settle down and then return home. Not surprisingly, runaway and transient youths were selective in their travels, frequently moving to attractive and appealing locations. A report entitled "Transients in December 1934" suggested that many youths were attracted to the city of Jacksonville (Florida) because of the mild weather and the local resort attractions (Bremner, 1974). The city of Dallas also took in many young transients coming to the legendary southwest, while numerous younger adolescents were drawn to Los

Angeles because of the motion picture studios, by a desire to see the Pacific Ocean, and by the winter climate.

John Burkhart studied transient boys in Cleveland, Ohio, during the 1930s. He reported that "when they first start out on the road, the majority of these boys are honestly seeking employment . . . but meeting rebuff after rebuff, they become hardened and bitter" (Bremner, 1974: 32). A special U.S. House Select Committee was established to investigate interstate migration, particularly out of concern for the transient girl. A report by Mary Vorse about the Scottsboro case also provide a descriptive account of runaway and transient lifestyles during the 1930s (Vorse, 1933).

During the past five or six decades, many young runaway have been categorized as law breakers and delinquents. Historically, police officials and juvenile court officers have had the responsibility of controlling these youths (Levine and Levine, 1969). Since the turn of the century, the mental health profession has also played a significant role in working with runaway children. Ever since Lightner Witmer started the first psychological clinic for children and William Healey opened the first psychiatric clinic in 1909 as part of the juvenile court of Chicago, psychiatrists and clinical psychologists have become important agents of treatment and control (Goldenberg, 1971). These professionals have not only become responsible for identifying and classifying deviant or pathological behavior but in developing therapeutic remedies as well. Although there has been considerable controversy and differences of opinion regarding the cause and meanings of runaway behavior, by 1970 the American Psychiatric Association officially categorized running away as a mental disorder (Jenkins, 1971).

During the 1940s and 1950s, runaway activity was present but not well publicized. World War II and the Korean conflict were responsible for many runaway episodes. It was not until the countercultural youth movement in the 1960s, however, that running away reached the heart of America's consciousness. The youth culture which developed in urban centers around the country—in Cambridge, New York, Washington, San Francisco, and Berkeley—attracted thousands of runaways (Ambrosino, 1971).

It was a new consciousness . . . a new medium of human relations. A magnet drawing together all the freaky, hip, unhappy, young, happy, curious, criminal, gentle, alienated, weird, fustrated, far-out, artistic, lonely, lovely people to the same place at the same time [Rubin, 1970: 56].

What made this such an extraordinary occurrence was the fact that many, perhaps even a majority, of these youths were from comfortable middle- and upper-class families. Unlike most of their predecessors who, over the years, have frequently come from poor families, these runaways were both leaving and rejecting considerable material comforts, educational advantages, and future professional prospects. Instead, these youths often adopted a simple gypsy lifestyle with few possessions, little money, and even less interest in succeeding in the existing social order. For many of these adolescents, self-exploration, self-expression, drug experimentation, sexual freedom, and communal living were attractive and exciting alternatives to living at home (Kaufman et al., 1969).

By the latter part of 1967, the first runaway programs in America were initiated in several large cities which had experienced a large influx of young people. Project Place and Bridge over Troubled Waters in Boston were among the first of these service programs working with countless runaway and street children in Massachusetts. Other service projects like Runaway House in Washington, D.C., and Huckleberry's in San francisco shared a common purpose of assisting these teenagers, many of whom were under 16. Providing service to and being advocates for these adolescents became a central focus of these programs.

Although the youth scene began to change by early 1970s as the "flower age" faded, young people continued to leave home in great numbers. The United States Senate Subcommittee on Juvenile Delinquency, for example, estimated that the total number of runaway children in the year 1972 exceeded one million.

Until 1974, when the Runaway Youth Act was approved by the President, there had never been federal legislation that specifically recognized or provided funding for young people who had run away from home. (The legislation during the Depression years was aimed at all transient people.) The Congress reported:

> The number of juveniles who leave and remain away from home without parental permission has increased to alarming proportions, creating a substantial law enforcement problem for the communities inundated and significantly endangering the young people who are without resources and live on the street [U.S. Congress, Senate, 1972: 6].

It may be correctly argued that only when the runaway youth issue reached "middle America" did it become an issue of considerable public attention and concern.

During the intervening years, running away from home has remained a major social phenomenon, although most youths have tended to stay in closer proximity of their hometown or state as compared with the more transient patterns of the late 1960s. One intention of another piece of youth legislation, the Juvenile Justice and Delinquency Prevention Act of 1974, has been to decriminalize status offenses such as running away. Progress to date has been sporadic and uneven, and some critics feel that, despite the stated intentions, many procedures and labeling tendencies continue today.

When viewed in a historical perspective, it is apparent that children from poor families have often run away to escape poverty. For many adolescents, running away has been a response to an unhealthy family or work situation, and at times it has been a problem-solving behavior. Since early colonial days, running away has been synonymous with seeking adventure, romance, and one's fortune. Last but not least, running away has been an expression of independence, often marking a passage into adulthood. Periods of great social economic, cultural, and political change have always fostered runaway behavior, and periods of war have also contributed to this syndrome.

There is a great need to narrow the existing gap of knowledge and understanding concerning runaway children. Being neither a creation of the turbulent 1960s nor a minor passing fad, the concept of the adolescent period in our society, specifically runaway adolescents, is now and will continue to be a major concern for years to come. Presently, our society most often labels runaway children as either psychopathological or delinquent (or perhaps both). Yet a review of the history of running away in America provides much contradictory evidence (Shellow et al., 1967; Walker, 1975).

While running away may be an indication of inadequate social or psychological development for limited numbers of youths, there is reason to believe that within our historical perspective the behavior may be understood as a natural reaction to certain predictable societal forces and even as a positive response to serious problems.

FOOTNOTES

1. The terms "adolescent," "children," and "youth" are used interchangeably throughout this article.

REFERENCES

Abbot, E.
1908 "A study of the early history of child labor in America." Amer. J. of Sociology 14: 15-38.

Ambrosino, L.
1971 Runaways. Boston: Beacon.

Aries, P.
1962 Centuries of Childhood. New York: Alfred A. Knopf.

Borstein, D. J.
1965 The Americans. New York: Random House.

Bremmer, R. H.
1974 Children and Youth in America; Volume III. Cambridge, MA: Harvard University Press.
1970 Children and Youth in America, Volume I. Cambridge, MA: Harvard University Press.

Goldenberg, I. I.
1971 Build Me a Mountain. Cambridge: MIT Press.

Greeley, H.
1850 Hints Toward Reform. New York: Harper & Row.

Handlin, O.
1951 The Uprooted. Boston: Little, Brown.

Jenkins, R. L.
1971 "The runaway reaction." Amer. J. of Psychiatry, 128, 2: 168-173.

Kaufman, J., J. R. Allen, and L. J. West.
1969 "Runaways, hippies, and marijuana." Amer. J. of Psychiatry 126: 163-166.

Levine, M. and A. Levine
1969 A Social History of Helping: Clinic, Court, School and Community. New York: McGraw-Hill.

Mack, J. W.
1909 "The juvenile court." Harvard Law Rev. 23: 104-122.

Platt, A. M.
1969 The Child Savers: The Invention of Delinquency. Chicago: Univ. Of Chicago Press.

Rubin, J.
1970 Do It. New York: Simon and Schuster.

Shellow, R., J. R. Schamp, E. Liebow, and E. Unger.
1967 "Suburban Runaways of the 1960's." Monographs of the Society for Research in Child Development 32, 3, Serial No. 111.

Sherburn, A.
1831 Memoirs. Providence, R. I.

Shurtleff, N. (ed.)
1854 Massachusetts Records: Records of the Governor and Company of Massachusetts Bay. five Volumes: 1628-1685.

Thernstrom, S.
1964 Poverty and Progress: Social Mobility in a Nineteenth Century City. Cambridge, MA: Harvard University Press.

Vorse, M. H.
1933 "How Scottsboro happened." New Republic 74.

Walker, D. K.
    1975 Runaway Youth, an Annotated Bibliography and Literature Overview. Washington, DC: Office of the Assistant Secretary for Planning and Evaluation, Department of Health, Education and Welfare.

Witke, C.
    1939 We Who Built America. Cleveland: Press of Western Reserve University. U.S. Congress, Senate.

U.S. Congress, Senate.
    1972 Runaway Youth. Hearings before the Subcommittee to Investigate Juvenile Delin quency of the Committee on the Judiciary. 92nd Congress, 1st session. Legislative hear ings on S. 2829, the "Runaway Youth Act." January 13-14.

20

Poverty has been a major cause of family crises throughout history. The pages of history are permeated by tales of horror that befell families with inadequate incomes. Poverty has been a factor in the existence of infanticide, in the mental and physical retardation of children, in the uprooting of families, and in family desertion by mothers, fathers, and children.

In this stimulating article, Elaine T. May suggests that, in a cruel twist of historical destiny, while the spread of affluence lifted many Americans into the middle class and eliminated most economic causes of family decay, it led to the increase in another form of family dislocation: divorce. May argues that increased affluence led to greater expectations on the part of women, particularly middle class wives, and, consequently, to increased pressure on their husbands to provide them with the varied delights offered by a consumer-oriented society. The interactions between economic expectations and psychological pressures, according to May, fostered a startling rise in the divorce rate by 1920.

Do you agree? Are economic conditions primary factors in male-female conflicts? Or are they symptoms of more fundamental problems?

The Pressure to Provide:
Class, Consumerism, and Divorce in
Urban America, 1880-1920

Elaine Tyler May

In an era of massive production of consumer goods, what determines the normative standard of living, and what constitutes the necessities of life? These questions became increasingly difficult to answer during the decades surrounding the turn of the century, when profound economic changes ushered in corporate America. Scholars have documented a number of crucial developments, including standardized industrial technology, a mushrooming national bureaucracy, a shorter work week, and increased wages. Some observers hail these changes for providing security and material abundance to enhance the home and enrich private life. Others lament the loss of the craft tradition, and the intrinsic satisfactions that went with it. Still others claim that consumerism was a ploy to buy off workers and women, making them complacent while discouraging effective unionization and political action.[1] But, as yet, no study has used empirical data to probe the impact of these developments on American families, or determined how they affected individuals on different levels of the class order. This article examines and compares the effects of heightened material aspirations upon wealthy, white-collar, and blue-collar Americans. While the rising standard of living may have enhanced family life for some among the comfortable classes, it often wreaked havoc in the homes of those who could not afford the fruits of abundance. It is no accident that the emergence of the affluent society paralleled the skyrocketing of the American divorce rate.

One way to explore the way in which prosperity took its toll is to examine the casualties themselves. I have used hundreds of divorce cases filed during these years to uncover some of the economic problems that plagued American marriages. The samples include 500 litigations from Los Angeles in the 1880s, and another 500 from 1920. A comparative sample includes 250 divorces filed throughout New Jersey in 1920. The proceedings cover a developing west-coast city with little manufacturing, and an eastern industrial state with a large rural population. Within the samples are individuals from virtually every ethnic group and occupational category. By comparing the accusations mentioned in the 1880s and in 1920, we can determine the effects of economic change over time, during these crucial transitional years. The testimonies of the litigants in these cases reveal the limits of abundance, and suggest that no class or locale was immune to the ill effects of rising material aspirations. . . .[2] Although the percentage of cases filed on the grounds of "neglect to provide" did not rise significantly between the two samples taken, these problems did become more complicated in the later decades. The Lynds found a similar development in Muncie, Indiana. In spite of the fairly constant rate of neglect complaints in divorce litigations from 1890 to the 1920s, "economic considerations figure possibly more drastically than formerly as factors in divorce."[3]

At first glance, this appears rather perplexing. The nation was more prosperous in the later period than the earlier, and the standard of living was rising steadily for all classes. Moreover, women found greater opportunities to work, and both males and females experienced increasing wages and more free time off the job. During the same years, an unprecedented abundance of consumer goods became available on a mass level. Presumably, these developments would contribute to easing tensions between husbands and wives rather than creating them, while fostering a more pleasant, expressive, and comfortable existence. However, with the standard of living rising, and affluence filtering down to a greater proportion of the population, the "provider" was often expected to fulfill the increased demands sparked by widespread prosperity.

The evidence in the divorce proceedings suggests that this was not a major problem in the 1880s. Although financial conflicts appeared often, there was no controversy over what constituted the necessities of life. Either a husband supported his family, or he did not. Virtually all of the cases in the early sample that dealt with issues of neglect were clear-cut. If a man did not provide enough food, clothing, and shelter for his wife to live comfortably, she was entitled to a divorce. No husband questioned that; and no quarrels ensued over what his obligation entailed.

One typical case was that of Mary and Emmet Hickey. They were married in 1882, at Virginia City, Nevada. During their three-year marriage, they had one child, and Emmet worked as a teamster in Los Angeles. Their community property consisted of a small amount of household furiture worth $100. The basic problem in the marriage was Emmet's inability to fulfill his role as provider. When Mary requested money for "the necessities of life for herself and little child, her husband, disregarding his duties as a husband toward the wife, cruelly told her that he would not give her a dollar . . . if she did not like it, she could leave him and go elsewhere." To make matters worse, his behavior was hardly genteel; he swore often, calling her a "lying bitch" and a "bastard." As she was a "weak, frail woman," his behavior seriously impaired her health.[4] In a similar case, Christina Adams claimed that her husband, a miner, "never earned one cent," never provided for her, and told her, "You don't know enough to spend money. You don't know enough to buy your own clothes." To add to his other insults, when she requested two dollars for shopping, he replied, "I will shit you two dollars."[5]

In the 1880s, divorcing wives complained if their mates failed to provide for them. But they did not complain about how much their husbands provided. By 1920, however, it was no longer clear precisely what constituted adequate support on the part of a husband, and a number of bitter conflicts erupted over the issue. Money problems affected marriages of the wealthy as well as the poor. . . .

The Keagys, for example, were an affluent Los Angeles couple who lived together only seven months. John Keagy was a dentist with a good deal of property, and his wife Zella was also fairly wealthy in her own right. According to John, Zella had a monthly income of $75 (although John did not say the source), plus six lots in Alabama, bank accounts, stocks, and diamonds. She had been married previously, and had a daughter. The evidence suggests that she was widowed, although that is not entirely clear. Apparently, John and Zella had a rather stormy relationship. Throughout their charges and countercharges of cruelty, humiliation, violence, and insult, they had a running debate over financial matters. Zella felt neglected. She complained to a friend that John "did not appreciate her enough, she didn't like the house he furnished her, that her house in Alabama was so fine, and that her first husband would have sacrificed anything for her." She requested a divorce, $500 in fees, and $75 per month alimony. Denying the charges, John filed a cross-complaint on the grounds of cruelty, claiming that Zella "proceeded to run bills against him, without justification, which were not for the necessities of life." Finally, Zella was granted a divorce, and the bitter financial conflict ended with a property agreement. In this case, money may not have been the primary issue, but it certainly aggravated an already bad marriage. In spite of their wealth, John and Zella Keagy could not agree on an appropriate level of expenditure.[6]

Another example suggests how a wife's material desires might put strains upon a marriage, if a husband's income was adequate but not enormous. Edward and Louise Atkinson were a middle-class couple who married in Brooklyn in 1910. During their ten-year marriage, they spent several years living apart, and had constant quarrels over money matters. Finally, Edward filed for a divorce. Aside from Louise's alleged adultery, her husband claimed that she "spent money freely and extravagantly and with utter disregard of his circumstances." Although they had no children, he gave her his $35 per week salary, keeping only $1 to buy tobacco and other small items for himself. From 1915 to 1917, she remained in New York, refusing to join him in California. At the same time, she corresponded with other men who gave her money.

One bone of contention between the two was Louise's fetish for pet dogs. Once she wrote to Edward, asking him for $75 for another dog, which she "would rather have than an evening gown." Complaining of the sacrifices she had made for her negligent husband, she bemoaned the loss of one of her animals: "I sold Peggy to buy you a suit." In another letter, she claimed that he owed her money, for "there is no Tom [reference unclear, perhaps her lover] here to take care of me, and I am not well enough to work."

Edward Atkinson considered his wife's material desires quite outrageous. But apparently she found a paramour who was more inclined to cater to her tastes for the trappings of elegance and high culture. He wrote her slick letters about fancy hotels where she could stay on New York's Fifth Avenue, learn painting "from a good teacher and meet artistic people," and frequent his luxurious new club house, which was "most comfortable in every way." At the same time, she wrote to her husband in California that she was in a dire situation: "Now, I am in need, do I have to make out an itemized bill, or do you have enough *manhood* to do the proper and decent thing towards me?" According to Louise, this meant "weekly payments until such time as you figure you have done your duty." She then told him to go ahead with the divorce, she will not object. The court apparently had no sympathy for her alleged difficulties, and granted Edward the divorce. Nevertheless, Louise's pleas are revealing. Not only did she consider herself "in need," but she equated her husband's ability to provide for her desires—however eccentric—with his very "manhood." For Louise Atkinson, manhood and duty meant taking care of women—and in the proper style.[7]

This equation reflected more than the demand of an outraged wife. It symbolized a much larger phenomenon that had evolved with the maturation of industrial society. Women who placed heavy demands upon their husbands were not merely selfish or lazy. Although these were the years of women's presumed "emancipation," females still faced limited options outside the home. Middle-class wives in particular may have felt restless as well as powerless. While their numbers in the work force increased, it was still considered undesirable for a married woman to work. If a wife did seek employment, she did not have access to the most lucrative, prestigious, and rewarding occupations. Most jobs available to women were routine and monotonous, with low pay and few chances for advancement.

What was left, then, to give these married females personal satisfaction? Even at home they may have felt a sense of uselessness. Childbearing and household responsibilities utilized less of a woman's creative energies as the birth rate declined and labor-saving devices proliferated. New avenues for self-expression had to be explored. The economy offered little in the way of jobs; yet it provided seemingly unlimited possibilities for consumerism. Indeed, female emancipation found its most immediate expression not in the work force, but in the realms of styles and leisure pursuits. These were purchasable, provided one had the means. If wives began spending to adorn their homes and themselves, it may have reflected their constraints elsewhere. It is no wonder that, for some women, this gave rise to an obsession with material goods and private indulgence. Thus, they turned the full force of their pent-up energies to these endeavors.[8]

With limited financial resources of their own, women often looked to men to provide the means for their consumption desires. This pressure was one of many new challenges facing 20th-century males. While public notice focused on new female activities, parallel shifts that affected men went virtually unnoticed. Males continued to work, their clothing styles remained practically unaltered, and their public behavior did not change dramatically. Yet they were experiencing a subtle transformation in sex-role expectations that, while not as obvious as the new status of women, was no less profound.

For white-collar men, the most far-reaching changes came with the maturation of the corporate system. The engulfing bureaucracies stabilized many uncertainties of the earlier era, and offered at least a modicum of security. The 20th-century businessman was less likely to enter business on his own, with the full burden of success or failure resting on his shoulders. If one followed the rules, he would advance up the hierarchy in a steady, predictable manner, and reach a moderate level of success and prosperity. There may have been few examples of men making a fortune overnight within the modern system; but, in fact, the Carnegies of the previous era served as little more than encouragement to fantasies. The top of the ladder was virtually closed then as well as later.[9] However, successful men had been models of 19th-century striving. In spite of new rewards, the corporations took away some of the unique triumphs of individual enterprise.

With the mechanization of industry, increasing production, the declining work week, and a rising standard of living, the benefits were obvious. In terms of purely material considerations, the corporate economy offered abundance and leisure. The tragedy, however, was that the aspiration for affluence was more widespread than the luxurious life itself. Even if an individual entered the white-collar ranks, he still faced enormous pressures to advance and succeed. Supplying increased demands necessitated continual striving. This was difficult enough for relatively successful businessmen, but infinitely more so for employees with modest salaries, or for petty proprietors without the cushion of corporate security.

We know from national statistics that the white-collar level of society shifted away from self-employed businessmen to corporate bureaucrats and clerical workers. Our Los Angeles samples reflect a similar trend. These white-collar group, possibly more than any other level in society, were striving for upward mobility, afraid of slipping down the socioeconomic ladder, and concerned with deriving the fruits of their labor in tangible material goods. Arno Mayer has suggested that, historically, the petite bourgeoisie was possibly the most insecure and status-conscious level in western nations. This group had its own unique aspirations and cultural forms geared toward emulating the more affluent groups above them. If this premise holds for 20th-century America, and I believe it does, then petty proprietors facing competition from large corporations, as well as rank and file white-collar workers, would be feeling these pressures most intensely. . . .[10]

Looking at the divorce samples from Los Angeles, we find that, by 1920, the low-white-collar level is overrepresented, compared to its proportion of the general population. In the later sample, the proportion of divorces granted to the wealthy classes declined dramatically as the more bureaucratic clerical and sales categories mushroomed. At the same time, the percentage of petty proprietors in the work force shrank; but these small businessmen remained heavily overrepresented in the divorce samples. Those who remained among the entrepreneurial ranks may well have felt new pressures. As large chains and department stores began drawing local patrons and customers away from independent enterprises, owners of small shops and businesses may have faced increasing insecurity. To add to these burdens, many of them had to purchase goods from larger firms, making them dependent upon a national marketing system. Undersold by large competitors who often controlled production and supply as well as distribution, and bound by wholesale merchandise prices, they may have tried to cut costs by turning to family labor. This was not always a satisfactory solution, especially if proprietors of small concerns had to cope with diminishing returns as well as increasing consumer demands. It is perhaps no wonder that this group had more than its share of divorce.

Unfortunately, relatively few of the divorce litigants articulated how financial and status considerations affected their marriages and their lives. As with virtually every complex issue that eroded these relationships, we must glean insights from a handful of cases where evidence is rich and detailed. In terms of material considerations, we are able to discern a pattern of discontent for each of the major socioeconomic levels represented.[11] As we saw in the two cases cited above, affluence did not preclude the possibility of money squabbles. The leisured wife of a man with means might make a quasi-career out of purchasing goods and adorning herself and her abode. Even wealthy husbands may have reacted against frivolous or wasteful expenditures. But if a man's income was consistently a measure below his wife's aspirations for comfortable living, the tension could become chronic and destroy a marriage that otherwise might have survived.

In the divorce proceedings, conflicts over status and social mobility stand out in bold relief, particularly among white-collar families on the west coast. It is here that we can best perceive the intensified pressures placed upon men to supply heightened material desires. Norman Shinner, for example, admitted that he deserted his wife after five years of marriage because of his "inability to support her in the manner she desired on my salary, and on this account we could not live together in an amiable manner." Rather than struggling to meet up to his wife's aspirations, Norman Shinner simply left.[12]

Although these pressures were particularly acute for the lower middle-class, they were also severe for workers. Financial difficulties among working-class couples, however, were qualitatively different from those facing white-collar families. Laborers faced a double-edged problem. They may have felt the same status anxieties as petty proprietors or rank and file bureaucrats, but it was often difficult for them to make ends meet. Blue-collar families lived with the uncertainties of a fluid labor market and usually lacked the cushion of corporate security. Weak or non-existent labor unions left them virtually unprotected. This is not to deny the fact that some of the abundance filtered down among the working classes. By 1900, their improved circumstances prompted Samuel Gompers, when asked if he thought the conditions of workers were worsening, to reply, "Oh, that is perfectly absurd."[16] In our samples, we find that financial conflicts among blue-collar families actually decreased somewhat between 1880 and 1920. However, their percentage of the total number of litigants increased markedly. This may reflect a number of factors. It is possible that in the 1880s, the very price of a divorce precluded legal action for many blue-collar couples. When they did come to court, nearly one-third of them included money conflicts among their complaints. By 1920, more workers may have been able to afford a divorce, and the wives might have been less likely to complain of financial desperation. Yet status and spending concerns might well have helped erode these unions as well. To add to the problem of meeting basic needs, working-class families also shared new consumer desires with their more affluent peers. But for those with meager incomes, luxuries were out of the question, and the affluence they saw everywhere around them only served to heighten frustrations.

Working-class couples, then, faced compounded difficulties. Often the breadwinner's earnings were inadequate and his job insecure. Moreover, he was subject to the same sorts of demands for mass-produced goods as his white-collar contemporaries. One of the crucial features of the consumer-oriented economy was the way it transcended class boundaries. On one level, this contributed to a certain superficial "classless" quality. But, on another level, it served to homogenize tastes in a society where wealth remained unequally distributed. Once self-esteem and validation came to rest upon supplying material goods, those on the bottom rungs would be considered less worthy. We have seen that Louise Atkinson, the middle-class woman in the case cited earlier, had tastes that outdistanced her husband's ability as well as willingness to provide. Yet her evaluation of his very "manhood" rested on this function of his income. For working-class women, the situation may have been less frivolous and more desperate. Nevertheless, the equation still held.

Alberta Raschke was a blue-collar wife in Los Angeles with a five-year-old daughter. She filed for a divorce on the grounds of desertion and neglect, claiming that her husband forced her to rely on her parents' charity. The couple married in Indiana in 1913, and separated four years later. At some point, Alberta came to California and William remained in Chicago. In a letter, she accused him of refusing to support her, and claimed that she was in a "weakened condition." "You have had ample time to *make a man of yourself* in all these six years, if you cared for your wife and baby, instead of driving a wagon for $12 a week. You would not take work offered you at $21 a week, so it is not because you could not find better. I stood for all the terrible abuse you gave me, and went without the very necessities of life to see if you would not come to your senses, but now I am tired of waiting and have decided to file suit for divorce . . . I am as ever Alberta."[17]

Although Alberta Raschke probably had a valid complaint, the pressure put upon William to "make a man" of himself may have been unfair. It is not clear why he did not take the job allegedly offered to him for more pay, but perhaps he simply enjoyed what he was doing. The conflict between working at a job one liked and working for money may have ultimately led to this divorce. Although William Raschke apparently found the lower paying job more satisfying, as far as his wife was concerned the primary purpose of his work was to make money. Undoubtedly, it was not easy for this women to live on $12 a week with a five-year-old child. However, the equation of manhood with the ability to provide placed a particularly heavy burden on a working-class husband.

Oscar Lishnog faced similar difficulties. He married Martha in Chicago in 1908, and had four children prior to their Los Angeles divorce. While the Lishnogs appeared to be a fairly comfortable suburban family, financial strain ultimately caused their union to collapse. Oscar was in the insurance and real estate business, working as an employee or salesman rather than executive or proprietor. His income was steady but modest. He spent some time living apart from his family while working in San Pedro; nevertheless, Oscar and Martha exchanged frequent loving, chatty, but slightly distant letters to each other. He sent her money, she tried to save, and they express affection for one another. Now and then Martha would tell Oscar to "mind the store and not waste time or money." Revealing her material aspirations, she wrote that many of her neighbors owned automobiles, for there was no street car line nearby. This suggests that their Los Angeles home was in a fairly new suburban development, removed from the downtown district and transportation network. Martha also reminded her husband that she was paying mortgage on the house, and the "kids want a hammock." She usually closed with affection, saying she was "waiting for him."

But in 1920, Martha filed for divorce on the grounds of willful neglect, saying that Oscar spent his $35 per week salary in "riotous living away from his family," squandering his money while depriving his wife and children. Claiming that she was not skilled in any vocation, Martha said she had to rely on the charity of friends. She asked for custody of the children. Oscar denied the charges, insisting that he earned only $21 per week and gave it all to his wife except a small amount for living expenses. He asked that the divorce be denied, and, assuming that they would remain living apart, requested joint custody of the children. Nevertheless, the court granted Martha the divorce, plus custody, $9 per week for the children, and $3 per month for her "personal recreation." This final item, though minimal in amount, suggests that courts were willing to designate some money for amusements and consumption within the category of necessities—which men were required to provide. Whatever other problems may be hidden from our view that contributed to this couple's woes, it is clear that money was a sore spot for a long time. Oscar's salary was hardly abundant, and he was finally unable to supply the demands of his wife and children to maintain their suburban lifestyle.[13]

Perhaps one of the most telling of these cases was the Los Angeles divorce of Margaret and Donald Wilton. She was a devout midwestern Protestant whose marriage to her clerk husband lasted two years. At one point, she wrote to her estranged spouse, hoping to be reconciled. She recommended that he read some bible passages relating to the duties of husbands and wives, and promised to be a "good Christian wife." In a revealing passage at the end, she wrote, "I heard something about you that made my heart sing with joy; you have climbed another rung on the ladder of success. I am proud to know it, dear. . . . " In spite of Donald's improved status, their marriage was beyond repair. After a rather bitter case, Margaret Wilton was granted a divorce.[14]

Families such as the ones mentioned above may not have suffered severe deprivation. But, like other 20th-century couples, they faced a greater potential for disappointment when a modicum of luxury became the anticipated norm. As the standard of living continued to climb, the golden age of affluence seemed imminent, and it was anticipated with almost religious fervor. For much of the American population, increasing prosperity appeared as a signal from the Divine that the culmination of progress was at hand. One observer perceived, "To most people a millenium implies spiritual overtones. So does the standard of living."[15] For a male provider, then, inability to keep up with this sanctified progress meant failure and damnation.

In general, working-class wives were less obsessed with status considerations and more concerned with bread and butter issues. Most blue-collar divorces that included money difficulties revolved around basic needs, similar to the conflicts that surfaced in the 1880s proceedings. These problems erupted frequently in New Jersey, where the majority of divorces were among blue-collar couples. It is important to keep in mind that New Jersey only permitted divorces on the grounds of adultery and desertion—not financial neglect. Nevertheless money was at the heart of many New Jersey litigations. In fact, a number of these couples struggled, quite literally, just to keep a roof over their heads. . . .

A severe housing shortage in urban areas placed serious strains on several marriages. Providers with meager earnings often found themselves unable to provide a home. Numerous couples lived with parents or other relatives, or moved from one form of lodging to another. For these couples, the inability to acquire adequate housing was the fundamental issue that destroyed their marriages. The Shafers were one such family. "I want one thing," pleaded Anna Shafer to her husband. "Won't you please come back and make a home for me, I don't care if it is only two rooms, if you can afford to pay for two rooms." They had been married since 1910, when they ran away together to Hoboken, New Jersey. Anna claimed that William deserted her three years later. She said that her husband was "a drinking man who never made a home or provided for her and their child," although he worked for an insurance company. Anna was granted a divorce and restored to her maiden name.

The same problems ended the marriage of Harris and Catherine Martin, two blue-collar workers in Newark. "I told him I would go anyplace with him as long as he could furnish me with a home," explained Catherine. "I didn't care where it was, even if it was only one room and I was alone." But after three months they separated, and Catherine was granted a divorce plus the return of her maiden name.[18]

Lack of housing and insecure work also disrupted the marriage of a Jewish couple in New Jersey. Sarah and Morris Dubin, who married in 1910, and had one child that died. Morris was a tailor by trade, but was unable to practice his craft. Instead, he worked for the railroad, and as a cook in a sanitarium. It appears that this duo had a rather stormy marriage, with Morris deserting now and then and Sarah continually begging him to make a home for her. Whenever she asked, "Why won't you make me a home and support me?" he replied, "I won't and can't live in Newark with you." Newark was particularly plagued by the housing shortage at this time, which aggravated the situation for Morris, who was unable to find work that utilized his tailoring skills. But the court had little mercy. The interviewer concluded that Morris was "apparently one of those people who find it difficult to settle down and perform his obligations for any length of time." Sarah won her suit and the return of her maiden name.[19]

Although a chronic shortage of basic needs eroded most of these blue-collar marriages, a number of working-class couples quarreled over consumer spending and status concerns as well. A few cases illustrate how squabbles might ensue over how money should be spent. Emma Totsworth was 19 when she married David Totsworth, a 22-year-old machinist, in Jersey City. Five years later she deserted. When asked about their difficulties, David said they argued "over different things, like going out and clothes, no clean clothes and all around jealousy. Simple meanness. She spent money on clothes that should have gone for eating." It appears that David Totsworth preferred to see his hard-earned income used for less frivolous items.[20]

Charles and Ada Davis were plagued by similar problems. They were married in New Jersey in 1902 and had one child. After nine years, Ada deserted and went to New York. Apparently Charles, a railroad brakeman, never managed to provide for her in the style that she wanted. According to the interviewer, Ada became "dissatisfied with her surroundings and complained of the style of life her husband afforded her. She wouldn't speak or recognize her husband sometimes for days at a time. Finally she left, saying she wanted to live where she wanted to, and also wanted him to support her." Charles' brother stood up for the aggrieved husband, saying that he "always worked steadily and was a good provider for his home and did everything he could for his wife and family that a man could do under his circumstances." But apparently it was not enough. Charles testified that Ada "insisted upon telling me how much more the neighbors had than she had, and what the neighbor's husband did, and what they didn't do. I told her that if she would stop listening to outsiders and live for me and our little girl as she had done up to that time, everything could be very nice and we could get along." But Ada's dissatisfaction increased until she finally left, and Charles was granted a New Jersey divorce on the grounds of desertion.[21]

These blue-collar couples were plagued by status anxieties. Both Emma Totsworth and Ada David had aspirations for material goods beyond the reach of their husbands' pay checks. Some wives not only held their spouses' incomes in disdain, they also looked down upon the work itself. Olivia Garside was a New Jersey housekeeper bent on feverish social climbing. After 26 years of marriage and three children, she finally left her husband Frederick, a machinist, who could not supply the lifestyle she craved. According to Frederick,

> My wife never considered me her equal. She told me this shortly after her marriage, and she was never satisfied with anything I might undertake to do and that I was not as neat appearing as a professional man. She would say my conversation wasn't as it should be and she felt I was socially beneath her. I have always turned over every cent I made to my wife outside of my traveling expenses. I have never been intoxicated in my life. I would very often work overtime and on Sundays around the neighborhood to earn a few dollars more. My wife always complained I wasn't making enough money.

This husband took pride in his work, his efforts to support his wife, his sobriety and discipline. But to his wife, he lacked polish and grace—and the ample income to go with it. The court granted Frederick a divorce on the grounds of desertion.[22]

The evidence in these cases suggests that mass consumption was not necessarily a positive outgrowth of the society's industrial development, even though it held the potential for increased financial security and a more comfortable lifestyle. Rather, these marital conflicts represent a failure or inability to come to terms with the changing economic order. For affluent couples, tensions emerged over how the family's resources should be spent. For those among the lower-white-collar ranks, status considerations clashed with limited incomes, creating enormous pressures upon the family breadwinner. For many working-class couples, mass consumption remained virtually out or reach, contributing to a greater sense of economic insecurity and heightened frustrations.

The testimonies of divorce litigants reflect the discrepancy between material desires and reality, for it was difficult to meet the soaring demands put before every consumer's eyes. Perhaps many Americans did indeed benefit from new opportunities created by the mature industrial system. But among those whose marriages fell apart during these years, and undoubtedly among thousands more whose thoughts and feelings are beyond the reach of scholars, there was a great deal of disappointment, disillusion, and despair that the good life they had hoped for could not be grasped.

FOOTNOTES

1. See, for example, C. Wright Mills, *White Collar* (New York, 1956); Robert S. and Helen Merrell Lynd, *Middletown* (New York, 1956). Chapters IV through VIII; Stuart Ewen, *Captains of Consciousness: : Advertising and the Social Roots of the Consumer Culture* (New York, 1977); Edward Kirkland, *Dream and Thought in the Business Community, 1860-1900* (New York, 1956); Daniel Miller and Guy Swanson, *The Changing American Parent* (New York, 1958). For a discussion of the wholarly debate, see Donald Meyer, "Churches and Families," in William McLaughlin, ed., *Religion in America* (Boston, 1968).

2. This is part of a larger study in progress tentatively entitled "The Pursuit of Happiness: Marriage and Divorce in America, 1880-1920."

3. In 1870, there were 1.5 divorces for every 1,000 marriages. By 1920, the figure had increased to 17 divorces per every 1,000 marriages. See Paul H. Jacobson, *american Marriage and Divorce* (New York, 1959), 21, 90; Lynd and Lynd, *Middletown,* 80-81, 126. Nationally, the percentage of divorces granted for "neglect to provide" rose steadily from 1870 to 1930, and then declined up to 1950. See Jardson, *american Marriage and Divorce,* 126.

4. Case 4191, Los Angeles County Archives, 1885. Names have been changed in all of the

cases cited.

5. Case 2773, Los Angeles, 1883.
6. Case D251, Los Angeles, 1920.
7. Case D127, Los Angeles, 1920.
8. This is more fully elaborated in my study in progress, "the Pursuit of Happiness."
9. For discussions of social mobility in America, see, for example, Stephan Thernstrom, *Poverty and Progress* (Cambridge, Mass., 1964), and *The Other Bostonians* (Cambirdge, mass., 1973); William Miller, ed., *Men in Business: Essays on the Historical Role of the Entrepreneur* (New York, 1962), esp. articles by Miller, Frances Gregory, and Irene Neu; Reinhard Bendix and Seymour M. Lipset Howton. An intriguing exception is reported by Herbert G. Gutman in "The Reality of the Rags to Riches Myth: The Case of the Paterson, New Jersey Locomotive, Iron and Machinery Manufacturers, 1830-1880," in Stephan Thernstrom and Richard Sennett, eds., *Nineteenth Century Cities* (New Haven, 1969).
10. Arno Mayer, "The Lower Middle Class As Historical Problem," *Journal of Modern History* 47, No. 3 (September, 1975), 409 to 436.
11. Table 2 gives the total number of cases from which these patterns were drawn. Although few in number, these cases show striking variations.
12. Case D385, Los Angeles, 1920.
13. Case D177, Los Angeles, 1920.
14. Case D386, Los Angeles, 1920.
15. Edward Chase Kirkland, *Industry Comes of Age* (New York, 1961), 403.
16. Testimony of Samuel Gompers, *Report of the Industrial Commission* VII, 645, in Kirkland Industry, 402.
17. Case D258, Los Angeles, 1920., emphasis added.
18. Case G-60-402, New Jersey, 1920; Case H-60-193, New Jersey, 1920.
19. Case H-60-186, New Jersey, 1920.
20. Case H-60-186, New Jersey, 1920.
21. Case Z-60-202, New Jersey, 1920.
22. Case H-60-215, New Jersey, 1920.

As a nation of immigrants Americans have been peculiarly sensitive to the problems generated by migration. Especially during the period of the great migrations from southern and eastern Europe, from the last-third of the nineteenth century to the First World War, commentators often depicted ethnic families as incapable of managing the stresses on family cohesiveness spawned by city life. The prophecies of doom were, as we now realize, premature: ethnicity survived because it was married to ethnic family values that immigrants and their descendants tenaciously clung to.

But no success is absolute. Family stress is inseparable from the process of migration. In his powerful autobiography, Piri Thomas depicted the strain and pain inherent in his family's migration from Puerto Rico to Spanish Harlem in the 1940s. As this short but hard-hitting excerpt shows, non-white immigrants, in sharp contrast to the white ethnics, were confronted with the ubiquitous American race problem. In Thomas's case, he was faced with the double indemnity of being both Puerto Rican and black (his mother was white, his father black). The suffering he experienced because of this, and the strain it placed upon the daily life of his family, were both considerable.

Mean Streets:
Identity and Family Life
in Spanish-Harlem

Piri Thomas

I had two colored cats, Crutch and Brew, for tight *amigos*. All the time I heard them talk about Jim Crow and southern paddies'* way-out, screwed-up thinking. Crutch told me once that he was sitting on the curb down South where he used to live and some young white boys passed in a car and yelled out to him, "Hey, nigger, git outta that gutter and climb down the sewer where all you black niggers belong."

*Paddy is a slang word for white man.

It really bugged me, like if they had said it to me. I asked Crutch if he knew any colored cats that had been hung. "Not person'ly," he said, "but my daddy knew some." He said it with a touch of sadness hooked together with a vague arrogance.

Crutch was smart and he talked a lot of things that made sense to any Negro. That was what bothered me—it made a lot of sense to me.

"You ain't nevah been down South, eh, Piri?" Crutch had asked me.

"Uh-uh. *Nunca*, man. Just read about it, and I dug that flick *Gone with the Wind*."

"Places like Georgia and Mississippi and Alabama. All them places that end in i's an' e's and' a whole lotta a's. A black man's so important that a drop of Negro blood can make a black man out of a pink-asshole, blue-eyed white man. Powerful stuff, that thar white skin, but it don't mean a shit hill of beans alongside a Negro's blood."

Yeah, that Crutch made sense.

The next day I looked up at the faces of the people passing by my old stoop. I tried to count their different shades and colors, but I gave it up after a while. Anyway, black and white were the most outstanding; all the rest were in between.

I felt the fuzz on my chin and lazily wondered how long it'd be before I'd have one like Poppa. *I look like Poppa*, I thought, *we really favor each other*. I wondered if it was too mean to hate your brothers a little for looking white like Momma. I felt my hair—thick, black, and wiry. Mentally I compared my hair with my brothers' hair. My face screwed up at the memory of the jillion tons of stickum hair oils splashed down in a vain attempt to make it like theirs. I felt my nose. "Shit, it ain't so flat," I said aloud. But mentally I measured it against my brothers', whose noses were sharp, straight, and placed neat-like in the middle of their paddy fair faces.

Why did this have to happen to me? Why couldn't I be born like them? I asked myself. I felt sort of chicken-shit thinking like that. I felt shame creep into me. It wasn't right to be ashamed of what one was. It was like hating Momma for the color she was and Poppa for the color he wasn't. . . .

My daydreaming was splintered by my brother José kicking at the door in sheer panic. "Hey, who's in there?" he yelled.

"Me, man, me," I yelled back. "Whatta ya want?"

"Let me in. I gotta take a piss so bad I can taste it."

"Taste good?" I asked softly.

"Dammit, open up!"

I laughed, and reached out a dripping hand and flipped the latch. José rushed in like his behind was on fire. His face had a pained look on it. "Chris-sus sake," he said, "you made me piss all over my pants."

"It'll dry, man, it'll dry."

"Aggh," he said as he relieved himself. "That feels good."

I looked at my brother. *Even his peter's white, I* thought, *just like James's. Only ones got black peter is Poppa and me, and Poppa acts like his is white, too.*

"Poppa's home."

"Yeah. Hand me the towel, simple."

"Damn, Piri, you made me piss all over my pants," José said again. He pulled back the towel he was offering me and began to wipe his pants with it.

"Man, turkey, what you doin'?" I said. "You drying that piss and I gott my face with that towel."

"It'll dry, man, it'll dry."

I yanked the towel outta his hand and carefully wiped with what seemed to part he hadn't used. "You know somethin', José?" I said.

"What? Jesus, I hope this piss don't stink when it dries."

"I'm goin' down South."

"Where?"

"Down South."

"What for?"

"Don't know all the way," I said, "except I'm tryin' to find somethin' out."

"*Down South!*" He said it like I was nuts.

"*Si.* I want to see what a *moyeto's* worth and the paddy's weight on him," I said.

"Whatta ya talking about? You sound like a *moto* who's high on that *yerba* shit. And anyway, what's the spade gotta do with you?"

"I'm a Negro."

"You ain't no nigger," José said.

"I ain't?"

"No. You're a Puerto Rican."

"I am, huh?" I looked at José and said, "Course, you gotta say that.' Cause if I'm a Negro, then you and James is one too. And that ain't leavin' out Sis and Poppa. Only Momma's an exception. She don't care what she is."

José didn't look at me. He decided that looking at the toilet bowl was better. "So whatta you got to find out, eh?" he said. "You're crazy, stone loco. We're Puerto Ricans, and that's different from being *moyetos.*" His voice came back very softly and his hand absent-mindedly kept brushing the drying wet patch on his pants.

"That's what I've been wanting to believe all along, José," I said. "I've been hanging on to that idea even when I knew it wasn't so. But only pure white Puerto Ricans are white, and you wouldn't even believe that if you ever dug what the paddy said."

"I don't give a good shit what you say, Piri. We're Puerto Ricans, and that makes us different from black people."

I kept drying myself even though there was nothin' to dry. I was trying not to get mad. I said, "José, that's what the white man's been telling the Negro all along, that 'cause he's white he's different from the Negro; that he's better'n the Negro or anyone that's not white. That's what I've been telling myself and what I tried to tell Brew."

"Brew's that colored guy, ain't he?" José said.

"Yeah—an' like I'm saying, sure there's stone-white Puerto Ricans, like from pure Spanish way back—but it ain't us. Poppa's a Negro and, even if Momma's *blanca,* Poppa's blood carries more weight with Mr. Charlie," I said.

"Mr. Charlie, Mr. Charlie. Who the fuck is he?"

"That's the name Brew calls the paddies. Ask any true *córazon* white motherfucker what the score is," I said.

"I'm not black, no matter what you say, Piri."

I got out of the shower and sat on the edge of the tub. "Maybe not outside, José," I said. "But you're sure that way inside."

"I ain't black, damn you! Look at my hair. It's almost blond. My eyes are blue, my nose is straight. My mother-fuckin' lips are not like a baboon's ass. My skin is white. White, goddamit! White! Maybe Poppa's a little dark, but that's the Indian blood in him. He's got white blood in him and—"

"So what the fuck am I? Something Poppa an' Momma picked out the garbage dump?" I was jumping stink inside and I answered him like I felt it. "Look, man, better believe it, I'm one of 'you-all.' Am I your brother or ain't I?"

"Yeah, you're my brother, and James an' Sis, and we all come out of Momma an' Poppa—but we ain't Negroes. We're Puerto Ricans, an' we're white."

"Boy, you, Poppa and James sure are sold on that white kick. Poppa thinks that marrying a white woman made him white. He's wrong. It's just another nigger marrying a white woman and making her as black as him. That's the way the paddy looks at it. The Negro just stays black. Period. Dig it?"

José's face got whiter and his voice angrier at my attempt to take away his white status. He screamed out strong, "I ain't no nigger! You can be if you want to be. You can go down South and grow cotton, or pick it, or whatever the fuck they do. You can eat that cornbread or whatever shit they eat. You can bow and kiss ass and clean shit bowls. But—I—am—*white!* And you can go to hell!"

"And James is *blanco*, too?" I asked quietly.

"You're damn right."

"And Poppa?"

José flushed the toilet chain so hard it sounded as if somebody's neck had broken. "Poppa's the same as you," he said, avoiding my eyes, "Indian."

"What kinda Indian?" I said bitterly. "Caribe? Or maybe Borinquén? Say, José, didn't you know the Negro made the scene in Puerto Rico way back? And when the Spanish spics ran outta Indian coolies, they brought them big blacks from you know where. Poppa's got *moyeto* blood. I got it. Sis got it. James got it. And, mah deah brudder, you-all got it! Dig it! It's with us till game time. Like I said, man, that shit-ass poison I've been living with is on its way out. It's a played-out lie about me—us—being white. There ain't nobody in this fucking house can lay any claim to bein' paddy exceptin' Momma, and she's never made it a mountain of fever like we have. You and James are like houses—painted white outside, and blacker'n a mother inside. An' I'm close to being like Poppa—trying to be white on both sides."

José eased by me and put his hand on the doorknob.

"Where you going?" I said. "I ain't finished talking yet."

José looked at me like there was no way out. "Like I said, man, you can be a nigger if you want to," he said, as though he were talking with a ten-ton rock on his chest. "I don't know how you come to be my brother, but I love you like one. I've busted my ass, both me and James, trying to explain to people how come you so dark and how come your hair is so curly an'—"

I couldn't help thinking, *Oh, Crutch, you were so right. We shouldn't have moved to Long Island.* I said, "You and James hadda make excuses for *me?*" I looked at the paddy in front of me. "Who to?" I said. "Paddies?"

Lights began to jump into my head and tears blurred out that this was my brother before me. The burning came up out of me and I felt the shock run up my arm as my fists went up the side of his head. I felt one fist hit his mouth. I wondered if I had broken any of his nice white teeth.

José fell away and bounced back with his white hands curled into fists. I felt the hate in them as his fists became a red light of exploding pain on my tender, flat-nose. *Oh, God!* I tried to make the lights go away. I made myself creep up a long sinking shit-hole agony and threw myself a José. The bathroom door flew open and me, naked and wet with angry sweat, and José, his mouth bleedin', crashed out of the bathroom and rolled into the living room. I heard all kinds of screaming and chairs turning over and falling lamps. I found myself on top of José. In the blurred confusion I saw his white, blood-smeared face and I heard myself screaming, "You bastard! Dig it, you bastard. You're bleeding, and the blood is like anybody else's—red!" I saw an unknown face spitting blood at me. I hated it. I wanted to stay on top of this unknown what-was-it and beat him and beat him and beat him and beat him and *beat beat beat beat beat*—and feel skin smash under me and—and—and—

I felt an arm grab me. It wasn't fair; it wasn't a *chevere* thing to do. In a fair rumble, nobody is supposed to jump in. "Goddammit, are you crazy?" a voice screamed. "Goddamn you for beating your brother like that. My God!—"

I twisted my head and saw Poppa. And somewhere, far off, I heard a voice that sounded like Momma crying, "What's it all about? What's it all about? Why do brothers do this to each other?"

I wanted to scream it out, but that man's arm was cutting my air from sound. I twisted and forced out, "Lemme go, Poppa. *Coño,* let me go!" And the arm was gone. I stayed on bended knees. My fists were tired and my knuckles hurt at this Cain and Abel scene. As the hurting began to leave me, I slowly became a part of my naked body. I felt weak with inside pain. I wondered why.

"José, José," Momma screamed, and I wondered why she didn't scream for me, too. Didn't she know I had gotten hurt the worst?

"Why in God's name?" Poppa was saying.

Fuck God! I thought.

"Why in God's name?"

I looked at Poppa. "'Cause, Poppa," I said, "him, you and James think you're white, and I'm the only one that's found out I'm not. I tried hard not to find out. But I did, and I'm still copping out to." I got up from my knees. "Poppa," I added, "what's wrong with not being white? What's so wrong with being *Tregeño?* Momma must think it's great, she got married to you, eh? We gotta have pride and dignity, Poppa; we gotta walk big and bad. I'm me and I dig myself in the mirror and it's me. I shower and dig my peter and it's me. I'm black, and it don't make no difference whether I say good-bye or *adiós*—it means the same."

Nobody said anything; everyone just stood there. I said, "I'm proud to be a Puerto Rican, but being Puerto Rican don't make the color." Still there was silence. "I'm going," I said.

"Where?" Poppa asked.

"I don't know . . ."

"He's going down South," said José, sitting on the floor with his head in his hands and the almost-blond hair, the good, straight hair that could fall down over his forehead.

"*Where?*" Poppa asked.

I looked at José and felt sorry for me. I looked at the wall and said, "Down South. I joined the merchant marine and me and Brew's going, and—"

"Who? Brew? That's that colored boy, ain't it?" Poppa said.

"—and I wanna find out what's happening, and . . ."

I wondered why everything I was saying didn't sound like it was so important to anybody, including me. I wondered why James wasn't there. I wondered why Sis wasn't there . . .

I walked away. Momma put her hand on me and she asked, "Why does it hurt you so to be *un Negrito?*"

I shook my head and kept walking. I wished she could see inside me. I wished she could see it didn't hurt—so much.

Among the most formidable challenges to family stability are natural and man-made catastrophes. Earthquakes, floods, nuclear holocausts, and even automobile accidents can undermine family cohesiveness. It is commonly assumed that such crises ultimately engender a renewed sense of cohesiveness among families and communities: after the initial shock people draw closer together to protect one another against the common "enemy."

This is not necessarily true, as the noted sociologist Kai T. Erikson demonstrates in the following article. With great insight, clarity, and empathy Erikson presents the social and personal devastation caused by a monstrous flood that tore through a mountain mining community in West Virginia in 1972. Drawing on the testimony of survivors, Erikson shows that the stability of both family and community are inextricably linked to the individual's ecological surrounding, and that feelings of personal, familial, or communal wholeness are inseparable from the cultural and psychological meanings people give to their physical environments. By destroying the physical contours of this community the flood also destroyed the existential terrain that linked the person to his family and community. Instead of bringing people closer together, the devastating flood resulted in increases in crime, adultery and divorce.

Why do some disasters create such havoc on the family while others have the opposite effect?

Everything in its Path:
The Buffalo Creek Flood
and Family Trauma in Appalachia

Kai T. Erikson

Well, it was Saturday morning. I was watching television and we got a flash that a twenty-foot wall of water ripped through Buffalo Creek hollow. I tried to get in touch with my family but the lines were all busy. I tried calling the State Police, but I couldn't get ahold of them. I tried the Red Cross and they did not know any details of it. I kept trying until about twelve or one o'clock. I finally got in touch with the State Police, you know, and I asked exactly where the flood hit. He told me everything in Buffalo Creek was either gone or destroyed. So I went home and packed a couple of shirts and pants and stuff and started coming home, hitchhiking. I arrived on Sunday morning, I don't remember exactly when, and I went over to the high school first. That's where all the people were at. I asked a couple of friends if they'd seen my parents, and they said no. I went over to the hospital and talked to some of the people over there where my mother used to work in the kitchen, and the lady over there thought my mother was in the morgue and my brother and dad were missing. I asked the lady where the morgue would be at and she told me in an old warehouse up there at Proctor. Then I started up Buffalo Creek, but they stopped me at Man and told me I could not go up the creek. I backtracked and went up the side of the mountain and went up the creek on my own. As I was going up through there I realized how bad it was then because I seen people taking bodies out of the creek and laying them beside the road. Right below where I live I seen a friend's house and they had three bodies in front of it. I went on up and finally got to the warehouse in Proctor and started in there and seen all them people there and I couldn't believe it. I turned back and went home to be sure, because I didn't want to go in there half messed up. I didn't really want to go in there and see what I thought I was going to see, I guess. I seen a neighbor of mine and asked him if he'd seen my mother and dad and asked him if they got out of the water. He said he seen them that morning and he said he was pretty sure they got out. So I just sat down and let it all out, you know. I started crying and stuff like that. After about an hour, just setting there, I met them in front of our house as they were coming up from Accoville. . . . We was walking around like everybody else, you know, looking for friends. We got to Amherstdale and they was just taking this young girl out of a bunch of debris. We seen her, and—well—we decided just to come back home. We went back home and went upstairs and stayed in our house. . . . The worst thing about the flood to me was walking across the mountain not knowing if I was going to find my mother in the morgue or find her home safe. And seeing that little girl being drug out of that pile of debris and her blond hair falling back on her shoulders. That's the two things I really think about. And when I dream, that's what I dream about.

Once the dead were lifted out of the wreckage and the injured were taken to hospitals, cleaning up became the big problem. In the upper half of the hollow this meant bulldozing the debris into great mounds so that it could be burned, while homes in precarious condition were marked with huge X's by the State Department of Health and were leveled by the Army Corps of Engineers. In the lower half of the hollow, however, where most of the houses were at least standing, cleaning up meant trying to dispose of an incredible mess.

The water was halfway up my curtains. Everything was full of mud and water. The mud was way up in the wardrobes, and the clothes, they wasn't no good. All the furniture was turned over except the sink and stove and stuff that was hooked up. My living-room floor had torn loose at the end and all my living-room furniture was handing in the creek. Everything was wet and black. I went into the bathroom and stepped on a body at the door, so I just got out of there.

Well, there was mud all over the house, no place to sleep. There was mud in the beds, about a foot and a half of it on the floors. And I had all that garbage. It was up over the windows. In the yard I had poles and trees and those big railroad ties from where they had washed out at Becco—furniture, garbage cans, anything that would float in the water. They was all around the house and caught in the fence.

Both of the above speakers were middle-aged women, the first married to a disabled miner and the second widowed and alone. The carnage they were surveying those first hours after the flood would turn out to be their lonely burden.

Eventually, of course, the debris was cleared away from houses like these, the muck hauled away, the sewerage restored, the walls scrubbed clean, the yards stripped of rubbish so that grass might one day try to force its way through a drying crust of sludge. But a smell still hung in the air more than a year later and the warped boards continued to emit streaks of oily black mud from the deposits that had caked under the floors and between the walls.

When the initial rescue and cleanup operations had been completed, the valley was little more than a long black gash, devastated almost beyond recognition. But most of its inhabitants were still here. A few had left the creek for a time to seek shelter with relatives elsewhere; others were gathering what possessions they had left in order to move away permanently. But the majority found a precarious niche somewhere in the hollow itself and hung on—staying with friends, camping out in the school gymnasium, or trying to make the most of scarred and twisted homes. The most serious recovery problem, then, was finding adequate quarters for the many refugees, scattered as they were all over the territory they had once called home, and it was in response to this emergency that the most important outside agency of all moved into Buffalo Creek.

This was the U.S. Department of Housing and Urban Development. HUD went to work providing mobile homes for everyone without accommodations of their own, placing most of them on vacant lots in the general vicinity of Buffalo Creek and permitting them to be occupied rent-free for a year. The idea itself was sound in principle and the agency did a remarkable job of administering it. Within a short span of time HUD had established thirteen trailer camps, supplied almost seven hundred mobile homes, and found shelter for close to twenty-five hundred persons, half the original population of Buffalo Creek. Yet the long-range costs of this program turned out to be a good deal higher than anyone had anticipated. HUD assigned applicants to vacant spaces on a first-come, first-served basis, the theory being that people should be moved under a secure roof as soon as possible. The net result of this procedure, however, was to take a community of people who were already scattered all over the hollow, already torn out of familiar neighborhoods, and make that condition virtually permanent. Most of the survivors found themselves living among relative strangers a good distance from their original homes, and although they continued to be within commuting range of old friends and churches and stores, they felt alien and alone. In effect, then, the camps served to stabilize one of the worst forms of disorganization resulting from the disaster by catching people in a moment of extreme dislocation and freezing them there in a kind of holding pattern.

There were other complications, too, and we'll come to them later. But for more than two years, Buffalo Creek lay in a kind of suspension, unable to forget the dark torments of the past and unable to plan a brighter future. "You know what it's like?" said one survivor. "It's like you were watching the best movie ever made and it stops for a commercial or something like that. And the commercial just goes on and on and on . . ."

So most of the survivors remained on or near Buffalo Creek. But they were a very long way from home. . . .

As other people on Buffalo Creek were to discover, even the closest family groups had trouble maintaining their old intimacy in the wake of the flood. Deborah said:

> *My family is just different. We were always a happy family and a close family. We worked together, my girls and I. We did our housework together. We did our baking together and our cooking together, and we done our sewing together. Just everything we done together. But since this all happened, it seems like one is one way and one's another. They want to pull one way and me the other. I can't get nowhere with them. I can't do nothing with them.*

And Wilbur added:

> *My whole family is a family of fear. Fear of rain, storms, wind, or hail. If it will just cloud up, my family all want to get to higher ground, but there's no place around that I can go to that'll beat where I am. And my wife, she's about to run us all off. She is so nervous and she is so upset, she don't take no interest in what we've got. It's not there. In other words, our house is just a place to stay. It's not a home. And we don't have no neighbors, that's the whole lot of it.*

". . . no neighbors, that's the whole lot of it." Deborah and Wilbur have lost a home to which they were attached, lost whatever tone and rhythm kept the family intact, lost a feeling that they were secure in their surroundings, lost the sense, even, that they were fully alive. And a crucial feature in that pattern of loss seems to be the absence of a meaningful community setting. What had it been like before? Wilbur:

> *We all just seemed, in that vicinity, like one big family. We raised our children with our neighbor's children, they was all raised up together, and if your children wasn't at my house on a weekend from Friday to Sunday, mine was at your house with your children. And that's the way we raised our children, we raised them together, more or less like brothers and sisters. The whole community was that way.*
>
> *Back before this thing happened, you never went up the road or down it but what somebody was ahollering at you. I could walk down the road on a Saturday morning or a Sunday morning and people would holler out their door at me, and maybe I would holler back at them, maybe go sit down and have us a cup of coffee or a cigarette or something. And there'd be half a dozen families would just group up and stand there and talk. But anymore you never see nobody out talking to one another. They're not friendly like they used to be. It's just a whole different life, that's all. . . .*

Those survivors who had thought the matter through and consulted the stirrings of their inner selves often found that they were privately holding others to account for what happened, and this realization, in turn, became but another source of guilt.

At that time I had tremendous feelings of guilt over the death of my mom and dad. I felt like it was my fault. And then I blamed my husband, I guess, in a way, because his mom and dad both got out and mine didn't. And I didn't even want him near me.

That's why I can understand some of those couples breaking up, you know.

As you know, my wife and I had a most crucial time in our marriage as a result of her father's death. Our marriage was on the verge of breaking up, our sex life had completely diminished. She was very hostile and had taken on a hardened attitude that I couldn't understand. At the visit with Dr. Lee, we discovered that she was holding me responsible for her father drowning in the flood. Since that time, things are a lot better between us.

Now both of these speakers are unusually insightful and both had had the benefit of a round or two of professional counseling, but much the same thought was expressed by others in somewhat more muted way.

Well, I'm irritable, I know that. So is my wife. We have had disagreements in the past, of course, but now we're both irritable and we fight at each other a lot. And I think the flood's the very cause of it, because it never happened before. Sometimes I get the impression she thinks I caused the flood.

Since the disaster there have been many separations and divorces. I have had to live the last seven and a half months without my family. We have separated and have filed for divorce. Since the disaster my wife has acted very strange toward me, like I was the one who caused the disaster.

Ever since that flood, I drink a pretty good bit. Me and my wife, all we do is argue. I've even accused her—I said, "Why didn't you get my mom out?" Her family got out of the flood, see, and they got some more people out, but not my mom. So I was drinking and everything and I ran my wife off. And then her mommy came to talk to me about it and I ran her off, too.

I hated my husband at first. I just thought, as a man, he should have known more about dams around the mines. More or less, I just kind of blamed him for my sister's and her children's death.

And so the circle closes. People punish themselves for not being able to protect their families, for not being able to rescue their neighbors, or, worse, for not being able to recall that they even cared enough to attempt a rescue; and those awful moments of self-doubt are easily converted into a readiness to blame others. It is a hard burden to carry, all the more so for a people who do not have much in the way of psychiatric advice and would not be sure how to use it if they did, and it eats away at the sense of communion that once held people together. . . .

In most disasters, according to available reports, the initial state of shock wears off quickly. Two of the most experienced students of human disasters state flatly that "disasters do not generally have disabling emotional consequences or leave numbing mental health problems among any large numbers of their victims." One reason for this outcome, they suggest, is that victims are invariably outnumbered by non-victims in situations like this, leaving a more or less intact community into which those affected by the disaster can be gradually reabsorbed. On Buffalo Creek, of course, the victims outnumbered the non-victims by so large a margin that the community itself has to be counted a casualty.

The lack of a discernible wave of euphoria, then, as well as the inability of the survivors to recover from the initial effects of the "disaster syndrome" had something to do with conditions local to Buffalo Creek; and in order to follow that line of approach properly, we should again look for particular themes in the larger syndrome.

Before doing so, however, one reservation should probably be noted in passing. I am talking about a syndrome here, by which I mean that the experience of the disaster and its aftermath was generally shared by all the survivors. But this does not suggest that the suffering itself was quantitatively the same for everyone, and, in reading the material to follow, it may be worth keeping in mind that people living in the higher reaches of the hollow saw a great deal more destruction than those living farther down, and that women may be more distressed on the average than men, if only because the men can fall back, if weakly, on the fellowship of work. These differences are not great, however, because everybody on Buffalo Creek, regardles his or her exposure to the black water, was implicated in the loss of communality, and in that regard, at least, all were hurt in much the same way. This does not appear to have become a new basis for community, as has so often been the case in other disasters, but it has certainly contributed to the leveling tendency already pronounced along the creek.

One further note before we move on to the particular themes. It is quite likely that the survivors' memories of the old community are somewhat idealized, partly because it is natural for people to exaggerate the standard against which they measure their present distress, and partly because the past always seems to take on a more golden glow as it recedes in the distance. It is important to remember and to make an allowance for that idealization, but it is also important to remember that the ideal tone of those memories, whatever its basis in fact, has now become the only relevant reality to the people of Buffalo Creek. One way to convey the sharpness of one's pain is to contrast it with a climate that may never have existed in quite the form it is remembered, but the need to do this is itself a strong indication of how deep that pain must be.

MORALE AND MORALITY

The Buffalo Creek survivors face the post-disaster world in a state of severe demoralization, both in the sense that they have lost much of their individual morale and in the sense that they have lost (or fear they have lost) most of their moral anchors.

The lack of morale is reflected in a weary apathy, a feeling that the world has more or less come to an end and that there are no longer any compelling reasons for doing anything. People are drained of energy and conviction, in part because the activities that once sustained them on an everyday basis—working, caring, playing—seem to have lost their direction and purpose in the absence of a larger communal setting. They feel that the gound has gone out from under them.

People don't know what they want or where they want to go. It is almost as though they don't care what happens anymore.

My husband and myself used to enjoy working and improving on our home, but we don't have the heart to do anything anymore. It's just a dark cloud hanging over our head. I just can't explain how we feel.

I don't know. I just got to the point where I just more or less don't care. I don't have no ambition to do the things I used to do. I used to try to keep things up, but anymore I just don't. It seems I just do enough to get by, to make it last one more day. It seems like I just lost everything at once, like the bottom just dropped out of everything.

I don't have the heart to work. I don't know. I just don't feel like it. It used to tickle me to get ready to go to work, but now it seems like I've got a dread on my mind or something.

The clinical name for this state of mind, of course, is depression, and one can hardly escape the conclusion that it is, at least in part, a reaction to the ambiguities of post-disaster life in the hollow. Most of the survivors never realized the extent to which they relied on the rest of the community to reflect back a sense of meaning to them, never understood the extent to which they depended on others to supply them with a point of reference. When survivors say they feel "adrift," "displaced," "uprooted," "lost," they mean that they do not seem to belong to anything and that there are no longer any familiar social landmarks to help them fix their position in time and space. They are depressed, yes, but it is a depression born of the feeling that they are suspended pointlessly in the middle of nowhere. "It is like being all alone in the middle of a desert," said one elderly woman who lives with her retired husband in a cluster of homes. As she talked, the voices of the new neighbors could be heard in the background; but they were not *her* neighbors, not *her* people, and the rhythms of their lives did not provide her with any kind of orientation.

This failure of personal morale is accompanied by a deep suspicion that moral standards are beginning to collapse all over the hollow, and in some ways, at least, it would appear that they are. As so frequently happens in human life, the forms of misbehavior people find cropping up in their midst are exactly those about which they are most sensitive. The use of alcohol, always problematic in mountain society, has evidently increased, and there are rumors spreading throughout the trailer camps that drugs have found their way into the area. The theft rate has gone up too, and this has always been viewed in Appalachia as a sure index of social disorganization. The cruelest cut of all, however, is that once close and devoted families are having trouble staying within the pale they once observed so carefully. Adolescent boys and girls appear to be slipping away from parental control and are becoming involved in nameless delinquencies, while there are reports from several of the trailer camps that younger wives and husbands are meeting one another in circumstances that violate all the local codes. A home is a moral sphere as well as a physical dwelling, of course, and it would seem that the boundaries of moral space began to collapse as the walls of physical space were washed down the creek. The problem is a complex one. People simply do not have enough to do, especially teen-agers, and "fooling around" becomes one of the few available forms of recreation. People have old memories and old guilts to cope with, especially the seasoned adults, and drinking becomes a way to accomplish that end. And, for everyone, skirting the edges of once-forbidden territory is a way to bring new excitement and a perverse but lively kind of meaning into lives that are otherwise without it.

A widow in her forties speaking of her sixteen-year-old daughter:

And then she started running with the wrong crowds. She started drinking. She started taking dope. And feelings wasn't the same between her and I. Before the flood it wasn't like that at all.

A retired miner in his sixties speaking of himself:

> *I did acquire a very bad drinking problem after the flood which I'm doing my level best now to get away from. I was trying to drink, I guess, to forget a lot of things and get them moved out of my mind, and I just had to stop because I was leading the wrong way. I don't know what the answer is, but I know that's not it. I don't want to drink. I never was taught that. I've drunk a right smart in my life, but that's not the answer.*

And a woman in her late twenties who had recently moved out of the largest of the trailer camps:

> *There was all kinds of mean stuff going on up there. I guess it still does, to hear the talk. I haven't been back up there since we left. Men is going with other men's wives. And drinking parties. They'd play horseshoes right out by my trailer, and they'd play by streetlight until four or five in the morning. I'd get up in the morning and I'd pick up beer cans until I got sick. The flood done something to people, that's what it is. It's changed people. Good people has got bad. They don't care anymore. "We're going to live it up now because we might be gone tomorrow," that's the way they look at it. They call that camp "Peyton Place," did you know that? Peyton Place. I was scared to death up there. I don't even like to go by it. . . .*

The inability of people to come to terms with their own isolated selves is counterpointed by an inability to relate to others on an interpersonal, one-to-one basis. Human relations along Buffalo Creek took their shape from the expectations pressing in on them from all sides like a firm but invisible mold; they had been governed by the customs of the neighborhood, the traditions of the family, the ways of the community. And when the mold was stripped away by the disaster, something began to happen to those relationships. This was true of everyday acquaintances; it was doubly true of marriages.

No act in life seems more private, more intimate, than the decision by two people to get married, particularly in this age when we celebrate the distance we have come since the times of arranged marriages. It is true, of course, that people "select" their own mates now, whatever that may mean. But there are other ways to arrange marriages than becoming a formal partner to the contract—spoken and unspoken encouragements that pass among families and friends beforehand, as well as a million other hints and suggestions that become a part of the marriage scene afterward. While we do not know very much about those subtle chemistries, it is clear enough that marriage, too, is something of a community affair. It is validated by the community, witnessed by the community, commemorated by the community, and every married couple in the world knows something about the pressures exerted on that union by interests outside of it. In one sense, then, a marriage between two persons lies in a kind of gravitational field. The human particles who form the union are held together by interpersonal charges passing between them, but they are also held together by all the other magnetic forces passing through the larger field; and when the outer currents and tensions lose their force, the particles find that the inner charge, the interpersonal bond, begins to fade as well. Wholly devoted husbands and wives were to discover on Buffalo Creek that they did not know how to care for each other or to work together as a team or even to carry on satisfactory conversations when the community was no longer there to provide the context and set the cadence.

So some of these marriages limp along, the particles remaining in a kind of proximity even though the charge seems entirely exhausted. "My marriage? It's just like a job," said one women bitterly. Said another:

> *Our marriage is just there. We care for each other, but it's like a fixture in life. We're married, and that is it. We don't seem to have the time for each other anymore. If I sit down and try to tell him something, he turns the TV on and me off. We're just not a close unit like we were.*

But other marriages—a large number of them, apparently—are breaking up altogether, the particles drifting farther and farther apart.

> *It's tore up I don't know how many marriages. The divorce list is as long as your arm. There's been hundreds of them, I bet, and remarriages and things. Like I said, I had a cousin who divorced her husband and then my other cousin married him. And now she's seeing him again. I don't know, people are just going around in circles.*

> *Many marriages have broken up that seemed secure before the flood. My husband and I can agree on only one thing: we won't go back to Lorado. When the time comes to buy us a house, we both agree that we will face a major problem in our marriage. I hope we can agree on where to live. If not, then we many have to come to a parting of the ways after twenty-six years of marriage.*

> *My husband and I, we was happy before the flood. We got along real good, other than just a few quarrels that never amounted to nothing. But after the flood we had fights, and it was constantly we were quarreling about something or other. We had fights. He would hit me and he would choke me and he would slap me around.*

All of this is reflected, as one might reasonably expect, in a decreasing ability to get along sexually. Studies of emotional stress have suggested that a decline in sexual interest is only to be expected after moments of extreme dislocation, and the pattern has certainly held here. But it has held too long. As the people of the hollow prepared to commemorate the second and then the third anniversary of the flood, they were still reporting all manner of trouble in this sensitive area, and one has to conclude that the absence of viable community supports has helped prolong what might otherwise have been a transitory problem. The following comments of a young couple are a fair sample of what people from every part of the hollow said in formal interviews or in chance conversations.

> *You wanted to know how the disaster has affected our lives. Well, we haven't had much time for play since the flood. We have had to readjust to many new homes, and we didn't feel like having any fun. Really, we just haven't been a complete family since the flood. I was just unable to be whole woman and wife to my husband and even now we don't seem to enjoy our relations like we once did.*

> *I was robbed of my sex life, if that's what you're getting at. I enjoyed sex before the flood, but now I don't. I still feel for my wife. I don't want nothing to ever happen to her, and I think she feels the same way about me. Even though we sleep in*

separate bedrooms, there is never a night goes by that I don't go in to her and tell her good night. But I don't have any desire for sex with her.

Older couples, too, expressed the same complaints, although sometimes in the heartier language of people who have known the ways of bedrooms for thirty or more years.

Well, male and female—you have to get in a mood for something like that. He quarrels at me and he fusses at me. He says I got another man because it don't interest me whatsoever. The memories come back when I least expect them. So you might as well throw a bucket of ice water on me. It's no good.

The difficulties experienced by so many married couples in relating to each other spread to the rest of the family as well. In the same way that wives and husbands stare at each other across the breakfast table and wonder how to strengthen and reconfirm their relationship, other members of the family find that intimacy and gentleness are hard to sustain in an emotional atmosphere as dry as this one. The general community validated those bonds and gave them shape, and people do not really know how to keep them intact by deliberate expressions of affection or by conscious offers of support. For one thing, as we noted earlier, people are very absorbed in their own problems.

Each person in the family is a loner now, a person alone. Each of us is fighting his own battles. We just don't seem to care for each other anymore.

But even when heroic attempts are made, old familial bonds reaching across generations or within generations seem to break noiselessly as the various particles, drifting now in a dead gravitational field, slowly separate.

The family is not what they was. They're not the same people they was. Before—I don't know how you'd put this—but there was love in the home. Of course we had arguments like everybody else does once in a while, maybe over something that doesn't amount to anything. But now it seems like each one is a different person, an individual by himself or herself, and there's just nothing there.

My children are changed. I sit and try to talk to them, tell them they are a family and should love each other and treat each other like brothers and sisters. But most of the time they treat each other like enemies. They're always on the firing line at each other. It's always screaming and yelling.

My grandchildren. It used to be we was the loveliest people you ever seen. We was, together. Now my grandchildren won't hardly give me a look. I don't know what's wrong. They seem like they are moody or something. My grandson there, used to be he loved me better than anything, and now he won't even look at me. He don't want to be around me. One of the grandaughters, too, is about the same. She has spells that way. I don't know. I can't understand it. . . .

But that only begins to explain the difficulty, for most of the survivors are still in the general vicinity of Buffalo Creek, strewn around the area, to be sure, but still within reach of one another. There are those who seem to maintain a permanent storm alert and hesitate to let others wander too far away from the safety of home.

The people who are here don't get out and do things like they used to. Before the flood, the men worked on old cars or got together and talked for hours at a time. Now it's just for a few minutes at a time, and it seems everyone wants their children to stay close to home.

Well, my children. When I let them go anyplace I expect them back at a certain time, and if they are late, I panic. I always worry that something will happen to them while they are gone. I fear for the safety of my children. I used to be a reasonable person, but now I magnify those fears a hundred times more than I used to. . . .

The feeling that something terrible is apt to happen (or maybe even that something terrible *should* happen) often began on the very day of the flood.

We picked up a little kid that morning and put him in the back of the truck. He looked at me—he was covered with mud from his head to his toe—he looked at me and said, "Mister, are you going to kill me?" And I didn't know what to do. We just put him in the back of the truck and put a blanket around him. He didn't have a stitch of clothes on and he was just covered with mud.

And it was still one of the main themes stalking those young minds a year and even two or three years later.

On the morning the dam broke, he kept asking daddy, "Are we going to die too?" He saw the bodies of some of the people. Now, every time it rains, he asks us, "Are we going to get drowned now?"

My daughter, who was four years old at the time of the flood, has really had a time. She's very nervous. Right after the flood we were at my sister's house and everyone walked out of the room she was in. We heard her screaming and ran in there. She just kept screaming and was talking all over, crying that everybody had left her there. We were a long time quieting her down. She still won't go in a room by herself. We have to sleep with her because she tries to run out and tries to climb the walls. If she's outside and hears a loud noise, we have to run to her because she goes all to pieces. When it rains she won't leave our side.

Both my children have changed since the flood. My son will not go to bed at night without plenty of clothes on because he says that if the dam breaks again he doesn't want to get cold. When it rains, he sets his shoes beside the door and asks me if we are going to go up on the hill. My daughter was small then, but she has a certain hostility toward everyone. She seems to want to hurt everyone. She is bright for her age, but she acts very much older than what she is. She liked to play with dolls before the flood, but now she punches out their eyes and pulls their arms off. She calls her daddy on her play phone now when it rains and tells him to come get her because the dam is breaking. They both seem to be carrying a burden too heavy for children their ages. They seem to be worried all the time.

My little girl, she wakes up at night and all you can do is sit and hold her, just hold her in your arms until she hushes screaming—not crying, screaming—"The water's going to get us, Mommy, the water's going to get us." My boy is the same way. At night you can be laying in the bedroom and him in his room and all of a sudden he'll hit the wall. You go in there an he's rolling all over the bed. Sometimes he goes onto the floor.

These children moved from infancy to childhood in the embrace of an elaborate network of aunts, uncles, grandparents, and other people, some of the latter attached by bonds of kinship but most of them attached only by ties of neighborhood. Communality, to them, meant a continuing atmosphere of warmth and concern, and their fears were obviously aggravated by the abrupt disappearance of that surrounding. Parents try to fill the vacuum, of course, but they are low on such resources themselves and cannot substitute for all the other people who once made up their children's social world. . . .

The people of Buffalo Creek come from a land where dreams are thought to have special portent, so they may have been prepared for the fact that the black water would come back to haunt them at night. Most of those dreams are hazy reenactments of scenes witnessed on the day of the disaster or general dramatizations of the horror they provoked. As one might expect, children, both known and unknown, play a prominent part in those dreams.

My sister's got a baby about a year old, and I dreamed that we lived in the hollow and water was coming out of there. She had come down to the house and she was getting out of the car and she dropped the baby. She made it to the steps in the yard, but the baby went down and was trying to get hold of the fence. There's a wire fence there and the baby was trying to get hold of it and pull itself out. We never did find it.

I've had bad dreams, too. I had one dream three times about water. One time it would be black, and the next time it would be clear. I'd have a baby in my arms, and I'd go so far in this water and it would keep getting deeper, and then I would get fear. I'd start smothering and I'd head back the other way. And this baby were in my arms. I don't know whose baby it was. . . .

Section Six:

Social Policy and the Family

The American family has been characterized at one time or another as small and mobile, or geographically rooted and extended. The commonality between these two strikingly different portraits of the family has been the persistence of both the myth and the reality of self-sufficiency. This description developed early in our history. To be sure, there were numerous single-parent households, often a result of the hazzards of childbirth. diseases unknown to early medical science, and early death. These forgotten families along with the aged, the infirm, and the orphaned, often bore the stamp of limited government intervention—a life of bare subsistence. These families, moreover, remained lost because the gaze of many nineteenth century Social Darwinians (who defined the limits of domestic respectability) was cast away from those passive-dependent family remnants who were deemed in capable of going it alone. There was, as a counterpoint, the frontier family: the sturdy yeoman farmer who carved a home out of the wilderness for his wife and his children. This household was patriarchal—a mini-despotism where everyone's needs were met within the domus. And there was also the three generation family whose increased membership provided enough hands to complete the arduous but often necessary chores of day-to-day living. These "havens in a heartless world" with father positioned at the head of the household, parents posessing control over their children's discipline and education, everyone pulling together, provided a myth more often then the reality of family self-sufficiency paraleiling our social ideology of individual self-sufficiency. Whether fact or fancy, the family was not to enjoy Eden for long. The onslaught of modernity, urbanization, and industrialization tugged at the boundaries of the family, forcing the abandonment of self-sufficiency to a veritable army of family interventionists—educators, justices, law enforcement agents, physicians, psychologists, and social workers. No longer self-sufficient in practice, the family clung to its last remaining life-line, the ideology of self-sufficiency. Under the guise of strengthening the sagging family would-be do-gooders and family engineers buried their patients under an avalanche of prescriptions and remedies. The vulnerability of the family increased even more when family engineers increasingly came armed with the power of the State! And so the story goes . . . today we hear the outcry of neoconservativism, calling for less government interference and restoration of the home. Can the family survive without the continued support of the State? Will the family become obsolete as a mediator between the outside world and its members if it becomes more dependent? Is the State an intruder or a friend of the family? Does the State protect the interests of all families equally?

By 1920, America had become an urban nation. by 1980, America had become a suburban nation. In New York, for example, more people live in the suburbs than in the central cities.

{22} *Such rapid suburbanization could not have been achieved without the active support of the Federal Government. The establishement of the Federal Housing Authority, for example, made low interest mortgages available to families seeking more pastoral setting than city pavement could provide. Curiously, however, the "great migration" was predominently white, and the many suburban communities remained white. Was the government discriminating in its lending policies? Was the government colluding with private racist interests by barring access for blacks seeking the suburban dream?*

In a revealing essay, Hugh Wilson addresses the strains and frustrations black families experience when they confront ghettoization all over again, when they seek to provide a decent environment for their members, and confront the exclusivity of the charmed circles of local government.

Black Families and the Suburban Dream*

Hugh Wilson

Writing in 1903, W.E.B. Dubois commented that " . . . the problem of the Twentieth Century is the problem of the color line." (DuBois, 1969). That problem has moved from the rural south to the urban North and is now settling uneasily on America's suburbs. It is indicative of the relationship of blacks to suburbs that until quite recently, the bulk of the extensive literature on the subject dealt with the constraints to black suburbanization and attempts to breach the white curtain, rather than black adjustment to surburban living. This article is an analysis of the process of black suburbanization, particularly the history, constraints, and adjustment of blacks to suburban life; it closes with policy recommendations focusing on the issue of black suburban migration.

SUBURBANIZATION

The modern American suburb—a sprawling, nuclear-family based, auto-culture—grew out of a convergence of public policies, private needs, and modern technology after World War II. But it was explicit governmental policies that made it possible for modern suburbia to exist through the Federal Housing Administration (FHA) and Veteran's Administration (VA) providing low interest mortgages and loans

*I wish to thank the editors, particularly Mel Albin, for their assistance in preparing this manuscript.

for homes, and federally subsidized highways permitting greater distance between home and the workplace (Wattel, 1958; Schnore, 1958; Marsh and Kaplan, 1976).

The preference of large segments of the population for suburban living in the past decades has resulted in the 1970 census heralding America as a suburban nation (U.S. Census, 1974). The 1980 Census will likely indicate that suburbs and nonmetropolitan areas have continued to grow at the expense of central cities.

While America was being "suburbanized," however, blacks were restricted in their attempts to take full advantage of suburban housing opportunities by explicit federal housing policies and by extensive concerted private discrimination. Since the 1930's, the federal government was aggressive in articulating a discriminatory housing policy. The FHA led the way, detailing this policy in its official manuals. In one FHA manual it was suggested that, "If a neighborhood is to retain stability, it is necessary that properties shall be continued to be occupied by the same social and racial classes" (Abrams, 1966:75). The FHA was so concerned with neighborhood stability that "incompatible racial elements" were to be excluded by racial covenants or deed restrictions, rigid zoning requirements and by the placement of black families in the same zoning categories as stables and pigpens. If all this failed and blacks did infiltrate, the FHA suggested *resegregating* black children in "another school with pupils of their same social class" (Abrams, 1966:76).

Federal mortgage policies (FHA & VA) were overtly racist until 1948. Between 1948 and the 1960's, federal mortgage insurance remained a white homebuyers' program through informal guidelines. Up until the 1960's only 2% of FHA insured loans were directed at black families (Falk and Franklin, 1976). The Federal Home Loan Bank System, the regulatory agency for savings and loans associations, supported the FHA in implementing discriminatory housing policies (Abrams, 1965).

One cannot over-estimate the influence of federal governmental policies in creating and maintaining segregated residential patterns in America in general and in suburbia in particular. In this instance, at least, state intervention arose from reactionary rather than liberal impulses and was geared towards denying an identifiable group access to the market place.

The private sector of the housing industry—brokers, builders, lending institutions—worked in concert with the government to limit black access to suburban housing. Until 1950, the National Association of Real Estate Boards (NAREB) had guidelines prohibiting their agents from selling homes to blacks in choice suburban locations. Indeed, blacks with money were closeted along with other undesirables such as bootleggers, call girls, madames, and gangsters in NAREB guidelines (Abrams, 1966). And while these explicit guidelines were shelved after 1950, they were replaced by more subtle practices such as racial steering by white real estate brokers and denial of listings of available housing in white areas to black brokers (U.S. Commission on Civil Rights, 1974). Private mortgage lending institutions also discriminated against black families. A 1972 study by an Advisory Committee to the Department of Housing and Urban Development found that mortgage lending institutions maintained separate lending policies for blacks and whites (U.S. Commission on Civil Rights, 1974). Thus, at least in the field of housing, the private and public sectors were in accord that suburbia was to be white terrain.

BLACK SUBURBANIZATION

Despite the formidable forces arrayed against them, black families have been a part of the suburbanization process. From the early 1900's until World War II, blacks have lived in the suburbs, generally in predominantly black enclaves like Kinloch outside St. Louis, Robbins outside Chicago, and Lincoln Heights outside Cincinnati. These early black suburbs grew because of a number of factors. Some were service enclaves for black domestics and gardeners situated along suburban railroad lines. Some were enclaves close to industrial activity. Some were "rural tribes" encircled by white suburban expansion. Others were black middle class enclaves created as havens from the city. But for whatever reason early black suburbs grew, they all had one thing in common: physical and social isolation from white suburbia (Rose, 1976; Farley, 1976; Douglas, 1970).

From the close of World War II to 1970, blacks moved to the suburbs at generally the same rate as whites (Pendleton, 1973; Connolly, 1973). While blacks moved to the suburbs for the same reason as whites, their destinations were different. Black suburbanization after World War II meant reghettoization as the segregated patterns which existed in the central cities were replicated in the suburbs, these new black suburban ghettos developed through three principle patterns. First, expansion of black city ghettos into nearby older white suburban communities across the municipal border. Second, expansion of black suburban concentrations creating black ghettos. Third, the creation of predominantly black suburban housing developments (Farley, 1976; Connolly, 1973).

BLACK EXPERIENCES IN SUBURBIA

Blacks, like whites, move to the suburbs for familistic reasons. They see the suburbs as a better place than cities to raise a family and to educate children (Handlin, 1962; Bell, 1958). However, there are some difference in family experiences among blacks and whites. Nearly two-thirds of all black suburban families are two-parent families compared to over four-fifths of white suburban families and one half of black central city families. Nearly one third of black suburban families are female single parent compared to nearly one half of black urban families and one tenth of white suburban families (U.S. Census). Significantly higher separation and divorce patterns among black suburban families, compared to white families, account for the large number of female single parent families. These high separation and divorce patterns are probably due in part to the social isolation engendered by resegregation patterns, the ongoing strain attendant upon a permanent two-income family, and anger at the hollowness of the suburban dream for blacks. These factors might exacerbate normal intra-family tensions to the point where dissolution of the marriage becomes the only feasible alternative.

Black suburban families also differ from white suburban families with respect to size. Black suburban families average 3.77 members compared to 3.2 for whites. Among two-parent families, blacks also exhibit a larger family size than whites, 3.9 members to 3.39. And while white suburban families are declining in size, black suburban families' size remains stable (U.S. Census, 1980a). The disparity in family size results from the increase of young black families with children in black migration pools, the slower pace with which blacks leave home to set up new households and the aging of the white population.

The homeowning drive is very strong among black suburbanites. Nearly two-thirds of all black suburban families live in homes compared to about four-fifths of white suburban families. Black families however, tend to depend on the existing housing pool rather than on newly constructed housing for homeownership. This very often leads to black families living in homes that are older and of lower value than those of white homeowners (Farley, 1976; Lake, 1979). Living in older suburban housing, however, sometimes necessitates home improvement loans from banking institutions that are less than sympathetic to black family aspirations. The result could be increased economic strains. Black suburbanites also rate their housing and neighborhood lower than do their white counterparts (Clay, 1979).

Proportionately, black suburban families are twice as likely to be renters as white suburban families (U.S. Census, 1980a). There are several reasons for this disparity between black and white homeownership and renting patterns, including racial discrimination and differential financial ability. A more telling reason is found in the difficulty that black single parent families have in securing housing. Sixty-two percent of white female single parents are homeowners compared to forty-two percent of black female single parents. There are certain undesirable consequences of the high percentage of renters among black female head of families. Despite the fact that many female-headed families rent private homes as opposed to apartments, black female-headed families are disproportionately represented among apartment renters. Thus cramped living quarters result in diminished privacy and increased family tensions. Black suburbanites, nevertheless, tend to identify strongly with suburbia, preferring it to the city (Blumberg and Lalli, 1966; Nelson, 1980).

Black suburban families have a higher median income than blacks in central cities but not as high as white suburban families (Grier, 1973; Connolly, 1973). The black median income in suburbia is aided considerably by the fact that black families have significantly higher percentages of two-income households than do whites (Connolly, 1973; Grier, 1973; Wilson and Ridgeway, 1980). Although white suburban women, in general, have increased their participation in the labor force in the 1970's, black suburban women in general still outstrip them (U.S. Census, 1979).

For black suburban women, working has been a necessity rather than a liberating force. Most black families could not have made the move without two incomes and cannot survive, after the move, without two incomes. The high percentage of female-headed black families also necessitates increased labor force participation.

Between 1970 and 1979, the black suburban population increased almost 50% compared to an 11.7% increase for whites and a 14.3% increase for all suburbanites. This brought the black share of the suburban population in 1979 to 5.8% compared to 4.8% in 1970 (U.S. Census, 1980b). But recent black migrants to suburbia are somewhat different than earlier black migrants. These black newcomers are of a higher socio-economic and educational status than black central city residents and black suburbanites in general. Whereas 14.2% of black suburban males in the civilian labor force held professional, managerial or sales jobs, 23.2% of black males who moved to suburbia between 1975 and 1978 held such jobs. While suburbanites had a median education of 12.2 school years, black migrants to the suburbs from adjacent central cities between 1975 and 1978 had a median education of 12.4 school years and black migrants from non-adjacent central cities had a median education of 12.7 school years (U.S. Census, 1979). Thus, if higher status blacks from central cities continue to migrate to the suburbs, as is the current trend, the suburban black population will begin to take on more of the educational and socio-economic coloration of their white suburban environment.

SOME PROBLEMS CONFRONTING BLACK
FAMILIES LIVING IN SUBURBIA

There might be an overarching black framework within which blacks view the outside world. However, there are sub-frameworks, based on class orientation, sectional biases, and territorial affinities, which account for the differing concerns of suburban and urban black families. Being of a higher socio-economic status, suburban black families generally have less fears about negotiating the annual economic winds, although they are susceptible to the general economic strains attendant upon living in older communities with increasing property taxes and shrinking tax bases.

Black families generally appear to live in unincorporated areas which allows them little control over their local political destinies. However, there are indications that high status blacks are more likely to manipulate the suburban political system to achieve group goals (Rabinovitz and Siembilda, 1977).

Black children, since they live in segregated neighborhoods where the neighborhood school is a sacred institution, very often end up in a segregated school setting for extended periods of time. Not until junior high or high school do some black suburban children interact scholastically with their white peers (Dworkin, 1968). One should not conclude from this that black children necessarily sustain irreparable damage to their self-esteem. In fact, there are numerous supports in middle class black families that could mitigate the harsher effects of segregated education.

But the major implication for black families in suburbia is what occurs at the end of the suburban move. Blacks have consistently indicated a preference for mixed or interracial residential areas. Those who express strong preferences for all-black residential arrangements do so to avoid the trauma of racial strife (Pettigrew, 1973). Thus for most black families who make the suburban move in the hope of experiencing an integrated living environment, the social and psychic damage of continued segregation must be considerable. For some black families, however, the harsh effects of the segregated suburban move was lessened by a previous move to the residential outskirts of the city, allowing for a period of adaptation to segregated quasi-suburban living.

DISSCUSSION AND PUBLIC
POLICY RECOMMENDATIONS

The rate of black suburbanization in the future will depend on the level of black income, the availability of housing in suburbia, the role of real estate brokers, the attitude of lending institutions and their policies toward black homeowners, the attitude of white homeowners and most importantly, federal housing policies.

According to the RAND Corporation, black males earn three-fourths of the salaries of white males, a far cry from equality, but a substantial rise above the 1947 figure of 50%. Rand also found that black women now earn as much as white women (*New York Post, 1978*). This combined economic advance will allow blacks more housing options in the suburbs, however, the housing market, especially in the Northeast suburbs, has been tight with fewer and fewer housing starts. This will affect blacks only because a slower rate of turnover will slow the housing supply for blacks. Blacks generally buy existing housing rather than new housing. But all it takes is for a few blacks to move into an all white community and presto, a fresh supply of housing!

Real estate brokers play a key role in determining the number and location of black families within suburbia. As guardians of white society, brokers will generally steer blacks to "their own kind" while keeping white areas for white replacements. Brokers are the social agents who decide on exclusivity, the unofficial arms of suburban municipalities in their efforts to maintain "racial integrity" of neighborhoods.

Although there have been a number of attempts to make brokers legally accountable for their actions the future remains in doubt.

Lending institutions, as pointed out earlier, still take race into account when determining loan applications and the terms under which those loans will be granted. It is still unusual for banks to give black families mortgages to buy homes in white neighborhoods. Like brokers, they act as unofficial guardians of "lily-white" communities. Blacks, in fact, are two to three times more likely to be turned down for mortgages than whites despite similar income and credit records (*Newsday, 1980*).

Federal housing policy, historically a major cause of suburban housing segregation, has attempted over the past decade or so, to atone for past behavior. A number of new federal housing programs have attempted to expand the black population in the suburbs (Falk and Franklin, 1976). The Fair Housing Act of 1968 also helped to create a climate of government support for equal access to housing. However, federal housing policy as currently constituted—placing the emphasis on low and moderate income housing for blacks in suburbia—is sadly misplaced and is a waste of governmental energy. Government intervention is not the problem but rather the focus of that intervention.

The major strategy advanced by governmental activists, in conjunction with civil rights leaders and liberal scholars, is, to "open up the suburbs". This would be done by changing exclusionary zoning laws to allow the building of low and moderate income housing, giving poor and working class minorities in the central cities a chance for decent housing and an opportunity for employment in one of the many businesses that have left the aging inner cities for the greener pastures of suburbia. In their estimation, this creation of low and moderate income housing, especially if placed within middle and upper income communities, would lead to racial, social and economic integration (Downs, 1973; Davidoff and Brooks, 1976).

"Opening up the suburbs" to the poor unfortunately, is neither a politically nor economically feasible strategy to increase the black population of suburbia at this time. It is not clear that blacks would be able to improve their economic lot by a move to suburbia (Harrison, 1974; Frieden, 1972). The problem of poor blacks securing jobs is not one of supply but one of discrimination in hiring and promotion. Until union halls are "opened up" blacks will continue to have a disproportionate share of their population unemployed.

On the question of erecting low and moderate income housing in suburbia, the courts have spoken with numerous tongues, alternately expressing support and opposition (Falk and Franklin, 1976). Public and private efforts at constructing low and moderate income housing in suburbia have been notably unsuccessful. And even when low and moderate income housing *is* built, it generally houses the elderly rather than low income blacks (Haar and Iatridis, 1974; Greenhouse, 1973). If building low and moderate income housing is seen as one way of exporting urban problems to suburbia in order for suburban areas to bear their fair share of the metropolitan region's problems, then we are doing the poor a gross disservice. The construction of the decision-making process in suburbia, based on fragmented governmental units concerned with hoarding resources, *and on the family as the economic unit capable of taking care of all its basic needs*—transportation, health care, employment—mitigates against providing for the needs of the poor. Suburban policy-making, unlike urban policy-making is not based on the concept of redistributive justice, that is, on the use of taxation as an income *transfer mechanism*. In the suburbs, the tax system is seen as a *collaborative mechanism* used by residents to provide for those hard services that the family unit cannot provide, e.g., police, sewer, sanitation. In short, it is expected that by the time one reaches suburbia, one does not need social services.

The fragmented nature of the suburban governmental system, and the spatial arrangement of suburban housing, would, on the basis of logistics alone, preclude the creation of the kind of extensive infra-structure—public transportation, public health care, job training—that would be necessary for poor urban families to survive, much less rise, in suburbia. The funds needed to build such a system would best be directed at rebuilding an already existing infra-structure in the central cities and to provide jobs for minorities that would contribute to upward mobility.

Those blacks who are poor and who live in suburbia have not benefied from their locational situation. Suburban residence works to keep poor blacks in a state of constant poverty. These blacks experience high unemployment, low reading scores among black children, high social service costs, and complete physical isolation from suburban resources. Placing poor blacks from central cities in suburbia will *only* result in increasing the poor black population in suburbia. What is clear is that the condition of being poor and powerless does not change whether one lives away from or beside the rich. While there may be psychological pluses and minuses to different spatial relationships between rich and poor, the overriding economic conditions do not change as a result of proximity or distance.

Given the current political, social and spatial arrangement of America's suburbs, black middle class families should be the focus of governmental intervention. Because middle class blacks are quite capable of coping with the fragmented governmental system of suburbia—like their white middle class counterparts they provide their own transportation, health care, employment, education, etc.—they would not need the creation of a costly service infrastructure. Their desire to move to the suburbs is evident in the increasing percentage of the suburban population they represent. This group is primed to move and would benefit greatly from government policy targeted to their needs.

At the same time, the federal government, though an infusion of money and expertise into the cities, should attempt to assure the opportunity for poor and working-class blacks to become upwardly mobile so that suburbia will be an option in the future. Federal action would involve incentives to businesses to remain in cities, increased funding to central city schools and colleges, serious monitoring of union halls to prevent discriminatory practices, and aid in helping central city blacks to b   decent urban housing.

THE FUTURE OF BLACK SUBURBANIZATION

The rate of black suburbanization has increased largely without government support. Those blacks whom government sought to introduce to suburban living are still locked into central city ghettos. Those blacks whom governmental policy ignored have persevered and are now testing out the dream. However, with or without governmental intervention, black suburbanization will probably continue at a faster rate than white suburbanization.

With this continued rise, what kind of experiences will blacks undergo in the suburbs of the 1980s? If history is any indication, blacks entering the suburbs in the future will be largely middle-class and will repeat the housing patterns of their compatriots who preceded them in the fifties, sixties, and seventies. They will gravitate towards predominantly black communities in the inner suburbs, either by choice or by racial steering. Even if the majority of the policy recommendations suggested in the previous section are implemented, it is quite likely that blacks would still remain largely segregated in suburbia. Certainly there would be a significant number of blacks entering the suburbs and obtaining decent housing, but they would not necessarily experience social dispersal.

Governmental programs can guarantee middle-class blacks freedom of access to a multiplicity of housing, but they cannot change long, ingrained personal prejudices that see blacks—all blacks—as, at best, an inferior class, and, at worst, as a sub-human species. It does not matter that black middle-class suburbanites show as much passionate concern as white middle-class suburbanites about rising property taxes, crabgrass, downzoning, low- and moderate-income housing, rising college tuition, and property values. It does not matter that black suburbanites are beginning to "look" more and more like white suburbanites on the socio-economic scale. Blacks might share the same values, the same dreams, the same concerns. They just don't share the binding cement—the same skin color. Structural changes might be no match for attitudinal and behavioral rigidities and might result not in integrated suburban communities but in a series of communities in perpetual racial transition.

It is here that we must think the unthinkable. If we cannot legislate "integrated communities" (except in new towns where the developer's total control guarantees any desired racial and economic mix), then "integration housing strategies" should be reformulated into solely "housing strategies." These would provide blacks with freedom of access to all housing and if, and when, the community turns predominantly black, would prohibit redlining by banks, in order to maintain the existing standard of housing.

Perhaps at some future date the prejudices of whites will be moderated and "white flight" will be removed from the sociological jargon. Maybe . . . but one suspects that race will continue to be the most inflammatory issue among suburban whites for a long time to come.

REFERENCES

Abrams, Charles
  1965 *The City is The Frontier*. Harper & Row: New York.

Abrams, Charles
  1966 "The Housing Problem and the Negro". *Daedalus* 95: 64-76.

Bell, Wendell
  1958 "Social Choice, LIfe Styles and Suburban Residence". pp. 225-247 in William Dobriner (ed) *Community* New York: Putnam and Sons.

Blumberg, Leonard and Michael Lalli
  1966 "Little Ghettoes: A study of Negroes in the Suburbs" *Phylon* 27: 117-131.

Burby, Raymond J III and Shirley F. Weiss
  1976 "Public Policy for Integration . . . the Case For New Communities "*Urban Law Journal* 11: 101-129.

Clay, Phillip L.
  1979 "The Process of Black Suburbanization "*Urban Affairs Quarterly* 14: 405-424.

Connolly, Harold X
  1973 Black Movement Into the Suburbs *"Urban Affairs Quarterly* 9: 91-111.

Davidoff, Paul and Mary E. Brooks
  1976 "Zoning Out the Poor" pp. 135-166 in Philip C. Dolce (ed) *Suburbia: The American Dream and Dilemma* Garden City: Doubleday.

Dobriner, William
  1963 *Class in Suburbia* Englewood Cliffs: N.J: Prentice-Hall, Inc.

Douglas, Harlan Paul
1970 *The Suburban Trend* New York: Johnson Reprint Corporation

Downs, Anthony
1973 *Opening Up the Suburbs,* New Haven: Yale University Press.

DuBois, W.E.B.
1969 *The Souls of Black Folks New York: Signet.*

Dworkin, Rosalind J.
1968 "Segregation and Suburbia" pp. 190-234 in R.W. Mack (ed) *Our Children's Burden* New York: Random House

Farley, Reynolds
1976 "The Changing Distribution of Negroes Within the Metropolitan Areas: The Emergence of Black Suburbs" pp. 333-351 in Robert T. Ernst & Law: Rev. Hugg (ed) Black America: Geographic Perspectives, Garden City: Doubleday.

Frieden, Bernard J.
1972 "Blacks in Suburbia: The Myth of Better Opportunities" pp. 31-49 in Lowdon Wingo (ed) *Minority Perspectives* Resources for the Future: Washington, D.C.

Greenhouse, Linda
1973 "Accord Reached on Bill to Cut Urban Development Unit's Power *"New York Times* Sunday, May 20:28.

Grier, Eunice S.
1973 *Black Suburbanization in Metropolitan Washington: Characteristics of Black Suburbanites.* Washington, D.C.: The Washington Center for Metropolitan Studies.

Haar Charles and Dimitrius Iatridis
1974 *Housing the Poor in Suburbia.* Cambridges, Mass: Balinger Publishing Co.

Handlin, Oscar
1962 "Motives for Negro Migration to the Suburbs" pp. 125-130 in *The Newcomers* Garden City, N.Y.: Doubleday anchor

Harrison, Bennett
1974 *Urban Economic Development: Suburbanization, Minority Opportunity and the Condition of the Central City* Washington, D.C.: Urban Institute

Lake, Robert
1979 "Racial Transition and Black Homeownership" *Annals of the American Academy of Political and Social Science* 441: 142-156.

March, Margaret S. and Samuel Kaplan
1976 "The Lure of the Suburbs" pp. 37-58 in Dolce (ed).

Nelson, Kathryn
1980 "Recent Suburbanization of Blacks: How Much, Who, And Where", *Journal of the American Planning Association* 46: 287-300.

Newsday
1979 "Realtors ruled Liable in Sterring" Wednesday, April 18:5.

Newsday
1980 "Tear Down the Racial Barriers to Mortgages" Sunday, August 24:3 Ideas Section.

Pendleton, William W.
1973 "Blacks in Suburbs" pp. 171-184 in Masotti & Hadden (ed).

Rose, Harold M.
1976 "The All-Negro Town: It's Evolution and Function" pp. 352-367 in Ernst and Hugg (ed).

Falk, David and Herbert M. Franklin
1976 *Equal Housing Opportunity: The Unfinished Federal Agenda* Washington, D.C. The Potomac Institution.

Schnore, Leo F.
1958 "The Growth of Metropolitan Suburbs" pp. 26-44 in Dobriner (ed).

Schwartz, Joel
1976 "The Evolution of the Suburbs" in Dolce (ed).

Timnick, Lois

1978 "Blacks Close Payroll Gap But Parity Still Far Off" New York Post, May 10:64.

Wattel, Harold
1958 "Levittown: A Suburban Community" pp. 287-313 in Dobriner (ed).

Wilson, Hugh and Sally Ridgeway
1980 *Moving Beyond the Myth & Women in the Suburbs* Garden City, N.Y.: Institute for Suburban Studies.

U.S. Commission on Civil Rights
1974 *Equal Opportunity in Suburbia* Washington, D.C.

1979 *Current Population Reports* Series p. 20 No. 331 "Geographical Mobility: March 1975-March 1978 "Washington, D.C.: U.S. Government Printing Office.

U.S. Bureau of the Census
1974 *Statistical Abstact of the United States: 1974* (99th ed) Washington, D.C. 1978.

U.S. Bureau of the Census
1980a *Current Population Reports* Series p. 20 No. 352 "Household and Family Characteristics: March 1979 "Washington, D.C.: U.S. Government Printing Office.

U.S. Bureau of the Census
1980b *Current Population Reports Series p-20, No. "Population Profile of the United States: 1979 "Washington, D.C.: U.S. Government Printing Office.*

Social services have always carried the stigma of irresponsibility, lack of autonomy, and degradation for those families unfortunate enough to depend on them. These services were deemed necessary by policy-makers to protect the indigent, the infirm, widows, single parents, and others who could not be absorbed into the labor force for a variety of reasons. The myth of the sturdy middle class, by contrast, has put pressure on those parents who have struggled to "make ends meet" without the intervention of the state. The wealthy provide many of the essential family services for themselves, possessing the resources to employ governesses, cooks, physicians, and more to ease the burdens of family living.

Kenneth Keniston raises three questions: what services do all families need; what family services must the government provide to insure minimal equality between social classes; and at what cost?

Services Families Need

Kenneth Keniston

As Mr. and Mrs. Henderson pull into their driveway, three people await them and their new baby girl. Two are the Hendersons' older children; the other, a serious woman dressed in white, is the nurse the Hendersons have hired to help them care for the infant for the first two weeks she is home. The Hendersons live in a large house, and on Tuesdays and Fridays a woman comes in to do the heavy cleaning. Mrs. Henderson is usually there when her children come home from school in mid-afternoon, but on days when she has to be away, she arranges for baby-sitting with a high school senior down the block or with Mrs. Murphy, an elderly neighbor. She also relies on these two to baby-sit on evenings when she and her husband go out.

The Hendersons consider themselves concerned parents. One of them usually goes to PTA meetings, and Mrs. Henderson regularly consults with their pediatrician, who sees the children several times a year for checkups, immunizations, and routine care. The Hendersons have asked their attorney to set up a trust fund so that a college education for their children will be assured.

The Hendersons are normal middle-class members of their community whom their friends and neighbors consider independent, up-standing citizens. Are these the kind of people who need the help of social services in raising their children or keeping their family intact? When we think about providing services to families, does a picture of the Hendersons come to mind? Probably not. The word "services" in this country has come to be associated with public charity and government intervention in the lives of families considered too poor, too unstable, or too incompetent to manage to raise their children themselves.

This is a myth. People like the Hendersons, whom no one regards as poor, unstable, or incompetent, have plenty of help in raising their children—much of it in services they need and use as much as do families on welfare or families where both parents work but earn low incomes. Of course the *names* of those services—by which we signal whether we find them stigmatizing and distasteful or perfectly normal and acceptable—are often radically different. When the Hendersons had their first child, the live-in nurse they had at home for two weeks not only fed, bathed, changed, and kept watch over the baby but gave Mrs. Henderson helpful suggestions on caring for him. If this same advice had been provided as a service to a poor mother, it would have been called "parent training"—a not-so-subtle label that implies the parent would be inadequate without the training. For a poor family, Mrs. Henderson's cleaning woman would be referred to as providing "homemaker services." Nursery school would be "developmental day care" or Head Start. Afternoon baby-sitting would be "after-school child care." Calling the pediatrician would mean "finding medical services," and for poor children, most routine visits to the doctor would be termed "screening, diagnosis, and treatment." The equivalent of the Hendersons' attorney would be found at a local legal services program, although this lawyer would more likely be engaged in tenant-landlord disputes than setting up a college trust fund.

Are a cleaning woman, nursery school, advice from the nurse, baby-sitting, and the annual eye exam the signs of a failing family? Of course not. Are a need for homemaker services, child care, early education, parent training, and health services signs of parental inadequacy? Of course not. As we have said throughout this book, it is a natural feature of family life that parents today need the help of various other hands in raising their children. The difference between the services the Hendersons receive and those that poor families currently get is more than a matter of labels; it is also a matter of quality. For example, the publicly paid legal services lawyer simply does not have the time in his over-crowded day to give his clients anything like the kind of attention that the Hendersons' lawyer gives them. The quality of legal service for the poor rarely approaches what the more prosperous can afford to buy, and this difference holds true across the board. Mrs. Henderson seldom has to spend more than forty minutes with one of her children at the pediatrician's office. But if she were relying on a public clinic where no appointments are possible, she and her child might spend as long as five hours waiting to see a doctor whom they never met before and could expect never to see again.

Why should human services be most available to those well-off enough to buy them, when all families need them? In most communities, we have a model of one very expensive service that most parents use without having to "buy"—namely, public school. The same impulses that led us to create one school system for rich and poor alike should extend to other social services that families need in order to bring up their children.

"Services" is the catchall term for many of the kinds of help that parents use now that life is not the simple family affair it was on eighteenth-century farms. When we say "services," we mean the help provided families on an ordinary day by teachers, nurses, bus drivers, pediatricians, nutritionists, or social workers. At times, families may also need the help of employment counselors for unemployed parents or their teen-age children, housing or real estate agents to find a place for the family to live, a homemaker while the mother is sick, a psychologist to diagnose a child's learning problem, a lawyer if a child is unjustly expelled from school, and people who can make referrals to all of these. Families with unusual and more serious problems, whether a severely handicapped child or a parent who physically abuses a child, need help even more urgently. Some of these families and others as well may be unable to care for their children, so at the extreme end of the range of services we must include in our list the people and places that deal with children who are separated from their families: institutions for the delinquent and the severely handicapped, and foster care and adoption.

We do not believe that government can provide services to fill all the needs of all the families in the country. Instead, the long-term goal should be to enable families themselves to choose and pay for the services they want. But government does have a positive and active role to play. This chapter examines what is wrong with the family services currently provided at public expense and describes the characteristics we would like to see embodied in a new system.

We believe that families should have access to services without stigma or barriers based on race or class. We also believe that services should be provided as an integrated network, so that instead of isolated programs for children, we have coordinated national and local systems to support families, giving them maximum choice of which services will best strengthen their ability to cope with the problems of living. Parents should participate in planning and running services; services should make full use of parents and others as paraprofessionals and volunteers. Finally, as we will discuss in Chapter 9 on legal protection, we believe this country is currently spending a great deal of money on repair rather than on prevention. This emphasis should be reversed and every measure taken to save families before they reach the breaking point. A decent system of child care relieves some of the problems of child abuse and makes foster care a less frequent necessity; good family planning makes some health services superfluous; counseling, homemaking, and other services can sometimes make the difference that is needed to forestall removing children from a troubled family. An ounce of prevention often costs less than a later "cure."

If all families need help in raising their children, how are the families with very low incomes to find it and pay for it? Two broad strategies are possible.

The first is enabling parents to purchase the services they need on the open market. The goal of this strategy is to increase the purchasing power of families by ensuring work at a decent wage, by income supplements, or by social insurance that provides extra financial support in times of crisis or special need.

The second possible strategy is for the government to organize, provide, and pay for services for those who need them. The public school system exemplifies this approach, as do the direct (and usually free) services provided by welfare and health departments to their clients.

Our emphasis in earlier chapters on the overriding importance of full, fair, and flexible employment and of income supports indicates our preference for providing

American families with the wherewithal for choosing and paying for the services they need. This strategy leaves in the hands of parents, rather than the government, crucial choices about whose help they want, where they go for help, and how much they want to pay. It is consistent with the high value we place on giving parents the maximum possible control over how they raise their children.

But providing the wherewithal to parents is not always enough. Although full and fair employment, income supports, and childhood disability insurance would take us a long way toward ensuring that all families have the help they need, a free market by itself will not produce the full range of family services or get them to all families who need them.

Some crucial needs of society require government initiative, action, and regulation to support and protect individual family choices. Services like fluoridation or inoculation against epidemics, for example, should be provided to whole populations, not left entirely to individual choice on a free-market basis. Orphans, victims of child abuse, and juvenile offenders require services that no one in their families can or will pay for. Certain geographic areas have trouble attracting the services they need; for example, we do not have an overall shortage of doctors in this country, but there are precious few licensed physicians in rural areas or inner cities. Research and development in the service field is unlikely to be done adequately by private providers alone. Nor will the cost of services remain low or the quality high without some government support for monitoring. Professional judgements about the need for services—a stay in a mental institution, removal of a child from a family, an appendectomy—are hard for parents to question, especially in the middle of a crisis. Given this widespread control of both demand and supply by professional providers in many services, some public assurance of control over cost and quality is necessary, either through regulation or through the provision of less costly or better quality services.

Government has a critical role to play in helping create and support some services, maintaining the quality of services, public or private, and keeping their costs within reasonable and affordable limits. We do not advocate government monopoly of services, much less dispensing services to American families on a take-it-or-leave-it basis. Our goal throughout is to enlarge the range of choices that parents have.

SERVICES WE HAVE NOW

The present array of publicly supported services for families and children has developed over decades of emphasis on particular problems, such as the need to fund foster homes for children whose families cannot care for them, or to immunize children against diphtheria or polio. Some of these services are funded and operated entirely at the local or state level; others are managed at the state level with large federal subsidies in the form of revenue sharing or block grant funds (which basically provide money without dictating forms); a few, such as Head Start and Title I, are funded by the federal government. One survey of federal programs in 1972 showed 280 specifically designed to help families and children, administered by twenty different federal agencies. All but twenty-five of these programs provided services as their major function.[1]

Contrary to popular belief, many of these federally supported programs are not directed only toward poor children and their families. Some programs, such as school lunches, are available to all, but those who can afford to are required to pay some or all of the cost. Still other services focus on particular human needs without regard for ability to pay, including education for the handicapped, childhood lead-paint-poisoning control, centers for runaway youths, and programs for the prevention of drug and alcohol abuse.

Other programs, though nominally aimed at the disadvantaged, define "disadvantaged" very broadly. For example, the Appalachian Child Development Program helps all children in a disadvantaged region of the country; Title I of the Elementary and Secondary Education Act helps low-achieving children living in an economically deprived area whatever their family's income. In fact, over three-quarters of the federal programs for families and children listed in 1972 were not intended primarily for the poor, and 35.6 percent of these were completely unrestricted, meant to benefit all comers, including middle-class children like the Hendersons' if they needed them.[2]

Despite the number of direct service programs to help families cope with their needs, the federal investment in these services is a small proportion of the federal budget. In 1976, the entire budget for family services (as opposed to tax exemptions, deductions, and cash transfers) amounted to about $30 billion; of this amount, $4 billion went to the public school system and $16.3 billion went for such health expenditures as Medicaid, much of it, of course, spent on adult family members. Nutrition programs, including food stamps (not a service proper) and the national school lunch program, accounted for $5.6 billion.[3]

However important these programs are in specific cases, the problems that have accompanied their piecemeal development are well known: as a nation, we have an inadequate, uncoordinated, and incomplete patchwork of family support services. Services provided at public expense are failing to support families in a number of ways:

Services are unavailable to many who need them. Children entering school are eligible to be screened and treated for physical and emotional problems (basically, what the Hendersons' children get at a checkup with the pediatrician) under the government's Early and Periodic Screening, Diagnosis and Treatment program. In the first nine years of the program, however, fewer than one-quarter of those eligible had actually been screened. Some states have actually screened as few as 1 percent; the most active state annually screens only 39 percent of eligible children. Furthermore, of the approximately 2.2 million screened children who proved to need treatment, only about 50 percent ever received it.[4]

Since 1968, federal Vocational Education Amendments have required that at least 10 percent of vocational education funds be spent on handicapped and retarded children. But since these funds are expended through the public schools, some 128,000 children who are in state-run institutions do not benefit from them.[5]

A federal program supports special educational services for poor children. Some states and school districts have used these funds to pay for health services related to learning such as diagnostic testing, eyeglasses, and hearing aids. But poor children must be in special classes to be eligible for these health services. If a low-income family had five nearsighted children, only two of whom were in special classes, only those two would be eligible for eyeglasses.[6]

Services are fragmented. A young mother on welfare who becomes pregnant can seek prenatal care from her local health department clinic, but when it is time for the birth, she will be transferred (theoretically with her records but most likely without them) to a public hospital, where she will encounter entirely new faces and a new set of documents. The pediatrician who examines the new baby there will never see the child again. Instead, the young mother now has to take her baby to a "well-child" clinic—but not the same place where she got prenatal care. The well-child clinic unfortunately will not take care of a sick child, so when the baby falls ill she must take the infant to a private physician, whose fee will be paid by the welfare department, or to a hospital emergency room. If the child is found to have a handicapping condition, the child will be eligible for crippled children's services, but these will often be provided at still another place, and paid for with public health funds, which require a whole new set of eligibility determinations. This process, all too typical, would discourage almost any parent from getting that baby the medical care it is entitled to.[7]

Services do not encourage families to stay together. For many years, in order to get welfare, poor families had to prove that the father was absent from the house, which encouraged many poor families to separate or lie. Recognizing this, the federal government in 1972 passed an "unemployed fathers" provision which gave states the option of giving AFDC* assistance to families with two parents. But, as of mid-1976, almost half the states had not adopted this provision.[8]

Families with temporary problems such as the illness of a parent may need help caring for their children. Child care during the day in another home or a center is the remedy that disrupts the family least; temporary foster care is more disruptive; placing children in institutions is the most traumatic of all. Yet close relatives who take a child in at times of family stress do not qualify for the payments most welfare programs give to unrelated foster parents; so when money to support the child is a major factor, this federal service policy encourages parents to place their children with strangers or in an institution.**

Most services are designed only to treat problems, not prevent them. The Child Lead-Based Paint Poisoning Control Program was enacted to help communities combat the poisoning that each year kills between 300 and 400 children and irreversibly damages the brains of 6,000 more. But program funds can be used only to remove lead paint from apartments where children have already been found poisoned.[12]

Medicaid programs in twenty-one states deny prenatal care to first-time mothers, even though studies have indicated that, compared with those who do get care, mothers who receive no prenatal care are three times more likely to give birth to infants with low birth weights, a condition associated with almost half of all infant deaths and with birth defects.[13]

Services are underfunded. The 1976 appropriation for federal child welfare expenditures (which is not AFDC but funds to help state and local welfare agencies provide protective services meant to prevent public dependency and neglect) was more than $200 million short of the authorization enacted by Congress.[14] The appropriations for Title I of the Elementary and Secondary Education Act have never matched the authorizations; in fiscal 1977, the appropriations covered the equivalent of an estimated 39 percent of those children judged to be in need in that year.[15]

Recognizing that educating handicapped children can place an extra financial

[ed. note] *AFDC means Aid to Families with Dependent Children

**The least disruptive solution is also the least expensive to society. Foster care costs approximately twice as much as care in a child's own family, and institutional care cost at least twice as much as foster care.[9] Yet in 1976, 73 percent of federal child welfare service expenditures were for services to children in foster homes, and less than 10 percent could be identified for day-care services.[10] Average monthly payments for AFDC foster care in five sample states in April, 1976, were, respectively, $91, $137, $141, $155, and $180; by contrast, average monthly payments for child-care institutions in these same states were $709, $1,015, $1,032, $1,165 and $992.[11]

burden on public schools, the federal government enacted the Education for All Handicapped Act in 1972. But the total amount of money authorized for this purpose for fiscal 1978 will amount to only about $17.50 for every handicapped child in the nation.[16]

Services stigmatize. Overall, the second-class nature of services for the poor is the biggest stigma of all. Specific instances add insult to injury: children who need services but receive them because a court judges them to be "persons in need of supervision" or "children in need of services" may later find that the stigma of their court records outweighs the benefits of any services they get. For example, in forty-seven states truants from school may get services by being institutionalized; but their records may later close job opportunities even if they go back to school.[17]

When the federal government required Head Start programs to make at least 10 percent of their enrollment handicapped children, many programs merely labeled as handicapped 10 percent of the children already enrolled, in order to receive federal funds.[18]

PRINCIPLES FOR CHANGE

Given these problems, it is small wonder that publicly provided social services have received a bad name among both taxpayers and recipients. Yet these problems are not inevitable. The way we provide services to families in this country could be very different if we started from different principles.

1) *Universal Access* As long as we care about the growth and development of this nation's children, services for all who need them must be the first principle. This means services that are open to every one—whatever race they are, whatever income they have, wherever they live, and whatever languages they speak. The public has an interest in seeing that everyone has services available and that these meet federal standards of fairness and quality, even if they are privately provided. When the public decides that a service is essential and will be publicly financed for all users, as with education, then everyone should have equal access and get equal benefits. We believe that health care should fall into this category. . . .

Whenever services are in short supply, we believe that priority should be given to families where the well-being of the child and the integrity of the family are in greatest jeopardy for lack of services. For example, if daytime child-care places are in short supply, children with special developmental, emotional, and educational needs should have a high priority. If homemaker services are scarce, families that require these services to prevent placing their children outside the home should have first claims. In practice, we believe this will mean that priority will most often be given to families at the lower end of the income scale, to families who cannot afford to seek the service from private providers.

The same principles—the well-being of the child and the integrity of the family—should determine priorities for the creation of new services when these are needed. And the community itself should determine its own local priorities, within broad federal guidelines, since the unmet service needs of Harlem are likely to be quite different from those of rural Nebraska.

2) *Racial and Economic Integration* Services should foster, as much as possible, the racial, class, and cultural integration of different families. Having black and white, middle-class and poor children in the same program not only teaches children about diversity but also builds the breadth of political support that is necessary to sustain adequate support for most services. Integration will be fostered most by

making service programs universally available, regardless of family income. In addition, this goal will be helped by better consolidation and coordination of services. Community service centers, for example, ought to be organized to serve families with battered children, children who do not speak English, or children who may need special help to prepare for school—all problems that cut across the lines of race and class.

3) *Convenience and Coordination* In order to use a service, many families need "secondary support services" such as transportation, baby-sitting, someone who will answer their questions on the telephone, interpreters for those who do not speak English, and public information to let them know what is available. Most current service programs use all their funds for their own basic functions, with nothing left to provide other kinds of help that will enable families to make use of the services. Secondary support services make other family services accessible and contribute to their efficacy well out of proportion to their cost. Therefore, there should be one place where families can go to find out about the available services they may need, to get proper referrals to the correct services, to make appointments, and to get needed transportation or baby sitters. To provide this, a referral-and-appointment center should exist in every town, county, or neighborhood, depending on the size of the area and the population involved.

Where possible, clusters of related services should be located together or close by each other—on the model of the county courthouse—so that families can go to one location for a variety of related services. When new services are added, they should build on existing service systems that are well accepted. Schools, for example, might also be used for providing health and early screening services.

Coordination should also take place at the federal level, and the government should review the standards it has already set for programs, eliminating discrepancies and conflicting regulations for similar services provided by several agencies.

4) *Maximum Choice* Service systems should strive to provide families with the widest possible range of options so that they can choose which services will help them most and which provider will suit them best. An illness of one parent may require a visiting nurse, a homemaker, or temporary day care, but families should not be forced to put their children into day care because nurses or homemakers are not available. If they do choose day care, various types should be available: family, group, or center care.

5) *Parent Participation* Obviously, a good program for migrant-worker families would not be identical to a good program for middle-class suburbanites. The ethnic and cultural traditions of families and communities should be taken into account when organizing and delivering family services. In order to ensure that differences in child rearing and other family patterns are reflected accurately and sensitively in social programs, and to check remote bureaucracies, services should require inclusion of families in policy making, monitoring, and helping run the day-to-day program.

6) *Paraprofessionals and Volunteers* While good professionals—doctors, teachers, social workers, and the like—are important in diagnosing problems and providing services of all kinds, services should also draw on a range of paraprofessionals and volunteer help. The United States has enormous resources in parents, youths, and senior citizens. Using them as volunteers and paid paraprofessionals should be encouraged—and, in federally supported programs, mandated—in order to keep costs down, open up career options for the unemployed or those who choose to work in human services, and make service programs familiar and politically popular in the communities that use them.

7) *Prevention and Keeping Families Intact* A rational and unified system of services should put the prime stress on preventive services and those that disrupt family life the least. It should be as easy for families to go to a clinic for diagnosis and treatment of a mild problem as to the emergency room after the problem has become a serious condition. It should be more attractive for overburdened parents to use day-care and counseling services before they reach the point of harming their child than court-mandated services after the fact.

ACCOUNTABILITY: INCREASING PARENTS' CONTROL

These principles we have sketched out are essentially standards of fairness and quality that we would like to see applied to all service programs, not only those that are government run.[19] Just as restaurants have to meet minimum standards of public health and are not allowed to discriminate against racial minorities, so private service programs should not be allowed to fall below uniform levels. Federally determined standards for all services, some of which we will outline below, should be put into effect nationwide through legislation, where appropriate, and through agency regulations and executive orders as well.

Traditionally, people who provide services, at least those publicly funded, have had to account to their bosses, not their clients, for how well they are doing their job. This means that a father has very little say in how his daughter's day-care center is run, even though he may know more about the center's shortcomings and successes than the bureaucrat to whom they are supposedly being reported. We believe that the traditional enforcement of standards by administrative fiat must be balanced by giving authority and responsibility to the level where the service works. This is why there should be parent representation—which also serves the other purposes outlined above—as well as federal supervision. And parents should be involved in assessing more than just how programs are performing the job they set out to do.

At present, many agencies that operate services do some self-monitoring. Schools, hospitals, and counseling centers, for example, may undertake surveys of the number of people who need their service; they may plan whether to have one center or six; they may count how many of the people who need the service are getting it; they may try to survey how much the service is helping its clients. But in essence this is similar to a business auditing its own books, a practice long outlawed because of the obvious conflicts of interest. To reduce such ethical conflicts, in recent years some service programs supported with public funds have been required to hire outside evaluators. The trouble is that most such evaluators are profit-making consulting firms who know that if they deliver an evaluation of "poor" this year, next year the agency may give its evaluation business to someone else. The result is evaluations that all too often play things safe.

We propose that federal regulations take away from service operators such planning and assessment functions as overall coordination with other similar services, needs surveys, coverage surveys and evaluations, and require communities to set up "consumers councils" with heavy representation of parents to perform these auditing jobs. The councils should receive enough federal support to purchase technical assistance such as surveys. Their responsibility should extend to an area no greater than an efficient service "basin," that is, an area about the size of a school district. These councils will have to be independent of any organization that itself provides services. Also, they should be concerned with different services and different approaches to the same service, so they do not in effect become advocates for any single kind of solution of service needs. Since experience shows that getting parents and clients in general to participate effectively is far from simple, experimental versions of these councils should be tested.

Consumers' councils would first of all assess the need for services in their area of responsibility; second, survey how well programs are reaching people with those needs; and third, evaluate how well programs are actually alleviating the problems they were set up to solve, and whether they meet federal standards. Although the councils would not have the staff to do evaluations themselves, they should have the responsibility of choosing the contractor for every program assessment.

The fact that this kind of quality auditing is a yet undeveloped field, with none of the familiar devices that by now make the auditing of double-entry bookkeeping routine, should not be a barrier to beginning. However rudimentary the beginning standards that are developed, the benefits of auditing quality on a regular basis will be well worth the difficulty in creating the systems to do it.

The most important tool for making programs accountable for quality is accurate data open to those who evaluate the service and to individuals or groups who wish to challenge a provider of services. Within the bounds of respecting privacy, federal standards should open for public scrutiny the internal information necessary to evaluate how effectively each service program plans and how well it is performing.

At the national level as well, data on the conditions and needs of American families and children must be improved. Most of the major national data-collection systems, such as the National Bureau of the Census and Bureau of Labor Statistics, ask questions about problems, which at least begins to define what services are needed. But these data systems make no effort to connect the conditions for which they gather data to the coverage provided by federal programs to find out whether existing programs are even in place and trying to help.[20]

For example, the National Health Examination Survey (the single major source of national estimates on health conditions among children) produces a dozen or more reports every year on a wide and growing range of specific illnesses and symptoms.[21] But when it surveyed school-age children for vision deficiencies and asked whether they had corrective lenses, it did not ask why children who needed them did not have them, nor did it ask how recently the children had received a vision examination at school. Similarly, a special Health and Nutrition Examination Survey (HANES) series which determined the incidence of nutritional deficiencies among children and young adults did not ask whether the children received school lunches.[22] The Bureau of Labor Statistics in its national survey of employment and earnings asks whether an unemployed family head sought work in the last month but not whether federal programs are supplying assistance to the family or, if so, what programs or in what amount.[23]

While these data-collection systems should not be deflected from their primary mission of collecting information on national conditions regardless of what programs are in operation, adding a few questions to the existing forms could greatly improve the information available to people who design and monitor child and family services. The data should be presented in reports that emphasize the impact that programs have on children. Regular state-of-the-family and state-of-the-children reports should become routine.

Furthermore, everyone—from administrators of federal programs to members of

Congress—will have a far clearer view of service needs and coverage, as well as the impact that services are having, once consumers' councils are able, under federal standards, to hold programs responsible for keeping up-to-date, accurate, and complete internal management records about the operation and effectiveness of service programs.

We believe that the responsibility for watching over standards and performance belongs primarily in two places: at the federal level where the federal intent was formulated, and at the level where the program functions—namely, with the programs' clients who serve on the consumers' council. Neither of these alone can do an effective job of monitoring because federal officials often have no idea of local needs and preferences, and consumers' councils may ignore federal standards and thereby neglect some of the local populations.

What about state and local governments, where there are many agencies with responsibility for services? Unfortunately, many problems with current federally funded services originate with state or local governments, whose officials are not necessarily interested in either the programs or the principles but may instead be using the services for political ends or may simply want the federal money to use for something else. Block grants made to states with no strings attached often fall under the administration of state or local government, and with poor results, for recent history shows that local or state government control does not always produce the programs that Congress intended when it voted for funds.[24]

There are some hard conflicts between providing local control and assuring that federal standards are met. An example of this is the way that local interests dominated by sectionalism, provincialism, and outright bias and discrimination have often resisted federal enforcement of antidiscrimination requirements and other attempts to strike a fairer balance between the haves and the have-nots. Federal revenue sharing may be a convenient way to provide financial relief to hard-pressed local governments, but it can seriously undercut the enforcement of federal discrimination provisions. It also makes it easier for special interest groups with political strength to dictate how the money will be spent, while those who need services but have no political clout go wanting. For example, between the start of the federal revenue-sharing program in 1972 and early 1975, municipalities spent 44 percent of their revenue-sharing funds on public safety, 15 percent on public transportation, and 13 percent on environmental protection but only 15 percent on health and a mere 1 percent on social services for the poor and aged.[25] In many cases, communities elected to drop services that were once provided with federal money as soon as revenue sharing with local control gave them the choice.* A recent study of thirty-

*We do not advocate the retention of every current categorical aid program in its present form. On the contrary, consolidation of related programs and the integration of program functions (such as auditing, impact evaluation, needs assessment, and case monitoring) across programs and providers are both highly desirable administrative reforms. What is essential is that the consolidated programs also gain the kind of administrative mechanisms that will keep their efforts forcused on the needs their original categorical versions were meant to fill in the first place. Unless both administrative reforms are installed simultaneously, consolidation of programs will mean only the stultification of national purpose in a morass of local interests. The needed administrative mechanisms are discussed later in this chapter.

In practice, state plan mechanisms have unfailingly broken down. Part of the problem is that in the early years of a new program, the federal agency does not yet have the experience to set up any but formalistic criteria for measuring the adequacy of a state plan. For example, since 1974, the regulations for Title XX have required states to determine which services families need, but as of 1976 the federal government had no specific standards for how the states should go about determining this.

seven cities reported that only seven used any revenue-sharing funds to replace any terminating federal programs.[26] In essence, local governments decided to supplant local with federal funds to hold down local taxes instead of providing servies.

Changes can be made at the state level, however, that will improve the delivery of services. In recent years, many major federal service programs have begun requiring states to submit a permanent or annual plan for providing and coordinating certain services. Such plans are required for Title XX of the Social Security Act, Aid for the Education of Handicapped Children, Vocational Education, the delinquency prevention services funded under the Law Enforcement Assistance Administration, and host of other laws. In some instances, state plans are the only part of an entire program that has to measure up to any specific standards about the substance of the program. Thus, the standards that the states have to meet in preparing their plans are virtually the only tool federal agencies have for keeping accountable the people who spend billions of federal dollars.

We endorse the process of requiring state service plans, but urge that it be strengthened. The federal government should insist that state plans include all of the following elements, only a few of which are now required even in the best plans:

1) assessments of what services are needed in the state, where and who actually is being served;

2) an identification of agencies and groups that could provide the service in question;

3) an internal system for reporting on the management of the program operations;

4) plans for how the program is to be evaluated;

5) mechanisms that allow the agency involved to follow the cases of individual children or families and be held responsible for their continued treatment.

6) Most important, each state plan should spell out ways services can be monitored by outsiders and clients, including ways for citizens to participate in planning; grievance and complaint mechanisms for people who use the service; and various forms of technical assistance for agencies providing services run by parents and community organizations, so they can compete for contracts and funds with more experienced governmental and private providers.

Our proposals for firm accountability reflect a conservative view of the role of government. Government, we believe, should enable the simplest units possible—individuals and families—to make their own choices and control the shape of their own lives. In seeking to ensure that federal law is enforcd on behalf of families and children, we are essentially recommending family empowerment. Moreover, poor

---

A more basic problem is that when a state plan is submitted, public comment often is allowed only during a brief period, usually ninety days. There is no requirement for hearings, and no requirement that any public comments be evaluated by the federal agency that gives the state its funds. Even if public groups or groups of beneficiaries had a decent forum, there is never funding or technical support for them to prepare careful analysis of the state plans that are proposed. Even if they had staff, time, and money, there is no requirement that the state give the public access to the data and information it used in the planning process. The result is that public participation is reduced to a charade in which individuals and community groups knowledgeable about their local areas but without access to resources, information, or a neutral forum helplessly try to out-argue a statewide bureaucracy.

enforcement and poor implementation of laws that are already on the books have contributed powerfully to current gaps in family services and to the widespread belief that government does not mean to do what is says. Firm accountability can help reverse this trend.

LIMITING THE PUBLIC COST

Who should pay for family services and how is a key question for family members, taxpayers, and legislators. Even "free" services such as public education must ultimately be paid for. In the same way, publicly provided family services have to be paid for, either directly by the user or indirectly by users and nonusers through taxes. Furthermore, the public purse is not bottomless.

At present, most properous American families such as the Hendersons pay for almost all of the services they use from their own pockets. Those who live in or near poverty can sometimes call upon services provided by taxes or by private charity, although too often they simply go without the help they need. Those in the middle do the best they can with what they earn.

If the proposals put forward earlier for jobs, income supports, and childhood disability insurance are implemented, that will mean that all families of four in which one member is able to work will have an income above half the median—at least $8,400 per year in 1974 dollars (see page 109). Not just people at the guaranteed job level, but almost all families up to an income of about $18,000 will have more after-tax income than they do under our current system. Child-care costs will be fully deductible from taxable income, which—under the credit tax we offered as an example—means an indirect federal subsidy of 50 percent. Single parents will either receive support payments from the absent parent or an income supplement administered through the tax system. Flexible work practices will make it possible for parents to combine child rearing and work outside the home with less complicated and less expensive child-care provisions, and a reformed tax system will mean that those who choose this will not be paying prohibitive implicit tax rates. Childhood disability insurance will protect families against the financial catastrophe of rearing a disabled child, enabling them to pay for special service like transportation just as the family with health insurance now pays hospital bills. A national health system, proposed in the next chapter, will guarantee all American families, regardless of income, good health care.

These broad changes would reduce the cost of services to federal, state, and local budgets by enabling parents to pay the expenses of services from their own income or insurance.

We have repeatedly emphasized our preference for directly supporting families rather than bureaucracies. But as we also emphasized, government has to play an assertive role in ensuring that parents have control over the services they use. Furthermore, no one but government can guarantee equity of treatment, access for those who need the service, and good quality. Government must also be largely responsible for planning and for seeing that new programs are designed and tried out. As far as the costs of services are concerned, this means several things:

1) Public funds are necessary to develop national, regional, and local surveys of families' and children's needs and to create appropriate plans for meeting those needs.

2) In many cases, government must provide the start-up costs, and the costs of

training new workers, for family services that are needed but not available now. For example, public support will be important for creating information-and-referral centers; public monies should help train homemakers who can help families passing through special transitions, or child-care workers for day-care centers.

3) Public monies are needed to fund demonstration centers and to evaluate the effects of existing programs. In the continuing discussion of the most desirable forms of nonfamilial child care of very young children, for example, federally funded demonstration and evaluation studies should play a major role.

4) Public funds are needed for consumers' councils to monitor family services and ensure that they meet standards of quality and requirements about parent participation, that they are financially accountable, and that they adhere to general legal requirements.

5) Public support will be needed for some secondary support and access services such as transportation to get people to the services they need.

6) Public funds and enforcement action will be needed to ensure more equitable access to the services families need. For example, ensuring that rural, poor, and non-white families have access to needed services that are now maldistributed will require federal action and, in some cases, federal funds to pay construction, training, and start-up costs in underserved communities.

7) In the foreseeable future, there are bound to be some families who cannot pay the full cost of all the services they urgently need. In such cases, we advocate subsidizing a portion of the costs which the family cannot pay from earnings, income supplements, or insurance benefits. The method of payment adopted by community mental health centers, in particular, has much to recommend it. In such centers, a wide variety of mental health services are available to all who need them. Users who can afford it pay the full costs of the services they receive. For those of limited means, payments are adjusted according to the incomes and assets of the family, with the public subsidizing the remainder. Of course, unless the use of sliding-scale subsidies is carefully adjusted, it will create the very high implicit tax rates for certain users that are a feature of the present system we are eager to see left behind. For if a family will lose, say, $500-worth of several services when an earner in the family gets a $500 raise, they are, implicitly, paying a 100-percent tax on the raise.

We should emphasize that there are important choices to be made in the balance between public subsidies for family services and direct public support of family income. In the short run, we recognize the need for services with at least some of their ongoing operating costs paid from public funds. Until we have full employment and a strong system of income supports, families in need will have to rely on a complementary mix of earnings from work, transfer payments, and subsidized services.

In the long run, we believe the goal should be to enable families themselves to pay for the help they need in raising children, keeping subsidization of the operating costs of public services as limited as possible. Only in areas such as health care and education do we support the full payment of service costs from public revenues.

We have indicated that we believe government has a major role to play in the creation, evaluation, coordination, and planning of services. And government must alway be ready and able to step in to help families afford necessary help that they cannot fully pay for. But the overriding long-term goal of family policy should be to put even more families in the position of the Hendersons, to give them the financial and political power to select and control the services they receive.

FOOTNOTES

1. Sheldon H. White, et al., *Federal Programs for Young Children* Washington, D.C.: Department of health, Education and Welfare, 1972, Appendix IIIC, pp. 2-3.
2. *Ibid.*
3. Program categorization and budget estimates were derived from unpublished materials developed at the Congressional Budget Office for a "Children's Budget" for fiscal year 1976. All calculations were done by the Carnegie Council on Children.
4. These data are from federal reports on the progress of states' implementation of Early and Periodic Screening. Diagnosis and Treatment (EPSDT) and from a year-long field study of how the program is working by the Children's Defense Fund, reported in *EPSDT: Does It Spell Health Care for Poor Children?* Washington, D.C.: Children's Defense Fund, 1977.
5. 20 U.S.C.A. § 1262 (b) (3) and U.S. Department of Commerce, Bureau of the Census, *Statistical Abstract of the United States, 1975,* 96th edition. Washington, D.C.: Government Printing Office, Table 62, p. 45. There is also some question as to whether the 10 percent set aside is actually reaching handicapped and retarded children who are in public schools because the Office of Education has not monitored or reported the results publicly.
6. From research conducted for *Children Out of School in America.* Cambridge, Mass.: Children's Defense Fund, 1974.
7. Nathan Glazer, "Paradoxes of Health Care," *The Public Interest, Winter, 1971, pp. 62-77.*
8. *Public Assistance Statistics, June, 1976,* SRS, National Center for Social Statistics, Nov. 1976, p. 1.
9. Paul E. Mott, "Foster Care and Adoptions: Some Key Policy Issues," prepared for the Subcommittee on Children and Youth of the United States Senate Committee on Labor and Public Welfare, Washington, D.C.: Government Printing Office, 1975, pp. 1-2.
10. Unpublished preliminary figures for Fiscal Year 1976, Child Welfare Expenditures under Title IV-B. Washington, D.C.: Social and Rehabilitation Service, October, 1976.
11. *Public Assistance Statistics, April 1976.* Washington, D.C.: National Center for Social Statistics, August, 1976, Table 12, p. 22.
12. Statistics on incidence of leadpaint poisoning come from Frederick Green, M.D., "Getting Ready for National Health Insurance: Shortchanging Children," statement before the Subcommittee on Oversight and Investigations of the United States House Committee on Interstate and Foreign Commerce, October 7, 1975; see also *Catalog of Domestic Assistance,* program number 13.266, 42 U.S.C. 480.
13. *Monthly Vital Statistics Report, Summary Report, Final Natality Statistics,* National Center for Health, Education and Welfare, Washington, D.C.: Government Printing Office, 1973, p. 8; and *America's Children, 1976, A Bicentennial Assessment.* Washington, D.C.: National Council of Organizations for Children and Youth, 1976, p. 34.
14. Compare the fiscal year 1977 appropriation of $56.5 million with an authorization for fiscal year 1977 of $266 million (Title IV-B, 420, Social Security Act). This trend has continued since the budget authorization for Title IV, Part B was increased in 1969; see *More Can Be Learned and Done About the Well-Being of Children.* Washington, D.C.: U.S. General Accounting Office, April 9, 1976, pp. 4-5.
15. In Title I funding, the proportion of the authorized funding for local school programs actually appropriated is called the "rateable reduction." That figure was projected to be 39 percent for fiscal 1977 by HEW's Office of Education. It has never exceeded 46 percent since 1970 census data was first used as the basis of distribution (in 1973). Figures were supplied by Caroline Horner of the Title I staff of the Office of Education. A National Institute of Education survey in 1976 indicated that school districts actually spread the limited funds more thinly over the eligible population, so that 50 to 70 percent of eligible children receive some diluted Title I services.
16. Public Law 94-142 established a very complex formula for determining the amount of federal aid provided to the local schools of each state for the education of handicapped children. For fiscal year 1978, the first year of full operation of this law, the following rough calculations will apply: the law authorizes 5 percent of the national average per-pupil expenditure (in the preceding year, fiscal 1977) per handicapped child *served* by the schools in the previous year. The average per-pupil expenditure in fiscal 1977 will be about $1,400, so the authorization will by 70 federal dollars per child previously served. Half of this amount is reserved for the continuation of older state-selected research and demonstration projects, so only about $35 per child served in 1977 will be available to local schools in fiscal 1978.

The most recent estimates of the percent of all handicapped children served by public school programs (Nicholas Hobbs, *The Futures of Children: Categories, Labels, and Their Consequences,* report of the Project on Classification of Exceptional Children. San Francisco: Jossey-Bass, 1975) are that only 51 percent of the retarded, 40 percent of the emotionally disturbed, 24 percent of the learning disabled, and 20 percent of the hearing impaired are reached. Assuming that at least half of all handicapped children were served in 1977 (which is very optimistic in the light of the OCD figures just given), in 1978 the $35 of federal aid will have to be spread over two children—one served the previous year, and one not yet reached. About 50 percent of the funds must be spent to seek out the least served, according to a recent Bureau of the Education of the Handicapped ruling, in any case.

Thus there will be about $17.50 per handicapped child available in the first year of this program. The P.L. 94-142 formula will gradually increase this amount over the following four years to a rate equal to 30 percent of the average per pupil expenditure (if all handicapped children are finally reached), but the very low funding in the first year of the program will have already set a precedent for inadequate levels of service.

17. *Children Out of School in America, op. cit.* Appendix J. p. 226.

18. See correspondence of Rims Barber, David Rice, and Charles E. Jenkins, Directors, Mississippi Head Start, to Senator Jacob Javits cited in *Children Out of School in America op. cit.,* p. 108.

19. The importance of public standards applying to private service programs cannot be underestimated. In 1972, during a five-day period, of 2,084 requests to social welfare agencies for services from families with children under eighteen, 1,663 (79.8 percent) were directed to private voluntary agencies. (Barbara L. Haring, *1972 Census of Requests for Child Welfare Services.* New York: Child Welfare League of America, Inc., December, 1972, p. 8)

20. The exception is the Current Population Reports of the Bureau of the Census for which the family income reporting surveys (series P-60) do make a strong effort to identify sources (including federal sources) of income received by low-income families. It is no coincidence that many family-oriented policy analyses and proposals draw upon the Current Population Reports for their cost and incidence estimates.

21. See, for example, National Center for Health Statistics, *Vital and Health Statistics,* "Visual Acuity of Children," Series 11, No. 101, Washington, D.C.: Government Printing Office, February, 1970.

22. See, for example, Sidney Abraham, *Preliminary Findings of the First Health and Nutrition Examination Survey, United States, 1971-72: Anthropometric and Clinical Findings,* Washington, D.C.: Government Printing Office, April 1975.

23. *BLS Handbook of Methods for Survey and Studies,* Bulletin 1711, Bureau of Labor Statistics, Washington, D.C.: Government Printing Office, 1971, Chapter 1. Also see any issue of the Bureau's monthly *Employment and Earnings.*

24. See, for example, Wayne A. Clark, *Discrimination in General Revenue Sharing in the South,* Atlanta, Ga.: Southern Governmental Monitoring Project, Southern Regional Council, Dec., 1975, pp. 5-6.

25. Morton H. Sklar, "The Impact of Revenue Sharing on Minorities and the Poor," in *Revenue Sharing: A Selection of Recent Research,* Subcommittee on Intergovernmental Relations of the U.S. Senate Committee on Government Operations. Washingtion, D.C.: Government Printing Office, March 1975.

26. Richard P. Nathan, et al., *Monitoring Revenue Sharing.* Washington, D.C.: Brookings Institution, 1975, pp. 211-213.

For sometime now we have been beset by those who sound the death knell for the American family. According to Christopher Lasch, the continued erosion of parental authority and the delegation of authority to other agencies have dissolved the bond of discipline and affection between generations. Unable to evaluate their parents' authority because they have become their friends, the young become more and more susceptible to cultural and social forces outside of the home, and to the authoritarian control of the state. Society itself has taken over the role of socialization to increase its control.

Has the family lost control of the socialization function? Is the authoritarian state the result of family dynamics as Lasch contends?

Authority and the Family: Law and Order in a Permissive Society

Christopher Lasch

PARENTS AND CHILDREN

The erosion of parental authority and the delegation of discipline to other agencies have created in the American family a growing gap between discipline and affection—something of the same result that has been brought about by deliberate design in the Israeli kibbutz and other experiments in communal living. In the kibbutz, according to its admirers, the child sees his parents only in "affectional" settings, while toilet training and other forms of discipline are entrusted to the socialized agencies of child rearing. This arrangement supposedly spares the family the conflicts that arise when the same persons exercise love and discipline.[1] In America the family still supervises the child's early development, but new modes of child care have lowered the temperature of family life and reduced overt tensions. Parents accept their obsolescence with the best grace they can muster, voluntarily relegating themselves to the background of their children's lives. They do all they can to make it easy for the younger generation to surpass the older, while secretly dreading the rejection that usually follows. The children return neither solicitude nor resentment, nor does anyone expect them to. On the contrary, everyone assumes that children will painlessly escape emotional entanglements with their parents, and the older generation cooperates in this escape by making few demands it can back up. Mothers worry about losing their sons, but sons seldom worry, at least explicitly, about losing their mothers. Fathers spontaneously abdicate in favor of sons-in-law. Parents represent the useless past. Raising and holding children, not escaping from parents, are the dominant themes of domesticity in a culture which assumes that children will put family attachments behind them without passing through an emotional crisis.

Recent studies of American youth show how closely practice conforms to this ideal, at least on the surface. Again and again, young people assure interviewers that relations with their parents are free of tension, that their families are "abnormally normal," and that even their parents' cool detachment provokes no bitterness on their own part.[2] Yet the rise in student suicide, drug addiction, and impotence immediately casts doubt on this agreeable picture. It does not require a high order of psychoanalytic sophistication to penetrate the bland surface of family life and to uncover deep-seated fears and resentment. The same students who complain of parental neglect—if indeed they complain at all—dream of their parents as devouring, murderous monsters. Some accuse their parents simultaneously of indifference and of intense, suffocating attention to the child's every whim. Young people routinely deplore the absence of their fathers, only to conjure up fantasies of relentless persecution by fathers whose knowledge of their victims' movements extends to the smallest detail.

On the surface, American youth seem to experience no strong sexual attachment to either parent; yet their dreams and fantasies bring to light feelings of rage and desire, which can be traced back to the earliest stages of infancy. Thus while they describe their mothers as cool and remote, their deeper fears center on a completely different kind of mother, alluring and castrating at the same time: a terrifying mother with a vagina full of teeth.[3]

Popular culture embodies the same split, so pronounced in psychiatric interviews, between conflicting images of parenthood—between the untroubled emotional surface of family life and the rage beneath. Films, comic strips, and popular novels—in particular, the many novels of adolescent revolt, patterned after J. D. Salinger's *Catcher in the Rye*—ridicule the "manifest" father, and authority in general, while depicting "latent" father-figures as sinister, aggressive, and utterly unprincipled in their persecution of the hero or heroine.[4] Often the parents have divorced, leaving the child to fend for himself. Alternately, they preserve the emotional intensity of their marriage at the child's expense. In either case, they hover in the background of the child's existence. In the enormously popular comic strip *Peanuts,* parents have vanished completely from the world of childhood—an anomaly recaptured, in more sinister form, in William Golding's *Lord of the Flies,* a novel that has enjoyed a long vogue among high school students and undergraduates.

If parents attempt to intervene in their children's lives, family comedies depict them as objects of amusement or contempt. Thus Mother ineffectually attempts to uphold old-fashioned ideas of decorum and refinement, which Father collaborates with the younger generation in subverting. Father's well-meaning attempts to instruct, befriend, or discipline the young lead to situations that expose his incompetence. Having nothing of value to pass on to his sons, he reserves most of his affection, what there is of it, for his daughters.[5] Yet he makes no attempt to keep his daughter to himself. He makes way for her suitors without complaint, even encouraging their courtship. According to Martha Wolfenstein and Nathan Leites, the ease with which fathers welcome sons-in-law as boon companions exposes another important theme in American popular culture: the sharing of a woman by two friends or "buddies." As sex becomes more casual, the jealousy of the male subsides. He not only tolerates promiscuity in his women but finds it titillating, largely because women know how to keep promiscuity within the bounds of what is called sexiness.[6]

On the surface, then, children in American popular culture painlessly escape the crippling entanglements with their parents that have obsessed so much of the world's literature. On the rare occasions when a strong father appears in the story, his part of the story takes place offstage, as if Americans found it impossible to imagine a strong father in action. But things are not so simple after all—even in popular fantasies not noted for their emotional complexity and moral depth. The nighttime world of melodrama, mystery, crime, and intrigue, which alternates with the family sit-com as the setting for most popular "entertainment," projects onto the comic strip or television screen a shadowy dreamworld in which deeper emotions come to the surface. The melodrama of crime brings to quasi-consciousness a sinister father-image, buried but not forgotten, in the disguise of a criminal, a "lord of the underworld," or a law-enforcement officer who commits crimes in the name of justice. In The *Godfather,* the identification of the father with the master-criminal becomes unmistakable, but in a more tenuous form it has always provided the excitement on which the popular thriller depends for its appeal to a mass audience.

A stock situation in films and novels of crime arises when the hero is wrongly suspected and falsely accused of the very crimes committed by his surrogate father. The regularity with which crime stories return to the theme of false accusation suggests that the latent father-image consists of the son's own repressed wishes projected onto the father. The gangster-father perpetrates the crimes the son would like to commit and then blames them on his son. The unfairness of his accusation expresses the popular belief that mere wishes are harmless and should never be punished. Only incompetent or criminal authorities propose to do so. The drama of the divided self, in which the superego attacks the ego for entertaining forbidden impulses, does not interest the producers of American popular culture. Instead, they externalize not only the superego, in the form of falsely accusing authorities, but the forbidden wishes themselves, now attributed to those same authorities and vicariously gratified even as the hero remains incorruptibly innocent. Self-accusations become the accusations of others, and the son's wish to get rid of his father is translated into the father's determination to make the son one of his victims. Danger comes from without, not from within.

The externalization of dangerous impulses makes the whole world seem dangerous and forbidding; it reinforces the realistic perception that public safety has objectively deteriorated in almost every sector of American society. "The hero of the melodrama," as Wolfenstein and Leites have observed, "is surrounded by an almost completely dangerous world—danger replacing the guilt of divine vengeance which have oppressed and pursued other dramatic heroes."[7] The unpredictability of the outer world has become a recurrent theme not only in melodrama but in all of modern literature. The sense of man's isolation and loneliness reflects the collapse of public order and the loss of religion; but the waning of public order and of religion itself reflects the waning of parental authority and guidance. Without this guidance, according to Alexander Mitscherlich, the world becomes "totally inaccessible and incalculable, continually changing shape and producing sinister surprises."[8]

Modern man faces the world without the protection of kings, priests, and other more or less benevolent father-figures; but he could accept their loss if it had helped him to develop inner resources of his own. Unable to internalize authority, however, he projects forbidden impulses outward and transforms the world into a nightmare. Authorities, inevitably modeled on the divided father, present themselves as either incompetent or malevolent. Accordingly, the individual appears to be justified in his efforts, not to overthrow or succeed them, but to bypass them: to undertake "investigations" of his own, in his capacity of "private eye" or investigative reporter, into the crimes they seek to conceal; to resort to private violence in the tradition of the vigilante; or simply to make endless protestations of his own innocence.

THE NORMALIZATION OF THE ABNORMAL

Divided perceptions of authority, which figure so prominently both in psychiatric testimony and in popular culture, presumably originate not only in the structure of American society but more immediately in the family, which mediates between society and the individual. But how can the family give rise to such deeply conflicting views of itself? The father's absence—the structural feature of the American family that has attracted the attention of so many observers—might explain why children so often complain of parental neglect and why popular fantasy relegates parents to the background, but it hardly seems at first sight to explain the fantasy of paternal persecution and revenge. The fantasy of maternal suffocation might be accounted for, on the other hand, by the hypothesis that "Mom" has emerged as the dominant parent in the father's absence; but in that case, why do children see her at the same time as a figure remote, detached, ineffectual, and indifferent to their needs?

All such explanations make too crude and direct a connection between sociology and psychology, between the structure of family and its reverberations in mental life. They assume that everyday perceptions of the family more or less accurately reflect its structure and emotional content. They fail to distinguish between conscious and unconscious ideas. Complaints of parental indifference, which alternate with the claim that generational conflict plays little part in domestic life, embody conscious perceptions of the family, while the fear of devouring, castrating parents survives from infancy at a deeper psychic level. The remoteness and self-effacement of the American parent, the desexualization of motherhood, and the coolness that has come to characterize domestic relations only superficially ease the younger generation's break with the older. At a deeper level, old conflicts live on. Indeed, they become more deadly, precisely because of the social changes which have diminished the emotional intensity of family life, made it easier for the young to break with their parents, and thus smoothed the transition from childhood to maturity. The softening of the more explicit manifestations of generational conflict merely guarantees the persistence of that conflict in a more primitive psychological form.

Every society imposes certain prohibitions on the young and teaches them how to cope with the ambivalent emotions those prohibitions evoke. It enforces its rules in such a way that the young make the rules their own, neither submitting to them passively nor ignoring them. When adults have confidence in their ability to instruct the young, they do not allow their children's putative needs, as defined by the young themselves, to determine the entire content of education. Nor can they afford to take the child's rights and wishes into account at every point. On the other hand, neither can they ignore those wishes. "Obedience must not be taken for granted and must not be enforced by unilateral communication from above to below; instead, conscious consideration must be given to the weaker party, [who] will one day be the stronger."[9] Without this consideration, the child experiences authority as pure force and learns only that superior strength will always prevail.

An excess of permissiveness, strangely enough, does not necessarily soften this impression. The child who scorns his parents as weak and indecisive—who forms the most tenuous ties to his parents and pushes them without much difficulty into the background of his mind—conjures up another set of parents in his fantasies. Since those other parents so largely represent the creation of the child's unconscious thought—projections of his unconscious wishes and the fears that go with them—they appear to be as vengeful and punitive, as terrifyingly arbitrary and unjust, as the real-life parents are helpless, reasonable, and bland. The remoteness of the older generation does not mean that children form no vivid impressions of their parents; it only means that those ideas will seldom be tested against everyday experience. The child's fantasies go unchecked; he invents a supremely seductive, castrating mother and a fantasy-father who is remote, vindicative, and all-powerful. He sees the world to be starkly divided between power and impotence, and reduces all questions of justice and morality to questions of strength.

The pathology of the bourgeois family, subjected to penetrating scrutiny by psychoanalysis just as the bourgeois family was giving way to a new type of domesticity, provides a glimpse into the psychic structures that are now becoming typical, normal. According to Freud, the infant's sexual feelings and fantasies center first around the intake of nourishment, then around the retention and elimination of his feces, and only later around genital sensations. The child enters the genital or phallic stage of his development only when he has been forced to give up oral and anal gratification—to feed and evacuate according to his parents' pleasure instead of his own. At this point, he becomes aware of his father as a rival for the sexaul favors of his mother and dreams of taking his place.

Sometimes, however, the fear and guilt aroused by these fantasies overwhelm the child, and he represses his genital wishes with particular severity. Still enthralled by the earliest associations aroused by his mother, those of nursing at the breast, he fears that his genital desires will themselves be governed by oral-sadistic impulses. The aggressive impulses inevitably directed against the mother, which originate in her frustration of the child's oral and anal pleasures, become so intense that they threaten to dominate every other activity. Under these conditions, the penis presents itself to the child's mind as a dangerous weapon, the presence of which in the mother's vagina makes the vagina itself a dangerous place by association. In the child's fantasies, she becomes a vampire, a devouring bird with an open beak. "This dread of the mother is so overwhelming," writes Melanie Klein, "because there is combined with it an intense dread of castration by the father."[10] These fears make the thought of sexual intercourse intolerably menacing. Unable to allow himself the fantasy of taking the father's place, the child can make his mother a love-object only by disowning his phallic desires, idealizing the breast and the mother-baby relationship, and attempting to restore the oral dependence of infancy.

Having projected fears of his own destructiveness onto his parents, the child then incorporates these monsters into his own psyche. He thinks of himself as containing alien aggressors that threaten to destroy him from within. The fear of persecution coexists with hypochondria, fear of the devouring presences inside his own body. These alien forces seem to threaten not only the child's health but the internalized image of the nurturing mother. The child regresses from object-love to narcissism; this regression tends to abolish the object itself, just as it does in the similar psychic process of mourning, in which the mourner reconciles himself to the loss of a loved object by internalizing it. In both cases, however, the object not only lives on in the ego but overwhelms it. The ego itself becomes an object, not only of love but also of anger, aggression, and murderous impulses that can lead even to suicide.[11] Impotence, hypochondria, depression, and suicide form part of the same psychic configuration, which originates in the intense anxiety associated with the child's own destructive impulses. The fear that he cannot protect his loved internal objects from danger, and that their death means the end of his own life, constitutes "the fundamental anxiety of the depressive individual."[12]

In the heyday of the bourgeois family, the very structure of the family helped the child to overcome these anxieties—the analysis and treatment of which, accordingly, belonged to the realm of abnormal psychology. As everyday contact with the parents diminished the intensity of early fantasies about them, the child acknowledged rivalry with his father, turned his aggression outward, and took up in fantasy (and later, in sublimated form, in actual practice) the struggle to displace the father. The emotional structure of the contemporary family, however, increasingly militates against such an outcome. The parents remain too shadowy and remote to challenge the child's primitive fantasies about them. Since the content of those fantasies reflects anxieties aroused by oral-sadistic impulses, the child internalizes his parents not as objects of genital love but as projections of his own destructiveness. He sees the father not as a rival but as an all-powerful avenger, the mother alternately as breast and *vagina dentata*. What Melanie Klein wrote of one of her patients, a ten-year-old boy who imagined his mother a "vampire," now has a wider application: "The fear and guilt relating to his destructive phantasies moulded his whole emotional life."[13] The students recently interviewed by Herbert Hendin, both those suffering from severe psychic disturbances and those whom psychiatry would consider healthy and normal, all seek to repress their aggressive impulses for fear that those impulses, once unleashed, will destroy everything in sight. These young people can "conceive of no competition that [does] not result in someone's annihilation."[14] The flight from competition in all areas of life, so striking a feature of the youth culture of the sixties and seventies and so often justified in the name of principle, originates in a murderous rage.

The so-called counterculture, hailed for its subversion of established conventions, merely gives ideological sanction to the retreat from rage, rivalry, and strong emotions in general. The counterculture's quest for emotional detachment, put forward as a program of emotional liberation, reflects a deeply held belief, rooted in the psycho-dynamics of the contemporary family and much more pervasive than the counterculture itself, that strong feelings lead to self-destruction. New ideas of sexual liberation—the celebration of oral sex, masturbation, and homosexuality—spring from the prevailing fear of heterosexual passion, even of sexual intercourse itself. The repudiation of monogamy expresses an accurate understanding of the destructive effects of possessive individualism extended to the emotional realm, of the jealousy that confuses love with emotional ownership. Yet it also expresses a rejection of intimacy and a search for sex without emotion—the "zipless fuck" in which "no one is trying to prove anything or get anything out of anyone."[15]

The contemporary cult of sensuality implies a repudiation of sensuality in all but its most primitive forms. The fascination with personal relations, which becomes increasingly intense as the hope of political solutions recedes, conceals a thoroughgoing disenchantment with personal relations. Ideologies of impulse gratification and pleasure seeking gain the ascendancy at the very moment that pleasure loses its savor. A narcissistic withdrawal of interest from the external world underlies both the demand for immediate gratification—resoundingly endorsed by advertising, mass promotion, and the health industry—and the intolerable anxiety that continually frustrates this demand. The more the "liberated" man clamors for fulfillment, the more he succumbs to hypochondria, to melancholy, or to a suicidal self-hatred that alternates, not with occasional heights of rapture, but with a chronic mild depression, the dominant mood of the times.

CORRUPTION AS A FORM OF SOCIAL CONTROL

The organized assault on the superego, which has liberated pleasure only to transform it into another form of pain, reflects the devaluation of authority in modern society. Those who wield authority—fathers, teachers, magistrates, and priests—have all suffered a loss of "credibility." Unable to inspire loyalty or even to command obedience, they have had to allow their subordinates a greater range of pleasures—and also a greater range of crimes and misdemeanors—than they would once have tolerated. But just as the seeming triumph of the pleasure principle masks a new submission to reality, so a permissive society has invented new forms of political repression or perfected old ones, notably force, bribery, intimidation, and blackmail. The dissolution of authority brings not freedom but new forms of domination. . . .

The new mode of social control avoids conflicts and direct confrontations between authorities and the people on whom they seek to impose their will. Because confrontations provoke arguments about principle, the authorities whenever possible delegate discipline to someone else, so that they themselves can pose as friendly helpers. The diffusion of discipline even within the family provides the new forms of control with a solid basis in the individual's early experience. Having been taught from infancy to measure his demands not against abstract moral standards but against reality, the child submits all more willingly to the reality principle as an adult. His own view of the world corresponds to the view of those who seek to control him.

In a study of the American high school, Edgar Z. Friedenberg found that high school students regard social control as "a technical problem, to be referred to the right expert for solution."[16] In response to a series of hypothetical problems in social control, Friedenberg's subjects rejected both libertarian and openly authoritarian solutions, justifying their preference for social engineering on pragmatic rather than moral grounds. Thus if a teacher finds an unruly student smoking in the washroom, he should neither "beat him coolly and with emotional restraint" or publicly humiliate him, on the one hand, nor ignore the offense, on the other hand, as a minor infraction that should not add to the student's reputation as a troublemaker. Having rejected authoritarian solutions for reasons that were "cautiously bureaucratic rather than indignantly humane," the students voted overwhelmingly that the offender should be sent to the school psychiatrist. Beating him would make him more unmanageable than ever, whereas the psychiatric solution, in effect, would enlist his own cooperation in the school's attempt to control him.

When authority presents itself as benevolence and questions about the exercise of power disguise themselves in the language of psychiatry, traditional political responses become inappropriate and traditional safeguards ineffective.[17] Thus a judge who pronounces a defendant incompetent to stand trial, on the advice of professional psychiatrists, ostensibly protects the defendant's rights, although in fact his ruling may have the opposite effect. In many cases, courts have proceeded to incarcerate the "mentally incompetent," in effect, without a trial. The court assigns the defendant to a hospital for the criminally insane until he can establish his competence to stand trial, failing which he can be reconfined for an indeterminate period of time. The psychiatric perversion of the concept of incompetence nullifies the rights of the accused—the right to a trial on his guilt or innocence, the right to a sentence of determinate duration, and the right not to be tried twice for the same offense—in the name of medical assistance. Even if the "patient" sees through the disguise, he finds that medical tyranny yields to resistance even more reluctantly than political tyranny. He could prove his innocence, even in a rigged system of justice, more easily than he can establish his mental competence. The very tenacity with which he insists on his innocence may be taken as evidence of mental derangement, especially if he has what amounts to a criminal record—a history of psychic disorder. "This patient still denies or keeps on repeating his denial of having committed the crime," runs the psychiatric verdict, "and he still insists upon his innocence." In the doctors' eyes, the patient's refusal to incriminate himself becomes a form of self incrimination in its own right. . . .

The younger generation itself has adopted this view of things. Friedenberg's students "believe that enforcement of regulations, rather than any internal stability or homeostasis, is what keeps society from breaking down into disorder." They regard law not as a body of authoritative commandments but as "an indispensable technique for controlling behavior." This distinction goes to the root of the contemporary situation; it explains the growing devotion to "law and order" in a permissive society. The demand for law and order, which at first sight appears to attempt a restoration of moral standards, actually acknowledges and acquiesces in their collapse. Law enforcement comes to be seen as the only effective deterrent in a society that no longer knows the difference between right and wrong. The campaign to empty law of moral content—to banish the ideas of right and wrong and to replace them with an ethic of human relations—has had an unintended consequence. Divorced from the concept of justice, the law becomes nothing more than an instrument by means of which authorities enforce obedience. In former times, men regarded law as the moral consensus of the community—a means of "setting up categories," in Friedenberg's words, "under which society could subsume and isolate those whom it defined as miscreant." Today they see law merely as a means of controlling behavior. "Neglect law enforcement and the social structure decays."[18]

The prevalence of this view does not mean, however, that subjects and citizens regard authorities as "essentially benign" or hesitate "to discuss the possibility," in Friedenberg's words, "that a social institution . . . might be hostile or destructive in its purpose."[19] On the contrary, official protestations of benevolence elicit contempt or cynical indifference. "Apathy," widely deplored by political scientists and other observers of the political scene, greets all public statements in a society saturated with public lies. The official pretense that officials only want to "help" is rightly regarded as the biggest lie of all. People submit to the rules of social life, then, because submission usually represents the line of least resistance, not because they believe in the justice of the rules or the good intentions of those who promulgate them. The public takes it for granted that power corrupts those who wield it, but it regards this fact not with indignation but with a resigned sense of its inevitability. Disbelief in official pretensions, which formerly might have aroused resistance to the state, becomes another form of obedience, another acknowledgment of the way things are. Men submit not to authority but to reality.

If submission rests not on loyalty to a moral consensus but simply on a belief in the need for law enforcement, it rests on a shaky foundation. Men break the rules whenever the opportunity presents itself, not only because infractions of the rules so often go undetected, but also because authorities themselves conspire with offenders to overlook such violations. The contempt for authority, which leads to rising rates of crime and to the "legitimation of the ripoff," originates in part in the ease with which authorities can be corrupted.[20] Yet the corruptibility of authority serves in a curious way to strengthen the hand of those who wield power. The official who winks at an offense puts the offender in his debt. Moreover, he exposes the offender to blackmail. He keeps people in line precisely by overlooking their transgression, a technique of control that closely resembles the "flattery of the lie," by means of which industrial supervisors assert power over subordinates by tolerating falsehood and inefficiency.[21] Lawbreaking contributes to law enforcement. The complicity between the criminal and the crime fighter, the subordinate and the superior, the violators of rules and the enforcers of rules, contributes to the maintenance of order by keeping troublemakers in a state of chronic uneasiness.[22] Repeated humiliations—the other side of flattery—lower their self-esteem, while the constant threat of disclosure creates fears more painful than disclosure itself. The threat of punishment exceeds punishment in its horror.

The family serves the social order even in the dissolution of its authority. It teaches the child his first lessons in the corruption of authority and thereby exposes him, at an impressionable age, to prevailing modes of social control. The "absence of the father," so often alluded to by students of the family but so little understood in its psychic repercussions, creates in the child a chronic fear of punishment; and although the threat loses its practical force through repeated deferral, it continues to reverberate in the child's fantasies. Precisely because the father's absence allows early fantasies to persist unmodified by later experience, the child fears the terrible vengeance that his father can inflict even while he scorns the everyday father who never inflicts it. The divided perception of parental authority carries over into social action. On the one hand, authorities invite contempt because they allow so many violations of their own rules; on the other hand, they threaten to exact a terrifying revenge at some unspecified moment in the future. As the postponement of gratification loses its force as a form of social control, the postponement of punishment takes its place. Deferred retribution represents the price paid for undeferred gratification. . . .

Today the state controls not merely the individual's body but as much of his spirit as it can preempt; not merely his outer but his inner life as well; not merely the public realm but the darkest corners of private life, formerly inaccessible to political domination. The citizen's entire existence has now been subjected to social direction, increasingly unmediated by the family or other institutions to which the work of socialization was once confined. Society itself has taken over socialization or subjected family socialization to increasingly effective control. Having thereby weakened the capacity for self-direction and self-control, it has undermined one of the principal sources of social cohesion, only to create new ones more constricting than the old, and ultimately more devastating in their impact on personal and political freedom.

FOOTNOTES

1. Bruno Bettelheim, *Children of the Dream* (New York, 1969), pp. 36, 74n, 97, 130, 171, 262; see also Melford E. Spiro, *Children of the Kibbutz* (New York, 1965) [1958], chaps. 2, 4. According to Bettleheim, the founders of the kibbutz movement misunderstood Freud to be saying that "parents should never have any but good times with their children." The same fear of ambivalent attachments, based in part on the same misunderstanding of Freudian theory, can be seen in the American family today. But it is precisely the conjunction of love and constraint that enables a child to grow up and to accept the constraints of adulthood without losing the capacity for love. It is true that children do grow up in the kibbutz and in fact develop into remarkably "well-adjusted" adults; but it is precisely their "adjustment," their "ability to work well with others," their attachment to the peer group, their fear of being alone, their alienation from the past (since "there is no permanence in human relations except with the peer group"), and their lack of introspection and of a highly developed inner life which may provide an ominous foretaste of our future.

2. Hendin, *Age of Sensation,* p. 34.

3. Ibid., pp. 34, 47, 72, 75, 79, 96-98, 108, 116, 129-130, 215, 267, 289, 292, 297.

4. The distinction between "manifest" and "latent" images of parents derives from Martha Wolfenstine and Nathan Leites, *Movies: A Psychological Study* (New York, 1970 [1950]), chap. 2, a penetrating psychoanalytic interpretation on which I have relied heavily in the following argument.

5. It may be objected that the strength of the father-daughter connection is nothing new in American culture. According to Page Smith, *Daughters of the Promised Land: Women in American History* (Boston, 1970), it has been a prominent theme ever since the eighteenth century: "The father-daughter relationship . . . was the principal source of much of the energy and ambition that American women displayed," (p. 66). The novelty lies in the father's unpossesive attitude toward his daughter. The attack on jealousy, focused initially on the relations between lovers, now extends to the relations between parents and children as well.

6. Wolfenstein and Leites, *Movies,* pp. 25-46.

7. Ibid., p. 168.

8. Alexander Mitscherlich, *Society Without the Father* (New York, 1970), p. 160.

9. Ibid., pp. 174-175. See also Jacques Ellul, *The Political Illusion,* translated by Konrad Kellen (New York, 1967), p. 211: "The contemporary orientation is that the child must learn without pain, that it must have agreeable, seductive work, that it must not even notice that it is working, and that in class the teacher must be really a sort of game leader, a permissive leader with whom there is no conflict." Ellul goes on to argue that the elimination of conflict between teacher and pupil, or between parent and child, "radically falsifies the child's participation in social life and keeps his personality from developing." It is in the course of such conflicts that the pupil learns and grows, providing, of course, that "in this conflict the teacher knows that his role is not to bully, crush, or train children like animals."

10. Melanie Klein, "Early Stages of the Oedipus Complex" (1928), in *Contributions to Psycho-Analysis, 1921-1945* (New York, 1964), p. 206.

11. See Sigmund Freud, "Mourning and Melancholia" (1917), *Standard Edition* 14: 161-163.

12. Klein, "The Oedipus Complex in the Light of Early Anxieties" (1945), in *Contributions,* p. 362. I have made heavy use of this essay in the foregoing analysis.

13. Ibid. p. 346.

14. Hendin, *Age of Sensation,* p. 167.

15. Erica Jong, *Fear of Flying* (New York, 1973), pp. 10-14.

16. Edgar Z. Friedenberg, *Coming of Age in America* (New York, 1965), p. 76.

17. Both Thomas S. Szasz, *Psychiatric Justice* (New York, 1965), and Nicholas N. Kittrie, *The Right to Be Different* (Baltimore, 1971), discuss this problem in detail. But the liberal, pluralist critique of "psychiatric justice" and its underlying "medical model" of mental disorder need to be deepened, extended, and in some ways revised. Not only does this argument depend on an indefensible distinction between somatic sickness (regarded as genuine sickness requiring medical intervention) and social deviance (which Szasz contends is misleadingly labeled sickness for purposes of social control), but it also assumes that the answer to the medicaliza-

tion of justice is made society more tolerant of deviance—for example, by getting psychiatrists to admit that homosexuality is not a "sickness." What looks at first like a radical attack on the therapeutic sensibility turns out to be an objection merely to a particularly rigid form of it. by redefining psychiatry not as medicine but as the management of interpersonal relations, these revisionists would extend what remains a therapeutic view of life into all social relations. Their cure is that staple of post-Freudian psychiatric practice, universal understanding. But it is precisely this universal understanding, sympathy, and tolerance (which in any case does not conceal the persistence of intolerance at a deeper level) that reflect the collapse of moral con--sensus, the collapse of distinctions between right and wrong, the collapse of moral authority, and the shift from the old civic religion to the new antireligion of the therapeutic.

How and why the critique of "psychiatric justice" needs to be revised is suggested by a sentence from the introduction to Kittrie's *Right to Be Different,* which, as its title indicates, adopts the perspective of Szasz, but with a dawning awareness of its inadequacy. Kittrie first notes that the "therapeutic state" redefines crime as sickness in order to enforce conformity in the guise of benevolence (against which we have no legal defenses). He then goes on to say that although his book is addressed to the problems growing out of this medical revolution, "as this volume neared completion, the fear of societal excesses, which still remains very real, is somewhat dulled by yet another and opposite surge towards a 'permissive society,' where even fundamental needs of social order and organization fail to achieve broad public consensus and suppport." It remains only to note that it is precisely the collapse of "public consensus" that turns law into an agency for the mechanical enforcement of rules and regulations. Such a concept of law is quite compatible with the notion that those who get out of line are sick and need "treatment."

18. Friedenberg, *Coming of Age,* p. 77.
19. Ibid., p. 82.
20. See Arnold A. Rogow, *The Dying of the Light* (New York, 1975), chap. 2, "The Decline of the Superego," on the legitimation of the ripoff, the collapse of corporate loyalties, new patterns of child rearing based on bribery, and the increasing prevalence of language associated with primary-process thinking.
21. On the "flattery of the lie" in the enforcement of bureaucratic patterns of superordination and subordination, see Thomas S. Szasz, *The Myth of Mental Illness* (New York, 1961), pp. 275-276.
22. Thus law reinforces advertising, which tries to keep the consumer chronically anxious, uneasy, and fearful.

ABOUT THE EDITORS

Dominick Cavallo earned a Ph.D. in American history from the State University of New York at Stony Brook, and has taught at Howard University and the University of Rhode Island. Currently he teaches American history at University College, Adelphi University. He has published articles on the history of American education, the life of Jane Addams, and American millennialism. His book, *Muscles and Morals: Organized Playgrounds and Urban Reform, 1880-1920* was published by the University of Pennsylvania Press in 1981.

Mel Albin is a member of the Department of Political Studies at Adelphi University. Professor Albin has published articles in, and has taught, both family history and public policy and the family. He is the editor of *New Directions in Psychohistory: The Adelphi Papers in Honor of Erik H. Erikson* (Lexington: D.C. Heath, 1980) and recently authored with Gerald Heeger, "Political Turmoil and the Polities of the Third World," in *The Yearbook of World Affairs* (London: Maxwell Publishers, 1981)